Lecture Notes in Computer Science　11895

Commenced Publication in 1973
Founding and Former Series Editors:
Gerhard Goos, Juris Hartmanis, and Jan van Leeuwen

Services Science

Subline of Lectures Notes in Computer Science

Sami Yangui · Ismael Bouassida Rodriguez ·
Khalil Drira · Zahir Tari (Eds.)

Service-Oriented Computing

17th International Conference, ICSOC 2019
Toulouse, France, October 28–31, 2019
Proceedings

 Springer

Editors
Sami Yangui ⓘ
Laboratory for Analysis and Architecture
Toulouse, France

Ismael Bouassida Rodriguez
National Engineering School of Sfax
Sfax, Tunisia

Khalil Drira ⓘ
Laboratory for Analysis and Architecture
Toulouse, France

Zahir Tari ⓘ
RMIT University
Melbourne, VIC, Australia

ISSN 0302-9743   ISSN 1611-3349 (electronic)
Lecture Notes in Computer Science
ISBN 978-3-030-33701-8   ISBN 978-3-030-33702-5 (eBook)
https://doi.org/10.1007/978-3-030-33702-5

LNCS Sublibrary: SL2 – Programming and Software Engineering

This Springer imprint is published by the registered company Springer Nature Switzerland AG
The registered company address is: Gewerbestrasse 11, 6330 Cham, Switzerland

Preface

The 17th International Conference on Service-Oriented Computing (ICSOC 2019) took place in Toulouse, France, during October 28–31, 2019. It aimed at bringing together academics, industry researchers, developers, and practitioners to report and share ground-breaking work in the area of Service-Oriented Computing (SOC). The objective of ICSOC 2019 was to foster cross-community scientific excellence by gathering experts from various disciplines, such as business-process management, distributed systems, computer networks, wireless and mobile computing, cloud computing, cyber-physical systems, Internet of Thing (IoT), networking, scientific workflows, services science, data science, management science, and software engineering. This edition of ICSOC built upon a history of a successful series of previous editions in Hangzhou (Zhejiang, China), Malaga (Spain), Banff (Alberta, Canada), Goa (India), Paris (France), Berlin (Germany), Shanghai (China), Paphos (Cyprus), San Francisco (California, USA), Stockholm (Sweden), Sydney (Australia), Vienna (Austria), Chicago (USA), Amsterdam (the Netherlands), New York (USA), and Trento (Italy).

The conference attracted papers co-authored by researchers, practitioners, and academics from different countries. We received 183 research and industry paper submissions from countries across all continents. Each paper submission was carefully reviewed by at least three members of the Program Committee (PC), followed by discussions moderated by a senior PC member who made a recommendation in the form of a meta-review. The PC consisted of 172 world-class experts in service-oriented computing and related areas (142 PC members and 22 senior PC members) from different countries across all continents. Based on the recommendations, and the discussion, 28 papers (15%) were accepted as full papers. We also selected 10 short papers (6%) and 7 posters (4%), as well as 2 invited papers from prominent researchers.

The program we assembled is reflective of the breadth and depth of the research and applications of SOC, with contributions in the following areas:

- Service Engineering
- Run-time Service Operations and Management
- Services and Data
- Services in the Cloud
- Services for the Internet of Things
- Services in Organizations, Business, and Society
- Services at the Edge

In addition, we were honored to have three prominent players in academic and industrial research areas who gave keynote addresses at ICSOC 2019:

- "State of Permissionless and Permissioned Blockchains: Myths and Reality," by Dr. C. Mohan, IBM Almaden Research Center in Silicon Valley, San Francisco, CA, USA

- "The infrastructure, from physical servers to containers and beyond, what is the next breakthrough?" by Dr. Pierre Rognant, Thales Alenia Space, Toulouse, France
- "Developing AI Systems New challenges for Software Engineering," by Prof. Ivica Crnkovic, Chalmers University, Gothenburg, Sweden

In addition to the technical program consisting of the keynote talks, the main research track, the industry track, the PhD symposium, the demo session and poster sessions, the scope of ICSOC 2019 was broadened by 5 workshops:

- The 15th International Workshop on Engineering Service-Oriented Applications and Cloud Services (WESOACS 2019)
- The 4th International Workshop on Adaptive Service-oriented and Cloud Applications (ASOCA 2019)
- The 4th International IoT Systems Provisioning & Management for Context-Aware Smart Cities (ISYCC 2019)
- The first edition of Towards Blockchain-Based Collaborative Enterprise (TBCE 2019)
- The first edition of Smart daTa integRation And Processing on Service based environments (STRAPS 2019)

We are grateful to the members of the PC as well as the meta-reviewers for helping us to provide valuable and timely reviews. Their efforts enabled us to put together a high-quality technical program for ICSOC 2019. We are indebted to the local arrangements team of LAAS-CNRS for the successful organization of all conference, social, and co-located events. The ICSOC 2019 submission, review, and proceedings process was extensively supported by the Conftool Conference Management System. We are grateful to their technical support.

We would also like to acknowledge all the members of the Organizing Committee and all who contributed to make ICSOC 2019 a successful event. We also acknowledge the prompt and professional support from Springer, who published these proceedings in printed and electronic volumes as part of the *Lecture Notes in Computer Science* series. Most importantly, we would like to thank all authors and participants of ICSOC 2019 for their insightful work and discussions!

November 2019

Sami Yangui
Ismael Bouassida Rodriguez
Khalil Drira
Zahir Tari

Organization

General Chairs

Albert Zomaya   University of Sydney, Australia
Djamal Benslimane   Université de Lyon, France

Program Committee Chairs

Sami Yangui   LAAS-CNRS, France
Khalil Drira   LAAS-CNRS, France
Zahir Tari   RMIT University, Australia

Industry Chairs

Samir Tata   LinkedIn, USA
Emna Mezghani   Orange Labs, France

Workshop Chairs

Sami Yangui   LAAS-CNRS, France
Athman Bouguettaya   University of Sydney, Australia
Xiao Xue   Tianjin University, China

Demonstration Chairs

Noura Faci   Université de Lyon, France
Qi Yu   Rochester Institute of Technology, USA
Walid Gaaloul   Télécom SudParis, France

PhD Symposium Chairs

Zhangbing Zhou   University of Geosciences in Beijing, China
Nathalie Hernandez   Université Toulouse 2, France
Elisa Y Nakagawa   Universidade de Sao Paulo, Brazil

Panel Chairs

Nicolas Van Wambeke   Thales Alenia Space, France
Richard Chbeir   Université de Pau et des Pays de l'Adour, France

Finance Chair

Bernd Krämer   Fern University, Germany

Publication Chair

Ismael Bouassida Rodriguez   University of Sfax, Tunisia

Publicity Chairs

Nicolas Seydoux   LAAS-CNRS, France
Ilhem Khlif   University of Sfax, Tunisia
YiWen Zhang   Anhui University in Hefei, China
Manel Abdellatif   École Polytechnique de Montréal, Canada

Web Chairs

Nour El-Houda Nouar   LAAS-CNRS, France
Fatma Raissi   LAAS-CNRS, France
Josue Castañeda Cisneros   LAAS-CNRS, France

Steering Committee

Boualem Benatallah   UNSW, Australia
Fabio Casati   University of Trento, Italy
Bernd Krämer   Fern University, Germany
Winfried Lamersdorf   University of Hamburg, Germany
Heiko Ludwig   IBM, USA
Mike Papazoglou   Tilburg University, The Netherlands
Jian Yang   Macquarie University, Australia
Liang Zhang   Fudan University, China

Senior Program Committee

Benatallah Boualem   UNSW, Australia
Bouguettaya Athman   The University of Sydney, Australia
Canal Carlos   University of Malaga, Spain
Casati Fabio   University of Trento, Italy
Dustdar Schahram   TU Wien, Austria
Franch Xavier   Universitat Politcnica de Catalunya, Spain
Ghose Aditya   University of Wollongong, Australia
Hacid Mohand   University of Lyon, France
Pahl Claus   Free University of Bozen-Bolzano, Italy
Paoli Flavio   University di Milano Bicocca, Italy
Pautasso Cesare   University of Lugano, Switzerland
Pernici Barbara   Politecnico di Milano, Italy

Rossi Gustavo	UNLP, Argentina
Ruiz-Corts Antonio	University of Sevilla, Spain
Sheng Michael	Macquarie University, Australia
Tai Stefan	TU Berlin, Germany
Tata Samir	Engineering Manager at LinkedIn, USA
Vukovic Maja	IBM Research, USA
Weske Mathias	HPI, University of Potsdam, Germany
Yang Jian	Macquarie University, Australia
Yin Jianwei	Zhejiang University, China
Zhang Liang	Fudan University, China

Program Committee

Abdelkarim Erradi	Qatar University, Qatar
Alena Buchalcevova	University of Economics, Czech Republic
Alex Norta	Tallinn University of Technology, Estonia
Allel Hadjali	ENSMA, France
Alvaro Arenas	IE Business School, Spain
Andrzej Goscinski	Doctor, Australia
Anne Ngu	Texas State University, USA
Antonio Brogi	University of Pisa, Italy
Antonio Bucchiarone	Fondazione Bruno Kessler, Italy
Anup Kumar Kalia	IBM T. J. Watson Research Center, USA
Aviv Segev	University of South Alabama, USA
Azadeh Ghari Neiat	University of Sydney, Australia
Bedir Tekinerdogan	Wageningen University, The Netherlands
Brahim Medjahed	University of Michigan, USA
Bruno Defude	Télécom SudParis, France
Carla Mouradian	Concordia University, Canada
Carlos E. Cuesta	Rey Juan Carlos University, Spain
Chihab Hanachi	IRIT Laboratory, Toulouse University, France
Chi-Hung Chi	CSIRO, Australia
Christian Zirpins	Karlsruhe University of Applied Sciences, Germany
Christoph Bussler	Google, Inc., USA
Claude Godart	University of Lorraine, France
Cristina Cabanillas	Vienna University of Economics and Business, Austria
Dalila Chiadmi	EMI, Morocco
Daniela Grigori	Université Paris-Dauphine, France
Danilo Ardagna	Politecnico di Milano, Italy
David Bermbach	TU Berlin, Germany
Diptikalyan Saha	IBM Research, India
Domenico Bianculli	University of Luxembourg, Luxembourg
Ebrahim Bagheri	Ryerson University, Canada
Efstratios Georgopoulos	University of Peloponnese, Greece
Ejub Kajan	State University of Novi Pazar, Serbia
Elena Navarro	Castilla-La Mancha, Spain

Elisa Yumi Nakagawa	Universidade de São Paulo, Brazil
Emna Mezghani	Orange Labs, France
Erik Wittern	IBM Research, USA
Ernesto Exposito	UPPA-LIUPPA, France
Fairouz Fakhfakh	ReDCAD, Tunisia
Faiza Belala	LIRE Laboratory Constantine 2 University, Algeria
Faouzi Ben Charrada	University of Tunis El Manar, Tunisia
Flavia Coimbra Delicato	Federal University of Rio de Janeiro, Brazil
Flavio Oquendo	IRISA, UMR CNRS, Université Bretagne Sud, France
Florian Daniel	Politecnico di Milano, Italy
Floriano Zini	Free University of Bozen-Bolzano, Italy
Francois Charoy	University of Lorraine, France
Frank Leymann	University of Stuttgart, Germany
Fuyuki Ishikawa	National Institute of Informatics, Japan
George Feuerlicht	University of Technology, Australia
George Pallis	University of Cyprus, Cyprus
George Spanoudakis	City University London, UK
Gerald Kotonya	Lancaster University, UK
Gianluigi Zavattaro	University of Bologna, Italy
Gowri Sankar Ramachandran	CCI, University of Southern California, USA
Guadalupe Ortiz	University of Cadiz, Spain
Guiling Wang	North China University of Technology, China
Hai Dong	RMIT University, Australia
Hai Jin	HUST, China
Haithem Mezni	Taibah University, Tunisia
Hamid Reza Motahari-Nezhad	EY - AI Lab, USA
Hanchuan Xu	Harbin Institute of Technology, China
Helen Paik	UNSW, Australia
Ignacio Silva-Lepe	IBM, Mexico
Ilhem Khlif	University of Sfax Redcad Research Laboratory, Tunisia
Iman Saleh	University of Miami, USA
Imen Abdennadher	ReDCAD, Tunisia
Ioannis Stamelos	Aristotle University of Thessaloniki, Greece
Ismael Bouassida Rodriguez	University of Sfax, Tunisia
Javier Cubo	University of Malaga, Spain
Jean Paul Arcangeli	University Toulouse 3, France
Jean-Michel Bruel	University Toulouse 2, France
Jian Yu	Auckland University of Technology, New Zealand
Jianmin Wang	Tsinghua University, China
Jianwu Wang	University of Maryland, USA
Jin Xiao	IBM T. J. Watson Research Center, USA
Joao E. Ferreira	Universidade de São Paulo, Brazil
John Grundy	Monash University, Australia

Joyce El Haddad	Université Paris-Dauphine, France
Juan Boubeta-Puig	University of Cadiz, Spain
Juan Manuel Murillo	University of Extremadura, Spain
Jun Han	Swinburne University of Technology, Australia
Jun Shen	University of Wollongong, Australia
Jun Wei	Institute of Software, Chinese Academy of Sciences, China
Kais Klai	University of Paris 13, France
Khalil Drira	LAAS Toulouse, France
Lamia BenAmor	Redcad, Tunisia
Lars Braubach	Hochschule Bremen, Germany
Lars Moench	University of Hagen, Germany
Laura Gonzalez	Universidad de la Republica, Uruguay
Lawrence Chung	The University of Texas at Dallas, USA
Liang Chen	Sun Yat-Sen University, China
Liang Zhang	Fudan University, China
Lijie Wen	Tsinghua University, China
Lionel Seinturier	University of Lille, France
Luciano Baresi	Politecnico di Milano, Italy
Manfred Reichert	University of Ulm, Germany
Marcelo Fantinato	Universidade de São Paulo, Brazil
Marco Aiello	University of Stuttgart, Germany
Maria Maleshkova	University of Bonn, Germany
Mark Little	Red Hat, UK
Massimo Mecella	Sapienza Università di Roma, Italy
Matthias Galster	University of Canterbury, New Zealand
Maude Manouvrier	Université Paris-Dauphine, France
Michael Mrissa	InnoRenew CoE, University of Primorska, Slovenia
Mike Papazoglou	University of Tilburg, The Netherlands
Mohamad Kassab	Pennsylvania State University, USA
Mohamed Lamine Kerdoudi	University of Biskra, Algeria
Mohamed Mohamed	IBM Almaden Research Center, USA
Mohamed Sellami	Télécom SudParis, France
Mohammad Abu-Lebdeh	Concordia University, Canada
Monica Vitali	Politecnico di Milano, Italy
Mu Qiao	IBM Almaden Research Center, USA
N. D. Gangadhar	M S Ramaiah University of Applied Sciences, India
Nanjangud C. Narendra	Ericsson Research, India
Naouel Moha	UQAM, Canada
Nathalie Hernandez	University of Toulouse 2, France
Nawal Guermouche	Université de Toulouse, France
Nesrine Khabou	Redcad, Tunisia
Nirmit Desai	IBM T J Watson Research Center, USA
Noura Faci	Université Lyon 1, CNRS, France
Okba Tibermacine	University of Biskra, Algeria

Uwe Zdun	University of Vienna, Austria
Vasilios Andrikopoulos	University of Groningen, The Netherlands
Walid Gaaloul	Télécom SudParis, France
Walter Binder	University of Lugano, Switzerland
Weiliang Zhao	Macquarie University, Australia
Willem-Jan van den Heuvel	Tilburg School of Economics and Management, The Netherlands
Wing-Kwong Chan	City University of Hong Kong, Hong Kong, China
Wolfgang Reisig	Humboldt-Universität zu Berlin, Germany
Xianzhi Wang	University of Technology Sydney, Australia
Xiao Xue	Tianjin University, China
Yan Wang	Macquarie University, Australia
Yehia Taher	University of Versailles-St-Quentin-en-Yvelines, France
Ying Zou	Queen's University, Canada
Zahir Tari	RMIT University, Australia
Zakaria Maamar	Zayed University, UAE
Zaki Malik	Texas A & M University, USA
Zhangbing Zhou	China University of Geosciences, Beijing, China
Zhiyong Feng	Tianjin University, China
Zhiyong Feng	Tianjin University, China
Zhongjie Wang	Harbin Institute of Technology, China

Additional Reviewer

Lamia BenAmor

Contents

Services and Data

Services in the Cloud

Services on the Internet of Things

Short Papers

Service Engineering

An Empirical Study of GraphQL Schemas

Erik Wittern[1]([✉]), Alan Cha[1], James C. Davis[2], Guillaume Baudart[1],
and Louis Mandel[1]

[1] IBM Research, Yorktown Heights, USA
{witternj,lmandel}@us.ibm.com, {alan.cha1,guillaume.baudart}@ibm.com
[2] Virginia Tech, Blacksburg, USA
davisjam@vt.edu

Abstract. GraphQL is a query language for APIs and a runtime to
execute queries. Using GraphQL queries, clients define precisely what
data they wish to retrieve or mutate on a server, leading to fewer round
trips and reduced response sizes. Although interest in GraphQL is on
the rise, with increasing adoption at major organizations, little is known
about what GraphQL interfaces look like in practice. This lack of knowledge makes it hard for providers to understand what practices promote
idiomatic, easy-to-use APIs, and what pitfalls to avoid.

To address this gap, we study the design of GraphQL interfaces in
practice by analyzing their schemas – the descriptions of their exposed
data types and the possible operations on the underlying data. We base
our study on two novel corpuses of GraphQL schemas, one of 16 commercial GraphQL schemas and the other of 8,399 GraphQL schemas mined
from GitHub projects. We make available to other researchers those
schemas mined from GitHub whose licenses permit redistribution. We
also make available the scripts to mine the whole corpus. Using the two
corpuses, we characterize the size of schemas and their use of GraphQL
features and assess the use of both prescribed and organic naming conventions. We also report that a majority of APIs are susceptible to denial
of service through complex queries, posing real security risks previously
discussed only in theory. We also assess ways in which GraphQL APIs
attempt to address these concerns.

Keywords: GraphQL · Web APIs · Practices

1 Introduction

GraphQL is a *query language* for web APIs, and a corresponding *runtime* for
executing queries. To offer a GraphQL API, providers define a *schema* containing the available data *types*, their *relations*, and the possible *operations* on that
data. Clients send *queries* that precisely define the data they wish to retrieve
or mutate. The server implementing the GraphQL API executes the query, and
returns exactly the requested data. Figure 1 shows, on the left, an example query
for GitHub's GraphQL API [12]. It aims to retrieve the description of the

© Springer Nature Switzerland AG 2019
S. Yangui et al. (Eds.): ICSOC 2019, LNCS 11895, pp. 3–19, 2019.
https://doi.org/10.1007/978-3-030-33702-5_1

graphql-js repository owned by graphql. The query, in case that this owner is an Organization, further requests the totalCount of all members of that organization, and the names of the first two of them. The right hand side of Fig. 1 shows the response produced by GitHub's GraphQL API after executing that query,[1] which contains exactly the requested data.

```
1   query {                                          1   { "data": {
2     repository(name: "graphql-js", owner: "graphql") {   2     "repository": {
3       description                                  3       "description": "A reference imple...",
4       owner {                                      4       "owner": {
5         ... on Organization {                      5         "membersWithRole": {
6           membersWithRole(first: 2) {              6           "totalCount": 4,
7             totalCount                             7           "nodes": [
8             nodes {                                8             {"name": "Member 1"},
9               name                                 9             {"name": "Member 2"}
10            }                                      10          ]
11  } } } } }                                        11  } } } } }
```

Fig. 1. Example of a GraphQL query (left), and corresponding JSON response (right).

GraphQL is seeing adoption at major organizations thanks in part to its advantages for performance and usability. In some use-cases, allowing users to precisely state data requirements using GraphQL queries can lead to fewer request-response roundtrips and smaller response sizes as compared to other API paradigms, e.g., REST-like APIs [16]. GraphQL prescribes a statically *typed* interface, which drives developer tooling like GraphiQL, an online IDE helping developers explore schemas and write and validate queries [2], or type-based data mocking for testing services [3]. Major organizations have begun to embrace it, including GitHub [12], Yelp [10], The New York Times [11], or Shopify [13].

As any new technology is deployed, users begin to follow useful patterns and identify best practices and anti-patterns. Our aim is to shed light on emerging GraphQL uses and practices, in the spirit of similar studies for REST(-like) APIs [18,22,23]. By studying technological practices in the GraphQL context, we benefit the entire GraphQL community: Our study will help GraphQL providers build idiomatic, easy-to-use GraphQL APIs, and avoid pitfalls others have experienced before. Our findings also inform tool developers about the practices that are more (and less) important to support. Obviously GraphQL consumers will benefit from the resulting well-designed GraphQL APIs and effective tool support. And finally, our contributions may influence the evolution of GraphQL itself, as we highlight challenges that the specification may eventually address.

Specifically, the contributions of this work are:

– We present two novel GraphQL schema corpuses, derived respectively from commercial GraphQL deployments and open-source projects (Sect. 3). We make parts of the open-source corpus – as permitted by schema licenses – publicly available for other researchers [30], and also share the scripts to reproduce the whole open-source corpus [29].

---

[1] We anonymized the returned names.

– We analyze our corpuses for common schema characteristics, naming conventions, and worst-case response sizes, and describe practices that address large responses (Sect. 4).

In brief, we find that: (1) There are significant differences between commercial and open-source schemas; (2) Schemas commonly follow naming conventions, both documented and not; (3) A majority of schemas have large worst-case response sizes, which schema developers and endpoint providers should consider; and (4) Mechanisms to avoid these large response sizes are applied inconsistently.

2   Background

As sketched above, a schema describes the types of data offered by a GraphQL API, the relations between those types, and possible operations on them. In this section, we outline selected concepts related to GraphQL schemas. GraphQL providers can define schemas either programmatically using libraries like graphql-js [6], or they can define them declaratively using the *Schema Definition Language* (SDL). Figure 2 shows an example schema defined in the SDL.

```
1    schema {
2      query: Query
3      mutation: Mutation
4    }
5    type Mutation {
6      createOffice(input: OfficeInput!): Office
7    }
8    type Query {
9      company(id: ID!): Company
10   }
11   type Company {
12     id: ID!
13     name: String
14     address: String
15     age: Int @deprecated(reason: "No longer relevant.")
16     offices(limit: Int!, after: ID): OfficeConnection
17   }
```

```
1    type OfficeConnection {
2      totalCount: Int
3      nodes: [Office]
4      edges: [OfficeEdge]
5    }
6    type OfficeEdge {
7      node: Office
8      cursor: ID
9    }
10   type Office {
11     id: ID!
12     name: String
13   }
14   input OfficeInput {
15     name: String!
16   }
```

Fig. 2. Example of a GraphQL schema in the Schema Definition Language (SDL).

The schema defines *fields* query and mutation, one of which forms the entry for any valid query. Every GraphQL schema must contain a Query operation type, which in this case is the Query object type. According to this schema, queries can retrieve a company field that returns a Company identified by an id *argument* of type ID (the character "!" indicates that the argument is required). The returned Company again allows queries to retrieve its id, name, address, age, and/or offices. The latter requires the user to limit the number of offices returned. Offices, implementing the *connections pattern* for pagination [7], are related to a company via an OfficeConnection, that contains information about the totalCount of offices of that company, and grants access to them directly via the nodes field or indirectly via the edges field. Querying for an OfficeEdge allows users to obtain a cursor that they can use (in subsequent queries) to precisely slice which offices to retrieve from a Company via the after argument.

```
query { company(id: "n3...") { offices(limit: 10, after: "mY...") { edges: {
    cursor
    node { name }
} } } }
```

The schema further allows to mutate data via the createOffice field. The data about the office to create is defined in a dedicated input object type called OfficeInput and passed as an argument. A corresponding query may look like:

```
mutation { createOffice(input: { name: "A new office" }) {
    id
} }
```

In GraphQL, basic types like String, Int, or Boolean are called *scalars*, sets of predefined strings are called *enums*, and complex types that contain fields are called *object types* (e.g., Company in Fig. 2). GraphQL further allows developers to define *interfaces* that can be implemented by object types or extended by other interfaces, and *unions* which state that data can be of one of multiple object types. For example, in line 5 of Fig. 1, ... on Organization is a *type condition* that queries fields on the interface RepositoryOwner returned by field owner only if the owner happens to be an Organization. Beyond queries that retrieve data, GraphQL schemas may also define a root Mutation operation type, whose fields define possible mutations, e.g., to create, edit, or delete data. Input for mutations is defined using arguments, which are (lists of) scalars, enums, or *input* object types. Finally, GraphQL schemas may contain *directives* that define metadata or behavioral changes associated with field, type, argument or even the whole schema definitions. For example, in Fig. 2 the field age in type Company is marked with a directive as deprecated. This information could, for example, be displayed by documentation tooling. Tools or clients can send an *introspection* query to retrieve the latest schema from a GraphQL API.

After defining their GraphQL schema, to offer a GraphQL API a provider must build a mapping between the data types defined in the schema and their representation in the back-end storage system(s). The provider does this by implementing a *resolver function* for each field defined in the schema, which can retrieve or mutate the corresponding data. Resolver functions can, for example, interact with databases, other APIs, or dynamically compute a result — GraphQL is agnostic to their implementation. To execute a query, a GraphQL runtime validates it against the schema, and then in sequence calls all resolver functions required to fulfill the query.

Although a schema definition does not tell us everything about a GraphQL API (e.g., how its resolver functions are implemented), GraphQL schemas can still tell us about GraphQL practices. For example, from a GraphQL schema we can learn the characteristics of the corresponding GraphQL API, the nature of possible queries to its API, and the conventions followed in designing it. Schema definitions thus comprise useful research artifacts. In the next section we discuss the schema definitions we sampled to understand these and other topics.

3   Data: Two Novel GraphQL Schema Corpuses

We created two corpuses of GraphQL schemas: one from introspecting publicly accessible commercial GraphQL APIs (Sect. 3.1), and the other from mining GitHub for GraphQL schema definitions (Sect. 3.2). Figure 3 illustrates the GraphQL schema populations we sampled to create these corpuses.

Fig. 3. Schema corpuses used in this work. A subset of all GraphQL schemas is defined using the SDL rather than programmatically. We mine the subset hosted on GitHub. Schemas in our commercial corpus can be defined either way, and may be hosted (privately) on GitHub.

In both corpuses, we included only schemas that are parsable (e.g., written in valid SDL syntax) and complete (e.g., contains a *query operation* and definitions of all referenced types). We checked these constraints using the *parsing* and *validation* capabilities offered by the graphql-js reference implementation [6], thus ensuring that schemas can be processed and analyzed without risking runtime errors. We make available the schemas in the open-source corpus – considering the constraints for redistributing them defined in their licenses [30]. We also make available the scripts to collect the whole open-source corpus [29]. These scripts contain the schema reconstruction logic described in Sect. 3.2.

3.1   Commercial Corpus (Schemas Deployed in Practice)

Our commercial corpus (16 schemas) represents GraphQL schemas written and maintained by professional software developers for business-critical purposes. This corpus allows us to reason about GraphQL practices in industry.

To identify commercial GraphQL APIs, we started with the community-maintained list provided by *APIs.guru* [1].[2] We manually assessed the documentation for all 33 of the "Official APIs" listed on May 1st 2019 to remove demo interfaces and non-commercial APIs. We then used introspection to collect these commercial GraphQL schemas. After discarding invalid schemas (validity is defined in Sect. 3.2), we obtained our final corpus of 16 valid, unique GraphQL schemas maintained by commercial websites. The corpus includes, among others, schemas of prominent GraphQL APIs like GitHub, Shopify, Yelp, and BrainTree.

---

[2] We submitted a pull request adding several public GraphQL APIs that were missing from the *APIs.guru* list, but that we found using web searches. The *APIs.guru* maintainers accepted the pull request and we included those schemas in this analysis.

3.2 Open-Source Corpus (Schemas in GitHub Projects)

Our open-source corpus (8,399 schemas) provides another perspective on GraphQL practices, depicting (ongoing) development efforts and privately-deployed APIs. For this corpus, we aimed to collect schema definitions written in the SDL (cf. Sect. 2) and stored in a GitHub project. Figure 4 summarizes the stages of our data-collection methodology.

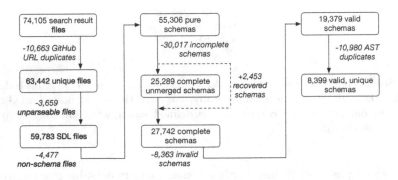

Fig. 4. Filters to construct the open-source schema corpus.

We used GitHub's code search API to obtain **search result files** that likely contain schemas on May 21st 2019 using this query:

```
type extension:graphql extension:gql
    size:<min>..<max> fork:false
```

The pieces of this query have the following meaning. The *search term* `type` is used in any non-trivial schema in the GraphQL SDL. The *extensions* `.graphql` and `.gql` are common file suffixes for the GraphQL SDL. The *file sizes* `<min>` and `<max>` partitioned the search space by file size in order to work around GitHub's limit on code search query results. We omitted project forks to avoid duplicates.

We removed duplicates by URL to obtain **unique files**. We filtered unparsable files per the graphql-js [6] reference implementation to obtain **SDL files**. The GraphQL SDL can describe not only schemas, but also executables like queries, mutations, or subscriptions (e.g., the query in Fig. 1) or a mixture of both. Because we are only interested in schemas, we obtained **pure schemas** by removing any files that contain executables, a.k.a. *executable definitions* [14].

These steps left us with parsable SDL files, but not all are **complete**.[3] We observed that some schemas contain reference errors, e.g., because they are divided across multiple files for encapsulation. Supposing that a repository's complete schema(s) can be produced through some combination of its GraphQL files, we used heuristics to try to reconstruct these *partitioned schemas*, thus

---

[3] A *complete* schema (1) contains a *query operation* (a *SchemaDefinition* node [15] or a *Query* object type [8]), and (2) defines all referenced types and directives.

adding **recovered schemas** back to our data. For every schema that contains a *query operation* but also reference errors, we searched for the missing definitions in the repository's other GraphQL files. When we found a missing type in another file, we appended that file's contents to the current schema.[4] We repeated this process until we obtained either a complete schema or an unresolvable reference. Of the 30,017 **incomplete schemas**, there are 5,603 that contain an *query operation*, meaning they can form the basis of a merged schema, and from these schemas, we were able to recover 2,453 schemas (43.8% success rate). This success rate suggests that *distributing GraphQL schema definitions across multiple files is a relatively common practice.*

We obtained **valid schemas** by removing ones that could not be validated by the graphql-js reference implementation, and finally **valid, unique schemas** by removing duplicates by testing for abstract syntax tree (AST) equivalence. We discarded about half of the remaining schemas during deduplication (Fig. 4). Inspection suggests many of these schemas were duplicated from examples.

Our final open-source schema corpus contains 8,399 valid, unique GraphQL Schema Definition files, 1,127 of which were recovered through merging.[5] Although all of these schemas are valid, some may still be "toy" schemas. We take a systematic approach to identify and remove these in the analysis that follows.

4   Schema Analysis: Characteristics and Comparisons

In this section, we analyze our GraphQL schema corpuses. We discuss schema metrics, characterize the corpuses, and compare and contrast them. Specifically, we analyze some general characteristics (Sect. 4.1), identify naming conventions (Sect. 4.2), estimate worst-case query response sizes (Sect. 4.3), and measure the use of pagination, a common defense against pathological queries (Sect. 4.4).

Because our purpose is to understand GraphQL practices in open-source and in industry, we extracted a subset of the GitHub corpus called the "GitHub-large" (GH-large) corpus that is comparable in complexity to the commercial corpus. This distinction is useful for measurements that are dependent on the "quality" of the schema, e.g., worst-case response sizes and defenses, though for studies like trends in naming conventions we think it is appropriate to also consider the full GitHub corpus. In future analyses, other measures of quality could be considered to segment the data, for example the number of stargazers of the associated GitHub repository.

We identified the GitHub-large corpus using a simple measure of schema complexity, namely its number of distinct definitions (for types, directives, operations etc.). As shown in Fig. 5, the smallest commercial schema contains 8 definitions,

---

[4] If multiple possible definitions were found, we broke ties under the assumption that developers will use the directory hierarchy to place related files close to each other.

[5] We collected data in November 2018 using the same methodology, and found 5,345 unique schemas, 701 of which resulted from merging. This reflects a growth of 57% in half a year.

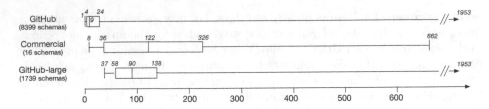

Fig. 5. Distributions of schema complexity (number of definitions) in the GitHub, commercial, and GitHub-large schema corpuses. Whiskers show min and max values and the boxes show the quartiles.

while half of the GitHub corpus contains 9 or less definitions. To avoid a bias toward these toy schemas and to accommodate the small sample size of the commercial corpus, we conservatively define a GitHub schema as *large* if it is at least as complex as the first quartile of the commercial corpus (i.e., has more than 36 definitions). We include separate measurements on this GitHub-large corpus (1,739 schemas, 20.7% of the GitHub corpus, 10 of which were recovered through merging). The complexity distribution of the GitHub-large corpus is not perfectly aligned with the commercial corpus, but it is a better approximation than the GitHub corpus and allows more meaningful comparisons of open-source and industry GraphQL practices.

4.1   Schema Characteristics

First, we provide a reference for what GraphQL schemas look like in practice. This snapshot can inform the design of GraphQL backends (e.g., appropriately sizing caches) as well as the development of the GraphQL specification (e.g., more and less popular features). We parsed each schema using the graphql-js reference implementation [6] and analyzed the resulting AST.

Table 1 shows clear differences among all three corpuses. Not surprisingly, commercial and GitHub-large schemas are larger, containing more object and

Table 1. Characteristics & Features used in schema corpuses.

	Commercial (16)	GitHub (8,399)	GH-large (1,739)
Median object types (OTs)	60	6	35
Median input OTs	44	6	43
Median fields in OTs	3	3	3
Median fields in Input OTs	2	3	3
Have interface types	11 (68.8%)	2,377 (28.3%)	1,395 (80.2%)
Have union types	8 (50.0%)	506 (6.0%)	330 (19.0%)
Have custom directives	2 (12.5%)	160 (1.9%)	26 (1.5%)
Subscription support	0 (0.0%)	2,096 (25.0%)	1,113 (64.0%)
Mutation support	11 (68.8%)	5,699 (67.9%)	1,672 (96.1%)

input object types. The sizes of individual object and input object types, however, look similar in all corpuses. In terms of feature use, commercial schemas apply interface types, union types, and custom directives most frequently, followed by GitHub-large schemas and then GitHub schemas. Conversely, GitHub-large schemas have mutation and subscription[6] support most frequently, followed by GitHub schemas and then commercial schemas.

Analyzing multiple corpuses provides a fuller picture of GraphQL practices. For example, suppose you were to propose changes to the GraphQL specification based solely on one of these corpuses, e.g. to identify little-used features as deprecation candidates. Considering only commercial schemas, subscription support appears to be unpopular (none of the commercial schemas offer subscriptions), so subscriptions might be a deprecation candidate. But the GitHub-large corpus tells a different story: subscriptions are offered in 64% of the GitHub-large schemas. Considering only the GitHub-large corpus instead, you might conclude that custom directives are a deprecation candidate (only 1.5% of GitHub-large schemas use them), even though 12.5% of the commercial corpuses use them. In both cases a single-corpus analysis is misleading, showing the value of our multi-corpus analysis.

> **Finding 1:** Commercial and GitHub-large schemas are generally larger than GitHub schemas. Reliance on different GraphQL features (e.g., unions, custom directives, subscription, mutation) varies widely by corpus.

4.2 Naming Conventions

Naming conventions help developers understand new interfaces quickly and create interfaces that are easily understandable. In this section we explore the prescribed and organic naming conventions that GraphQL schema authors follow, e.g. common ways to name types, fields, and directives. Table 2 summarizes our findings. We focus on the proportion of schemas that follow a convention *consistently*, i.e., the schemas that use them in all possible cases.

Prescribed Conventions. GraphQL experts have recommended a set of naming conventions through written guidelines [4] as well as implicitly through the example schemas in the GraphQL documentation [5]. These prescribed conventions are: (1) Fields should be named in camelCase; (2) Types should be named in PascalCase; and (3) Enums should be named in PascalCase with (4) values in ALL_CAPS.

We tested the prevalence of these conventions in real GraphQL schemas[7]. As shown in Table 2, these prescribed conventions are far from universal. The only prescribed convention that is frequently used in all three corpuses is (3) Pascal-Case enum names, exceeding 80% of schemas in each corpuses and over 95% in

---

[6] Subscriptions permit clients to register for continuous updates on data.

[7] For simplicity, we tested for camelCase and PascalCase names using only the first letter. A more sophisticated dictionary-based analysis is a possible extension.

Table 2. The proportion of schemas that consistently adhere to prescribed (upper part) and organic (lower part) naming conventions. In rows marked with a † we report percentages from the subsets of schemas that use any enums, input object types, or mutations, respectively.

	Commercial (16)	GitHub (8,399)	GH-large (1,739)
camelCase field names	12.5%	53.9%	8.2%
PascalCase type names	62.5%	91.8%	82.1%
PascalCase enum names †	81.3%	96.8%	96.4%
ALL_CAPS enum values †	56.3%	35.7%	12.1%
Input postfix †	23.1%	71.6%	68.2%
Mutation field names †	9.1%	49.3%	62.9%
snake_case field names	0.0%	0.5%	0.1%

the GitHub and GitHub-large corpuses. In contrast, (1) camelCase field names are only common in GitHub schemas, (2) PascalCase type names are common in GitHub and GitHub-large schemas and less so in commercial schemas, and (4) ALL_CAPS enum values appear in more than half of commercial schemas, but are unusual in the GitHub and GitHub-large schemas.

Organic Conventions. Next we describe "organic" conventions[8] that we observed in practice but which are not explicitly recommended in grey literature like the GraphQL specification or high-profile GraphQL tutorials.

Input Postfix for Input Object Types. Schemas in our corpuses commonly follow the convention of ending the names of input object types with the word Input. This convention is also followed in the examples in the official GraphQL documentation [5], but the general GraphQL naming convention recommendations do not remark on it [4]. In GraphQL, type names are unique, so the Input postfix is often used to associate object types with related input object types (e.g., the object type User may be related to the input object type UserInput).

Mutation Field Names. Developers commonly indicate the effect of the mutation by including it as part of the field name. These names are similar to those used in other data contexts: update, delete, create, upsert, and add.

snake_case Field Names. Of the non-camelCase field names in the GitHub corpus, 90.3% follow snake_case (determined by the presence of an underscore: "_"), covering 30.6% of all field names and used in 37.3% of all schemas in the GitHub corpus. However, barely any schema across all corpuses uses this convention throughout.

---

[8] These conventions are "organic" in the sense that they are emerging naturally without apparent central direction. There could, however, be some hidden form of direction, e.g. many projects influenced by the same team or corporation.

In general, the observed organic conventions are much more common in GitHub and GitHub-large schemas than in commercial schemas.

> **Finding 2:** GraphQL experts have recommended certain naming conventions. We found that PascalCase enum names are common in all three corpuses, and PascalCase type names are common in the GitHub and GitHub-large corpuses, but other recommendations appear less consistently. In addition, we observed the relatively common practice of input postfix and mutation field names in the GitHub and GitHub-large corpuses. We recommend that commercial API providers improve the usability of their APIs by following both recommended and "organic" conventions.

4.3 Schema Topology and Worst-Case Response Sizes

Queries resulting in huge responses may be computationally taxing, so practitioners point out the resulting challenge for providers to throttle such queries [24,25]. The size of a response depends on three factors: the schema, the query, and the underlying data. In this section, we analyze each schema in our corpuses for the worst-case response size it enables with pathological queries and data.

A GraphQL query names all the data that it retrieves (cf. Fig. 1). Provided a schema has no field that returns a list of objects, the response size thus directly corresponds to the size of the query. On the other hand, if a field can return a list of objects (e.g., **nodes** in Fig. 1), nested sub-queries are applied to all the elements of the list (e.g., **name** in Fig. 1). Therefore, nested object lists can lead to an explosion in response size.

From the schema we can compute K, the maximum number of nested object lists that can be achieved in a query. For example, if **Query** contains a field **repos: [Repo]**, and **Repo** contains a field **members: [User]** then $K = 2$. Without access to the underlying data, we assume that the length of all the retrieved object lists is bounded by a known constant D.[9]

Polynomial Response. For a query of size n, the worst-case response size is $O\big((n - K) \times D^K\big)$ — at worst polynomial in the length D of the object lists. The proof is by induction over the structure of the query. As an illustration, consider the worst-case scenario of a query with maximum number of nested lists, K. Since the query must spend K fields to name the nested lists, each object at the deepest level can have at most $(n - K)$ fields and will be of size at most $(n - K)$. Each level returns D nested objects, plus one field to name the list. The size of each level k starting from the deepest one thus follows the relation: $s_k = D \times s_{k-1} + 1$ with $s_0 = (n - K)$. The response size is given by the top level K: $s_K = (n - K) \times D^K + \frac{D^K - 1}{D - 1}$, that is, $O\big((n - K) \times D^K\big)$.[10]

---

[9] In practice, the size of retrieved object lists are often explicitly bounded by slicing arguments (e.g., **first: 2** in Fig. 1). See also Sect. 4.4.

[10] In Table 3, we use the slightly relaxed notion $O(n \times D^K)$.

Exponential Response. If the schema includes a cycle containing list types (e.g., a type `User` contains a field `friends:[User]`), the maximum number of nested object lists is only bounded by the size of the query, i.e., $K < n$.[11] In that case the worst-case response size becomes $O(D^{n-1})$, that is, exponential in the size of the query. Consider for example the following query that requests names of third degree friends (size $n = 4$ and nesting $K = 3$). If every user has at least ten friends, the size of the response is $1 + 10 \times (1 + 10 \times (1 + 10 \times 1)) = 1111$.

```
query { friends(first: 10) { friends(first: 10) { friends(first: 10) { name } } } }
```

Table 3. Worst-case response size based on type graph analysis, where n denotes the query size, and D the maximum length of the retrieved lists.

Worst-case response		Commercial (16)	GitHub (8,399)	GH-large (1,739)
Exponential	$O(D^{n-1})$	14 (87.5%)	3,219 (38.3%)	1,414 (81.3%)
Polynomial	$O(n \times D^6)$	0 (0.0%)	6 (0.1%)	4 (0.2%)
Polynomial	$O(n \times D^5)$	0 (0.0%)	9 (0.1%)	4 (0.2%)
Polynomial	$O(n \times D^4)$	0 (0.0%)	34 (0.4%)	7 (0.4%)
Polynomial	$O(n \times D^3)$	1 (6.3%)	186 (2.2%)	40 (2.3%)
Quadratic	$O(n \times D^2)$	1 (6.3%)	785 (9.3%)	88 (5.1%)
Linear	$O(n \times D)$	0 (0.0%)	3,112 (37.1%)	182 (10.5%)
Linear	$O(n)$	0 (0.0%)	1,048 (12.5%)	0 (0.0%)

Results. We implemented an analysis for schema topographical connectedness based on the conditions for exponential and polynomial responses sizes outlined above, and applied it to our schema corpuses. As shown in Table 3, the majority of commercial (100.0%), GitHub (50.5%), and GitHub-large (89.5%) schemas have super-linear worst-case response sizes. This finding is of course not altogether surprising, as the key to super-linear response sizes is a particular and intuitive relational schema structure, and the purpose of GraphQL is to permit schema providers to describe relationships between types. However, the implication is that GraphQL providers and middleware services should plan to gauge the cost of each query by estimated cost or response size, or otherwise limit queries.

> **Finding 3:** The majority of commercial, GitHub, and GitHub-large schemas have super-linear worst-case response sizes, and in the commercial and GitHub-large corpuses, they are mostly exponential. Providers need to consider throttling requests to their APIs to avoid the negative consequences of expensive queries, whether malicious or inadvertent.

---

[11] In GraphQL the first field is always `query`, and cannot be a list type.

4.4   Delimiting Worst-Case Response Sizes Through Pagination

Queries with super-linear response sizes can become security threats, overloading APIs or even leading to denial-of-service. For commercial GraphQL providers, exponential response sizes pose a potential security risk (denial of service). Even polynomial response sizes might be concerning — e.g., consider the cost of returning the (very large) cross product of all GitHub repositories and users.

The official GraphQL documentation recommends that schema developers use one of two *pagination* techniques to bound response sizes [7]: **Slicing** refers to the use of numeric arguments to index a subset of the full response set. The **connections pattern** introduces a layer of indirection to enable more complex pagination. The addition of *Edge* and *Connection* types allows schema developers to indicate additional relationships between types, and to paginate through a concurrently updated list (cf. schema described in Sect. 2).

Analysis. We used heuristics relying on names of fields and types to identify the use of pagination patterns within schemas.

For slicing, we identify fields that return object lists and accept numeric *slicing arguments* of scalar type Int. In our corpuses these arguments are commonly named first, last, and limit, or size. We use the presence of arguments with these names as an indication that slicing is in use. We differentiate schemas that use such arguments for slicing consistently, for some fields, or not at all.

For the connections pattern, we check schemas for types whose names end in Connection or Edge as proposed in the official GraphQL docs [7]. We again check for the use of slicing arguments on fields that return connections.

Table 4. Use of slicing arguments and connections pattern.

	Comm. (16)	GitHub (8,399)	GH-large (1,739)
Have fields returning object lists	16 (100.0%)	7,351 (87.5%)	1,739 (100.0%)
...with no slicing arguments	10 (62.5%)	5,335 (63.5%)	385 (22.1%)
...with slicing args. sometimes	6 (37.5%)	1,771 (21.1%)	1,265 (72.7%)
...with slicing args. throughout	0 (0.0%)	245 (2.9%)	89 (5.1%)
Have types with names matching			
/Edge$/ and /Connection$/	9 (56.3%)	2,073 (24.7%)	1,365 (78.5%)
...with no slicing arguments	1 (6.3%)	1,397 (16.6%)	1,073 (61.7%)
...with slicing args. sometimes	2 (12.5%)	48 (0.6%)	31 (1.8%)
with slicing args. throughout	6 (37.5%)	628 (7.5%)	261 (15.0%)

Results. Using our heuristics, Table 4 summarizes the use of the pagination patterns in our corpuses. In no corpus are these pagination patterns used consistently, strengthening the threat of the worst-case responses discussed in Sect. 4.3. For the schemas that do use pagination patterns, the commercial and GitHub-large schemas tend to use the more complex yet flexible connections pattern, while slicing alone is used inconsistently across all schemas.

> **Finding 4:** No corpus consistently uses pagination patterns, raising the specter of worst-case response sizes. When pagination patterns are used, commercial and GitHub-large schemas tend to use the connections pattern, while slicing is not used consistently. Our worst-case findings from Sect. 4.3 urge the wider adoption of pagination.

5   Related Work

Our work is most closely related to that of Kim et al., who also collected and analyzed GraphQL schemas [21]. They analyzed 2,081 unique schemas mined from open-source repositories on GitHub. Our works are complementary. We use different mining techniques and conduct different analyses. For **mining**, to identify GraphQL schemas on GitHub, both works queried the GitHub API for filenames with GraphQL-themed substrings. We additionally proposed a novel schema stitching technique to repair incomplete schemas, which permitted us to recover thousands of schemas that their methodology would discard (Sect. 3.2). In **analysis**, we compared multiple corpuses, while they focused solely on schemas obtained from GitHub and did not distinguish between the larger and smaller schemas therein. Where our analyses overlap, our findings agree: in our GitHub schema corpus we report similar proportions of schemas using mutations (we: 67.9%, they: 70%) and subscriptions (we: 25.0%, they: 20%). Similarly, in our GitHub corpus we found a similar proportion of schemas with type cycles (we: 38.3%, they: 39.7%). Our analyses of naming conventions, worst-case response sizes, and pagination are novel.

Our worst-case response size analysis (Sect. 4.3) benefits from the work of Hartig and Pérez. They complemented the GraphQL specification [17] with a formal description for key parts of GraphQL [19,20]. They also proved the existence of GraphQL schema-data (graph) combinations on which a query will have exponential-sized results (cf. [20, Propositions 5.2 and 5.3]) and gave an upper bound for the response size (cf. [20, Theorem 5.4]). In comparison, our analysis in Sect. 4.3 explicitly identifies object lists as the cause of the response size explosion, and we use this observation to provide a tighter upper bound.

The remaining academic literature on GraphQL focuses on the challenges of creating a GraphQL API. Several research teams have described their experiences exposing a GraphQL API or migrating existing APIs to GraphQL [16, 27,28]. Others have described automatic techniques for migration [31] and testing [26].

Our work is similar in spirit to studies of REST(-like) APIs, which have focused on API design best practices [22,23] or assessed API business models [18]. Because of the paradigmatic differences between GraphQL and REST (single endpoint, typed schema, queries formed by clients, etc.), this work complements existing ones.

6   Threats to Validity

Construct Validity. In Sect. 4.3 we assume that response size is the primary measure of query cost. We leave to future work a more fine-grained analysis dependent on backend implementation details (e.g. resolver function costs).

Internal Validity. Our name-based analyses depend on heuristics which could be inaccurate, although they are grounded in the grey literature where possible.

External Validity. Our corpuses may not be representative of the true state of GraphQL schemas in practice, affecting the generalizability of our results. The commercial corpus contains the 16 public commercial GraphQL APIs we could identify, well short of the 100+ companies that use GraphQL (presumably internally) [9]. We restricted the open-source corpus to statically defined schemas stored in GitHub. By analyzing the "GitHub large" schemas separately, we provide a better understanding of both (1) methodologically, the risks of treating all GitHub schemas alike, and (2) scientifically, the properties of larger schemas.

7   Conclusions

GraphQL is an increasingly important technology. We provide an empirical assessment of the current state of GraphQL through our rich corpuses, novel schema reconstruction methodology, and novel analyses. Our characterization of naming conventions can help developers adopt community standards to improve API usability. We have confirmed the fears of practitioners and warnings of researchers about the risk of denial of service against GraphQL APIs: most commercial and large open-source GraphQL APIs may be susceptible to queries with exponential-sized responses. We report that many schemas do not follow best practices and thus incompletely defend against such queries.

Our work motivates many avenues for future research, such as: refactoring tools to support naming conventions, coupled schema-query analyses to estimate response sizes in middleware (e.g. rate limiting), and data-driven backend design.

Acknowledgments. We are grateful to A. Kazerouni and B. Pirelli for their feedback on the manuscript, and to O. Hartig for a helpful discussion.

References

1. APIs-guru/graphql-apis: A collective list of public GraphQL APIs. https://github.com/APIs-guru/graphql-apis
2. GraphiQL: An in-browser IDE for exploring GraphQL. https://github.com/graphql/graphiql
3. GraphQL Faker. https://github.com/APIs-guru/graphql-faker
4. GraphQL Style conventions. https://www.apollographql.com/docs/apollo-server/essentials/schema.html#style
5. Introduction to GraphQL. https://graphql.org/learn/

6. JavaScript reference implementation for GraphQL. https://github.com/graphql/graphql-js
7. Pagination. http://graphql.github.io/learn/pagination/
8. Schemas and Types. https://graphql.org/learn/schema
9. Who's using GraphQL? http://graphql.org/users
10. Introducing Yelp's Local Graph (2017). https://engineeringblog.yelp.com/2017/05/introducing-yelps-local-graph.html
11. React, Relay and GraphQL: Under the Hood of The Times Website Redesign (2017). https://open.nytimes.com/react-relay-and-graphql-under-the-hood-of-the-times-website-redesign-22fb62ea9764
12. GitHub GraphQL API v4 (2019). https://developer.github.com/v4/
13. GraphQL and Shopify (2019). https://help.shopify.com/en/api/custom-storefronts/storefront-api/graphql/
14. GraphQL Current Working Draft: Schema (2019). https://facebook.github.io/graphql/draft/#sec-Executable-Definitions
15. GraphQL Current Working Draft: Schema (2019). https://facebook.github.io/graphql/draft/#sec-Schema
16. Brito, G., Mombach, T., Valente, M.T.: Migrating to GraphQL: a practical assessment. In: 2019 IEEE 26th International Conference on Software Analysis, Evolution and Reengineering (SANER), pp. 140–150. IEEE (2019)
17. Facebook Inc.: GraphQL. Working Draft, June 2018. https://facebook.github.io/graphql/
18. Gamez-Diaz, A., Fernandez, P., Ruiz-Cortes, A.: An analysis of RESTful APIs offerings in the industry. In: Maximilien, M., Vallecillo, A., Wang, J., Oriol, M. (eds.) ICSOC 2017. LNCS, vol. 10601, pp. 589–604. Springer, Cham (2017). https://doi.org/10.1007/978-3-319-69035-3_43
19. Hartig, O., Pérez, J.: An initial analysis of Facebook's GraphQL language. In: CEUR Workshop Proceedings (2017)
20. Hartig, O., Pérez, J.: Semantics and complexity of GraphQL. In: Conference on World Wide Web (WWW) (2018)
21. Kim, Y.W., Consens, M.P., Hartig, O.: An empirical analysis of GraphQL API schemas in open code repositories and package registries. In: Proceedings of the 13th Alberto Mendelzon International Workshop on Foundations of Data Management (AMW), June 2019
22. Palma, F., Gonzalez-Huerta, J., Moha, N., Guéhéneuc, Y.-G., Tremblay, G.: Are RESTful APIs well-designed? Detection of their linguistic (Anti)Patterns. In: Barros, A., Grigori, D., Narendra, N.C., Dam, H.K. (eds.) ICSOC 2015. LNCS, vol. 9435, pp. 171–187. Springer, Heidelberg (2015). https://doi.org/10.1007/978-3-662-48616-0_11
23. Petrillo, F., Merle, P., Moha, N., Guéhéneuc, Y.-G.: Are REST APIs for cloud computing well-designed? An exploratory study. In: Sheng, Q.Z., Stroulia, E., Tata, S., Bhiri, S. (eds.) ICSOC 2016. LNCS, vol. 9936, pp. 157–170. Springer, Cham (2016). https://doi.org/10.1007/978-3-319-46295-0_10
24. Rinquin, A.: Avoiding n+1 requests in GraphQL, including within subscriptions
25. Stoiber, M.: Securing your GraphQL API from malicious queries
26. Vargas, D.M., et al.: Deviation testing: a test case generation technique for GraphQL APIs (2018)
27. Vázquez-Ingelmo, A., Cruz-Benito, J., García-Peñalvo, F.J.: Improving the OEEU's data-driven technological ecosystem's interoperability with GraphQL. In: Proceedings of the 5th International Conference on Technological Ecosystems for Enhancing Multiculturality - TEEM 2017, pp. 1–8 (2017)

28. Vogel, M., Weber, S., Zirpins, C.: Experiences on migrating RESTful web services to GraphQL. In: Braubach, L., et al. (eds.) ICSOC 2017. LNCS, vol. 10797, pp. 283–295. Springer, Cham (2018). https://doi.org/10.1007/978-3-319-91764-1_23
29. Wittern, E., Cha, A., Davis, J.C., Baudart, G., Mandel, L.: GraphQL schema collector. https://doi.org/10.5281/zenodo.3352421, accessible at https://github.com/ErikWittern/graphql-schema-collector
30. Wittern, E., Cha, A., Davis, J.C., Baudart, G., Mandel, L.: GraphQL Schemas. https://doi.org/10.5281/zenodo.3352419, accessible at https://github.com/ErikWittern/graphql-schemas
31. Wittern, E., Cha, A., Laredo, J.A.: Generating GraphQL-Wrappers for REST(-like) APIs. In: Mikkonen, T., Klamma, R., Hernández, J. (eds.) ICWE 2018. LNCS, vol. 10845, pp. 65–83. Springer, Cham (2018). https://doi.org/10.1007/978-3-319-91662-0_5

Automating SLA-Driven API Development with SLA4OAI

Antonio Gamez-Diaz[✉], Pablo Fernandez, and Antonio Ruiz-Cortes

Universidad de Sevilla, Seville, Spain
{antoniogamez,pablofm,aruiz}@us.es

Abstract. The OpenAPI Specification (OAS) is the *de facto* standard to describe RESTful APIs from a functional perspective. OAS has been a success due to its simple model and the wide ecosystem of tools supporting the SLA-Driven API development lifecycle. Unfortunately, the current OAS scope ignores crucial information for an API such as its Service Level Agreement (SLA). Therefore, in terms of description and management of non-functional information, the disadvantages of not having a standard include the vendor lock-in and prevent the ecosystem to grow and handle extra functional aspects.

In this paper, we present SLA4OAI, pioneering in extending OAS not only allowing the specification of SLAs, but also supporting some stages of the SLA-Driven API lifecycle with an open-source ecosystem. Finally, we validate our proposal having modeled 5488 limitations in 148 plans of 35 real-world APIs and show an initial interest from the industry with 600 and 1900 downloads and installs of the SLA Instrumentation Library and the SLA Engine.

1 Introduction

In the last decade, RESTful APIs are becoming a clear trend as composable elements that can be used to build and integrate software [7,18]. One of the key benefits this paradigm offers is a systematic approach to information modeling leveraged by a growing set of standardized tooling stack from both the perspective of the API consumer and the API provider.

Specifically, during the last years, the *OpenAPI Specification*[1] (OAS), formerly known as *Swagger* specification, has become the *de facto* standard to describe RESTful APIs from a functional perspective providing an ecosystem

---

[1] https://github.com/OAI/OpenAPI-Specification.

This work is partially supported by the European Commission (FEDER), the Spanish Government under projects BELI (TIN2015-70560-R) and HORATIO (RTI2018-101204-B-C21), and the FPU scholarship program, granted by the Spanish Ministry of Education, Culture and Sports (FPU15/02980).

S. Yangui et al. (Eds.): ICSOC 2019, LNCS 11895, pp. 20–35, 2019.
https://doi.org/10.1007/978-3-030-33702-5_2

that helps the developer in several aspects of the API development lifecycle[2]. As an example, from the API provider perspective, there are tools that aim to automate the server scaffolding, an interactive documentation portal creation or the generation of unit test cases; from the perspective of the consumer, there are tools to automate the creation of API clients, the security configuration or the endpoints discovery and usage [1,15,16].

However, as APIs are deployed and used in real settings, the need for non-functional aspects is becoming crucial. In particular, the adoption of Service Level Agreements (SLAs) [13] could be highly valuable to address significant challenges that the industry is facing, as they provide an explicit placeholder to state the guarantees and limitations that a provider offers to its consumers. For example, these limitations (such as *quotas* or *rates*) are present in most common industrial APIs [3] and both API providers and consumers need to handle how they monitor, enforce or respect them with the consequent impact in the API deployment/consumption.

In this paper, we address the challenge of SLA modeling and management in APIs by providing the following contributions:

– SLA4OAI, an open SLA specification that is integrated with the OpenAPI Specification joint with a Basic SLA Management Service (i.e., a minimum definition of endpoints required for the SLA enforcing in the APIs) that can be used to promote the vendor independence.
– A set of tools to support the different activities of the API development lifecycle when it becomes aware of the existence of an SLA.
– An initial validation over 5488 limitations in 35 of real-world APIs showing the expressiveness coverage and the potential evolution roadmap for the specification.

The rest of the paper is structured as follows: in Sect. 2, we describe the related work and motivate the need for our proposal. In Sect. 3 we describe in brief words the OpenAPI Specification focusing on its extension's capabilities. In Sect. 4 we describe our SLA4OAI model proposal. In Sect. 5 we show the ecosystem of tools that have been built around our proposal. In Sect. 6 we validate our proposal by modeling 5488 limitations in 35 of real-world APIs. Finally, in Sect. 7 we show some remarks and conclusions.

2   Motivation and Related Work

The software industry has embraced integration as a key challenge that should be addressed in multiple scenarios. In such a context, the proliferation of APIs is a reality that has been formally analyzed: in [14], authors performed an analysis of more than 500 publicly-available APIs to identify the different trends in the current industrial landscape. Specifically, regarding the *documentation*, there is a clear trend with respect to the functional description of the service: during

---

[2] https://openapi.tools.

the last years, the OpenAPI Specification has consolidated as a *de-facto* standard to define the different functional properties an API provides. For instance, in [12], authors study on the presence of dependency constraints among input parameters in web APIs in industry.

With such a consolidated market of APIs, non-functional aspects are also becoming a key element in the current landscape. In [3], authors analyze a set of the 69 real APIs in the industry to characterize the variability in its offerings, obtaining a number of valuable conclusions about real-world APIs, such as: (i) Most APIs provide different capabilities depending on the tier or plan of the API consumer is willing to pay. (ii) Usage limitations are a common aspect all APIs describe in their offerings. (iii) Limitations over API requests are the most common including quotas over static periods of times (e.g., *1.000 request each natural day*) and rates for dynamic periods of times (*3 request per second*). (iv) Offerings can include a wide number of metrics over other aspects of the API that can be domain-independent (such as the number of returned results or the size in bytes of the request) or domain-dependent (such as the CPU/RAM consumption during the request processing or the number of different resource types). Based on these conclusions, we identify the need for non-functional support in the API development life-cycle and the high level of expressiveness present in the API offerings.

From the perspective of the API development life-cycle, the lack of a standard spec for non-functional aspects integrated with existing standards OpenAPI, prevents the tooling ecosystem to grow and provide support advanced issues: as an example, to support the API consumer, it could be possible to develop tools to automate the generation of SLA-aware API clients able to self-adapt the request rate to the API limitations; to support the API provider, it could be possible to create of SLA-aware API testers enriching the habitual tests with information about limitations in order to analyze the actual performance capabilities to decide the maximum number of API consumers to be allowed with a certain SLA that explicitly states the limitations in their usage. We have analyzed the most prominent academic and industrial proposals that aim to the definition of SLAs in both traditional web services and cloud scenarios in order to outline their scope and limitations. Specifically, in Table 1, we have considered 7 aspects to analyze in each SLA proposal, namely: **F1** determines the format in which the document is written; **F2** shows whether the target domain is web services; **F3** indicates if it can model more than one offering (i.e., different operations of a web service); **F4** determines if it allows modeling hierarchical models or overriding properties and metrics; **F5** shows whether temporal concerns can be model (e.g., in metrics); **F6** indicates if there exists a tool for assisting users to model using this proposal; **F7** determines if there exists a tool/framework for enacting the SLA.

Based on this comparison of the different SLA models, we highlight the following conclusions: (i) None of the specifications provides any support or alignment with the OpenAPI Specification; (ii) Most of the approaches provide a concrete syntax on XML, RDF (some of them they even lack concrete syntax) and there is no explicit support to YAML or JSON serializations. (iii) An important number of proposals are complete, but others leave some parts open to being implemented by practitioners. (iv) Besides the fact that a number of proposals are that aims to model web services, they are focused on traditional SOAP web services rather than

Table 1. Analysis of SLA models

Name	F1	F2	F3	F4	F5	F6	F7
SLAC [19]	DSL					✓	✓
CSLA [9]	XML		✓			✓	
L-USDL Ag. [6]	RDF	✓	✓		†	✓	
rSLA [17]	Ruby	✓		✓	✓		✓
SLAng [10]	XML	✓					
WSLA [11]	XML	✓	✓		✓		
SLA* [8]	XML	✓	✓		✓		
WS-Ag. [2]	XML	✓	✓	✓	†		

† Supported with minor enhancements or modifications.

RESTful APIs. In this context, they do not address the modeling standardization of the RESTful approach: i.e., the concept of a resource is well unified (a URL), and the amount of operations is limited (to the HTTP methods, such as GET, POST, PUT and DELETE). This lack of support of the RESTful modeling prevents the approaches to have a concise and compact binding between functional and non-functional aspects. (v) They do not have enough expressiveness to model limitations such as quotas and rates, for each resource and method and with complete management of temporally (static/sliding time windows and periodicity) present in the typical industrial API SLAs. (vi) Most proposals are designed to model a single offering and they mostly lack support to modeling hierarchical models or overriding properties and metrics (F4); in such a context, they cannot model a set of tiers or plans that yield a complex offering that maintains the coherence by model and instead they rely on a manual process that is typically error-prone. (vii) finally, the ecosystem of tools proposed in each approach (in the case of its existence) is extremely limited and that aims to be solely as a prototype; moreover, they apparently are not integrated into a developer community nor there is evidence of this usage by practitioners in the industry.

In order to overcome the limitations of existing approaches, the main goals of this paper can be summarized as follows: (i) An interoperable model fully-integrated with leading API description language (OAS) to express the API limitations. (ii) an initial ecosystem of tools to provide support to different parts of the SLA-Driven API development lifecycle. (iii) validation of this model in real-world scenarios to assess its expressiveness.

3 OAS in a Nutshell

In this section, we briefly present the OpenAPI Specification (OAS), considering its goals, structure and extension capabilities. OAS, formerly known as Swagger, is a vendor-neutral, portable and open specification for the functional deception of APIs. It is promoted by the OpenAPI Initiative (OAI), an open source consortium hosted by The Linux Foundation and supported by a growing number of leading industry stakeholders, such as Google, IBM, Microsoft or

Oracle, amongst others. Both API clients and vendors are able to benefit from the formal definition using the OAS: from the clients' point of view, they can use any tool from the extensive ecosystem created around the OAI; conversely, from the vendors' point of view, they can generate interactive documentation portals, create auto-generated prototypes and perform automatic API monitoring and testing. Specifically, as a minimum content, an OAS document should describe a set of aspects including *API general information* (such as title, description and version), a list of *Resources*, *Paths* and *Methods* allowed, and set of *Schemas* (following the JSON-schema specification) to identify the structure of the data to be exchanged with the API (e.g., a resource structure). In order to have a more concise description, it is possible to reuse definitions of schemes by means of the *$ref* constructor as proposed in the JSON-schema standard. Complementary, API provider can include optional elements such as the different *API endpoints*, where the API can be accessed. This is especially useful in scenarios with different endpoints for development and production stages.

```
1   openapi: 3.0.0
2   info:
3    title: Simple petstore API
4    description: ...
5    version: ...
6    x-sla: ./pets-plans.yaml
7   servers:
8   - url: ....
9   paths:
10   /pets:
11    get:
12     description: ...
13     parameters: ..
14     responses:
15      200:
16       description: pet response
17       content:
18        application/json:
19         schema:
20          $ref: "#/components/schemas/pet"
21    post:
22     ...
23   components:
24    schemas:
25     pet:
26      title: pet model
27      ...
```

Listing 1.1. RESTful API in OAS

```
1   context:
2    id: plans
3    sla: '1.0'
4    type: plans
5    ...
6   infrastructure: ...
7   metrics:
8    requests:
9     type: integer
10    format: int64
11    description: #requests
12    resolution: consumption
13  ...
14  plans:
15   free:
16    pricing:
17     cost: 0
18     currency: USD
19     billing: monthly
20    quotas:
21     /pets:
22      post:
23       requests:
24        - max: 100
25         period: daily
26    rates:
27     /pets:
28      get:
29       requests:
30        - max: 2
31         period: secondly
32         scope: tenant
33   pro:
34    ...
```

Listing 1.2. SLA written in SLA4OAI

As an example, Listing 1.1 shows an OAS fragment from a basic RESTful API that corresponds with a single endpoint (*/pets*) and two methods. Lines 9–22 describe the definition of the *pet* resource including the *GET* and *POST* methods for retrieving and creating resources; specifically, line 11 starts modeling the *GET* method with a *description* and the *parameters* that the request might be able to handle and *responses* section (lines 14–20) describe the model of a successful HTTP response (i.e., status code *200*) returning a *pet* resource conforming with the appropriate schema reference (line 20). Finally, in lines 24–27, the data model (schema) of the pet object is being defined. A key feature of the OAS is the capability of being extended with the definition of custom properties starting with *x-*, paving the way for customizing or adding additional features according to specific business needs. As an example, line 6 shows the use of the *x-* extension point to include a reference to the SLA description of the API following our proposal (c.f., Sect. 4).

4 Our Proposal

4.1 SLA4OAI Language

SLA4OAI[3] is a language which provides a model for describing SLA in APIs in a vendor-neutral way by means of extending the main specification. This proposal is open for evolution based on the discussion with the community and other partners of the OpenAPI Initiative, hosted by the Linux Foundation. For the sake of completeness, always refer to the online version so as to have a complete reference of the language.

The figure available online[4] depicts an abstract syntax of an SLA4OAI description. Starting with the top-level placeholder (denoted as *SLA4OAI Document* in the figure) we can describe basic information about the *context*, the *infrastructure* endpoints that implement the Basic SLA Management Service, the *metrics* and a default value for *quotas, rates, guarantees* and *pricing*.

Context contains general information, such as the *id*, the *version*, the URL pointing to the *api* OAS document, the *type* and the *validity* of the document; in this context, the *type* field can be either *plans* or *instance* and it indicates whether the document corresponds with the general plan offering or it correspond with a specific SLA agreed with a given customer. The *Metrics* enables the definition of custom metrics which will be used to define the limitations, such as the number of requests, or the bandwidth used per request. For each metric, the *type, format, unit, description*, and *resolution* should be defined. The *Plan configuration* (configuration parameters for the service tailored for the plan), availability (availability of the service for this plan expressed via time slots using the ISO 8601 time intervals format), and the rest of the elements that will override the default with plan-specific values: quotas, rates and guarantees, pricing. In this context, it is important to highlight that the *Plan* section maps the structure in the OAS document to attach the specific limitations (quotas or rates) for each path and method. Specifically, after defining the *configuration*, the *availability, pricing, guarantees*, the limitations *quotas* and *rates* can be modeled; particularly, the limitations are described in the *Limit* with a *max* value

---

[3] https://sla4oai.specs.governify.io.

[4] https://isa-group.github.io/2019-05-sla4oai/files/sla4oai_diagram.png.

that can be accepted, a *period* (i.e., secondly, minutely, hourly, daily, monthly or yearly) and the *scope* where they should be enforced; as an extensible scope model, we propose two possible initial values (*tenant* or *account* as default) corresponding with a two-level structure: a limitation or guarantee with a tenant scope will be applicable to the whole organization while an account scope would be applicable to each specific user or account (typically with a different API key) in the organization.

Considering the features of the existing SLA proposals previously analyzed and available in the online appendix, SLA4OAI is a proposal serialized using the YAML/JSON syntax (F1) specifically designed for web services (F2), concretely, RESTful APIs. It is able to model one or more offerings (F3) in a hierarchical model (F4) since *plans* can override the default values for the limitations. Furthermore, our proposal takes into account the temporality (F5), since each limitation is scoped to a precise period of time and each plan has its own *availability* information. Finally, as stated in following sections, SLA4OAI has a set of tools for assisting users to write the model (F6) and an initial ecosystem of tools to support parts of the development lifecycle (F7).

Let us consider the aforementioned example (as modeled in Listing 1.1) to be extended with a basic SLA: as a provider, it would be useful to limit, on the one hand, the number of requests a consumer is allowed to make in a static window (quota) of 1 day depending on the plan purchased and, on the other hand, the requests allowed to be made in a sliding window (rate), differing from GET and POST methods to avoid the API saturation derived from abusive customers. Specifically, Listing 1.2 illustrates the model in SLA4OAI of the limitations of this example API: in lines 14–34 the *free* and *pro* plans are being modeled. Focusing on the first, line 15 define a specific *plan* by its limitations *quotas* (lines 20–25) and *rates* (lines 26–32). For instance, a quota of 100 POST requests over the resource */pets* in a static window of 1 day is defined in lines 23–25. Conversely, a rate of 2 requests per second is defined for */pets* GET requests (lines 29–32). Finally, note that line 4 indicates that this document is for describing *plans*. Whenever a client accepts a specific plan, *type* field would become an *instance* one. It is interesting to highlight the *scope: tenant* (line 32) in the rates for the GET request represents a limitation for the whole consumer organization affecting all the accounts of the organization, while the rest of the quotas and rates are enforced on a default per-account basis.

4.2   SLA-Driven API Development Lifecycle

In spite of the fact that each organization could address the API development lifecycle with slightly different approaches, a minimal set of activities can be identified: a first activity corresponds with the actual *Functional Development* of the API implementing and testing the logic; next a *Deployment* activity where the developed artifact is configured to be executed in a given infrastructure; finally, once the API is up and running, an *Operation* activity starts where the requests from consumers can be accepted. This process is a simplification that can be evolved to add intermediate steps (such as testing) or to include an evolutive cycle where different versions are deployed progressively. In order to incorporate SLAs in this process, we expand this basic lifecycle where both API Provider and API Consumer can interact (as depicted in Fig. 1).

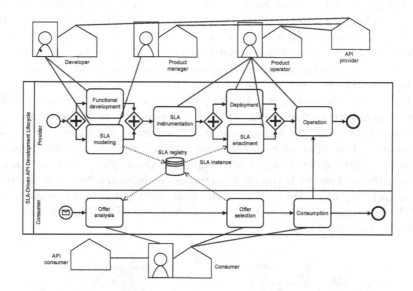

Fig. 1. SLA-Driven API development lifecycle

Specifically, from the provider's perspective, the *Functional Development* can be developed in parallel with a *SLA modelling* where the actual SLA offering (type *plans*) is written and stored in a given *SLA Registry*. Once both the functional development and the SLA modeling has concluded, the *SLA instrumentation* must be carried out, where the tools and/or developed artifacts are parameterized so they can adjust their behavior depending on a concrete SLA and provide the appropriate metrics to analyze the SLA status. Next, while the *deployment* of the API takes place, a parallel activity of *SLA enactment* is developed where the deployment infrastructure should be configured in order to be able to enforce the SLA before the API reaches the *operation* activity.

Complementary, from consumer's perspective, once the provider has published the SLA offering (i.e., *Plans*) in the *SLA Registry*, it starts the *offer analysis* to select the most appropriate option (*offer selection* activity) and to create and register its actual SLA (type *instance*); finally, the API *Consumption* is carried out as long as the API is the *Operation* activity and its regulated based on the terms (such as quotas or rates) defined in the SLA.

In order to implement this lifecycle, it is important to highlight that the *SLA instrumentation*, *SLA enactment* and *Operation* activities should be supported by an SLA enforcement protocol that aims to define the interactions for *checking* if the consumption of the API for a given consumer is allowed (e.g., it meets the limitations specified in its SLA) and to gather the actual values of the *metrics* from the different deployed artifacts that implement the API.

4.3   Basic SLA Management Service

The *Basic SLA Management Service* (BSMS) is a basic non-normative API description to provide basic support for the SLA enforcing protocol as motivated in the SLA-Driven API development lifecycle (c.f., Sect. 4.2) and addresses the following features: (i) Checking the current state of a given SLA (SLA Check). (ii) Reporting metrics to calculate the current state of a given SLA (SLA Metrics). To this end, this BSMS proposal represents a descriptive interface that could be implemented in different technologies and acts as a decoupling mechanism to the underlying infrastructure that actually provides support to the development lifecycle.

Moreover, the definition of a BSMS paves the way to define multiple SLA enforcing architectures that could be selected depending on the performance or technological constraints of a given scenario. Specifically, Figs. 2 and 3 represent an overview of two different SLA enforcing architectures: on the one hand, the *Standalone* enforcing define an SLA instrumentation as part of the API with a direct communication with the SLA management infrastructure; on the other hand, a *Gateway* enforcing relays on the front load balancer to connect with the SLA management infrastructure so a potential set of API instances do only provide the functional logic.

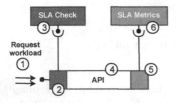 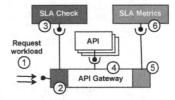

Fig. 2. Standalone SLA enforcing arch.   **Fig. 3.** Gateway SLA enforcing arch.

In order to illustrate the interactions and behavior of each component implementing (or interacting with) the BSMS, we will focus on the *Gateway* enforcing architecture (See Fig. 3) as it is a more complete scenario:

1. Requests will pass through the API Gateway until they are directed to the node that will serve it (step 1).
2. The API Gateway query the SLA Check component to determine if the request is authorized to develop the actual operation based on the appropriate SLA (step 2).
   (a) If it is authorized, the actual API is invoked and the response is returned (step 3).
   (b) If it is not authorized, a status code and a summary of the reason (as generated by the SLA check component) is returned (step 3).
3. After the consumption ends (step 4), the metrics are sent to the SLA Metrics component (step 5). This component is in charge of updating the status of the agreement with the new metrics introduced (step 6). This new information

could be processed to determine the SLA state that should be taken into account in further requests.

In the following subsections, we overview the interface and the expected behavior of the SLA Check and SLA Monitor components; a complete description of the proposed API is available online[5].

SLA Check. This component should support the verification process to decide whether an API request can be satisfied based on the current state of its SLA. In particular, it should provide two different endpoints:

- A query (*GET*) operation over the */tenants* path in order to locate the SLA scope and the SLA id that should regulate the consumption based on a given token (typically an API key sent by the consumer as a query or header parameter). The SLA scope should determine the actual tenant (the consumer organization that has signed the SLA) and the account (that belongs to the consumer organization).
- A verification (*POST*) operation over the */check* path in order verify whether a specific request can be done; specifically, it will respond true or false to notify the provider if it is: (i) Acceptable to fulfill the request (positive case), or on the contrary; (ii) Not acceptable and then, the request should be denied (negative case); in such a case, it could include optional information describing the reason for the SLA violation. Concerning the HTTP status code, in a general case, a negative response should correspond with standard *403 Forbidden*; if the denial reason is rate/quota limit enforcement, then the recommendation is to use *429 Too Many Requests* and include rate limit information as metadata into the consumer response to explain the denial of service: as an example it could include the actual metric computation, the limit or a future timestamp when the rate/quota will be reset for the given consumer.

It is important to note that, while a complete interaction with the SLA Check component involves the invocation to both endpoints, in demanding scenarios, a local API key cache can be introduced in order to avoid the first query over the */tenants* path.

SLA Metrics. This component should implement a mechanism for metric gathering in order to support the analysis of SLA fulfillment. In particular, it should provide a storage (*POST*) operation over the */metric* path in order to register a certain metric. In addition to the actual metric value, as mandatory elements, it should also include information about the metric context including the *SLA Scope*, the *SLA Id* and the *sender* (i.e., the specific API instance or API Gateway generating the metric).

The metrics can correspond with a standard set of well-defined domain-independent metrics such as *request count* or *response time*, or domain-dependent metrics such as a certain payload attribute (e.g., the size of a specific parameter).

---

[5] https://sla4oai.specs.governify.io/operationalServices.html.

Since metrics flow could be dense in the same scenarios a buffering can be introduced; to this respect, the SLA Metric component should allow reception of multiple metrics values in a single operation. Consequently, metrics can be grouped in batches or sent one by one to fine-tune performance versus real-time SLA tracking in each scenario.

5   Tool Support

The SLA-Driven API development lifecycle, depicted in Fig. 1 and explained in Sect. 4.2, should be assisted by a set of tools during certain activities. Since we seek to provide a fully-fledged language, we provide an initial working implementation of these tools [4]. Specifically, for the *SLA modeling* activity we present the *SLA Editor* for hiding the complexity of the language to the end user. The concrete implementation of the *SLA instrumentation* activity is provided in the *SLA Engine*, an implementation of the *Basic SLA Management Service*, defining the */metrics* and */check* endpoints. On the one hand, for the *Standalone* SLA enforcing architecture, we support the *SLA instrumentation* and *SLA enactment* activities with the *SLA Instrumentation Library* in a Node.js module; on the other hand, for the *Gateway* SLA enforcing architecture, a complete *SLA-Driven API Gateway* is provided as a service.

SLA Editor. In modeling tasks, supporting tools are commonly provided to the users. In this scenario, we provide the *SLA editor*[6], for the *SLA modeling* activity in the SLA-Driven API development lifecycle. *SLA editor* is a user-friendly and web-based text editor specifically developed for assisting the user during the modeling tasks, including auto-completion, syntax checking, and automatic binding. It is possible to create plans (e.g., free and pro) with quotas and rates. Clicking on the + sign, the user is able to select the path and method (previously defined in the OAS document) for entering the value of the limitation. Note that custom metrics can also be defined at the bottom, however, the calculation logic is left open for a specific implementation.

SLA Engine. Whereas the BSMS (c.f., Sect. 4.3 defines the interaction flows and the endpoints */check* and */metric*, a reference implementation should be provided in order to properly carry out the *SLA instrumentation* activity in the SLA-Driven API development lifecycle. The *SLA Engine*, thus, provides a concrete implementation which also includes a particular way to handle SLA saving/retrieving tasks. Specifically, *Monitor*[7] is an implementation of the *Metrics* BSMS service and *Supervisor*[8], of the *Check* service.

The *Monitor* service exposes a POST operation in the route */metrics* for gathering the metrics collected from other different services. It can collect a

---

[6] https://designer.governify.io.
[7] http://monitor.oai.governify.io/api/v1/docs.
[8] http://supervisor.oai.governify.io/api/v1/docs.

set of basic metrics and send them to a data store for aggregation and later consumption. The metrics can be grouped in batches or sent one by one to fine-tune performance versus real-time SLA tracking.

The *Supervisor* service has a POST */check* endpoint for the verification of the current state of the SLA for a given operation in a certain scope. For each request, this service will evaluate the state of the SLA and will respond with a positive or negative response depending on whether a limitation has been overcome. In addition, this service also implements (outside the scope of the BSMS) these additional endpoints: GET/POST */tenants*, GET/POST */slas* and PUT/DELETE *slas/<id>* for managing both users (tenants and accounts) and SLA4OAI documents themselves.

SLA Instrumentation Library. Despite the fact that the BSMS defines the interaction flows between the endpoints, the concrete implementation of these interactions is left open for the activities of *SLA instrumentation* and *SLA enactment* of the SLA-Driven API development lifecycle. The tool that we present aims to cover this lack in the *Standalone* SLA enforcing architectures. Specifically, we present an SLA Instrumentation Library for Node.js[9], which is a middleware (i.e., a filter that intercepts the HTTP requests and perform transformation if necessary) written for Express, the most used Node.js web application framework. This middleware intercepts all the inbound/outbound traffic to perform the BSMS flow.

Specifically, *Monitor* is an implementation of the *Metrics* BSMS service and *Supervisor*, of the *Check* service, as explained in the SLA Engine section.

Once the API uses the SLA Instrumentation Library, a new endpoint */plans* is added. It creates a provisioning portal for clients to purchase a plan. Once the customer purchases (or simply selects, in case of the free ones) a plan, this customer will get an API-key, acting as a bearer token for HTTP authentication.

SLA-Driven API Gateway. A more transparent way to implement the interaction flows defined is the BSMS is achieved by using an *SLA-Driven API Gateway*[10]. We provide an open-source implementation for deploying SLA-Driven API Gateways using any *SLA Engine* and supporting the *SLA instrumentation* and *SLA enactment* activities of the SLA-Driven API development lifecycle in a *Gateway* SLA enforcing architecture.

Particularly, we provide as a service, an online preconfigured instance (using the aforementioned SLA Instrumentation Library) of an SLA-Driven API Gateway. API providers are only required to enter: (i) The real endpoint of their API; (ii) A URL pointing to the SLA4OAI document. Once an API is registered, the SLA-Driven API Gateway exposes a public and SLA-regulated endpoint, as well as the */plans* endpoint for the provisioning portal. Clients who have selected a plan will get an API-key from the portal that will be as a bearer token to consume the SLA-regulated API.

---

[9]   https://www.npmjs.com/package/sla4oai-tools.
[10]   https://gateway.oai.governify.io.

6   Validation

In this section, we describe how we have evaluated our proposal. In particular, the goal of the evaluation was to answer the following research questions:

RQ1: How expressive is our SLA4OAI model in comparison to real-world APIs' SLAs We want to know whether the SLA4OAI model that we use is expressive enough to model a wide variety of real-world SLAs and which are the characteristics of the SLAs that we are not able to express.

RQ2: Which difficulties appear when modeling SLAs defined are expressed in natural language? All real-world APIs' SLAs are expressed in natural language. Therefore, before checking their limitations, it is necessary to formalize them. With this question, we examine the problems that may appear in this step.

RQ3: What is the reception of our SLA4OAI model and tools in the community? Besides this proposal has not been officially published, it is publicly available in our code and artifact repositories (such as NPM). We wonder whether our proposal is being used by a set of external users and how large this set is.

RQ1: Expressiveness of SLA4OAI. To evaluate the expressiveness of the SLA4OAI proposal, we have modeled the limitations of a set of APIs. For selecting this set we considered the work of [3], where the authors analyzed a set of 69 APIs from two of the largest API directories, Mashape (now integrated into RapidAPI) and ProgrammableWeb, studying 27 and 41 respectively.

For our evaluation, we have manually selected a subset of these APIs, giving, as a result, a number of 35 APIs whose modeling using SLA4OAI is challenging (i.e., the 27 ones from RapidAPI have the same expressiveness, as the authors noted). Specifically, have modeled 5488 limitations (quotas/rates) over 7055 combinations of metrics (e.g., number of requests) and periods (e.g., secondly, monthly) in 148 plans of 35 real-world APIs. We provide a workspace[11] with the 35 modeled APIs and the statistical analysis that we have performed. Focusing on these limitations, the quotas use to be defined over custom metrics based on their business logic (e.g., credits spent by request, the number of returned results or the storage consumed). On the other hand, rates are mostly defined over the number of requests. In both cases, APIs usually define their limitations over one or two different metrics. Finally, regarding the periods, both limitations are usually over just one period: *monthly* for quotas, and *secondly* for rates.

RQ2: Modeling Issues. During the modeling process we have noticed a few issues, namely: (i) When an overage exists (i.e., one can overcome the limitation value by paying an extra amount of money per request), the quotas are *soft*, that is, the service is still accessible, but this situation should be taken into account. (ii) Sometimes plans in real APIs are the result of an aggregation of other plans. For instance, one can buy a *base plan* with N requests/s, but, purchasing an upgrade, it is possible to reach the N+1 requests/s. (iii) Using

---

[11] https://isa-group.github.io/2019-05-sla4oai.

more than one period for limitations. For instance, (1000 requests/month and 100 requests/week). Despite the fact that it is supported in SLA4OAI, it is not present in the current reference implementation. (iv) Some limitations use a custom period by means of defining the amount and unit, for example, every 5 min, every 2.5 months, etc. (v) In a few APIs, especially for trial plans, *forever* periods are often used.

RQ3: SLA4OAI Interest in the Community. Despite the SLA4OAI extension and tools have not been widely announced nor promoted, we have disclosed the tooling ecosystem into the main public NodeJS artifact repository (i.e., NPM) and this platform provides a set of analytics, refering to individual installations[12], of the usage since it was published. Specifically, based on its data, it is observed that the SLA Instrumentation Library has been downloaded and installed more than 600 times[13] while the SLA Engine was downloaded more installed than 1900 times. Furthermore, several industry members of the Open API Initiative (including Google or PayPal) have expressed their interest in this proposal and to promote a working group for evolving and extending the SLA4OAI proposal [5].

7   Conclusions

The current *de facto* standard for modeling functional aspects of RESTful APIs, the OpenAPI Specification, ignore crucial non-functional information for an API such as its Service Level Agreement (SLA). This lack of a standard to define the non-functional aspects leads to vendor lock-in and it prevents the open tool ecosystem to grow and handle extra functional aspects. In this paper, we pioneer in extending OAS to define a specific model for SLAs description and we provide an initial set of open-source tools that leverage the pre-existing OAI ecosystem in order to automate some stages of the SLA-Driven API lifecycle. Our proposal has been validated in terms of expressivity in 35 real-world APIs and, in spite of the lack of promotion, the initial metrics of usage of the tools proof an interest from the industry.

As future work, the modeling issues identified in Sect. 6 spot the potential improvements of SLA4OAI specification and the ecosystem of tools, namely: (i) Incorporate the concept of *hard/soft* limitation types. (ii) Add the definition of custom periods, rather than limiting them to a fixed set of values. (iii) Design a process for creating composite plans on the top of simpler ones. (iv) Improve the reference implementation of the tools to support more than one period in each limitation. From a community perspective, based on the interest received in the industry, we are in the process of creating an official working group for the industrial members in OAI to incorporate more feedback from the industry and

---

[12] Details about how this calculation is being made is available at http://bit.ly/npm-calculation.

[13] https://npm-stat.com/charts.html?package=sla4oai-tools.

define a coordinated mechanism of evolution for future versions of the current SLA4OAI proposal.

References

1. Acharya, M., Xie, T., Pei, J., Xu, J.: Mining API patterns as partial orders from source code. In: ESEC-FSE 2007, p. 25. ACM Press, New York (2007)
2. Andrieux, A., et al.: Web Services Agreement Specification (WS-Agreement) (2004)
3. Gamez-Diaz, A., Fernandez, P., Ruiz-Cortes, A.: An analysis of RESTful APIs offerings in the industry. In: Maximilien, M., Vallecillo, A., Wang, J., Oriol, M. (eds.) ICSOC 2017. LNCS, vol. 10601, pp. 589–604. Springer, Cham (2017). https://doi.org/10.1007/978-3-319-69035-3_43
4. Gamez-Diaz, A., Fernandez, P., Ruiz-Cortes, A.: Governify for APIs: SLA-Driven ecosystem for API governance. In: ESEC-FSE 2019. ESEC/FSE 2019, Tallin, Estonia. ACM (2019)
5. Gamez-Diaz, A., et al.: The role of limitations and SLAs in the API industry. In: ESEC-FSE 2019. ESEC/FSE 2019, Tallin, Estonia. ACM (2019)
6. Garcia, J.M., Fernandez, P., Pedrinaci, C., Resinas, M., Cardoso, J., Ruiz-Cortes, A.: Modeling service level agreements with linked USDL agreement. IEEE TSC 10(1), 52–65 (2017)
7. Harms, H., Rogowski, C., Lo Iacono, L.: Guidelines for adopting frontend architectures and patterns in microservices-based systems. In: Proceedings of the 2017 11th Joint Meeting on Foundations of Software Engineering, pp. 902–907 (2017)
8. Kearney, K.T., Torelli, F., Kotsokalis, C.: SLA*: an abstract syntax for service level agreements. In: GRID, pp. 217–224. IEEE, October 2010
9. Kouki, Y., Alvares de Oliveira, F., Dupont, S., Ledoux, T.: A language support for cloud elasticity management. In: CCGrid 2014, pp. 206–215. IEEE, May 2014
10. Lamanna, D.D., Skene, J., Emmerich, W.: SLAng: a language for defining service level agreements. In: FTDCS, pp. 100–106, January 2003
11. Ludwig, H., Keller, A., Dan, A., King, R.: A service level agreement language for dynamic electronic services. In: WECWIS 2002, pp. 25–32. IEEE Computer Society (2002)
12. Martin-Lopez, A., Segura, S., Ruiz-Cortes, A.: A catalogue of inter-parameter dependencies in restful web APIs. In: Yangui, S., et al. (eds.) ICSOC 2019. LNCS, vol. 11895, pp. 399–414. Springer, Cham (2019)
13. Muller, C., Gutierrez Fernandez, A.M., Fernandez, P., Martin-Diaz, O., Resinas, M., Ruiz-Cortes, A.: Automated validation of compensable SLAs. IEEE TSC, 1 (2018)
14. Neumann, A., Laranjeiro, N., Bernardino, J.: An analysis of public REST web service APIs. IEEE TSC, 1 (2018)
15. Nguyen, T.N., et al.: Complementing global and local contexts in representing API descriptions to improve API retrieval tasks. In: ESEC/FSE 2018, pp. 551–562. ACM Press, New York (2018)
16. Reinhardt, A., Zhang, T., Mathur, M., Kim, M.: Augmenting stack overflow with API usage patterns mined from GitHub. In: ESEC/FSE 2018, pp. 880–883 (2018)
17. Tata, S., Mohamed, M., Sakairi, T., Mandagere, N., Anya, O., Ludwiga, H.: RSLA: a service level agreement language for cloud services. In: CLOUD, pp. 415–422, June 2017

18. Thomas Fielding, R.: Architectural styles and the design of network-based software architectures. Ph.D. thesis, University of California, Irvine (2000)
19. Uriarte, R.B., Tiezzi, F., De Nicola, R.: SLAC: a formal service-level-agreement language for cloud computing. In: UCC, pp. 419–426. IEEE, December 2014

On Observability and Monitoring of Distributed Systems – An Industry Interview Study

Sina Niedermaier[1], Falko Koetter[2](✉), Andreas Freymann[2],
and Stefan Wagner[1]

[1] Institute of Software Technology, University of Stuttgart, Stuttgart, Germany
{sina.niedermaier,stefan.wagner}@iste.uni-stuttgart.de
[2] Fraunhofer Institute for Industrial Engineering IAO, Fraunhofer IAO,
Stuttgart, Germany
{falko.koetter,andreas.freymann}@iao.fraunhofer.de

Abstract. Business success of companies heavily depends on the availability and performance of their client applications. Due to modern development paradigms such as DevOps and microservice architectural styles, applications are decoupled into services with complex interactions and dependencies. Although these paradigms enable individual development cycles with reduced delivery times, they cause several challenges to manage the services in distributed systems. One major challenge is to observe and monitor such distributed systems. This paper provides a qualitative study to understand the challenges and good practices in the field of observability and monitoring of distributed systems. In 28 semi-structured interviews with software professionals we discovered increasing complexity and dynamics in that field. Especially observability becomes an essential prerequisite to ensure stable services and further development of client applications. However, the participants mentioned a discrepancy in the awareness regarding the importance of the topic, both from the management as well as from the developer perspective. Besides technical challenges, we identified a strong need for an organizational concept including strategy, roles and responsibilities. Our results support practitioners in developing and implementing systematic observability and monitoring for distributed systems.

Keywords: Monitoring · Observability · Distributed systems · Cloud · Industry

1 Introduction

In recent years, many IT departments have successfully migrated their services to cloud computing [21]. Still, challenges for cloud adoption remain regarding the operation and holistic monitoring of such services [16]. While conventional IT infrastructure can be monitored with conventional monitoring solutions, cloud environments are more dynamic and complex [1], resulting in a gap [12] between the complexity of distributed systems and the capability of monitoring tools to manage that complexity.

© Springer Nature Switzerland AG 2019
S. Yangui et al. (Eds.): ICSOC 2019, LNCS 11895, pp. 36–52, 2019.
https://doi.org/10.1007/978-3-030-33702-5_3

Emerging trends like Internet of Things (IoT) and microservices further increase the complexity, making monitoring a significant barrier for adoption of these technologies [13].

While newly emerged software tools try to bridge this complexity gap, the way forward for many companies is unclear. We found that there is no research matching new solutions and technologies to different application areas, problems and challenges. While a plethora of new technologies and approaches exists, companies need to be able to relate these technologies to the challenges they face. Processes and good practices are necessary to incorporate new solutions into existing enterprise architectures as well as emerging cloud architectures.

To address this need, we conducted an industry interview study among different stakeholders involved in monitoring, including service managers, DevOps engineers, software providers, and consultants. From the semi-structured interviews, we extracted contemporary challenges, requirements, and solutions.

2   Related Work

To provide context to the survey described in this work, the related work investigates (1) current approaches to bridging the gap between distributed system complexity and monitoring capability as well as (2) preceding surveys regarding monitoring and observability (see Fig. 1).

IEEE defines *monitoring* as the supervising, recording, analyzing or verifying the operation of a system or component [10].

The term *Observability* originates in control system theory and measures the degree to which a system's internal state can be determined from its output [7]. In cloud environments, observability indicates to what degree infrastructure and applications and their interactions can be monitored. Outputs used are for example logs, metrics and traces [18].

Yang et al. [24] investigate the capturing of service execution paths in distributed systems. While capturing the execution path is challenging, as each request may cross many components of several servers, they introduce a generic end-to-end methodology to capture the entire request. During our interviews we found a need for transparency of execution paths as well as more generally interdependencies between services.

The current trend towards more flexible and modular distributed systems is characterized by using independent services, such as micro- or web services. While systems consisting of web services provide better observability than monolithic systems, services have the potential to enhance their observability and monitoring by giving relevant information about their internal behaviour. Sun et al. [23] deal with the challenge that web service definitions do not have any information about their behaviour. They extend the web service definition by adding a behaviour logic description based on a constraint-based model-driven testing approach. During our interviews we identified that the behaviour especially of third-party services needs to be more clearly communicated to assess the impact on service levels and to detect and diagnose faults.

Besides monitoring individual service calls, it is important to predict the runtime performance of distributed systems. Johng et al. [11] show that two techniques, benchmarking and simulation, have shortcomings if they are used separately and introduce and validate a complementary approach. Their approach presents a process which maps benchmark ontologies of simulations. This prove to be inexpensive, fast and reliable. Similarly, Lin et al. [14] propose a novel way of root cause detection in microservice architectures utilizing causal graphs. In our interviews we found that performance is often only known when a system goes live, as the interdependencies between different services and their individual performance are not assessed beforehand.

Gupta et al. [8] addresses runtime monitoring on continuous deployment in software development as a crucial task, especially in rapidly changing software solutions. While current runtime monitoring approaches of previous and newly deployed versions lack in capturing and monitoring differences at runtime, they present an approach which automatically discovers an execution behaviour model by mining execution logs. Approaches like this that gather information automatically instead of necessitating manual definition are crucial with growing complexity and dynamics of distributed systems.

These works show that for research on closing the complexity gap between cloud environments and their monitoring is ongoing. However, these solutions are not yet widely adopted in practice. When adopting new technology to industry application, non-functional requirements such as usability, configurability and adaptability increase in importance.

In the following preceding surveys in the context of monitoring and observability (2) are described.

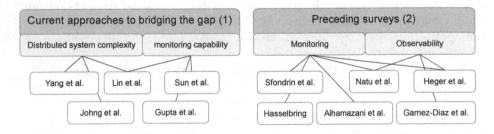

Fig. 1. Overview on the related work

Aceto et al. [1] conducted a comprehensive cloud monitoring survey in 2013, detailing motivations, then-current tool support and open challenges. They identified the need for scalability, robustness and flexibility. The survey correctly predicted the rise in complexity and dynamics of cloud architectures and propose actions to handle these such as root-cause-detection, filtering/summarizing of data, and cross-layer/cross-platform monitoring. Similarly, another early survey of cloud monitoring tools by Fatema et al. [5] identifies capabilities such as scalability, robustness, interoperability and customizability to find a gap between necessary capabilities and existing tools.

Sfondrin et al. [21] conducted a survey of 62 multinational companies on public cloud adoption. While use of public cloud infrastructure is on the rise, barriers like security, regulatory compliance, and monitoring remain. Regarding monitoring, the survey has shown that half of the companies rely solely on their cloud providers' monitoring dashboard. Participants noted a crucial need for quality of service monitoring integrated with their monitoring tool.

Similarly, Knoche and Hasselbring [13] conducted a survey of German experts on microservice adoption. Drivers for microservice adoption are scalability, maintainability and development speed. On the other hand, barriers to adoption are mainly operational in nature. Operations department resist microservices due to the change in their tasks. On the technical level, running distributed applications prone to partial failures and monitoring them is a significant challenge.

Gamez-Diaz et al. [6] performed an analysis of RestFUL APIs of cloud providers, identifying requirements for API governance and noting a lack of standardization.

While not an empirical study, Natu et al. [16] show monitoring challenges of holistic cloud applications. Scale and complexity of applications is identified as a main challenge. Related to observability, incomplete and inaccurate views of the total system as well as fault localization are other identified challenges.

Heger et al. [9] give an overview of the state-of-the-art in application performance monitoring (APM), describing typical capabilities and available APM software. They found APM to be a solution to monitoring and analyzing cloud environments, but note future challenges in root cause detection, setup effort and interoperability. APM cannot be understood as a purely technical topic anymore but needs to incorporate business and organizational aspects as well.

Alhamazani et al. [2] give an insight into commercial cloud monitoring tools, showing state-of-the-art features, identifying shortcomings and, connected with that, future areas of research. Information aggregation across different layers of abstraction, a broad range of measurable metrics and extensibility are seen as critical success factors. Tools were found to be lacking in standardization regarding monitoring processes and metrics.

Comparing preceding surveys regarding monitoring and observability (2) to our work, these surveys focus either on drivers and challenges or on available solutions (in science and commercial tools). In comparison, our study takes a holistic approach. We provide empirical industry-focused research with in-depth interviews, where we combine different perspectives in order to find out which emerging solutions and strategies are used by companies and to what degree they overcome the existing challenges. This is necessary to gauge the adoption of new technologies in practice. Moreover, it comprises which challenges these technologies address and which challenges emerge in adoption or are unsolved.

3   Scope and Research Method

Study Design: To structure our research, we applied the five-step case study research process as described by Runeson and Hoest [19]. Our research objective can be defined as follows: *Analysis of the contemporary challenges of monitoring and operating distributed systems for the purpose of deducting requirements and mapping existing solutions and strategies from the viewpoint of different stakeholders of monitoring systems and tool providers.* Table 1 summarizes the research questions:

Table 1. Overview of the research questions

RQ1	Which contemporary challenges exist in monitoring distributed systems?
RQ2	Which requirements do stakeholders have for a monitoring and observability concept for distributed systems?
RQ3	What are technical and organizational strategies and solutions in companies?

To answer our research questions, we applied the qualitative method of semi-structured interviews. They allow us to explore the individual challenges stated by the participants and to analyze the underlying relations by providing a basic agenda. At the same time, interviews enable dynamic interaction based on the background of our experts and their responses [22].

In total, we conducted 28 semi-structured interviews of 45 min on average. The interviews were completed between February and April 2019. To achieve a balanced distribution of interviewees, first, we considered users using monitoring solutions and tool providers offering monitoring solutions (see Table 2). Second, we ensured that solution providers and users are related to different domains and focus to get diverse perspectives of monitoring solutions. Apart from the tool providers, we covered further domains such as software and IT service, IoT, telecommunication, insurance, and IT consulting. The users have been selected from different points of view in the application stack and different roles like DevOps and support engineers along with product owners and managers. The recruiting of participants was achieved by personal industry contacts as well as by acquisition on developer conferences.

Preparation for Data Collection: To conduct the semi-structured interviews, we created an interview guide [17]. The guide is structured in different thematic blocks to group the individual questions. The interviewees were pre-informed about scope and procedure of the interviews. Besides the information to treat their transcripts as confidential, we asked to record the interviews to create transcripts if permitted. Moreover we informed them about the possibility to review their transcript to assent to the information given in the interview.

Data Collection: From the 28 interviews, 15 were conducted 'face to face' and 13 via remote communication. The interviews were held in German, except for two interviews in English. While 21 interviews have been audio recorded, for the remaining interviews two researchers created protocols to reduce researcher bias. During the interviews, we loosely followed the interview guide accordingly

Table 2. Overview about participants and companies

CID	Domain	Staff	EID	Expert role	Focus
C1	IoT	>100T	E1	Product Owner	APM Solution
			E2	Lead Architect	Cloud Infrastructure
			E3	Product Owner	Connectivity Backend
			E4	Service Manager	Support and Operation of IoT Solution
			E5	Cloud Architect	IoT Backend
C2	IoT	100-1T	E6	IoT Consultant/Architect	Consulting of IoT Projects
			E7	Open Source Developer	Cloud Service
			E8	DevOps Engineer	Cloud Service
			E9	DevOps Architect	Cloud Service
			E10	Product Owner	Cloud Service
			E11	Project Lead	IoT Project
C3	IoT	10T-100T	E12	Manager	IoT Platform
C4	IoT	10T-100T	E13	IoT Solution Owner	Cloud Service
C5	Telecom	10T-100T	E14	Product Owner	Monitoring Platform
C6	Software and IT Services	>100T	E15	Former Chief Technology Officer	Software Development and Operations Tool
			E16	Technical Lead IT-Operations	Operation Solution and Event Management
C7	Applied Research	100-1T	E17	DevOps Engineer	Insurance Service
			E18	Developer	Front- and Backend of Fleet Management
C8	Tool Provider	1T-10T	E19	Sales Engineer	APM Solution
C9	Tool Provider	10T-100T	E20	Strategic Officer	Infrastructure Monitoring Tool
			E21	Support	Infrastructure Monitoring Tool
C10	Tool Provider	100-1T	E22	Developer and Architect	Infrastructure Monitoring Tool
C11	Tool Provider	100-1T	E23	Developer	Monitoring Tool
C12	IT Service Insurance	1T-10T	E24	Divisional Director Monitoring	Performance-Monitoring
C13	IT Consulting	1-25	E25	Developer and Architect	IT Consulting Monitoring
C14	IT Consulting	100-1T	E26	Chief Executive Officer	Business Process Monitoring
C15	Software and IT Services	10T-100T	E27	Solution Architect	Open Source Technology Provider
C16	Software and IT Services	10T-100T	E28	Developer	Cross-Stack Instrumentation for Monitoring and Debugging

*CID = Company ID, *EID = Expert ID

to the answers and to the participants' focuses. After manually transcribing the interviews, we sent the transcripts to the participants for review, where they had the possibility to correct unintended statements or remove sensitive data.

Data Analysis: For the analysis of the individual transcripts, we encoded the material to extract important categories regarding our research goal. For this purpose, we followed Mayring's approach of qualitative content analysis [15]. We openly encoded the transcripts by applying inductive category development, where we analyzed the transcripts on sentence level. Usually, one code was assigned to different sentences in a transcript and furthermore one sentence could be assigned to more than one code. During analysis we formed hierarchies of codes and sub-codes. In several iterations, the codes were revised, split or merged.

4 Results and Discussion

This section presents the aggregated findings from the interview analysis with the focus on our research questions defined in Sect. 3. We created a hierarchy of categories as an abstraction of the codes defined during the analysis of the transcripts. This paper presents the top-level hierarchy of the identified challenges, requirements, and solutions. In the following, we describe the different codes generated according to the research questions and illustrate the answers given for the codes with some exemplary statements from the experts (see EID Table 2).

4.1 Challenges

The first research question (RQ1) aims to understand the challenges our participants deal with in the field of distributed systems and which implications are further related with these challenges. We identified a set of nine challenges (Cx) and their corresponding implications which are described in the following.

Increasing dynamics and complexity (C1): The emerging trend of microservice architectures, cloud deployments, and DevOps increase the complexity of distributed systems. While the individual complexity of a microservice is reduced, the complexity of the interdependencies of microservices and the dynamic components within a distributed system cause more operational effort. This dynamic environment is not manageable manually and traditional approaches such as Configuration Management Database (CMDB) [4] are not sufficient anymore: *"CMDB are often based on polling and get the state of the system once a week. In one week, a lot has happened in the cloud system, which a CMDB can not cover."* (E16). This issue does not only include cloud native microservice architectures but also historically grown systems, where an overview of service the dependencies is missing. In addition, some participants stated an underestimation of the dynamic complexity of their systems. This caused that in case of a problem (especially for the diagnosis of context dependent or non-permanent faults) the average duration for detection and recovery took too long.

Heterogeneity (C2): Todays distributed systems consist of several layers: from application to infrastructure technologies like containers, VMs or even serverless environments. These layers are developed and operated by heterogeneous teams. Moreover, as stated by our participants, systems often contain legacy and modern service technology in parallel, where additional tooling is necessary to integrate legacy components. With regard to multi-tenant systems, some participants experienced a noisy-neighbour-effect, where one tenant monopolizes resources and negatively affect other tenants on the same infrastructure. However, in this case the participants were not able to separate views among different tenants. In terms of technological heterogeneity and speed of innovation, the participants had divisive opinions. For distributed systems developer can choose the most suitable technology on the one hand, but on the other hand, the technological heterogeneity complicates the consistent application of monitoring tools. Furthermore, other participants have criticized the speed of innovation and some require a slow-down of technology hypes by defining regulations. The heterogeneity in these different areas is leading to a missing overview of the overall system, it's individual components and the requests processed.

Company culture and mindset (C3): Most of the participants believe that culture and mindset aspects referring to monitoring are essential. Several even stated that this aspect is more challenging than technical aspects. Furthermore, some interviewees also mentioned that a holistic transparency to apply monitoring is often not intended. This gives for instance rise to danger of being blamed in retrospect for a failure. Often, the participants described that teams do not have an overview outside of their own area, for example of the business context of their service. This caused isolated monitoring and operation concepts without context to customer solutions and related requirements. Overall, collaboration and communication between teams and the perspective from which they develop and operate their services are often weakly pronounced. This illustrates the following statement (E22): *"It is usually not the ignorance or the inability of people in the company, but the wrong point of view. Often the developers are so buried in their problem environment, so engrossed in their daily tasks that they can no longer afford to change themselves."*

Lack of central point of view (C4): Participants stated limited possibilities in terms of visibility and dependencies to other services and teams. This results in turn in a missing system-wide overview. E6 describes for instance such situation: *"If it comes to problems such that there are many user complains because the system is not working properly, everyone went for troubleshooting. Due to the lack of an overview, it was difficult to diagnose the faults. It took several escalation rounds and teleconferences to discuss where the fault is located."* At the same time, we identified a lack of a responsible persons in charge to generate overall views and thus to enable individual teams to collaborate. Another point mentioned is the missing transparency about the impact on availability and performance of integrated components from 3rd parties which are often part of a distributed system. Due to the fact that for such components service parameters are usually not accessible, blind spots remain and prevent an overall monitoring.

Flood of data (C5): Participants mentioned the overwhelming flood of data coming from the distributed system, which is constantly in change. The identified challenge is to create meaningful conclusions from customer alerts and how to prioritize them. This shows the following statement (E17): *"The volume and amount of alerts are currently challenging, we are not able to prioritize the customer impacting ones."* Moreover, for problems, where one request has to be handled by multiple components that are developed by independent teams, it is very complex to identify the location of faults, including the responsibilities to fix it. In more detail, many participants described the complexity in correlation of metrics and timestamped logs from multiple services which is often accompanied by insufficient metadata. In addition, participants stated an absence of a comprehensible dashboard that enables navigable views through the data.

Dependency on experts (C6): The process of fault detection and diagnosis, which are often manually performed, seems to be highly dependent on knowledge of individual experts about design and behaviour of the systems. As the following statement from E11 illustrates, these experts appear as a 'source to debug': *"This form of troubleshooting depends highly on the expert knowledge of the team members [...]. Mostly, the knowledge about the structure of the service is currently more crucial than a monitoring which specifically indicates 'search at this point'."* This challenge again outlines the missing systematic development of monitoring systems in supporting humans in fault detection and diagnosis.

Lack of experience, time and resources (C7): Many participants described the challenge of mastering microservice technologies and the DevOps paradigm, which require additional effort for operation, but at the same time, skilled DevOps engineers are missing. Especially, the short time to market results in a prioritization of features and in a disregard of non-functional requirements like availability or performance. Most participants mentioned the limited time as reason for an iterative, often reactive development of system observability and monitoring.

Unclear non-functional requirements (C8): According to the interviewees, non-functional requirements like availability and performance, also referred to as Quality of Service (QoS) or Service Levels (SL), are often not or insufficiently defined and controlled. In addition, some participants commented that teams are often not aware of their major QoSs as well as of their importance in the context of what needs to be measured and monitored. The related reasons for that is due to missing or unprecise customer requirements or due to the lack of awareness regarding the importance of non-functional requirements (E6): *"It is very important to think about service levels or KPls and to define them in a certain way. This is often underestimated. In many projects it can be determined that the project managers only have a purely technical view of the system without being aware of the availability and performance that is needed."* Another reason we identified is the complexity to define overall availability and performance goals, which then have to be converted into goals for component services. This is further intensified by time constraints that lead to reactive implementations as stated in the following statement (E6): *"Many development teams are under pressure to bring the service to market as quickly as possible. So the teams usually start developing without specific customer requirements and end up in production without any systematically derived requirements."* The lack of requirement definitions leads in turn to missing feedback loops (E4): *"[...] where the quality control in the service provision is missing"*.

Reactive implementation (C9): As stated in several interviews, the unclear requirements and the lack of sufficient indication and control often leads to failure. In these cases, the development of monitoring was triggered by an failure in production, where the teams recognized a lack of observability to diagnose customer failure or even to detect them. In fact, customers often received inadequate service levels. In several examples, the teams were occupied only with troubleshooting, which in turn resulted into ad-hoc solutions, instead of creating systematically derived monitoring solutions. Moreover, we identified that teams run into same problems, where labor-intensive development of monitoring for individual services are created and synergy effects of sharing knowledge, expertise and good practices are not used. A further reason for reactive implementation is that during development, the developers did not have enough knowledge about the complex interactions in production and therefore blind spots remained until operation.

4.2   Requirements and Solutions

Regarding RQ 2 and RQ 3, the following requirements (Rx) and possible solutions (Sx) are listed. Rx and Sx have been extracted from the interviews. The mapping of the previous described challenges, the corresponding requirements as well as the solutions are shown in Fig. 2.

Holistic approach (R1): Along with C4, the interview participants stated that they characterize monitoring *"[...] as holistic problem and try to come up with a holistic approach to ensure observability [...]"* (E28). Therefore, it is necessary to enable collaboration and communication along different system layers and teams. We worked out that a common and central view is required which assists the implementation of a system-wide diagnosis and fault detection. One solution stated by interviewees is an event management system (S1), also referred as 'manager of managers', that enables an overall view of the system state. This allows to correlate events for event reduction. Other solutions mentioned are topology managers and architecture discovery modeling (S2). These enable to dynamically map transactions to underlying infrastructure components. Moreover, distributed tracing (S3) was emphasized as solution, which records the execution path of a request at runtime by propagating request IDs [20]. This solution enables to capture causal relationship among events on the execution path. It allows to create a *"[...] bird's eye view, to find out what is going on with*

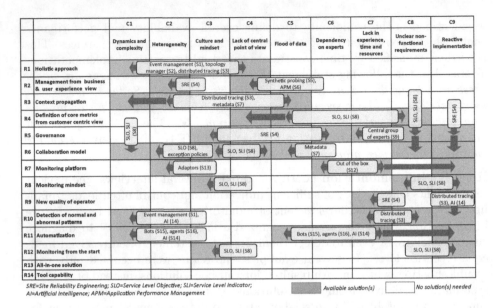

Fig. 2. Overview of challenges, requirements and solutions

a user request [...]" (E28). Distributed tracing can also be applied for diagnosis of 3rd party components where source code is not available. Hence, the participants mentioned that the instrumentation in order to propagate trace IDs through individual services, developed by different teams, is at the moment not consistently assured.

Management from business and user experience view (R2): Several participants described the trend moving from isolated monitoring of individual services to a context dependent view from the perspective of a customer or business application. In addition, some stated to apply Google's approach of Site Reliability Engineering (SRE) (S4) (E28): *"With our SRE approach in mind, we care about the user experience and these are the golden paths we want to improve. I do not necessarily care about what is going on underneath, as soon as the user is not experiencing any errors, latency or unlikely indicators."* SRE [3] takes aspects of software engineering and applies them to infrastructure and operations problems with a focus on customer experience. Moreover, several interviewees stated to perform synthetic probing. This is known as end-to-end monitoring (S5) that enables emulation of real user behaviour to measure and compare its availability and performance. In general, many participants referred to apply Application Performance Management (APM) (S6) which comprises methods, techniques, and tools to continuously monitor the state of a system from an application-centric view. The APM allows diagnosing and resolving especially performance-related problems.

Context propagation (R3): To provide a holistic approach and to be able to detect customer impacting events context propagation is needed. The system propagates relevant context in form of metadata, such as IDs or tags along the execution flow of a request through services. Alongside with distributed tracing (S3), adding metadata (S7) to metrics and logs are further examples. This helps to localize the underlying fault in the flood of data generated by the systems by providing contextual information (E28): *"With context propagation, you can easily point to the root cause of the issues. For example, there is some additional latency and you can see that this other particular database call is causing the additional latency. You can automatically inspect and ping the right time and component [...]".*

Definition of core metrics from customer centric view (R4): A way to systematically define metrics for individual services is the concept of establishing service level metrics. Some participants apply Service Level Objectives (SLO) and Service Level Indicators (SLI) (S8) as part of a SRE approach. While SLOs describe business objectives by defining the acceptable downtime of a service from a user perspective, the SLI in turn enables to tie back metrics to the business objectives. The interviewees express an essential need for a systematic definition of these metrics, but at the same time they struggle with their implementation (E28): *"It is a lot of work to figure out the right SLO, which is a very long process. Not everybody is interested in this. [...] It is hard to introduce this concept at a later time. This is creating tension in teams, because they are saying: "This is not what you have promised us". But the problem is, if nobody actually formulated what the promise was."*

Governance (R5): To foster the previous requirements, several participants outlined the need for a governance that defines a strategy including roles, responsibilities, processes and technologies for monitoring and observability. This should comprise clear formulations of a minimal set of indicators that have to be monitored from every service. A further requirement is to claim observability of a service as an acceptance criteria for development and operation. The participants mentioned that developing and applying governance needs several iterations and has to be continuously adapted in terms of the company strategy. Especially for services running in the cloud, guidelines have to be defined because *"Cloud is standardization"* (E16). Concurrently some participants criticized the introduction of tooling standards and a slow-down of development by oversized governance regulations. Some companies already have an own department and group of specialists with the central responsibility of monitoring (S9). To provide a strategy, participants mentioned to align their governance to SRE principles and guidelines (S4), which in some examples already evolved into a self-regulating system. A commonly mentioned issue addresses the creation of community of a practice (S10) to share good practices and lessons learned.

Collaboration model (R6): Some participants described a collaboration model as an essential base for communication and efficient diagnosis processes along different teams. As part of that, exception policies and taxonomies for anomalies (S11) need to be defined. To efficiently work together during diagnosis metadata (S7), capturing the causal relationships and providing context are needed. Moreover, some participants stated that a (E28): *"[...] common language, called SLO and SLI"* (S8) is base for their team collaboration.

Monitoring platform (R7): Several interviewees required a unified monitoring platform to increase operational efficiency. This includes out of the box (S12) and standardized components which can be used modularly and are customizable to specific needs of the individual services. Monitoring and its default setup also needs to enable the *"democratization of data"* (E19), for example to offer a standard API to deploy adaptors (S13) for different technologies. This default can therefore *"[...] create a kind of governance that is not strict."* (E20).

Monitoring mindset (R8): The prerequisite is to increase the importance of observability and monitoring of distributed systems. Without an increasing awareness, isolated ad-hoc solutions will remain, which do not enable sufficient service provisioning and diagnostics. One mentioned solution to increase the importance of non-functional attributes, like availability and performance, can be reached by setting and controlling SLOs (S8). Thereby, stability and feature development can be controlled from management perspective. Further, the participants outlined a need to equalize functional and non-functional requirements.

New quality of operator (R9): Many participants mentioned a lack of academic education of the operators. Accordingly, operators need to increase their skills especially of being able to cope with automation tasks. Achieving this, the company has to increase the awareness of monitoring and to promote proper responsible operators. Some participants highlighted the need for Site Reliability Engineers (SRE) (S4), who are able to work on operation and infrastructure tasks as well as software engineering aspects.

Detection of normal and abnormal patterns (R10): Nearly all interviewees spoke about anomaly detection as an important task for monitoring to differ between what is normal and abnormal behaviour. Different solutions are mentioned, such as event management (S1), to correlate events from different parts of the system. For correlating events, predictive analytics and artificial intelligence (AI) (S14) are in use. Some participants discussed the problem of differentiating normal behaviour of a service. In this context, some participants considered distributed tracing (S3) to indicate performance measures and iteratively develop guarantees for their services by setting service levels. The most advanced method for anomaly detection is AI (S14). Almost all participants appreciated its enormous potential to master the complexity and the flood of data generated by distributed systems. However, many interviewees pointed out that sufficient preconditions for the use of AI are still missing in practice. Primarily, the right data has to be collected, the quality of data has to be ensured, the context needs to be propagated and data has to be stored centrally. Concerns in terms of the cost value ratio of AI approaches and their reliability remain (E28): *"I don't know if we will ever have a solution that we can rely on confidently"*.

Automation (R11): The increasing dynamics and complexity within distributed systems, caused by the upcoming microservice architecture and shorter lifecycles of components, is not manually controllable as a whole any more. Therefore, automation is indispensable to observe and monitor a distributed system. Especially recurring problems can be automatically solved and basic monitoring techniques can be automatically implemented. Bots (S15) and agents (S16) can realize automation, as they act by themselves. In combination with AI (S14), bots and agents can be more efficient and more precise in their tasks such as collection and analysis of traffic data.

Monitoring from the start (R12): Monitoring is a prerequisite for any development and operation. Many interviewees indicated to consider monitoring from the start. It should be the part of any design. Some participants quote to integrate SLOs and SLIs (S8) *"[...] in the design time. As soon as there is a new service you have a section in the design doc., where you can see these are the promises, they may change over time to reduce toil. We start the conversation very early on."* (E28). This might enhances the awareness for monitoring and can change the company culture towards a monitoring mindset. While IT departments should see monitoring as an integrated part, the management needs to be the key driver to implement such a mindset.

All-in-one solution (R13): Solutions covering all monitoring functionalities in one solution were mentioned in the interviews. However, the reality shows that such solutions do not exist. In the best case, the market offers solutions which provide basic functionalities for monitoring such as performance measurement or logging. In more detail, they often provide the capability to easily expand the solutions, for instance by combining and integrating other software solutions. This can also comprise new standards, technologies and other already existing solutions. Hence, all-in-one solutions represent in this context a combination of several solutions and technologies. Nevertheless, to realize such an encompassing solution, it needs to avoid or substitute isolated solutions with standard monitoring software, open standards and modern technologies to reach an encompassing solution in the future.

Tool Capabilities (R14): In this paragraph, we summarized different tool capabilities, mainly non-functional requirements, mentioned by the participants. An often stated requirement is real-time monitoring, where changes and impacts are being directly monitored without delay. Therefore, the necessary information can be provided for appropriate response (e.g. real-time alerts to reduce reaction time). A further requirement addresses the use of open standards (e.g. JSON or standard monitoring functionalities), which is motivated by being adaptable and flexible due to new technologies and standards. This also fosters the maintainability and portability of monitoring solutions by being easily transferable to other distributed systems. Associated with that, scalability is of a particular importance to cope with large and dynamic distributed systems. While the management of the dynamics within a distributed system needs to be addressed, reliability and availability of the monitoring is highly demanded. For example, health functionalities, such as the current status of the system, needs to be available all the time. Moreover, tools need to support multi-tenant management. This requirement specifically addresses the ability of tenant specific views and individual permission management. A further mentioned aspect is the importance of the security of the monitoring tools itself. The more agents are used and the higher the integration depth is, the more 'backdoors' might be open and the higher the possible negative impact could be. Thus, security aspects such as prevention actions need to be realized. A minimally invasive approach needs to be followed, where the changes in an existing system are limited. This might be opening just a minimum of relevant ports. In addition, a careless deployment and configuration of monitoring agents have been mentioned as potential problems which might causes instability and an increasing network load.

5 Threats to Validity

For **internal validity**, there is a risk that the participants did not state the true situation or their opinion. However, this risk is rather small, because we were ensuring the anonymity of the interviews and the participants seemed not to be worried to talk about negative aspects of their product or company. Another threat to internal validity are potentially misunderstood concepts used within the questions. Therefore, we provided additional explanations for important concepts. Otherwise, we asked questions to clarify terms used by the participants that could have a domain or company specific meaning. To reduce researcher bias and therefore to increase the interpretation validity, every transcript was reviewed by at least one additional researcher. Furthermore, our participants had the chance (and took it) to adjust statements in their transcript that were incorrect, indistinct or contained sensitive data.

To increase **external validity**, we asked participants not exclusively based in Germany but also participants coming form international companies with diversity in terms of domain and size. Additionally, with our participants we are covering different roles, coming from different layers of the application stack as well as including providers of monitoring solutions and consultants advising companies and teams in integrating monitoring solutions. Therefore, it was possible to generate an overall view of the complex relations in terms of technical and organizational aspects leading to challenges as well as requirements and solutions. Still, as we performed qualitative research, we do not claim our results to be generalizable.

6 Conclusion

Our research objective was to explore challenges, requirements and contemporary good practices as well as solutions in terms of monitoring and observability of distributed systems. Therefore, we conducted interviews with 28 software professionals from 16 organizations. We identified that monitoring and the observability of distributed systems is not purely a technical issue anymore but becomes a more cross-cutting and strategic topic, critical to the success of a company which offers services. Development and deployment paradigms of microservices, DevOps and cloud are creating maximal independence and specialization resulting in isolated monitoring and observability solutions, not allowing to manage a service from a customer or business centric view. Most companies have already solutions and good practices in place, but in many cases they remain isolated approaches due to siloed company structures. With reference to the findings of the contemporary state of practice, we see a need for further work on good practices and real world-examples for aligning business goals with technical metrics to break down silos and enable efficient development and operation. Furthermore, researchers can take these results into account for designing industry-focused methods.

References

1. Aceto, G., Botta, A., de Donato, W., Pescapè, A.: Cloud monitoring: a survey. Comput. Netw. **57**(9), 2093–2115 (2013)
2. Alhamazani, K., et al.: An overview of the commercial cloud monitoring tools: research dimensions, design issues, and state-of-the-art. Computing **97**(4), 357–377 (2015)
3. Beyer, B., Jones, C., Petoff, J., Murphy, N.R.: Site Reliability Engineering: How Google Runs Production Systems. O'Reilly Media Inc., Sebastopol (2016)
4. Colville, R.J.: CMDB or configuration database: know the difference (2006)
5. Fatema, K., Emeakaroha, V.C., Healy, P.D., Morrison, J.P., Lynn, T.: A survey of cloud monitoring tools: taxonomy, capabilities and objectives. J. Parallel Distrib. Comput. **74**(10), 2918–2933 (2014)
6. Gamez-Diaz, A., Fernandez, P., Ruiz-Cortes, A.: An analysis of RESTful APIs offerings in the industry. In: Maximilien, M., Vallecillo, A., Wang, J., Oriol, M. (eds.) ICSOC 2017. LNCS, vol. 10601, pp. 589–604. Springer, Cham (2017). https://doi.org/10.1007/978-3-319-69035-3_43
7. Gopal, M.: Modern Control System Theory, 2nd edn. Halsted Press, New York (1993)
8. Gupta, M., Mandal, A., Dasgupta, G., Serebrenik, A.: Runtime monitoring in continuous deployment by differencing execution behavior model. In: Pahl, C., Vukovic, M., Yin, J., Yu, Q. (eds.) ICSOC 2018. LNCS, vol. 11236, pp. 812–827. Springer, Cham (2018). https://doi.org/10.1007/978-3-030-03596-9_58
9. Heger, C., van Hoorn, A., Mann, M., Okanovic, D.: Application performance management: state of the art and challenges for the future. In: Proceedings of the 8th ACM/SPEC International Conference on Performance Engineering (ICPE 2017). ACM (2017)
10. IEEE: IEEE Standard Glossary of Software Engineering Terminology (1990). https://ieeexplore.ieee.org/document/159342
11. Johng, H., Kim, D., Hill, T., Chung, L.: Estimating the performance of cloud-based systems using benchmarking and simulation in a complementary manner. In: Pahl, C., Vukovic, M., Yin, J., Yu, Q. (eds.) ICSOC 2018. LNCS, vol. 11236, pp. 576–591. Springer, Cham (2018). https://doi.org/10.1007/978-3-030-03596-9_42

12. Kinsella, J.: The cloud complexity gap: making software more intelligent to address complex infrastructure. https://www.cloudcomputing-news.net/news/2015/jun/17/cloud-complexity-gap-making-software-more-intelligent-address-complex-infrastructure/

13. Knoche, H., Hasselbring, W.: Drivers and barriers for microservice adoption– a survey among professionals in Germany. Enterp. Model. Inf. Syst. Architect. (EMISAJ)–Int. J. Conceptual Model. **14**(1), 1–35 (2019)

14. Lin, J., Chen, P., Zheng, Z.: Microscope: pinpoint performance issues with causal graphs in micro-service environments. In: Pahl, C., Vukovic, M., Yin, J., Yu, Q. (eds.) ICSOC 2018. LNCS, vol. 11236, pp. 3–20. Springer, Cham (2018). https://doi.org/10.1007/978-3-030-03596-9_1

15. Mayring, P.: Qualitative Content Analysis: Theoretical Foundation, Basic Procedures and Software Solution (2014)

16. Natu, M., Ghosh, R.K., Shyamsundar, R.K., Ranjan, R.: Holistic performance monitoring of hybrid clouds: complexities and future directions. IEEE Cloud Comput. **3**(1), 72–81 (2016)

17. Niedermaier, S., Koetter, F., Freymann, A., Wagner, S.: Interview guideline on observability and monitoring of distributed systems (2019). https://doi.org/10.5281/zenodo.3346579

18. Picoreti, R., Pereira do Carmo, A., Mendonça de Queiroz, F., Salles Garcia, A., Frizera Vassallo, R., Simeonidou, D.: Multilevel observability in cloud orchestration. In: 2018 IEEE 16th International Conference on DASC/PiCom/DataCom/CyberSciTech, pp. 776–784, August 2018

19. Runeson, P., Höst, M.: Guidelines for conducting and reporting case study research in software engineering. Empirical Softw. Eng. **14**(2), 131 (2008)

20. Sambasivan, R.R., Shafer, I., Mace, J., Sigelman, B.H., Fonseca, R., Ganger, G.R.: Principled workflow-centric tracing of distributed systems. In: Proceedings of the Seventh ACM Symposium on Cloud Computing, pp. 401–414. ACM (2016)

21. Sfondrini, N., Motta, G., Longo, A.: Public cloud adoption in multinational companies: a survey. In: 2018 IEEE International Conference on Services Computing (SCC), pp. 177–184, July 2018

22. Singer, J., Sim, S.E., Lethbridge, T.C.: Software engineering data collection for field studies. In: Shull, F., Singer, J., Sjøberg, D.I.K. (eds.) Guide to Advanced Empirical Software Engineering, pp. 9–34. Springer, London (2008). https://doi.org/10.1007/978-1-84800-044-5_1

23. Sun, C., Li, M., Jia, J., Han, J.: Constraint-based model-driven testing of web services for behavior conformance. In: Pahl, C., Vukovic, M., Yin, J., Yu, Q. (eds.) ICSOC 2018. LNCS, vol. 11236, pp. 543–559. Springer, Cham (2018). https://doi.org/10.1007/978-3-030-03596-9_40

24. Yang, Y., Wang, L., Gu, J., Li, Y.: Transparently capturing execution path of service/job request processing. In: Pahl, C., Vukovic, M., Yin, J., Yu, Q. (eds.) ICSOC 2018. LNCS, vol. 11236, pp. 879–887. Springer, Cham (2018). https://doi.org/10.1007/978-3-030-03596-9_63

Integrating Geographical and Functional Relevance to Implicit Data for Web Service Recommendation

Khavee Agustus Botangen[1(✉)], Jian Yu[1], Sira Yongchareon[1],
LiangHuai Yang[2], and Quan Z. Sheng[3]

[1] School of Engineering, Computer, and Mathematical Sciences,
Auckland University of Technology, Auckland, New Zealand
{khavee.botangen,jian.yu,sira.yongchareon}@aut.ac.nz
[2] School of Computer Science and Technology, Zhejiang University of Technology,
Hangzhou, China
yang.lianghuai@gmail.com
[3] Department of Computing, Macquarie University, Sydney, Australia
michael.sheng@mq.edu.au

Abstract. Designing efficient and effective Web service recommendation, primarily based on usage feedback, has become an important task to support the prevalent consumption of services. In the mashup-API invocation scenario, the most available feedback is the implicit invocation data, i.e., the binary data indicating whether or not a mashup has invoked an API. Hence, various efforts are exploiting potential impact factors to augment the implicit invocation data with the aim to improve service recommendation performance. One significant factor affecting the context of Web service invocations is geographical location, however, it has been given less attention in the implicit-based service recommendation. In this paper, we propose a recommendation approach that derives a contextual preference score from geographical location information and functionality descriptions. The preference score complements the mashup-API invocation data for our implicit-tailored matrix factorization recommendation model. Evaluation results show that augmenting the implicit data with geographical location information and functionality description significantly increases the precision of API recommendation for mashup services.

Keywords: Recommendation · Location · Topic model · Implicit feedback · Matrix factorization

1 Introduction

The growing number and diversity of Web services present challenges in the discovery and selection of appropriate services to construct service compositions [2,10]. Service recommendation techniques have been explored to handle such

This work is supported in part by Key Project of the National Natural Science Foundation of China (No. 61832004 and 61672042).

challenges, and since the explicit QoS information is considered one of the key criteria in service recommendation, collaborative QoS prediction has been the main focus of various research works [9,12]. But oftentimes, the most realistic and best available data is the *implicit* user-service invocation, which simply tells whether a user has invoked a service or not. We propose in this paper a context-aware collaborative filtering service-recommendation approach that deals with the implicit mashup-API invocation scenario, i.e., a mashup uses an API. We explore two contextual factors that may influence the invocation preference for an API. By contextual factors, we mean those surround information stretching beyond the mashup-API invocation matrix. These contextual factors are the *geographic locations* and *functional characteristics* of mashups and APIs. From these two factors, we respectively derive the geographical and functional relevance scores for a certain mashup-API invocation. This paper has the following main contributions: (1) the mapping of geographical location information into geographical relevance scores; (2) the mapping of textual descriptions into functional relevance scores; and (3) the integration of the geographical and functional relevance scores as impact factors to the implicit mashup-API invocation data that is utilized by our matrix factorization recommendation model.

2   Deriving Geographical and Functional Relevance

To demonstrate our approach, we utilize one of the largest repositories of APIs and mashups – the ProgrammableWeb. We extract a dataset that comprises the mashup-API invocation matrix: 5,691 mashups and 1,170 APIs, with only 10,737 mashup-API invocations, which shows a very low matrix density of 1.6×10^{-3}. Afterwards, we derive the geographical and functionality information to establish the degrees of preference for the implicit mashup-API invocations.

Mashups and APIs are situated in various geographical locations, e.g., city, country, or autonomous system. Each location provides the mashup-API invocation a certain operational context which can be different in every other location. We formulate two assumptions in the mashup-API service invocation scenario: (i) there is a better quality of service invocations in shorter geographic distances, hence, a higher preference should be given to a potential API that is located closer to the mashup; and (ii) the preference of mashup m for a potential API a reflects the preferences of m's neighboring mashups. When a is invoked by m's neighboring mashup n, we expect that a provides *better* quality of service invocation to n. When m is geographically close to n, it is likely to get that same (better) quality of invocation when m invokes a. We define a geographical similarity function that transforms the distance d_{ui} between the geolocations of a mashup u and a potential API i into a similarity value:

$$geosim_{ui} = 1 - \left(\left(\frac{1}{1 + e^{(-1 \cdot \frac{d_{ui}}{\delta})}} \cdot 2 \right) - 1 \right) \tag{1}$$

where δ is the dispersion factor that approximates the decrease rate of the similarity value as the distance d_{ui} increases, and d_{ui} is computed using the inverse

Haversine formula. Our similarity function should satisfy two constraints: (i) the function is equal to 1 when $d_{ui} = 0$, and (ii) the function tends to be 0 as the distance d_{ui} increases.

Given a mashup u and a potential API i, we get the list of nearest neighbors of mashup u: $M(u) = \{m \mid m$ is within k distance from u, and m invokes $i\}$. Then, we compute the geographical similarity between each m and u: $geosim_{um}$. We aggregate the geographical similarity of u with all its neighbors into a mashup context similarity:

$$consim_u = \frac{1}{\mid M(u) \mid} \sum_{m \in M(u)} geosim_{um} \tag{2}$$

The geographical relevance score between a mashup u and API i aggregates the $geosim_{ui}$ and $consim_u$: $g_s(u, i) = geosim_{ui} \times consim_u$.

Then, for each mashup/API in the dataset, we aggregate its description, category, and tags into a mashup/API document. We use the Latent Dirichlet Allocation (LDA) topic model [1] to analyze each document and obtain the associated topic distribution. We define the functionality relevance score between a mashup m_u and an API a_i as the similarity of the topic distributions of m_u: θ_u, and a_i: θ_i. We compare the topic distributions using the Jensen-Shannon divergence method: $JSD\left(\theta_u\|\theta_i\right) = 0.5 \times D\left(\theta_u\|M\right) + 0.5 \times D\left(\theta_i\|M\right)$, where $M = 0.5 \times (\theta_u + \theta_i)$, and $D(.\|.)$ is the Kullback-Leibler divergence. Hence, the functionality relevance score of m_u and a_i is defined as: $f_s(m_u, a_i) = 1 - JSD\left(\theta_u\|\theta_i\right)$.

3   The Recommendation Model

Adapting the collaborative filtering approach that integrates preference degrees to implicit feedback [3], our matrix factorization model augments the implicit mashup-API invocation pairing r_{ui} with the unified preference score $p_{ui} = g_s(u, i) \times f_s(u, i)$. With a non-zero entry $r_{ui} = 1$, we believe that i is preferred in u. Otherwise, a zero entry $r_{ui} = 0$ indicates a negative or none preference. We associate these beliefs with varying preference degrees which indicate the levels of confidence we have. We use a variable c_{ui} to hold our confidence for r_{ui}, and is calculated as follows: $c_{ui} = 1 + \alpha p_{ui}$. For every mashup-API pair r_{ui}, we have a minimal confidence that increases with the preference score p_{ui}. The larger the preference score for an $r_{ui} = 1$, the higher our confidence will be. The increase rate in our confidence is set through the linear scaling factor α. Increasing or decreasing α will respectively increase or decrease the confidence variability among the preferences. Setting $\alpha = 200$ has given good results in our experiments. It is worth noting that if $r_{ui} = 0$, then $p_{ui} = 0$, giving us a minimal confidence $c_{ui} = 1$. We compute the latent factors (i.e., $x_u \in \mathbb{R}^d$ for each mashup u, and $y_i \in \mathbb{R}^d$ for each API i), by minimizing a confidence weighted sum of squared errors loss function:

$$L = \min_{x_*, y_*} \sum_{u,i} c_{ui}(r_{ui} - x_u^T y_i)^2 + \lambda\left(\sum_u ||x_u||^2 + \sum_i ||y_i||^2\right) \tag{3}$$

where $\lambda\left(\sum_u ||x_u||^2 + \sum_i ||y_i||^2\right)$ is an L2 regularization term to reduce overfitting the training data.

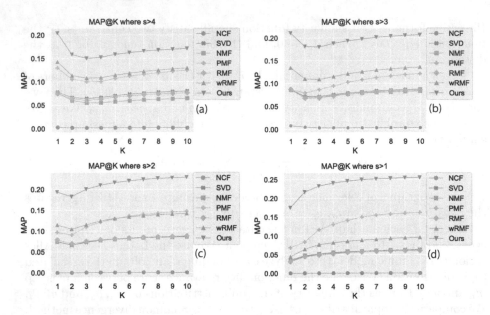

Fig. 1. MAP@K scores comparison.

4 Evaluation

Using the Mean Average Precision (MAP@K) metric, we evaluate the recommendation performance of our approach against some baseline prediction methods: the neighbor-based CF (NCF [11]), the SVD-based MF (SVD [8]), the non-negative MF (NMF [5]), the regularized MF (RMF [4]), the weighted regularized MF (wRMF [7]) which is a variant of RMF, and the probabilistic MF (PMF [6])which is considered a probabilistic extension of SVD.

To create the training data, we hide an n equal number of interactions of each mashup in the mashup-API interaction matrix (i.e., the corresponding entries become 0). The test data contains all the mashups, each with the n invoked APIs (i.e., the APIs associated with the hidden interactions). We then evaluate the MAP of the top K recommended APIs with regard to those hidden ones.

In the derivation of MAP scores, we create four settings of training data: $s > 4$, $s > 3$, $s > 2$, and $s > 1$, where s is the number of APIs in a mashup. In the setting $s > 3$, for instance, we only consider those mashup rows invoking more than 3 APIs. Each setting has its test cases with varying sizes of the training-test split. For example, the setting $s > 3$ has 3 test cases: $t = \{3, 2, 1\}$, where each t corresponds to the number of APIs in the test set of each mashup. The training-test split varies with t. Figure 1 illustrates the MAP@K evaluation results of the various methods in the four dataset settings. Each setting shows the average scores from the test cases, e.g., Fig. 1(b) which corresponds to the setting $s > 3$, plots the average MAP@K of its 3 test cases. Our method outperforms the baseline methods in all four settings in terms of precision on the top-10 recommendations.

5   Conclusion and Future Work

In this paper, we leverage the matrix factorization technique to not just consider invocation patterns but also recognize the varying degree of preferences behind the binary mashup-API invocation data. We combine the geographical and functional relevance scores and integrate them as preference degrees to the mashup-API invocations in our implicit-tailored matrix factorization model. During the training process, we can make full use of the geographic locations and functional descriptions of mashups and APIs, besides the implicit invocation data.

We are conducting more experiments to ascertain the impact of the key model parameters, as well as the individual components of the relevance scores. We also aim (i) to consider the proximity among neighboring APIs in the geographical relevance model, and (ii) to integrate into our recommendation model additional contextual information such as social relationships among the neighboring mashups and APIs.

References

1. Blei, D.M.: Probabilistic topic models. Commun. ACM **55**(4), 77–84 (2012)
2. Bouguettaya, A., et al.: A service computing manifesto: the next 10 years. Commun. ACM **60**(4), 64–72 (2017)
3. Hu, Y., Koren, Y., Volinsky, C.: Collaborative filtering for implicit feedback datasets. In: 8th International Conference on Data Mining, pp. 263–272. IEEE (2008)
4. Koren, Y., Bell, R., Volinsky, C.: Matrix factorization techniques for recommender systems. Computer **42**(8), 30–37 (2009)
5. Luo, X., Zhou, M., Xia, Y., Zhu, Q.: An efficient non-negative matrix-factorization-based approach to collaborative filtering for recommender systems. IEEE Trans. Industr. Inf. **10**(2), 1273–1284 (2014)
6. Mnih, A., Salakhutdinov, R.R.: Probabilistic matrix factorization. In: Advances in Neural Information Processing Systems, pp. 1257–1264 (2008)
7. Pan, R., et al.: One-class collaborative filtering. In: 8th International Conference on Data Mining, pp. 502–511. IEEE (2008)
8. Symeonidis, P., Zioupos, A.: Matrix and Tensor Factorization Techniques for Recommender Systems, vol. 1. Springer, New York (2016). https://doi.org/10.1007/978-3-319-41357-0
9. Wu, H., Yue, K., Li, B., Zhang, B., Hsu, C.H.: Collaborative QoS prediction with context-sensitive matrix factorization. Future Gener. Comput. Syst. **82**, 669–678 (2018)
10. Yao, L., Wang, X., Sheng, Q.Z., Benatallah, B., Huang, C.: Mashup recommendation by regularizing matrix factorization with API co-invocations. IEEE Trans. Serv. Comput. (2018). https://doi.org/10.1109/TSC.2018.2803171
11. Zheng, Z., Ma, H., Lyu, M.R., King, I.: WSREC: a collaborative filtering based web service recommender system. In: IEEE International Conference on Web Services, pp. 437–444. IEEE (2009)
12. Zheng, Z., Zhang, Y., Lyu, M.R.: Investigating QoS of real-world web services. IEEE Trans. Serv. Comput. **7**(1), 32–39 (2014)

Towards Automated Microservices Extraction Using Muti-objective Evolutionary Search

Islem Saidani[1], Ali Ouni[1(✉)], Mohamed Wiem Mkaouer[2], and Aymen Saied[3]

[1] ETS Montreal, University of Quebec, Montreal, QC, Canada
islem.saidani@ens.etsmtl.ca, ali.ouni@etsmtl.ca
[2] Rochester Institute of Technology (RIT), Rochester, NY, USA
mwm@se.rit.edu
[3] Concordia University, Montreal, QC, Canada
m_saied@encs.concordia.ca

Abstract. We introduce in this paper a novel approach, named *MSExtractor*, that formulate the microservices identification problem as a multi-objective combinatorial optimization problem to decompose a legacy application into a set of cohesive, loosely-coupled and coarse-grained services. We employ the non-dominated sorting genetic algorithm (NSGA-II) to drive a search process towards optimal microservices identification while considering structural dependencies in the source code. We conduct an empirical evaluation on a benchmark of two open-source legacy software systems to assess the efficiency of our approach. Results show that *MSExtractor* is able to find relevant microservice candidates and outperforms recent three state-of-the-art approaches.

Keywords: Microservices · Search-based software engineering · Legacy decomposition · Microservices architecture

1 Introduction

In this paper, we introduce a novel approach namely *MSExtractor*, that formulate the microservices extraction problem as a multi-objective combinatorial optimization problem to decompose an OO legacy application into a set of cohesive, loosely-coupled microservices. We employ the Non-dominated Sorting Genetic Algorithm II (NSGA-II) [1], as search method to drive the decomposition process and find the near-optimal trade-off between two objectives: (1) minimize coupling (inter-service dependencies), and (2) maximize cohesion (intra-services dependencies) while leveraging the structural information embodied in the source code. MSExtractor aims at supporting software developers and architects by providing a decision-making support in their design decisions for their microservices migration.

We conduct an empirical study to evaluate our approach on a benchmark of two open source Java legacy applications. Results show that MSExtractor is able

© Springer Nature Switzerland AG 2019
S. Yangui et al. (Eds.): ICSOC 2019, LNCS 11895, pp. 58–63, 2019.
https://doi.org/10.1007/978-3-030-33702-5_5

to extract cohesive and loosely coupled microservices with higher performance than three recent state-of-the-art approaches.

2   Approach

We formulate the automated extraction of microservices from a legacy application as a combinatorial optimization problem, in which a search algorithm explores alternative combinations of classes from an input legacy system. Given legacy system composed of a set of classes to be decomposed into microservices, there are many ways in which the microservice boundaries can be drawn leading to different possible class combinations. The problem is a graph partitioning problem, which is known to be NP-hard and therefore seems suited to a metaheuristic search-based techniques [2].

To identify such instances of candidate microservices, MSExtractor proceeds to (i) create a set of new empty microservices, and (ii) assign each class to a unique microservice. The process should assign each class to exactly one microservice, and have no empty microservices. Then, MSExtractor uses NSGA-II [1] in order to find the optimal solutions that provide the best trade-off between our two objective functions.

Figure 1 shows a simple microservices decomposition example. A simple solution $X = \{1, 1, 2, 3, 1, 1, 2\}$, for example, denotes a decomposition of seven classes into three microservices. The classes $InitFilter$, $IPBanFilter$ and $User$ are in the microservice m_1, $Product$, $CarItem$ and $Category$ are in m_2, and finally, $Order$ and $Catalog$ are in m_3. Moreover, different class dependencies exist in order to implement the required functionalities by the microservice. An appropriate decomposition should maximize the cohesion within a microservice while minimizing coupling between the extracted microservices.

1	1	3	2	2	3	1
InitFilter	IPBanFilter	CalendarTag	FileContent	MediaFile	CalendarModel	User

Fig. 1. An example of a microservice decomposition solution (snippet) from JPetstore.

Source code dependencies are widely used in software engineering to measure how strongly related are the elements of a software system, i.e., methods, classes, packages, etc. [3]. MSExtractor is based on a combination of structural measures to detect the dependencies among classes. In a nutshell, structural dependency for two given classes represents the shared method calls between them. We use two popular structural measurements to define our fitness objectives.

Objective Functions. To evaluate the quality (i.e., the fitness) of a candidate microservices decomposition solution, we define a fitness function that evaluates multiple objective and constraint dimensions. Each objective dimension refers to a specific value that should be either minimized or maximized for a solution to be considered "better" than another solution. In our approach, we optimize the three following objectives:

1. **Cohesion:** The cohesion objective function is a measure of the overall cohesion of a candidate microservices decomposition. The cohesion of a candidate microservice m is denoted by $Coh(m)$ and defined as the complement of the average of all pairs of classes belonging to the microservice m. Then, the cohesion objective function corresponds to the average cohesion value of all microservice candidates in a decomposition. This objective function should be maximized to ensure that each candidate microservice contains strongly related classes and does not contain classes that are not part of its functionality.

2. **Coupling:** The coupling objective function measures the overall coupling among the microservice in a decomposition $\mathcal{M}$. We define the coupling between two microservices m_1 and m_2 as the average similarity between all possible pairs of classes from m_1 and m_2. The coupling objective function corresponds to the average coupling measures between all possible pairs of microservices in the decomposition. This objective function is to be minimized. The lower the coupling value between all candidate microservices, the better is the decomposition quality.

3   Empirical Evaluation

In this section, we present the results of our evaluation for the proposed approach, MSExtractor. The goal of this evaluation is to assess the efficiency of our approach in identifying appropriate microservices and compare it with available state-of-the-art approaches. This study aims at answering the following research question:

- **RQ1.** To what extent can MSExtractor identify relevant microservices?

Empirical Setup. To evaluate our approach, we conduct an experimental study on a benchmark of two legacy web applications namely JPetstore[1], and Springblog[2]. To answer RQ1, we employ four evaluation metrics to assess the quality of the identified microservices based on measuring their *functional independence*. This measure assesses the extent to which microservices exhibit a bounded context and present their own functionalities with low coupling to other microservices. In particular, four metrics were commonly used in recent studies [4–6] to assess the quality of Web service interfaces.

- **CHM** *(CoHesion at Message level):* CHM is inspired by LoC_{msg}, a widely used metric to measure the cohesion of a service at the message level [4–6].

---

[1] https://github.com/mybatis/jpetstore-6.
[2] https://github.com/Raysmond/SpringBlog.

- **CHD** *(CoHesion at Domain level):* CHD is inspired by LoC_{dom}, a widely used metric to measure the cohesion of a service at the domain level [4,5].
- **OPN** *(OPeration Number):* OPN computes the average number of public operations [4,7] exposed by an extracted microservice to other candidate microservices. The smaller OPN is, the better.
- **IRN** *(InteRaction Number):* IRN represents the number of method calls among all pairs of extracted microservices [4,8]. The smaller is IRN, the better is the quality of candidate microservices as it reflects loose coupling.

State-of-the-Art Comparison. We evaluate the performance of our approach, we compare it against three recent state-of-the-art approaches, namely *FoME* [4], *MEM* [9], and *LIMBO* [10]. We selected these three state-of-the-art methods as they use different decomposition techniques, and have been selected in recent comparative studies [4].

Table 1. The results achieved by MSExtractor, FoME, MEM, and LIMBO.

System	Metric	MSExtractor	FoME	MEM	LIMBO
Jpetstore	CHM	**0.5–0.6**	0.7–0.8	**0.5–0.6**	**0.5–0.6**
	CHD	**0.6–0.7**	**0.6–0.7**	**0.6–0.7**	**0.6–0.7**
	OPN	28	**22**	39	68
	IRN	**33**	35	48	329
SpringBlog	CHM	**0.5–0.6**	0.7–0.8	0.6–0.7	0.6–0.7
	CHD	**0.6–0.7**	0.8–0.9	0.8–0.9	0.7–0.8
	OPN	10	**7**	21	147
	IRN	**21**	26	30	238

3.1 Results

Table 1 presents the achieved results by each of the approaches, *MSExtractor*, and the compared approaches, *FoME* [4], *MEM* [9], and *LIMBO* [10]. The metrics CHM and CHD reflect the cohesion of the identified microservices, while the metrics OPN and IRN reflect the coupling. Higher cohesion metrics values indicate better performance while lower coupling metrics values indicate better performance. The cohesion results are provided in the form of an interval, e.g., [0.5–0.6], instead of specific values since slight differences between CHM or CHD values are not significant. We observe from the table that our approach, MSExtractor, outperforms the three competing approaches in the two studied systems, in the majority of metrics. In particular, for smaller systems such as JPetStore (24 classes), the achieved results on the four metrics are comparable. Indeed, this system represents a relatively smaller search space where deterministic approaches may achieve high performance. For larger systems, such as Roller and `JForum` (340 and 534, respectively), there is a clear superiority achieved by MSExtractor compared to the three compared approaches in terms of both CHM and CHD, as well as IRN.

We can also observe from Table 1 that FoME tends to provide better results in terms of OPN in three out of the two systems. This superiority is justified by the fact that FoME excludes a relatively important number of classes that are not covered by the dynamic analysis scenarios. These excluded classes will be, in turn, excluded from the candidate microservices. Obviously, ignoring a number of classes may improve coupling, but would provide functionally incomplete microservice candidates. These classes are generally related to exceptions, e.g., the classes *MailingException*, *FilePathException*, *BootstrapException* from the project `Roller`, or to other third-party or no-behavior classes, e.g., *YoutubeLink-Transformer*, *MessageHelper*, and *SecurityConfig* from the project `Springblog`. Such exclusion of classes from microservices would result in an incomplete architecture and would require a manual inspection by developers performing the migration.

4   Conclusions and Future Work

In this paper, we proposed MSExtractor, a novel approach that tackles the microservices extraction problem and formulates it as a multi-objective combinatorial optimization problem. Specifically, MSExtractor employs the non-dominated sorting genetic algorithm (NSGA-II) to drive a search process towards an optimal decomposition of a given legacy application while considering structural dependencies in the source code. Our evaluation demonstrates that MSExtractor is able to extract cohesive and loosely coupled services with higher performance than three recent state-of-the-art approaches.

As we only focused on the identification of microservices boundaries, we plan in our future work to investigate the other steps of the migration process towards containerization and pre-deployment configuration of our microservices candidates. We also plan to evaluate our approach form developers and software architects perspective on more systems. We also plan to consider non-functional criteria that are essential in the context of microservices architecture, including the scalability and availability of the system. We further plan on challenging the effectiveness of NSGA-II, being the main search algorithm used in MSExtractor, by performing a comparative study with other popular search algorithms, namely the Non-dominated Sorting Genetic Algorithm II (NSGA-II) [1], and Strength Pareto Evolutionary Algorithm 2 (SPEA2) [11].

References

1. Deb, K., Pratap, A., Agarwal, S., Meyarivan, T.: A fast and elitist multiobjective genetic algorithm: NSGA-II. IEEE Trans. Evol. Comput. **6**(2), 182–197 (2002)
2. Mkaouer, W., et al.: Many-objective software remodularization using NSGA-III. ACM Trans. Softw. Eng. Methodol. (TOSEM) **24**(3), 17 (2015)

3. Chidamber, S.R., Kemerer, C.F.: A metrics suite for object oriented design. IEEE Trans. Softw. Eng. **20**(6), 476–493 (1994)
4. Jin, W., Liu, T., Zheng, Q., Cui, D., Cai, Y.: Functionality-oriented microservice extraction based on execution trace clustering. In: 2018 IEEE International Conference on Web Services (ICWS), pp. 211–218. IEEE (2018)
5. Athanasopoulos, D., Zarras, A.V., Miskos, G., Issarny, V., Vassiliadis, P.: Cohesion-driven decomposition of service interfaces without access to source code. IEEE Trans. Serv. Comput. **8**(4), 550–562 (2015)
6. Ouni, A., Wang, H., Kessentini, M., Bouktif, S., Inoue, K.: A hybrid approach for improving the design quality of web service interfaces. ACM Trans. Internet Technol. (TOIT) **19**(1), 4 (2018)
7. Adjoyan, S., Seriai, A.-D., Shatnawi, A.: Service identification based on quality metrics object-oriented legacy system migration towards SOA. In: SEKE: Software Engineering and Knowledge Engineering (2014)
8. Newman, S.: Building Microservices: Designing Fine-grained Systems. O'Reilly Media, Sebastopol (2015)
9. Mazlami, G., Cito, J., Leitner, P.: Extraction of microservices from monolithic software architectures. In: 2017 IEEE International Conference on Web Services (ICWS) (2017)
10. Andritsos, P., Tzerpos, V.: Information-theoretic software clustering. IEEE Trans. Softw. Eng. **31**(2), 150–165 (2005)
11. Zitzler, E., Laumanns, M., Thiele, L.: SPEA2: improving the strength Pareto evolutionary algorithm, TIK-report, vol. 103 (2001)

Towards Automated Planning
for Enterprise Services: Opportunities
and Challenges

Maja Vukovic[1]($\boxtimes$), Scott Gerard[1], Rick Hull[1], Michael Katz[1], Laura Shwartz[1],
Shirin Sohrabi[1], Christian Muise[1], John Rofrano[1], Anup Kalia[1],
Jinho Hwang[1], Dang Yabin[2], Ma Jie[2], and Jiang Zhuoxuan[2]

[1] IBM T.J. Watson Research Center, Yorktown Heights, USA
{maja,sgerard,lshwartz,ssohrab,rofrano,jinho}@us.ibm.com,
{michael.katz1,christian.muise,anup.kalia}@ibm.com
[2] IBM China Research Lab, Beijing, China
{dangyb,bjmajie,jzxjiang}@cn.ibm.com

Abstract. Existing Artificial Intelligence (AI) driven automation solutions in enterprises employ machine learning, natural language processing, and chatbots. There is an opportunity for AI Planning to be applied, which offers reasoning about action trajectories to help build automation blueprints. AI Planning is a problem-solving technique, where knowledge about available actions and their consequences is used to identify a sequence of actions, which, when applied in a given initial state, satisfy a desired goal. AI Planning has successfully been applied in a number of domains ranging from space applications, logistics and transportation, manufacturing, robotics, scheduling, e-learning, enterprise risk management, and service composition. In this paper, we discuss experience in building automation solutions that employ AI planning for use in enterprise IT and business services, such as change and event management, migration and transformation and RPA composition. We discuss challenges in adoption of AI planning across the enterprise from implementation and deployment perspectives.

Keywords: Enterprise services · Change and event management · Migration · AI planning

1 Introduction

For the past several years there has been a focus on AI driven automation in services business, with successful solutions that employ Machine Learning (ML), Natural Language Processing (NLP), and chatbots. We believe there is also an opportunity to apply AI Planning in multiple domains e.g., to accelerate migration processes and IT service management (ITSM), speed up creation of RPA solutions and to further enhance chatbots.

AI Planning offers a capability to reason about possible action trajectories to help build automation blueprints. We discuss use cases in services business, proposed framework and challenges to adoption of AI planning.

© Springer Nature Switzerland AG 2019
S. Yangui et al. (Eds.): ICSOC 2019, LNCS 11895, pp. 64–68, 2019.
https://doi.org/10.1007/978-3-030-33702-5_6

2   Use Cases

AI Planning offers automated means to schedule, re-plan when needed and manage the design phase of migration processes [8], and can be further used to dynamically assemble (and reassemble) sequences of actions that drive the migration execution process. We also see an opportunity for AI planning in IT Service Management, such as event management, change management, and service management. Similarly, one catalyst for exploring the use of AI Planning in the process specification area is the field of Robotic Process Automation (RPA), and more broadly workflow management.

The general idea of using AI Planning to orchestrate services was explored in the Web Services area [10]. Hoffmann et al. [6] provides a first exploration of how planning can be applied in connection with SAP-based business processes. In task-oriented conversation scenarios, bots are designed to follow a pre-defined dialog flow to respond to user's intents, collect information, take actions and fulfill the user predefined task. But in many business scenarios, tasks are complex and difficult to define as a logical flow, and this opens an opportunity for AI planning.

3   Framework for AI Planning in Enterprise

There are two phases in the application of AI Planning to business domains. At design time: the domain is explored, the problem is specified, stakeholders validate the expected value, the solution is designed, and the implementation is built. Typically at run time, the implementation is executed, plans are created on-demand, and are recreated as unforeseen events occur plan actions are executed, and the implementation is refined as necessary. The design time vs. run time distinction is somewhat variable. Specifically, if the domain is both stable (unchanging) and well understood, it is possible that plans can be generated once during design time and then used repeatedly throughout run time. In this case, a Subject Matter Experts (SME) might review and refine the plan before it is used for repeated execution. Also, in this approach the plans typically include conditionals, so that a single plan can accommodate variations that will arise as the plan is applied to different real-world cases.

Figure 1 illustrates how a Planning capability can be situated in an overall process automation scenario. Starting from the bottom center, the figure shows a library of re-usable configurable items, including micro-robots, decisioning capabilities, and manual tasks. The engines for the configurable items are shown at the bottom, including the ML-based decisioning components, the Robot Engines (from various vendors), and the rules engine. The configurable items are callable using REST APIs, gRPC APIs, or similar. The meta-data about the configurable items is based on a World Model that supports generic business processes (e.g., supporting notions of process flows and conditionals) and also the application at hand (e.g., including data structures for the different business entity types that progress through the process). There is also meta-data about the client environment (e.g., system configuration information).

When applying AI Planning for process specification there is a design-time variant, where the plan is created in advance and includes conditionals, and a run-time variant, where planning is preformed dynamically, at the beginning and/or in the middle of process execution. The design-time variant is appropriate when developing a process that will be run many times (e.g., invoice processing, supply chain management, report generation) or where a manual validation and refinement of the automatically generated plan is desired. The run-time variant is useful for handling exceptional situations. Figure 1 shows Planning Engines in two places, corresponding to the use of design-time or run-time planning.

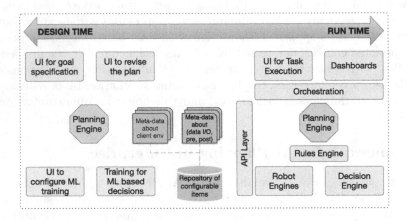

Fig. 1. High-level framework

Finally, the top layer of the figure shows the main user interface capabilities of the framework. These include, for design-time planning, a UI for specifying the goals to be achieved, and also for reviewing and refining the generated plans and process schemas. For both design-time and run-time planning there are UIs for end-user task performance and for monitoring and reporting.

4   Challenges in AI Planning for Enterprise

Non-experts rarely are familiar with the existing planning tools and their formalisms. For example, tools that provide a provably optimal solution might be of interest for some tasks, while tools that provide a solution of increased quality in an anytime manner can be desired in other cases. Thus, there is a clear benefit in removing the burden of choosing the right tool from the non-expert user.

The work on planning portfolios, where multiple planners for the same computational problem are exploited to derive a meta-planner for that computational problem is one step in that direction [4,9,12]. Across computational problems, aside of educating the user, not much has been done so far. One possible step in that direction is creating a single entry point that receives a planning task and returns solutions for multiple computational problems, emphasizing the differences in solution quality, consumed resources, and solution guarantees. That way, the user will be able to make an intelligent decision about the actual computational problem and the respective (meta-)planner to use.

Per computational problem, the performance issues may be tackled by introducing additional planners, and making the choice of the actual planner task dependent. Performance can improve gradually, with every additional planner added to the meta-planner.

Since planning domains often ignore large parts of the actual problem at hand, all too often, the obtained solutions are not fully applicable in the real world. Further, since planning tools are not easily maintained by generalists, it might be beneficial to minimize the actual planning at the critical path of an application.

To ease the entry into planning for the general crowd, it might be beneficial to focus on a small set of domains of specific interest, such as IT service management. In these domains, specific tools can be created to extract the knowledge needed in order to create the planning model. Creating such tools will reduce the barrier to using planners for these applications.

Difficulty of modeling planning tasks is one of the major obstacles to using planners, there are research efforts on developing tools that help with generic, domain-independent modeling, such as itSIMPLE [14]. Other possibilities may include the use of Mind Maps, a graphical representation of concepts and relations, to address the knowledge engineering challenge. The domain knowledge can be encoded by one or more Mind Maps connected by the same concept used in multiple Mind Maps. The system can then translates the Mind Maps into an AI planning problem automatically [13]. It is also possible to learn the causal relation between the concepts in order to build the Mind Maps automatically from scratch or augment or validate existing ones [5].

Another area for research is how to develop systems that automatically learn the actions that comprise the domain descriptions. The goal would be to learn both the actions themselves coupled with preconditions and effects. Predicates would need to be consistent across all the atomic actions. Some early work is being done on learning the actions from SMEs (e.g. generating high level descriptions and approximated preconditions and effects, prompting the SME to refine them); business process information is extracted from text-based descriptions using natural language processing [3,7,11].

5 Conclusion

We presented use cases of AI planning as means of automating IT and Business services. We introduced key elements of an overarching framework, which brings together planning at design and runtime phases. We then outline key research challenges to full adoption of AI planning for automation in the Enterprise, including lack of tooling that enables seamless and automated development of world models, coupled with generic planning models. Future work will focus on integration of planning and learning.

Acknowledgments. We thank our colleagues: Stefan Pappe, Arvind Viswanathan, Valentina Salapura, Sridrar Thiruvengadam, Boby Philip, Sharon Alvarado Brenes, Joaquin Eduardo Bonilla Arias, and Sussana Ting.

References

1. Ninth International Planning Competition (IPC-9): planner abstracts (2018)
2. Proceedings of the Thirty-Third AAAI Conference on Artificial Intelligence (AAAI 2019). AAAI Press (2019)
3. van der Aa, H., Leopold, H., Reijers, H.A.: Detecting inconsistencies between process models and textual descriptions. In: Business Process Management - 13th International Conference, BPM 2015, Innsbruck, Austria, 31 August - 3 September, 2015, Proceedings, pp. 90–105 (2015)
4. Cenamor, I., de la Rosa, T., Fernández, F.: IBaCoP-2018 and IBaCoP2-2018. In: Ninth International Planning Competition (IPC-9): planner abstracts [1], pp. 9–10
5. Hassanzadeh, O., et al.: Answering binary causal questions through large-scale text mining: An evaluation using cause-effect pairs from human experts. In: IJCAI19 (2019)
6. Hoffmann, J., Weber, I., Kraft, F.M.: Sap speaks PDDL: exploiting a software-engineering model for planning in business process management. J. Artif. Int. Res. **44**(1), 587–632 (2012). http://dl.acm.org/citation.cfm?id=2387933.2387946
7. Hull, R., Nezhad, H.R.M.: Rethinking BPM in a cognitive world: transforming how we learn and perform business processes. In: BPM 2016, Rio de Janeiro, Brazil, 18–22 September 2016, Proceedings (2016)
8. Jackson, M., Rofrano, J.J., Hwang, J., Vukovic, M.: Blueplan: a service for automated migration plan construction using AI. In: Service-Oriented Computing - ICSOC 2018 Workshops, Hangzhou, China, November 2018, Revised Selected Papers (2018)
9. Katz, M., Sohrabi, S., Samulowitz, H., Sievers, S.: Delfi: Online planner selection for cost-optimal planning. In: Ninth International Planning Competition (IPC-9): planner abstracts [1], pp. 57–64
10. Narayanan, S., McIlraith, S.A.: Simulation, verification and automated composition of web services. In: Proceedings of the 11th International Conference on World Wide Web, WWW 2002, pp. 77–88. ACM, New York (2002)
11. Nezhad, H.R.M., Akkiraju, R.: Towards cognitive BPM as the next generation BPM platform for analytics-driven business processes. In: Business Process Management Workshops - BPM 2014 International Workshops, Eindhoven, The Netherlands, 7–8 September 2014, Revised Papers, pp. 158–164 (2014)
12. Sievers, S., Katz, M., Sohrabi, S., Samulowitz, H., Ferber, P.: Deep learning for cost-optimal planning: task-dependent planner selection. In: Proceedings of the Thirty-Third AAAI Conference on Artificial Intelligence (AAAI 2019). [2]
13. Sohrabi, S., Katz, M., Hassanzadeh, O., Udrea, O., Feblowitz, M.D., Riabov, A.: IBM scenario planning advisor: plan recognition as AI planning in practice. AI Commun. **32**(1), 1–13 (2019)
14. Vaquero, T.S., Romero, V., Tonidandel, F., Silva, J.R.: itSIMPLE 2.0: an integrated tool for designing planning domains. In: Boddy, M., Fox, M., Thiébaux, S. (eds.) Proceedings of the Seventeenth International Conference on Automated Planning and Scheduling (ICAPS 2007), pp. 336–343. AAAI Press (2007)

Run-Time Service Operations and Management

A Model for Distributed Service Level Agreement Negotiation in Internet of Things

Fan Li[✉][iD], Andrei Palade[✉], and Siobhán Clarke[✉][iD]

Trinity College Dublin, College Green, Dublin, Ireland
{fali,paladea,Siobhan.Clarke}@scss.tcd.ie

Abstract. Internet of Things (IoT) services can provide a comprehensive competitive edge compared to traditional services by leveraging the physical devices' capabilities through a demand-driven approach to provide a near real-time state of the world. Service provision in such a dynamic and large-scale environment needs to cope with intermittent availability of service providers, and may require negotiation to agree on Quality of Service (QoS) of a particular service. Existing negotiation approaches for IoT require a centralised perspective of the environment, which may not be practical given the scale and autonomy of service providers that rely on sensors deployed various environments to deliver their services. We propose a negotiation mechanism that uses distributed service brokers to dynamically negotiate with multiple IoT service providers on behalf of service consumers. The framework uses a hierarchical architecture to cluster service information and to manage the message flows during the negotiation process. Simulation results demonstrate the feasibility and efficiency of our proposal.

Keywords: Internet of Things · Distributed SLA negotiation · Negotiation protocol

1 Introduction

The IoT envisions that a large number of physical, potentially mobile devices, connected over the Internet, may provide a near real-time state of the world. The capabilities of each device can be abstracted through a well-defined interface and provided as a service [24]. Compared to traditional (cloud-based) services, service provisioning in such a dynamic and large-scale environment needs to cope with the intermittent availability of service providers, and may have flexible service quality demands and pricing options [8]. For example, compared to a weather forecasting application, a fire detection application has more stringent QoS demands on a smoke detection service and a temperature service. If a pay-as-you-go model is used, the same services can be delivered to different users with different service properties or QoS, by reconfiguring the services [5,14].

Mission-critical applications in transportation, health care, and emergency response services, require certain QoS guarantees to be provided to successfully

© Springer Nature Switzerland AG 2019
S. Yangui et al. (Eds.): ICSOC 2019, LNCS 11895, pp. 71–85, 2019.
https://doi.org/10.1007/978-3-030-33702-5_7

deliver their services to stakeholders [23]. Traditionally, such applications have relied on a Service Level Agreement (SLA), which is a contract-like concept that formalizes the obligations and the guarantees of involved parties in the context of a particular service provisioning [13]. To tailor a service based on user's demand, and resolve possible conflicts between a service provider and consumer, a dynamic negotiation process is required where both parties express their own demands and preferences to arrive at a consensus before the actual service delivery. The output of this process is used to generate an SLA [21].

Compared to traditional (cloud-based) services, research on SLA negotiation in the IoT is still in the preliminary stage [17,19]. Because of the scale and the intermittent availability of geographically distributed service providers, the existing proposals do not address the negotiation problems that emerge because of frequent disconnections between service providers and insufficient awareness of local context such as service location [16]. The IoT is dynamic nature in terms of service providers' availability and mobility, unpredictable device status, and unstable wireless network conditions. Also, the data transmissions between devices and cloud, and the spontaneous interactions amongst devices may produce an enormous number of messages or events, which may further cause network congestion and reduce event processing capability. A lightweight negotiation protocol that considers the communication problems in a dynamic environment is needed for run-time IoT service negotiation. In our previous work, we assume a middleware is deployed on a set of edge devices, which uses a decentralized negotiation protocol to negotiate with candidate service providers on behalf of consumers [11]. The services are registered in the gateways that receive the registration requests, and the negotiation requests are forwarded by gateways to their neighbours until the request can be solved, or the maximum hop is reached. The simulation result shows that the purely decentralized architecture is not efficient enough to address large-scale and dynamic issues. Also, this experiment does not consider users' spatial requirements.

In this paper, we propose IoT-Negotiate, a negotiation model that enables distributed service brokers connected through an overlay network to manage the service information and control message flows during the negotiation process. The model uses a hierarchical topology to address the communication challenges in the environment, performs location-based data distribution and replication to enable an efficient message forwarding, and conducts distributed SLA negotiation with candidate service providers.

The remainder of this paper is organised as follows. Section 2 summarises the related work. Section 3 introduces the IoT-Negotiate mechanism. Section 4 describes the hierarchical overlay network of IoT-Negotiate and introduces the overlay network creation algorithm. Section 5 presents the service distribution mechanism. Section 6 illustrates the distributed SLA negotiation process. Section 7 details the experimental setup and evaluation results and Sect. 8 concludes the paper with a discussion about future research directions.

2   Related Work

Existing literature on SLA negotiation is limited, especially for dynamic, large-scale environments such as IoT. As one of the key area of building a negotiation component [26], the negotiation protocol has been discussed in different cloud projects. For instance, a set of messages were designed for QoS negotiation when delivering composite services [23]. However, this proposal moved the burden of negotiation from the end user to each atomic service. Karl Czajkowski *et. al.* [4] presented the Service Negotiation and Acquisition Protocol (SNAP) for negotiating access to different resources in a distributed system. However, it is too heavyweight and not flexible enough for automatic negotiation. Nabila *et. al.* [9] illustrated the generic alternating offers protocol proposed by Rubinstein, for bargaining between agents. Based on that, a set of extensions has been proposed to address different negotiation issues such as multilateral negotiation [2], or semantic-based approach [18]. FIPA Contract Net Interaction Protocol [6] (CNP) is another commonly-used negotiation protocol, which supports recursive negotiation to find a compromise [28]. Smith [22] described the semantics of exchanged information among the nodes in a distributed system under the assumption that each node can communicate with every other node. Misura et al. [16] proposed a cloud-based mediator platform where automatic negotiation is performed to find the conditions of data provision that are acceptable to application providers. Gaillard et al. [7] outlined a centralized SLA management component in WSN to guarantee the QoS parameters. However, this framework relies on human intervention to finish the negotiation process. Mingozzi et al. presented an SLA negotiation framework for M2M application [15]. However, the paper does not specify the detail of the negotiation mechanism, and the single request-reply interaction is insufficient for multi-round negotiation.

3   System Model

Consider a smart city environment where service providers deploy their services on resource-constrained, potentially mobile devices to capture data from the surrounding physical environment. Such service providers can provide a comprehensive competitive edge compared to traditional service provisioning techniques by leveraging the available services through a demand-driven approach to enable new applications for citizens such as real-time monitoring applications (e.g., traffic and real-time public transport services monitoring, particle concentration or noise pollution detection). Such services are generally developed using various approaches and technologies, and provide various QoS levels. SLA negotiation procedures may be required to achieve certain guarantees about the QoS of the application. Also, given the scale the environment, an automated procedure may be required as a manual approach may not be practical. To automate SLA negotiation for an urban-scale environment, we propose IoT-Negotiate, which is a distributed negotiation framework deployed on a set of devices deployed at the edge of the network. These devices can be mobile such a mobile handset or

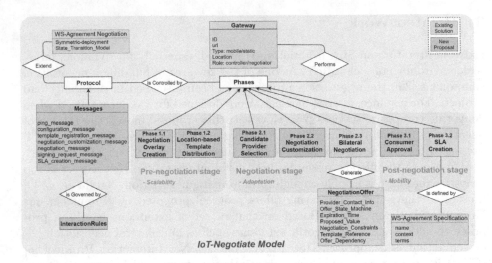

Fig. 1. IoT-negotiate ontology

fixed such as a workstation connected through WiFi or Ethernet. We refer to the devices as gateways. The negotiation procedure is performed by the fixed gateways because they are likely to have more stable and reliable network connections, whilst the mobile gateways are only used for forwarding messages.

To enable the demand-driven service provisioning vision, the service providers are required to provide the service properties with default values in SLA templates and publish the templates to the market. An SLA template is defined as $\text{SLAT} = \langle At_{id}, A_c, At_t, N_i, T, C \rangle$, consisting of template id At_{id}, agreement context A_c, template temporality At_t, negotiation information N_i, terms T (e.g., location, QoS, price, etc.) and constraints C, which can be regarded as a blueprint to create a valid negotiation offer based on user-specific demands [10]. Figure 1 shows the ontology of our proposed IoT-Negotiate model.

The IoT-Negotiate model composed of three stages: pre-negotiation, negotiation, and post-negotiation. Seven types of messages are designed to support different phases in the three stages:

Definition 1. *Ping message, which is defined as: $Ping = <S_{id}, R_{id}, \text{"hello"}>$, consisting of the sender identifier S_{id}, receiver identifier R_{id} and a "hello" string.*

Definition 2. *Configuration message, which is defined as: $Cf_{msg} = <O_p, S_{id}, R_{id}, m, ttl, Route>$, consisting of an operation code O_p, sender identifier S_{id}, receiver identifier R_{id}, message content m, the maximum number of hops ttl, and a routing table Route.*

Definition 3. *Template registration message, which is defined as: $Tr_{msg} = <O_p, SP_{id}, S_t>$, consisting of an operation code O_p, service provider identifier SP_{id}, and a template S_t.*

Definition 4. *Negotiation customize message, which is defined as:* $Nc_{msg} = <Ni_{id}, Nr_{id}, cnt, S_t>$, *consisting of the negotiation initiator identifier* Ni_{id}, *negotiation responder identifier* Nr_{id}, *negotiation context cnt (e.g., negotiation protocol, SLA schema, deadline, etc.), and the referred template* S_t.

Definition 5. *Negotiate message, which is defined as:* $Ng_{msg} = <S_{id}, R_{id}, O, O_p, m>$, *consisting of the sender identifier* S_{id}, *receiver identifier* R_{id}, *negotiation offers* O, *operation code* O_p *and message content* m.

Definition 6. *Signing request message, which is defined as:* $Sr_{msg} = <G_{id}, SC_{id}, O_a, Route>$, *consisting of the gateway identifier* G_{id}, *the consumer identifier* SC_{id}, *a list of acceptable offers* O_a, *and a routing table Route.*

Definition 7. *Mobile entity locating message, which is defined as:* Ml_{msg} $= <S_{id}, R_{id}, E_{id}, m, O_p>$, *consisting of the sender identifier* S_{id}, *the receiver identifier* R_{id}, *the entity identifier* E_{id}, *message content* m, *and operation code* O_p.

Definition 8. *SLA creation message, which is defined as:* $Sc_{msg} = <Ai_{id}, Nr_{id}, O_a>$, *consisting of the agreement initiator identifier* Ai_{id}, *agreement responder identifier* Ar_{id}, *and an offer signed by the service user* O_a. *The response should contain the reference of new pending SLA instance.*

In the **pre-negotiation** stage, a logic hierarchical negotiation overlay network (HNON) is dynamically created by exchanging ping and configuration messages (Phase 1.1, Sect. 4). The HNON manages SLA templates and controls the message flow during the negotiation process. The SLATs submitted by service providers are distributed in HNON according to service locations using template registration messages. The location-based message forwarding mechanism (Phase 1.2, Sect. 5) is designed based on the assumption that service providers are more likely to appear or move around the areas that are close to the advertised service location. If a gateway detects a local stored SLAT has the potential to meet QoS requirements, the gateway has a bigger chance to directly connected to the service provider (i.e. candidate service provider) to start a bilateral negotiation.

The **negotiation stage** begins when a user submits the request through a negotiation message. The message contains an offer expected by the user, which specifies the requested service location, QoS requirements and negotiation constraints. The message is forwarded to the gateways that are close to the requested location over the HNON. The gateways compare the request with local stored SLATs according to a unified SLA ontology (e.g., the WIoT-SLA ontology [10]) to search for candidate services (Phase 2.1). Once a candidate service is detected, a negotiation customization message (Phase 2.2) is sent to the service provider to initialize the negotiation instance before the bilateral negotiation (Phase 2.3). After the negotiation, the entity locating message may be used to locate mobile consumers if they cannot be contacted at the moment (Sect. 6).

In the **post-negotiation stage**, the negotiation results from different brokers are aggregated and the most optimized solution is selected and sent to the

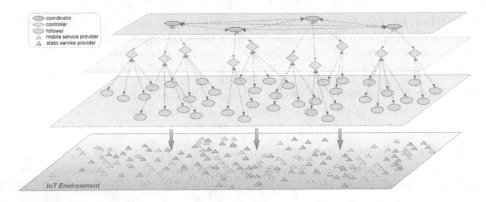

Fig. 2. Hierarchical negotiation overlay network

user through a signing request message (Phase 3.1). Once the negotiation result is approved by the user (i.e., the message is digitally signed), an SLA creation message is sent to the corresponding service provider to create a pending SLA (Phase 3.2).

4   Hierarchical Negotiation Overlay Network (HNON)

The HNON is a logistic negotiation overlay built upon the actual network topology. Figure 2 shows the three-layered structure of the proposed HNON. Each static gateway distributed in the environment is assigned to at least one of the following roles: follower, controller or coordinator. Each follower has a controller and each controller is associated with a coordinator. Followers compose the bottom layer of the overlay, which only work as brokers under the control of their controllers. Controllers compose the middle layer, which divides the environment into a set of sub-areas. Each controller can be regarded as a small data centre in the sub-area. It collects its followers' information and replicates local registered templates. The sub-area is referred to as the controller's range, which is roughly estimated by the maximum distance between the controller and its followers. The top layer is comprised of coordinators, which are directly connected with each other through the internet. A coordinator can be regarded as the access point of its controllers. In this hierarchical architecture, the follower layer guarantees a timely bilateral negotiation with service providers, the controller layer allocates negotiation tasks and improves the efficiency of template match-making process. The coordinator layer propagates messages over different sub-areas.

To create the HNON, the key requirement is to automatically assign different roles to gateways based on the network topology. To maximize the communication efficiency, we enforce that in each sub-area, the gateways which have the maximum number of wireless connections are assigned as controllers. Since the network topology is unknown for each gateway initially, the static gateways first broadcast ping messages through WiFi to identify their neighbouring gateways. Based on the number of replies, each gateway acquires the connection information and exchange this information with neighbours. As can be seen in Algorithm 1, each gateway initially caches itself as the controller and sends the controller's information through a configuration message (O_p is set to CIM) to search for a gateway that has the maximum number of connections in the nearby area (Line 1–6 in Algorithm 1(a)). Then, it waits for messages from other gateways and updates the cache if the controller specified in the received message has more connections than the cached one, or a shorter route has been detected for the same controller. If the cache is updated and the TTL message has not been reached, the controller's information is further propagated to neighbours (Line 2–17 in Algorithm 1(b)). Here the message's TTL controls the message propagation range, which is also the range of each sub-area. When the message propagation time is due, it sends a verification to the controller through a Cf_{msg} whose O_p is set to CVM (Line 7–10 in Algorithm 1(a)). The controller saves the follower's information and updates its range (Line 18–21 in Algorithm 1(b)). If the controller can not access to the Internet, it multicasts a Cf_{msg} (O_p is set to RIM) to neighbours to search for an internet-connected gateway in the sub-area, and sends a verification to it when the time is due (Line 13–22 in Algorithm 1(a)). Once a gateway is allocated as a new coordinator, it saves controllers' information and collects other coordinators' information by broadcasting a Cf_{msg} (O_p is set to FRM) through the Internet (Line 23–26 in Algorithm 1(a), Line 22–35 in Algorithm 1(b)).

5   Location-Based Template Distribution

As we mentioned in Sect. 3, the location-based template distribution mechanism is performed when a service provider advertises its service by sending the SLA template to a nearby gateway through a Tr_{msg} (O_p is set to ADV). The template is forwarded over the HNON and stored in the gateways that are within or close to the service location. Figure 3 shows the template distribution process, the message is first forwarded to a coordinator. The coordinator computes the distance between the service location and its controllers' locations, and forwards the message to controllers whose range is within the service coverage (O_p is set to $CREG$). Controllers compute the distance between service location and their followers' locations, cache the follower that has minimum distance and reply the distance to its coordinator. The coordinator caches the controller that has the minimum distance, adds the distance (d_f) to the message content and sends the message to other coordinators (O_p is set to TRG). If the coordinator does not have any controllers whose range is within the service coverage, the d_f is set as the minimum distance between the service location and its controllers' locations. Other coordinators perform the same process and reply the minimum distance if it is not greater than the d_f specified in the received message. When time is due, the originating coordinator forwards the template to the cached controller if there is no reply (O_p is set to $FREG$), or forwards the template to the coordinator that replies minimum d_f (O_p is set to $RREG$). Then the template is further forwarded to the cached follower so that it can be saved in the

---

Algorithm 1: HNON Creation Algorithm (a) - Message Sender

1 Cache itself as controller;
2 Create Cf_{msg} ($Cf_{msg}.m$ ←cached controller info, $Cf_{msg}.O_p$←CIM);
3 Set Timer T;
4 Send Cf_{msg} to neighbours;
5 /* Waiting for responses */
6 **if** receives a reply: Check if the cached controller needs to be updated;
7 **if** T expires **and** the cached controller is not itself:
8   Create Cf_{msg} ($Cf_{msg}.m$ ←self info, $Cf_{msg}.O_p$ ←CVM);
9   Mark itself as a follower, send Cf_{msg} to cached controller;
10   **if** receives the ACK: Save controller's identifier and routing info;
11 **if** T expires **and** the cached controller is itself:
12   Mark itself as a controller;
13 **if** current gateway is a controller **and** no Internet connection:
14   Create Cf_{msg} ($Cf_{msg}.m$ ←self info, $Cf_{msg}.O_p$ ←RIM);
15   Set Timer T;
16   Send Cf_{msg} to neighbours;
17   /* Waiting for responses */
18   **if** receives a reply: Check if the cached coordinator needs to be updated;
19   **if** T expires:
20   Create Cf_{msg} ($Cf_{msg}.m$ ←self info, $Cf_{msg}.O_p$ ←RVM);
21   Send Cf_{msg} to cached coordinator;
22   **if** receives the ACK: Save coordinator's identifier and routing info;
23 **if** current gateway is a controller **and** have Internet connection:
24   Create Cf_{msg} ($Cf_{msg}.m$ ←self info, $Cf_{msg}.O_p$ ←FRM);
25   Mark itself as a coordinator, broadcast Cf_{msg};
26   **if** receives a reply: Add the responder to coordinator list;

---

gateway that closest to the service location (O_p is set to REG). All the registered templates are also replicated in corresponding controllers. If a service provider is mobile and specifies a flexible service location, the SLA template is stored in the gateway that receives the request. The provider re-submits the request when moving more than a pre-defined distance. All the registered templates are periodically checked by gateways to remove the ones that are out of date or the providers are unreachable. Also, a provider can change their offerings after registration by submitting a new template with the same identifier but different creation timestamp. The updated template is submitted to a nearby gateway through a Tr_{msg} (O_p is set to UPD). Similarly, this message is forwarded to a coordinator and multicasted to all coordinators. Each coordinator forwards the message to its controllers to detect if the originating template is stored in their local areas and update it if so. If the service location is changed in the updated template, the same template distribution process will be performed to search for the closest gateway, and the old template will be deleted.

Algorithm 2: HNON Creation Algorithm (b) - Message Receiver

1 /* listening configuration messages */
2 **if** $Cf_{msg}.O_p$ =CIM:
3   resvCon ← Cf_{msg}.getMessageContent().getControllerConnections();
4   resvRoute ← Cf_{msg}.getRoute();
5   **if** resvCon > cached controller's connections:
6   Update cache with received controller's info;
7   Set state into active;
8   **else if** Cf_{msg} specifies a shorter route for a same controller:
9   Update cache with resvRoute;
10   Set state into active;
11   **else:** Set state into inactive;
12   **if** state is active **and** TTL is not reached :
13   Add self identifier to resvRoute;
14   Create Cf_{msg} ($Cf_{msg}.m$ ←cached controller info, $Cf_{msg}.O_p$←CIM, resvRoute);
15   Send Cf_{msg} to neighbours;
16   Set state into inactive;
17   **else:** Set state into inactive;
18 **if** $Cf_{msg}.O_p$ =CVM:
19   Mark itself as a controller, update range;
20   Mark sender as a follower, save follower's identifier, location and route;
21   Send back ACK;
22 **if** $Cf_{msg}.O_p$ =RIM:
23   **if** current gateway has internet connection:
24   Reply with self identifier and routing info;
25   **else if** TTL is not reached:
26   add self identifier to message's routing table;
27   forward the message to neighbours;
28 **if** $Cf_{msg}.O_p$ =RVM:
29   Mark itself as a coordinator, mark sender as a controller ;
30   Save controller's identifier, location, range and route;
31   Send back ACK;
32 **if** $Cf_{msg}.O_p$ =FRM:
33   **if** current gateway is a coordinator:
34   Save sender's identifier;
35   Reply with self identifier;

6   Distributed SLA Negotiation

The SLA negotiation process is mainly composed of three phases: (i) request forwarding and template match-making; (ii) negotiation customization with the candidate service providers; (iii) distributed bilateral negotiation and mobile consumer locating.

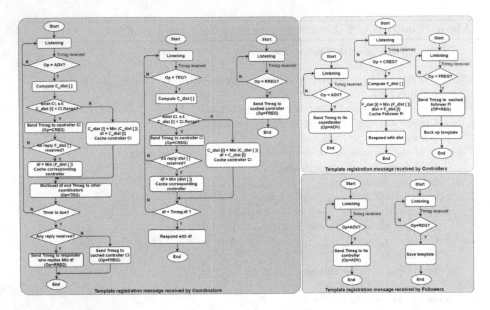

Fig. 3. Processing of template registration messages

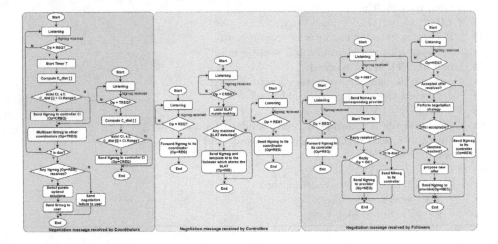

Fig. 4. Processing of negotiation messages

6.1 Negotiation Request Forwarding

Figure 4 shows the location-based request forwarding mechanism: a user submits a request through a negotiation message (O_p is set to REQ). The message is first forwarded to the coordinator layer (O_p is set to $TREQ$), then propagated to the controllers whose range covers the requested location (O_p is set to $CREQ$). Controllers match the request with local backup templates to search for the candidate services that have the potential to satisfy all the QoS requirements and forward the providers' information to the followers that actually store the templates (O_p is set to *INS*) to initialize the negotiation instance. Based on the negotiation information provided in the template, the follower sends a customization message to the provider's negotiation interface to test provider's availability and customize the negotiation context (i.e. negotiation protocol, SLA schema, template). Then the follower generates an initial offer according to the constraints specified in the request and the template. The bilateral negotiation phase starts when the follower sends the offer to the service provider through a negotiation message (O_p is set to *NEG*). During the phase, follower negotiates with the service provider by exchanging offers in an orderly way [25]. Each time a new offer is proposed by the service provider, the follower makes decisions (i.e., accept/reject the received offer, or propose a new offer) according to a predefined negotiation strategy[1]. The bilateral negotiation stops when the deadline is reached, or an offer is accepted. During the negotiation customization or consumer approval phase, it is possible that the WiFi-connected mobile negotiating parties (i.e., service providers or users) move to another place and lose the original network connection. The mobile entity locating message is created and sent to the local controller to detect the negotiation parties (O_p is set to *INQ*). The local controller propagates the message to its followers (O_p is set to *FINQ*) and each follower sends a ping message to the entity to test the connection. If any follower receives an ACK, it forwards the message content to the entity. Otherwise, the local controller forwards the message to its coordinator(O_p is set to *RINQ*), the coordinator propagates the message to its other controllers (O_p is set to *CINQ*) to detect the entity in different managed sub-areas. If the consumer cannot be connected in any sub-area, the coordinator forwards the message to other coordinators (O_p is set to *NINQ*) to start an exhaustive searching over the whole network. This design guarantees that the entity locating process is firstly performed in the local sub-area, then the nearby sub-areas, and then the whole network.

7   Evaluation

To test the performance of IoT-Negotiate model, we implemented it using *Simonstrator* [20], which is a peer to peer simulator for distributed mobile applications. The environment is configured as Dublin city center where a set of static gateways are randomly distributed and connected through WiFi. 50% gateways have Internet connections. Service providers (mobile or static) and consumers (mobile) are initialized randomly in the environment. The consumers and autonomous service providers are connected to the network by WiFi while web service providers connect with the Ethernet. Based on an existing OWLS-SLR dataset [1] and the IoT services examples proposed in related literature [3,27], we create 436

---

[1] The discussion of negotiation strategy is out of this paper's scope, more details about the evaluation of received offers and the corresponding decision-making model can be found in [12].

service prototypes which specify the service name, domain information, functional and non-functional properties (i.e., location and QoS parameters). Based on the prototypes, we generated different SLA templates for each provider by randomly assigning values to negotiable QoS parameters based on a predefined variation range. The variation range guarantees that the conflict between the service provider and a consumer is resolvable. In other words, it guarantees a successful negotiation if the services provider receives the request. In this experiment, the maximum hop of messages is set to 8 and the negotiation timeout is set to 2 min. Considering the possible network congestion, gateways use the UDP send-and-reply mode to send messages, the maximum time to wait for the reply is 2 s. Since the autonomous service providers are likely to be online and offline at any time, the *Churn* model provided by *Simonstrator* to model the connectivity of peers is adopted to simulate the availability of hosts, and the mobile entities follow a random movement pattern with a pre-defined moving speed varying from 16.7 m/s to 27.8 m/s (i.e., car speed).

Figure 5(a) shows the simulation results when the number of static gateways increases from 50 to 250 while the number of service providers is set to 150 (i.e., 50 mobile service providers and 100 static service providers). 100 consumers periodically submit requests to nearby gateways within 100 min. The negotiation result is evaluated using three metrics: template registration accuracy, percentage of successful negotiation, and the percentage of signing request messages received by the user. The template registration accuracy measures if the template has been correctly registered into the proper gateways. If the distance between the service location and the registering gateway is within 500 m, we regard it as a correct registration. The percentage of successful negotiations measures the ability to achieve a successful negotiation when potential solutions are existing in the environment. Since we adopt a negotiation strategy that guarantees a successful negotiation when consumers and providers have overlapped negotiation space, this metric measures if a candidate service provider can be successfully detected and contacted with. The percentage of signing request messages received by the user measures the efficiency of the mobile entity locating mechanism when returning the negotiation result back to the user.

The simulation result shows that the registration accuracy is around 75% when there are only 50 gateways deployed in the environment. The incorrect registrations are mainly caused by two reasons: (i) some controllers cannot find any coordinators to propagate messages. When we increase the percentage of internet-connected gateway from 50% to 90%, the registration accuracy increases to 97.2%. This is also approved by the result that the registration accuracy improves as the number of deployed gateways increasing. (ii) the SLA templates are more likely to be forwarded to the controllers that have large ranges, but the gateway finally registers the template may not be the closest gateway. This implies that the SLA templates may be stored in incorrect places if the gateways are not evenly distributed. The success rate is not as high as we expected: the percentage of successful negotiations is only about 31.7% when there are 150 gateways deployed in the environment. The main reason that causes the

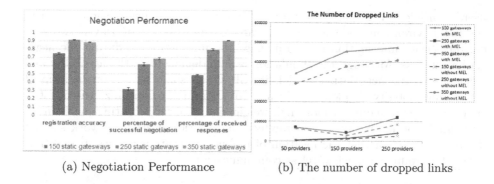

(a) Negotiation Performance   (b) The number of dropped links

Fig. 5. Simulation result

negotiation failures is negotiation timeout, which includes following situations: (i) mobile entities can not connect to any gateway during the negotiation process, or the area they are moving around does not have any internet-connected gateway;(ii) the candidate service is not registered in the right place since the controller which receives the registration request can not find a coordinator to propagate the request. When we increase the percentage of internet-connected gateway from 50% to 90%, the success rate increases from 31.7% to 72%. If we assume a majority of gateways are internet-connected, this result is acceptable. However, if most of the gateways are WiFi-connected, increasing the number of gateways can reduce the type of failures to some extent but can not eliminate the negative impact because the mobile entity locating mechanism highly relies on the interactions between gateways of different layers. Any lost response may cause a large number of simultaneous interactions when the number of gateways is large, which further increases the risk of losing packages. Figure 5(b) shows the comparison of the number of dropped links with and without mobile entity locating process (MEL). This result implies that the current mobile entity locating mechanism is not lightweight enough to locate entities that move fast in the environment. A mechanism that can trace and manage mobile negotiating entities may be more efficient to address the communication problem.

However, compared to our previous work, by adopting the hierarchical negotiation overlay network, we have decreased the maximum negotiation time from 10 min to 2 min, and the users' spatial requirements are considered as well.

8   Conclusion and Future Work

In the IoT environment, there is potential for a range of different types of devices to provide their functionalities as services and tailor the services' properties based on user-specific requirements. However, the demand-driven IoT service provisioning requires an SLA negotiation between consumers and service providers. In a distributed large-scale environment like the IoT, a middleware that can automatically negotiate with candidate service providers on behalf of users is needed. This paper proposes a distributed SLA negotiation model in the IoT environment, which uses a hierarchical negotiation overlay network to cluster service information and to manage the message flows during the negotiation process. Although the simulation results demonstrate the feasibility and efficiency of the negotiation model, it still shows some limitation in term of addressing mobility problems. In future work, we plan to optimize the negotiation model by designing a more lightweight mobile entity locating mechanism. This might be improving the hierarchical negotiation overlay network so that it can trace and predict the location of mobile negotiation parties in real-time without introducing much wireless communication.

Acknowledgment. This work was funded by Science Foundation Ireland (SFI) under grant 13/IA/1885.

References

1. OWLS-SLR - Datasets. http://lpis.csd.auth.gr/systems/OWLS-SLR/datasets.html
2. Aydoğan, R., Festen, D., Hindriks, K.V., Jonker, C.M.: Alternating offers protocols for multilateral negotiation. In: Fujita, K., et al. (eds.) Modern Approaches to Agent-based Complex Automated Negotiation. SCI, vol. 674, pp. 153–167. Springer, Cham (2017). https://doi.org/10.1007/978-3-319-51563-2_10
3. Cabrera, C., Palade, A., Clarke, S.: An evaluation of service discovery protocols in the internet of things. In: Proceedings of the Symposium on Applied Computing, pp. 469–476. ACM (2017)
4. Czajkowski, K., Foster, I., Kesselman, C., Sander, V., Tuecke, S.: SNAP: a protocol for negotiating service level agreements and coordinating resource management in distributed systems. In: Feitelson, D.G., Rudolph, L., Schwiegelshohn, U. (eds.) JSSPP 2002. LNCS, vol. 2537, pp. 153–183. Springer, Heidelberg (2002). https://doi.org/10.1007/3-540-36180-4_9
5. Elfatatry, A., Layzell, P.: Negotiating in service-oriented environments. Commun. ACM **47**(8), 103–108 (2004)
6. FIPA, F.f.I.P.A.: FIPA Contract Net Interaction Protocol Specification. Architecture (SC00029H), 9 (2002). http://www.mit.bme.hu/projects/intcom99/9106vimm/fipa/XC00029E.pdf
7. Gaillard, G., Barthel, D., Theoleyre, F., Valois, F.: Service level agreements for wireless sensor networks: a WSN operator's point of view. In: 2014 IEEE/IFIP Network Operations and Management Symposium (NOMS), pp. 1–8. IEEE (2014)
8. Grubitzsch, P., Braun, I., Fichtl, H., Springer, T., Hara, T., Schill, A.: ML-SLA: multi-level service level agreements for highly flexible IoT services. In: 2017 IEEE International Congress on Internet of Things (ICIOT), pp. 113–120. IEEE (2017)
9. Hadidi, N., Dimopoulos, Y., Moraitis, P.: Argumentative alternating offers. In: McBurney, P., Rahwan, I., Parsons, S. (eds.) ArgMAS 2010. LNCS (LNAI), vol. 6614, pp. 105–122. Springer, Heidelberg (2011). https://doi.org/10.1007/978-3-642-21940-5_7
10. Li, F., Cabrera, C., Clarke, S.: A WS-agreement based SLA ontology for IoT services. In: Issarny, V., Palanisamy, B., Zhang, L.-J. (eds.) ICIOT 2019. LNCS, vol. 11519, pp. 58–72. Springer, Cham (2019). https://doi.org/10.1007/978-3-030-23357-0_5

11. Li, F., Clarke, S.: Service negotiation in a dynamic IoT environment. In: Proceedings of the Service-Oriented Computing Workshop (ICSOC) (2018)
12. Li, F., Clarke, S.: A context-based strategy for SLA negotiation in the IoT environment. In: 2019 IEEE International Conference on Pervasive Computing and Communications Workshops (PerCom Workshops). IEEE (2019)
13. Ludwig, H., Keller, A., Dan, A., King, R.P., Franck, R.: Web service level agreement (WSLA) language specification, pp. 815–824. IBM Corporation (2003)
14. Menascé, D.A.: QoS issues in web services. IEEE Internet Comput. **6**(6), 72–75 (2002)
15. Mingozzi, E., Tanganelli, G., Vallati, C.: A framework for QoS negotiation in things-as-a-service oriented architectures. In: 2014 4th International Conference on Wireless Communications, Vehicular Technology, Information Theory and Aerospace & Electronic Systems (VITAE), pp. 1–5. IEEE (2014)
16. Misura, K., Zagar, M.: Internet of Things cloud mediator platform. In: 2014 37th International Convention on Information and Communication Technology, Electronics and Microelectronics (MIPRO), pp. 1052–1056. IEEE (2014)
17. Palade, A., et al.: Middleware for Internet of Things: an evaluation in a small-scale IoT environment. J. Reliable Intell. Environ. **4**, 3–23 (2018)
18. Ragone, A., Di Noia, T., Di Sciascio, E., Donini, F.M.: Alternating-offers protocol for multi-issue bilateral negotiation in semantic-enabled marketplaces. In: Aberer, K., et al. (eds.) ASWC/ISWC -2007. LNCS, vol. 4825, pp. 395–408. Springer, Heidelberg (2007). https://doi.org/10.1007/978-3-540-76298-0_29
19. Razzaque, M.A., Milojevic-Jevric, M., Palade, A., Clarke, S.: Middleware for Internet of Things: a survey. IEEE Internet Things J. **3**(1), 70–95 (2016)
20. Richerzhagen, B., Stingl, D., Rückert, J., Steinmetz, R.: Simonstrator: simulation and prototyping platform for distributed mobile applications. In: Proceedings of the 8th International Conference on Simulation Tools and Techniques (SIMUTOOLS), pp. 99–108. ACM, August 2015
21. Saravanan, K., Rajaram, M.: An exploratory study of cloud service level agreements-state of the art review. KSII Trans. Internet Info. Syst. **9**(3) (2015)
22. Smith, R.G.: The contract net protocol: high-level communication and control in a distributed problem solver. IEEE Trans. Comput. **12**, 1104–1113 (1980)
23. Swiatek, P., Rucinski, A.: Iot as a service system for eHealth. In: 2013 IEEE 15th International Conference on e-Health Networking, Applications & Services (Healthcom), pp. 81–84. IEEE (2013)
24. Thoma, M., Meyer, S., Sperner, K., Meissner, S., Braun, T.: On IoT-services: survey, classification and enterprise integration. In: 2012 IEEE International Conference on Green Computing and Communications (GreenCom), pp. 257–260. IEEE (2012)
25. Waeldrich, O., Battré, D., Brazier, F.F., Clark, K., Oey, M., Papaspyrou, A., Wieder, P., Ziegler, W.: WS-Agreement Negotiation Version 1.0, p. 04 (2011)
26. Yao, Y., Ma, L.: Automated negotiation for web services. In: 2008 11th IEEE Singapore International Conference on Communication Systems. ICCS 2008, pp. 1436–1440. IEEE (2008)
27. Zanella, A., Bui, N., Castellani, A., Vangelista, L., Zorzi, M.: Internet of things for smart cities. IEEE Internet Things J. **1**(1), 22–32 (2014)
28. Zulkernine, F., Martin, P., Craddock, C., Wilson, K.: A policy-based middleware for web services SLA negotiation. In: 2009 IEEE International Conference on Web Services. ICWS 2009, pp. 1043–1050. IEEE (2009)

Edge User Allocation with Dynamic Quality of Service

Phu Lai[1], Qiang He[1(✉)], Guangming Cui[1], Xiaoyu Xia[2],
Mohamed Abdelrazek[2], Feifei Chen[2], John Hosking[4], John Grundy[3],
and Yun Yang[1]

[1] Swinburne University of Technology, Hawthorn, Australia
{tlai,qhe,gcui,yyang}@swin.edu.au
[2] Deakin University, Burwood, Australia
{xiaoyu.xia,mohamed.abdelrazek,feifei.chen}@deakin.edu.au
[3] Monash University, Clayton, Australia
john.grundy@monash.edu
[4] The University of Auckland, Auckland, New Zealand
j.hosking@auckland.ac.nz

Abstract. In edge computing, edge servers are placed in close proximity to end-users. App vendors can deploy their services on edge servers to reduce network latency experienced by their app users. The edge user allocation (EUA) problem challenges service providers with the objective to maximize the number of allocated app users with hired computing resources on edge servers while ensuring their fixed quality of service (QoS), e.g., the amount of computing resources allocated to an app user. In this paper, we take a step forward to consider dynamic QoS levels for app users, which generalizes but further complicates the EUA problem, turning it into a dynamic QoS EUA problem. This enables flexible levels of quality of experience (QoE) for app users. We propose an optimal approach for finding a solution that maximizes app users' overall QoE. We also propose a heuristic approach for quickly finding sub-optimal solutions to large-scale instances of the dynamic QoS EUA problem. Experiments are conducted on a real-world dataset to demonstrate the effectiveness and efficiency of our approaches against a baseline approach and the state of the art.

Keywords: Resource allocation · Edge computing · Quality of Service · Quality of Experience · User allocation

1 Introduction

Mobile and Internet-of-Things (IoT) devices, including mobile phones, wearables, sensors, etc., have become extremely popular in modern society [4]. The rapid growth of those devices have increased the variety and sophistication of software applications and services such as facial recognition [21], interactive gaming [6], real-time, large-scale warehouse management [7], etc. Those applications usually require intensive processing power and high energy consumption. Due to the limited computing capabilities and battery power of mobile and IoT devices,

S. Yangui et al. (Eds.): ICSOC 2019, LNCS 11895, pp. 86–101, 2019.
https://doi.org/10.1007/978-3-030-33702-5_8

a lot of computing tasks are offloaded to app vendors' servers in the cloud. However, as the number of connected devices is skyrocketing with the continuously increasing network traffic and computational workloads, app vendors are facing the challenge of maintaining a low-latency connection to their users.

Edge computing – sometimes often referred to as *fog computing* – has been introduced to address the latency issue that often occurs in the cloud computing environment [3]. A usual edge computing deployment scenario involves numerous edge servers deployed in a distributed manner, normally near cellular base stations [16]. This network architecture significantly reduces end-to-end latency thanks to the close proximity of edge servers to end-users. The coverage areas of nearby edge servers usually partially overlap to avoid non-serviceable areas – the areas in which users cannot offload tasks to any edge server. A user located in the overlapping area can connect to one of the edge servers covering them (*proximity constraint*) that has sufficient computing resources (*resource constraint*) such as CPU, storage, bandwidth, or memory. Compared to a cloud data-center server, a typical edge server has very limited computing resources, hence the need for an effective and efficient resource allocation strategy.

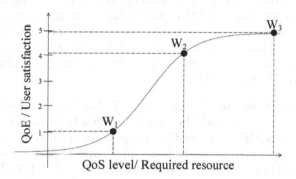

Fig. 1. Quality of Experience - Quality of Service correlation

Naturally, edge computing is immensely dynamic and heterogeneous. Users using the same service have various computing needs and thus require different levels of quality of service (QoS), or computational requirements, ranging from low to high. Tasks with high complexity, e.g. high-definition graphic rendering, eventually consume more computing resources in an edge server. A user's satisfaction, or quality of experience (QoE), varies along with different levels of QoS. Many researchers have found that there is a quantitative correlation between QoS and QoE, as visualized in Fig. 1 [2,8,15]. At one point, e.g. W_3, the user satisfaction tends to converge so that the QoE remains virtually unchanged at the highest level regardless of how high the QoS level is.

Consider a typical game streaming service for example, gaming video frames are rendered on the game vendor's servers then streamed to player's devices. For the majority of players, there is no perceptible difference between 1080p and 1440p video resolution on a mobile device, or even between 1080p and UHD from a distance farther than 1.5x the screen height regardless of the screen size [17]. Servicing a 1440p or UHD video certainly consumes more resources (bandwidth, processing power), which might be unnecessary since most players are likely to be satisfied with 1080p in those cases. Instead, those resources can be utilized to serve players who are currently unhappy with the service, e.g. those experiencing poor 240p or 360p graphic, or those not able to play at all due to all nearby servers being overloaded. Therefore, the app vendor can lower the QoS requirements of high demanding users, potentially without any remarkable downgrade in their QoE, in order to better service users experiencing low QoS levels. This way, app vendors can maximize users' overall satisfaction measured by their overall QoE. In this context, our research aims at allocating app users to edge servers so that their overall QoE is maximized.

We refer to the above problem as a *dynamic QoS edge user allocation* (EUA) problem. Despite being critical in edge computing, this problem has not been extensively studied. Our main contributions are as follows:

- We define and model the dynamic QoS EUA problem, and prove its $\mathcal{NP}$-hardness.
- We propose an optimal approach based on integer linear programming (ILP) for solving the dynamic QoS EUA and develop a heuristic approach for finding sub-optimal solutions to large-scale instances of the problem efficiently.
- Extensive evaluations based on a real-world dataset are carried out to demonstrate the effectiveness and efficiency of our approaches against a baseline approach and the state of the art.

The remainder of the paper is organized as follows. Section 2 provides a motivating example for this research. Section 3.1 defines the dynamic QoS problem and proves that it is $\mathcal{NP}$-hard. We then propose an optimal approach based on ILP and an efficient sub-optimal heuristic approach in Sect. 4. Section 5 evaluates the proposed approaches. Section 6 reviews the related work. Finally, we conclude the paper in Sect. 7.

2   Motivating Example

Using the game streaming example in Sect. 1, let us consider a simple scenario shown in Fig. 2. There are ten players $u_1, ..., u_{10}$, and four edge server $s_1, ..., s_4$. Each edge server has a particular amount of different types of available resources ready to fulfill users' requests. A server's resource capacity or player's resource demand are denoted as a vector $\langle CPU, RAM, storage, bandwidth \rangle$. The game vendor can allocate its users to nearby edge servers and assign a QoS level to each of them. In this example, there are three QoS levels for the game vendor to choose from, namely W_1, W_2 and W_3 (Fig. 1), which consume $\langle 1, 2, 1, 2 \rangle$, $\langle 2, 3, 3, 4 \rangle$, and $\langle 5, 7, 6, 6 \rangle$ units of $\langle CPU, RAM, storage, bandwidth \rangle$, respectively. Players' corresponding QoE, measured based on Eq. 3, are $1.6, 4.09$, and 4.99, respectively. If the server's available resources are not limited then all players will be able to enjoy the highest QoS level. However, a typical edge server has relatively limited

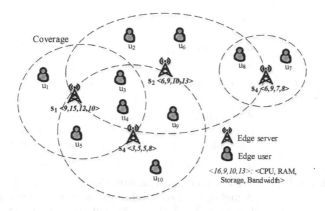

Fig. 2. Dynamic QoS EUA example scenario

resources so not everyone will be assigned W_3. The game provider needs to find a player - server - QoS allocation so that the overall user satisfaction, i.e. QoE, is maximized.

Let us assume server s_2 has already reached its maximum capacity and cannot serve anymore players. As a result, player u_8 needs to be allocated to server s_4 along with player u_7. If player u_8 is assigned the highest QoS level W_3, the remaining resources on server s_4 will suffice to serve player u_7 with QoS level W_1. The resulting total QoE of those two players is 1.6+4.99 = 6.59. However, we can see that the released resources from the downgrade from W_3 to W_2 allows an upgrade from W_1 to W_2. If players u_7 and u_8 both receive QoS level W_1, players' overall QoE is 4.09 + 4.09 = 8.18, greater than the previous solution.

The scale of the dynamic QoS EUA problem in the real-world scenarios can of course be significantly larger than this example. Therefore, it is not always possible to find an optimal solution in a timely manner, hence the need for an efficient yet effective approach for finding a near-optimal solution to this problem efficiently.

3   Problem Formulation

3.1   Problem Definition

This section defines the dynamic QoS EUA problem. Table 1 summarizes the notations and definitions used in this paper. Given a finite set of m edge servers $\mathcal{S} = \{s_1, s_2, ..., s_m\}$, and n users $\mathcal{U} = \{u_1, u_2, ..., u_n\}$ in a particular area, we aim to allocate users to edge servers so that the total user satisfaction, i.e. QoE, is maximized. In the EUA problem, every user covered by edge servers must be allocated to an edge server unless all the servers accessible for the user have reached their maximum resource capacity. If a user cannot be allocated to any edge servers, or is not positioned within the coverage of any edge servers, they will be directly connected to the app vendor's central cloud server.

Table 1. Key notations

Notation	Description
$\mathcal{S} = \{s_1, s_2, ..., s_m\}$	finite set of edge server s_j, where $j = 1, 2, ..., m$
$\mathcal{D} = \{CPU, RAM, storage, bandwidth\}$	a set of computing resource dimension
$c_j = \langle c_j^1, c_j^2, ..., c_j^d \rangle$	$d-$dimensional vector with each dimension c_j^k being a resource type, such as CPU or storage, representing the available resources of an edge server s_j, $k \in \mathcal{D}$
$\mathcal{U} = \{u_1, u_2, ..., u_n\}$	finite set of user u_i, where $i = 1, 2, ..., n$
$\mathcal{W} = \{W_1, W_2, ..., W_q\}$	a set of predefined resource level W_l, where $l = 1, 2, ..., q$. A higher resource level requires more resource than a lower one $W_l < W_{l+1}$. We will also refer to a resource level as a QoS level.
$w_i = \langle w_i^1, w_i^2, ..., w_i^d \rangle$	$d-$dimensional vector representing the resource amount demanded by user u_i. Each vector component w_i^k is a resource type, $k \in \mathcal{D}$. Each user can be assigned a resource level $w_i \in W$
$\mathcal{U}(s_j)$	set of users allocated to server s_j, $\mathcal{U}(s_j) \subseteq \mathcal{U}$
$\mathcal{S}(u_i)$	set of user u_i's candidate servers – edge servers that cover user u_i, $\mathcal{S}(u_i) \subseteq \mathcal{S}$
s_{u_i}	edge server assigned to serve user u_i, $s_{u_i} \in \mathcal{S}$
$cov(s_j)$	coverage radius of server s_j

A user u_i can only be allocated to an edge server s_j if they are located within s_j's coverage area $cov(s_j)$. We denote $\mathcal{S}_{u_i}$ as the set of all user u_i's candidate edge servers – those that cover user u_i. Take Fig. 2 for example, users u_3 and u_4 can be served by servers s_1, s_2, or s_3. Server s_1 can serve users u_1, u_3, u_4, and u_5 as long as it has adequate resources.

$$u_i \in cov(s_j), \forall u_i \in \mathcal{U}; \forall s_j \in \mathcal{S} \tag{1}$$

If a user u_i is allocated to an edge server, they will be assigned a specific amount of computing resources $w_i = (w_i^d)$, where each dimension $d \in \mathcal{D}$ represents a type of resource, e.g. CPU, RAM, storage, or bandwidth. w_i is selected from a predetermined set $\mathcal{W}$ of q resource levels, ranging from low to high. Each of those resource levels corresponds to a QoS level. The total resources assigned to all users allocated to an edge server must not exceed the available resources on that edge server. The available computing resources on an edge server $s_j, s_j \in \mathcal{S}$ are denoted as $c_j = (c_j^d), d \in \mathcal{D}$. In Fig. 2, users u_1, u_3, u_4, and u_5 cannot all receive QoS level W_3 on server s_1 because the total required resources would be $\langle 20, 28, 24, 24 \rangle$, exceeding server s_1's available resources $\langle 9, 15, 12, 10 \rangle$.

$$\sum_{u_i \in \mathcal{U}(s_j)} w_i \le c_j, \quad \forall s_j \in \mathcal{S} \tag{2}$$

Each user u_i's assigned resource w_i corresponds to a QoS level that results in a different QoE level. As stated in [2,8,15], QoS is non-linearly correlated with QoE. When the QoS reaches a specific level, a user's QoE improves very trivially regardless of a noticeable increase in the QoS. For example, in the model in Fig. 1, the QoE gained from the W_2-W_3 upgrade is nearly 1. In the meantime, the QoE gained from the $W_1 - W_2$ upgrade is approximately 3 at the cost of a little extra resource. Several works model the correlation between QoE and QoS using the sigmoid function [10,12,20]. In this research, we use a logistic function (Eq. 3), a generalized version of the sigmoid function, to model the QoS - QoE correlation. This gives us more control over the QoE model, including QoE growth rate, making the model more generalizable to different domains.

$$E_i = \frac{L}{1 + e^{-\alpha(x_i - \beta)}} \tag{3}$$

where L is the maximum value of QoE, β controls where the QoE growth should be, or the mid-point of the QoE function, α controls the growth rate of the QoE level (how steep the change from the minimum to maximum QoE level is), E_i represents the QoE level given user u_i's QoS level w_i, and $x_i = \frac{\sum_{k \in \mathcal{D}} w_i^k}{|\mathcal{D}|}$. We let $E_i = 0$ if user u_i is unallocated.

Our objective is to find a user-server assignment $\{u_1, ..., u_n\} \longrightarrow \{s_1, ..., s_m\}$ with their individual QoS levels $\{w_1, ..., w_n\}$ in order to maximize the overall QoE of all users:

$$maximize \sum_{i=1}^{n} E_i \tag{4}$$

3.2 Problem Hardness

We can prove that the dynamic QoS EUA problem defined above is $\mathcal{NP}$-hard by proving that its associated decision version is $\mathcal{NP}$-complete. The decision version of dynamic QoS EUA is defined as follows:

Given a set of demand workload $\mathcal{L} = \{w_1, w_2, ..., w_n\}$ and a set of server resource capacity $\mathcal{C} = \{c_1, c_2, ..., c_m\}$; for each positive number Q determine whether there exists a partition of $\mathcal{L}' \subseteq \mathcal{L}$ into $\mathcal{C}' \subseteq \mathcal{C}$ with aggregate QoE greater than Q, such that each subset of $\mathcal{L}'$ sums to at most $c_j, \forall c_j \in \mathcal{C}'$, and the constraint (1) is satisfied. By repeatedly answering the decision problem, with all feasible combination of $w_i \in \mathcal{W}, \forall i \in \{1, ..., n\}$, it is possible to find the allocation that produces the maximum overall QoE.

Theorem 1. *The dynamic QoS EUA problem is $\mathcal{NP}$.*

Proof. Given a solution with m servers and n users, we can easily verify its validity in polynomial time $\mathcal{O}(mn)$ – ensuring each user is allocated to at most one server, and each server meets the condition of having its users' total workload less or equal than its available resource. Dynamic QoS EUA is thus in $\mathcal{NP}$ class.

Theorem 2. PARTITION $\leq_p$ *dynamic QoS EUA. Therefore, dynamic QoS EUA is $\mathcal{NP}$-hard.*

Proof. We can prove that the dynamic QoS EUA problem is $\mathcal{NP}$-hard by reducing the PARTITION problem, which is $\mathcal{NP}$-complete [9], to a specialization of the dynamic QoS EUA decision problem.

Definition 1 (PARTITION). *Given a finite sequence of non-negative integers $\mathcal{X} = (x_1, x_2, ..., x_n)$, determine whether there exists a subset $\mathcal{S} \subseteq \{1, ..., n\}$ such that $\sum_{i \in \mathcal{S}} x_i = \sum_{j \notin \mathcal{S}} x_j$.*

Each user u_i can be either unallocated to any edge server, or allocated to an edge server with an assigned QoS level $w_i \in \mathcal{W}$. For any instance $\mathcal{X} = (x_1, x_2, ..., x_n)$ of PARTITION, construct the following instance of the dynamic QoS problem: there are n users, where each user u_i has two 2-dimensional QoS level options, $\langle x_i, 0 \rangle$ and $\langle 0, x_i \rangle$; and a number of identical servers whose size is $\langle C, C \rangle$, where $C = \dfrac{\sum_{i=1}^{n} x_i}{2}$. Assume that all users can be served by any of those servers. Note that $\langle x_i, 0 \rangle \equiv \langle 0, x_i \rangle \equiv w_i$. Clearly, there is a solution to dynamic QoS EUA that allocates n users to two servers *if and only if* there is a solution to the PARTITION problem. Because this special case is $\mathcal{NP}$-hard, and being $\mathcal{NP}$, the general decision problem of dynamic QoS EUA is thus $\mathcal{NP}$-complete. Since the optimization problem is at least as hard as the decision problem, the dynamic QoS EUA problem is $\mathcal{NP}$-hard, which completes the proof.

4   Our Approach

We first formulate the dynamic QoS EUA problem as an integer linear programming (ILP) problem to find its optimal solutions. After that, we propose a heuristic approach to efficiently solve the problem in large-scale scenarios.

4.1   Integer Linear Programming Model

From the app vendor's perspective, the optimal solution to the dynamic QoS problem must achieve the greatest QoE over all users while satisfying a number of constraints. The ILP model of the dynamic QoS problem can be formulated as follows:

$$\text{maximize} \sum_{i=1}^{n} \sum_{j=1}^{m} \sum_{l=1}^{q} E_l x_{ijl} \tag{5}$$

$$\text{subject to: } x_{ijl} = 0 \qquad \forall l \in \{1, ..., q\}, \forall i, j \in \{i, j | u_i \notin cov(s_j)\} \tag{6}$$

$$\sum_{i=1}^{n} \sum_{l=1}^{q} W_l^k x_{ijl} \leq c_j^k \ \forall j \in \{1, ..., m\}, \forall k \in \{1, ..., d\} \tag{7}$$

$$\sum_{j=1}^{m} \sum_{l=1}^{q} x_{ijl} \leq 1 \qquad \forall i \in \{1, ..., n\} \tag{8}$$

$$x_{ijl} \in \{0, 1\} \qquad \forall i \in \{1, ..., n\}, \forall j \in \{1, ..., m\}, \forall l \in \{1, ..., q\}$$

x_{ijl} is the binary indicator variable such that,

$$x_{ijl} = \begin{cases} 1, & \text{if user } u_i \text{ is allocated to server } s_j \text{ with QoS level } W_l \\ 0, & \text{otherwise.} \end{cases} \quad (9)$$

The objective (5) maximizes the total QoE of all allocated users. In (5), the QoE level E_l can be pre-calculated based on the predefined set $\mathcal{W}$ of QoS levels $W_l, \forall l \in \{1, ..., q\}$. Constraint (6) enforces the *proximity constraints*. Users not located within a server's coverage area will not be allocated to that server. A user may be located within the overlapping coverage area of multiple edge servers. *Resource constraint* (7) makes sure that the aggregate resource demands of all users allocated to an edge server must not exceed the remaining resources of that server. Constraint family (8) ensures that every user is allocated to at most one edge server with one QoS level. In other words, a user can only be allocated to either an edge server or the app vendor's cloud server.

By solving this ILP problem with an Integer Programming solver, e.g. IBM ILOG CPLEX[1], or Gurobi[2], an optimal solution to the dynamic QoS EUA problem can be found.

4.2 Heuristic Approach

However, due to the exponential complexity of the problem, computing an optimal solution will be extremely inefficient for large-scale scenarios. This is demonstrated in our experimental results presented in Sect. 5. Approximate methods have been proven to be a prevalent technique when dealing with this type of intractable problems. In this section, we propose an effective and efficient heuristic approach for finding sub-optimal solutions to the dynamic QoS problem.

Heuristic 1. GREEDY

1: **procedure** ALLOCATEEDGEUSERS($\mathcal{S}, \mathcal{U}$)
2:     **for each** $u_i \in \mathcal{U}$ **do**
3:         $\mathcal{S}_{u_i} \leftarrow \{s_j \in \mathcal{S} | u_i \in cov(s_j)\}$;
4:         **if** $\mathcal{S}_{u_i} \neq \emptyset$ **then**
5:             $s_{u_i} \leftarrow \text{argmax}_{s_j \in \{0\} \cup \mathcal{S}_{u_i}} \{s_j : c_j \geq W_1\}$;
6:             $w_i \leftarrow \text{argmax}_{W_l \in \{0\} \cup \mathcal{W}} \{W_l : W_l \leq c_j\}$;
7:         **end if**
8:     **end for**
9: **end procedure**

The heuristic approach allocates every user $u_i \in \mathcal{U}$ one by one (line 2). For each user u_i, we obtain the set $\mathcal{S}_{u_i}$ of all candidate edge servers that cover that user (line 3). If the set $\mathcal{S}_{u_i}$ is not empty, or user u_i is covered by one or more edge

---

[1] www.ibm.com/analytics/cplex-optimizer/.
[2] www.gurobi.com/.

servers, user u_i will then be allocated to the server that has the most remaining resources among all candidate servers (line 5) so that the server will be most likely to have enough resources to accommodate other users. In the meantime, user u_i is assigned the highest QoS level that can be accommodated by the selected edge server (line 6).

The running time of this greedy heuristic consists of: (1) iterating through all n users, which costs $\mathcal{O}(n)$, and (2) sorting a maximum of m candidate edge servers for each user, which costs $\mathcal{O}(m \log m)$, to obtain the server that has the most remaining resources. Thus, the overall time complexity of this heuristic approach is $\mathcal{O}(nm \log m)$.

5 Experimental Evaluation

In this section, we evaluate the proposed approaches by an experimental study. All the experiments were conducted on a Windows machine equipped with Intel Core i5-7400T processor(4 CPUs, 2.4 GHz) and 8 GB RAM. The ILP model in Sect. 4.1 was solved with IBM ILOG CPLEX Optimizer.

5.1 Baseline Approaches

Our optimal approach and sub-optimal heuristic approach are compared to two other approaches, namely a random baseline, and a state-of-the-art approach for solving the EUA problem:

– *Random*: Each user is allocated to a random edge server as long as that server has sufficient remaining resources to accommodate this user and has this user within its coverage area. The QoS level to be assigned to this user is randomly determined based on the server's remaining resources. For example, if the maximum QoS level the server can achieve is W_2, the user will be randomly assigned either W_1 or W_2.
– *VSVBP*: [18] models the EUA problem as a variable sized vector bin packing (VSVBP) problem and proposes an approach that maximizes the number of allocated users while minimizing the number of edge servers needs to be used. Since VSVBP does not consider dynamic QoS, we randomly preset users' QoS levels, i.e., resource demands.

5.2 Experiment Settings

Our experiments were conducted on the widely-used EUA dataset [18], which includes data of base stations and end-users within the Melbourne central business district area in Australia. In order to simulate different dynamic QoS EUA scenarios, we vary the following three parameters:

– Number of end-users: We randomly select $100, 200, ..., 1,000$ users. Each experiment is repeated 100 times to obtain 100 different user distributions so that extreme cases, such as overly sparse or dense distributions, are neutralized.

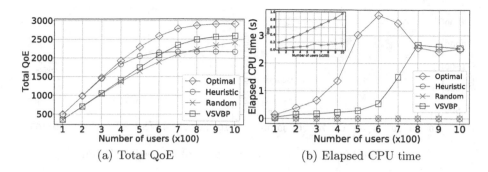

(a) Total QoE

(b) Elapsed CPU time

Fig. 3. Experiment set #1 results

- Number of edge servers: Say the users selected above are covered by m servers, we then assume $10\%, 20\%, ..., 100\%$ of those m servers are available to accommodate those users.
- Server's available resources: The server's available computing resources is generated following a normal distribution $\mathcal{N}(\mu, \sigma^2)$, where $\sigma = 1$ and the average resource capacity of each server $\mu = 5, 10, 15, ...50$ in each dimension $d \in \mathcal{D}$.

Table 2 summarizes the settings of our three sets of experiments. The possible QoS level, for each user is preset to $\mathcal{W} = \{\langle 1, 2, 1, 2\rangle, \langle 2, 3, 3, 4\rangle, \langle 5, 7, 6, 6\rangle\}$. For the QoE model, we set $L = 5, \alpha = 1.5$, and $\beta = 2$. We employ two metrics to evaluate our approaches: (1) overall QoE achieved over all users for effectiveness evaluation, and (2) execution time (CPU time) for efficiency evaluation.

Table 2. Experiment Settings

	Number of users	Number of servers	Server's available resources
Set #1	$100, 200, ..., 1000$	70%	35
Set #2	500	$10\%, 20\%, ..., 100\%$	35
Set #3	500	70%	$5, 10, 15, ..., 50$

5.3 Experimental Results and Discussion

Figures 3, 4, and 5 depict the experimental results of three experiment sets 1, 2, and 3, respectively.

(1) Effectiveness: Figures 3, 4, and 5(a) demonstrate the effectiveness of all approaches in experiment sets 1, 2, and 3, measured by the overall QoE of all users in the experiment. In general, Optimal, being the optimal approach, obviously outperforms other approaches across all experiment sets and parameters. The performance of Heuristic largely depends on the computing resource availability, which will be analyzed in the following section.

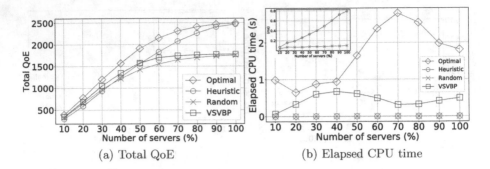

(a) Total QoE   (b) Elapsed CPU time

Fig. 4. Experiment set #2 results

In experiment set 1 (Fig. 3(a)), we vary the number of users starting from 100 and ending at 1,000 in steps in 100 users. From 100 to 600 users, Heuristic results in higher total QoE than Random and VSVBP. Especially in the first three steps (100, 200, and 300 users), Heuristic achieves a QoE almost as high as Optimal. This occurs in those scenarios because the available resource is redundant and therefore almost all users receive the highest QoS level. However, as the number of users continues to increase while the amount of available resources is fixed, the computing resource for each user becomes more scarce, making Heuristic no longer suitable in these situations. In fact, from 700 users onwards, Heuristic starts being outperformed by Random and VSVBP. Due to being a greedy heuristic, Heuristic always tries to exhaust the edge servers' resources by allocating the highest possible QoS level to users, which is not an effective use of resource. For example, one user can achieve a QoE of 4.99 if assigned the highest QoS level W_3, which consumes a resource amount of $\langle 5, 7, 6, 6 \rangle$. That resource suffices to serve two users with QoS levels W_1 and W_2, resulting in an overall QoE of $1.6 + 4.09 = 5.69 > 4.99$. Since a user's QoS level is randomly assigned by Random and VSVBP, these two methods are able to user resource more effectively than Heuristic in those specific scenarios.

A similar trend can be observed in experiment sets 2 and 3. In resource-scarce situations, i.e. number of servers ranging from 10%–40% (Fig. 4(a)), and server's available resources ranging from 5–25 (Fig. 5(a)), Heuristic shows a nearly similar performance to Random and VSVBP (slightly worse in a few cases) for the same reason discussed previously. In those situations, the performance difference between Heuristic and Random/VSVBP is not as significant as seen in experiment set 1 (Fig. 3(a)). Nevertheless, the difference might be greater if the resources are more limited, e.g. 1,000 users in both experiment sets 2 and 3, an average server resource capacity of 20 in set 2, and 50% number of servers in set 3.

As discussed above, while being suitable for resource-redundant scenarios, Heuristic has not been proven to be superior when computing resources are limited. This calls for a more effective approach to solve the dynamic QoS problem under resource-scarce circumstances.

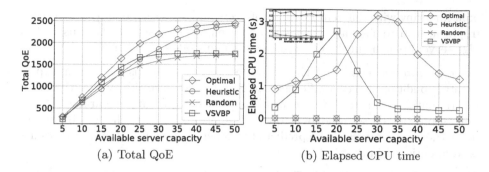

(a) Total QoE   (b) Elapsed CPU time

Fig. 5. Experiment set #3 results

(2) Efficiency: Figures 3, 4, and 5(b) illustrate the efficiency of all approaches in the study, measured by the elapsed CPU time. The execution time of Optimal follows a similar pattern in all three experiment sets. As the experimental parameters increase from the starting point to a point somewhere in the middle – 600 users in set 1, 70% number of servers in set 2, and 30 average server resource capacity in set 3 – the time quickly increases until it reaches a cap of around a hefty 3 seconds due to being $\mathcal{NP}$-hard. The rationale for this is that the complexity of the problem increases as we keep adding up more users, servers, and available resource, generating more possible options and solutions for Optimal to select from. After passing that mid-point, the time gradually decreases at a slower rate then tends to converge. We notice that this convergence is a reflection of the convergence of the total QoE produced by Optimal in each corresponding experiment set. After the experimental parameters passing the point mentioned above, the available resource steadily becomes more redundant so that more users can obtain the highest QoS level without competing with each others, generating less possible options for Optimal, hence running faster.

In experiment sets 1 and 2, the execution time of Heuristic grows gradually up to just 1 milliseconds. However, it does not grow in experiment set 3 and instead stabilizes around 0.5–0.6 ms. This is because the available resource does not impact the complexity of Heuristic, which runs in $\mathcal{O}(nm\log m)$.

5.4   Threats to Validity

Threat to Construct Validity. The main threat to the construct validity lies in the bias in our experimental design. To minimize the potential bias, we conducted experiments with different changing parameters that would have direct impact on the experimental results, including the number of servers, the number of users, and available resources. The result of each experiment set is the average of 100 executions, each with a different user distribution, to eliminate the bias caused by special cases such as over-dense or over-sparse user distributions.

Threat to External Validity. A threat to the external validity is the generalizability of our findings in other specific domains. We mitigate this threat by experimenting with different numbers of users and edge servers in the same geographical area to simulate various distributions and density levels of users and edge servers that might be observed in different real-world scenarios.

Threat to Internal Validity. A threat to the internal validity is whether an experimental condition makes a difference or not. To minimize this, we fix the other experimental parameters at a neutral value while changing a parameter. For more sophisticated scenarios where two or more parameters change simultaneously, the results can easily be predicted in general based on the obtained results as we mentioned in Sect. 5.3.

Threat to Conclusion Validity. The lack of statistical tests is the biggest threat to our conclusion validity. This has been compensated for by comprehensive experiments that cover different scenarios varying in both size and complexity. For each set of experiments, the result is averaged over 100 runs of the experiment.

6   Related Work

Cisco [3] coined the fog computing, or edge computing, paradigm in 2012 to overcome one major drawback of cloud computing – latency. Edge computing comes with many new unique characteristics, namely location awareness, wide-spread geographical distribution, mobility, substantial number of nodes, predominant role of wireless access, strong presence of streaming and real-time applications, and heterogeneity. Those characteristics allows edge computing to deliver a very broad range of new services and applications at the edge of network, further extending the existing cloud computing architecture.

QoE management and QoE-aware resource allocation have long been a challenge since the cloud computing era and before that [13]. Su et al. [22] propose a game theoretic framework for resource allocation among media cloud, brokers and mobile social users that aims at maximizing user's QoE and media cloud's profit. While having some similarity to our work, e.g. the brokers can be seen as edge servers, there are several fundamental architectural differences. The broker in their work is just a proxy for transferring tasks between mobile users and the cloud, whereas our edge server is where the tasks are processed. In addition, the price for using/hiring the broker/media cloud's resource seems to vary from time to time, broker to broker in their work. We target a scenario where there is no price difference within a single service provider. [11] investigates the cost - QoE trade-off in virtual machine provisioning problem in a centralized cloud, specific to video streaming domain. QoE is measured by the processing, playback, or downloading rate in those work.

QoE-focused architecture and resource allocation have started gaining attraction in edge computing area as well. [5] proposes a novel architecture that integrates resource-intensive computing with mobile application while leveraging mobile cloud computing. Their goal is to provide a new breed of personalized, QoE-aware services. [1,19] tackle the application placement in edge computing environments. They measure user's QoE based on three levels (low, medium, and high) of access rate, required resources, and processing time. The problem we are addressing, user allocation, can be seen as the step after application placement. [14] focuses on computation offloading scheduling problem in mobile clouds from a networking perspective, where energy and latency must be considered in most cases. They propose a QoE-aware optimal and near-optimal scheduling scheme applied in time-slotted scenarios that takes into account the trade-off between user's mobile energy consumption and latency.

Apart from the aforementioned literature, there are a number of work on computation offloading or virtual machine placement problem. However, they do not consider QoE, which is important in an edge computing environment where human plays a prominent role. Here, we seek to provide an empirically grounded foundation for the dynamic QoS/QoE edge user allocation problem, forming a solid basis for further developments.

7 Conclusion

App users' quality-of-experience is of great importance for app vendors where user satisfaction is taken seriously. Despite being significant, there is very limited work considering this aspect in edge computing. Therefore, we have identified and formally formulated the dynamic QoS edge user allocation problem with the goal of maximizing users' overall QoE as the first step of tackling the QoE-aware user allocation problem. Having been proven to be $\mathcal{NP}$-hard and also experimentally illustrated, the optimal approach is not efficient once the problem scales up. We therefore proposed a heuristic approach for solving the problem more efficiently. We have also conducted extensive experiments on real-world dataset to evaluate the effectiveness and efficiency of the proposed approaches against a baseline approach and the state of the art.

Given this foundation of the problem, we have identified a number of possible directions for future work with respect to QoE such as dynamic QoS user allocation in resource-scarce or time-varying situations, user's mobility, service migration, service recommendation, just to name a few. In addition, a finer-grained QoE model with various types of costs or network conditions could be studied next.

Acknowledgments. This research is funded by Australian Research Council Discovery Projects (DP170101932 and DP18010021).

References

1. Aazam, M., St-Hilaire, M., Lung, C.H., Lambadaris, I.: Mefore: QoE based resource estimation at fog to enhance QoS in IoT. In: 2016 23rd International Conference on Telecommunications (ICT), pp. 1–5. IEEE (2016)
2. Alreshoodi, M., Woods, J.: Survey on QoE\QoS correlation models for multimedia services. arXiv preprint arXiv:1306.0221 (2013)

3. Bonomi, F., Milito, R., Zhu, J., Addepalli, S.: Fog computing and its role in the internet of things. In: Proceedings of the First Edition of the MCC Workshop on Mobile Cloud Computing, pp. 13–16. ACM (2012)

4. Cerwall, P., et al.: Ericsson Mobility Report. Ericsson, Stockholm (2018). https://www.ericsson.com/en/mobility-report/reports/november-2018

5. Chen, M., Zhang, Y., Li, Y., Mao, S., Leung, V.C.: EMC: emotion-aware mobile cloud computing in 5G. IEEE Netw. **29**(2), 32–38 (2015)

6. Chen, X.: Decentralized computation offloading game for mobile cloud computing. IEEE Trans. Parallel Distrib. Syst. **26**(4), 974–983 (2015)

7. Ding, B., Chen, L., Chen, D., Yuan, H.: Application of RTLS in warehouse management based on RFID and wi-fi. In: 2008 4th International Conference on Wireless Communications, Networking and Mobile Computing, pp. 1–5. IEEE (2008)

8. Fiedler, M., Hossfeld, T., Tran-Gia, P.: A generic quantitative relationship between quality of experience and quality of service. IEEE Netw. **24**(2), 36–41 (2010)

9. Garey, M.R., Johnson, D.S.: Computers and Intractability, vol. 29. wh freeman, New York (2002)

10. Hande, P., Zhang, S., Chiang, M.: Distributed rate allocation for inelastic flows. IEEE/ACM Trans. Netw. (TON) **15**(6), 1240–1253 (2007)

11. He, J., Wen, Y., Huang, J., Wu, D.: On the cost-QoE tradeoff for cloud-based video streaming under Amazon EC2's pricing models. IEEE Trans. Circuits Syst. Video Technol. **24**(4), 669–680 (2013)

12. Hemmati, M., McCormick, B., Shirmohammadi, S.: QoE-aware bandwidth allocation for video traffic using sigmoidal programming. IEEE MultiMedia **24**(4), 80–90 (2017)

13. Hobfeld, T., Schatz, R., Varela, M., Timmerer, C.: Challenges of QoE management for cloud applications. IEEE Commun. Mag. **50**(4), 28–36 (2012)

14. Hong, S.T., Kim, H.: QoE-aware computation offloading scheduling to capture energy-latency tradeoff in mobile clouds. In: 2016 13th Annual IEEE International Conference on Sensing, Communication, and Networking (SECON), pp. 1–9. IEEE (2016)

15. Hoßfeld, T., Seufert, M., Hirth, M., Zinner, T., Tran-Gia, P., Schatz, R.: Quantification of YouTube QoE via crowdsourcing. In: 2011 IEEE International Symposium on Multimedia, pp. 494–499. IEEE (2011)

16. Hu, Y.C., Patel, M., Sabella, D., Sprecher, N., Young, V.: Mobile edge computing-a key technology towards 5G. ETSI White Pap. **11**(11), 1–16 (2015)

17. Lachat, A., Gicquel, J.C., Fournier, J.: How perception of ultra-high definition is modified by viewing distance and screen size. In: Image Quality and System Performance XII, vol. 9396, p. 93960Y. International Society for Optics and Photonics (2015)

18. Lai, P., et al.: Optimal edge user allocation in edge computing with variable sized vector bin packing. In: Pahl, C., Vukovic, M., Yin, J., Yu, Q. (eds.) ICSOC 2018. LNCS, vol. 11236, pp. 230–245. Springer, Cham (2018). https://doi.org/10.1007/978-3-030-03596-9_15

19. Mahmud, R., Srirama, S.N., Ramamohanarao, K., Buyya, R.: Quality of experience(QoE)-aware placement of applications in fog computing environments. J. Parallel Distrib. Comput. (2018)

20. Shenker, S.: Fundamental design issues for the future internet. IEEE J. Sel. Areas Commun. **13**(7), 1176–1188 (1995)
21. Soyata, T., Muraleedharan, R., Funai, C., Kwon, M., Heinzelman, W.: Cloudvision: real-time face recognition using a mobile-cloudlet-cloud acceleration architecture. In: 2012 IEEE Symposium on Computers and Communications (ISCC), pp. 59–66. IEEE (2012)
22. Su, Z., Xu, Q., Fei, M., Dong, M.: Game theoretic resource allocation in media cloud with mobile social users. IEEE Trans. Multimedia **18**(8), 1650–1660 (2016)

Automatic Business Process Model Extension to Repair Constraint Violations

Xavier Oriol[2][(✉)], Giuseppe De Giacomo[1], Montserrat Estañol[2,3],
and Ernest Teniente[2]

[1] Sapienza Università di Roma, Rome, Italy
degiacomo@dis.uniroma1.it
[2] Universitat Politècnica de Catalunya, Barcelona, Spain
{oriol,estanyol,teniente}@essi.upc.edu
[3] Barcelona Supercomputing Center, Barcelona, Spain

Abstract. Consider an artifact-centric business process model, containing both a data model and a process model. When executing the process, it may happen that some of the data constraints from the data model are violated. Bearing this in mind, we propose an approach to automatically generate an extension to the original business process model that, when executed after a constraint violation, repairs the contents of the data leaving it in a new consistent state.

Keywords: BPMN · UML · Data-aware processes · Integrity constraints repair

1 Introduction

Artifact-centric business process modeling has been recognized as an appropriate approach to specify the two main assets of any organization, i.e. information (data as defined through the artifacts managed by the business) and processes (services offered by the organization to perform its business) [14,15].

Despite the variety of existing proposals to specify artifact-centric Business Process Models (BPMs), there is a large consensus that any of them must contain at least a conceptual model for data, such as a UML class diagram [11], and a model for the processes, such as BPMN [8,28]. Linking data and processes along these two models has shown to be a feasible and practical way to achieve automatic executability of BPMs [5].

Furthermore, a data model always includes a set of *integrity constraints*, i.e. conditions that each state of the information base must satisfy. These constraints can be specified either graphically (such as multiplicity constraints) or textually (for instance by means of OCL constraints or SQL assertions).

The BPM states the order of execution of activities to successfully perform a business and also the effect of each executed activity over the contents of the information base (i.e. the object insertions and deletions performed by that activity over the classes in the data model). Clearly, this effect might violate some of the constraints in the data model.

S. Yangui et al. (Eds.): ICSOC 2019, LNCS 11895, pp. 102–118, 2019.
https://doi.org/10.1007/978-3-030-33702-5_9

Handling integrity constraints in the data model itself provides several advantages over manually programming them inside the BPM. Indeed, each constraint can be violated by different activities, and it is very difficult to manually identify all possible situations that may induce such violations. This makes programming manually the treatment of constraints an error-prone task and, thus, it should be avoided as much as possible. Therefore, we assume here that the execution of an activity in the BPM can raise an integrity constraint violation. A naive approach to deal with these violations would consist in forbidding the execution of the activity that caused the violation. However, this is not always appropriate because the actions entailed by the activity might have already happened in the real world. Thus, not performing this activity would end up with an information system that no longer represents the real world.

To overcome this situation, there is an alternative approach aimed at repairing the constraint violation, so that the activity can be executed anyway. This is achieved by means of performing additional updates, other than the ones explicitly specified by the activity. Therefore, under this approach, both the state of the real world and the contents of the information system will coincide and be consistent.

Since constraints can be repaired in several ways, the user (i.e. the person executing the process) should choose the most appropriate action in each situation. However, the chosen repair might lead to another violation which, in turn, requires additional repairing. Choosing repairs blindly can make the user get into a complicated sequence of violations/repairs which, known in advance, would have led him/her to make a better decision in the first place.

To properly deal with this phenomenon, we realized that the sequence of actions required to repair a constraint can be seen as a process. Then, all potential sequences of repairing actions may be modeled as a BPM itself. Therefore, given a constraint violation, we build a BPM that shows all possible ways to repair it. Then, the user may use this extended model to select the proper repairing actions by having a global sense of all the repair implications. By inspecting the model, the user can see which is the shortest path to reach consistency, which is the way to avoid a certain undesired repairing action, etc., and choose the repair(s) accordingly.

Given an artifact-centric BPM, where the data is described through a data model containing integrity constraints and the behavior of the activities is described in terms of modifications over the previously mentioned data model, we can automatically compute, at compile time, the whole chain of activities that, when executed, repairs a constraint violation. Therefore, we can extend the original BPM model by considering the flow of additional activities that have to be performed to preserve an integrity constraint. This extension can be computed for each activity of the original BPM and, since the computation can be done at compile time, it does not negatively impact the performance of the original process execution.

Moreover, by modelling the repairing process as a BPM, the process designer may customize these models at compile time to forbid some undesired paths/activities. Then, the final process model obtained can be used at execution time, by the user, to repair constraint violations when they occur. In particular, the user executes the original process as usual (e.g., through a CASE tool). However, when an integrity violation is detected, the current execution of the process stops, and the user starts executing the corresponding BPM extension to repair the violation caused by the last activity execution. When, the user has finished executing the extension, he/she can continue executing the original BPM, with the guarantee that no constraint is being violated.

2   Generating Violation Handling Extensions in BPM

We will illustrate our approach by means of the BPMN diagram in Fig. 1, together with the UML class diagram in Fig. 2. The UML diagram specifies that employees work in and manage projects. Additionally, there is a *subset* constraint stating that each manager of a project should work in it.

The process model begins when creating a new project. Then, the user can either provide employee information, in order to add him to the project (*Add Employee*) or not (the process ends). If the former, the user then can choose to provide (another) project in order to delete this employee from it (*Delete From Project*), or not. In any case, the flow goes back to the option of adding another employee to the recently created project. Hence, the message events in the BPMN diagram correspond to user-provided input, and not to evaluation of expressions using process data. This is why we use Event-Based Gateways. Note that there may be other processes in the company for hiring managers or performing other tasks, which are not shown here.

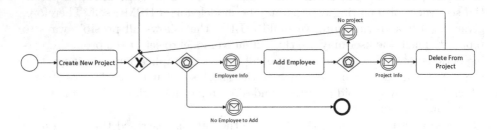

Fig. 1. Initial BPMN diagram

When executing any process activity, a violation of a constraint can occur. For example, when executing *Delete From Project* the *subset* constraint may be violated (i.e. a manager of the project is not one of its employees any more). Naturally, we could reject such activity to avoid the violation, but it may likely happen that this deletion has already taken place in the real world and cannot be undone. Thus, a reactive behavior has to be applied. We can repair that constraint by removing this employee as a manager of the project. However, this additional removal might in turn violate the minimum cardinality constraint

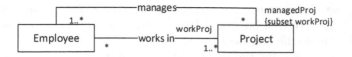

Fig. 2. Class diagram for the BPMN diagram in Fig. 1

stating that each project needs at least one manager, thus forcing the execution of more updates to preserve the consistency of the information base. This is the difficulty of the problem of integrity constraint repairing.

Fortunately, the constraints that might be violated when repairing other constraints can be determined at compile time; i.e., we can identify them by inspecting the constraints' definition itself, without considering the information contents. Indeed, several approaches build a dependency-graph showing this relation among the constraints [21,24]. Thus, the idea is that, to repair a constraint violation C and ensure that no other constraint has been violated, we have to repair C, check the constraints pointed out by C and repair them if necessary (which might require inspecting and repairing other constraints, recursively).

For instance, in our example we would be able to determine that the subset constraint might violate the minimum cardinality constraint requiring one manager for each project. Thus, after repairing the subset constraint, we should check, and possibly repair, such cardinality constraint.

In essence, our idea is that we can see the dependency graph as a BPMN diagram establishing which activities have to be carried out (and in which order) to repair a constraint violation. That is, each activity in the diagram stands for an update to apply to repair a constraint violation. Then, this activity is followed by those additional activities that repair the constraint that might have been violated because of the previously applied data update. When we reach the final BPM end event, we are sure that the initially violated constraint has been repaired, and that it has been repaired in such a way that no other constraint is being violated.

More in detail, our method uses the following steps which will be further explained in the remainder of this section:

1. *Translating integrity constraints into RGDs.* Repair-generating dependencies (RGDs) are logic formulas that, given a database state and a data update, derive new updates that must be applied to repair a constraint violation [22]. In this step, we translate the constraints into the corresponding RGDs.
2. *Building the dependency-graph of RGDs.* When executing RGDs to derive new updates, one RGD can cause the violation of another constraint, thus triggering the execution of another RGD. In the dependency-graph, we explicitly show this interaction, i.e., which RGDs might trigger other RGDs.
3. *Associating each activity to the affected part of the dependency-graph.* Given a BPMN activity, its execution might only violate some constraints, thus triggering only some specific RGDs from the dependency-graph. In this step, we automatically prune all those RGDs that can never be triggered.

4. *Translating the dependency-graph fragment into a BPMN diagram.* Intuitively, RGDs are translated as BPMN activities and the dependency-graph edges determine the flow between them.

5. *Customization.* Finally, the BPM designer may decide to prune some of the suggested ways to repair a constraint in the BPM. Indeed, our method generates all possible activities that might be applied to repair a violation. However, it might be the case that some of them are not desirable in the domain. In this step, we show how to prune undesired repairs.

In this way, given any BPM activity, we compute its BPM extension which guarantees that, when executed, it checks and repairs all violations that might occur. This extension could be integrated in the original BPM through a CASE tool, and can be used at runtime to repair constraint violations through a process executor, such as [5]. In this paper, we leave the part of showing the extension as further work, and concentrate on generating the extension and executing it. Furthermore, although we use the BPMN and UML notations, it is worth to mention that other languages, such as *service blueprints* for instance, might be used as long as they are detailed enough to be executed [10]. In particular, we only need these notations to be translatable into first-order logics, which is the base framework of our approach. Finally, one limitation of our approach is that two tasks cannot be executed simultaneously, as they might interact to cause a constraint violation. In such cases, they should be serialized.

2.1   Translating Constraints into RGDs

RGDs are logic formulas that, given a database state and a set of updates, derive new updates in order to repair a constraint violation [22]. Every UML/OCL constraint gives raise to several RGDs, each one capturing a different way to violate/repair it. For instance, consider the subset constraint stating that if x *Manages* y, then x *WorksIn* y. This constraint gives raise to the following RGDs:

$$\iota Manages(x,y) \wedge \neg WorksIn(x,y) \rightarrow \iota WorksIn(x,y) \qquad (1)$$

$$Manages(x,y) \wedge \delta WorksIn(x,y) \rightarrow \delta Manages(x,y) \qquad (2)$$

$$\iota Manages(x,y) \wedge \delta WorksIn(x,y) \rightarrow \bot \qquad (3)$$

The first RGD states that if we insert that x *manages* y ($\iota Manages(x,y)$), when x *is not working in* y ($\neg WorksIn(x,y)$), then, we must insert that x *works in* y ($\iota WorksIn(w,y)$) to guarantee the consistency of the new state after the update. Similarly, the second RGD states that if we delete some worker x from y, s.t. x was managing y, then, we must also delete that x no longer manages y. Finally, the third RGD asserts that, if we insert some manager x into y and we delete x as working in y, there is an irreparable violation, since these are two contradictory events (a manager of a project should work in it) that are executed simultaneously. Generally, any RGD with $\bot$ in the head cannot be repaired.

Not all RGDs are deterministic since some violations can be repaired in different ways. RGDs capture this indeterminism through disjunctions and existential variables in their head. E.g., consider the cardinalities from our UML diagram stating that each employee works at least in one project, and that each project has, at least, one manager. These constraints give raise, respectively, to the following RGDs:

$$Employee(x) \wedge \delta WorksIn(x,y) \wedge \neg OtherWorksIn(x) \rightarrow \delta Employee(x) \vee \iota WorksIn(x,y') \quad (4)$$
$$OtherWorksIn(x) \leftarrow WorksIn(x,z) \wedge \neg \delta WorksIn(x,z)$$

$$Project(y) \wedge \delta Manages(x,y) \wedge \neg OtherManager(y) \rightarrow \delta Project(y) \vee \iota Manages(x',y) \quad (5)$$
$$OtherManager(y) \leftarrow Manages(z,y) \wedge \neg \delta Manages(z,y)$$

Intuitively, RGD 4 detects a violation when we delete employee x from project y, and x does not work for any other project. In this case, we should choose between deleting the employee x, or adding a new project y' where he is working. Note that the decision is indeterministic. Moreover, choosing the project y' is also indeterministic since it can take different values. A similar condition with projects and managers is stated by RGD 5.

Some RGDs can be simplified by taking into account that, given a particular domain, some events cannot ever happen. Indeed, we can consider that projects are never deleted from the system. Thus, the literal $\delta Project$ can be safely deleted from the head of the RGD 5, leading to a new formula:

$$Project(y) \wedge \delta Manages(x,y) \wedge \neg OtherManager(y) \rightarrow \iota Manages(x',y) \quad (6)$$
$$OtherManager(y) \leftarrow Manages(z,y) \wedge \neg \delta Manages(z,y)$$

The structural updates (i.e., insertions or deletions) that cannot happen in a domain can be extracted from the UML class diagram itself. When a class/association A is considered to be *add-only*, this means that the event of deleting an instance of A cannot take place. Similarly, if a class/association A is considered to be *frozen*, no insertion nor deletion update can occur in its population.

The problem of obtaining RGDs from UML/OCL constraints, and simplifying them, is already solved in [22]. For our purposes, we consider only constraints written in the UML/OCLuniv subset [20]. Roughly speaking, UML/OCLuniv is the subset of UML/OCL where all constraints are universally quantified (i.e., no OCL *exists* operator is allowed), with the exception of UML min. cardinalities. We impose this limitation because: (1) RGDs from UML/OCLuniv constraints generate repairs of only one single structural event, which are easier to translate to BPMN activities, and (2) the termination of the repair process is guaranteed (while, in general OCL constraints, the repair process is undecidable) [20].

2.2   Building the Dependency-Graph of RGDs

Given a set of RGDs, we can build a dependency-graph that shows which RGDs may trigger other RGDs. Indeed, consider the case in which we delete some worker x from project y, when x was manager of y. In this situation, RGD 2 states that we have to additionally delete x as a manager of y. However, if we do so, it might be the case that the project y has no manager, thus triggering RGD 6, which states that we should add a new manager to it.

This *triggering relationship* between RGDs can be depicted graphically in several ways. For our purposes, we choose the one from [21]. Briefly, for each RGD, the left-hand side is depicted as a vertex (called *constraint-vertex*), and the different structural events from the right-hand side are depicted also as vertices (called *repair-vertex*). There is an arrow from an RGD constraint-vertex to each of its corresponding repair-vertices that indicates that, when the condition stated in the constraint-vertex is satisfied, one of its repair-vertices should be executed. Then, there is also an edge from a repair-vertex to each of the constraint vertices that might have been violated because of its execution.

The grey part of Fig. 3 shows the dependency-graph of RGDs 1, 2, 3, 4 and 6, together with other RGDs that will be used in the rest of the paper[1]. Note that there is, as expected, a triggering relationship between 2 and 6.

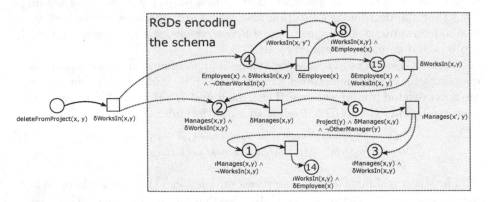

Fig. 3. Fragment of the dependency-graph showing constraint-vertices as circles, repair-vertices as squares, and triggering relationships with dashed-edges between both.

In general, there is a triggering relationship between the repair vertex R of a RGD to the constraint vertex C of another RGD if R and C have a structural event (i.e. an update operator) in common. Indeed, this means that the repair of the first constraint is applying some update that can potentially violate the second constraint. We could also apply some optimizations to remove some triggering relationships [21], but we leave them out due to space limitations.

2.3   Associating Activities to the Dependency-Graph

We start with a graph showing which constraints can be violated when repairing other constraints, and we want to know now which constraints can be violated when executing a BPMN activity in the process model. This is achieved by

---

[1] We do not include all the generated RGDs for easier understandability.

specifying the BPMN activity as an RGD, include this RGD in the dependency-graph, and identify the RGDs in the original graph reachable from it.

A BPMN activity can be seen as an RGD whose repair is, in fact, the execution of the update it specifies. For instance, consider the BPMN activity *delete from project*, from Fig. 1, stating the deletion of an employee from a project given by parameter. This BPMN activity can be written as the RGD:

$$deleteFromProject(x, y) \rightarrow \delta WorksIn(x, y) \tag{7}$$

This way of specifying BPMN activities is already used in [5], where an automatic translation from BPMN activities written with OCL constraints into these RGDs is given. Now, this RGD can be incorporated in the dependency-graph, as shown in Fig. 3, and indicate its triggering relationships, i.e. those RGDs with a constraint-vertex containing the structural events applied in the BPMN activity. In our running example, this new RGD would point to RGDs 2 and 4 since they have the $\delta WorksIn$ predicate in common.

Thus, the RGDs possibly affected by the execution of the BPMN activity correspond to the fragment of the dependency-graph reachable from the RGDs encoding the activity. In our example, these correspond to the RGDs seen so far, but, in a real case, they would likely be a subset of all the RGDs in the graph. Intuitively, this is because the execution of some activity affecting one part of the diagram will not necessarily propagate its effects to the whole diagram.

The rest of the RGDs, i.e., those that are not reachable from the RGD encoding the activity, are removed. They correspond to constraints that can never be violated when executing and repairing the main activity. Thus, they can be safely removed from the graph.

2.4 Translating the Dependency-Graph into a BPMN Diagram

Now, we translate the relevant part of the pruned dependency-graph we have just obtained into a BPMN diagram. The basic idea of the translation is that constraint-vertices are translated to BPMN gateway events that allow a user to choose between the available repairs, and any repair-vertex becomes a single BPMN activity that applies the repair itself. Then, these BPMN activities are followed either by an OR-gateway which points out to the (BPMN translation of) constraint-vertices that may have been violated because of the repair applied, or by an end-event in case none of the constraints can be actually violated.

More precisely, the translation of a constraint-vertex depends on the number of repair-vertices it has. If there is no repair, the constraint-vertex becomes a BPMN error event which means that, if we reach the violation of such constraint in the way captured by the constraint-vertex, there is no possible way to repair it and an error is thrown. If there is a single repair, the constraint-vertex becomes the BPMN-activity that applies its unique repair. If there is more than one potential repair, the constraint-vertex is translated to an event-gateway that enables the user to choose his preferred way to repair the violation (Fig. 4).

```
BPMN translateGraph(Dependency-graph g, ConstraintVertex startCV){
    Map<ConstraintVertex, BPMN-Node> c-map = new Map();
    Map<RepairVertex, BPMN-Activity> r-map = new Map();
    //    Creating the BPMN and adding the start/final node
    BPMN bpmn = new BPMN();
    BPMN-StartEvent start = new BPMN-StartEvent();
    BPMN-EndEvent end = new BPMN-EndEvent();
    //    Translating Constraints
    for(ConstraintVertex cv: g.getConstraintVertices()){
        Set<BPMN-Activity> repairingActivities = new Set();
        for(RepairVertex rv: cv.getRepairVertices()){
            BPMN-Activity repairActivity = createRepairActivity(rv);
            repairingActivities.add(repairActivity);
            r-map.put(rv, repairActivity);
        }
        BPMN-Node cv-node;
        if(repairingActivities.isEmpty()) cv-node = new BPMN-ErrorEvent();
        else if(repairingActivities.size() == 1)
                cv-node = repairingActivities.pop();
        else cv-node = new BPMN-EventGateway(repairingActivities);
        c-map.put(cv, cv-node);
        bpmn.add(cv-node);
    }
    //    Adding the start
    start.addNext(c-map.get(startCV));
    //    Link repairs to Constraints
    for(RepairVertex rv: g.getRepairActivities()){
        Map<Condition, BPMN-Node> bpmn-cons = new Map();
        for(ConstraintVertex cv: rv.getNextConstraintVertices()){
            bpmn-cons.put(cv.getViolationCondition(), c-map.get(cv));
        }
        if(bpmn-cons.isEmpty()) r-map.get(rv).addNext(end)
        else {
            BPMN-Node bpmn-or = new BPMN-OrGateway(bpmn-cons);
            if(bpmn-cons.size() == 1) bpmn-or = c-map.get(bpmn-cons.get(1))
            bpmn-or.addDefault(end);
            r-map.get(rv).addNext(bpmn-or)
}}}
```

Fig. 4. Algorithm for obtaining the BPMN diagram from the dependency-graph (Java-like notation used)

The translation of a repair-vertex always produces a unique activity that applies the changes that repair the constraint. This activity may require user input to choose the value for the existential variables. In this case, the BPMN activity is represented as a *receive task*. As an example, consider the case of RGD 2 where we have a repair vertex which inserts a new Manager x' to the project. In case a user wants to repair this RGD by means of this x' insertion, we need the user to explicitly choose a specific value for this x'.

After applying a repair, it may be the case that other constraints are violated. If this is the case, *several* constraints may need to be repaired. The OR-gateway is in charge of checking this. If no violation occurs, the flow continues to the end event. Otherwise, one (or several) path(s) will be activated. These paths will lead to the corresponding constraint-vertices so that the violations can be repaired.

This is guaranteed by the guard conditions in the OR-gateway's outgoing flows. That is, an outgoing flow pointing to the (BPMN translation of a) constraint vertex c has, as a guard, the logic condition encoded in c. Thus, the unique way to execute an activity that repairs a violation (or leads to an error event) is through the guard that first checks the constraint. So, these activities only take place when the update needs to be applied.

Note that we do not use OR-joins for synchronizing the activities execution. Intuitively, such synchronization is not necessary since each path execution represents a different violation repair for some particular values, and such repair for those particular values is independent from the rest of violations/repairs. We capture this behaviour using OR-gateways without OR-joins for ease of readability. However, if the user prefers to avoid this kind of diagrams, since OR-gateways are usually synchronized with OR-joins, our method can be adapted to replace these OR gateways by a combination of XORs and tasks.

The translation process of our approach is formalized in Algorithm 4. This algorithm has two input parameters: the (relevant part of) the dependency graph, together with the constraint-vertex representing the BPMN activity that triggers all the repairing procedure, and thus, behaves as the starting activity. As output, the algorithm provides the resulting BPMN diagram. It is easy to see that the algorithm runs in polynomial time w.r.t the input.

In Fig. 5 we show the result of applying the previous algorithm to our running example. In this BPMN we see that when executing *deleteFromProject* it may happen that we satisfy all the constraints, or that we need to delete the worker as a manager (to satisfy the subset constraint), or that we need to choose between: (1) deleting him as an employee or (2) including him in a new project (to satisfy the minimum cardinality constraint stating that each employee works in at least one project).

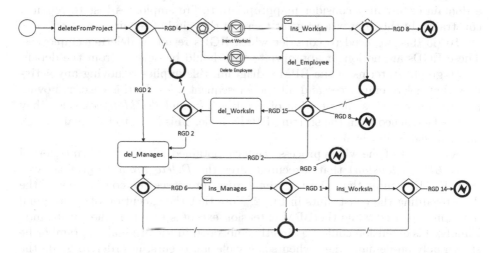

Fig. 5. BPMN diagram for repairing activity deleteFromProject in case of a violation

Although it does not happen in our running example, we should note that the BPMN diagram might have cycles. This is the case when a constraint C_1 can be repaired in such a way that violates a constraint C_2, and when repairing C_2

we might end violating C_1 again. These cycles require special attention since, in the general case, they are a source of an infinite BPM execution.

However, limiting the constraint language to be UML/OCLuniv ensures that, at runtime, these cycles do not execute forever. That is, at some point, the guard that checks if one of these activities has to be executed is going to be false, and thus, the user will not be able to loop forever. Roughly speaking, this is because, when repairing a UML/OCLuniv constraint violated by some object a of class A, we only need to create instances of a class different than A. Moreover, if those other instances violate another constraint, it is guaranteed that they will create instances of a class different than A and their current one. In general, when repairing UML/OCLuniv constraints we will never create instances of already visited classes. Thus, since the number of different classes is finite, all the constraints will eventually be repaired in a finite number of steps. A more detailed explanation of the finiteness of the computation, based on the chase algorithm termination, is given in [20].

2.5   Customization

The obtained BPMN diagram represents all possible ways to repair the various constraints that can eventually be violated by the activity execution. This is due to the fact that RGDs capture all possible ways to repair a constraint [22], and all the RGDs are represented in the BPMN diagram.

However, it might be the case that some of the proposed repairs are not desirable in the domain of the problem. For instance, in our running example, a domain expert may consider inappropriate to fire employees just to repair a constraint. In this context, we want to avoid this kind of repair.

To do this, we need to consider which RGDs result in deleting employees. These RGDs are no longer appropriate and should be deleted from the dependency graph. In terms of the BPMN diagram, this implies removing any activities that delete employees and all the subsequent ones. In this case, removing *del_Employee* causes the deletion of *del_WorksIn* and *del_Manages* since they cannot be reached from the starting BPMN node. This leads to the final BPMN diagram shown in Fig. 6.

As a result of the whole process, we have obtained a BPM diagram (referred to as *BPM extension*) that, executed after the *Delete From Project* activity from Fig. 1, ensures that *Delete From Project* preserves the consistency of the data regarding the constraints in Fig. 2. Note that the execution of the original diagram is paused while the BPM extension executes to repair the constraints. Finally, this extension could be directly embedded in the original diagram, or be shown only on-demand, i.e., when some violation occurs, in order to guide the user to repair the violations due to this activity.

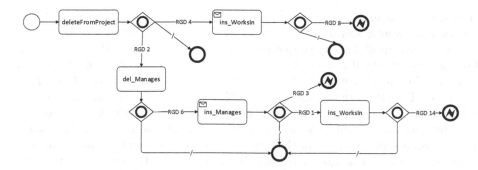

Fig. 6. Customized BPMN diagram for repairing the deleteFromProject activity

3 Executing BPM Extensions to Repair Violations

We first explain how our generated BPM extension is executed, with special emphasis on the interpretation of OR-gateways. Then, we use an existing BPM executor to run our generated extension to show the feasibility of our approach.

3.1 Business Process Extension Execution Semantics

Intuitively, the BPMN language is based on token semantics [16]. Each diagram node consumes and generates tokens. Roughly, when a process begins its execution, a token is generated by its start event for each of its outgoing flows. Each activity activates when a token reaches one of its incoming flows. When finishing its execution, the activity generates a token for each of its outgoing flows. When a token reaches an OR-gateway, all the conditions of the gateway's outgoing flows are analyzed. The gateway places a token on each outgoing flow whose condition evaluates to true. If no condition is true, then, a token is placed in the default flow. For our purposes, this intuitive token semantics suffices, but it is worth mentioning that they can be formalized by means of petri-nets [7].

The key idea of our approach is that, when running our BPM extension, each token will correspond to a different constraint violation. Since there are several constraints that can be violated simultaneously, when executing the BPM extension, there might be several tokens alive simultaneously.

The generation of these tokens is done by the OR-gateways. An OR-gateway generates a token for each outgoing flow satisfying the corresponding guard-condition. Thus, since the guard-conditions evaluate to true when there is a violation, the OR-gateway will generate, for each detected violation, a new token in the corresponding outgoing flows. Then, each of these tokens will trigger the execution of the activity that repairs the violation. After the activity's execution, another OR-gateway checks for more violations and generates the corresponding tokens. If no violation occurs, the OR-gateway generates a token in its default path, which leads to the end event, since no more repairs are needed.

For instance, when running the BPMN example of Fig. 6, we start with only one token placed in the activity *deleteFromProject*. This activity represents the structural event in the original process model that can lead to the violation of several constraints, and thus, to the execution of their repairing activities.

Once this initial activity is executed, the token reaches an OR-gateway. This OR-gateway checks if the employee who has been unassigned from the project is assigned to another project; if this is not the case, the activity *ins_WorksIn* is executed. The OR-gateway also checks if the employee was the manager of the initial project, and if this is the case, the *del_Manages* activity is executed.

The execution of the process terminates when all the tokens have reached the end events, or when one of them arrives into an error end event. In the first case, the process terminates because it has repaired all the violations and thus, the database is valid again. In the second case, the process terminates because it has found a violation that cannot be repaired[2].

It is worth mentioning that, in our approach, we consider that an OR-gateway can generate several tokens pointing to the same activity. This is the case when a constraint is violated several times by means of several data. For instance, consider that the *deleteFromProject* activity, instead of just deleting one worker given by parameter from some project, deletes several workers from different projects (i.e., its input parameter is a list of workers instead of just one). In this case, we might need to execute the activity *del_Manages* several times (one time for each worker that was also managing the project), similarly to [4]. In any case, note that the tokens that need to be spawned by an OR-gateway can be automatically generated by means of a query into the database that obtains the data that violates a particular constraint.

For our purposes, we do not commit the database changes established by the execution of those activities until all the tokens have successfully reached the end-event. That is, all the updates are delayed to be applied in a unique transaction at the end of the execution of the repairing-process rather than one at a time. There are two reasons behind this: (1) to avoid database rollbacks in case one of the tokens reaches an error event, (2) it is known that applying the events one at a time loses the information of the previously-applied events, which might result in changes which contradict past events (e.g., deleting, at the end of the process, a tuple that was inserted previously to repair some violation) [25]. In order to be able to check the constraints through database queries, these delayed changes are temporally stored in some auxiliary database tables.

3.2   Prototype Tool Implementation

In order to show the feasibility of our approach, we have implemented a prototype tool by means of adapting our previous version of the OpExec Java library [5]. OpExec is a Java library capable of parsing and executing BPMN activities. Since OpExec is not meant to control the BPM flow neither provide a GUI (indeed, controlling the BPM flow and bringing a GUI is a different problem [6]),

---

[2] Following the BPMN standard, we use the common behavior of terminating the whole process instance when we reach an unhandled error event. Other possibilities are allowed [16].

we have to simulate the BPM flow of the original process programmatically. For the BPM extensions, however, we have extended OpExec to parse and execute the condition gateways that checks the current database state, and leads the execution to the corresponding next activity. This adaptation can be downloaded at http://www.essi.upc.edu/~xoriol/opexec/.

Using this library, a BPM-user can effectively repair the violations that take place when executing its activities. For instance, consider the case of two different employees working and managing two different projects. In such case, removing the first employee from his project leads to a constraint violation. Our adapted library detects this situation, and forces the execution of the activities which make the data consistent again. That is, it applies the sufficient activities to remove the first employee from the first project, adds it to the second project, removes him as a manager from the project, picks the second employee and makes her manager of the first project, and includes her as a worker from the first project. A test file to check this behavior is available at the previous website.

4   Related Work

There are several approaches to model artifact-centric BPM, ranging from more flexible approaches [17] - which use condition-action rules instead of a BPMN, for instance - to procedural ones, such as ours, which establish a clear order for task execution [4,11,27]. To the best of our knowledge, there are no previous works which deal with constraint repair in artifact-centric process models and which generate an extension of the original model to carry out the repairs.

4.1   Constraint Repair

In the conceptual modeling literature, there are quite a lot of proposals for incrementally evaluating constraints [3,12,26]. Using these techniques, it is possible to efficiently identify when the execution of some activity leads to a constraint violation. However, none of them is able to derive the repairing activities that need to be applied, as we do.

In a different way, some approaches are meant to, given a schema with some constraints, build operations for inserting/deleting/updating instances in the schema, and completing the behavior of the operation with additional updates to satisfy all the constraints [1,23].

However, we argue that these approaches of compiling all the repairing actions into a single activity are more limited than ours. Indeed, our approach generates a process, rather than a single activity, and a process can naturally encode recursive repair actions by means of adding a cycle in the BPMN diagram. However, the proposals defined in [1,23] lacks recursion, thus, these approaches might hang because of infinitely unfolding the recursion into a single method.

4.2   Compliance in Business Process Models

There are several approaches to verify and/or validate the correctness of artifact-centric business process models, such as [4,11,13,14,27]. However, these works focus on the correctness of the model as a whole and checking if it fulfills certain desirable properties. Note that this is different from our proposal, where we detect potential integrity constraint violations and find ways to repair them.

Similarly, [18] applies constraint programming to detect errors in data constraints without the need for an information base, taking the data flow through the process into consideration. However, the approach does not generate repairs for these constraints.

On the other hand, there are other works dealing with process compliance at design-time [2,9] and runtime [19], but without considering data. For instance, [2] focuses on detecting violations of task order execution and proposes repairs. Similarly, [9] checks the process's compliance with several patterns, such as existence, absence or separation-of-duties, determining the reason behind each violation. On the other hand, [19] detects constraint violations at runtime and proposes several strategies to deal with them, but does not generate any repairs.

5   Conclusions

We have proposed an approach to automatically extend a business process model to include, at compile time, the activities that might repair constraint violations. We take as a starting point an artifact-centric BPM, represented by a UML class diagram (with OCL integrity constraints) to model the data; and a BPMN diagram to model the tasks and their execution order.

As further work, we would like to study the generation of BPM extensions for full OCL constraints rather than OCLuniv ones, and to analyze the usage of BPMN reasoning tools to optimize our generated BPMN diagrams. Another area of interest is the development of heuristics or an aid to help choose the best repair when there are different repair options available.

References

1. Albert, M., Cabot, J., Gómez, C., Pelechano, V.: Automatic generation of basic behavior schemas from UML class diagrams. Softw. Syst. Model. **9**(1), 47–67 (2010)
2. Awad, A., Smirnov, S., Weske, M.: Resolution of compliance violation in business process models: a planning-based approach. In: Meersman, R., Dillon, T., Herrero, P. (eds.) OTM 2009. LNCS, vol. 5870, pp. 6–23. Springer, Heidelberg (2009). https://doi.org/10.1007/978-3-642-05148-7_4
3. Bergmann, G.: Translating OCL to graph patterns. In: Dingel, J., Schulte, W., Ramos, I., Abrahão, S., Insfran, E. (eds.) MODELS 2014. LNCS, vol. 8767, pp. 670–686. Springer, Cham (2014). https://doi.org/10.1007/978-3-319-11653-2_41
4. Borrego, D., Gasca, R.M., López, M.T.G.: Automating correctness verification of artifact-centric business process models. Inf. Softw. Technol. **62**, 187–197 (2015)

5. De Giacomo, G., Oriol, X., Estañol, M., Teniente, E.: Linking data and BPMN processes to achieve executable models. In: Dubois, E., Pohl, K. (eds.) CAiSE 2017. LNCS, vol. 10253, pp. 612–628. Springer, Cham (2017). https://doi.org/10.1007/978-3-319-59536-8_38
6. Diaz, E., Panach, J.I., Rueda, S., Pastor, O.: Towards a method to generate GUI prototypes from BPMN. In: 12th International Conference on Research Challenges in Information Science (RCIS), pp. 1–12, May 2018
7. Dijkman, R.M., Dumas, M., Ouyang, C.: Semantics and analysis of business process models in BPMN. Inf. Softw. Technol. **50**(12), 1281–1294 (2008)
8. Dumas, M., Rosa, M.L., Mendling, J., Reijers, H.A.: Fundamentals of Business Process Management. Springer, Heidelberg (2013). https://doi.org/10.1007/978-3-662-56509-4
9. Elgammal, A., Turetken, O., van den Heuvel, W.-J., Papazoglou, M.: Root-Cause analysis of design-time compliance violations on the basis of property patterns. In: Maglio, P.P., Weske, M., Yang, J., Fantinato, M. (eds.) ICSOC 2010. LNCS, vol. 6470, pp. 17–31. Springer, Heidelberg (2010). https://doi.org/10.1007/978-3-642-17358-5_2
10. Estañol, M., Marcos, E., Oriol, X., Pérez, F.J., Teniente, E., Vara, J.M.: Validation of service blueprint models by means of formal simulation techniques. In: Maximilien, M., Vallecillo, A., Wang, J., Oriol, M. (eds.) ICSOC 2017. LNCS, vol. 10601, pp. 80–95. Springer, Cham (2017). https://doi.org/10.1007/978-3-319-69035-3_6
11. Estañol, M., Sancho, M., Teniente, E.: Ensuring the semantic correctness of a BAUML artifact-centric BPM. Inf. Softw. Technol. **93**, 147–162 (2018)
12. Falleri, J., Blanc, X., Bendraou, R., da Silva, M.A.A., Teyton, C.: Incremental inconsistency detection with low memory overhead. Softw. Pract. Exper. **44**(5), 621–641 (2014)
13. Gonzalez, P., Griesmayer, A., Lomuscio, A.: Verification of GSM-based artifact-centric systems by predicate abstraction. In: Barros, A., Grigori, D., Narendra, N.C., Dam, H.K. (eds.) ICSOC 2015. LNCS, vol. 9435, pp. 253–268. Springer, Heidelberg (2015). https://doi.org/10.1007/978-3-662-48616-0_16
14. Hariri, B.B., Calvanese, D., De Giacomo, G., Deutsch, A., Montali, M.: Verification of relational data-centric dynamic systems with external services. In: PODS 2013, pp. 163–174. ACM (2013)
15. Hull, R.: Artifact-centric business process models: brief survey of research results and challenges. In: Meersman, R., Tari, Z. (eds.) OTM 2008. LNCS, vol. 5332, pp. 1152–1163. Springer, Heidelberg (2008). https://doi.org/10.1007/978-3-540-88873-4_17
16. ISO: ISO/IEC 19510:2013 Information technology - Object Management Group Business Process Model and Notation (2013)
17. Leno, V., Dumas, M., Maggi, F.M.: Correlating activation and target conditions in data-aware declarative process discovery. In: Weske, M., Montali, M., Weber, I., vom Brocke, J. (eds.) BPM 2018. LNCS, vol. 11080, pp. 176–193. Springer, Cham (2018). https://doi.org/10.1007/978-3-319-98648-7_11
18. López, M.T.G., Gasca, R.M., Pérez-Álvarez, J.M.: Compliance validation and diagnosis of business data constraints in business processes at runtime. Inf. Syst. **48**, 26–43 (2015)
19. Maggi, F.M., Montali, M., Westergaard, M., van der Aalst, W.M.P.: Monitoring business constraints with linear temporal logic: an approach based on colored automata. In: Rinderle-Ma, S., Toumani, F., Wolf, K. (eds.) BPM 2011. LNCS, vol. 6896, pp. 132–147. Springer, Heidelberg (2011). https://doi.org/10.1007/978-3-642-23059-2_13

20. Oriol, X., Teniente, E.: OCL$_{univ}$: expressive UML/OCL conceptual schemas for finite reasoning. In: Mayr, H.C., Guizzardi, G., Ma, H., Pastor, O. (eds.) ER 2017. LNCS, vol. 10650, pp. 354–369. Springer, Cham (2017). https://doi.org/10.1007/978-3-319-69904-2_28

21. Oriol, X., Teniente, E.: Simplification of UML/OCL schemas for efficient reasoning. J. Syst. Softw. **128**, 130–149 (2017)

22. Oriol, X., Teniente, E., Tort, A.: Computing repairs for constraint violations in UML/OCL conceptual schemas. Data Knowl. Eng. **99**, 39–58 (2015)

23. Pastor-Collado, J.A., Olivé, A.: Supporting transaction design in conceptual modelling of information systems. In: Iivari, J., Lyytinen, K., Rossi, M. (eds.) CAiSE 1995. LNCS, vol. 932, pp. 40–53. Springer, Heidelberg (1995). https://doi.org/10.1007/3-540-59498-1_236

24. Queralt, A., Teniente, E.: Verification and validation of conceptual schemas with OCL constraints. ACM Trans. Softw. Eng. Methodol. **21**(2), 13:1–13:41 (2012)

25. Teniente, E., Olivé, A.: Updating knowledge bases while maintaining their consistency. VLDB J. **4**(2), 193–241 (1995)

26. Uhl, A., Goldschmidt, T., Holzleitner, M.: Using an OCL impact analysis algorithm for view-based textual modelling. ECEASST **44**, 1–20 (2011)

27. Weber, I., Hoffmann, J., Mendling, J.: Beyond soundness: on the verification of semantic business process models. Distrib. Parallel Databases **27**(3), 271–343 (2010)

28. Weske, M.: Business Process Management: Concepts, Languages, Architectures. Springer, Heidelberg (2007). https://doi.org/10.1007/978-3-642-28616-2

N2TM: A New Node to Trust Matrix Method for Spam Worker Defense in Crowdsourcing Environments

Bin Ye, Yan Wang$^{(\boxtimes)}$, Mehmet Orgun, and Quan Z. Sheng

Macquarie University, Sydney, Australia
bin.ye@students.mq.edu.au,
{yan.wang,mehmet.orgun,michael.sheng}@mq.edu.au

Abstract. To defend against spam workers in crowdsourcing environments, the existing solutions overlook the fact that a spam worker with guises can easily bypass the defense. To alleviate this problem, in this paper, we propose a Node to Trust Matrix method (N2TM) that represents a worker node in a crowdsourcing network as an un-manipulable Worker Trust Matrix (WTM) for identifying the worker's identity. In particular, we first present a crowdsourcing trust network consisting of requester nodes, worker nodes, and transaction-based edges. Then, we construct WTMs for workers based on the trust network. A WTM consists of trust indicators measuring the extent to which a worker is trusted by different requesters in different sub-networks. Moreover, we show the un-manipulable property and the usable property of a WTM that are crucial for identifying a worker's identity. Furthermore, we leverage deep learning techniques to predict a worker's identity with its WTM as input. Finally, we demonstrate the superior performance of our proposed N2TM in identifying spam workers with extensive experiments.

Keywords: Crowdsourcing · Trust · Spam worker identification

1 Introduction

Crowdsourcing is a novel problem-solving model that organizes anonymous and scalable *workers* to solve the tasks published by *requesters* in the form of an open call [8]. In a crowdsourcing platform, a requester (service demander) publishes a group of tasks to be available for all the undefined workers (service providers) in the form of an open call, and then a worker whose answer is approved in a task by the answer approval mechanism (such as a voting-based mechanism or a verification-based mechanism) will be rewarded [24]. Due to its cost-effectiveness, crowdsourcing has been widely applied in various human intelligence tasks, such as tagging images, translation, and prediction. In the meantime, a trust crisis exists in crowdsourcing environments because spam workers could flood the tasks with junk answers [7,9,22,28]. In particular, spam workers could cheat for rewards by submitting random answers to as many tasks as possible [21]. In addition, a sufficient number of spam workers can uniformly submit an incorrect answer to a task, and thus manipulate the incorrect answer to be approved as a correct answer under the voting-based consensus mechanisms [17]. Moreover, prior studies, e.g., [20,22], have indicated that spam workers with different cheating strategies (e.g., randomly answer, uniformly answer and selectively answer) may co-exist in a task.

S. Yangui et al. (Eds.): ICSOC 2019, LNCS 11895, pp. 119–134, 2019.
https://doi.org/10.1007/978-3-030-33702-5_10

A well-known spam attack was reported in the DARPA Shredder Challenge 2013, where the team that first completed five jigsaw puzzles would win the prize of US $50,000. In this attack, spam workers sabotaged the crowdsourcing processes of a team from the University of California San Diego when the team had reached the second place [19].

In crowdsourcing environments, spam worker defense has become a top-priority but it is an extremely challenging problem [7]. The low or even free transaction fee [3] and the high degree of user anonymity [28] in most crowdsourcing platforms make it easy for workers to masquerade as "honest" workers via low-cost collusions [1].

In general, a spam worker can possess two types of guises:

- **G1 (Manipulated Trust):** a spam worker obtains a high answer approval rate that is widely applied as a trust indicator in crowdsourcing environments, by colluding with some requesters to manipulate the transaction outcomes in shadow tasks [10]. A *shadow task* is one whose answer is preset and revealed to the colluding spam workers beforehand, which ensures the spam workers can succeed in the task.
- **G2 (Fake Trust Link):** a spam worker colludes with some requesters and workers who are trusted by some honest workers and requesters [25]. Such a spam worker can indirectly link himself/herself to honest requesters and then mount attacks in the tasks published by these honest requesters.

To defend against the spammers in general online environments rather than crowdsourcing environments, such as e-commerce and P2P networks, two categories of trust-aware defense models have been widely discussed: *trust value-based defense models* (Category 1) and *trust feature-based defense models* (Category 2). In Category 1, the existing models commonly suggest that a trust value calculated from a worker's historical transaction records can truly indicate the worker's reliability in future tasks [7,12,27]. However, in crowdsourcing environments, these models are vulnerable to the spam workers who possess manipulated trust values from many "successful" transactions (i.e., guise **G1**). In Category 2, several studies have suggested limiting the number of spammers in general online environments. However, to the best of our knowledge, there is a lack of studies to effectively identify spam workers in crowdsourcing environments. Though, in P2P networks, SybilLimit [26] and SybilInfer [5] can constrain the number of spammers with guise **G1** by investigating trust network-based features, they cannot precisely identify a specific worker's identity. Moreover, in crowdourcing environments, a spam worker with guise **G2** can render these conventional trust feature-based defense models ineffective.

To address the problem discussed above, in this paper, we propose a novel Node to Trust Matrix method (N2TM), and combine it with learning algorithms to achieve effective spam worker identification.

Target Problem. Effective defense against spam workers with both guises **G1** and **G2** in crowdsourcing environments.

Our Approach. We propose a novel method that represents a Node as a Trust Matrix (N2TM) for identifying spam worker (see Fig. 1). N2TM firstly represents each worker as a trust network-based feature set called Worker Trust Matrix (WTM), and then predicts each worker's identity by using a deep learning-based model taking its WTM as input. To the best of our knowledge, in the literature, N2TM is the first proposal to

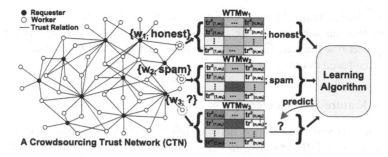

Fig. 1. A Worker Trust Matrix (WTM) encapsulates the global trust network-based features of the worker and thus is exploited by machine learning algorithms for further prediction.

investigate trust network-based representation for identifying spam workers in crowd-sourcing environments.

Contributions. (1) We first propose a requester taxonomy and a worker taxonomy. Then, we formulate a Crowdsourcing Trust Network (CTN) where the requesters and workers are connected via transaction-based edges with trust values.

(2) We then propose a novel Node as Trust Matrix method (N2TM) that represents each worker as a novel Worker Trust Matrix (WTM). A worker's WTM contains the transaction-based trust links of the worker in sub-CTNs starting from different requesters and thus is a global set of trust network-based features of the worker.

(3) We further illustrate that a WTM possesses the un-manipulable property and the usable property that are critical for effective spam worker identification.

(4) We apply deep learning techniques for predicting a worker's identity by taking the worker's WTM as input. We demonstrate the effectiveness of our proposed model in extensive experiments over four datasets.

2   Related Work

2.1   Trust Value-Based Defense in Crowdsourcing

On crowdsourcing platforms, such as Amazon Turk, a worker's overall answer approval rate has been commonly used to evaluate his/her trust level [15]. Taking geographical factors into account, a location-aware trust value-based defense model is proposed by [13] to assess a worker's trust level. Furthermore, a sequential performance-based defense model named H2010e is proposed by [27] to ascertain if a worker is trustworthy. In addition, a worker's performance in gold-standard tasks with known answers is used to evaluate the worker's reliability in a crowdsourcing data analytics system (CDAS) proposed in [12]. Moreover, the consistency of each pair of workers in answering tasks is leveraged to detect random and uniform spam workers by [21]. In [7], based on consistency, the disagreement level of a worker's answers in past tasks is used to assess the worker's trust. Taking contextual factors into account, CrowdTrust [24] calculates the task type-aware trust and the task reward amount-aware trust for selecting trustworthy workers. CrowdDefense [25] suggests that a worker is trustworthy if the worker's three trust values calculated from a trust network are all above the averages. However, the existing trust value-based defense models proposed in crowdsourcing environments commonly overlook the case in which spam workers with guise **G1** can easily bypass the trust value-based defense.

2.2 Trust Feature-Based Defense

Trust features derived from a trust network have been widely applied for defending against spammers in P2P networks. In P2P networks, SybilLimit [26] reduces the maximum number of permitted spammers in a user network to $g * w$, where g is the number of attack edges and w is the mixing time of the user network. SybilInfer [5] detects spammers by directly estimating the minimum-quotient cut between honest networks and a spam network. Essentially, this method leverages Bayesian inference with the knowledge of a known honest user to detect spam users. SybilRank [4] infers a user's reliability based on the distributed trust scores assigned by verified users to the user. SybilDefender [23] identifies a user as a spammer if he/she tightly links to a very few users. The effectiveness of these studies is based on a basic assumption that the number of attack edges is relatively small. However, this assumption can be hardly supported in crowdsourcing environments because a spam worker can easily obtain many attack edges via collusions (i.e., guise **G2**).

From the perspective of machine learning, Louvain [2] and Infomap [18] leverage clustering to detect communities in bipartite networks. Deepwalk [16] represents each node as a unique embedding that contains latent features for further classifying nodes in a social network. However, these models ignore the fake trust links, i.e., guise **G2**, and hence are vulnerable to spam workers who tightly connect with honest communities via fake trust links.

3 Problem Formulation

3.1 A Requester Taxonomy

Based on requesters' transaction behaviours, we define three types of requester identities:

(1) *Honest Requester:* a requester who publishes normal tasks and fairly verifies, approves, and rewards the answers submitted by workers.

(2) *Grey Requester:* a requester who publishes normal tasks when he/she is not colluding with other workers but publishes shadow tasks to assist his/her colluding workers to obtain a good reputation (i.e., guise **G1**) and attack edges (i.e., guise **G2**).

(3) *Spam Requester:* a requester who only publishes shadow tasks to assist his/her colluding workers to obtain guises **G1** and **G2**.

3.2 A Worker Taxonomy

Based on workers' transaction behaviours, we define three types of worker identities:

(1) *Honest Worker:* a worker who submits answers that are believed by himself/herself as the correct answers.

(2) *Grey Worker:* a worker who honestly behaves in some tasks to obtain a good reputation and trust links to honest requesters but colludes with some spam requesters and grey requesters in shadow tasks.

(3) *Spam Worker:* a worker who colludes with spam requesters and grey requesters in shadow tasks to obtain both a manipulated good reputation (i.e., guise **G1**) and fake trust links (i.e., guise **G2**). Then, a spam worker may follow an arbitrary cheating strategy to submit junk answers in tasks published by honest requesters.

Based on the above discussion, we know that a spam worker generally colludes with his/her accomplices to obtain a good reputation and fake trust links for further mounting attacks in the tasks published by honest requesters. However, a spam worker's behaviours for obtaining the guises are permanently recorded in a Crowdsourcing Trust Network (CTN). Below, we discuss the components of constructing a CTN.

3.3   Crowdsourcing Trust Network (CTN)

Direct Trust The *answer approval rate* has been widely adopted as a trust metric in crowdsourcing platforms (e.g., Amazon Turk). Thus, we apply the answer approval rate of worker w_j in the tasks published by requester r_i to indicate the direct trust $dt_{(r_i,w_j)}$ between r_i and w_j, i.e., $dt_{(r_i,w_j)} = \frac{n_{apv(r_i,w_j)}}{n_{sub(r_i,w_j)}}$, $0 \leq dt_{(r_i,w_j)} \leq 1$. Here, $n_{sub(r_i,w_j)}$ denotes the total number of the answers submitted by w_j in the tasks published by r_i, and $n_{apv(r_i,w_j)}$ denotes the number of the approved answers submitted by w_j in the tasks.

Trust Edge. A trust edge connects a requester r and a worker w who directly trust each other, i.e., $dt_{(r,w)} \geq \varepsilon$.

Distrust Edge. A distrust edge connects a requester r and a worker w who directly distrust each other, i.e., $dt_{(r,w)} < \varepsilon$.

In practice, the threshold ε can be set as the value of the average answer approval rate of honest workers in normal tasks. In this paper, we set $\varepsilon = 0.9$ as it is commonly applied in Amazon Turk.

Construction of a Crowdsourcing Trust Network (CTN). As a crowdsourcing user may have the roles of both a *requester* and a *worker,* we use two separate nodes to represent a user's worker role and requester role, respectively. Based on the direct trust values between requesters and workers, requesters and workers can be connected via trust edges or distrust edges to construct a bipartite trust network. Note that, there are no edges between any two requesters in the trust network because they cannot transact with each other. Likewise, there are no edges between any two workers in the trust network. Therefore, *one hop* in a path in the trust network contains two intermediate nodes of a worker and a requester, respectively (e.g., r_1-w_1-r_2-w_2 in Fig. 2), which is different from the concept of one hop in social networks. Let $R = \{r_i\}_{i=1}^{|R|}$ denote the set of all the requester nodes, $W = \{w_j\}_{j=1}^{|W|}$ denote the set of all the worker nodes, $TE = \{te_k\}_{k=1}^{|TE|}$ denote the set of all the trust edges, and $DTE = \{dte_k\}_{k=1}^{|DTE|}$ denote the set of all the distrust edges.

Then, a crowdsourcing trust network (CTN) can be represented as $CTN(R \cup W, TE \cup DTE)$. The construction of such a trust network only requires the transaction records that are available in most of the existing crowdsourcing platforms, e.g., Amazon Turk. Thus, technically, it is easy to construct such a trust network in practice.

Note that, a spam worker can obtain a manipulated trust value and fake trust links via collusions, however, the trust and distrust edges generated during the collusions are all permanently recorded in the CTN. This critical characteristic is taken into account in the design of our novel worker trust representation called Worker Trust Matrix (WTM), which is discussed in the next section.

3.4 Problem Definition

Input: (1) A $CTN(R \cup W, TE \cup DTE)$; (2) a small worker set $U \subset W$, and in U the workers' identities have been manually verified; and (3) a large worker set $V = W - U$ where workers' identities need to be predicted.
Output: The predicted identities of the workers in V.

4 The Node to Trust Matrix (N2TM) Method

In this section, we present the method to represent a Node to a Trust Matrix (N2TM). As we focus on defending against spam workers, each worker node is represented as a Worker Trust Matrix (WTM). We then illustrate the critical properties of a WTM for effectively identifying a worker's identity.

4.1 Trust and Distrust in Paths

Trustworthy Path. Based on an intuitive trust inference method [6], i.e., a friend's friend is a friend, we define a trustworthy path as the one where each pair of directly connected nodes consists of a requester and a worker who directly trust each other. Thus, a **trustworthy path** $tp^k_{(r_i, w_j)}$ is a k-hop path that starts from a requester r_i and ends at a worker w_j, in which each edge is a trust edge.

Positive Trust Indicator. In a k-hop sub-CTN that starts from requester r_i, if there exist k-hop trustworthy paths ending at worker w_j, we calculate the *positive trust indicator positrust*$^k_{(r_i, w_j)}$ of w_j in the sub-CTN. In particular, a trustworthy path only contains trust edges, which indicates each pair of directly connected nodes trust each other. Accordingly, the worker w_j is trusted by the requester r_i in these trustworthy paths. As such, we apply the sum of all the direct trust values $\{dt\}$ in the trustworthy paths between r_i and w_j to represent the *positrust*$^k_{(r_i, w_j)}$ in Eq. (1):

$$positrust^k_{(r_i, w_j)} = \sum_{tp^k_{(r_i, w_j)} \in TP^k_{(r_i, w_j)}} \sum_{dt \in DT^{tp^k_{(r_i, w_j)}}} dt, \tag{1}$$

where, $TP^k_{(r_i, w_j)}$ denotes the set of all the k-hop trustworthy paths between r_i and w_j, and $DT^{tp^k_{(r_i, w_j)}}$ denotes the set of all the direct trust values in a trustworthy path $tp^k_{(r_i, w_j)}$. Note that, if $TP^k_{(r_i, w_j)} = \emptyset$, $positrust^k_{(r_i, w_j)} = 0$.

Untrustworthy Path. Accordingly, following the rule that the friends' enemy is enemy, we define an untrustworthy path $utp^k_{(r_i,w_j)}$ as a k-hop path that starts from a requester r_i and ends at a worker w_j, where each edge is a trust edge except that the one between the last requester in the path and the worker w_j is a distrust edge.

Trust Penalty. In a k-hop sub-CTN starting from requester r_i, if there exist k-hop untrustworthy paths ending at worker w_j, we calculate the trust penalty $penalty^k_{(r_i,w_j)}$ of w_j in the sub-CTN. In particular, as only the worker w_j is connected to a requester via a distrust edge in each of the untrustworthy paths, w_j is distrusted by r_i in these paths. As such, we apply the sum of all the direct trust values dt on the trust edges and the distrust degrees $(1 - dt_e)$ on the distrust edges in the untrustworthy paths between r_i and w_j to represent $penalty^k_{(r_i,w_j)}$ in Eq. (2):

$$penalty^k_{(r_i,w_j)} = \sum_{utp^k_{(r_i,w_j)} \in UTP^k_{(r_i,w_j)}} \sum_{dt \in DT^{utp^k_{(r_i,w_j)}}} dt + 1 - dt_e, \qquad (2)$$

where, $UTP^k_{(r_i,w_j)}$ denotes the set of all the k-hop untrustworthy paths between r_i and w_j, $DT^{utp^k_{(r_i,w_j)}}$ denotes the set of all the direct trust values in the trust edges in an untrustworthy path $utp^k_{(r_i,w_j)}$, and dt_e denotes the direct trust value on the distrust edge in $utp^k_{(r_i,w_j)}$. Note that, if $UTP^k_{(r_i,w_j)} = \emptyset$, $penalty^k_{(r_i,w_j)} = 0$.

4.2   Construction of a Worker Trust Matrix

Trust Trace. A trust trace $tr^k_{(r_i,w_j)}$ aggregates both the positive trust indicator and the trust penalty of worker w_j in a k-hop sub-CTN starting from requester r_i to measure the extent to which the worker w_j is trusted by the requester r_i in the sub-CTN, which is calculated by Eq. (3):

$$tr^k_{(r_i,w_j)} = \frac{positrust^k_{(r_i,w_j)} - penalty^k_{(r_i,w_j)}}{\sum_{tp^k \in TP^k_{r_i}} \sum_{dt \in DT^{tp^k}} dt}, \qquad (3)$$

where, $TP^k_{r_i}$ denotes the set of all the k-hop trustworthy paths that start from requester r_i and end at any worker. The sum of all direct trust values in $TP^k_{r_i}$ is applied as the denominator in Eq. (3) as it is the total trust information given by r_i in the k-hop sub-CTN. Essentially, $tr^k_{(r_i,w_j)}$ leverages the frequencies by which the worker w_j appears in the k-hop trustworthy paths and the k-hop untrustworthy paths that start from the requester r_i for measuring the extent to which the worker w_j is trusted by the requester r_l in the k-hop sub-CTN.

Worker Trust Matrix (WTM). Given a target worker w_t, we compute the trust traces between w_t and all the requesters in sub-CTNs with different hops to obtain a global trust feature set for representing the worker, i.e., a Worker Trust Matrix (WTM). For example, in Fig. 2, we first compute the trust traces of w_t in the sub-CTNs that start from r_1 and end with 0 to m ($m \geq 1$) hops, i.e., $TR_{(r_1,w_t)} = \{tr^0_{(r_1,w_t)}, tr^1_{(r_1,w_t)}, ...,$ $tr^m_{(r_1,w_t)}\}$. Here, m is the maximum hop of all the sub-CTNs. Likewise, the trust trace

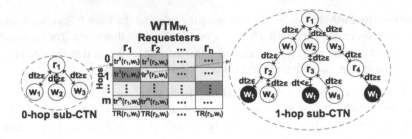

Fig. 2. An example of a WTM for a target worker w_t

set TR between w_t and each of other requesters can be obtained. Taking each TR of w_t as one column of WTM_{w_t}, we obtain $WTM_{w_t} = \{TR_{(r_1,w_t)}, TR_{(r_2,w_t)}, ..., TR_{(r_n,w_t)}\}$. WTM_{w_t} contains all the trust relations between w_t and all the requesters in sub-CTNs with different hops, and thus is a global trust feature set of worker w_t. Below, we illustrate that such a global trust feature set also possesses (1) the *un-manipulable* property and (2) the *usable* property that are critical for identifying a worker's identity.

4.3 Properties of a Worker Trust Matrix

The Un-manipulable Property of a WTM. We use θ_w, ρ_w, and τ_w to represent the probabilities by which a worker w can obtain a trust edge to an honest requester, a grey requester, and a spam requester, respectively. Given a spam worker sw, we have $\theta_{sw} < \rho_{sw} < \tau_{sw}$ because sw can easily succeed in a shadow task published by a spam requester or a grey requester while it is hard for sw to have a junk answer approved in a normal task published by an honest requester or a grey requester. By contrast, we have $\theta_{hw} > \rho_{hw} > \tau_{hw}$ because it is easier for an honest worker hw to succeed in a normal task than in a shadow task. We know as a fact that it is not possible for sw to behave as an honest worker in all the transactions to make $\theta_{sw} < \rho_{sw} < \tau_{sw}$ become $\theta_{sw} > \rho_{sw} > \tau_{sw}$. Therefore, sw cannot manipulate its WTM_{sw} determined by $\theta_{sw} < \rho_{sw} < \tau_{sw}$ to be the same as an honest worker's WTM_{hw} determined by $\theta_{hw} > \rho_{hw} > \tau_{hw}$. Likewise, a grey worker gw with $\theta_{gw} \leq \rho_{sw} \leq \tau_{sw}$ also cannot manipulate WTM_{gw} to be the same as WTM_{hw}. Therefore, a WTM is *un-manipulable*.

The Usable Property of a WTM. Below, we prove the usable property of a WTM.

Theorem 1. *Given any honest worker hw_i, grey worker gw_j, and spam worker sw_k, there exists a function $\phi(\cdot)$ that satisfies $\phi(WTM_{hw_i}) \neq \phi(WTM_{gw_j})$, $\phi(WTM_{gw_j}) \neq \phi(WTM_{sw_k})$, and $\phi(WTM_{hw_i}) \neq \phi(WTM_{sw_k})$.*

Proof. Let $\mathcal{F}$, $\mathcal{G}$ and $\mathcal{S}$ denote the distribution functions of the trust trace sets TRs between a worker and all the honest requesters $HR = \{hr_l\}_{l=1}^{|HR|}$, all the grey requesters $GR = \{gr_p\}_{p=1}^{|GR|}$, and all the spam requesters $SR = \{sr_u\}_{u=1}^{|SR|}$, respectively. Given a worker w_t's WTM_{w_t}, as the values of the trust traces in WTM_{w_t}

depend on to whom w_t links via trust edges, the probabilities θ_{w_t}, ρ_{w_t}, and τ_{w_t} by which w_t can obtain a trust edge to an honest requester, a grey requester, and a spam requester are the latent parameters of $\mathcal{F}$, $\mathcal{G}$, and $\mathcal{S}$, respectively. Hence, we obtain that $WTM_{hw_i} = \{TR_{(hr,hw_i)} \sim \mathcal{F}(\theta_{hw_i}), TR_{(gr,hw_i)} \sim \mathcal{G}(\rho_{hw_i}), TR_{(sr,hw_i)} \sim \mathcal{S}(\tau_{hw_i})\}$, $WTM_{gw_j} = \{TR_{(hr,gw_j)} \sim \mathcal{F}(\theta_{gw_j}), TR_{(gr,gw_j)} \sim \mathcal{G}(\rho_{gw_j}), TR_{(sr,gw_j)} \sim \mathcal{S}(\tau_{gw_j})\}$, and $WTM_{sw_k} = \{TR_{(hr,sw_k)} \sim \mathcal{F}(\theta_{sw_k}), TR_{(gr,sw_k)} \sim \mathcal{G}(\rho_{sw_k}), TR_{(sr,sw_k)} \sim \mathcal{S}(\tau_{sw_k})\}$, respectively. As a worker's identity determines its transaction behaviours, and vice versa, the probabilities by which a worker can obtain a trust edge to an hr, a gr or an sr satisfy $\theta_{hw_i} > \theta_{gw_j} > \theta_{sw_k}$, $\rho_{hw_i} < \rho_{gw_j} < \rho_{sw_k}$, and $\tau_{hw_i} < \tau_{gw_j} < \tau_{sw_k}$. Thus, there must exist a function $\phi(\cdot)$ that satisfies $\phi(WTM_{hw_i}) \neq \phi(WTM_{gw_j})$, $\phi(WTM_{gw_j}) \neq \phi(WTM_{sw_k})$, and $\phi(WTM_{hw_i}) \neq \phi(WTM_{sw_k})$.

Based on the above inequality relations among $\phi(WTM_{hw_i})$, $\phi(WTM_{gw_j})$, and $\phi(WTM_{sw_k})$ proved in Theorem 1, a worker can be classified into the correct identity type once knowing the ϕ. Therefore, we conclude that a WTM contains the *usable* property for effectively identifying spam workers.

5 Spam Worker Identification Model

Our proposed model consists of (1) a random walk-based WTM estimation algorithm, and (2) a convolutional neural network (CNN)-based classifier.

5.1 WTM Estimation Algorithm

Ideally, $WTM_{w \in W}$ can be exactly calculated by traversing all the paths in a CTN. However, the complexity of a traversal algorithm exponentially increases with the degree of a node. Thus, we devise a random walk-based algorithm with a lower complexity to estimate WTMs. In particular, in each round of a random walk, we update the trust traces of all the workers in a randomly searched path. The algorithm terminates when the number of searching rounds exceeds the maximum round number rod_{max} or the change of WTMs converges. The algorithm's worst time complexity is $O(rod_{max} * hop_{max} * de)$, where hop_{max} is the maximum number of hops in a searching path, and de is the maximum degree of a node.

5.2 CNN-based Classifier

A WTM contains the latent spatial features because the trust traces in a column in a WTM derive from the sub-CTNs starting from the same requester. As CNNs are effective in discovering spatial features [11], we devise a six-layer convolutional network CLnet-6 to learn WTMs for correctly classifying workers with different identities. Compared to Lnet-5, CLnet-6 contains one more layer after the input layer for standardizing WTMs. **Probabilistic Classifier.** Let WM denote the weight matrix, b denote the bias vector, $WI = \{HW, GW, SW\}$ denote the worker identity set, and $\otimes$ denote the operations in CLnet-6. Given a WTM'_{w_k}, the probability that $w_k \in WI_i$ is defined as a stochastic variable $P(Y = WI_i | WTM'_{w_k}, WM, b) = \frac{e^{\otimes WTM'_{w_k} * WM_i + b_i}}{e^{\sum_j \otimes WTM'_{w_k} * WM_j + b_j}}$.

Loss Function. Given $WTM_{w_i \in U}$ with workers' identities, the log-likelihood is calculated as $L(W, b, WTM_{w_i \in U}) = \sum_{i=1}^{|U|} \log \left(P(Y = WI^{(w_i)} | WTM_{w_i}, WM, b) \right)$. In CLnet-6, we adopt the negative log-likelihood as the loss, i.e., $l(W, b, WTM_{w_i \in U}) = -L(W, b, WTM_{w_i \in U})$.

Training Operations. (1) *Standardization:* We normalize each element in $WTM_{w_k \in W}$ by 4:

$$WTM_{w_k}(i, j) = \frac{WTM_{w_k}(i, j) + avg(WTM) - min(WTM)}{max(WTM) + avg(WTM) - min(WTM)} \tag{4}$$

where, $avg(WTM)$ denotes the average trust trace values in all the WTMs, $min(WTM)$ denotes the minimal trust trace value in all the WTMs, and $max(WTM)$ denotes the maximal trust trace value in all the WTMs.

(2) *Convolution:* The size of a receptive field of a filter function is set as $\beta * \gamma$. In particular, for each $\beta * \gamma$ area X in a feature map, we calculate an output: $o = \tanh(X * WM_c + b_c)$, where $WE_c \in R^{\beta * \gamma}$ is weight matrix and b_c is bias.

(3) *Sub-sampling:* Given a feature map, the sub-sampling operation extracts the sampling information from the map to reduce the computation in the next operations and also provides the robustness of position. Max-pooling is applied in sub-sampling because it can effectively reduce the dimensions of intermediate representations [11]. Given a feature map with size $m' * n'$, we firstly partition the map into l non-overlapping regions with size $\frac{m'}{l} * \frac{n'}{l}$. In each region, the maximum value is selected and then mapped to the corresponding feature map in the next layer.

(4) *Parameter Update:* in CLnet-6, we apply the *Stochastic Gradient Descent* (SGD) with mini batches to update the parameters because it can effectively reduce the time consumption. Let lr denote the learning rate, then the parameters are updated as follows: $WE = WE - lr * \frac{\partial l}{\partial WE}$ and $b = b - lr * \frac{\partial l}{\partial b}$.

6   Experiments

6.1   Data Preparation

To evaluate the effectiveness of our model in identifying a worker's identity, we first conduct experiments on a CTN constructed from the complete transaction records of a real-world crowdsourcing processing dataset *wiki-RfA*[1]. Furthermore, to evaluate the effectiveness of our model in identifying spam workers who possess different degrees of guises **G1** and **G2**, we conduct experiments on three CTNs constructed based on three semi-synthetic datasets generated from a real-world dataset *soc-sign-epinions*[2].

(1) *wiki-RfA:* this dataset records the crowdsourcing processes of administrator elections on wikipedia, where voters (workers) submit votes (answers) in one or more of the elections for an administrator (a requester). Based on the ground truth of *wiki-RfA*

---

[1] https://snap.stanford.edu/data/wiki-RfA.html
[2] https://snap.stanford.edu/data/soc-sign-epinions.html

(i.e, the final result after multiple elections), we manually verified the identities of 1,880 workers, and found 1,418 honest workers, 48 grey workers, and 414 spam workers.

(2) *soc-sign-epinions 1-3: soc-sign-epinions* contains the complete transaction-based trust relations between reviewers (workers) and review verifiers (requesters) without spam workers possessing guises **G1** and **G2**. Thus, based on *soc-sign-epinions*, we generate three semi-synthetic datasets *soc-sign-epinions 1-3* to contain spam workers with different degrees of guises **G1** and **G2** and construct their CTNs. In particular, all spam workers are first granted with high trust values (i.e., guise **G1**). In addition, the percentages of the fake trust edges (i.e., guise **G2**) in all the edges of a spam worker are set as 10%, 30% and 50%, respectively in the three datasets. In each dataset, we randomly generate workers based on the definition of a grey worker. The percentage of the spam workers and grey workers in all the workers is commonly set to be less than 10%.

Table 1. The Comparison of different models in identifying workers with different identities

Datasets	Models	Honest Worker			Grey Worker			Spam Worker		
		Precision	Recall	F-Measure	Precision	Recall	F-Measure	Precision	Recall	F-Measure
wiki-RfA	**Our model**	**0.9986**	**0.9831**	**0.9908**	**0.9537**	**0.9952**	**0.9740**	**0.9231**	**1**	**0.96**
	Deepwalk	0.7812	0.8504	0.8143	0.2535	0.1956	0.2208	0.1667	0.0590	0.0872
	SybilDefender	0.7708	0.1031	0.1819	-	-	-	0.0313	0.8709	0.0604
	H2010e	0.7426	1	0.8599	-	-	-	0	0	0
	AMT	0.7426	1	0.8599	-	-	-	0	0	0
soc-sign-epinions 1	**Our model**	**1**	**1**	**1**	**0.9459**	**1**	**0.9722**	**1**	**0.9444**	**0.9714**
	Deepwalk	1	0.9970	0.9985	0.4615	0.3529	0.4000	0.4211	0.5714	0.4849
	SybilDefender	0.9153	0.0620	0.1161	-	-	-	0.0370	0.9167	0.0711
	H2010e	0.9245	1	0.9608	-	-	-	0	0	0
	AMT	0.9245	1	0.9608	-	-	-	0	0	0
soc-sign-epinions 2	**Our model**	**1**	**1**	**1**	**0.9079**	**0.9857**	**0.9452**	**0.9859**	**0.9091**	**0.9459**
	Deepwalk	1	0.9907	0.9953	0.68	0.5	0.5763	0.6170	0.8286	0.7073
	SybilDefender	0.8704	0.0537	0.1012	-	-	-	0.0753	0.9481	0.1395
	H2010e	0.8559	1	0.9223	-	-	-	0	0	0
	AMT	0.8559	1	0.9223	-	-	-	0	0	0
soc-sign-epinions 3	**Our model**	**1**	**1**	**1**	**0.6923**	**0.9643**	**0.8060**	**0.9787**	**0.7931**	**0.8762**
	Deepwalk	1	0.9935	0.9968	0.1667	0.067	0.0952	0.6216	0.8846	0.7302
	SybilDefender	0.9048	0.0648	0.1209	-	-	-	0.0598	0.9310	0.1124
	H2010e	0.9104	1	0.9531	-	-	-	0	0	0
	AMT	0.9104	1	0.9531	-	-	-	0	0	0

6.2 Compared Models

To evaluate the effectiveness of our proposed trust feature-based model in defending against spam workers, we first compare our model with two representative *trust value-based defense models* (i.e., AMT and H2010e). In the *trust feature-based defense models*, there is a lack of studies in crowdsourcing environments. Thus, we compare our model with two promising models (i.e., SybilDefender [23] and Deepwalk [16]) that can be adapted to crowdsourcing. In this paper, we do not consider some models with strict synthetic conditions that cannot be fairly compared with our model without these settings, e.g., CrowdDefense [25] that presets all requesters' reputations and a group of trustworthy requesters.

All of the above models have been reviewed in the Related Work section.

AMT: a model applied in Amazon Turk, which uses the overall answer approval rate to judge if a worker is trustworthy [15].

H2010e: a model that leverages a worker's sequential performance for differentiating between spam workers and honest workers [27].

SybilDefender: a model that investigates the frequently appearing nodes in the random walks starting from trust seeds for identifying spammers [23].

Deepwalk: a model that leverages SkipGram [14] to learn latent representations of nodes from a social network for classification [16].

Moreover, in order to find out whether WTMs is a promising representation for learning algorithms to identify spam workers. In addition to our proposed CLnet-6, we also apply two representative learning algorithms, i.e., Logistic Regression and Multiple Perceptron on our proposed WTM. The classic SVMs inherently perform a binary classification, thus, we do not directly apply them to our problem with three types of worker identities.

6.3 Parameter and Measure Settings

In all the experiments, 2-fold cross validation is used. In the training of CLnet-6, the batch size is set as 5% of the total number of training samples, and the number of two feature maps in convolutional layers are set as 20 and 50, respectively. The maximum number of training epochs is set as 150. All the experiments are implemented by using Theano in a Ubuntu 16.04.1 system with 16 GB RAM. To measure the effectiveness of each model, we calculate the precision, the recall and the F-measure values.

6.4 Experimental Results

Result 1-1 (Effectiveness Comparison in *wiki-RfA*). First, our model with WTMs as input is the best one in identifying honest workers. Our model delivers the highest F-measure value of 0.9908 which is 15.22% higher than the best result delivered by the comparison models. Interestingly, all the four comparison models deliver satisfactory precision values in identifying honest workers (see Table 1). Regarding the effectiveness in identifying grey workers, our model possesses the highest F-measure value of 0.974, which is higher than that of the second best model Deepwalk by 341.12%. Most importantly, our model performs best in identifying spam workers in terms of both precision and recall. The precision value and the recall value of our model are 0.9321 and 1, respectively, which are about 4.5 times and 14.5 times higher than the best results delivered by all the four compared models.

Result 1–2 (Effectiveness Comparison in *soc-sign-epinions 1-3*). When the spam workers possess different degrees of guises **G1** and **G2**, i.e., the percentage of the fake trust edges in all the edges of a spam worker increases from 10% to 50% with a step of 20%, our model maintains the highest F-measure values in identifying all types of workers (see Table 1). Regarding the effectiveness in identifying grey workers in *soc-sign-epinions 1-3*, our model possesses the highest F-measure values. On average, the F-measure value of our model in identifying grey workers is 0.9078, improving the best result delivered by all the four compared models by 154.14%. Most importantly, regarding the effectiveness in identifying spam workers with different degrees of guises **G1** and **G2** in the three datasets, the F-measure values of our model are as high as 0.9714, 0.9459, and 0.8762, respectively, which are 100.33%, 33.73%, and 19.99% higher than those of the second best model Deepwalk.

Analysis: (1) In the *wiki-RfA* dataset, the four compared models cannot effectively identify spam workers, which demonstrates that spam workers in real-world crowdsourcing environments may possess guises **G1** and **G2** and thus can bypass the general defense models. (2) The superior performance of our model on both *wiki-RfA* and *soc-sign-epinions 1-3* datasets results from the fact that WTM is un-manipulable and contains the usable trust network-based features for identifying workers' identities.

Result 2 (Comparison of Different Learning Algorithms with WTMs as Input): Figures 3(a)–(d) depict the test errors of different learning algorithms that all take WTMs as input in 200 epoches of training. As Stochastic Gradient Descent (SGD) training is applied, we can see some fluctuations at the early stages of training. In Figs. 3(a)–(d), the lowest test errors are always delivered by the CLnet-6 over all the four datasets among the 200 epoches. Though the Logistic Regression and the Multiple Perceptron converge to the satisfied errors, the minimal errors achieved by CLnet-6 are 0.0138, 0.0021, 0.0078, and 0.0135, which are still 84.15%, 66.67%, 43.98%, and 13.33% lower than the minimum test errors delivered by the Logistic Regression and Multiple Perceptron, respectively.

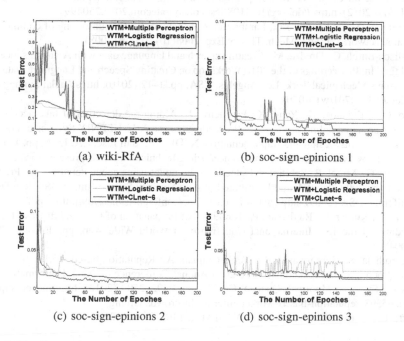

(a) wiki-RfA

(b) soc-sign-epinions 1

(c) soc-sign-epinions 2

(d) soc-sign-epinions 3

Fig. 3. The Comparison of test errors of different learning algorithms with WTMs as input

Analysis: (1) All the three learning algorithms converge to the satisfied testing errors which shows that WTM is a type of effective representations containing usable trust features for identifying a worker's identity. (2) A WTM contains trust traces derived from the sub-CTNs starting from the same requester. Thus, it possesses the latent spatial features that enable our proposed CNN-based CLnet-6 outperform other two classic learning algorithms.

7   Conclusion

In this paper, we have proposed a novel Node to Trust Matrix (N2TM) method which generated input for the proposed learning algorithm CLnet-6 to effectively predict a worker's identity. The experiments have demonstrated the superior performance of our model in identifying spam workers over several state-of-the-art methods. The performance of our supervised learning-based model still highly depends on the training data containing ground truth, therefore we plan to extend our model with unsupervised learning techniques to identify both spam workers and spam requesters.

References

1. Allahbakhsh, M., Ignjatovic, A., Benatallah, B., Beheshti, S., Bertino, E., Foo, N.: Reputation management in crowdsourcing systems. In: Proceeding of the 2012 International Conference on Collaborative Computing: Networking, Applications and Worksharing, pp. 664–671 (2012). https://doi.org/10.4108/icst.collaboratecom.2012.250499
2. Blondel, V.D., Guillaume, J.L., Lambiotte, R., Lefebvre, E.: Fast unfolding of communities in large networks. J. Stat. Mech. Theory Exp. **2008**(10), 10008 (2008)
3. Callison-Burch, C., Dredze, M.: Creating speech and language data with Amazon's mechanical turk. In: Proceedings of the 2010 Workshop on Creating Speech and Language Data with Amazon's Mechanical Turk, Los Angeles, USA, pp. 1–12 (2010). https://aclanthology.info/papers/W10-0701/w10-0701
4. Cao, Q., Sirivianos, M., Yang, X., Pregueiro, T.: Aiding the detection of fake accounts in large scale social online services. In: Proceedings of the 2012 USENIX Symposium on Networked Systems Design and Implementation, NSDI 2012, San Jose, CA, USA, pp. 197–210 (2012), https://www.usenix.org/conference/nsdi12/technical-sessions/presentation/cao
5. Danezis, G., Mittal, P.: Sybilinfer: Detecting sybil nodes using social networks. In: Proceedings of the 2009 Network and Distributed System Security Symposium, NDSS, San Diego, California, USA (2009). http://www.isoc.org/isoc/conferences/ndss/09/pdf/06.pdf
6. Guha, R., Kumar, R., Raghavan, P., Tomkins, A.: Propagation of trust and distrust. In: Proceedings of the 13th International Conference on World Wide Web, pp. 403–412. ACM (2004)
7. Jagabathula, S., Subramanian, L., Venkataraman, A.: Reputation-based worker filtering in crowdsourcing. In: Proceeding of the 2014 Annual Conference on Neural Information Processing Systems, Montreal, Quebec, Canada, pp. 2492–2500 (2014). http://papers.nips.cc/paper/5393-reputation-based-worker-filtering-in-crowdsourcing
8. Jeff, H.: The rise of crowdsourcing. Wired Mag. **14**(6), 1–4 (2006)

9. Karger, D.R., Oh, S., Shah, D.: Iterative learning for reliable crowdsourcing systems. In: Proceeding of the 2011 Annual Conference on Neural Information Processing Systems, Granada, Spain, pp. 1953–1961 (2011). http://papers.nips.cc/paper/4396-iterative-learning-for-reliable-crowdsourcing-systems

10. KhudaBukhsh, A.R., Carbonell, J.G., Jansen, P.J.: Detecting non-adversarial collusion in crowdsourcing. In: Proceedings of the 2014 Second AAAI Conference on Human Computation and Crowdsourcing, HCOMP, Pittsburgh, Pennsylvania, USA (2014). http://www.aaai.org/ocs/index.php/HCOMP/HCOMP14/paper/view/8967

11. LeCun, Y., Bengio, Y., Hinton, G.: Deep learning. Nature 521(7553), 436–444 (2015)

12. Liu, X., Lu, M., Ooi, B.C., Shen, Y., Wu, S., Zhang, M.: Cdas: A crowdsourcing data analytics system. PVLDB 5(10), 1040–1051 (2012). http://vldb.org/pvldb/vol5/p1040xuanliuvldb2012.pdf

13. Mashhadi, A.J., Capra, L.: Quality control for real-time ubiquitous crowdsourcing. In: Proceedings of the 2011 International Workshop on Ubiquitous Crowdsouring, pp. 5–8. ACM (2011)

14. Mikolov, T., Chen, K., Corrado, G., Dean, J.: Efficient estimation of word representations in vector space. CoRR abs/1301.3781 (2013). http://arxiv.org/abs/1301.3781

15. Peer, E., Vosgerau, J., Acquisti, A.: Reputation as a sufficient condition for data quality on Amazon mechanical turk. Behav. Res. Methods 46(4), 1023–1031 (2014)

16. Perozzi, B., Al-Rfou, R., Skiena, S.: Deepwalk: online learning of social representations. In: The Proceeding of 2014 ACM SIGKDD International Conference on Knowledge Discovery and Data Mining, KDD 2014, New York, NY, USA, pp. 701–710 (2014). https://doi.org/10.1145/2623330.2623732

17. Raykar, V.C., Yu, S.: Eliminating spammers and ranking annotators for crowdsourced labeling tasks. J. Mach. Learn. Res. 13, 491–518 (2012). http://dl.acm.org/citation.cfm?id=2188401

18. Rosvall, M., Bergstrom, C.T.: Maps of random walks on complex networks reveal community structure. Natl. Acad. Sci. 105(4), 1118–1123 (2008)

19. Stefanovitch, N., Alshamsi, A., Cebrian, M., Rahwan, I.: Error and attack tolerance of collective problem solving: the darpa shredder challenge. EPJ Data Sci. 3(1), 13 (2014)

20. Tran, D.N., Min, B., Li, J., Subramanian, L.: Sybil-resilient online content voting. In: Proceedings of the 2009 USENIX Symposium on NSDI, Boston, MA, USA, pp. 15–28 (2009). http://www.usenix.org/events/nsdi09/tech/full_papers/tran/tran.pdf

21. Vuurens, J.B.P., de Vries, A.P.: Obtaining high-quality relevance judgments using crowdsourcing. IEEE Internet Comput. 16(5), 20–27 (2012). https://doi.org/10.1109/MIC.2012.71

22. Vuurens, J.B., de Vries, A.P., Eickhoff, C.: How much spam can you take? An analysis of crowdsourcing results to increase accuracy. In: ACM SIGIR Workshop on Crowdsourcing for Information Retrieval, CIR11, pp. 21–26 (2011)

23. Wei, W., Xu, F., Tan, C.C., Li, Q.: Sybildefender: a defense mechanism forsybil attacks in large social networks. IEEE Trans. Parallel Distrib. Syst. 24(12), 2492–2502 (2013). https://doi.org/10.1109/TPDS.2013.9

24. Ye, B., Wang, Y., Liu, L.: Crowd trust: a context-aware trust model for worker selection in crowdsourcing environments. In: Proceeding of the 2015 IEEE International Conference on Web Services, ICWS 2015, New York, NY, USA, pp. 121–128 (2015). https://doi.org/10.1109/ICWS.2015.26

25. Ye, B., Wang, Y., Liu, L.: Crowddefense: a trust vector-based threat defense model in crowdsourcing environments. In: Proceeding of the 2017 IEEE International Conference on Web Services, ICWS 2017, Honolulu, HI, USA, pp. 245–252 (2017). https://doi.org/10.1109/ICWS.2017.39

26. Yu, H., Gibbons, P.B., Kaminsky, M., Xiao, F.: Sybillimit: a near-optimal social network defense against sybil attacks. IEEE/ACM Trans. Netw. **18**(3), 885–898 (2010). https://doi.org/10.1109/TNET.2009.2034047
27. Yu, H., Shen, Z., Miao, C., An, B.: Challenges and opportunities for trust management in crowdsourcing. In: Proceeding of the 2012 IEEE/WIC/ACM International Conferences on Intelligent Agent Technology, IAT 2012, Macau, China, pp. 486–493 (2012). https://doi.org/10.1109/WI-IAT.2012.104
28. Yuen, M., King, I., Leung, K.: A survey of crowdsourcing systems. In: 2011 IEEE Conference on Privacy, Security, Risk and Trust (PASSAT) and on Social Computing (SocialCom), Boston, MA, USA, pp. 766–773 (2011). https://doi.org/10.1109/PASSAT/SocialCom.2011.203

QoS Value Prediction Using a Combination of Filtering Method and Neural Network Regression

Soumi Chattopadhyay[1(✉)] and Ansuman Banerjee[2]

[1] Indian Institute of Information Technology, Guwahati, India
soumi61@gmail.com
[2] Indian Statistical Institute, Kolkata, India

Abstract. With increasing demand and adoption of web services in the world wide web, selecting an appropriate web service for recommendation is becoming a challenging problem to address today. The Quality of Service (QoS) parameters, which essentially represent the performance of a web service, play a crucial role in web service selection. However, obtaining the exact value of a QoS parameter of service before its execution is impossible, due to the variation of the QoS parameter across time and users. Therefore, predicting the value of a QoS parameter has attracted significant research attention. In this paper, we consider the QoS prediction problem and propose a novel solution by leveraging the past information of service invocations. Our proposal, on one hand, is a combination of collaborative filtering and neural network-based regression model. Our filtering approach, on the other hand, is a coalition of the user-intensive and service-intensive models. In the first step of our approach, we generate a set of similar users on a set of similar services. We then employ a neural network-based regression module to predict the QoS value of a target service for a target user. The experiments are conducted on the WS-DREAM public benchmark dataset. Experimental results show the superiority of our method over state-of-the-art approaches.

1 Introduction

With the proliferation of emerging technologies in the era of Internet-of-Things (IoT), the number of web services is increasing day by day. The existence of a large number of competing, functionally equivalent web services in world wide web, makes the problem of recommending an appropriate service for a specific task, quite challenging in recent times. A number of different factors may actually influence the process of recommendation [4,19,20]. The QoS parameter (e.g., response time, throughput, reliability, availability) being the representative of the performance of a web service is one of the key factors that may have an impact on service recommendation. However, the value of a QoS parameter of a web service varies across time and users. Therefore, obtaining the exact QoS that a user will witness during invocation is a difficult task. Prediction plays an important role in this context to obtain a close enough approximate QoS value

© Springer Nature Switzerland AG 2019
S. Yangui et al. (Eds.): ICSOC 2019, LNCS 11895, pp. 135–150, 2019.
https://doi.org/10.1007/978-3-030-33702-5_11

for recommendation. Quite evidently, the task of prediction is recognized as one of the fundamental research challenges in the domain of services computing.

In this paper, we address the problem of predicting the QoS value of a service for a given user by leveraging the past user-service QoS invocation profiles consisting of the QoS values of a set of services across different users. A significant number of research articles exist in literature which deal with this problem. Collaborative filtering [3,15] is one of the most popular methods adopted in this domain to predict the missing value. The collaborative filtering technique is classified into two categories: memory-based and model-based. The memory-based collaborative filtering comprises the computation of either the set of similar users [3] or the set of similar services [14] or the combination of them [25] followed by the computation of average QoS values and the computation of the deviation migration. However, these approaches suffer from the problem of the sparsity of the user-service invocation matrix. Therefore, model-based collaborative filtering is used which can deal with the sparsity problem. Matrix factorization [9,10,23] is a class of model-based collaborative filtering technique used for this problem. Though the contemporary approaches are able to predict the missing QoS value of a service for a target user, however, the prediction accuracy still is not quite satisfactory. Therefore, there is a scope for improving the prediction accuracy.

In this paper, we propose a new approach for predicting the QoS value of a service for a target user. Our method combines two primary techniques, i.e., collaborative filtering with a regression method, to come up with a solution. We first use the collaborative filtering technique to filter the set of users and services. Our filtering method is again a combination of the user-intensive and service-intensive filtering models. In user-intensive (service-intensive) filtering, we first find a set of similar users (services) from the given user-service invocation profile. We then find a set of similar services (users) from the user-service invocation profile corresponding to the set of users (services) obtained earlier. Once the filtering is done, we combine the results for further processing. Instead of computing the average QoS value and the deviation migration as done in the collaborative filtering approach, in our final step, we employ a neural network-based regression module to predict the QoS value of a service for a target user. We have shown the significance of each step of our proposal experimentally.

We have implemented our proposed framework and tested the performance of our approach on a public benchmark dataset, called WS-DREAM [24]. We have compared our method with state-of-the-art approaches. The experimental results show that our method achieves better performance in terms of accuracy as compared to others.

The contributions of this paper are summarized below:

(i) We propose a new approach for QoS prediction. On one side, our approach leverages the principle of collaborative filtering. On the other side, our approach takes advantage of the power of a neural network-based regression method.

(ii) We propose a filtering method, which is a combination of user-intensive and service-intensive models.

(iii) To find the set of similar users (and services), we propose a method based on unsupervised learning.

(iv) We have implemented our framework. A rigorous experiment has been conducted on the WS-DREAM dataset to establish our findings. The experimental results demonstrate that our method is more efficient in terms of prediction accuracy as compared to its contemporary approaches.

2 Related Work

A number of work [2,5,12,13,17] has been carried out in literature to address the problem of QoS value prediction. Collaborative filtering [15,16,21] technique is one of the key techniques used for the prediction. The collaborative filtering approach can be of two types: memory-based and model-based. The memory-based collaborative filtering approach uses the user-service invocation profile to find the set of similar users or services. Depending on the similarity finding method, the memory based collaborative filtering is again classified into two categories: user-intensive and service-intensive. In the user-intensive collaborative filtering method [3], a set of users similar to the target user is computed, while in the service-intensive filtering method [14], a set of services similar to the target service is computed. There are some research works [22,25] in literature, which combine both the user-intensive and service-intensive filtering techniques to obtain the predicted value. The main disadvantage of this approach is that the prediction accuracy decreases as data gets sparse. One possible solution to this problem is to employ model-based collaborative filtering. One such approach is matrix factorization [9,10,20,23], which is widely used to predict the QoS value of a service. In matrix factorization, the user-service QoS invocation matrix is decomposed into the product of two lower-dimensional rectangular matrices to improve the robustness and accuracy of the memory-based approach.

Although state-of-the-art approaches can predict the missing QoS values, however, they fail to achieve satisfactory prediction accuracy. Therefore, in this paper, we propose a novel approach to improve the prediction accuracy.

3 Overview and Problem Formulation

In this section, we formalize our problem statement. We begin with defining two terminologies as follows.

Definition 1 (QoS Invocation Log). *A QoS invocation log is defined as a 3-tuple $(u_i, s_j, q_{i,j})$, where u_i is a user, s_j is a web service and $q_{i,j}$ denotes the value of a given QoS parameter q when the user u_i invoked the service s_j.* ∎

Once a user invokes a service, the corresponding invocation log is recorded. The QoS invocation logs are stored in the form of a matrix. We now define the concept of a QoS invocation log matrix.

Definition 2 (QoS Invocation Log Matrix). *The QoS invocation log matrix $\mathcal{Q}$ is a matrix with dimension $n \times k$, where n is the number of users and k is the number of web services. Each entry of the matrix $\mathcal{Q}(i,j)$ represents $q_{i,j}$.* ∎

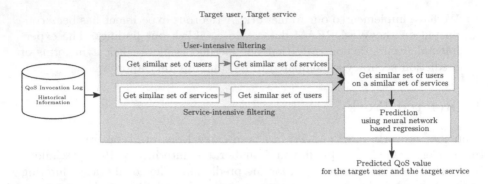

Fig. 1. Our proposed framework

Example 1. Consider $\mathcal{U} = \{u_1, u_2, u_3, u_4, u_5, u_6\}$ be a set of 6 users and $\mathcal{S} = \{s_1, s_2, s_3, s_4, s_5, s_6\}$ be a set of 6 web services. Table 1 represents the QoS invocation log matrix $\mathcal{Q}$ for the set of users $\mathcal{U}$ and the set of services $\mathcal{S}$. $\mathcal{Q}(i,j)$ represents the value of the response time (in millisecond) of $s_j \in \mathcal{S}$ during the invocation of s_j by $u_i \in \mathcal{U}$. Our objective, here, is to predict the value of the QoS parameter of a service for a user, where the user has never invoked the service in past. For example, here, we want to predict the value of $q_{1,3}$, which is marked by ? symbol.

Table 1. Example of QoS invocation log matrix

$\mathcal{S}$						
$\mathcal{U}$	s_1	s_2	s_3	s_4	s_5	s_6
u_1	0.25	0.3	0 ?	0.301	0	0.01
u_2	0.25	0.33	0.32	0.322	0.1	0
u_3	0.22	0.31	*0.29*	0	0.22	0.01
u_4	0	0	0.31	0.311	0.4	0.15
u_5	0.8	0	0	0.15	0.7	0.99
u_6	0	0	0	0.1	0	0.9

It may be noted that each entry of this matrix essentially represents a QoS invocation log. For example, consider the colored cell, which represents the QoS invocation log $(u_3, s_3, 0.29)$, i.e., the value of the response time of s_3 is 0.29 during the invocation of s_3 by u_3. ∎

It may be noted that if a user u_i has never invoked a service s_j, the corresponding entry in the QoS invocation log is $(u_i, s_j, 0)$. In other words, if $\mathcal{Q}(i,j) = 0$, this implies the user u_i has never invoked the service s_j. We now formulate our problem of QoS prediction. We are given the following:

- A set of users $\mathcal{U} = \{u_1, u_2, \ldots, u_n\}$.
- A set of web services $\mathcal{S} = \{s_1, s_2, \ldots, s_k\}$.
- For each user u_i, a set of invoked services $\mathcal{S}^i \subseteq \mathcal{S}$.
- For each service s_i, a set of users that invoked s_i, $\mathcal{U}^i \subseteq \mathcal{U}$.
- The QoS invocation log matrix $\mathcal{Q}$ for a given QoS parameter q.
- A target user u_x and a target web service s_y.

The objective of this problem is to predict the value of $q_{x,y}$. In the next section, we demonstrate our solution methodology in detail.

4   Detailed Methodology

Figure 1 illustrates the framework proposed in this paper. Our framework consists of 4 basic modules: (a) a user-intensive filtering module, (b) a service-intensive filtering module, (c) a module for combining the results obtained from the previous steps and (d) a neural network based regression module. Each of the user-intensive and the service-intensive filtering modules again consist of two submodules. Given a target user u_x and a target service s_y, in user intensive module, we first generate a set of users similar to u_x, say $USIM(u_x)$. In the next stage, we find a set of services similar to s_y on $USIM(u_x)$, say $SSIM(u_x, s_y)$. Similarly, in the service-intensive filtering module, we first generate a set of services similar to s_y, say $SSIM(s_y)$, followed by a set of users similar to u_x on $SSIM(s_y)$, say $USIM(s_y, u_x)$. Once we generate, $USIM(u_x)$, $SSIM(u_x, s_y)$, $SSIM(s_y)$ and $USIM(s_y, u_x)$, in our third module, we combine all of them to generate our final user-service QoS invocation log matrix $\mathcal{Q}_{SIM}$. In the final module, we employ a neural network based regression method on $\mathcal{Q}_{SIM}$ to predict the value of $q_{x,y}$. In the following subsections, we discuss each of these modules.

4.1   User-Intensive Filtering

This is the first module of our framework. In this module, we first find a set of users similar to the target user and then find a set of services similar to the target service on the previously computed user-set. We now discuss these two steps in detail.

Find Similar Users. Given a target user u_x, the objective of this step is to find a set of users similar to u_x. Since we do not have any contextual information about a user, the similarity between two users u_i and u_j is calculated from their service-invocation profiles. The key factors that are responsible for measuring the similarity between two users are enlisted below:

(i) The set of web services invoked by either the user u_i or the user u_j, i.e., $(\mathcal{S}^i \cup \mathcal{S}^j)$.

(ii) The set of common services invoked by the user u_i and the user u_j, i.e., $(\mathcal{S}^i \cap \mathcal{S}^j)$.

(iii) The correlation among the QoS values of the services in $(\mathcal{S}^i \cap \mathcal{S}^j)$.

Cosine similarity measure [3] is one such measure which takes all the above factors into account. We now define cosine similarity between two users.

Definition 3 (User Cosine Similarity $SIM_{CS}(u_i, u_j)$). *The cosine similarity between two users u_i and u_j is defined as follows:*

$$SIM_{CS}(u_i, u_j) = \frac{\sum\limits_{s_k \in \mathcal{S}^{i,j}} q_{i,k}\, q_{j,k}}{\sqrt{\sum\limits_{s_k \in \mathcal{S}^i} q_{i,k}^2}\sqrt{\sum\limits_{s_k \in \mathcal{S}^j} q_{j,k}^2}} \tag{1}$$

Where $\mathcal{S}^{i,j} = \mathcal{S}^i \cap \mathcal{S}^j$.   ∎

It may be noted that the numerator of the above expression is calculated on the set of common services invoked by u_i and u_j, while the denominator is calculated on the individual service invocation profiles of u_i and u_j. The overall expression essentially measures the QoS similarity between two users. Therefore, altogether the cosine similarity measure takes care of all the factors discussed above to compute the similarity between two users.

Given a target user u_x, we now discuss our algorithm to find the set of users similar to u_x. Algorithms 1 and 2 demonstrate our method of finding the similar users.

Algorithm 1. Find Similar Set of Users

1: Input $= \mathcal{U}, \mathcal{S}, \mathcal{Q}, u_x$
2: Output $= USIM(u_x)$
3: **for** each u_i and $u_j \in \mathcal{U}$ **do**
4:     Calculate $SIM_{CS}(u_i, u_j)$ and store it in a matrix called CosineUser(i, j);
5: **end for**
6: $USIM(u_x) =$ ClusterUsers(CosineUser, t);
7: return $USIM(u_x)$;

In the first step of Algorithm 1, we compute the similarity between each pair of users u_i and u_j in $\mathcal{U}$ using cosine similarity measure as defined in Definition 3. It may be noted, the above definition is commutative, i.e., $SIM_{CS}(u_i, u_j) = SIM_{CS}(u_j, u_i)$. We then perform a clustering to find the set of users similar to u_x. Our proposed clustering algorithm, i.e., Algorithm 2, is a variant of the classical DBSCAN algorithm [8]. The clustering method takes a threshold parameter t as an input. This threshold is a tunable parameter, which is used to decide whether two users are similar. If the similarity measure between $u_i \in \mathcal{U}$ and u_x is more than t, we consider them as similar users and add u_i in $USIM(u_x)$. Here, $USIM(u_x)$ represents the set of users similar to u_x. The transitive similarity between users is also considered in this algorithm. If a user u_i is similar to u_x and another user u_j is similar to u_i, we then add u_j to $USIM(u_x)$, since u_j is transitively similar to u_x. The main motivation behind considering the transitive similarity between users is as follows. The similarity between two users u_i and

u_j is highly dependent on the set of common services they invoked. If u_i and u_j do not invoke any common service, the similarity measure between u_i and u_j becomes 0. However, it may so happen u_j is not similar to u_x, because of less number of common service invocations. Again u_j is highly similar to u_k, which is similar to u_x. In that case, we should consider u_j as well.

Algorithm 2. ClusterUsers

1: Input = CosineUser, t
2: Output = $USIM(u_x)$
3: Add u_x in $USIM(u_x)$;
4: **repeat**
5:     **for each** new $u_i \in USIM(u_x)$ not considered earlier **do**
6:         **for each** $u_j \in \mathcal{U}$ **do**
7:             **if** $USIM_{CS}(u_i, u_j) \geq t$ **then**
8:                 Add u_j in $USIM(u_x)$, if not already added;
9:             **end if**
10:         **end for**
11:     **end for**
12: **until** no new user is added in $USIM(u_x)$;
13: return $USIM(u_x)$;

Example 2 Consider Example 1, where we want to predict the value of $q_{1,3}$. Table 2 shows cosine similarities between each pair of users in $\mathcal{U}$.

Table 2. Example of finding similar users in user-intensive filtering

$\mathcal{U}$	u_1	u_2	u_3	u_4	u_5	u_6
u_1	1	0.84	0.578	0.31	0.35	0.08
u_2		1	0.83	0.62	0.35	0.06
u_3			1	0.56	0.44	0.02
u_4				1	0.53	0.3
u_5					1	0.69
u_6						1

Consider the value of $t = 0.6$. Initially, $USIM(u_1)$ contains only u_1. Using the clustering algorithm discussed above, u_2 is added in $USIM(u_1)$, since $SIM_{CS}(u_1, u_2) = 0.84 > 0.6$. The similarity between u_2 and other users are checked further. Depending on the similarity measures, u_3 and u_4 are added further in $USIM(u_1)$. Therefore, $USIM(u_1) = \{u_1, u_2, u_3, u_4\}$.   ∎

In the next step of user-intensive filtering, we deal with $USIM(u_x)$ instead of $\mathcal{U}$, where $USIM(u_x) \subseteq \mathcal{U}$. Similarly, instead of dealing with the entire QoS invocation log matrix, we now consider $\mathcal{Q}_u$. $\mathcal{Q}_u$ is a sub-matrix of $\mathcal{Q}$, containing the rows for the users in $USIM(u_x)$.

Find Similar Services. This is the second step of the user-intensive filtering module. Given a target service s_y, the objective of this step is to remove the set of services dissimilar to s_y. The similarity between two services s_i and s_j can be inferred from the following information:

1. The set of common users who invoked s_i and s_j, i.e., $(\mathcal{U}^i \cap \mathcal{U}^j)$.
2. The correlation among the QoS values of s_i and s_j when invoked by the users in $(\mathcal{U}^i \cap \mathcal{U}^j)$.

We use Pearson Correlation Coefficient (PCC) [25] to measure the similarity between the services, since it takes care of all the above factors. We now define PCC similarity below:

Definition 4 (Service PCC Similarity $SIM_{PS}(s_i, s_j)$). *The PCC similarity between two services s_i and s_j is defined as follows:*

$$SIM_{PS}(s_i, s_j) = \frac{\sum\limits_{u_k \in \mathcal{U}^{i,j}} (q_{k,i} - \bar{q}_i)(q_{k,j} - \bar{q}_j)}{\sqrt{\sum\limits_{u_k \in \mathcal{U}^{i,j}} (q_{k,i} - \bar{q}_i)^2} \sqrt{\sum\limits_{u_k \in \mathcal{U}^{i,j}} (q_{k,j} - \bar{q}_j)^2}} \tag{2}$$

where $\mathcal{U}^{i,j} = \mathcal{U}^i \cap \mathcal{U}^j$; $\bar{q}_i = \frac{1}{|USIM(u_x)|} \sum\limits_{u_k \in USIM(u_x)} q_{k,i}$. ∎

It may be noted, the above definition is commutative, i.e., $SIM_{PS}(s_i, s_j) = SIM_{PS}(s_j, s_i)$.

We now use the same clustering technique as discussed above to find the set of services similar to s_y on the basis of $\mathcal{Q}_u$. The clustering algorithm generates $SSIM(u_x, s_y)$ as output, where $SSIM(u_x, s_y)$ represents the set of services similar to s_y. It may be noted that after this step, we have to deal with $SSIM(u_x, s_y)$ instead of $\mathcal{S}$. Accordingly we change the QoS invocation log matrix. We now consider $\mathcal{Q}_{us}$ instead of $\mathcal{Q}_u$. $\mathcal{Q}_{us}$ is a sub-matrix of $\mathcal{Q}_u$, containing the columns corresponding to the services in $SSIM(u_x, s_y)$. It may be noted, the size of $\mathcal{Q}_{us}$ is $|USIM(u_x)| \times |SSIM(u_x, s_y)|$.

4.2   Service-Intensive Filtering

This is the second module of our framework. In this step, we first find a set of services similar to the target service and then find a set of users similar to the target users on the previously calculated service-set. This method is philosophically similar to the user-intensive filtering method. Below, we discuss the steps of this method briefly.

Find Similar Services. Given a target service s_y, the aim of this step is to find a set of services similar to s_y. Since we do not have any contextual information about a web service, the similarity between two services s_i and s_j is measured from their user-service invocation profiles. As in the case of the user-intensive filtering method, we use the cosine similarity measure [3] to calculate the similarity between two services. We now define cosine similarity between two services as follows.

Definition 5 (Service Cosine Similarity $SIM_{CS}(s_i, s_j)$). *The cosine similarity between two services s_i and s_j is defined as follows:*

$$SIM_{CS}(s_i, s_j) = \frac{\sum\limits_{u_k \in \mathcal{U}^{i,j}} q_{k,i}\, q_{k,j}}{\sqrt{\sum\limits_{u_k \in \mathcal{U}^i} q_{k,i}^2}\sqrt{\sum\limits_{u_k \in \mathcal{U}^j} q_{k,j}^2}} \tag{3}$$

where $\mathcal{U}^{i,j} = \mathcal{U}^i \cap \mathcal{U}^j$. ∎

Once we calculate the cosine similarity between each pair of services in $\mathcal{S}$, we use the same clustering technique as discussed in Subsection 4.1 to find the set of services similar to s_y. The clustering algorithm returns $SSIM(s_y)$ as output, which is used in the next step of the service-intensive filtering method. It may be noted that $SSIM(s_y) \subseteq \mathcal{S}$ represents the set of services similar to s_y. Like earlier, we change the QoS invocation log matrix as well. Instead of considering the entire QoS invocation log matrix $\mathcal{Q}$, we now consider $\mathcal{Q}_s$. It may be noted, $\mathcal{Q}_s$ is a sub-matrix of $\mathcal{Q}$, containing the columns corresponding to the services in $SSIM(s_y)$.

Find Similar Users. Given a target user u_x, the objective of this step is to remove the set of users dissimilar to u_x. As in user-intensive filtering, we use Pearson Correlation Coefficient (PCC) [25] to measure the similarity between two users. We now define PCC similarity measure between two users as follows:

Definition 6 (User PCC Similarity $SIM_{PS}(u_i, u_j)$). *The PCC similarity between two users u_i and u_j is defined as follows:*

$$SIM_{PS}(u_i, u_j) = \frac{\sum\limits_{s_k \in \mathcal{S}^{i,j}} (q_{i,k} - \bar{q}_i)(q_{j,k} - \bar{q}_j)}{\sqrt{\sum\limits_{s_k \in \mathcal{S}^{i,j}} (q_{i,k} - \bar{q}_i)^2}\sqrt{\sum\limits_{s_k \in \mathcal{S}^{i,j}} (q_{j,k} - \bar{q}_j)^2}} \tag{4}$$

where $\mathcal{S}^{i,j} = \mathcal{S}^i \cap \mathcal{S}^j$ and $\bar{q}_i = \frac{1}{|SSIM(s_y)|} \sum\limits_{u_j \in SSIM(s_y)} q_{i,j}$. ∎

The remaining procedure to find the set of users similar to u_x on the basis of $\mathcal{Q}_s$ is same as earlier. The clustering algorithm returns $USIM(s_y, u_x)$ as output, where $USIM(s_y, u_x)$ represents the set of users similar to u_x. It may be noted that after this step, we have to deal with $USIM(s_y, u_x)$ instead of $\mathcal{U}$. Accordingly we change the QoS invocation log matrix. We now consider $\mathcal{Q}_{su}$ instead of $\mathcal{Q}_s$. $\mathcal{Q}_{su}$ is a sub-matrix of $\mathcal{Q}_s$, containing the rows for the users in $USIM(s_y, u_x)$. It may be noted, the size of $\mathcal{Q}_{su}$ is $|USIM(s_y, u_x)| \times |SSIM(s_y)|$.

4.3 Find Similar Set of Users on a Similar Set of Services

The objective of the third module of our framework is to combine the outputs of the user-intensive and service-intensive filtering methods. We take the intersection of the outputs to generate the final result. Consider $SIM(u_x)$ and $SIM(s_y)$ represent the final set of similar users and the final set of similar services respectively. These two sets are calculated as follows:

$$SIM(u_x) = USIM(u_x) \cap USIM(s_y, u_x) \tag{5}$$

$$SIM(s_y) = SSIM(u_x, s_y) \cap SSIM(s_y) \tag{6}$$

Finally, we consider the QoS invocation log matrix as $\mathcal{Q}_{SIM}$, which consists of the rows and columns corresponding to the users in $SIM(u_x)$ and the services in $SIM(s_y)$ respectively.

4.4   Prediction Using Neural Network Based Regression

This is the final module of our framework. Once we obtain the set of similar users $SIM(u_x)$ and the set of similar services $SIM(s_y)$, we employ a neural network based regression module [1] to predict the QoS value of the target service for the target user. Before feeding our data into the neural network, we preprocess the data. In the preprocessing step, we substitute all the 0 entries in $\mathcal{Q}_{SIM}$ by the corresponding column average, except the position that is going to be predicted. The main intuition behind this preprocessing step is as follows. Firstly, $\mathcal{Q}_{SIM}(i,j) = 0$ implies that the user u_i has never invoked the service s_j. Therefore, the 0 entry in $\mathcal{Q}_{SIM}$ does not actually depict the true value of $\mathcal{Q}_{SIM}(i,j)$. Secondly, the column average presents the average QoS values of s_j across all users in $SIM(u_x)$. Therefore, the average value is a better representative value than 0 for $\mathcal{Q}_{SIM}(i,j)$. The modified QoS log matrix is represented by $\mathcal{Q}'_{SIM}(i,j)$.

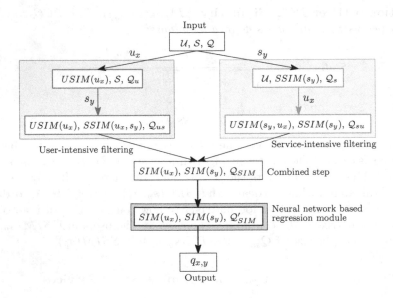

Fig. 2. Data flow in our framework

Finally, $\mathcal{Q}'_{SIM}$ is fed into the neural network. We train the neural network with the service invocation profiles of the following users: $SIM(u_x) \backslash \{u_x\}$. It may be noted that each training data corresponds to the service invocation profile of a specific user. For each training data, the input layer of the neural network consists of the QoS values of the services in $SIM(s_y) \setminus \{s_y\}$, and the output is the QoS value of s_y for the specific user. The objective is now to obtain the QoS value of s_y for u_x, given the service invocation profile (i.e., the QoS values of the services in $SIM(s_y) \setminus \{s_y\}$) of u_x as input. Figure 2 shows the data flow in our framework.

We now describe the neural network-based regression module [7] used in this paper. We use a linear regression to predict the missing QoS value, i.e., estimating Y, given X by formulating the linear relation between X and Y, as follows, $Y = wX + \beta$. To fit the linear regression line among data points, the weight vector w and bias β are tuned using a neural network architecture [6]. Here, we employ a feed-forward neural network with back propagation, where the weight values are fed forward, and the errors are calculated and propagated back. We use the *traingdx* as training function, since it combines the adaptive learning rate with gradient descent momentum training. *Learngdm* is employed as an adaptive learning function. The *Mean Squared Error (MSE)* measures the performance of the network to assess the quality of the net. *Hyperbolic tangent sigmoid* is used as the transfer function. The experimental setup of this neural network-based regression module is further discussed in Sect. 5.4.

5   Experimental Results

In this section, we demonstrate the experimental results obtained by our framework. We have implemented our framework in MATLAB R2018b. All experiments were performed on a system with the following configuration: Intel Core i7-7600U CPU @ 2.8 GHz with 16 GB DDR4 RAM.

5.1   DataSets

We use the WS-DREAM [24] dataset to analyze the performance of our approach. The dataset comprises of 5,825 web services across 73 countries and 339 web service users across 30 countries. The dataset contains 2 QoS parameters response time and throughput. For each QoS parameter, a matrix with dimension 339×5825 is given. We use the response time matrix to validate our approach.

Training and Testing DataSet. We divide the dataset into two parts: training set and testing set. We use a given parameter $d(0 \leq d \leq 1)$, called density, to obtain the training set. The density is used to denote the proportion of the QoS invocation logs used as the training dataset. For example, if the total number of QoS invocation logs is x and d is the density, the size of the training set then equals to $x \times d$, which is lesser than x. The remaining QoS invocation logs, i.e., $x \times (1 - d)$, are used as the testing dataset.

Each experiment is performed 5 times for each density value. Finally, the average results are calculated and shown in this paper.

5.2 Comparative Methods

We compare our approach with the following approaches from the literature:

- UPCC [3]: This method employs a user-intensive collaborative filtering approach for QoS prediction.
- IPCC [14]: This approach employs service-intensive collaborative filtering for QoS prediction.
- WSRec [22]: This method combines UPCC and IPCC.
- NRCF [16]: This method employs classical collaborative filtering to improve the prediction accuracy.
- RACF [21]: Ratio based similarity (RBS) is used in this work and the result is calculated by the similar users or similar services.
- RECF [25]: Reinforced collaborative filtering approach is used in this work to improve the prediction accuracy. In this method, both user-based and service-based similarity information are integrated into a singleton collaborative filtering.
- MF [11]: Matrix factorization based approach is used here for prediction.
- HDOP [18]: This method uses multi-linear-algebra based concepts of tensor for QoS value prediction. Tensor decomposition and reconstruction optimization algorithms are used to predict QoS value.

As discussed earlier in this paper, we propose a collaborative filtering approach followed by the neural network-based regression model (CNR). To show the necessity of each step of our approach, we further compare our method with the following approaches.

- NR: In this approach, we only consider the neural network-based regression model, without using any collaborative filtering method.
- CR: In this approach, we use the same collaborative filtering method as demonstrated in this paper. However, instead of using a neural network-based linear regression model, a simple linear regression module is used here to predict the QoS value.
- UCNR: In this approach, we use the user-intensive collaborative filtering method along with the neural network-based regression model.
- SCNR: In this approach, we use the service-intensive collaborative filtering method along with the neural network-based regression model.
- CNRWoV: This approach is same as CNR. The only difference here, we do not substitute the 0 entries in $\mathcal{Q}_{SIM}$ by the corresponding column average.
- CNRCC: In this approach, we use cosine similarity measure to find similar users and services for both user-intensive and service-intensive filtering methods.

5.3 Comparison Metric

We use *Mean Absolute Error (MAE)* [25] to measure the prediction error in our experiment. It may be noted that lower the value of MAE, better is the prediction accuracy.

Definition 7 (Mean Absolute Error (MAE)). *MAE is defined as follows:*

$$MAE = \frac{\sum\limits_{q_{i,j} \in TD} |q_{i,j} - \hat{q}_{i,j}|}{|TD|}$$

where, $q_{i,j}$ represents the ground truth QoS value of the jth service for the ith user in the testing dataset TD. $\hat{q}_{i,j}$ represents the predicted QoS value for the same. ∎

5.4 Configuration of Our Experiment

To generate the set of similar users and services, empirically we chose the user-threshold value between 0.5 to 0.6 and service-threshold value between 0.4 to 0.5 for our clustering methods. Later in this section, we show how the change of the threshold value impacts on the prediction quality.

For the neural network-based regression model, we used the following configuration in our experiment. We considered 2 hidden layers in the neural network. We varied the number of neurons in each hidden layer within the range [4, 128]. Finally, we obtained the best results for 16 neurons in the first hidden layer and 8 neurons in the second hidden layer. Among the hyper-parameters, the learning rate was set to 0.01 with momentum 0.9. The training was performed up to 1000 epochs or up to minimum gradient of 10^{-5}.

Table 3. Comparative study (MAE) on different prediction methods

Density	UPCC	IPCC	WSRec	NRCF	RACF	RECF	MF	HDOP	**CNR**
0.10	0.6063	0.7000	0.6394	0.5312	0.4937	0.4332	0.5103	0.3076	**0.2597**
0.20	0.5379	0.5351	0.5024	0.4607	0.4208	0.3946	0.4981	0.2276	**0.1711**
0.30	0.5084	0.4783	0.4571	0.4296	0.3997	0.3789	0.4632	0.1841	**0.0968**

We present partial comparative study from Fig. 3(a) due to space constraint

5.5 Analysis of Results

Figure 3(a) and (b) show a comparative study for QoS prediction by different approaches. Table 3 shows partial comparative results of Fig. 3(a) in a more quantitative way. From our experimental results, we have the following observations:

(i) It is evident from Table 3 and Fig. 3(a) that among all the approaches, our proposed approach (CNR) produces the best result in terms of the prediction accuracy, as CNR has the lowest MAE value among all the approaches for each density value.

(ii) It can also be observed from Table 3 and Fig. 3(a) and (b) that as the density increases, the value of MAE decreases. This is mainly because of the fact that as the density increases, the number of QoS invocation logs in the training dataset increases and thereby, the prediction accuracy increases.

(iii) Figure 3(b) shows the requirement of each step of our proposal. As is evident from the figure, CNR is better than NR, which explains the requirement of the collaborative filtering approach. CNR is also better than CR, which confirms the importance of the neural network-based regression model. On one side, CNR is better than UCNR, on the other side, CNR is better than SCNR, which indicates the necessity of our combine step. Further, we compare CNR with CNRWoV, which shows the significance of replacing 0 entries in Q_{SIM} by the corresponding column average.

In CNR, we use the cosine similarity measure followed by PCC (i.e., cosine + PCC). We have, therefore, further experimented our framework with other combinations of similarity measures, such as cosine+cosine, PCC+PCC, PCC+cosine, which did not work well in comparison with the cosine + PCC. In Fig. 3(b), we present only the result of CNRCC (i.e., cosine+cosine), which worked the second best.

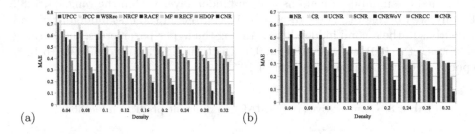

(a)   (b)

Fig. 3. Comparative study on different prediction methods

5.6   Impact of the Tunable Parameters on Our Experiment

In this subsection, we discuss the impact of the tunable parameters on the results obtained by our proposed method. We used 4 tunable threshold parameters in our experiments, i.e., a threshold value required to cluster the users and services in the user-intensive and service-intensive filtering steps. However, we used the same threshold value to cluster the users (services) in both the user-intensive and service-intensive filtering steps.

Figure 4(a) shows the variation of MAE (along the y-axis) with respect to the threshold (along the x-axis) required to cluster the services for a constant threshold (shown as legends in the graph) required for user clustering. Similarly, Fig. 4(b) shows the variation of MAE (along the y-axis) with respect to the the threshold (along the x-axis) required to cluster the users for a fixed threshold (shown as legends in the graph) required for service clustering.

From Fig. 4 (a) and (b), we have the following observations:

(i) As evident from both the figures, for the threshold value between 0.4 to 0.6, we obtain better results in terms of prediction accuracy.

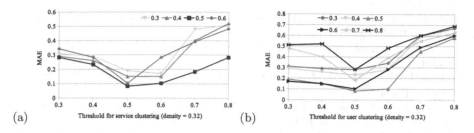

(a)

(b)

Fig. 4. Variation of MAE across the threshold used for (a) user clustering, (b) service clustering

(ii) For a very low value of the threshold, we may end up having the entire QoS logs in the training dataset. In this case, we obtain the same results as NR method.

(iii) For a very high threshold value, we end up having very less number of similar users and similar services which are insufficient to train the neural network-based regression model and thereby the prediction accuracy decreases.

In summary, as evident from our experiment, our proposed method outperformed the major state-of-the-art methods in terms of prediction accuracy.

6   Conclusion

In this work, we propose a method to predict the value of a given QoS parameter of a target web service for a target user. We leverage the collaborative filtering approach along with the regression method. We conducted our experiments on the WS-DREAM dataset. The experimental results show that our method is more efficient in terms of prediction accuracy than the past approaches. However, in this paper, we do not consider the fact that QoS parameters vary across time as well. Even for a single user, the QoS value of a service can be different across time. We wish to take up this task of QoS value prediction in a dynamic environment going ahead.

References

1. Adamczak, R., et al.: Accurate prediction of solvent accessibility using neural networks-based regression. Proteins Struct. Funct. Bioinform. **56**(4), 753–767 (2004)
2. Amin, A., et al.: An approach to forecasting qos attributes of web services based on arima and garch models. In: ICWS, pp. 74–81. IEEE (2012)
3. Breese, J.S., et al.: Empirical analysis of predictive algorithms for collaborative filtering. In: Uncertainty in Artificial Intelligence, pp. 43–52. Morgan Kaufmann Publishers Inc. (1998)
4. Chattopadhyay, S., et al.: A framework for top service subscription recommendations for service assemblers. In: IEEE SCC, pp. 332–339 (2016)

5. Chen, X., et al.: Personalized qos-aware web service recommendation and visualization. IEEE TSC **6**(1), 35–47 (2013)
6. Daniel, G.: Principles of Artificial Neural Networks, vol. 7. World Scientific, Singapore (2013)
7. Demuth, H., Beale, M.: Neural Network Toolbox, vol. 4. The MathWorks Inc., Boston (2004)
8. Ester, M., et al.: A density-based algorithm for discovering clusters in large spatial databases with noise. In: KDD, vol. 96, pp. 226–231 (1996)
9. Li, S., Wen, J., Luo, F., Ranzi, G.: Time-aware QoS prediction for cloud service recommendation based on matrix factorization. IEEE Access **6**, 77716–77724 (2018)
10. Li, S., et al.: From reputation perspective: a hybrid matrix factorization for QoS prediction in location-aware mobile service recommendation system. Mob. Inf. Syst. **2019**, 8950508:1–8950508:12 (2019)
11. Lo, W., et al.: An extended matrix factorization approach for qos prediction in service selection. In: IEEE SCC, pp. 162–169. IEEE (2012)
12. Ma, Y., et al.: Predicting QoS values via multi-dimensional QoS data for web service recommendations. In: ICWS, pp. 249–256. IEEE (2015)
13. Qi, K., et al.: Personalized QoS prediction via matrix factorization integrated with neighborhood information. In: SCC, pp. 186–193. IEEE (2015)
14. Sarwar, B.M., et al.: Item-based collaborative filtering recommendation algorithms. WWW **1**, 285–295 (2001)
15. Shao, L., et al.: Personalized qos prediction for web services via collaborative filtering. In: IEEE ICWS, pp. 439–446 (2007)
16. Sun, H., et al.: Personalized web service recommendation via normal recovery collaborative filtering. IEEE TSC **6**(4), 573–579 (2013)
17. Tang, M., et al.: Location-aware collaborative filtering for QoS-based service recommendation. In: ICWS, pp. 202–209. IEEE (2012)
18. Wang, S., et al.: Multi-dimensional QoS prediction for service recommendations. IEEE TSC **12**, 47–57 (2016)
19. Wu, C., Qiu, W., et al.: Time-aware and sparsity-tolerant QoS prediction based on collaborative filtering. In: IEEE ICWS, pp. 637–640 (2016)
20. Wu, H., et al.: Collaborative QoS prediction with context-sensitive matrix factorization. Future Gener. Comp. Syst. **82**, 669–678 (2018)
21. Wu, X., et al.: Collaborative filtering service recommendation based on a novel similarity computation method. IEEE TSC **10**(3), 352–365 (2017)
22. Zheng, Z., et al.: QoS-aware web service recommendation by collaborative filtering. IEEE TSC **4**(2), 140–152 (2011)
23. Zheng, Z., et al.: Collaborative web service QoS prediction via neighborhood integrated matrix factorization. IEEE TSC **6**(3), 289–299 (2013)
24. Zheng, Z., et al.: Investigating qos of real-world web services. IEEE TSC **7**(1), 32–39 (2014)
25. Zou, G., Jiang, M., Niu, S., Wu, H., Pang, S., Gan, Y.: QoS-aware web service recommendation with reinforced collaborative filtering. In: Pahl, C., Vukovic, M., Yin, J., Yu, Q. (eds.) ICSOC 2018. LNCS, vol. 11236, pp. 430–445. Springer, Cham (2018). https://doi.org/10.1007/978-3-030-03596-9_31

Harmonia: A Continuous Service Monitoring Framework Using DevOps and Service Mesh in a Complementary Manner

Haan Johng[1(✉)], Anup K. Kalia[2], Jin Xiao[2], Maja Vuković[2],
and Lawrence Chung[1]

[1] University of Texas at Dallas, Richardson, TX 75080, USA
{haanmo.johng,chung}@utdallas.edu
[2] IBM T. J. Watson Research Center, Yorktown Heights, NY 10598, USA
{Anup.Kalia,jinoaix,maja}@us.ibm.com

Abstract. Software teams today are required to deliver new or updated services frequently, rapidly and independently. Adopting DevOps and Microservices support the rapid service delivery model but leads to pushing code or service infrastructure changes across inter-dependent teams that are not collectively assessed, verified, or notified. In this paper, we propose Harmonia - a continuous service monitoring framework utilizing DevOps and Service Mesh in a complementary manner to improve coordination and change management among independent teams. Harmonia can automatically detect changes in services, including changes that violate performance SLAs and user experience, notify the changes to affected teams, and help them resolve the changes quickly. We applied Harmonia to a standard application in describing Microservice management to assist with an initial understanding and strengths of Harmonia. During the demonstration, we deployed faulty and normal services alternatively and captured changes from Jenkins, Github, Istio, and Kubernetes logs to form an application-centric cohesive view of the change and its impact and notify the affected teams.

Keywords: DevOps · Service Mesh · Microservice · Monitoring ·
Enterprise Cloud Management

1 Introduction

Software teams today are required to deliver new or updated services frequently, rapidly and independently. They look to DevOps to increase speed and frequency of service delivery by automating testing and deployment of services. Microservices, an architectural concept consisted of small-sized services that are independently deployable, scalable, and manageable, further helps the software teams to deliver services in a more rapid, incremental, and independent manner.

© Springer Nature Switzerland AG 2019
S. Yangui et al. (Eds.): ICSOC 2019, LNCS 11895, pp. 151–168, 2019.
https://doi.org/10.1007/978-3-030-33702-5_12

For example, Amazon and Netflix deploy thousands of times per day by using DevOps and Microservices [6,15].

Although adopting DevOps and Microservice design brings the aforementioned benefits, it also brings communication and collaboration challenges among independent software teams collectively contributing to changes in services over time. As each team pushes code or service infrastructure changes into the environment, its impacts on inter-dependent teams are not collectively assessed, notified, or verified. Rather they are present ad hocly across multiple data sources: code changes and commits can be detected through git, deployment configuration changes are visible through DevOps pipeline, runtime performance issues can be reported by Istio or Kubernetes depending on what is monitored. However, there is no correlation across changes in an application code, its configuration and runtime performance, especially when multiple independent services and development teams are involved. As a result, integration errors, misconfigurations, and security exposures may occur that are difficult to detect and trace across teams and resolve in a timely manner. Today's approach to detect and diagnose issues caused by changes through performance diagnosis or root-cause analysis is therefore time-consuming and reactive.

In this paper, we propose *Harmonia*[1] - a continuous service monitoring framework utilizing DevOps and Service Mesh in a complementary manner, as among the first of its kind to the best of our knowledge, to improve coordination and change management among independent teams. Harmonia can automatically detect code and infrastructure changes in services, including changes in code, configuration, deployment, and application performance. Furthermore, Harmonia can assess the impact of the changes to other services, and notify the changes to affected teams, whereby helping software teams resolve the changes quickly. More specifically, Harmonia offers an ontology alignment between DevOps logs and Service Mesh logs to utilize service deployment information from DevOps together with service run-time interaction information from Service Mesh. Harmonia supports declarative rules for detection and notifications to define what to detect and notify and whom to be notified. Thus, Harmonia takes a proactive approach to change management whereby defects and performance issues are detected as they occur, their impact across service components are assessed, and actions are taken by notifying both the teams (or team members) accountable for the change as well as impacted by the change.

To demonstrate Harmonia, we have built a capability to correlate logs from Github and Jenkins for DevOps and logs from Istio and Kubernetes for Service Mesh. We applied Harmonia to the Bookinfo application, which is a standard application in describing Istio for Microservices management and ran a simulation to comprehend the applicability of Harmonia and its strengths. During the simulation, we deployed faulty and normal services at regular intervals to observe whether Harmonia is able to capture the changes and notify them to the impacted teams correctly automatically. Our demonstration shows that, compared to existing DevOps and Service Mesh frameworks, Harmonia offers a

---

[1] Harmonia is the goddess of harmony and concord in Greek mythology.

better interpretability for software teams regarding service changes, the impact of the changes, and source of the changes in a timely manner, by representing service changes both in service deployment phase and in the run-time phase in a single view.

The rest of the paper is organized as follows, Sect. 2 provides related work, and Sect. 3 describes Harmonia. Section 4 presents our demonstration, followed by observations and discussions. In the end, a summary of contributions and future work are described.

2   Related Work

We discuss the related work on monitoring and root-cause analysis on microservices and DevOps.

In terms of monitoring, Heinrich et al. [9] highlight research directions in microservices with respect to performance-aware testing, monitoring and modeling services. Specifically they emphasize that due to frequent releases, extensive system and integration tests are not possible. Although canary deployments take care some aspect of the problem by releasing the deployment to a few set of users, however, such deployment process can be expensive and time-consuming. Pina et al. [19] propose an approach to monitor microservices by decoupling monitoring functionalities from function-oriented microservices. For monitoring they use Zuul an adapted gateway from Netflix. Fadda et al. [4] provide an approach to support microservices deployment in multi-cloud environments emphasizing on the quality of monitoring. Their proposed approach creates a knowledge base that mediates between the perspectives of the cloud provider and the application owner and a Bayesian network that enhances the provider's monitoring capabilities. Haselböck and Weinreich [8] propose guidance models for monitoring microservices. The models are derived from literature, previous work on monitoring distributed systems and microservice-based systems. Phipathananunth and Bunyakiati [18] provide Pink a framework that monitors microservices to assess non-functional properties such as session management, caching and security. The major focus with such monitoring base contributions is primarily tied to monitoring a service mesh. Such contributions do not connect service mesh with DevOps that have additional information on deployment. In case of service anomalies or abnormalities, such approaches may not trace microservices that might get impact nor can notify the teams in charge of the services together with recent deployment and program code change history on the services to help the teams to plan mitigation actions instantly.

In terms of root cause analysis, Lin et al. [16] propose Microscope to detect abnormal services with a ranked list of possible root causes. Wang et al. [20] propose CloudRanger that constructs causal graphs to determine the culprit services that are responsible for cloud incidents. Myunghwan et al. [14] provide MonitorRank that monitors historical and current time-series metrics of each sensor as its input along with the call graphs generated between the sensors to create an unsupervised model for ranking. Chen et al. [3] propose CauseInfer that creates a two-layer hierarchical causality graph from a distributed system to infer the root causes along the causal paths. Jayathilaka et al. [10] propose Roots that monitors a full-stack application to determine the root cause for an anomaly. It does so by analyzing previous workload data of the application and the performance of the internal PaaS services on which the application depends. Existing approaches to determine root causes are reactive based approaches, i.e., they identify a root cause after an anomaly has occurred. Also the current approaches do not consider logs generated from DevOps to pin point who is accountable for the root cause.

In DevOps, most of the contributions emphasize on utilizing microservices that facilitate rapid deployments of services. For example, Balalaie et al. [1] emphasize on how monolithic architecture can be broken down in to microservices considering microservices can quickly adapt to technological changes, reduce time-to-market and provision a better development team structuring around services. Zhu et al. [22] describe how DevOps can reduce time between committing a change to a system and the change being productionized ensuring high quality. Brunnert et al. [2] provide performance-relevant aspects of DevOps concept. Fitzgerald and Stol [5] propose BizDev that continuously assess business strategy and software development. Gupta et al. [7] propose an approach to automatically discover execution behavior models for the deployed and the new version using the execution logs. However, there seems a lack of studies on DevOps using service mesh that provides monitoring information of microservices and interactions among them. Without monitoring information, it is challenging to estimate the potential degree of impacts on other services before deploying updates and analyze the actual impacts after the deployment.

3   Harmonia - A Continuous Service Monitoring Framework

Harmonia is a continuous service monitoring framework that aims to reduce delays in communications among independent software teams regarding changes in services and impacts of the changes. Figure 1 shows the ontology of Harmonia. By using DevOps and Service Mesh in a complementary manner, Harmonia monitors changes in services by detecting violations of service level agreements (SLAs, e.g., latency SLA) together with impacted services after the changes are pushed. Harmonia further notifies software teams to assist them to take appropriate actions to remediate their services from the impact. The Harmonia rules define the following: *what to detect and notify* and *whom to be notified*. Each rule acts as a reference to let software teams customize the rule for their applications.

The underlying process in Harmonia consists of three steps as described in Fig. 2. In the first step, Harmonia aligns the ontologies obtained from the service deployment information i.e., from DevOps logs with run-time service interaction information obtained from Service Mesh logs to create an integrated body of knowledge. In the second step, once Harmonia detects changes in services from

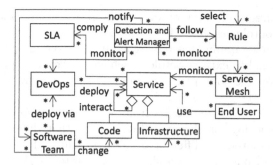

Fig. 1. The ontology of Harmonia for detecting and notifying changes in services.

DevOps logs, it traces the dependent services that might have recently interacted with the changed services. Harmonia does so by monitoring Service Mesh logs. Based on the detected changes, Harmonia notifies the changes to associated software teams that own the dependent services. In the third step, Harmonia detects SLA violations on services by monitoring Service Mesh logs after changes are pushed. Then, Harmonia traces recent changes on the problematic services, which are potential causes of the SLA violations, and notifies the change information to associated software teams.

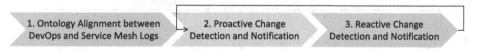

Fig. 2. The underlying process in Harmonia for detecting and notifying changes in services.

3.1 Ontology Alignment Among DevOps and Service Mesh Logs

DevOps is a framework to automate deployment and testing of services from development environments to production environments. Service Mesh is a framework for monitoring and managing interactions among (micro-) services. DevOps logs contain service deployment information such as logs for code push and service deployment. However, such logs do not include run-time service interaction information such as communications among services, latency between services and so on. On the other hand, Service Mesh logs contain run-time service interaction information but do not contain service deployment information. Without having the deployment information and run-time interaction information in a single view, software teams as of now manually inspect the impacts of changes, e.g., latency SLA violation, the source of such changes, software teams that might be impacted by the changes, their contacts, and notify them accordingly. Overall such process is time-consuming and the resultant delay in communication to appropriate software teams might delay the possible mitigation, thereby hurting the goal of frequent service delivery to production environments:

To create an integrated body of knowledge from DevOps and Service Mesh logs, we extract ontologies from both the logs and align them by common attributes. Work on log mining has researched in various domains [17]. For utilizing logs, it is essential to extract ontology, which is a set of important concepts, relationships among the concepts, and constraints, to understand what knowledge to utilize from the logs [11–13, 21].

We extract the DevOps ontologies from Jenkins logs and the Service Mesh ontologies from Istio logs as shown in Fig. 3. Note that different DevOps and Service Meshes can produce different ontologies. Thus, the ontology is *a* reference ontology and may not generalize to other frameworks. Nonetheless the underlying methodology to extract and align the onotologies remains the same.

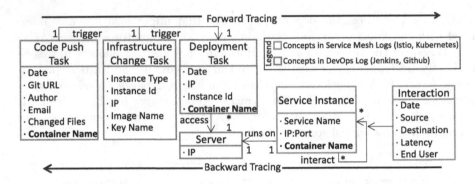

Fig. 3. The ontology alignment among DevOps and Service Mesh logs.

In DevOps logs are generated based on specific tasks such as code push and service deployment as stated earlier. We consider the code push task as pushing code to Github (a source code repository), containerizing the code to generate an image, and then pushing the image to Docker Hub (a container image repository). While pushing code to Github, the changed files and the committer's ID (email address) are recorded. The service deployment task is defined as accessing a server using a server IP via Secure Shell (SSH) and deploying a container image on a server. The logs of the code push task and the logs of service deployment task are aligned by a common attribute "Container Name".

The Service Mesh logs contain service instance information and interaction information among service instances. The service instance information contains a service name, an IP address, a port number and a container name. The interaction information contains an interaction date, a source service, a destination service, the latency of the interaction, and an end user who requested the interaction.

We align the ontologies (information) from DevOps and Service Mesh based on a common attribute "Container Name". By aligning the ontologies of DevOps and Service Mesh, we integrate service deployment and service interaction information. For example, if latency SLA is violated during interacting between two services, the destination service IP is mapped onto the IP of a deployment task. Then, the image name of the deployment task is mapped onto the image name of the code push task. From the code push task, we can trace the email address of the code committer.

3.2 Proactive Change Detection and Notification

For assisting in fast communication and collaboration among the independent software teams regarding changes in services, Harmonia automates detecting changes in services, tracing the dependent services that can be impacted by the changes, notifying the changes to appropriate teams.

To determine what to detect and notify and whom to be notified, Harmonia follows predefined detection and notification (reference-) rules. Each rule consists of a detection condition (C) and a notification action (A). We define each rule as $C \rightarrow A$. Either the condition or the action can be specialized to customize the rules as ($C' \rightarrow A$) or ($C \rightarrow A'$)

Suppose Team A in Fig. 4, is responsible for the *Review service* and deploys the *Review service* after changing the code, Harmonia detects the deployment change from the deployment task logs and changed files from the code push task logs. We consider *Review service* as a *depender* service. We assume that there are services that might be impacted by the changes in the depender service. We refer such services as the *Dependee* services. The dependency can be extracted from recent service interaction logs of Service Mesh. For example, in the Fig. 4, the *Product Page service* that recently sent requests to *the Review service* is considered as the dependee service. By tracing the deployment information of the dependee (*Product Page service*), Harmonia notifies the changes of the depender (*Review service*) to the committer of the dependee (*Product Page service*).

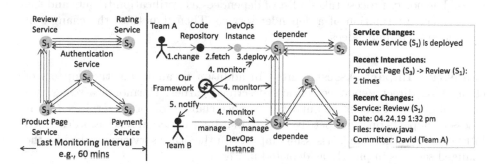

Fig. 4. Detecting changes and deployments of services and notifying to appropriate software teams.

We provide a reference rule (R_1) for the example scenario above as the following:

- **Condition** (C_1): The depender service (s) is deployed.

- **Action** (A_1): Notify the deployment and the change information of the depender service (s) to other teams responsible for the dependee services (d).

$$R_1 : deployed(s)_{C_1} \rightarrow \forall d \in dependee(s),\ notify(d, s)_{A_1} \tag{1}$$

Below, we refine the reference rule 1 (R_1) further. For example, if software teams responsible for the critical services (c), which are not direct dependees but had frequent interactions with the dependees, needs to be notified. Thus, we refine the rule as follows:

- **Condition** (C_1): The depender service (s) is deployed.
- **Action** (A_2): Notify the deployment and change information of the depender service (s) to teams responsible for the critical dependee services (c).

$$R_2 : deployed(s)_{C_1} \rightarrow (\forall d \in dependee(s),\ notify(d, s)_{A_1})$$
$$\land (\forall c \in (\neg dependee(s) \land dependee(d) \land is\_critical(s, c)),\ notify(c, s)_{A_2}) \tag{2}$$

To implement the reference rules, we define (reference-) heuristic translation algorithms associated with the rules in Algorithm 1 and 2. The *deployed* procedure describes the steps of detecting changes and deployments of services by using DevOps logs and Service Mesh logs in a complementary manner. We assume that the logs are represented in the JSON format. The deployed process takes logs from code push, deployment and run-time interaction, notifies the change and deployment information to dependees, and then returns a list of deployments including change information. The deployed process shows a forward tracing from code push logs to run-time interaction logs to get the dependees of the newly deployed services.

The *notify* procedure describes a backward tracing from service interaction logs to code push logs to extract contact email addresses of the dependee services. The notify process takes a list of dependees as notification targets and the deployment information of a depender service. Then it notifies the changes of the depender to dependees.

Transitive Impact Assessments. In addition to analyzing the impacts of changes on direct dependee services described earlier, Harmonia assesses two types of potential transitive impacts of service changes on other services. One is assessing impacts on a competitive service in using a common service as described in Fig. 5. The other one is assessing impacts on the other services invoked by the changed services implicitly as depicted in Fig. 6.

The difference between existing root-cause analysis approaches and our transitive impact assessment is the proactive change detection and notification. The root-cause analysis based approaches pinpoint the root-causes when multiple abnormal services are detected. In contrast, Harmonia considers newly changed services as root-causes and proactively infers the transitive impacts of the changes on other services.

Algorithm 1. A Heuristic Translation of *deployed* Condition to Code

1: *pushedList* ← *read(pushed.json)*;   ▷ Obtained from Jenkins and Github Logs
2: *deployedList* ← *read(deployed.json)*;   ▷ Obtained from Jenkins Logs
3: *interactionList* ← *read(interaction.json)*;   ▷ Obtained from Istio Logs
4: *namespaceList* ← *read(kubernetes.json)*;   ▷ Obtained from Kubernetes Logs
5: **procedure** DEPLOYED( )   ▷ Called regularly. Forward Tracing of Logs
6:     *deployments, dependeeList, pushedList*;
7:     **for each** *deployed* ∈ *deployedList* **do**▷ 1. Get recent changes and deployments
8:         **for each** *pushed* ∈ *pushedList* **do**
9:             **if** *pushed.containerName* == *deployed.containerName* **then**
10:                **if** *pushed.date* < *deployed.date* **then**
11:                    *pushedList.add(pushed)*;
12:            *deployed.put("changes", pushedList)*;
13:        **for each** *namespace* ∈ *namespaceList* **do**   ▷ 2. Get service names in production
14:            **if** *deployed.containerName* == *namespace.containerName* **then**
15:                *deployed.put("serviceName", namespace.instanceName)*;
16:        **for each** *interaction* ∈ *interactionList* **do**   ▷ 3. Get dependees
17:            **if** *interaction.destination* == *deployed.serviceName* **then**
18:                *dependeeList.add(interaction.source)*;
19:        *deployed.put("dependees", dependeeList)*;
20:        *deployments.put("deployments", deployed)*;
21:        *notify(dependeeList, deployed)*; ▷ 4. Notify the changes and deployments to dependees
22:     **return** *deployments*   ▷ A set of deployments

To assess the potential transitive impacts of service changes, we further define notations and rules for detecting and notifying service changes as below.

$$I = (\{S_{src}\}, \{S_{dst}\}, l, t), \quad S = (n, \{D\}), \quad D = (c_t, c_c, c_i) \tag{3}$$

The I is a set of individual interactions (i) within a time slot (T_{t-1}^t). Each interaction (i) consists of a source service (S_{src}), a destination service (S_{dstc}), an interaction latency (l), and a timestamp (t). Each service (S) is composed of a service name (n) and deployment information (D). The deployment information (D) involves a changed time (c_t), changed code information (c_c), and changed infrastructure information (c_i). The latency of a service interaction can be caused either by the changes in the source service or the changes in the destination service.

Figure 5 depicts a transitive impact assessment among competitive services. In this scenario, the service (S_3) and the service (S_5) are competing in invoking the common service (S_4), such as using a common API. A faulty change in the service (S_3) that occupies the service (S_4) with a longer period can impact the service (S_5). Harmonia detects the transitive relationship between competitive services by checking invoking sequences and latency propagations and then notifying service changes among the competitive services as described below:

Algorithm 2. A Heuristic Translation of *notify* Action to Code

1: **procedure** NOTIFY(*tagets, deployed*)	▷ Backward Tracing of Logs
2: **for each** *target* ∈ *targets* **do**	
3: **for each** *namespace* ∈ *namespaceList* **do**	▷ 1. Get container names of dependees
4: **if** *namespace.serviceName* == *target* **then**	
5: *target.put("containerName", namespace.containerName)*;	
6: **for each** *pushed* ∈ *pushedList* **do**	▷ 2. Get contacts of the dependees
7: **if** *pushed.containerName* == *target.containerName* **then**	
8: *sendEmail(pushed.email, deployed)*;	▷ 3. Send an Email with Deployment Information

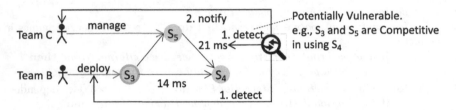

Fig. 5. A transitive impact assessment among competitive services.

– **Condition** (C_2): The interaction i_j (from S_j to S_m) and the interaction i_k (from S_k to S_m) have occurred within a time slot T^t_{t-1}. Service(S_j) and service (S_k) are competitive services that can impact each other in invoking the other service (S_m).

– **Condition** $(C_{1.1})$: Service (S_j) is deployed, which is an instance of C_1.

– **Condition** $(C_{1.2})$: Service (S_m) is deployed, which is an instance of C_1.

– **Action** $(A_{1.1})$: Notify the deployment and change information of service (S_j) to service (S_k) and service (S_m), which is an instance of A_1.

– **Action** $(A_{1.2})$: Notify the deployment and change information of service (S_m) to service (S_j) and service (S_k), which is an instance of A_1.

$$R_3 : (\forall i_j, i_k \in I^t_{t-1}, (i_j.S_{dst} = i_k.S_{dst}) \wedge (i_j.t < i_k.t) \wedge (i_k.l > i_j.l))_{C_2} \rightarrow$$

$$((i_j.S_{src}.D_{ct} \in T^t_{t-1})_{C_{1.1}} \rightarrow (notify(i_j.S_{src}.D, i_j.S_{dst}) \wedge notify(i_j.S_{src}.D, i_k.S_{src}))_{A_{1.1}}) \vee$$

$$((i_j.S_{dst}.D_{ct} \in T^t_{t-1})_{C_{1.2}} \rightarrow (notify(i_j.S_{dst}.D, i_j.S_{src}) \wedge notify(i_j.S_{dst}.D, i_k.S_{src}))_{A_{1.2}})$$

$$(4)$$

Figure 6 shows a scenario of a transitive impact assessment for services invoking the other services implicitly. In this scenario, the service (S_3) is not a direct dependee of the service (S_2) but implicitly invokes the service (S_2). If a change in the service (S_2) increases the interaction latency between the service (S_1) and the service (S_2), the service (S_3) can be impacted. Harmonia captures the transitive impacts for services invoking other services implicitly by checking invoking sequences and latency propagations and then notifying service changes among the competitive services as described below:

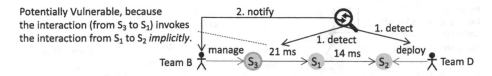

Fig. 6. A transitive impact assessment for services invoking the other services implicitly.

- **Condition** (C_3): The interaction i_j (from S_j to S_k) implicitly invokes the interaction i_k (from S_k to S_m).
- **Condition** $(C_{1.3})$: Service (S_m) is deployed, which is an instance of C_1.
- **Action** $(A'_{1.1})$: Notify the deployment and change information of service(S_m) to service (S_j) and service (S_k), which is an instance of specialization of A_1.

$$R_4 : \forall i_j, i_k \in I^t_{t-1}, ((i_j.S_{dst} = i_k.S_{src}) \wedge (i_j.t < i_k.t))_{C_3} \wedge (i_k.S_{dst}.D \in T^t_{t-1})_{C_{1.3}} \rightarrow$$
$$notify(i_k.S_{dst}.D, i_k.S_{src}) \wedge notify(i_k.S_{dst}.D, i_j.S_{src}))_{A'_{1.1}} \tag{5}$$

The proactive detection and notification rules aim to provide forewarning among independent software teams. If the systems are sensitive for reliability, the forewarning would help the independent software teams in communicating and collaborating with richer information before an abnormality on the system is detected.

3.3 Reactive Change Detection and Notification

DevOps software teams are required to deliver services more frequently and independently to production environments, thereby increasing complexity in communication and collaboration among the teams. For example, if SLA violations occurred after deploying services independently, it is timing consuming to pinpoint causes of the SLA violations and impacted services and to notify the causes to appropriate teams.

Consider the Product page service experiences a 3 s delay after the Team A has deployed a new Review service as shown in Fig. 7. Harmonia automatically detects the violations of the latency SLA when the Product Page service sents a request to the Review service, tracking recent changes in the Review service, and notifying the recent changes to the teams responsible for the Product Page service to assist them react to the violation of latency SLA and remediate it.

A reference rule (R_3) for the example scenario above is defined as below:

- **Condition** (C_2): The latency of interaction from a source service (s_{src}) to a destination service (s_{dst}) is higher than a latency SLA (l_{SLA}).
- **Action** (A_2): Notify the recent changes in the destination service (s_{dst}) to the teams responsible for the service (s_{dst}) and dependee services (d).

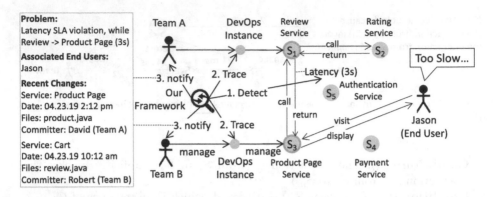

Fig. 7. Detecting SLA violations and impacted services and notifying recent changes in services to appropriate teams.

$$R_5 : \forall s_{dst} \in (latency(s_{src}, s_{dst}) > l_{SLA})_{C_2}) \rightarrow$$
$$notify(s_{dst}, s_{dst})_{A_2} \wedge (\forall d \in dependee(s_{dst}), \ notify(d, s_{dst})_{A_2}) \tag{6}$$

The latency of an interaction between two services can occur due to both changes in the source service and changes in the destination service. If dependees of the source service and the destination service need to be notified with the changes in source service and the destination service respectively, the reference rule 3 can be refined as below:

- **Condition** (C_2): The latency of interaction from a source service (s_{src}) to a destination service (s_{dst}) is higher than a latency SLA (l_{SLA}).
- **Action** (A'_2): Notify the recent changes in the source service (s_{src}) and destination service (s_{dst}) to the teams responsible for the dependees of source (d_{src}) and dependees of destination (d_{dst}).

$$R_6 : \forall s_{dst} \in (latency(s_{src}, s_{dst}) > l_{SLA})_{C_2}) \rightarrow$$
$$\forall d_{dst} \in dependee(s_{dst}), \ notify(d_{dst}, s_{dst})_{A_2} \wedge notify(s_{dst}, s_{dst})_{A_2} \tag{7}$$
$$\wedge \ \forall d_{src} \in dependee(s_{src}), \ notify(d_{src}, s_{src})_{A'_2} \wedge notify(s_{src}, s_{src})_{A'_2}$$

In Algorithm 3 for the rule R_4, the process for detecting violations of latency SLA and notifying appropriate teams, shows a backward tracing from run-time interaction logs to code push logs. The process assumes that the SLA specification is documented in the JSON. The process gets recent changes in the source and destination and then notify the changes to dependees of the source and destination.

Transitive Impact Assessments. In the transitive impact assessment phase, Harmonia pinpoints the root-causes of abnormal interactions, similar to the

---

Algorithm 3. A Heuristic Translation of *latency* Condition to Code

1: $SLA \leftarrow read(SLA.json)$;
2: **procedure** LATENCY( )
3:     $deployments \leftarrow depolyed()$;
4:     **for each** $interaction \in interactionList$ **do**
5:         **if** $interaction.latency > SLA.latency$ **then**
6:             **for each** $namespace \in namespaceList$ **do**
7:                 **if** $deployment.serviceName == interaction.destination$ **then**
8:                     $notify(interaction.destination, deployment)$;
9:                     $notify(interaction.destination.dependees, deployment)$;
10:                **if** $deployment.serviceName == interaction.source$ **then**
11:                    $notify(interaction.source, deployment)$;
12:                    $notify(interaction.source.dependees, deployment)$;

---

existing root-cause analysis based approaches. However, Harmonia goes beyond by providing richer information to software teams with an understanding of potential reasons why such abnormal interactions occurred. Harmonia additionally pinpoints and notifies recent code changes and infrastructure changes in abnormal services as a starting point of inspection, towards facilitating communication and collaborations among independent teams and fixing the issues more quickly.

For assessing the actual impacts among competitive services, Harmonia utilizes the rule (R_3) defined during the proactive detection and the notification phase. In the scenario described in Fig. 5, if the latency (l) of the interaction (i_j) (from service S_3 to service S_4) violates the latency SLA (l_{SLA}), Harmonia detects the code or infra changes and notifies to impacted teams. The detection and notification rules are specialized from the rule (R_3) and defined as below:

- **Condition** ($C_{2.1}$): The latency of interaction from a source service (S_{src}) to a destination service (S_{dst}) is higher than a latency SLA (l_{SLA}) in an interaction (i_j).
- **Condition** ($C_{2.2}$): The latency of interaction from a source service (S_{src}) to a destination service (S_{dst}) is higher than a latency SLA (l_{SLA}) in an interaction (i_k).

$$R_7 : \forall i_j, i_k \in I_{t-1}^t, C_2 \wedge (i_j.l > l_{SLA})_{C_{2.1}} \wedge (i_k.l > l_{SLA})_{C_{2.2}} \rightarrow A_{1.1} \wedge A_{1.2} \quad (8)$$

Similarly, Harmonia utilizes the rule (R_4) for the detection and notification rule for services invoking the other services implicitly. In the scenario described in Fig. 6, if the interaction between the service (S_1) and the service (S_2) violates the latency SLA due to a change in service (S_2), Harmonia detects the latency violations and notifies the change to impacted teams as defined below:

$$R_8 : \forall i_j, i_k \in I_{t-1}^t, C_3 \wedge C_{1.3} \wedge (i_j.l > l_{SLA})_{C_{2.1}} \wedge (i_k.l > l_{SLA})_{C_{2.2}} \rightarrow A_{1.1} \quad (9)$$

4 Harmonia in Action

To assist with an initial understanding of the applicability of Harmonia, we applied Harmonia to the Bookinfo application[2], which is adopted as an official sample application to describe the Istio framework, and compared the information collected from Harmonia with the information obtained from existing frameworks. The Bookinfo application displays the information of a book, including a description of the book, book details (ISBN, number of pages, etc.), and book reviews. The Bookinfo composed of four separate microservices - Product Page, Detail, Review, and Rating. Jenkins is adopted in our demonstration to build a sample DevOps pipeline, which consists of jobs for pushing code to Github, building and containerizing the code, and deploying the container.

4.1 Experimentation Setting

Four Github accounts are assigned to the Review service, the Detail service, and the Rating service. Each account is considered as a contact point of a software team that is responsible for a service. A total of 1200 visitors to the Bookinfo application are simulated. Sixty visitors per second are generated and access the Bookinfo application through a gateway service. Two types of Rating service are alternatively deployed every 10 s. We injected faulty code for causing delays from one second to seven seconds in communicating with the review service to one of the rating services. The other rating service works without causing delays. Harmonia collected the service deployment information and service interaction information every 10 s, detected violations of latency SLA, source of changes, and impacted services, notified the violations and changes to the four contacts. The latency SLA is given as one second. Then, we collected and compared the information from Harmonia, Github, Jenkins, Kubernetes, and Istio.

4.2 Observation and Discussion

Table 1 summarizes the experimentation results, showing a quantitative comparison with existing frameworks that measure the types of available information regarding service changes.

The Github logs captured the 20 times of code changes, including lines of changed code. The Jenkins logs captured the 20 times of code commitment history, containerization history of the code, and deployment history of the container. However, both Github and Jenkins have a lack of service run-time information after the deployments. The Kubernetes logs captured the 20 times of service container deployment history, and the Istio logs captured the number of visitors to the Bookinfo application, the total number of interactions among services, and the latency of the interactions. However, the Kubernetes and Istio do not capture the information of changes in the service containers that are newly deployed. Harmonia bridged the dichotomy between the DevOps tools

---

[2] https://istio.io/docs/examples/bookinfo/.

Table 1. A quantitative comparison with existing frameworks.

	Code changes	Service deployments	Problematic deployments	Visitors	Service interactions	SLA violations	Identified root-cause	Identified impact
Total # of Changes	20	20	10	1,200	10,753	932	220	712
Harmonia	20	20	10	1,200	10,753	932	220	712
Github	20	-	-	-	-	-	-	-
Jenkins	20	20	-	-	-	-	-	-
Kubernetes	-	20	-	-	-	-	-	-
Istio	-	-	-	1,200	10,752	932	-	-

and Service Meshes by extracting and aligning the logs from the tools. Additionally, based on the logs, Harmonia deduced ten problematic service deployments, 220 root-cause interactions that caused by problematic deployments, and 712 impacted interactions and notified the source of code changes and deployments that cause the violations. To evaluate whether root-cause of changes can be identified, refer to Fig. 6, we injected a faulty code in the rating service (S_2) (i.e., the root cause) which introduces delays in the interaction between the review service (S_1) and the rating service (S_2). The interaction impacts on the other interaction between the product page service(S_3) and the review service (S_1). Among the total of 932 abnormal interactions that violate the latency SLA, Harmonia detects the 220 interactions between the rating (S_2) and review (S_1) as root-cause interactions. The 712 impacted interactions represent the interactions between the product page (S_3) and the review page (S_1).

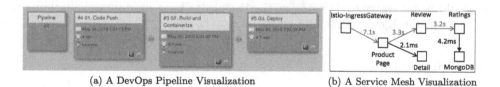

(a) A DevOps Pipeline Visualization   (b) A Service Mesh Visualization

Fig. 8. AS-IS visualizations of a DevOps pipeline and a service mesh

Figures 8 and 9 show a visual comparison between Istio, Jenkins, and Harmonia. The Jenkins pipeline described in Fig. 8a contains service deployment information, such as deployment date, code changes, etc., but rarely involves run-time service information after the deployments. On the other hands, as depicted in Fig. 8b, Istio visualizes the run-time interactions and latencies among services but has a lack of understanding about what kinds of service changes cause the latency variations.

As described in Fig. 9, Harmonia visualizes the service deployment information and run-time interaction information in a single view for helping independent software teams in understanding the impact of changes in services.

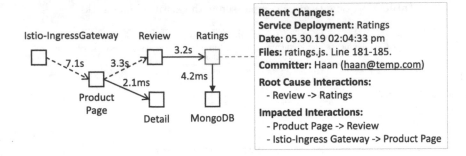

Fig. 9. A visualization of harmonia prototype

The Rating is colored red as the deployments of the Rating violated the latency SLA. The interaction between the Review and the Rating colored red with a solid line as it is a root-case interaction. The impacted interactions colored red with dotted lines.

4.3   Threats to Validity

Currently, as Harmonia understands an integrated body of knowledge from specific logs of Github, Jenkins, Istio, and Kubernetes, the Harmonia ontology is limited to be generalized. The Harmonia reference rule set for detection and notification is limited and straightforward yet to apply Harmonia to more diverse domains. In addition, Harmonia utilizes a centralized point of a knowledge base, whereas microservices build on independent teams with separation of concerns. It would be necessary to decentralize the knowledge base appropriately in terms of access control, ownership, and trust.

5   Conclusion

In this paper, we presented Harmonia - a continuous service monitoring framework using both DevOps and Service Mesh in a complementary manner, as among the first of its kind to the best of our knowledge, to facilitate communication and collaborations among DevOps software teams independently contributing to service changes. Harmonia offers a reference ontology alignment of DevOps logs and Service Mesh logs to have an integrated body of knowledge between service deployment information from DevOps that includes code and infrastructure changes of services and run-time service information from Service Mesh that captures run-time interactions among service along with its latency. Harmonia also offers detection and notification rules to enhance the understandability of the changes in services and impacts of the changes.

To generalize our approach, we are planning to expand the ontology to cover other DevOps and Service Mesh frameworks, such as Puppet, Chef, or Linke rd. To enhance the Harmonia reference rule set, we are also planning to consider more complex cases based on studying real application services in cloud-native production environments. We would also like to further evaluate to what extent can Harmonia notifications help development teams performing change management and diagnosis.

References

1. Balalaie, A., Heydarnoori, A., Jamshidi, P.: Microservices architecture enables DevOps: migration to a cloud-native architecture. IEEE Softw. **33**(3), 42–52 (2016)
2. Brunnert, A., et al.: Performance-oriented DevOps: a research agenda. CoRR abs/1508.04752 (2015). http://arxiv.org/abs/1508.04752
3. Chen, P., Qi, Y., Hou, D.: CauseInfer: automated end-to-end performance diagnosis with hierarchical causality graph in cloud environment. IEEE Trans. Serv. Comput. **12**(2), 214–230 (2019)
4. Fadda, E., Plebani, P., Vitali, M.: Monitoring-aware optimal deployment for applications based on microservices. Trans. Serv. Comput. 1–1 (2019)
5. Fitzgerald, B., Stol, K.J.: Continuous software engineering and beyond: trends and challenges. In: Proceedings of the 1st International Workshop on Rapid Continuous Software Engineering, pp. 1–9. ACM, Hyderabad (2014)
6. Forsgren, N., Kim, G., Kersten, N., Humble, J., Brown, A.: 2017 state of devops report. Puppet+ DORA
7. Gupta, M., Mandal, A., Dasgupta, G., Serebrenik, A.: Runtime monitoring in continuous deployment by differencing execution behavior model. In: Pahl, C., Vukovic, M., Yin, J., Yu, Q. (eds.) ICSOC 2018. LNCS, vol. 11236, pp. 812–827. Springer, Cham (2018). https://doi.org/10.1007/978-3-030-03596-9_58
8. Haselböck, S., Weinreich, R.: Decision guidance models for microservice monitoring. In: Proceedings of the International Conference on Software Architecture Workshops (ICSAW), pp. 54–61. IEEE (2017)
9. Heinrich, R., et al.: Performance engineering for microservices: research challenges and directions. In: Proceedings of the 8th ACM/SPEC on International Conference on Performance Engineering Companion, pp. 223–226. ACM, L'Aquila (2017)
10. Jayathilaka, H., Krintz, C., Wolski, R.: Performance monitoring and root cause analysis for cloud-hosted web applications. In: Proceedings of the 26th International Conference on World Wide Web, pp. 469–478. International World Wide Web Conferences Steering Committee, Perth (2017)
11. Johng, H., Kim, D., Hill, T., Chung, L.: Estimating the performance of cloud-based systems using benchmarking and simulation in a complementary manner. In: Pahl, C., Vukovic, M., Yin, J., Yu, Q. (eds.) ICSOC 2018. LNCS, vol. 11236, pp. 576–591. Springer, Cham (2018). https://doi.org/10.1007/978-3-030-03596-9_42
12. Johng, H., Kim, D., Hill, T., Chung, L.: Using blockchain to enhance the trustworthiness of business processes: a goal-oriented approach. In: 2018 IEEE International Conference on Services Computing (SCC), pp. 249–252. IEEE (2018)
13. Kalia, A.K., Xiao, J., Bulut, M.F., Vukovic, M., Anerousis, N.: Cataloger: catalog recommendation service for IT change requests. In: Maximilien, M., Vallecillo, A., Wang, J., Oriol, M. (eds.) ICSOC 2017. LNCS, vol. 10601, pp. 545–560. Springer, Cham (2017). https://doi.org/10.1007/978-3-319-69035-3_40
14. Kim, M., Sumbaly, R., Shah, S.: Root cause detection in a service-oriented architecture. In: Proceedings of the ACM SIGMETRICS/International Conference on Measurement and Modeling of Computer Systems, pp. 93–104. ACM, Pittsburgh (2013)

15. Len Bass, I.W., Zhu, L.: DevOps: A Software Architect's Perspective. Addison-Wesley Professional, Old Tappan (2015)
16. Lin, J., Chen, P., Zheng, Z.: Microscope: pinpoint performance issues with causal graphs in micro-service environments. In: Pahl, C., Vukovic, M., Yin, J., Yu, Q. (eds.) ICSOC 2018. LNCS, vol. 11236, pp. 3–20. Springer, Cham (2018). https://doi.org/10.1007/978-3-030-03596-9_1
17. Motahari, H., Benatallah, B., Saint-Paul, R., Casati, F., Andritsos, P.: Process spaceship: discovering and exploring process views from event logs in data spaces. Proc. VLDB Endow. **1**(2), 1412–1415 (2008)
18. Phipathananunth, C., Bunyakiati, P.: Synthetic runtime monitoring of microservices software architecture. In: Proceedings of 42nd Annual Computer Software and Applications Conference (COMPSAC), vol. 02, pp. 448–453 (2018)
19. Pina, F., Correia, J., Filipe, R., Araujo, F., Cardroom, J.: Nonintrusive monitoring of microservice-based systems. In: Proceedings of the 17th International Symposium on Network Computing and Applications (NCA), pp. 1–8. IEEE (2018)
20. Wang, P., et al.: Cloudranger: root cause identification for cloud native systems. In: Proceedings of 18th IEEE/ACM International Symposium on Cluster, Cloud and Grid Computing (CCGRID), pp. 492–502 (2018)
21. Xiao, J., Kalia, A.K., Vukovic, M.: Juno: an intelligent chat service for IT service automation. In: Liu, X., et al. (eds.) ICSOC 2018. LNCS, vol. 11434, pp. 486–490. Springer, Cham (2019). https://doi.org/10.1007/978-3-030-17642-6_49
22. Zhu, L., Bass, L., Champlin-Scharff, G.: Devops and its practices. IEEE Softw. **33**(03), 32–34 (2016)

Services and Data

ESDA: An Energy-Saving Data Analytics Fog Service Platform

Tiehua Zhang[1]([✉]), Zhishu Shen[2], Jiong Jin[1], Atsushi Tagami[2], Xi Zheng[3], and Yun Yang[1]

[1] School of Software and Electrical Engineering, Swinburne University of Technology, Melbourne, Australia
{tiehuazhang,jiongjin,yyang}@swin.edu.au
[2] KDDI Research, Inc., Fujimino-shi, Japan
{shen,tagami}@kddi-research.jp
[3] Department of Computing, Macquarie University, Sydney, Australia
james.zheng@mq.edu.au

Abstract. The volume of heterogeneous data collected through a variety of sensors is growing exponentially. With the increasing popularity of providing real-time data analytics services at the edge of the network, the process of harvesting and analysing sensor data is thus an inevitable part of enhancing the service experience for users. In this paper, we propose a fog-empowered data analytics service platform to overcome the frequent sensor data loss issue through a novel deep autoencoder model while keeping the minimum energy usage of the managed sensors at the same time. The platform incorporates several algorithms with the purpose of training the individual local fog model, saving the overall energy consumption, as well as operating the service process. Compared with other state-of-the-art techniques for handling missing sensor data, our platform specialises in finding the underlying relationship among temporal sensor data series and hence provides more accurate results on heterogeneous data types. Owing to the superior inference capability, the platform enables the fog nodes to perform real-time data analytics service and respond to such service request promptly. Furthermore, the effectiveness of the proposed platform is verified through the real-world indoor deployment along with extensive experiments.

Keywords: Fog computing · Service-oriented networking · Deep autoencoder · Energy-saving algorithm

1 Introduction

The rapid development of the Internet of Things (IoT) technologies has unleashed the immense potential of large-scale data analytics. In the meantime, the deluge of IoT data produced by these interconnected IoT objects becomes one of the critical enablers for enhancing the intelligent human living environments [17]. The ultimate goal of aiding ambient living experience and improving

© Springer Nature Switzerland AG 2019
S. Yangui et al. (Eds.): ICSOC 2019, LNCS 11895, pp. 171–185, 2019.
https://doi.org/10.1007/978-3-030-33702-5_13

quality of life continues to drive the success in the intersected field of IoT and service-oriented computing.

As the core component of IoT that are generally located at the edge of the network, various sensors take most of the credits in terms of forming the intelligent living environment. These massively heterogeneous, dynamic sensor data are facilitating a myriad of IoT applications in order to offer real-time, context-aware, and highly personalised service. Moreover, there is no doubt that in conjunction with the prosperity of IoT technology, the number of sensors is growing exponentially as well.

In the act of being an integral part of the IoT network, heterogeneous sensors always play an indispensable role in some prevailing IoT implementations including smart city, agriculture and building, etc. [6]. However, the amount of energy consumed by a large number of sensors is not negligible and thus attracts the attention from both academia and industry to come up with different energy conserving algorithms and frameworks to deal with this long-standing problem, yet converging to the common goal - to improve the sustainability of the IoT network involved heavily with sensors [5,13,18]. Apart from that, data loss is inevitable in IoT network due to sensors' inherent characteristics such as malfunction or battery exhaustion. This phenomenon severely compromises the quality of service (QoS) in some data-driven applications and poses a big challenge [1].

Most of the IoT applications are in favour of providing the data analytics service to some extent, taking advantage of the mature cloud computing is thus a preferable option. However, as the most commonly used approach nowadays, the colossal amount of data collected in the IoT network is simply transferred to the cloud servers for further processing and analysing, which has severe side effects on network performance and further causes communication overhead and network congestion. Also, the majority of IoT applications deployed on the cloud starts to concern the QoS being returned to the interested users, in which the service transmission latency contributes a significant part in service consumers' perception with regard to the overall performance of the service invocation. Apart from that, the arising challenges like cloud energy waste and data privacy issues also suggest that the reliance on traditional IoT-Cloud schema alone to provide various IoT services is no longer effective and efficient, and an alternative computing paradigm that could seal the gap between IoT devices and cloud to provide better quality of service is needed [6].

Fog computing is emerged under this circumstance to complement the inadequacy of the IoT-Cloud schema. The idea of extending the cloud to the edge of network closer to end users is considered as an alternative with the overarching goal of "off-loading" from the cloud where fog, as the proxy, could be equipped with not only computation power, but also storage and networking resources to accommodate various IoT applications. Most importantly, IoT applications could be deployed in fog rather than the conventional approach on either resource-constrained IoT devices or the remote cloud. In this regard, fog and cloud complement each other and encompass other IoT devices to form a seamless cloud-fog-things service continuum in which service could be disseminated [19].

Machine learning technologies, especially deep learning, have celebrated massive successes in domains of IoT and service-orientated computing owing to their adoptions in a wide range of IoT applications. The deployment of ubiquitous sensors has played a crucial role in IoT infrastructure to empower various real-time data analytic services such as health care monitoring, intrusive detection and smart building, etc. Applications provisioning such services require to collect, process, analyse and communicate enormous amount of sensor data consistently in order to provide the highly customisable services related to the sensed phenomena. However, these data-thirsty tasks are often plagued by the missing sensor data issue, which consequently compromises the performance of any learning algorithms [10]. While most of the data complementing algorithms and frameworks commonly fail to interpret underlying temporal data correlations and underestimate the high complexity of predicting multi-type sensor data [3], it is imperative to discover a powerful approach that could not only cope with the missing data but also respond to such service request promptly.

In this paper, we present a novel energy-saving data analytics fog service platform, namely ESDA, which serves the purpose of providing real-time, multi-type and large-scale data analytics services for IoT devices. More specifically, under the control of fog nodes, sensors no longer need to be constantly turned on to transmit sensed data upwards. Fog, instead, will initiate the in-fog learning process and use the trained local model to predict missed multi-type sensor data that are substantial for many service requesters. More importantly, the platform will automate the process of conserving energy cost of the platform by turning sensors into the sleep mode during the service operation.

The main contributions of this paper are as follows:

1. To better serve real-time services in IoT context, a fog-empowered energy saving data analytics platform is proposed. The fog can utilise dedicated computation and storage resources to facilitate real-time data analytics services. Besides, the platform offers a flexible deployment options through the selection of different energy saving patterns.

2. Taking advantage of the recurrent neural network (RNN), a novel fog-based deep encoder architecture is proposed to improve the accuracy of multi-type sensor data prediction, which takes the internal time-series correlation into account to enhance the inference accuracy.

3. An in-fog learning and predicting algorithm is designed and run at the fog layer, where each fog node will train the local model and ensure an acceptable data prediction accuracy to satisfy the need of data analytics services. Apart from that, an energy conserving algorithm is incorporated to minimise the overall energy consumption of the platform during the service operation.

4. Advantages of adopting the proposed platform are evaluated experimentally through a real-world indoor deployment, along with its effectiveness and applicability for many use cases in IoT environment empowered by fog computing.

The remainder of the paper is organised as follows. We review the related work on sensor data prediction and acquisition, deep learning based real-time data analytics and energy-saving approach in Sect. 2. In Sect. 3, we introduce the proposed fog service platform architecture followed by the detailed explanation of fog-enabled deep autoencoder (FEDA) and integrated algorithms. We then present the deployment of our real-world indoor testbed as well as the comprehensive experiments conducted in Sect. 4, and we draw the conclusion and point out the future work in Sect. 5.

2   Related Work

There are several previous efforts made towards developing methods in complementing missing sensor values and saving energy consumption in the IoT environment to fulfil different service needs.

The approaches to fill the incomplete data are actively studied in the area of image processing. The authors in [12] presented an unsupervised visual feature learning algorithm for image inpainting. By analogy with auto-encoders, this algorithm utilises convolutional neural networks (CNN) to generate the incomplete region of another arbitrary image based on the surrounding context of the incomplete part. In [8], the authors proposed a denoising autoencoder named Multimodal Autoencoder (MMAE) to handle the missing multimodal data. This method is an unsupervised learning technique using the deep neural network (DNN). The empirical evaluation verified that the MMAE could outperform the traditional principal components analysis (PCA) in prediction accuracy of the feature values from multiple missing modalities in the scale between 0 and 1.

Satisfactory performance of data prediction can eliminate the demand to periodically sending the original raw data to the cloud. The sensors whose data can be accurately predicted are permitted to sleep as long as possible during the network operation. Conceptually, the longer sleep time window that sensors are allowed to have, the more energy can be saved for the network. The critical task is how to precisely predict these incomplete data from sleeping or malfunctioning sensors [2]. For this reason, recently there are several works focusing on data prediction using machine learning for the IoT network: the authors in [11] developed a data prediction algorithm with an error-correction learning scheme. This algorithm is developed from recursive least squares (RSL) and is used to improve the value which is initially predicted by using a small number of data. The authors in [13] proposed a derivative-based prediction that uses a linear model to observe the trends of data in recently captured data to predict the future data. By analysing the latest data, this approach can produce a satisfactory model for predicting data in the short-term. However, frequent updates on trainable parameters of the model are required for holding this high accuracy in predicting long-term data trends. The authors in [15] introduced CNN to learn the correlation of the neighbouring sensor data to decide the sensors active/sleep status, i.e., the sensors whose data can be accurately predicted will be turned into the sleep mode in priority.

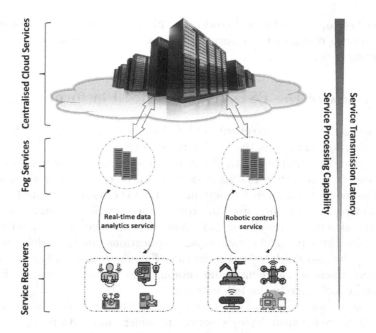

Fig. 1. Fog service architecture

However, with the rapid increase of the number of devices in the IoT environment, the heavy traffic volume generated by these sensors increases the processing burden on the cloud. Moreover, the expected connection latency leads to a degradation of the expectation of real-time data service. A potential solution is to place the service providers closer to end devices/users' side for the timely service provision process and reduce the redundant data communication to the cloud. For instance, the work [14] proved that for IoT environment like building energy management system, by utilising a collaborative fog platform for delivering data processing service in a real-time manner, a significant reduction of traffic volume to the cloud could be realised. Some works shift their attention to using resource-constrained IoT devices to fulfil the allegedly computation-intensive mission. For instance, the authors in [9] developed a light-weight, tree-based classification algorithm for data prediction on IoT devices. This algorithm learns a single, shallow, spare tree to reduce the required model size while forming a small number of prototypes data representing the entire data sets. This algorithm achieves high prediction accuracy while it can be executed on resource-constrained IoT devices, i.e., Arduino Uno board. Similarly, to reduce the data learning complexity, the authors in [4] proposed a k-nearest neighbour (k-NN)-based algorithm by using a spare projection matrix that projects all data sets into lower-dimension. One common issue for these two algorithms is that the model trained on a resource-scarce device is merely meant for the individual device, thus not suitable for providing data analytics service at a reasonable scale.

To the best of the authors' knowledge, this is the first work to propose a novel fog service platform to achieve prominent real-time data analytics in an energy-saving style.

3   Overview of the ESDA Fog Service Platform

A multi-tier fog service architecture can be observed in Fig. 1. Under this structure, end things/users act as the service requester/receivers, and fog nodes, on the other hand, are equipped with the computational and storage capability to enable a variety of real-time IoT services that can be activated on demand and delivered to the destination in a timely manner. In the service-oriented computing perspective, fog thus performs the role of the service provider. Besides, as the traditional service provider in IoT-Cloud schema, the cloud could still be the placeholder for a particular category of applications providing delay tolerant services, e.g., large-scale data backup service. This figure also well demonstrates what a hierarchical service continuum composed of IoT users/devices, fog and cloud visually looks like in the IoT network.

Since the service transmission latency drops with the shortening of the geographical distance between deployed service providers and end things/users (service requester/receiver), fog node could be placed in the vicinity of the raw data source in any autonomous environment. In a smart building scenario, multi-type sensors could interact directly with fog node in that area and feed raw data to the analytical applications running at the fog layer. Fog, at the same time, continually monitors the energy consumption status of each sensor to which it is connected, and utilises the energy-saving algorithm to put sensors to the sleep mode to extend their lifespan.

In the proposed ESDA fog service platform, a novel fog-enabled deep autoencoder model (FEDA), built on top of the long short term memory (LSTM)-based sequence-to-sequence structure [16], is adopted as the core part of the data analytics application to satisfy the real-time data service enquiries. The name "fog-enabled" comes from the fact that the whole training and inference process rely heavily on the support of the local fog nodes. Also, this platform fills in the gap concerning the missing sensor data when sensors are put into the sleep mode, recharging or malfunction. Afterwards, fog could respond to relevant IoT devices that depend on the returned service results to trigger corresponding actions, such as temperature change by air conditioner or luminous intensity adjustment by light controller.

Other than providing the reliable data analytics service, the platform also aims to accomplish the sustainability by taking an efficient energy utilisation. Both the in-fog learning algorithm for training the FEDA and the energy-saving algorithm are incorporated into the platform and explained in the following subsections.

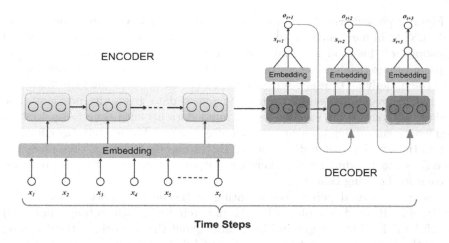

Fig. 2. FEDA model structure

3.1 Fog-Enabled Deep Autoencoder (FEDA)

An autoencoder is generally referred to as an unsupervised learning approach where a deep neural network tries to reconstruct an input X after the reconstruction error between the ground truth X and network output's X' is minimised through an optimizer. In this circumstance, the embedding layer is often presented in the compressed format and used as the compact representation of the data. One limitation of the traditional autoencoder is that the length of X' tends to be the same as X, which is not ideal for predicting the temporal data series that could end up being arbitrary length. Henceforth, we tend to leverage the LSTM-based sequence-to-sequence architecture as the fundamental part of our deep autoencoder owing to the capability of handling variable-length time series input and output another variable-length time series data.

The LSTM originally proposed in [7], enable several state variables, including hidden/control state h_t and memory cell state c_t to sustain the underlying correlation among temporal data, where t means a certain timestamp. A single LSTM unit's operations can be expressed as:

$$
\begin{aligned}
i_t &= \sigma\left(W_{xi}x_t + W_{hi}h_{t-1} + b_i\right) \\
f_t &= \sigma\left(W_{xf}x_t + W_{hf}h_{t-1} + b_f\right) \\
o_t &= \sigma\left(W_{xo}x_t + W_{ho}h_{t-1} + b_o\right) \\
g_t &= \phi\left(W_{xg}x_t + W_{hg}h_{t-1} + b_g\right) \\
c_t &= f_t \odot c_{t-1} + i_t \odot g_t \\
h_t &= o_t \odot \phi\left(c_t\right)
\end{aligned}
\tag{1}
$$

where σ is the sigmoidal non-linearity, ϕ is the tangent non-linearity and $\odot$ is the element-wise dot product. The weights and biases metrics for computing each gate values are represented as $W_{i,j}$ and b_j, respectively.

Figure 2 presents the graphical representation of FEDA model structure. We apply LSTM in both encoder and decoder parts of the RNN, and the principal philosophy of this model is that, for both encoder and decoder, the value at x_{t+1} timestamp depends on previous state h_t and previous output value x_t to learn the underlying time series correlation. In order to encompass the flexibility required to predict the arbitrary missing sensor data given any previous time window, we convert the variable-length input data up until timestamp t into a fixed length embedding layer first, which afterwards will be fed into the encoding part on the left. The last state generated by the encoding phase is then passed to the right - the decoding phase, where the output starting from $t+1$ is predicted for each forthcoming time step.

There are several points worth noting in the decoder part of the model. Firstly, since it could be multiple LSTM units (circles in each rectangle in Fig. 2) in each LSTM cell (rectangles in Fig. 2) throughout the network, in the decoding phase, the results generated by a number of LSTM units from a single LSTM cell, say n, is used as a mini-embedding vector whose size is equivalent to n. These mini-embedding vectors are then multiplied and added with their dedicated weight matrix W_{t+1} and bias b_{t+1}, respectively, to generate a single value (o_{t+1}) for that timestamp. Apart from that, the model generalises the coexistence of heterogeneous sensor data types, i.e., a multi-functional sensor can detect the value of temperature, humidity level, air pressure and luminous intensity at the same time in real world, and this sensor then produces four types of data repeatedly as the time elapses. To cope with that, each o_{t+1} is equipped with a trainable scalar variable s_{t+1} to scale the value of a specific data type up to its original magnitude as close as possible.

3.2 Integrated Algorithms

There are two main algorithms integrated into the platform designed with different purposes. The first one controls the process of fetching the preliminary trained model from the cloud based on historical backup data, communicating the controlled sensors to collect training data, and initiating the training process on each local fog node. The second one, on the other hand, focuses on the management of connected sensors per fog node, as well as carries out service operations from various service requesters. The details are broken down separately as Algorithms 1 and 2.

Algorithm 1 consists of two phases. Every fog node i ($i \in \mathcal{F}$) in phase one firstly checks the availability of local model $\mathcal{M}_{(i)}$, then it might use the preliminary pre-trained model from the cloud and restore it (lines 1–5 in Phase 1). As the preliminary model from the cloud is trained based on historical backup sensor data stored on the cloud, it does not reflect the real-time sensor reading in the environment and thus needs to be refined. The refinement process, in other words, can be addressed as the continuous in-fog training for the preliminary model. Each fog node collects sensor's reading in its managed area, then creates dataset $\mathcal{D}$ (lines 1–6 in Phase 2). To train the FEDA model used by each fog node, $\mathcal{D}$ needs to be split into two time series parts $\mathcal{D}_s$ and $\mathcal{D}_e$ randomly, where $\mathcal{D}_s$ is fed into the model as variable-length input mentioned in Sect. 3.1. In contrast, $\mathcal{D}_p$ corresponds to the predicted data series, and the reconstruction error $\mathcal{E}_{(i)}$ is calculated between $\mathcal{D}_p$ and $\mathcal{D}_e$ using a distance error measurement (lines 7–9), e.g., Root Mean Square Error (RMSE) used here. It is worth noting the relation between error $\mathcal{E}_{(i)}$ and hyperparameter θ, where θ is a system-level parameter defined to balance the trade-off between data reconstruction volume and energy consumption amount. It could be explained as error tolerance threshold. Fog will stop training the local model until the error is no greater than threshold θ (lines 10–13). The pick-up strategy of the threshold value will be demonstrated in Sect. 4.2.

Algorithm 1. In-fog learning algorithm

Phase 1: *Preliminary Model Fetch*

1: fog f_i $(i \in \mathcal{F})$ fetches the preliminary model $\mathcal{M}$ from the cloud
2: **if** $\mathcal{M}_{(i)}$ not exists **then**
3:     $\mathcal{M}_{(i)} \leftarrow \mathcal{M}$
4: **end if**
5: restore local model $\mathcal{M}_{(i)}$

Phase 2: *Local Model Refinement*

1: $\mathcal{D} \leftarrow \emptyset$
2: $\mathcal{S} \leftarrow$ sensors managed by fog f_i
3: **repeat**
4:     **for** $\forall s \in \mathcal{S}$ **do**
5:         $\mathcal{D}.add$(current reading of s)
6:     **end for**
7:     Separate $\mathcal{D}$ into two time series parts $\mathcal{D}_s$ and $\mathcal{D}_e$
8:     $\mathcal{D}_p \leftarrow \mathcal{M}_{(i)}(\mathcal{D}_s)$
9:     $\mathcal{E}_{(i)} \leftarrow \sqrt{\frac{1}{n} \sum_{t=1}^{n} (\mathcal{D}_{p,n} - \mathcal{D}_{e,n})^2}$
10:     **if** $\mathcal{E}_{(i)} > \theta$ **then**
11:         Feed $\mathcal{D}$ into $\mathcal{M}_{(i)}$ to continue training
12:     **end if**
13: **until** $\mathcal{E}_{(i)} \leq \theta$

Pseudocode in Algorithm 2 concerns on inactivating managed sensors in a time period to reduce the overall energy consumption of the platform, as well as resolving data analytics service request. To start with, fog nodes are aware of the local model $\mathcal{M}_{(i)}$ trained from Algorithm 1 and system-level hyperparameter θ. Based on the selection of threshold θ, the platform is assigned with the corresponding energy-saving pattern P, which is used to calculate sensor's sleep time T. In addition, variables t_i^{start} and t_i^{end} are adopted as the indicator of the sleep window (lines 1–6). During the service operation process, fog would receive periodic service request regarding the type and value of current sensor reading from different IoT equipments in every time interval t (lines 8–9). If a service request received falls into the sleep window of sensors, fog leverages $\mathcal{M}_{(i)}$ substantially to conduct the analytics service so that applicable results are able to be returned back regardless (lines 11 and 12). For example, inside a building, fog nodes may receive the temperature reading request from the air conditioner operating in the controlled area every minute to attain the thermal comfort. The sleep window needs to be re-calculated with the change of threshold θ along with energy-saving pattern P (line 17).

Algorithm 2. Energy-saving and service operating algorithm

1: **Energy-Saving** for $\forall f_i \in \mathcal{F}$
2:     $\mathcal{M}_{(i)} \leftarrow$ local model trained by fog f_i
3:     $P \leftarrow$ energy-saving pattern based on threshold value θ
4:     $\mathcal{S}_i \leftarrow$ sensors managed by fog f_i
5:     $T \leftarrow$ sleep time calculated based on P
6:     $(t_i^{start}, t_i^{end}) \leftarrow$ fog f_i de-activates $\mathcal{S}_i$ for T and records the sleep window
7: **Service Operation** for $\forall f_i \in \mathcal{F}$
8:     **Repeat** at every interval t
9:         $\mathcal{R}_{(i)} \leftarrow$ service requests sent to fog f_i at current interval t
10:        **for** $\forall r \in \mathcal{R}_{(i)}$ **do**
11:            **if** t falls into window between (t_i^{start}, t_i^{end}) **then**
12:                f_i employs $\mathcal{M}_{(i)}$ to conduct analytic service regarding r
13:            **else**
14:                f_i retrieves current sensor reading regarding r
15:            **end if**
16:        **end for**
17:    **Until** θ changes

---

4   Experiments

We present the real-world experimental settings in an indoor deployment as well as evaluation results in this section.

4.1   Experimental Setting

We introduce the building energy management system (BEMS) as the use case to evaluate our proposed platform. Figure 3 illustrates a deployment example of a BEMS application. The main objectives of BEMS include: 1. monitoring and managing the overall energy consumption; 2. constantly checking the indoor environment conditions (e.g., temperature, humidity) to ensure the comfort of occupants. Fog, as the placeholder of the application, acts as a real-time data analytics service provider to respond requests coming from various IoT devices.

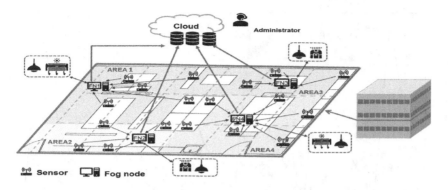

Fig. 3. Floor plan of real-world indoor deployment

Table 1. Setup parameters for experimental network

Parameters	Values
Sensor number	18
Network area size	162 m^2
Data collection interval	1 min
Data collection period	1 year
Data type	Temperature (Celsius), humidity (%), luminous intensity (Candela), barometric pressure (Pascal)

As mentioned earlier, the platform allows on setting of different energy-saving patterns aligned with the system-level parameter θ for versatile deployment scenarios, and such system-level parameters are controlled by system admin (demonstrated in Fig. 3). Apart from that, fog nodes remain connected to both sensors and other IoT devices such as humidifier, air conditioner and light, etc. to complete the service continuum. For example, in Fig. 3, as shown by blue arrows, fog nodes can send the analytics results straight to the air conditioning and lighting systems for adjusting the current status. It is worth mentioning that this real-world deployment happens inside an office building. The sensor (Texas Instruments CC2650 SensorTag) placement information is shown in Fig. 3, and the parameter details of the network topology are listed in Table 1.

4.2 Evaluation Results

It is of importance for applications such as BEMS deployed in the fog to provide real-time data analytics results as accurate as possible on which IoT service requester like air conditioner could faithfully rely and adjust the behaviour accordingly. We thus verify the effectiveness of the proposed platform through comprehensive experiments. To assess the performance of FEDA, three other state-of-the-art autoencoder variants are used as the benchmarks, including CNN encoder, DNN encoder as well as vanilla RNN. Two forms of comparisons are demonstrated here: real-world multi-type sensor data reading prediction at each

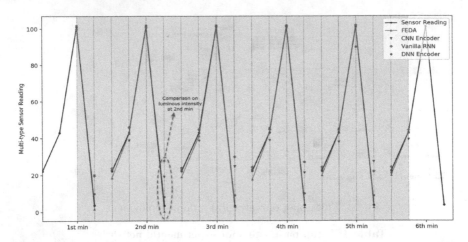

Fig. 4. Prediction on multi-type sensor reading (4 data types) (Color figure online)

time point, and the continuous single data type prediction in a given period. In addition, the experiment with regard to saving energy while retaining a satisfactory prediction result is demonstrated at last. In order to ensure a fair comparison, the Adam optimizer [8] is used across different learning techniques with the learning rate 0.001, which is observed to learn the fastest during the experiments.

Figure 4 displays the prediction results for multi-type sensor data reading at each time point. As stated in Table 1, each fog node collects managed sensor readings in 1 min interval for all four data types. To realise the test on the adopted learning model in terms of predicting heterogeneous data types all at once given a random length input, sensor reading in one time period has been randomly masked off indicating the loss of the data, and each model predicts on the lost heterogeneous data values, respectively. For each time interval (from 1 min to 6 min) in Fig. 4, sensors are set to read the surrounding phenomena in the order of temperature, humidity, barometric pressure, and then luminous intensity (four points connected into a line segment at every minute). The greyed-out area indicates the period when the mimic data loss happens (sensors in sleep or fault conditions), and the dashed-vertical line aligns with the prediction results for that data type generated among different models, e.g. dashed grey circle highlights on the prediction results on luminous intensity data type by different models at 2nd min. It could be observed that the green line with up-triangles markers (FEDA) generally have a closer distance to the ground truth sensor reading (black line with dots) on each data type at every time stamp compared with the other three.

Figure 5 amplifies the prediction results on each of the four data types in a 40 min time window, in which sensor data is mimicked to be missing from 10 to 30 mins. It is evident that for temperature, humidity and air pressure, the FEDA clearly outperforms other competitors, and even in the extreme case of luminous intensity where the value becomes 0 at some time point due to the office light

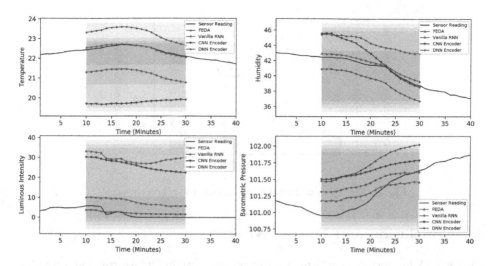

Fig. 5. Prediction on individual data type

being turned off at night, our model reserves a conservative prediction following the trend of the true sensor reading line. In general, both figures mentioned above verify that the novel FEDA model adopted in our proposed platform excels in delivering more accurate data analytics service from which the connected IoT service requesters could primarily benefit with better QoS.

The experiment result regarding the relation between the system-level error tolerance threshold θ and the total energy consumption in BEMS is shown in Fig. 6. The left y-axis in the graph represents the different values of θ after applying logarithm for better visualisation purpose, whereas the right y-axis tells the energy consumption by percentage (when energy consumption is 100%, all sensors are activated during the whole service operation period). The values of θ are derived from the calculated prediction errors using the test dataset. We conduct a grid search on θ and utilise four of them (errors calculated when 80%, 60%, 40% and 20% of total inactive times of all sensors, respectively) to form the corresponding energy-saving patterns (P1–P4), which is shown as the shared x-axis in the graph. It is as expected that the more sensors that are put into the sleep mode longer, the more reconstruction errors will be encountered, yet the less energy will be consumed for the whole system. We observe that the decrease of the θ is not strictly linear, and the slope between P2 and P3 is greater than other segments of the line. Henceforth, we adopt the threshold defined in P3 for both Algorithms 1 and 2, which empowers our platform to save energy consumption up to 40% while keeping an acceptable error tolerance. It is worth mentioning that the selection of patterns depends entirely on different use cases and deployment scenarios. For instance, if the platform is adopted in the smart agriculture use case where sensors and fog are placed in the geographically remote area, then the energy saving could come to the priority so as to extend the lifespan of energy-scarce sensors to a large extent, then the use of P1 might be more appropriate than others.

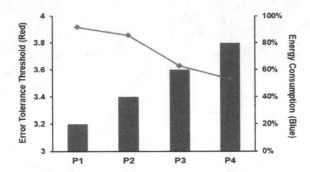

Fig. 6. Energy consumption and error tolerance threshold

5   Conclusion and Future Work

Our ESDA fog service platform is a low energy-cost IoT platform that provides real-time data analytics service and can be deployed in many scenarios. With the help of FEDA and in-fog learning, energy-saving algorithms, this platform could extend the lifespan of managed sensors without deteriorating much of the QoS thanks to the accurate data forecasting capability. We have deployed the platform into a real-world indoor IoT testbed and adopted BEMS to verify its effectiveness. The comprehensive experiment results demonstrate the superiority of the platform. The platform also enhances the flexibility by allowing to customise the error tolerance threshold θ to cater for different deployment requirements. Moving forward, we will investigate the possibility of using collaborative learning schema in this platform, where fog leverages each other's power to reach the consensus on the learning model.

Acknowledgements. This work is partly supported by Australian Government Research Training Program Scholarship, Australian Research Council Discovery Project Grant DP180100212 and NICT (Contract No. 19103), Japan.

References

1. Aldossary, S., Allen, W.: Data security, privacy, availability and integrity in cloud computing: Issues and current solutions. Int. J. Adv. Comput. Sci. Appl. **7**(4), 485–498 (2016)
2. Dias, G.M., Bellalta, B., Oechsner, S.: A survey about prediction-based data reduction in wireless sensor networks. ACM Comput. Surv. **49**(3), 58 (2016)
3. Gao, Z., Cheng, W., Qiu, X., Meng, L.: A missing sensor data estimation algorithm based on temporal and spatial correlation. Int. J. Distrib. Sens. Netw. **11**(10), 435391 (2015)
4. Gupta, C., et al.: ProtoNN: compressed and accurate kNN for resource-scarce devices. In: Proceedings of the 34th International Conference on Machine Learning, pp. 1331–1340. JMLR.org (2017)
5. Harb, H., Makhoul, A., Laiymani, D., Jaber, A.: A distance-based data aggregation technique for periodic sensor networks. ACM Trans. Sens. Netw. **13**(4), 32 (2017)

6. He, J., Wei, J., Chen, K., Tang, Z., Zhou, Y., Zhang, Y.: Multitier fog computing with large-scale IoT data analytics for smart cities. IEEE Internet of Things J. **5**(2), 677–686 (2018)
7. Hochreiter, S., Schmidhuber, J.: Long short-term memory. Neural Comput. **9**(8), 1735–1780 (1997)
8. Jaques, N., Taylor, S., Sano, A., Picard, R.: Multimodal autoencoder: a deep learning approach to filling in missing sensor data and enabling better mood prediction. In: Proceedings of the 7th International Conference on Affective Computing and Intelligent Interaction, pp. 202–208. IEEE (2017)
9. Kumar, A., Goyal, S., Varma, M.: Resource-efficient machine learning in 2 KB RAM for the Internet of Things. In: Proceedings of the 34th International Conference on Machine Learning, pp. 1935–1944. JMLR.org (2017)
10. Li, H., Ota, K., Dong, M.: Learning IoT in edge: deep learning for the Internet of Things with edge computing. IEEE Netw. **32**(1), 96–101 (2018)
11. Luo, X., Zhang, D., Yang, L.T., Liu, J., Chang, X., Ning, H.: A Kernel machine-based secure data sensing and fusion scheme in wireless sensor networks for the cyber-physical systems. Future Gener. Comput. Syst. **61**, 85–96 (2016)
12. Pathak, D., Krahenbuhl, P., Donahue, J., Darrell, T., Efros, A.A.: Context encoders: feature learning by inpainting. In: Proceedings of the IEEE Conference on Computer Vision and Pattern Recognition, pp. 2536–2544 (2016)
13. Raza, U., Camerra, A., Murphy, A.L., Palpanas, T., Picco, G.P.: Practical data prediction for real-world wireless sensor networks. IEEE Trans. Knowl. Data Eng. **27**(8), 2231–2244 (2015)
14. Shen, Z., Zhang, T., Jin, J., Yokota, K., Tagami, A., Higashino, T.: ICCF: an information-centric collaborative fog platform for building energy management systems. IEEE Access **7**, 40402–40415 (2019)
15. Shen, Z., Yokota, K., Tagami, A., Higashino, T.: Development of energy-efficient sensor networks by minimizing sensors numbers with a machine learning model. In: Proceedings of the IEEE International Conference on Pervasive Computing and Communications Workshops, pp. 741–746. IEEE (2018)
16. Sutskever, I., Vinyals, O., Le, Q.V.: Sequence to sequence learning with neural networks. In: Advances in Neural Information Processing Systems, pp. 3104–3112 (2014)
17. Tortonesi, M., Govoni, M., Morelli, A., Riberto, G., Stefanelli, C., Suri, N.: Taming the IoT data deluge: an innovative information-centric service model for fog computing applications. Future Gener. Comput. Syst. **93**, 888–902 (2019)
18. Trihinas, D., Pallis, G., Dikaiakos, M.D.: ADMin: adaptive monitoring dissemination for the Internet of Things. In: Proceedings of the IEEE Conference on Computer Communications, pp. 1–9. IEEE (2017)
19. Zhang, T., Jin, J., Yang, Y.: RA-FSD: a rate-adaptive fog service delivery platform. In: Pahl, C., Vukovic, M., Yin, J., Yu, Q. (eds.) ICSOC 2018. LNCS, vol. 11236, pp. 246–254. Springer, Cham (2018). https://doi.org/10.1007/978-3-030-03596-9_16

Leveraging AI in Service Automation Modeling: From Classical AI Through Deep Learning to Combination Models

Qing Wang[1]($\boxtimes$), Larisa Shwartz[1], Genady Ya. Grabarnik[2], Michael Nidd[3], and Jinho Hwang[1]

[1] IBM T.J. Watson Research Center, Yorktown Heights, NY 10598, USA
qing.wang1@ibm.com, {lshwart,jinho}@us.ibm.com
[2] Department of Math and Computer Science, St. John's University,
Queens, NY 11439, USA
grabarng@stjohns.edu
[3] IBM Research–Zurich, 8803 Rueschlikon, Switzerland
mni@zurich.ibm.com

Abstract. With the advent of cloud, new generations of digital services are being conceived to respond to the ever-growing demands and expectations of the market place. In parallel, automations are becoming an essential enabler for successful management of these services. With such importance being placed on digital services, automated management of these services – in particular, automated incident resolution – becomes a key issue for both the provider and the users. The challenge facing automation providers lies in variability and the frequently changing nature of the monitoring tickets that provide the primary input to automation. Despite the value of the correct automation at the correct time, it is also important to remember that triggering an incorrect automation may damage the smooth operation of the business. In this paper, we discuss AI modeling for automation recommendations. We describe a wide range of experiments which allowed us to conclude an optimal method with respect to accuracy and speed acceptable to service providers.

Keywords: Classical and deep learning models · Combination models · Multiclass text classification · AI for service automation

1 Introduction

Providing Service Management at scale requires automation. For decades, system administrators have had scripts to automate routine repairs, and have also employed automated monitoring systems to raise alerts when repair is called for. While some of these alert conditions require individual expert attention, service delivery professionals have confirmed that many of these conditions can be handled with the execution of the correct well-written script. These scripts

© Springer Nature Switzerland AG 2019
S. Yangui et al. (Eds.): ICSOC 2019, LNCS 11895, pp. 186–201, 2019.
https://doi.org/10.1007/978-3-030-33702-5_14

are combined into automation library for IBM Automation service. The first step in managing alert conditions is to filter and collect the alerts into the "trouble tickets" that act as work orders for repair. IBM service delivery teams have libraries of regular expressions that match ticket details to automation that may solve the problem. These regular expressions are applied to ticket raised by monitoring systems, which encode both specific fields (machine address, timestamp, severity, etc.) and also "free text" summary information.

In the normal course of business, new monitor systems are added, either through organic growth or by mergers and acquisitions. These new systems will usually be generating tickets about similar issues, so existing automation would often be appropriate for its resolution, but ticket formats may be sufficiently different to not match the corresponding regular expression. Figure 1 shows an example of two different ticket problems that were detected and auto-ticketed by the monitoring system, and subsequently successfully closed by the same automation. Over the course of several years IBM Global Services established around 25,000 regular expressions. This approach is very effective, but it is difficult to maintain. To assist IBM automation services we created "matching service" that utilizes artificial intelligence for choosing an automation for a monitoring ticket with ensuring the following challenge:

How does the matcher service effectively achieve and maintain high accuracy on noisy tickets while automatically adapting to an introduction of a new or changed ticket contents? Since executing an inappropriate automation on a server may cause damage, our recommendation has to be highly accurate. Informative, discriminating and independent features can greatly promote the performance of classification or regression algorithms, while irrelevant features decrease it. Unfortunately, real-world tickets (seen in Fig. 1) contain various time-format, numeric and domain-specific terms, and unknown text snippets that make them too noisy to be interpretable. Thus, effective feature-selection [1] often involving immense efforts on text preprocessing becomes a crucial step to make this learning task more efficient and accurate. Feature selection is performed manually for classical classification solutions [2], but the changes in ticket style and content over time means that optimal feature-selection will also change, leading to degraded performance. Reasonable techniques to address this issue include the direct use of deep neural networks [3–5] without manual feature-selection, or using convolutional neural networks as input for classical AI models (i.e., combination models) to automatically learn a generic feature representation.

In the course of our work with service delivery teams to improve automation, we have studied the use of Machine Learning (ML) to identify methodology that would help us to address the tickets that were not recognized by the existing rules. We have conducted a comparative study on a wide range of machine learning approaches including classical AI, deep learning and combination methods. They are described in details in Sect. 3. We have large volume of tickets from IBM Services which were successfully and automatically remediated, so we have large amount of task specific labeled dataset for our experiments.

ALERT_KEY	XXX_logairt_x072_aix		AUTOMATION	Disk Path Checker
AGENT	CUSTOMER_CODE	ALERT_GROUP	COMPONENT	OSTYPE
EIF Probe on xxxxxx	XXX	ITM_XXX_LOGFILEMONITOR_LOG_FILE	Computer System	Generic
TICKET_GROUP	PRIORITY	HOSTNAME	IP_ADDRESS	SUBCOMPONENT
I-XXX-XXX-DS	PX	XXX	XXX.XXX.XXX.XXX	Log
TICKET SUMMARY	LogEvent: Thu Apr 4 02:00:01 EDT2019,xxxxxx,pcmpath,disk,fib er adapters missing or failed on server		TICKET DESCRIPTION	4 xxxxxx GENERIC LOG /TMP/xxxxxx.LOG AIX is CRITICAL **
ALERT_KEY	XXX_erp_xlo2_std		AUTOMATION	Disk Path Checker
AGENT	CUSTOMER_CODE	ALERT_GROUP	COMPONENT	OSTYPE
EIF Probe on xxxxxx	XXX	ITM_XXX_LOGFILEEVENTS	Operating System	AIX
TICKET_GROUP	PRIORITY	HOSTNAME	IP_ADDRESS	SUBCOMPONENT
NUSN_XXDISTOPS	PX	XXX	XXX.XXX.XXX.XXX	ErrorReport
TICKET SUMMARY	Errpt log entry: xxxxxx 0404051519 P H - PATH HAS FAILED - hdisk21		TICKET DESCRIPTION	XXX.XXX.XXX.IBM.COM AIX ERRORREPORT /VAR/ADM/RAS/ERRLOG.HDISK2 1 UNIX is CRITICAL **

Fig. 1. Two different monitoring tickets and the same matching automation.

As we present in this paper, our initial solutions have performed extremely well on the labeled test data. A significant challenge when evaluating recommendations, however, is that this data is all taken from the tickets that were automated through regular expression match. When we apply these models to tickets that did not match any of those expressions, the only way to evaluate the recommendation is for a subject matter expert (SME) to review it. We have done this and, as we will present here, the results are very promising.

We have incorporated these models into "matching service" for IBM service delivery: automation service makes a call to matching service for the tickets that do not match any of the handcrafted rules. If our system identifies a ticket that our model strongly associates with an existing automation (for an audited set of automations that are deemed "safe" enough to run prospectively), that automation will be run. After it is run, the ticket condition is reevaluated, and the ticket is either resolved automatically or escalated.

This "matching service" is part of Cognitive Event Automation (CEA) framework [6] that focuses on service management optimization and automation with the goal of transforming the service management lifecycle to deliver better business outcomes through a data-driven and knowledge-based approach. The framework relies on novel domain specific techniques in data mining and machine learning to generate insights from operational context, among them generation of predictive rules, deep neural ranking, hierarchical multi-armed bandit algorithms, and combination models for the automation matching service that is the focus of this paper.

This paper presents the comprehensive performance comparison on a wide range of popular classical AI, deep learning and combination classifiers that has guided us in model selection for an IBM automation service implementation. We have established that under the time constraint, classical AI models perform best when size of training data is small but with the drawback that features must be hand-crafted. Deep learning models will also perform well when the training data is large enough, but combination models have the best performance for large dataset size and without a need for manual feature-engineering.

The remainder of this paper is organized as follows. An overview of the CEA system is presented in Sect. 2. In Sect. 3, we provide the mathematical formalization of the problem and methodologies. Section 4 describes a comparative study conducted over real-world ticket data to show the performance of the proposed methodologies. Finally, a systematic review of related work is presented in Sect. 5, and Sect. 6 concludes the work and provides directions for future research.

2   System Overview

2.1   Service Management Workflow

A typical workflow for service management usually includes six steps. (1) An anomaly is detected, causing the monitoring system to emit an event if the anomaly persists beyond a predefined duration. (2) Events from an entire environment are consolidated in an enterprise event management system, which makes the decision whether or not to create an alert and subsequently an incident ticket. (3) Tickets are collected by an IPC (Incident, Problem, and Change) system [7]. (4) A monitoring ticket is identified by automation services for potential automation (i.e., scripted resolution) based on the ticket description. If the automation does not completely resolve the issue, this ticket is then escalated to human engineers. (5) In order to improve the performance of automation services and reduce human effort on escalated tickets, the workflow incorporates an enrichment system like CEA that uses Machine Learning techniques [8–10] for continuous enhancement of automation services. Additionally, the information is added to a knowledge base, which is used by automation services as well as in resolution recommendation for tickets escalated to human engineers. (6) Manually created and escalated tickets are forwarded to human engineers for problem determination, diagnosis, and resolution, which is a very labor-intensive process.

2.2   System Architecture

The microservice is a new computing paradigm that overcomes the limitations of the monolithic architectural style. The microservice architecture consists of a collection of loosely coupled services, each of which implements a business function. The microservice architecture enables scalability, flexibility, and also continuous devops (development and operations) of large, complex applications. We use the microservices framework to support our data processing components.

Figure 2 illustrates the CEA system architecture. In general, the system consists of two types of services: offline processing services build a knowledge corpus and models; and inline processing services apply reasoning to gathered runtime data, using the models and knowledge corpus built offline. The offline processing services take advantage of AI that incorporates feedback loop analysis, automatically re-training models periodically or on demand if the monitoring system undergoes a significant change. The system continuously improves recommendations for automated resolution of monitoring tickets. The inline system has a number of services: Correlation and Localization Service (CLS) identifies clusters of symptoms attributable to a complex incident; Disambiguation of Root Causes (DRC) is built as a recommender system that enriches ticket data with possible root causes, identifies steps necessary for full diagnosis and provides optimal sequence of diagnostics and remediation steps using AI planning service. Finally, the ticket-automation matching service provides a service to identify the correct automation for a given ticket. The model built in this work allows the system to trigger the correct automation, despite the challenge of external influences that change ticket content and style over time.

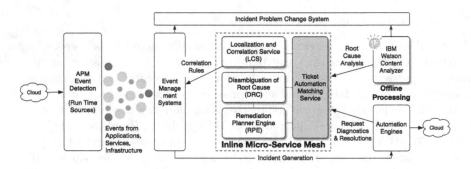

Fig. 2. CEA system architecture

3   Problem Definition and Methodology

In this section, we provide a mathematical formulation of the service automation modeling problem, followed by the description of proposed methodologies.

Based on a ticket's content, finding the best automation can be intuitively viewed as a multiclass text classification problem. A general framework for statistical learning (in particular for supervised learning) is as follows: a set of labeled training data $\mathcal{D} = \{(\mathbf{x}_t, y_t)\}_{t=1}^{N}$ is drawn independently according to a distribution $P(\mathbf{x}, y)$ on $(\mathbb{R}^d, Y)$, where $\mathbf{x}$, $\mathbf{x}_t \in \mathbb{R}^d$, y, $y_t \in Y = \{1, 2, \cdots, K\}$ is the ground truth class label for $\mathbf{x}_t$. For example, a ticket (seen in Fig. 1) can be represented by a set of features $\mathbf{x}$ using NLP techniques [11] and a known class label $y = \{Disk\ Path\ Checker\}$. We assume that $g(\mathbf{x}) : \mathbb{R}^d \mapsto Y$ be a prediction function.

A loss function $\ell : Y \times Y \mapsto \mathbb{R}$, usually a positive function, measures error between prediction and actual outcomes. Cross entropy loss (log loss), mean absolute error (L1 loss), and mean squared error (L2 loss) are three popular loss functions that calculate the error in different ways. Expectation L of ℓ by measure P is called expected loss:

$$L(g) = E_{(\mathbf{x},y)\sim P}[\ell(g(\mathbf{x}), y)].$$

The prediction function g is usually found from minimization of expected loss L:

$$g = \arg\min_{g} L(g). \tag{1}$$

Sometimes we choose g from a family of functions $g(\Theta)$, where Θ is a set of parameters. Equation 1 in this case becomes $\Theta^* = \arg\min_{\Theta} L(g(\Theta))$.

Let $p(k|\mathbf{x}) = P(Y = k|X = \mathbf{x})$ be the conditional probability of getting label k given $X = \mathbf{x}, k = 1, \ldots, K$. For equal misclassification costs the loss function $\ell(y, g(\mathbf{x})) = \chi(y \neq g(\mathbf{x}))$, with χ being indicator function of the set $\{y \neq g(\mathbf{x})\}$. Then the best classification (Bayes) rule minimizes expected misclassification

$$g_B(\mathbf{x}) = \arg\min_{k=1,\ldots,K}[1 - p(k|\mathbf{x})] = \arg\max_{k=1,\ldots,K} p(k|\mathbf{x}).$$

In order to solve the real-world challenge, we have conducted a comparative study on a wide range of machine learning approaches including classical AI, deep learning and combination methods. Figure 3 shows an overview of how different models are used to address multiclass text classification problem. In order to use classical AI models for this classification task, a feature extraction step must first transform the raw text data into informative feature vectors. In comparison, deep learning models can automatically perform feature engineering and classification tasks. Combination models unite the broad applicability of classical AI models with the automatic feature engineering of deep learning models to improve the performance. As background for the experimental design of Sect. 4, we will first outline a few classical AI learning algorithms, like support vector machines, ensemble methods, and deep learning approaches.

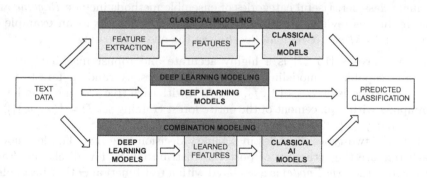

Fig. 3. Using modeling for the multiclass text classification: classical AI vs deep learning vs combination.

3.1   Classical AI: Support Vector Machines

Support Vector Machines (SVMs) are often considered as an efficient, theoretically solid and strong baseline for text classification problems [2]. SVMs were designed for binary classification. There are two main approaches for multi-class classification: one-vs.-all classifiers (OVA) [12] and multiclass SVMs [13]. One-vs.-all classifications simply construct K SVMs, where K is the number of classes, training k-th SVM with all of the training examples in the k-th class with positive labels, and all other examples with negative labels. In other words, the k-th SVM tries to find a hyperplane that satisfies the following constrained optimization problem:

$$\min_{\omega^k, b^k, \xi^k} \frac{1}{2}(\omega^k)^T(\omega^k) + C \sum_{t=1}^{N} \xi_t^k,$$

subject to:

$$(\omega^k)^T \phi(\mathbf{x}_t) + b^k \geq 1 - \xi_t^k, \text{ if } y_t = k,$$
$$(\omega^k)^T \phi(\mathbf{x}_t) + b^k \leq -1 + \xi_t^k, \text{ if } y_t \neq k,$$
$$\xi_t^k \geq 0, t = 1, 2, \cdots, n,$$

where ω is the weight vector, b is the intercept of the hyperplane, $\phi(\bullet)$ is the function mapping the feature vector $\mathbf{x}_t$ to a higher dimensional space and C is the penalty parameter. For a new text $\mathbf{x}$, the predicted $\hat{y}$ can be calculated as follows:

$$\hat{y} = \arg\max_{k=1,2,\cdots,K} ((\omega^k)^T \phi(\mathbf{x}) + b^k).$$

3.2 Classical AI: Ensemble Methods

Ensemble methods [14] are learning algorithms that train multiple classifiers, and then typically apply voting (weighted or unweighted) to make predictions for new data. It is well known that an ensemble method is generally more accurate than any single classifier. Useful categories of ensemble methods include *Bagging* and *Boosting*. In this review, we are considering *Random Forests* as an example of Bagging, and *eXtreme Gradient Boosting* as the one of Boosting.

Random Forests [15–17] is a highly accurate and robust machine learning algorithm, capable of modeling large feature spaces. A random forests is an ensemble of H decision trees $\{f_1, f_2, \cdots, f_H\}$, with each tree grown by randomly subsampling with replacement of the entire forest training set $\mathcal{D} = \{(\mathbf{x}_t, y_t)\}_{t=1}^{N}$, $\mathbf{x}_t \in \mathbb{R}^d$, and $y_t \in \{1, 2, \cdots, K\}$.

There are two types of nodes in a binary decision tree [18]. The leaf nodes of each tree are the estimates of posterior distribution p_k for all classes. Each internal node (i.e., *split node*) is associated with a test function Θ that best splits the space of training data. Often, Gini-impurity is used to choose the best test function Θ^*. During the training, each tree selects appropriate test functions and labels leaf node probabilities. For the evaluation, a test sample $\mathbf{x}$ is propagated through each tree leading to a classification probability $p_t(k|\mathbf{x})$ of the t-th tree. A forest's joint probability can be represented as follows:

$$p(k|\mathbf{x}) = \frac{1}{H} \sum_{h=1}^{H} p_h(k|\mathbf{x})$$

Therefore, given $\mathbf{x}$, the predicted class $\hat{y}$ is:

$$\underset{k=1,2,\cdots,K}{\arg\max}\ p(k|\mathbf{x})$$

eXtreme Gradient Boosting [19] has been widely recognized in many machine learning and data mining challenges and provided state-of-art results on many standard classification benchmarks. It is a tree ensemble model based on Gradient Boosting Machine and a set of Classification and Regression Trees (CARTs). Similar to RF, the final output is the sum of prediction of each tree with the given dataset $\mathcal{D}$.

$$\hat{y} = \sum_{h=1}^{H} f_h(\mathbf{x}), f_h \in \mathcal{F},$$

where K is the number of trees, $\mathcal{F}$ is the space of all possible CARTs, and f is an additive function in the functional-sapce $\mathcal{F}$. In order to learn the set of functions in the model, the objective function with a regulation term can be written as:

$$L = \sum_{t=1}^{N} l(y_t, \hat{y}_t) + \sum_{h=1}^{H} \Omega(f_h). \tag{2}$$

The loss function $l(\bullet)$ measures the difference between the target y_t and the prediction $\hat{y}_t$. The regularization function $\Omega(\bullet)$ penalizes the complexity of the model to avoid overfitting. Since the tree ensemble model including these functions (See Eq. (2)) cannot be easily solved by traditional optimization methods, XGboost is trained in an additive manner. For the multiclass classification problem, we construct K binary classifiers using XGBoost model [20] and subsequently apply OvA.

3.3 Deep Learning: Convolutional Neural Networks

In recent years, deep neural networks have brought about a striking revolution in computer vision, speech recognition and natural language processing.

Convolutional neural networks (CNNs), one of the most promising deep learning network methods, has achieved remarkable results in computer vision. It also has been shown to be effective in many NLP tasks, such as text categorization, spam detection, and sentiment analysis [4]. CNN performs well feature extraction and classification tasks without any preconfiguration (i.e., without selecting features manually).

For an m-word input text (padded where necessary) $\mathbf{s}_t = \{w_1, w_2, \cdots, w_m\}$ with a label y_t, $t = 1, 2, \cdots, n$, and $y_t \in \{1, 2, \cdots, K\}$, each word is embedded as a q-dimensional vector, i.e., word vectors $\mathbf{w}_1, \cdots \mathbf{w}_m \in \mathbb{R}^q$. The $m \times q$ representation matrix is fed into a convolutional layer with a filter $\alpha \in \mathbb{R}^{l \times q}$ sliding over the text to produce a feature map. Let $w_{i:i+l-1}$ denotes the concatenation of words $w_i, w_{i+1}, \cdots, w_{i+l-1}$ with a length l. A convolution feature is calculated as follows. $c_i = f(\alpha \cdot w_{i:i+l-1} + \beta)$, where $\beta \in \mathbb{R}$ ia a bias term and $f(\bullet)$ is a non-linear function. This filter α slides over the text $\{w_{1:l}, w_{2:l+1}, \cdots, w_{m-l+1:m}\}$ resulting in a convolution feature map $\mathbf{c}_\alpha = [c_1, c_2, \cdots, c_{m-l+1}]$. A maxpooling layer is followed to capture the most important feature $\hat{c}_\alpha = max\{\mathbf{c}\}$ as the feature corresponding to the particular filter α. In practice, numerous filters with varying window sizes are used to obtain multiple convolution features. Extracted features are passed to a fully connected softmax layer, whose output is the probability distribution over classification classes $\mathbf{o} = \{o_1, o_2, \cdots, o_K\}$. The predicted class is

$$\hat{y} = \underset{k=1,2,\cdots,K}{\arg\max} \{\mathbf{o}\}.$$

To avoid overfitting, dropout is employed.

In order to learn the parameters in this model, the objective loss function for mutlclass text classification is needed to be defined. Herein, we use the cross-entropy loss function:

$$\min_{\Theta} -\frac{1}{N} \sum_{t=1}^{N} \sum_{k=1}^{K} y_{t,k} \log(p_{t,k}),$$

where Θ denotes the parameters of the CNN model, $y_{t,k}$ is a binary indicator if class k is the correct classification for the t-th text, and $p_{t,k}$ is the predicted probability of text t is of class k through a softmax activation.

$$p_{t,k} = \frac{exp(g(\mathbf{s}_t; \theta_k))}{\sum_{k=1}^{K} exp((g(\mathbf{s}_t; \theta_k))}, \sum_{k=1}^{K} p_{t,k} = 1.$$

3.4   Combination Models

Figure 4 shows the overall architecture of combination models for multiclass text classification tasks. CNN is used for learning feature representation in many applications. Convolution feature filters with varying widths can capture several different semantic classes of n-grams by using different activation patterns [4]. A global maxpooling function induces behavior that separates important n-grams from the rest. We propose a combination model that replaces the softmax layer of CNN with classical AI models for multiclass text classification problems. In this model CNNs perform as an automatic feature extractor to produce the learned (i.e., not hand-crafted) feature vectors from large text data. These feature vectors used in the classical classification models to provide more precise and efficient classification performance [21].

When comparing methods, it is important to remember the preprocessing and feature extraction effort. The classical methods in Subsects. 3.1 and 3.2 require considerable effort for text preprocessing and feature extraction [5]. Ensemble methods also require either automatic feature extractors or manual selectors to transform the raw data into suitable internal feature vectors for further pattern recognition and classification [22]. These additional steps are not required for deep learning and combination models. Ability to evade preprocessing steps constitutes an important differentiation from classical methods.

4 Experiments

Executing an incorrect automation is potentially harmful to the service, so a classifier's recommendation has to be highly accurate.

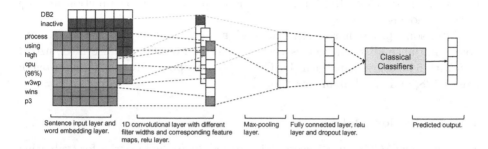

Fig. 4. Architecture of combination models on multiclass text classification tasks.

4.1 Dataset and Experimental Setup

Experimental ticket data is generated by a variety of monitoring systems and stored in the Operational Data Lake. This dataset contains $|\mathcal{D}| = 100,000$ tickets from Jan. 2019 to Apr. 2019, of which 80% is the training dataset, while the remaining are used for validation. There are 114 scripted automations (i.e., 114 classes/labels) in the dataset and a vocabulary V of size $|V| = 184,936$. To ensure validity of training, our ground truth dataset contains only tickets for which an automation was not only selected, but it also run and successfully resolved the ticket. Ticket information together with the automation name associated with the ticket constitutes the labeled dataset for training and testing.

The first step of preparing input data for the classical AI classifiers uses the bag of words method to represent feature vectors of each ticket after text preprocessing (stemming, lemmatization, stop words removal, etc.). Classical AI models usually work with relatively low-dimension attribute spaces, necessitating well-defined and highly informative attributes as coordinates of feature vectors. We use domain experts' assistance to determine such attributes for the dataset.

It is common to initialize deep learning models for NLP by using pre-trained word embeddings. This practice reduces the number of parameters that a neural network needs to discover from scratch. For the deep learning and combination models, it is a prevalent method to initialize pre-trained word vectors from an unsupervised neural language model to improve performance.

A weakness of this method lies with its ability to handle unknown or out-of-vocabulary (OOV) words. Our dataset (see Fig. 1) contains critical domain specific information such as various machine address, domain-specific terms, and unknown technical script snippets for which there are no pre-trained data.

A multilayer perceptron (MLP) is a deep artificial neural network composed of input layer, output layer and some number of hidden layers in between. In our case the layers are **word embedding layer, fully connected layer** and **dropout layer**. The introduction of a **dropout layer** is a regularization technique that reduces overfitting. CNN has an additional **convolutional layer**. Rectified Linear Unit (ReLU) is a commonly used activation function in deep learning models.

After some preliminary testing, we designed our primary experiments to randomly initialize all word vectors with a dimension of 300. We use filter size of 4, 5 with 64 feature maps each (for CNN only), dropout rate of 0.25, mini-batch size of 128, and epoch number of 20.

4.2   Evaluation Metrics

The accuracy (ACC) and F1-score (F1) are widely applied metrics for evaluating multiclass classifiers. We provide expression for the evaluation metrics in terms of Sect. 3, the problem definition, where $\mathcal{D} = \{(\mathbf{x}_t, y_t)\}_{t=1}^N$, y_t is one of K classes, and $g(\bullet)$ is the classifier. Multiclass accuracy is defined as an average number of correct predictions: $\mathrm{ACC} = P_{(\mathbf{x},y)\sim\mathcal{D}}[g(\mathbf{x}) = y]$. F1-score for 2 classes of outcome (0, 1), is the harmonic mean of precision and recall

$$F1 = (\frac{1}{2}(\frac{1}{precison} + \frac{1}{recall}))^{-1} = \frac{2C_{1,1}}{C_{1,1} + C_{0,1} + C_{1,1} + C_{1,0}}, \qquad (3)$$

where $C_{i,j}$ is a confusion matrix.

There are multiple ways to generalize Formula (3) to a multiclass F1-score. *Macro-averaged* F1-score (F1-macro), which emphasizes each class equally, has been demonstrated to be unbiased and provides an effective performance measure in multiclass settings [23]. For a classifier g, its (multiclass) confusion matrix $C[g] \in [0,1]^{K \times K}$ is defined as $C_{ij}[g] = P(y = i, g(\mathbf{x}) = j)$. Macro-averaged F1-score in terms of the confusion matrix can be written as:

$$F1_{macro}[g] = \frac{1}{K}\sum_{i=1}^{K} \frac{2 \times C_{ii}[g]}{\sum_{j=1}^{K} C_{ij}[g] + \sum_{j=1}^{K} C_{ji}[g]}.$$

4.3   Results and Discussions

A wide range of strong classifiers across supervised, unsupervised, deep and combination AI models are evaluated for their performance on a real-world multiclass classification task. To ensure the fairness of comparisons, the accuracy and F1 score for each model are calculated from the average results of 5-fold cross validation (CV). The comparison of performance of ACC, F1-macro and time cost has been shown in Table 1, where time cost is defined as the time required to train a good model on the dataset once for each model. The parameters in XGBoost are learning rate is 0.1, number of estimators is 100, booster is gradient boosting tree, and maximum depth is 4. For Random Forests, the number of estimators is 100 as well. All algorithms are implemented using Python 1.8. All empirical experiments are running on MacOS 10.14 with CPU only.

These results demonstrate that classical classification models such as SVM, Random Forests, and XGBoost have best performance on small datasets, but need handcrafted features. The training time for SVM increases exponentially with data size, while those of Random Forest and XGBoost increase linearly. Clearly, XGBoost has the best accuracy and F1-macro scores on the $4k$ dataset from Table 1.

Table 1. Performance comparison on **Accuracy (ACC(in percent %))**, **F1-macro (F1(in percent %))**, **Time Cost (t(in seconds))**.

Models	$|\mathcal{D}| = 4,000$			$|\mathcal{D}| = 20,000$			$|\mathcal{D}| = 100,000$		
	ACC(%)	F1(%)	t(s)	ACC(%)	F1(%)	t(s)	ACC(%)	F1(%)	t(s)
Linear SVM [24]	97.95	88.18	3.60	99.09	92.42	42.81	99.53	93.69	671.97
Decision Tree [25]	97.65	84.71	0.11	98.58	79.96	1.13	98.15	62.74	16.43
KNeighbors [26]	93.75	75.20	0.15	97.39	78.01	3.72	97.80	80.46	99.29
K-Means [27]	<50.00	–	78.01	<50.00	–	625.13	<50.00	–	5960.72
Random Forests [15]	97.65	89.26	1.15	99.05	92.28	13.25	99.29	93.39	251.26
XGBoost [19]	**98.50**	**91.79**	122.06	99.22	89.97	814.90	99.12	79.85	5345.62
MLP [3]	96.37	82.78	2.62	98.85	88.79	18.38	99.23	93.72	251.35
CNN [4]	97.12	81.10	8.65	98.92	88.40	52.87	99.39	93.16	601.11
CNN-SVM [21]	98.77	87.46	145.13	99.48	92.54	403.25	99.79	96.07	3019.69
CNN-Random Forests	98.75	87.92	148.24	99.54	90.01	148.24	**99.80**	**95.90**	1939.16
CNN-XGBoost [28]	93.50	67.41	260.19	97.70	72.15	1804.07	98.75	82.53	14035.91

Deep learning models perform better when the dataset is large, with the additional benefits that the models have a relatively short training time, and do not require feature engineering. Between deep learning models, CNN required more training time than MLP. And this can be attributed to the larger number of its parameters to learn.

Combination models have no need for handcrafted features, which allows them to support evolving sets of ticket templates and styles without the direct intervention of experts. Most of the combination models considered, CNN-SVM and CNN-Random Forests have better accuracy and F1-macro scores than SVM and Random Forests. This confirms that CNN models are good at automatically learning feature representation from a text data. CNN-Random Forest has the best overall performance among all the models including training time on a large dataset.

To summarize, we have explored a wide range of AI models and conducted a comparative study on our real-life data, aiming to provide guidance for model selection. While we find that all methods perform fairly well on different size datasets, the following insights have been learned from the experimental results:

1. Classical AI models perform well when the data size is small but they require handcrafted features.
2. Deep learning models achieve a better performance when the training data is large enough without feature engineering.

3. Combination models have the best performance on large dataset with no requirement for engineered features.

5   Related Work

The automation of service management [29] is largely achieved through the automation of subroutine procedures. Automated ticket resolution recommendation presents a significant challenge in service management due to the variability of services, and the frequently changing styles and formats for monitoring tickets that provide an input to automation.

Traditional recommendation technologies in service management focus on recommending the proper resolutions to a ticket reported by the system's user. Recently, Wang et al. [30] proposed a cognitive framework that enables automation improvements through resolution recommendations utilizing the ontology modeling technique. A deep neural network ranking model [31] was employed to recommend the best top-n matching resolutions by quantifying the qualify of each historical resolution. In [8,32], the authors leverage a popular reinforcement learning model (specifically, the multi-armed bandit model [9,33]) to optimize online automation through feedback in automation services.

Text classification, including binary text classification (e.g., sentiment classification and spam detection) and multiclass text classification are the fundamental tasks of Natural Language Processing [34]. The aim of text classification is to assign binary classes or multiple classes $m > 2$ to the input text. Traditional approaches of text classification directly use sparse lexical features, such as bag of words model [35] or n-gram language model [36] to represent each document, and then apply a linear or nonlinear method to classify the inputs. Many machine learning techniques have been developed for the multiclass text classification problem, such as Support Vector Machines (SVM), K-Nearest Neighbors (KNN) and ensemble methods (XGBoost and Random Forests). Most recently, deep learning models have achieved remarkable success in learning document representation from large-scale data. Convolutional neural network (CNN) [4] approach is a very effective to feature extraction, and long short-term memory (LSTM) [37] is powerful in modeling units in sequence. In [21,28], CNN-XGBoost and CNN-SVM models are used to improve the performance of image classification. We work with raw text data and use CNN in combination models for feature engineering.

Additional related work is provided in line with descriptions of relevant methods in Sect. 3.

6   Conclusion and Future Work

This paper addresses the automated management of digital services, more specifically an automated resolution of incidents. In the present context of an explosion of AI methods of multiple generations, it is important to choose optimal performing methods when implementing production systems.

In this paper we evaluate the performance of the three main types of the AI models: classical, deep learning and combination. Classical models include regular and ensemble methods. From a vast variety of existing methods, we have chosen those that are most promising in their class. For each model used, we have provided a short description and outlined its benefits and disadvantages.

We run wide range of experiments on real life data to find optimal modeling with respect to a number of metrics: accuracy, F1-macro score (measuring precision to recall ratio), running time and necessity of by-hand processing.

Our experimental results clearly show that under the time constraint, classical AI models perform best when the size of training data is small, and the combination methods are the best performing methods on large datasets of our data and they have no requirement for manual feature engineering. Following this conclusion, a Ticket Automation Matching Service has being implemented for the IBM Services production system.

For future work, we would like to employ the deep reinforcement learning method [22], transforming the backend offline model to an online one. Another important direction will be to build combination services that incorporate both deep learning and classical system together with common optimization problem and find global optimal parameters of the model.

References

1. Forman, G.: An extensive empirical study of feature selection metrics for text classification. J. Mach. Learn. Res. **3**, 1289–1305 (2003)
2. Joulin, A., Grave, E., Bojanowski, P., Mikolov, T.: Bag of tricks for efficient text classification, arXiv preprint arXiv:1607.01759 (2016)
3. Ruck, D.W., Rogers, S.K., Kabrisky, M.: Feature selection using a multilayer perceptron. J. Neural Network Comput. **2**(2), 40–48 (1990)
4. Kim, Y.: Convolutional neural networks for sentence classification, arXiv preprint arXiv:1408.5882 (2014)
5. Zhang, X., LeCun, Y.: Text understanding from scratch, arXiv preprint arXiv:1502.01710 (2015)
6. Shwartz, L., et al.: CEA: a service for cognitive event automation. In: Liu, X., et al. (eds.) ICSOC 2018. LNCS, vol. 11434, pp. 425–429. Springer, Cham (2019). https://doi.org/10.1007/978-3-030-17642-6_37
7. Zeng, C., Li, T., Shwartz, L., Grabarnik, G.Y.: Hierarchical multi-label classification over ticket data using contextual loss. In: 2014 IEEE NOMS (2014)
8. Wang, Q., Li, T., Iyengar, S., Shwartz, L., Grabarnik, G.Y.: Online IT ticket automation recommendation using hierarchical multi-armed bandit algorithms. In: Proceedings of the 2018 SIAM International Conference on Data Mining, SIAM, pp. 657–665 (2018)
9. Wang, Q., Zeng, C., Zhou, W., Li, T., Iyengar, S.S., Shwartz, L., Grabarnik, G.: Online interactive collaborative filtering using multi-armed bandit with dependent arms. IEEE Trans. Knowl. Data Eng. **31**, 1569–1580 (2018)
10. Zeng, C., Wang, Q., Wang, W., Li, T., Shwartz, L.: Online inference for time-varying temporal dependency discovery from time series. In: 2016 IEEE International Conference on Big Data (Big Data), pp. 1281–1290. IEEE (2016)

11. Kao, A., Poteet, S.R.: Natural Language Processing and Text Mining. Springer, London (2007). https://doi.org/10.1007/978-1-84628-754-1
12. Bottou, L., et al.: Comparison of classifier methods: a case study in handwritten digit recognition. In: International Conference on Pattern Recognition, p. 77. IEEE Computer Society Press (1994)
13. Hsu, C.-W., Lin, C.-J.: A comparison of methods for multiclass support vector machines. IEEE Trans. Neural Networks **13**, 415–425 (2002)
14. Dietterich, T.G.: Machine-learning research. AI Mag. **18**(4), 97–97 (1997)
15. Breiman, L.: Random forests. Mach. Learn. **45**(1), 5–32 (2001)
16. Liaw, A., Wiener, M., et al.: Classification and regression by randomforest. R News **2**(3), 18–22 (2002)
17. Prinzie, A., Van den Poel, D.: Random multiclass classification: generalizing random forests to random MNL and random NB. In: Wagner, R., Revell, N., Pernul, G. (eds.) DEXA 2007. LNCS, vol. 4653, pp. 349–358. Springer, Heidelberg (2007). https://doi.org/10.1007/978-3-540-74469-6_35
18. Santner, J., Unger, M., Pock, T., Leistner, C., Saffari, A., Bischof, A.: Interactive texture segmentation using random forests and total variation. In: BMVC, pp. 1–12. Citeseer (2009)
19. Chen, T., Guestrin, T.: XGBoost: a scalable tree boosting system. In: Proceedings of the 22nd ACM SIGKDD, pp. 785–794 (2016)
20. Madisetty, S., Desarkar, M.S.: An ensemble based method for predicting emotion intensity of tweets. In: Ghosh, A., Pal, R., Prasath, R. (eds.) MIKE 2017. LNCS (LNAI), vol. 10682, pp. 359–370. Springer, Cham (2017). https://doi.org/10.1007/978-3-319-71928-3_34
21. Sharif Razavian, A., Azizpour, H., Sullivan, J., Carlsson, S.: CNN features off-the-shelf: an astounding baseline for recognition. In: Proceedings of the IEEE Conference on Computer Vision and Pattern Recognition Workshops, pp. 806–813 (2014)
22. LeCun, Y., Bengio, Y., Hinton, G.: Deep learning. Nature **521**(7553), 436 (2015)
23. Narasimhan, H., Pan, W., Kar, P., Protopapas, P., Ramaswamy, H.G.: Optimizing the multiclass f-measure via biconcave programming. In: 2016 IEEE 16th International Conference on Data Mining (ICDM), pp. 1101–1106. IEEE (2016)
24. Boser, B.E., Guyon, I.M., Vapnik, V.N.: A training algorithm for optimal margin classifiers. In: Proceedings of the Fifth Annual Workshop on Computational Learning Theory, pp. 144–152. ACM (1992)
25. Quinlan, J.R.: Induction of decision trees. Mach. Learn. **1**(1), 81–106 (1986)
26. Cover, T.M., Hart, P.E., et al.: Nearest neighbor pattern classification. IEEE Trans. Inf. Theor. **13**(1), 21–27 (1967)
27. Hartigan, J.A., Wong, M.A.: Algorithm as 136: a k-means clustering algorithm. J. Roy. Stat. Soc. Ser. C (Appl. Stat.) **28**(1), 100–108 (1979)
28. Ren, X., Guo, H., Li, S., Wang, S., Li, J.: A novel image classification method with CNN-XGBoost model. In: Kraetzer, C., Shi, Y.-Q., Dittmann, J., Kim, H.J. (eds.) IWDW 2017. LNCS, vol. 10431, pp. 378–390. Springer, Cham (2017). https://doi.org/10.1007/978-3-319-64185-0_28
29. Wang, Q.: Intelligent data mining techniques for automatic service management. In: FIU Electronic Theses and Dissertations. FIU (2018). https://digitalcommons.fiu.edu/etd/3883
30. Wang, Q., Zhou, W., Zeng, C., Li, T., Shwartz, L., Grabarnik, G.Y.: Constructing the knowledge base for cognitive it service management. In: 2017 IEEE International Conference on Services Computing (SCC), pp. 410–417. IEEE (2017)

31. Zhou, W., et al.: Star: a system for ticket analysis and resolution. In: Proceedings of the 23rd ACM SIGKDD International Conference on Knowledge Discovery and Data Mining, pp. 2181–2190. ACM (2017)
32. Wang, Q., Zeng, C., Iyengar, S., Li, T., Shwartz, L., Grabarnik, G.Y.: AISTAR: an intelligent system for online IT ticket automation recommendation. In: 2018 IEEE International Conference on Big Data (Big Data), pp. 1875–1884. IEEE (2018)
33. Zeng, C., Wang, C., Mokhtari, S., Li, T.: Online context-aware recommendation with time varying multi-armed bandit. In: Proceedings of the 22nd ACM SIGKDD International Conference on Knowledge Discovery and Data Mining, pp. 2025–2034. ACM (2016)
34. Yang, Z., Yang, D., Dyer, C., He, X., Smola, A., Hovy, E.: Hierarchical attention networks for document classification. In: Proceedings of the 2016 Conference of the North American Chapter of the Association for Computational Linguistics: Human Language Technologies, pp. 1480–1489 (2016)
35. Zhang, Y., Jin, R., Zhou, Z.-H.: Understanding bag-of-words model: a statistical framework. Int. J. Mach. Learn. Cybern. 1(1–4), 43–52 (2010)
36. Brown, P.F., Desouza, P.V., Mercer, R.L., Pietra, V.J.D., Lai, J.C.: Class-based n-gram models of natural language. Comput. Linguist. 18(4), 467–479 (1992)
37. Hochreiter, S., Schmidhuber, J.: Long short-term memory. Neural Comput. 9(8), 1735–1780 (1997)

A Wearable Machine Learning Solution for Internet Traffic Classification in Satellite Communications

Fannia Pacheco[1]($\boxtimes$), Ernesto Exposito[1], and Mathieu Gineste[2]

[1] Univ Pau & Pays Adour, E2S UPPA, LIUPPA, EA3000,
64600 Anglet, France
{f.pacheco,ernesto.exposito-garcia}@univ-pau.fr
[2] Business Line Telecommunication, R&D départment, Thales Alenia Space,
31100 Toulouse, France
mathieu.gineste@thalesaleniaspace.com

Abstract. In this paper, we present an architectural framework to perform Internet traffic classification in Satellite Communications for QoS management. Such framework is based on Machine Learning techniques. We propose the elements that the framework should include, as well as an implementation proposal. We define and validate some of its elements by evaluating an Internet dataset generated on an emulated Satellite Architecture. We also outline some discussions and future works that should be addressed in order to have an accurate Internet classification system.

Keywords: Internet traffic classification · Machine Learning · Satellite Communications · Deep packet inspection

1 Introduction

Internet traffic classification is a group of strategies that aims at classifying the Internet traffic into predefined categories, such as normal or abnormal traffic, the type of application (streaming, web browsing, VoIP, etc) or the name of the application (YouTube, Netflix, Facebook, etc). Network traffic classification is important in Satellite communication principally to manage bandwidth resources and to ensure Quality of Service (QoS) requirements.

Traffic classification is widely implemented by Deep Parquet Inspection(DPI) solutions. Most of the commercial solutions use this technology for traffic management. DPI performs a matching between the packet payload and a set of stored signatures to classify network traffic. However, DPI fails when privacy policies and laws prevent accessing the packet content, as well as the case of protocol obfuscation or encapsulation. In order to overcome the former issues, Machine Learning (ML) emerged as a suitable solution, not only for the traffic classification task, but also for prediction and new knowledge discovery, among other things. In this context, statistical features of IP flows are commonly extracted and stored from network traces to generate historical data. In this way, different ML models can be trained with this historical data, and new incoming flows can be analyzed with such models.

S. Yangui et al. (Eds.): ICSOC 2019, LNCS 11895, pp. 202–215, 2019.
https://doi.org/10.1007/978-3-030-33702-5_15

In satellite networks, Internet traffic management is a key task due to it allows improving the QoS. Commonly, traffic data is captured from satellite Internet Service Providers (ISPs). The works in this area aim to classify and to analyze Internet traffic in large networks [6,12,14]. The principle is to deploy passive monitoring points in order to perform traffic classification. These monitoring points can be at routers [6] or points of presence (PoPs) [12] of large ISP networks. Another emerging approach is the use of Software-defined networks(SDNs) in satellite-terrestrial networks. In SDNs, traffic classification can be easily deployed in the SDN' master controllers as it is exposed in [1,8].

The authors outlined the complete process to achieve Internet traffic classification in the survey paper [10]. Therefore, this approach focuses its attention on developing a framework that can be deployed in a Satellite architecture. Such a framework comprises all the necessary elements to achieve the goal, as well as, additional components that should be integrated to assure a robust classification tool. We propose a hierarchical classification system based on ML, which treats encryption and flow patterns differently. We deploy the solution in a low level language that allows having an efficient and fast classification output. We also compare our approach with a well-known DPI solution called nDPI [2]. Finally, we set discussions about some important components that are in development; for instance, the treatment of tunneled connections and the evolution of the Internet network.

2   QoS Management in Satellite Communications

At this point, we start by introducing the general reference model to provide Satellite Communications. This model will serve us as guidance to find the requirements to integrate ML in such architecture. A common reference model of a multi-gateway Satellite architecture is shown in Fig. 1 [3]. This model is divided into two main blocks: Satellite access network and Satellite core network. On one hand, in the Satellite access network, a variety of network typologies can be used to the connectivity of the elements; these included the Satellite gateways and terminals. On the other hand, in the Satellite core network, an aggregate network allows interconnecting with other operators, corporations and Internet Service Providers (ISPs) through Points of Presence (PoPs).

Two main components of such model are described below:

- Satellite Terminal (ST): its function is to deliver broadband access to end-user equipment through IP routers and/or Ethernet switches.
- Satellite Gateway (GW): this component is in charge of deploying user plane functions such as packet routing and forwarding, interconnection to the data network, policy enforcement and data buffering. These functionalities are coordinated by the control and management systems of the Satellite network. The GW is composed of forwarding and returning link (FL and RL) subsystems, and a set of network functions. These network functions include the Performance Enhancing Proxy (PEP), switching and routing interfaces for the interconnection with the Satellite core network.

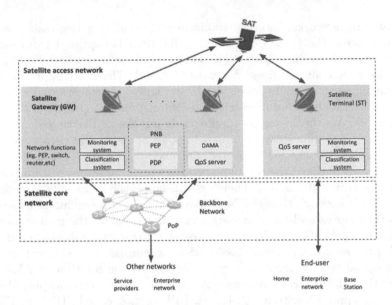

Fig. 1. Reference model of a multi-gateway Satellite network architecture.

One of the main objectives of this architecture is to provide a reliable communication system between different entities. However, improving the Quality of Service (QoS) and Quality of Experience (QoE) of their users is of paramount importance for network administrators. In principle, these last objectives can be achieved by manipulating the network functions. More specifically, a Policy Based Network (PBN) Architecture is deployed at this stage to perform traffic management [7]. In order to improve the QoS, one of the most common and accepted actions is to fulfill a set of requirements that can be executed by profiling Internet traffic [5,13]. This idea parts from the assumption that some Internet traffic is more sensitive to information loss and delay such as Internet calling or video conference. In contrast, Internet browsing or file downloads are less pruned to be affected by these error conditions.

Following this idea, the main goal of our proposal is to correctly profile the Internet communications, to later transmit this information to a PBN that will take the necessary actions for QoS management. Hence, in Fig. 2, we add two new elements to allow Internet traffic classification: Monitoring and Classification system. The resulting classification is forwarded to the PBN. In the figure above, we also show two basic components comprised by the PBN: (i) A Policy Decision Point (PDP) that takes decisions for itself and for other network elements. These decisions imply actions for enforcement when the conditions of a policy rule are met [15], and (ii) Policy Enforcement Point (PEP) which is a logical entity that enforces policy decisions [15]. Marked Internet traffic can be forwarded to the PDP, which in turn will identify the associated GWs or STs and determine if more bandwidth should be assigned. This last decision is sent to the PEP for its execution. In addition to this, a QoS server can be deployed to enforcing QoS for different flows directly, and not to the GWs and STs as the PEP does.

3 Architecture Design

Making an abstraction of the elements in a real Satellite network distribution, the primary steps to achieve Internet traffic classification in a Satellite Architecture are:

1. Intercept Internet traffic in the GW and ST through passive monitoring points.
2. Compute statistical features that define the Internet flows.
3. Send the extracted features to the Classification system and mark the flows with their QoS classes.
4. Forward the classification to the PDP that will take decisions in order to improve the QoS. Then the PEP and QoS server will execute those decisions.

In order to design the system, we use a software engineering tool called Capella[1]. This tool provides methodological guidance, intuitive model editing, and viewing capabilities for Systems, Software and Hardware Architects. In Capella, the Operational analysis and System analysis help finding and defining the requirements of the system. Whereas, the Logical and Physical architectures aim at developing the solution. Figure 2 shows a System Analysis viewpoint, focused on the GW actor, developing the requirement: Provide Internet traffic classification in Satellite Communications for QoS management. We will discuss as follows the functions associated to this system analysis.

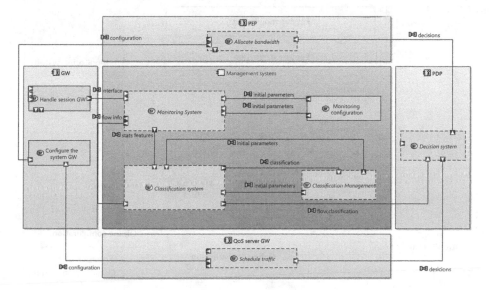

Fig. 2. System Analysis in the GW.

---

[1] https://www.polarsys.org/capella/.

3.1   Classification System

Particularly, this system proposes an automatic and logic process to analyze traffic in a hierarchical manner. The classification system is displayed in Fig. 3. Briefly speaking, the process starts performing the *Offline configuration* process in order to initialize the whole classification system (training process). In an online manner, the flow features pass through a *Flow discriminator 1 (D1)* that will be in charge of disjointing the non-encrypted/Encrypted flows from the tunneled flows. This separation will allow us to treat each technology differently. For instance, for the non-encrypted/Encrypted flows, classical ML models or DPI solutions (denoted as *Cl1*) can label the flows. Whereas, the tunneled flows will pass through another *Flow discriminator 2 (D2)* that separates the unitary (only one application within the tunnel) and the multiple (several applications at the same time in the tunnel). Finally, once the classifiers are actively working the *Online configuration* component is receiving information that can induce to change or to add models in the *Model repository*.

3.2   Monitoring System

Internet packets are captured to be organized into flows F. The construction of the flow is given in Fig. 4. In principle, all the flows are built matching the packet's headers, source (src) and destination (dst) IPs and ports. However, when $D1$ detected a multiplexed connection, the flow is broken into chunks of flows within a time interval, as seen in Fig. 4. Then, statistical based features are

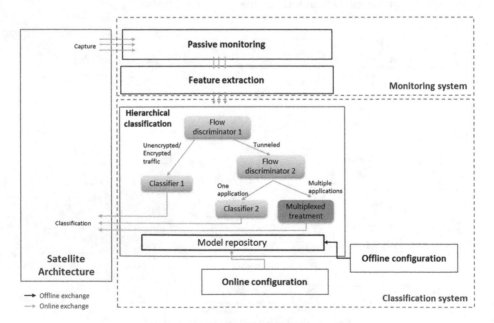

Fig. 3. Classification framework

computed for each flow in order to describe the communications. In brief, the properties computed are listed in Table 1. The passive monitoring and feature extraction processes were studied by the authors in [9,11]. The categorization of the packets (A, B, C, D, E and F) in Table 1 is obtained by studying the packet length distributions per class in the dataset.

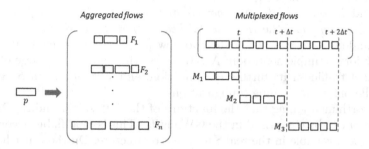

Fig. 4. Flow reconstruction.

Table 1. Result of the feature extraction process

Feature	Metric	Additional Information	Flow direction	Total
$pktlen\_[m]$	[m] of the packet lengths	"m" refers to the metric Mean, Std, Min and Max	F, F_{src} and F_{dst}	12
$iat\_[m]$	[m] of the inter-arrival time(iat)	-	F, F_{src} and F_{dst}	12
$pktlen\_[cat]\_[m]$	[m] of the packet lengths per [cat]	"cat" refers to the type of packet[a]	F, F_{src} and F_{dst}	72
$iat\_[cat]\_[m]$	[m] of the iat per [cat]		F, F_{src} and F_{dst}	72
$bytes\_[\Delta t]$	bytes per [Δt]	"Δt" is the time windows	F, F_{src} and F_{dst}	3
$pkt\_[\Delta t]$	packets counts per [Δt]	-	F, F_{src} and F_{dst}	3
Total				174

[a] A: pktlen $<= 170$, B: pktlen > 170 and pktlen $<= 902$, C: pktlen > 902 and pktlen $<= 1314$,D: pktlen > 1314 and pktlen $<= 1426$,E: pktlen > 1426 and pktlen $<= 1500$, F: pktlen > 1500

3.3 Classification Management

This component implements the offline and online reconfiguration. Regarding the *Online reconfiguration* component, this element will be in charge of evaluating the predictions performed by the classifiers. This is deployed in order to cope with the evolution of the network. Therefore, in an online manner, this component will evaluate if the traffic observed belongs to an existing QoS class; if so the classifier will "evolve" to offer more accurate predictions. This approach can be translated to a retraining process when new data is generated; nonetheless, there are another approaches based on clustering that could detect class evolution.

As a final note, the current investigation does not treat the *Online configuration* and *Multiplexed treatment* due to they involve more complex tasks that will be presented in future works.

4 Implementation Design

The implementation proposal is presented in Fig. 5, with the operational and physical architecture in the same viewpoint. The subsystems proposed in Fig. 5 will define the way in which the components of the *QoS management system* work. For instance, the *Offline configuration* will be developed by the *Training process* and *Historical data manager* components, the *Online configuration* by the *Model manager* and the *Incremental Learning Model(ILM) manager* components. In addition to this, we define two new physical components that will be necessary for the implementation: A *GW server* that will be in charge of taking the Internet traffic for its further classification, and a *Management Server* that will handle offline and online configurations.

It is worth mentioning that the functions of the *GW server* and the *Management Server* can be comprised in the GW entity. This is modifiable according to the resources available in the real Satellite Architecture. On the other hand, all the functions concerning the *Classification system* are comprised in *Framework*: which in turn is a library developed for this aim. For what concerns the *sniffer*, we use existing solutions such as Libcap[2] for performing the sniffing. Then, we add the *Flow reconstruction* and *Feature Extraction* behaviors. The ML models $D1$, $Cl1$, $D2$ and $Cl2$ will be selected in the experimental section.

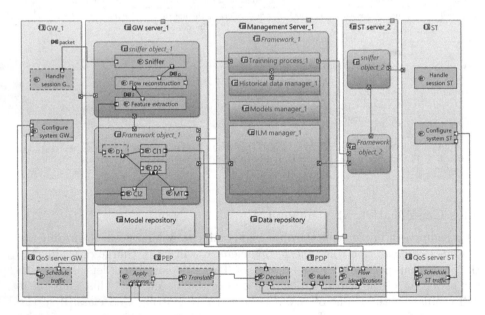

Fig. 5. System analysis in the GW.

---

[2] https://www.tcpdump.org/.

As additional comment, the reader can notice that the proposed implementation can be easily replicated in the ST component, as well as in different network components where packet monitoring is feasible.

5   Emulated Satellite Internet Traffic

This data set is a private dataset called SAT data. The model of a multi-gateway Satellite network in Fig. 6 with one ST and one GW was set over OpenSAND[3], which is a platform to emulate Satellite Communications. In addition to this, a VPN configuration is disposed between the ST and the GW, with the objective to emulate tunneled communications. Several applications were launched and captured by OpenBACH[4]. The user behavior was mimicked by using Selenium[5], which is a tool to test web applications.

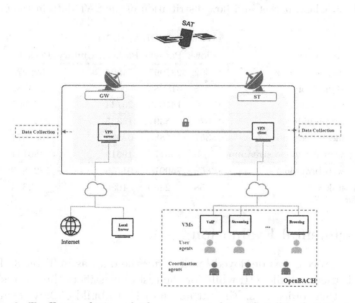

Fig. 6. Traffic emulation platform proposed in a Satellite Architecture.

The applications are launched in three main scenarios on the platform: (i) Internet traffic without the tunnel (ii) Unitary scenarios with the VPN: only one application at a time is launched, and (iii) Multiple scenarios with the VPN: several applications are launched at the same time. Additionally, some network configurations were imposed on OpenSand. For each scenario, the data collection process was performed in the GW and ST, before and after the VPN. In

---

[3] http://opensand.org/.

[4] https://www.openbach.org/.

[5] https://www.seleniumhq.org/.

this sense, all the possible transformations that the data perceived is recorded. The labeling process is performed per file and application launched. However, for the VPN tunnel, a special treatment was performed: for each packet getting into the tunnel a flag was used to mark the application launched. Therefore, the multiplexed connections are correctly labeled. This dataset is still in development. In this particular work, we used only the data captured in the GW with the applications in Table 2. These applications were launched differently to get a heterogeneous dataset; for instance, different codecs and websites were used for the VoIP and browsing applications, respectively. In Table 2, we show the flows captured per application and the amount of packets with and without the VPN. It is important to mention that the duration varies from 5 min up to 15 min. In addition to this, the experiments over the VPN were carried by using UDP as transport protocol.

Table 2. Class, packet and flow distribution of the SAT data in the GW.

		Without VPN		With VPN	
QoS class	Application	Flows	Packets	Packets: Unitary	Packets: Multiple
VoIP	facebook_voip	302	227997	74904	522275
	skype_voip	565	315281	60764	673780
	twinkle_voip	69	141663	26144	276995
Video	skype_video	579	925391	318335	2235781
	facebook_video	357	558880	162822	1000071
Streaming	youtube_video_streaming	760	158177	19619	486141
Browsing	web_browsing	6852	749979	91705	1824852
Unknown	unknown	58	2860	1080	2334

6   Experimental Evaluation

The training process was deployed by dividing the data as in Table 3. The complete data is used to build $D1$, while for the rest of classifiers the data is adapted according to their objectives. First at all, in order to build $Cl2$, we evaluate different time windows Δt to find the most adequate. Afterwards, we build the rest of the classifiers with different ML approaches. The best approaches are selected, and their average response time and accuracy are compared with nDPI.

Table 3. Data settings for building the classifiers.

Classifier	All data				
D1	Without VPN			With VPN	
Cl1	Unencrypted	Encrypted			
D2				unitary	multiple
Cl2				unitary	
MT					multiple

6.1 Classification System Results

Table 4 shows the results after evaluating different time windows for the unitary tunneled connections. The accuracy increase as Δt does; therefore, we compare the average number of packets evaluated for each application in Fig. 7. We can notice that for 5 ms and 10ms, the amount of packets is very low. To avoid this, the new window will be adjustable in the sense that $\Delta t = 10$ ms, but we wait until we have at least 20 packets to process.

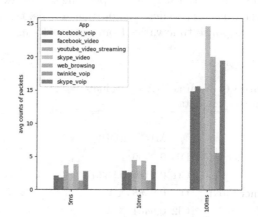

Table 4. Accuracy results for $Cl2$ varying Δt

Δt	Num. flow	Cl2
5 ms	167097	0.8982
10 ms	120395	0.9647
100 ms	26634	0.9673

Fig. 7. Average counts of packets for each Δt

On the other hand, the results in Table 5 show a comparison between several classifiers: Decision Tree (DT), Random Forest (RF), K Nearest Neighbors (KNN), Ada Boost, Voting and Extra Trees (ETs). The best performance is standing up in bold. We picked DTs for the flow discrimination tasks, while RF for the traffic classification task.

Table 5. Accuracy scores of several ML classifiers.

	DT	RF	KNN	AdaBoost	Voting	ETs
D1	**0.9999**	0.9999	0.9999	0.9999	0.9999	0.9999
Cl1	0.8876	**0.9186**	0.8617	0.7986	0.8941	0.8938
D2	0.9588	**0.9646**	0.9526	0.9584	0.9636	0.9638
Cl2	0.9321	**0.9401**	0.9209	0.8333	0.9358	0.9304

Following, the complete framework was implemented in C. The tree based models are built in sklearn[6] and parsed to C for faster Internet classifications,

---

[6] https://scikit-learn.org.

inspired by the work in [4]. These tests were performed on a PC with an i7-6700HQ CPU and 32 Gb RAM. The response time and accuracy are measured over the test set. We also evaluate nDPI for traffic classification.

In Table 6, we can notice that the C implemented models maintain their accuracy. In the unencrypted case, ML outperforms nDPI; while, for the encrypted case nDPI is unable to detect the class of an unitary session as $Cl2$ does. Regarding the response time of the classifiers, in Table 7, we can notice that fast Internet classifications are possible. It is important to mention that the model response time differs for each entry depending on how deep they go into the tree's branches until a leaf is reached. In addition to this, the packet processing and flow metering response time varies from 5 ms to 15 ms.

Table 6. Accuracy (Acc) evaluating the test data

		Acc	
		ML	nDPI
Unencrypted	D1	0.9999	1
	Cl1	0.9186	0.5830
Encrypted	D2	0.9588	X
	Cl2	0.9401	X

Table 7. Average response time in μs

		Time(μs)	
		ML	nDPI
Unencrypted	D1	2.867	1
	Cl1	5	6.6460
Encrypted	D2	2.717	X
	Cl2	5	X

6.2 About the Multiplexed Connections

We were able to divide the multiplexed connections between unitary and non unitary scenarios. We saw that the unitary scenarios can be classified by classical ML approaches. The scenario with multiple applications within a tunnel is challenge in this field. In order to illustrate the problem, we take the unitary tunneled flows of Skype, YouTube and Browsing; and its equivalent mixed tunneled flow. We represent them as a combination of types of packets (A:E from the source and 1:5 from the destination, using the packet lengths described in Table 1). We count the average number of packets for each combination within a time windows of 100ms and plot it into a heatmap. For instance, the flow "AAB1CAA" has AA:2, AB:1, B1:1 and CA:1. This representation is in Fig. 8. We can notice that the unitary tunneled connections have distinctively sequence of patterns that are merged in the mixed tunneled flow. It is important to say that the Skype pattern is maintained and might be identified. This illustration gives us an idea of how to decrypt the behavior within the tunneled connections by looking at the packet's patterns. However, the complexity grows when more than three applications are multiplexed in the tunnel.

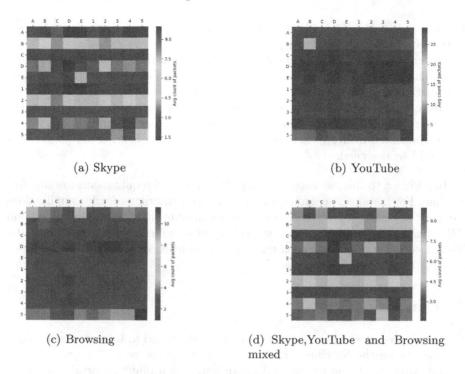

(a) Skype

(b) YouTube

(c) Browsing

(d) Skype, YouTube and Browsing mixed

Fig. 8. Heatmap representation of the flows with $\Delta t = 100\,\text{ms}$.

6.3   About the Evolution of Internet Traffic

Most of the publicly available datasets do not comprise all the existing applications on the Internet; in addition, the data collection process is tedious and expensive as remarked in [10]. One of the main deficiencies of ML in this field is handling with the evolution of the Internet traffic applications. If we consider some important QoS classes such as YouTube, NetFlix, Skype or Facebook video; as new incoming behavior, the classification accuracy might decrease considerably. Our architectural proposal comprises a component that should schedule retrainings of the models when the network administrators demand it. But also, an automatic approach can be set to continuously modify the trees of the RFs in the *Model repository* component. Such approach can be based on unsupervised methods for detecting the Internet evolution.

6.4   About the QoS Management

As we previously mentioned, it suffice to place the classification system over a network appliance that permits traffic monitoring. For instance, in the GW component, the classification output is forwarded to the PDP in order to perform the QoS management task. Depending on the classification output, QoS rules will be applied to trigger actions that will manage the Satellite resources. If a QoS rule is satisfied the traffic will be shaped as follows:

- Aggregate flows: the QoS rule is applied over all the incoming packets sharing the same tuple $(IP_{src}, IP_{dst}, port_{src}, port_{dst}, proto)$.
- Unitary tunneled flows: all the incoming packets of the unitary tunneled communications will be prioritized. However, this may be updated when the classification prediction of $D2$ or $Cl2$ changes in Δt.
- Multiplexed tunneled flows: we can think about prioritizing the tunnel as the unitary case. Nevertheless, in parallel, other less sensitive applications will be also benefited from this action. To avoid this, a classification per packet task should be designed.

In addition to this, we need to be sure that the QoS requirements are satisfied on time. For instance, according to [5], VoIP and Interactive video applications are very sensitive to delivery delays, to be specific they can tolerate around 100ms; whereas, another important class such as Video streaming around 10 s. We notice that the classification task can be achieved in 15 ms, giving sufficient time to treat those sensitive classes.

7   Conclusion

This work presented a ML system that can be integrated to Internet traffic architectures, being the Satellite Architecture our main interest. The proposal can be comparable with an existing DPI solution, which offers a portable software solution for Internet traffic inspection. We tested our approach in the GW component, with data captured from an emulated Satellite platform. This approach outperformed in accuracy and time a well-known DPI solution. We displayed the needs of having components that can deal with the evolution of the Internet network and the multiplexed connections, these last aspects are in development. Future works also include implementing the approach in the emulated Satellite platform, and tuning the framework proposed given different network conditions.

Acknowledgment. We want to thank the Centre National d'Études Spatiales (CNES), Toulouse, France for allowing us to use the SAT data, which is developed under the project R&T CNES: Application du Machine Learning au Satcom.

References

1. Bertaux, L., et al.: Software defined networking and virtualization for broadband satellite networks. IEEE Commun. Mag. **53**(3), 54–60 (2015)
2. Deri, L., Martinelli, M., Bujlow, T., Cardigliano, A.: nDPI: Open-source high-speed deep packet inspection. In: 2014 International Wireless Communications and Mobile Computing Conference (IWCMC), pp. 617–622 (2014)
3. Ferrús, R., Koumaras, H., et al.: Sdn/nfv-enabled satellite communications networks: opportunities, scenarios and challenges. Phys. Commun. **18**, 95–112 (2016). special Issue on Radio Access Network Architectures and Resource Management for 5G

 4. Garcia, J., Korhonen, T., Andersson, R., Västlund, F.: Towards video flow classi-
    fication at a million encrypted flows per second. In: 2018 IEEE 32nd International
    Conference on Advanced Information Networking and Applications (AINA), pp.
    358–365, May 2018
 5. ITU-T: End-user multimedia qos categories. Technical report, TELECOMMUNI-
    CATION STANDARDIZATION SECTOR OF ITU (2001)
 6. Jin, Y., Duffield, N., Erman, J., Haffner, P., Sen, S., Zhang, Z.L.: A modular
    machine learning system for flow-level traffic classification in large networks. ACM
    Trans. Knowl. Discov. Data **6**(1), 4:1–4:34 (2012)
 7. Moore, B., Ellesson, E., Strassner, J., Westerinen, A.: Policy core information
    model - version 1 specification, internet Engineering Task Force (IETF). https://
    tools.ietf.org/html/rfc3060
 8. Ng, B., Hayes, M., Seah, W.K.G.: Developing a traffic classification platform for
    enterprise networks with SDN: Experiences & lessons learned. In: 2015 IFIP Net-
    working Conference (IFIP Networking), pp. 1–9, May 2015
 9. Pacheco, F., Exposito, E., Aguilar, J., Gineste, M., Baudoin, C.: A novel statistical
    based feature extraction approach for the inner-class feature estimation using linear
    regression. In: 2018 International Joint Conference on Neural Networks (IJCNN),
    pp. 1–8, July 2018
10. Pacheco, F., Exposito, E., Gineste, M., Baudoin, C., Aguilar, J.: Towards the
    deployment of machine learning solutions in network traffic classification: a sys-
    tematic survey. IEEE Communications Surveys Tutorials, p. 1 (2018)
11. Pacheco, F., Exposito, E., Gineste, M., Budoin, C.: An autonomic traffic analy-
    sis proposal using machine learning techniques. In: Proceedings of the 9th Inter-
    national Conference on Management of Digital EcoSystems, MEDES 2017, pp.
    273–280 (2017)
12. Pietrzyk, M., Costeux, J.L., Urvoy-Keller, G., En-Najjary, T.: Challenging statis-
    tical classification for operational usage: the adsl case. In: Proceedings of the 9th
    ACM SIGCOMM Conference on Internet Measurement, IMC 2009, pp. 122–135
    (2009)
13. Siller, M., Woods, J.C.: QoS arbitration for improving the QoE in multimedia
    transmission. In: 2003 International Conference on Visual Information Engineering
    VIE 2003 (2003)
14. Trestian, I., Ranjan, S., Kuzmanovic, A., Nucci, A.: Googling the internet: profiling
    internet endpoints via the world wide web. IEEE/ACM Trans. Networking **18**(2),
    666–679 (2010)
15. Yavatkar, R., Pendarakis, D., Guerin, R.: A framework for policy-based admis-
    sion control, internet Engineering Task Force (IETF). https://tools.ietf.org/html/
    rfc2753

FAME: An Influencer Model for Service-Oriented Environments

Faisal Binzagr[1], Hamza Labbaci[2], and Brahim Medjahed[1(✉)]

[1] Department of Computer and Information Science,
University of Michigan - Dearborn, Dearborn, USA
{faisalb,brahim}@umich.edu
[2] Department of Computer Science, University of Tours, Tours, France
hemza.labbaci@univ-tours.fr

Abstract. We propose FAME (*inFluencer Apis in developer coMmuni-tiEs*), a multi-dimensional influencer model for APIs in service-oriented environments. We define influence as the extent to which an API is likely to be adopted in mashups and service-oriented applications. The proposed model helps providers increase the visibility of their APIs and developers select the best-in-class APIs. We extract more than eighteen textual and non-textual API features from various programming communities such as GitHub, StackOverflow, HackerNews, and ProgrammableWeb. We perform sentiment analysis to quantify developers' opinions towards using APIs. We introduce a cumulative API influence score to measure the influence of APIs across communities and categorize APIs into tiers based on their influence. We introduce a linear regression technique to predict the evolution of influence scores and correlate API features to those scores. We conduct experiments on large and real-world data-sets extracted from the above mentioned programming communities to illustrate the viability of our approach.

Keywords: API · Service-orientation · Mashup · Social content · Influencer · Developer community

1 Introduction

Service-oriented computing allows companies to break down capabilities and business functionalities into individual, autonomous services [5]. The last decade has seen a surge of services in the form of Web APIs (simply APIs) in a variety of domains [15]. The API economy is growing rapidly and companies are making APIs an integral part of their software development strategies. For instance, the ProgrammableWeb directory lists more than 22,200 APIs (as of August 2019). APIs enable developers to access hardware and software resources via Internet and Web-specific protocols. Using APIs accelerates the development of value-added applications (e.g., mashups) by providing reusable functionalities out-of-the-box. However, integrating multiple APIs created by diverse third parties requires a wide array of technical skills such as Web (e.g., REST), data management (e.g., JSON), programming (e.g., SDKs), and security (e.g., authentication) [12,15]. To overcome these challenges, developers often turn to

© Springer Nature Switzerland AG 2019
S. Yangui et al. (Eds.): ICSOC 2019, LNCS 11895, pp. 216–230, 2019.
https://doi.org/10.1007/978-3-030-33702-5_16

programming communities (e.g. `GitHub`) to share practices, knowledge, experience, and brainpower in solving intricate problems. For instance, `GitHub` reports (as of May 2019) having over 37 million users and 100 million repositories. Gathering and analyzing content about API usage and activities in existing communities (e.g., number of bugs, developer feedback, number of mashups) provides opportunities to better understand developers' interactions with APIs and detect relationships between APIs and mashups [5,13].

Combining social network analysis with service-oriented computing could bring novel insights to service selection, recommendation, and composition [4,5]. One particular research area that received significant attention in social computing is social *influence* [9]. Influencers have the power to impact the way others in the entire network behave or think [7]. Considerable work has been conducted to model influence or identify influencers in social media [6,7,11,16]. The research proposed in this paper approaches the concept of influencers from an API perspective. We define an API as *influential* if it is widely adopted in mashup and service-oriented application development. The more influence an API has, the more interest that API sparks to developers. We perceive API developers (both consumers and providers) in programming communities as social actors. API consumers use existing APIs to build mashups and service-oriented applications. They share experiences, feedback, and opinions about APIs in various ways such as participating in discussion forums, reporting bugs, and following APIs. API Providers are the developers that created the APIs available in the community. They publish important information about their APIs such as tutorials, articles, SDKs, libraries, new releases, and source code.

Analyzing social content to identify *influencer APIs* has several advantages. First, API consumers will be able to integrate the best-in-class APIs. For instance, the `ProgrammableWeb` directory lists more than fifty mapping APIs. Selecting the right API is time-consuming and may have an impact on future mashup maintenance and development [5]. Second, consumers may have different views on what makes an API relevant. Some consumers may value APIs with the least number of reported bugs. Others may consider the opinions expressed by peers toward the API as significant. Measuring influence based on various API features assists consumers in selecting APIs that are most suitable to their development style, needs, and requirements. Third, identifying influencer APIs enables providers to increase the visibility of their APIs and set up a strategy to reach out a larger audience of developers. Providers will be able to compare their API's influence with the influence of a competitor's API and pinpoint a plan of actions to promote their APIs. Some providers may, for example, decide to enhance their involvement in discussion forums, while others may choose to increase the number of articles and tutorials published about their APIs.

Developing an influencer model for service-oriented environments poses several research challenges. First, social data are scattered across multiple independent platforms and cannot be accurately obtained from one single source. For instance, the number of applications that use a given API is determined by looking at mashups listed in `ProgrammableWeb` and repositories hosted in `GitHub`. Besides, current platforms return API-related data in heterogeneous formats.

For example, posts in StackOverflow and commit comments in GitHub are textual and require natural language processing techniques. News articles in HackerNews and bug reports in Bugzilla are presented in proprietary formats. Other data such as the number of issues in GitHub, number of posts in StackOverflow, and number of followers on ProgrammableWeb are returned as atomic values on different scales. Second, the social content collected from existing communities deals with various aspects of the APIs. It covers both technical (e.g., number of SDKs) and non-technical (e.g., number of API followers) information. This includes information about the API itself (e.g., number of change logs representing the API's evolution), API consumption (e.g., number of projects that use the API), and API social activities (e.g., number of posts and articles related the API). A multi-dimensional influencer model that captures various API features is needed. Once API features are gathered and cleaned, it is important to determine the extent to which an API is influential and the features that have or do not have an impact on the API influence and, if so, to what degree. Third, newly developed APIs lack the social content necessary to assess their overall influence. Therefore, recommender systems based on API influence scores may omit to return such APIs. This may lead to the starvation of newly deployed APIs as they lack the required social presence. The proposed influencer model should allow bootstrapping the influence score of newly created APIs, hence overcoming the traditional cold start problem.

The identification of influential nodes in social networks has been the subject of many research efforts [6,7,11,16]. Existing research devoted to influencers in software ecosystems emphasizes on developers as influencers *not* APIs [3,10]. In this paper, we propose FAME (*inFluencer Apis in developer coMmunitiEs*), an influencer model for APIs in service-oriented environments. To the best of our knowledge, FAME is the first approach to consider APIs (instead of developers) as influencers in building mashups and service-oriented applications. The main contributions of this paper are summarized below:

- We propose an influencer model that extracts more than eighteen API features from multiple programming communities. The extracted features capture non-technical and technical information about APIs in various formats such as text, atomic values, and other proprietary structures. We perform sentiment analysis to quantify developers' opinions towards using APIs. We introduce a cumulative *API Influence Score* (AIS) to assess the influence of APIs in mashups and service-oriented applications. We also categorize APIs into tiers based on their influence scores.
- We predict the evolution of the influence scores of newly deployed and existing APIs using Non Negative Least Square (NLS) linear regression technique. We conduct an analytical study to determine the degree to which each extracted API feature impacts the influence score.
- We conduct experiments on four real-world programming platforms: GitHub, StackOverflow, HackerNews, and ProgrammableWeb. We categorize the extracted social content in five data-sets depending on the deployment dates

of the corresponding APIs (between 2005 and 2019). We compute the recall and precision of each data-set. Experiments reveal that the proposed approach can predict up to 87% influencer APIs with 71% precision.

The rest of this paper is organized as follows. Section 2 gives an overview of the proposed approach. Section 3 presents the FAME model for identifying and predicting influencer APIs. We describe experiments to evaluate our approach in Sect. 4. In Sect. 5, we overview related work. We conclude in Sect. 6.

2   The FAME Approach: An Overview

In this section, we give an overview of the proposed approach. We first introduce two scenarios to motivate our approach. Then, we describe FAME architecture for identifying and predicting influencer APIs.

2.1   Motivation

We describe two scenarios that illustrate the benefits and challenges of API influencer identification for consumers and providers. In both scenarios, we refer to two weather APIs: `Aeris Weather` (API_{AW}) and `World Weather Online` (API_{WWO}).

Scenario 1 (API Consumers) - Let us consider a developer, *Mary*, looking for a weather API to use in a mashup. A search on `ProgrammableWeb` returns API_{AW} and API_{WWO}. Since *Mary* has no prior experience programming with those APIs, she turns to developers in various programming communities to help her select the right one. *Mary* first looks at the features of API_{AW} and API_{WWO} on `ProgrammableWeb` (Table 1). Below is a summary of her findings. API_{AW} has more SDKs than API_{WWO}. The two APIs have approximately the same number of articles published on the platform. API_{WWO} has much more followers than API_{AW}. Because *Mary* is interested in mashup development. She learns that API_{WWO} is used in more mashups than API_{AW}. However, she finds only 2 and 11 mashups for API_{AW} and API_{WWO}, respectively. *Mary* then looks at the number of projects on `GitHub` that are relevant to the APIs. She noticed a much larger number of repositories related to API_{WWO} than API_{AW} (39 vs. 6). Similarly, API_{WWO} outperforms API_{AW} in terms of number of Wikis (428 vs. 3). However, less issues are reported by developers about API_{AW} than API_{WWO} (29 vs. 310). *Mary* is overwhelmed by the number of API features published on each platform. She is confused about the features to consider in order to decide about the API to use. She becomes even more frustrated when she parses the long texts posted under the reported issues and commit comments on `GitHub` to get a better idea about her peers' opinions about the APIs.

Table 1. Motivating scenarios

Platforms	Features	AerisWeather API	World Weather Online API
programmableweb	# of Articles	3	4
	# of SKDs	8	1
	# of Library	0	4
	# of Mashup	2	11
	# of Followers	126	271
	# of Changelog	21	19
GitHub	# of Repositories	6	39
	# of Commit	9	46
	#of Issues	29	310
	# of Wikis	3	428
Google Search Engine Index	By API name	14,000	42,400,000
	By API EndPoint	1,750	569,000
stackoverflow	# of Posts	4	41

Scenario 2 (API Providers) - The provider of API_{AW}, *John*, performs a Google search on API_{AW} and a competitor's API, namely API_{WWO}. A search by API endpoints returns more than 500,000 additional results for API_{WWO}. A second search by API names returned more than 42 million additional hits for API_{WWO}. *John* is concerned about the significant lack of popularity of his API compared to API_{WWO}. To increase the visibility of API_{AW} and promote its adoption, he looks at some of the features of API_{AW} and API_{WWO} on ProgrammableWeb, GitHub, and StackOverflow (Table 1). The aim is to come up with an action plan to increase the adoption of API_{AW} by developers. The following questions need to be answered as part of *John*'s action plan: how does he measure the influence of his API? which features are likely to have a higher impact on developers across programming communities to adopt API_{AW}? how are the different API features related to each other? which features does he need to improve in order to enhance API_{AW} influence?

2.2 Architecture

The FAME architecture is composed of three modules (Fig. 1): *Unstructured Data Extractor* (UDE), *Structured Data Extractor* (SDE), and the *FAME Model*. UDE extracts and analyzes unstructured (i.e., textual) API features from developer communities. Such features include commit comments in GitHub, posts in StackOverflow, and articles in ProgrammableWeb. UDE conducts sentiment analysis to quantify textual features as positive, neutral, or negative sentiment scores. Since the extraction and analysis of textual features is time consuming, UDE tasks are executed periodically and offline. *SDE* collects quantitative API features (e.g., number of repositories) from ProgrammableWeb, GitHub, and HackerNews. These features are extracted online (i.e., on demand) during the execution of an API influencer identification or prediction request. Since SDE-extracted features are measured on different scales, data normalization techniques are applied to adjust those features to a common scale. Once all features are extracted, cleaned, and normalized, the FAME model aggregates those features to determine the *API Influence Score* (AIS) of each API. The calculated scores are used to cluster APIs into tiers: nano (least influential), micro, mid-tier, mega, and celebrity (most influential). The FAME model also uses non-negative-least-square regression to figure out significant features and associate weights to those features. Such weights are used to predict the evolution of AIS scores and tweak API features in order to enhance API influence across communities.

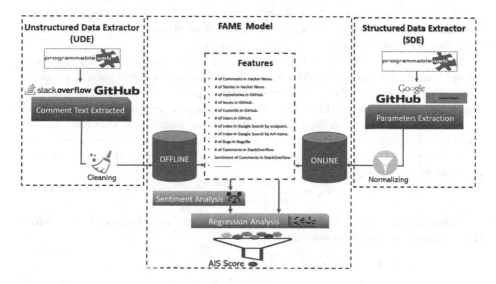

Fig. 1. FAME architecture

3 Influencer Identification and Prediction in FAME

In this section, we give details about the FAME approach for identifying and predicting influencer APIs. We first introduce the methods to extract both unstructured (i.e., textual) and structured features from programming community platforms (Sects. 3.1 and 3.2). Then, we describe the techniques for calculating *API Influence Scores* (AIS) and organizing APIs into influencer tiers based on AIS scores (Sect. 3.3). Finally, we present a linear regression-based model for predicting AIS scores (Sect. 3.4).

3.1 Unstructured Data Extractor (UDE)

UDE evaluates developers' sentiments toward APIs. It analyzes developers' feedback and computes scores of interest in APIs. UDE performs three major tasks:

data collection, data pre-processing, and sentiment analysis. The data collection task crawls and collects developers' textual data from `GitHub` (commit comments), `StackOverflow` (posts), and `ProgrammableWeb` (articles). As each one of these platforms exports large volumes of data, we define data extraction patterns based on API names, endpoints, and topics to sort out API-related content and speed-up data collection. The data pre-processing task cleans textual data from irrelevant information such as code snippets and hyperlinks.

Sentiment analysis is the main UDE task. It evaluates developers' opinions toward APIs. We use the Stanford NLP (Natural Language Processing) Parser[1]. The parser adopts recursive neural nets, a deep learning technique, to figure out text polarity (positive, neutral, negative). It returns a sentiment score, $sscore \in [-1, 1]$, along with text polarity. An $sscore$ closer to -1 denotes a negative sentiment. The sentiment is considered as positive if $sscore$ is closer to 1. An $sscore$ closer to 0 represents a neutral sentiment.

Some textual features may have higher user views than others. For instance, the sentiment of a post on an API with a large number of views should be given more importance than the sentiment of another post (on the same API) with a smaller number of views. Therefore, we associate a weight w_i for each textual feature f_i. Each weight value w_i correlates to the number of views on f_i. We normalize weights according to the following formula, where $viewsnumber_i$ and $Max(viewsnumber)$ represent the number of fi views and maximum number of views in all features:

$$w_i = \frac{viewsnumber_i}{Max(viewsnumber)}$$

Using the weight w_i and sentiment score $sscore_i$ of a feature f_i, we define the weighted sentiment as follows:

$$WeightedSentiment_i = w_i * sscore_i$$

Finally, we define the overall sentiment for a given API_j as the sum of the weighted sentiment of each extracted feature f_i divided by the total number of such features:

$$sentiment(API_j) = \frac{\sum WeightedSentiment_i}{TotalNumberOfExtractedFeatures}$$

3.2 Structured Data Extractor (SDE)

SDE collects structured API features from four programming community platforms: `ProgrammableWeb`, `GitHub`, `StackOverflow`, and `HackerNews`. By structured, we mean that the features are well formatted in the platforms and ready to extract/use. We rely on Selenium WebDriver[2], a framework that automates Web data extraction. The framework allows feature extraction using predefined parsing rules. A rule contains the URLs to load data from and keywords describing

---

[1] https://nlp.stanford.edu/.

[2] https://www.seleniumhq.org/projects/webdriver/.

APIs to filter data with. Data is parsed to extract features using DOM (Document Object Model)[3]. Table 2 summarizes all API features extracted by UDE and SDE.

Table 2. API features in developer communities

Platforms	Features	Description
programmableweb	# of Articles	The number of articles related to this API.
	# of SKDs	The number of SDKs available tools for consuming existing APIs.
	# of Library	The number of tools that, when installed, results in the provisioning a specific API.
	# of Followers	The number of users who follow the APIs.
	# of Changelog	The number of change Log which represents the APIs evolution history.
GitHub	# of Users	The number of users who mentioned the API name in their profiles.
	# of Commit	Number of commit that have mentioned the API name.
	#of Issues	Number of issues that have mentioned the API name.
	# of Topic	Number of Topics wikis that have mentioned the API name.
	# of Wikis	Number of wikis that have mentioned the API name.
Google Search Engine Index	By API name	The search index when we search by API name.
	By API EndPoint	The search index when we search by API endpoint.
Hacker News	# of Stories	Number of stories that have mentioned the API name.
	# of Comments	Number of comments that have mentioned the API name.
stackoverflow	# of post	Number of post (question /Answer) that have mentioned the API name.
	Average post view	The average view for all post related to specific API.
	Max post view	The maximum post view related to specific API.
	Average Sentiment	The average sentiment of all post related to API.

Another important factor that helps assess the influence of an API is its spread over the internet. A well distributed/spread API is usually indexed on many search engines, which increases its visibility and eases its access. For example, `Twitter` API is accessible via multiple resources such as tutorials, documentations, and videos. This makes the API more likely to attract developers. We run two kind of queries on `Google` search engine to measure the level of spread of an API. The first query counts the number of entries in the index that contain a given API name; the second query counts the number of entries containing a given API endpoint (Table 2).

The features retrieved by SDE are returned on different scales. For example, the number of issues reported for an API on `GitHub` may reach several hundreds; the number of SDKs available for an API on `ProgrammableWeb` is typically a one or two-digit value; the number of users interested in an API on `GitHub` may go beyond thousands. To normalize features on a common scale, we use the following formula:

$$\hat{x} = \frac{(x_{max} - x_{min}) * (r_{max} - r_{min})}{(x_{max} - x_{min})} + r_{min}$$

---

[3] https://www.w3.org/TR/WD-DOM/.

Where: $\hat{x}$ refers to the normalized value; x_{max} and x_{min} refer to the feature maximum and minimum values, respectively; r_{max} and r_{min} refer to the maximum and minimum new range values, 1 and 0 for our case.

3.3 API Influencer Score (AIS)

We define a metric, called *API Influence Score* (AIS), to model the degree to which community members use an API to develop mashups and service-oriented applications. For that purpose, we use the number of mashups and repositories that adopt the API on `ProgrammableWeb` and `GitHub`, respectively. However, some developers may display negative experiences using an API. To capture developers' opinions, the AIS score includes the average weighted sentiment. As shown in the formula given below, the AIS score is calculated using three of the API features extracted from community platforms (Table 2). The remaining extracted features are used to predict the AIS score as shown in Sect. 3.4. The AIS score is formally defined as follows:

$$AIS_{(i)} = \sum \#M_i + \#R_i + Sentiment(API_i)$$

Where: $\#M_i$ is the number of mashups that use APIi on `ProgrammableWeb`; $\#R_i$ is the number of repositories that use APIi on `GitHub`; Sentiment(API$_i$) is the overall sentiment on APIi as defined in Sect. 3.1.

Using the computed AIS scores, we define influencer tiers to categorize APIs according to their influence level. Figure 2b shows the five tiers: *Nano*, *Micro*, *Mid-Tier*, *Mega*, and *Celebrity*. Figure 2a depicts the distribution of all APIs across the five influence tiers. The *Nano* tier regroups the least influential APIs. APIs in this tier have a score below 0.015. This category has the highest proportion of APIs, with about 600 identified APIs. Examples of Nano APIs are `Blinksale`, `Plunker` and `MyWot`. The *Micro* tier contains APIs with a score between 0.015 and 0.15. `Hoiio Voice`, `Kiva` and `Songkick` are examples of APIs in this category. *Mid-Tier* refers to APIs with a score in the $[0.15, 0.5[$ range such

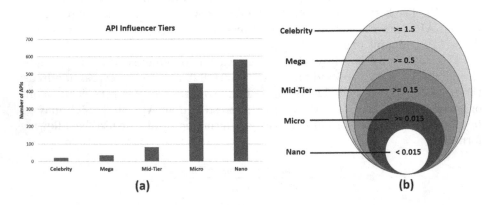

Fig. 2. Influencer tiers

as LinkedIn, Zillow and Evernote. *Mega* regroups APIs with a significant influence score $(AIS \in [0.5, 1.5[)$, such as Flickr, Last.fm, and Reddit. *Celebrity* represents APIs with the highest influence (AIS > 1.5). Celebrities appear in the highest number of mashups and repositories. They also subject to positive sentiments among developers. Examples of celebrities are Google Maps, Twitter and YouTube. Figure 2a shows that this tier has the lowest proportion of APIs, with about 20 identified APIs.

3.4   Influence Score Prediction

We compute the AIS score of an API using three features: number of mashups, number of repositories, and overall developers' sentiment. However, it is difficult for API providers to have direct control on those features to improve the adoption of their APIs by developers. To help API providers enhance the influence of their APIs, we conduct a statistical study to identify the most relevant API features that correlate the most to AIS scores. Once API providers understand which of the remaining features (other than number of mashups, repositories, and sentiment) impact the AIS score, they can come-up with a strategy to boost-up the influence of their APIs.

We use Non-Negative Least Squares (NNLS) regression [8] to learn a weight value for each API feature. NNLS assigns weights to features according to their correlation degree to AIS scores. The most relevant features are given high coefficients, while non relevant ones are given negative coefficients. NNLS replaces negative coefficients by 0. This will automatically get rid of non relevant features from the model. Figure 3 summarizes the coefficients assigned to each API feature. Features with the biggest coefficient values have the highest impact on AIS scores. For instance, the number of articles in ProgrammableWeb is strongly related to the AIS score. This shows that more articles published in the developer community may increase API influence. Figure 3 also states that StackOverflow features have little impact on AIS scores.

The next step is to define AIS prediction models. These models are useful to assign initial influence scores for newly deployed APIs, hence dealing with the traditional cold start problem. They also assist API providers in predicting the evolution of their API scores. We introduce three prediction models (Table 3). To evaluate and compare the models, we calculate the *adjusted R-squared* [14] and *Akaike Information Criterion* (AIC) [1]. The adjusted R-squared estimates the variance between predicted and real scores. AIC measures the goodness of the fit for the model. The model with the smallest AIC value and highest adjusted R-square is selected as the best-fitting model.

Table 3 summarizes our three prediction models. Model 1 uses all extracted features to predict the AIS score. It has a low adjusted R-squared value: 0.5788. Hence the model does not fit the trend perfectly. This is because AIS scores depend on developers' sentiments, which are hard to predict. To deal with this issue, we introduce the *adjusted AIS score* ($AIS_{adjusted}$). $AIS_{adjusted}$ is a variant of the original AIS score that eliminates developers' sentiments. The following formula computes API_i's adjusted AIS score.

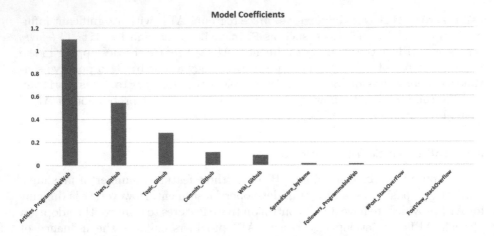

Fig. 3. Impact of API features on the AIS score

$$AIS_{adjusted_{(i)}} = \sum \#M_i + \#R_i$$

The second and third models predict the AIS adjusted scores. Model 3 uses all extracted features. Model 2 omits the features extracted from *StackOverflow* since our study shows that `StackOverflow` has little impact on API adoption across communities (Fig. 3). Both models display high adjusted R-squared: 0.77 for Model 2 and 0.78 for Model 3. The models also have low AIC values: 1346.347 for Model 1 and 1323.208 for Model 2. This makes both models suitable for predicting the adjusted AIS score, with a slight advantage to Model 3 as it uses more API features than Model 2.

4   Experiments

The goal of our experiments is to assess FAME's ability to accurately predict influencer APIs. We evaluate the second and third prediction models (Table 3) using five independent data-sets. The data-sets regroup APIs deployed during five different periods between 2005 to 2019. For each API, we compute the adjusted AIS score and use the models (2 and 3) to predict that score. We then compute the recall and precision for each data-set using both models.

The recall refers to the fraction of influencer APIs that are correctly identified within each data-set. It is the number of influencers that are successfully predicted divided by the number of all APIs that are identified as influencers. It can be also seen as the percentage of influencer APIs that are successfully predicted. Figure 4a shows that up to 86% and 88% of influencers are successfully recalled (i.e., predicted) by Model 2 and Model 3, respectively. Both models have a stable recall, but leveraging more features in Model 3 allows a better prediction than Model 2.

Table 3. Prediction models

	Prediction	Available Features	Number of Selected Features	Selected Features	Adjusted R-squared	AIC
Model 1	AIS	18 (SDA +UDA)	12 Features	➤ *ProgrammableWeb* #Articles, #Libraries, #Followers and ChangeLog ➤ *Google Search Engine* Spread Score by EndPoint ➤ *Hacker News* #Comments ➤ *GitHub* #Commits, #Users, #Wiki and #Topic ➤ *StackOverflow* #Post and Ave Post View	0.57	4400.073
Model 2	AIS-adjusted	15 (SDA)	7 Features	➤ *ProgrammableWeb* #Articles and #Followers ➤ *Google Search Engine* Spread Score by Name ➤ *GitHub* #Commits, #Users, #Wiki and #Topic	0.77	1346.347
Model 3	AIS-adjusted	18 (SDA+UDA)	9 Features	➤ *ProgrammableWeb* #Articles and #Followers ➤ *Google Search Engine* Spread Score by Name ➤ *GitHub* #Commits, #Users, #Wiki and #Topic ➤ *StackOverflow* #Post and Max(Post) View	0.78	1323.208

The precision checks the accuracy with which scores are predicted for APIs. It is the number of precisely predicted influencer APIs divided by all recalled APIs. It can be seen as the percentage of precisely recalled influencers. If the weight difference is less than a threshold value, the influencer is assumed to be precisely identified. We used 0.03 as a threshold; this value represents the average of the difference between the predicted and computed scores. Figure 4b shows that both models identify influencer APIs with up to 71% precision.

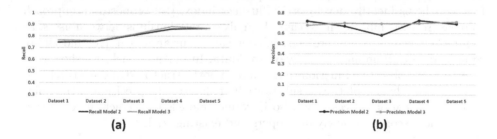

(a)   (b)

Fig. 4. Recall and precision

5 Related Work

The identification of influential nodes in distributed environments such as social networks and forums has been the subject of many research efforts [6,7,11,16]. Few research proposals [3,10] study influencers in software development. However, existing research considers developers as influencers *not* APIs. [11] proposes a methodology to identify influencer nodes that are likely to affect other nodes in social networks. It computes the centrality degree of nodes and analyzes node activities. [11] focuses on the position of nodes in the network. Our approach instead leverages both structured (e.g., number of mashups, number of articles) and unstructured (e.g., user feedback) across multiple developer platforms to identify influencers. We also show that influencer identification precision gets better as we leverage a larger number of features. [16] presents a study for finding influential authors on Twitter forums. It combines both user profile information and user interaction features with decision tree to identify influencer authors. Our approach identifies APIs as influencers *not* users. Moreover, we use a multi-objective function that combines multiple attributes collected from various sources. [7] proposes a study to understand influencers who lead development and dictate how projects evolve. It shows that analyzing influencer behaviors allows understanding the evolution of software ecosystem and even predict future evolution. The main focus of our approach is to identify influencer APIs and the attributes that contribute to their emergence, rather than assuming the existence of those influencers and studying their behavior. [2] shows that influence score depends on engagement, sentiment, and growth. [6] shows that originality and uniqueness of user content are crucial factors to identify influencers in Instagram. [2] and [6] rely mainly on social metrics to determine influencers. Our approach extends the analysis to encompass attributes from various sources. Besides, it considers APIs as influencers in programming platforms instead of users in social networks. [17] computes influence score for users across several social networks. It evaluates the quantity and quality of reactions a user action prompted to assess the extent to which the user is influential. [3] and [10] identify the most influential developers, repositories, technologies and programming languages in GitHub. [3] shows that the analysis of social networks, particularly the relations among developers, developers and repositories, and developers and followers helps identify developers' influencer index. [10] proposes an approach to measure user influence in Github. It analyzes relationships between users, as well as between users and projects. In contrast to our approach, [10] and [3] are restricted to GitHub and stackOverflow data. In our approach, we show that using a multi-objective function that combine both structured and unstructured features from diverse platforms substantially enhances the precision of the influencer identification process. We also introduce models to predict the evolution of influencer scores for newly developers and existing APIs.

6   Conclusion

We propose FAME (*inFluencer Apis in developer coMmunitiEs*), a novel approach for the identification and prediction of influencer APIs in service-oriented environments. To the best of our knowledge, FAME is the first influencer model that treats APIs as first-class citizens. We define influence as the degree to which an API is used in mashups and service-oriented applications. We extract and analyze several structured and unstructured features from various programming communities. We use the Stanford NLP parser to perform sentiment analysis and evaluate developers' opinions towards using APIs. Such opinions are expressed through posts in StackOverflow, commit comments in GitHub, and articles in ProgrammableWeb. We aggregate API features to compute influence scores and cluster APIs into influencer tiers according to those scores. We use Non-Negative Least Square (NNLS) regression to identify to most significant API features and predict the evolution of influence scores for newly deployed and existing APIs. Finally, we conduct extensive experiments on real-world and large data-sets extracted from multiple programming community platforms. Experiments reveal that the proposed approach predicts up to 87% influencer APIs.

References

1. Akaike, H.: A new look at the statistical model identification. In: Parzen, E., Tanabe, K., Kitagawa, G. (eds.) Selected Papers of Hirotugu Akaike. Springer Series in Statistics (Perspectives in Statistics), pp. 215–222. Springer, New York (1974). https://doi.org/10.1007/978-1-4612-1694-0_16
2. Arora, A., Bansal, S., Kandpal, C., Aswani, R., Dwivedi, Y.: Measuring social media influencer index-insights from facebook, twitter and instagram. J. Retail. Consum. Serv. **49**, 86–101 (2019)
3. Bana, R., Arora, A.: Influence indexing of developers, repositories, technologies and programming languages on social coding community github. In: 2018 Eleventh International Conference on Contemporary Computing (IC3), pp. 1–6 (2018)
4. Binzagr, F., Medjahed, B.: Crowdmashup: recommending crowdsourcing teams for mashup development. In: Pahl, C., Vukovic, M., Yin, J., Yu, Q. (eds.) ICSOC 2018. LNCS, vol. 11236, pp. 679–693. Springer, Cham (2018). https://doi.org/10.1007/978-3-030-03596-9_49
5. Bouguettaya, A., et al.: A service computing manifesto: the next 10 years. Commun. ACM **60**(4), 64–72 (2017)
6. Casaló, L.V., Flavián, C., Ibáñez-Sánchez, S.: Influencers on instagram: antecedents and consequences of opinion leadership. J. Bus. Res. (2018)
7. Farias, V., Wiese, I., dos Santos, R.P.: What characterizes an influencer in software ecosystems? IEEE Softw. **36**(1), 42–47 (2019)
8. Flammarion, N.: Stochastic approximation and least-squares regression, with applications to machine learning. PhD thesis, École Normale Supérieure, Paris, France (2017)
9. Gao, L., Yue, W., Xiong, X., Tang, J.: Discriminating topical influencers based on the user relative emotion. IEEE Access **7**, 100120–100130 (2019)
10. Hu, Y., Wang, S., Ren, Y., Choo, K.-K.R.: User influence analysis for github developer social networks. Expert Syst. Appl. **108**, 108–118 (2018)
11. Kim, E.S., Han, S.S.: An analytical way to find influencers on social networks and validate their effects in disseminating social games. In: 2009 International Conference on Advances in Social Network Analysis and Mining, ASONAM 2009, Athens, Greece, 20–22 July 2009, pp. 41–46 (2009)
12. Labbaci, H., Medjahed, B., Aklouf, Y., Malik, Z.: Follow the leader: a social network approach for service communities. In: Sheng, Q.Z., Stroulia, E., Tata, S., Bhiri, S. (eds.) ICSOC 2016. LNCS, vol. 9936, pp. 705–712. Springer, Cham (2016). https://doi.org/10.1007/978-3-319-46295-0_50

13. Liu, X., Kale, A., Wasani, J., (Cherie) Ding, C., Yu, Q.: Extracting, ranking, and evaluating quality features of web services through user review sentiment analysis. In: 2015 IEEE International Conference on Web Services, ICWS 2015, New York, NY, USA, 27 June–2 July 2015, pp. 153–160 (2015)
14. Miles, J.: R squared, adjusted R squared. Wiley StatsRef: Statistics Reference Online (2014)
15. Noor, T.H., Sheng, Q.Z., Ngu, A.H.H., Dustdar, S.: Analysis of web-scale cloud services. IEEE Internet Comput. **18**(4), 55–61 (2014)
16. Purohit, H., Ajmera, J., Joshi, S., Verma, A., Sheth, A.: Finding influential authors in brand-page communities. In: Sixth International AAAI Conference on Weblogs and Social Media (2012)
17. Rao, A., Spasojevic, N., Li, Z., Dsouza, T.: Klout score: measuring influence across multiple social networks. In: 2015 IEEE International Conference on Big Data (Big Data), pp. 2282–2289. IEEE (2015)

Latency-Aware Deployment of IoT Services in a Cloud-Edge Environment

Shouli Zhang[1,2,3]([✉]), Chen Liu[2,3], Jianwu Wang[4], Zhongguo Yang[2,3], Yanbo Han[1,2,3], and Xiaohong Li[1]

[1] Division of Intelligence and Computing, Tianjin University, Tianjin, China
zhangshoulia@163.com, xiaohongli@tju.edu.cn
[2] Beijing Key Laboratory on Integration and Analysis of Large-Scale Stream Data, North China University of Technology, Beijing, China
{liuchen, yangzhongguo, hanyanbo}@ncut.edu.cn
[3] Cloud Research Center, North China University of Technology, Beijing, China
[4] Department of Information Systems, University of Maryland, Baltimore County, Baltimore, MD 21250, USA
jianwu@umbc.edu

Abstract. Efficient scheduling of data elements and computation units can help to reduce the latency of processing big IoT stream data. In many cases, moving computation turns out to be more cost-effective than moving data. However, deploying computations from cloud-end to edge devices may face two difficult situations. First, edge devices usually have limited computing power as well as storage capability, and we need to selectively schedule computation tasks. Secondly, the overhead of stream data processing varies over time and makes it necessary to adaptively adjust service deployment at runtime. In this work, we propose a heuristics approach to adaptively deploying services at runtime. The effectiveness of the proposed approach is demonstrated by examining real cases of China's State Power Grid.

Keywords: Big IoT stream processing · Edge computing · Data overhead · Adaptive service deployment

1 Introduction

Today, lots of sensors have been deployed in various fields, producing large-scale sensor stream data. The typical stream data processing architecture nowadays relies on cloud-based data storage and processing techniques [1]. Such architecture may conceal big overhead of data movement and processing, and introduce latency that makes real-time data processing difficult to be achieved [2]. Edge computing has become attractive herein. It promotes that sensor data and its processing should be put close to the edge devices, as many of them have non-negligible computation capabilities [3, 4]. Many efforts have been made to integrate cloud and edge devices [5–7].

In our previous work [7], motivated by a real application scenario from the State Grid Corporation of China (SGCC), we tried to realize the cloud-edge integration with

© Springer Nature Switzerland AG 2019
S. Yangui et al. (Eds.): ICSOC 2019, LNCS 11895, pp. 231–236, 2019.
https://doi.org/10.1007/978-3-030-33702-5_17

proactive data services. Some lightweight services are moved to edge devices. The services collaborate to finish a task and form a data analysis flow by event routing. However, the data dependencies and data movement between services [8] introduce data overhead, both in terms of network traffic necessary to distribute the data, as well as extra storage space requirements. It can result in extra latency and become an important factor in making deployment decision. Besides, the data overhead can vary at runtime due to the uncertainty, fluctuation and spontaneous correlation of IoT streams. We intend to adapt to the fluctuation flexibly while scheduling composite deployments and satisfying other resource constraints.

In this paper, we propose an approach to dealing with the distinctive problem of deploying the variable stream dataflows with our former data service model. We propose a heuristics approach to adaptively deploying services at runtime through predicting the fluctuation. Based on the real datasets from SGCC, we evaluate our approach with two representative baseline approaches with extensive experiments to demonstrate the effectiveness.

2   Motivation Scenario and Problem

In China State Power Grid, the electric devices are apt to be affected by various disturbance sources and led to various power quality abnormal events, it is crucial to detect abnormal events and trigger protection on time. The China State Power Grid has deployed more than 20,000 sensors to monitor power quality. The real-time sensor stream data are collected and then transferred to the cloud via multi DATs[1]. DAT is one typical kind of edge devices that have remarkable but limited computing, storage and network capacity. With our previously proposed proactive data service model (PDS) [9], We have built a cloud-edge platform [7] which can reschedule some PDSs to DATs for realizing real-time detecting power quality abnormal events.

The service deployment strategy across cloud and edge directly affects the latency of an IoT application. Figure 1 shows different service deployment strategies for stream data analysis flow for identifying sources. The average latency of Fig. 1(a) is calculated as 513 ms, while the average latency of Fig. 1(b) is 350 ms. However, we find out that the overhead of data movement between services is large due to routing stream data among services. For example, as shown in Fig. 1(c), during the time range Δt_1, s_1 and s_5, s_2 and s_5, s_3 and s_6, the data overhead between them is 3.1 MB, 3.6 MB, and 3.8 MB respectively. Figure 1(c) is the service deployment strategy by considering the data overhead. Its latency is about 214 ms. It is smaller than above methods. This is because that the data overhead will result in latency both in terms of network traffic necessary to distribute the data, as well as extra storage space requirements. Deploying services with large data overhead on the same edge device can ignore the impact of this overhead on latency.

---

[1] DAT is the Data Acquisition Terminal are deployed on the electric transmission lines across the whole country. DAT is configured with a 32-bit embedded microprocessor, DSP chip, embedded Linux operation system and embedded JDK, etc.

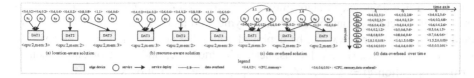

Fig. 1. Service deployment example with different approaches.

Furthermore, the data overhead can vary at runtime due to the peculiarities of uncertainty and fluctuation of sensor streams, which is as shown in Fig. 1(d). For example, based on service logs, we can predict that, during the time range Δt_2, the average data size between s_3 and s_6 changed to 0.14 MB, while the average data size between of s_4 and s_6 changed to 5.6 MB. The latency of Fig. 1(c) increased to 332 ms. Under this condition, the service deployment strategy should be reconfigured. A better deployment at this time is that, (s_4, s_6) should to be deployed onto DAT$_2$ after (s_3, s_6) have been finished. The latency of service redeployment is reduced to 221 ms.

3 The Adaptive Service Deployment Approach

The main idea to solve the problem in this paper is to adaptively deploy the services across cloud and edge at runtime according to the change of data overhead. The rationale is shown in Fig. 2.

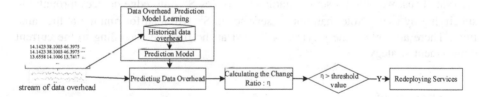

Fig. 2. The rationale of the approach.

The service monitoring system generates the real time data overhead of service, it can accumulate the factual data overhead value as historical data, and periodically trains the prediction model which is used to learn the change of data overhead. Then we can predict the data overhead in next time interval by the prediction model. For each service s_i, we construct a row vector $D(s_i) = \{d_1, d_2, \ldots d_l\}$ to represent the history of the data overhead in l consecutive time intervals. Our goal is to predict the values of $D(s_i)_{pre} = \{d_{l+1}, d_{l+2}, \ldots d_{l+k}\}$, where k is the number of predicted data overhead in next time intervals θ.

We define a change ratio as $\eta = \frac{\sum_{i=1}^{n} |d_{i+w} - d_i|}{n}$ for the data overhead which is the decision factor for service redeployment. Where d_i is the current value, d_{i+w} is the predicted value. If η has exceeded a given threshold value, it is the time to recalculate the deployment strategy by the deployment algorithm, then to redeploy the services.

The service deployment algorithm is realized based on the Genetic Algorithm. we use the binary coding composed of binary symbols 0 and 1 to encode the deployment candidates. If the service s_i can be deployed onto edge device, the $y_i = 1$, else $y_i = 0$. Thus $Y_i = \{y_1, y_2, \ldots y_i, \ldots y_n\}$ construct a chromosome, and a set of chromosomes form a population $\mathfrak{Y} = \{Y_0, \ldots Y_i, \ldots, Y_p\}$, p is the population size.

In every generation, an optimization function F gives the *fitness value F* for the jth chromosome Y_j in the population. In our approach, if the objective is to maximized the data overhead of subgraph with the constraint on resource consumption, the fitness function F can be defined as $F(Y_i) = \frac{1}{\sum_{s_i \in S} y_i \omega_{ij}}$, otherwise $F(Y_i) = \frac{1}{\sum_{s_i \in S} y_i \omega_{ij}} = 0$.

We use a roulette wheel to compute all the fitness value of chromosomes of the population. The chromosomes Y_j are chosen according to their probability by revolving a roulette in which the *j-th* part occupies percentage of it. We use $Pr(Y_j) = \frac{F(Y_j)}{\sum_{i=1}^{p} F(Y_i)}$ to represent the probability of selecting Y_j to produce new chromosomes for the next generation. We also use a penalty value of $\log_2(1 + \gamma F(Y_i))$ to each chromosome, for each constraint is violated.

For every generation, we repeat the steps: roulette wheel population selection from the previous generation's population; crossover to generate new chromosomes; mutation of these chromosomes and potential update of the best-fit chromosome based on fitness values for chromosomes in this population.

To realize the rationale, one challenge is that the cost of moving service from cloud to edge may be larger when repeatedly redeploying the services in very short time interval. Thus, we preset a set of candidate services S^C onto edge devices through the specifying by users. Note that, not all services in S^C will load for running at the same time. There are only some services will load at the runtime according to the current deployment strategy.

4　Experiment

The experiment environment is based on a cloud infrastructure and edge devices. 40 virtual machine (VM) instances interconnected with 1 GBs Ethernet to construct the cloud. 480 DATs are connected to the cloud with a bandwidth of 100 Mbps. The dataset in our experiment is the real sensor data collected from the power grid. There are total 5871 sensors. We have realized 1302 PDSs abstracts on cloud. We construct three kinds of SAGs using these PDSs: SAG_1 containing 10 PDSs as vertexes, SAG_2 containing 20 PDSs, SAG_3 holding 30 PDSs. We totally instantiate 620 SAGs based on three kinds of SAG.

We will conduct the following methods for stream processing: *the resource-aware approach (RA), the location-aware approach (LA), and our adaptive service deployment approach (ASDA)*. In the experiment, we vary the stream speed of sensors from 100, 200, 400, 800, to 1000 for services. We use the latency as the performance metrics.

Figure 3 shows the experiment results. The total average latency of *ASDA* is 32.19% less than RA. And the total average latency of *ASDA* is 18.35% less than *LA*. The experiment results prove that us method is more efficient than *RA* and *LA*. The reason is that *ASDA* can adaptively reconfigure the service deployment by predicting the fluctuation of data overhead between services. It helps to reduce the latency of SAGs by reducing the overhead of transferring and storing of stream data.

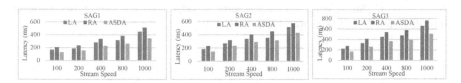

Fig. 3. Latency under different sensor streams

5 Conclusion

This paper proposed a distinctive problem of deploying the services in a cloud-edge environment to support the emerging real-time requirement of IoT applications. We have proposed a latency-aware approach to adaptively deploy services from cloud onto edge devices by predicting the fluctuation of data overhead. The effectiveness of the proposed approach is demonstrated by examining real cases of China's State Power Grid.

Acknowledgement. This work is supported by "National Natural Science Foundation of China (No:61672042), Models and Methodology of Data Services Facilitating Dynamic Correlation of Big Stream Data", "National Natural Science Foundation of China (No.61702014)", and "Beijing Natural Science Foundation (No. 4192020)".

References

1. He, B., Yang, M., Guo, Z., et al.: Comet: batched stream processing for data intensive distributed computing. In: Proceedings of the 1st ACM Symposium on Cloud Computing, Indianapolis, Indiana, USA, 2010, pp. 63–74. ACM (2010)
2. da Silva Veith, A., de Assunção, M.D., Lefèvre, L.: Latency-aware placement of data stream analytics on edge computing. In: Pahl, C., Vukovic, M., Yin, J., Yu, Q. (eds.) ICSOC 2018. LNCS, vol. 11236, pp. 215–229. Springer, Cham (2018). https://doi.org/10.1007/978-3-030-03596-9_14
3. Ahmed, A., Ahmed, E.: A survey on mobile edge computing. In: 10th IEEE International Conference on Intelligent Systems and Control, Coimbatore, India, pp. 1–8 (2016)
4. Shi, W., Jie, C., Quan, Z., et al.: Edge computing: vision and challenges. IEEE Internet Things J. **3**(5), 637–646 (2016)
5. Xu, X., Huang, S., Feagan, L., et al.: EAaaS: edge analytics as a service. In: 2017 IEEE International Conference on Web Services (ICWS). IEEE Computer Society (2017)

6. Varghese, B., Wang, N., Li, J., et al.: Edge-as-a-service: towards distributed cloud architectures. Adv. Parallel Comput. **32**, 784–793 (2017)
7. Zhang, S., Liu, C., Han, Y., et al.: Seamless integration of cloud and edge with a service-based approach. In: 2018 IEEE International Conference on Web Services (2018)
8. Ravindra, P., Khochare, A., Reddy, S.P., Sharma, S., Varshney, P., Simmhan, Y.: ECHO: An Adaptive Orchestration Platform for Hybrid Dataflows across Cloud and Edge. In: Maximilien, M., Vallecillo, A., Wang, J., Oriol, M. (eds.) ICSOC 2017. LNCS, vol. 10601, pp. 395–410. Springer, Cham (2017). https://doi.org/10.1007/978-3-319-69035-3_28
9. Han, Y., Liu, C., Su, S., et al.: A proactive service model facilitating stream data fusion and correlation. Int. J. Web Serv. Res. **14**(3), 1–16 (2017)

Trusted Data Integration in Service Environments: A Systematic Mapping

Senda Romdhani[1], Nadia Bennani[2], Chirine Ghedira-Guegan[4],
and Genoveva Vargas-Solar[3(✉)]

[1] University of Lyon, CNRS, University of Lyon 3, LIRIS, Lyon, France
senda.romdhani@univ-lyon3.fr
[2] LIRIS, INSA-Lyon, Villeurbanne, France
nadia.bennani@insa-lyon.fr
[3] University Grenoble Alpes, CNRS, Grenoble INP, LIG-LAFMIA,
38000 Grenoble, France
genoveva.vargas@imag.fr
[4] University of Lyon, CNRS, IAE - University of Lyon 3, LIRIS, Lyon, France
chirine.ghedira-guegan@univ-lyon3.fr

Abstract. This paper identifies and discusses trends and open issues regarding the use of trust in data-provisioning service environments, especially cloud environments. Applying a systematic review method [2], we propose a classification scheme used to provide a quantitative view of current trust solutions insisting in open issues. Finally, using analysis results, we give the general lines of an approach for improving data provisioning in multi-cloud using Service Level Agreement (SLA) and proposing the notion of multi-level trust.

Keywords: Trust · Data-provisioning services · Service environments · Multi-cloud · Service level agreement

1 Introduction

In recent years, data-provisioning service environments ranging from Service Oriented Architectures (SOA) and cloud architectures have become widely used provisioning environments [1]. The cloud eases the provisioning by providing dynamically scalable and virtualized resources as services [3] under a pay as you go model. The process of making data available in trustworthy conditions using the cloud is significantly challenging. Particularly because services are deployed under multi-tenant and multi-layer configurations.

In order to illustrate these challenges, let us consider the following e-health scenario. Assume that, for preparing a surgery, a doctor needs to have information about her patient including laboratory analysis, blood pressure etc. This information is produced by several actors participating in patients medical control (e.g., chemist, cardiologist, smart devices etc.). Consider that these actors use different clouds for storing and giving access to their data. A data integration tool can provide a global vision of these data to the doctor guided by quality

Funded by SUMMIT (http://summit.imag.fr) of the Auvergne Rhone Alpes region.

requirements specified in SLA. The challenge lies in consuming and composing data from cloud services with different SLA properties (e.g., QoS, reliability) and that provide data under different conditions and quality properties (e.g., timeliness, security). These properties depend on the way data services were developed and on those added by the clouds where they are deployed (e.g. availability, data replication, security measures etc.). Besides, the offered QoS specified in SLAs generally fluctuates due to the uncertainty and dynamics of the cloud and this explains the need for a quality warranty.

Guiding the data integration process by adding a trust management dimension as quality warranty should overpass the QoS uncertainty and improve the integration's result. Thus, by evaluating the trust level of data provisioning services and their composition it is possible to perform a reliable integration process.

The objective of our research being to identify the trends and open issues regarding trusted data integration, we deem necessary first conducting a comprehensive analysis on trust in data-provisioning service environments especially in the cloud and on the role of SLA in providing trust. In this context, the main contribution of this paper is a classification scheme that results from applying a systematic review method [2] which consists of 5 inter-dependant steps including: (i) Setting a research scope, (ii) retrieving candidate research papers from online databases, (iii) selecting relevant papers to answer research questions, (iv) defining a classification scheme, and (v) Performing statistical analysis. Based our systematic review study we propose the general lines of aspects to be considered for providing a trusted data integration solution by composing trustworthy provisioning services on multi-cloud settings. The remainder of this paper is as follows: Sect. 2 describes our mapping study. Section 3 gives a quantitative analysis, identifies open issues and present our solution. Section 4 concludes the paper and discusses future work.

2   Trust Challenges in Service Based Data-Provisioning

The aim of our systematic mapping is to (i) Categorize and quantify research contributions on trust in service environments and especially cloud computing. (ii) Categorize the key contributions of SLA-based research works. (iii) Discover open issues and limitations in existing work. Our study is guided by three research questions:

RQ1. How have published papers on trust evolved towards the cloud and other service environments? This question is devoted to identify trust solutions evolution towards the cloud, the research trends and contributions.

RQ2. What are the most and the least addressed evaluation targets and how are they combined? Trust can be associated to different entities defined as evaluation target. This question aims to determine the frequency of addressing entities implied in the data integration process in service environments and whether trust has been simultaneously considered for more than one entity.

RQ3. Have SLAs been used and how was it related to trust? The question aims to determine whether SLA's have been used to evaluate trust and if so, expose contributions.

2.1 Conducting Papers' Search and Screening

This step consisted in collecting papers from three online databases: IEEE, ACM, and Science Direct. A set of keywords was chosen using taxonomies and topics from conferences considered influential in the scientific community. We used the following general query for searching papers and retrieved a total of 3351 papers.

Trust AND (*multi-cloud* OR *cloud* OR *service*)

As a result of the filtering process specified in the review method, only 446 papers were included. Note that this study is normally influenced by various factors like the choice of keywords used to define the query, the way they are combined into a conjunctive and disjunctive expression and the selection of databases.

2.2 Key-Wording Using Abstracts

This step consists in analyzing selected papers and key-wording using frequent terms derived from abstracts. First, the frequent terms are considered as facets and then each facet is organized into dimensions forming a classification scheme. Our scheme defines 5 facets for classifying trust challenges[1]:

Evaluation Environment: This facet proposes 3 dimensions to classify data-provisioning service environments including, *single cloud*, *multi-cloud* (e.g. hybrid cloud, collaborative clouds etc.) and *service environment* (e.g. SOA).

Evaluation Target: According to our study a (trust) evaluation target can be a *service provider*, a *service user*, a *composite service*, a *service* or *data*.

SLA: Groups dimensions describing the actions performed on SLAs w.r.t trust evaluation solutions namely works that *extend SLA* or that propose some *trust evaluation metrics* or strategies for computing and *monitoring* SLA.

Contribution: Groups the dimensions that characterize the type of contributions in papers. It classifies proposals into five dimensions, namely, models, frameworks, methods, approaches and tools.

Validation Approach: This facet include 5 dimensions namely *experiments*, *comparisons*, *benchmarks*, *scenarios* and *use cases*.

2.3 Data Extraction and Mapping Process: Quantitative Analysis

RQ1. How have published papers on trust evolved towards the cloud and other service provisioning environments? Combining the facets Contribution, Evaluation Environment and Validation Approach, we observe contributions' trends on trust in the cloud (Fig. 1). The resulting bubble chart shows that most research

---

[1] For more information and references please use this link: https://drive.google.com/drive/folders/17SW_e8kbrROtpu0VTjNnqN9u1vQ3scdp?usp=sharing.

papers propose trust models and that experimentation (77%) is the most used way for validating models. According to our study, few solutions address trust in multi-cloud environments (5,8%).

RQ2. What are the most and the least addressed evaluation targets in each service environment and how are they combined? The facets Evaluation, Environment and Evaluation Target (Fig. 2) put the lights on the frequency of addressing each evaluation target per service environment. We can observe that most research contributions focused on evaluating the trustworthiness of services (35% cloud services). The results also show that little attention has been given to composite services and data and that are mostly addressed for a single cloud and other service environments. It seems that trust in data integration remains an open issue when combined with multi-cloud.

Some papers addressed trust evaluation on more than one evaluation target simultaneously. Nevertheless, this multi-evaluation concerns at best two-levels.

RQ3. Were SLAs used in these publications and how was it related to trust? According to our quantitative analysis, we found that only 25 papers used SLA for trust evaluation. The facets SLA and Evaluation Environment give elements for determining which actions have been applied on SLA in each environment (Fig. 2). The results shows that about 50% of proposals defined a set of SLA trust metrics. We can see that 10 papers proposed an SLA monitoring solution. These contributions are mostly deployed on single cloud. We can conclude from the results that there is merely no added new dimensions in SLA specific for trust evaluation and that papers tend to use the standard SLA form.

3   Open Issues and Outlook

Our systematic review shows that trust is an important property considered by proposals dealing with data provision, services, and the (multi)-cloud. Still, there are open issues regarding trusted data integration as it remains unexplored in multi-cloud environments. As explained in our scenario, data integration combines trust issues from data (data providers) and from the integration process itself which uses composite services and the cloud. Thereby we conclude that trusted data integration on multi-cloud is important and must consider 3 trust levels: data, service and cloud. Yet, current trust solutions do not cover the 3 trust levels simultaneously (see Sect. 2). Our work will propose a trusted data service composition algorithm based on SLA to compute query results considering all the chain trustworthiness. We also identify as promising research area the need of enhancing SLA beyond cloud resources quality. To do so, it is important to identify the set of data integration requirements and the missing information in SLA that can lead to a three-dimensional trust solution.

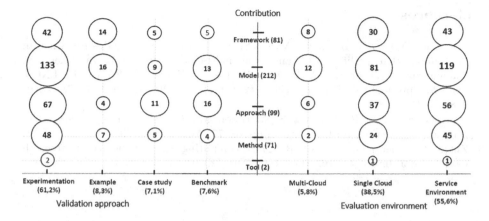

Fig. 1. Contribution trends on trust in the cloud

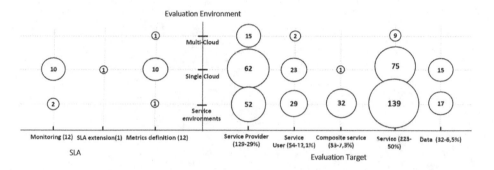

Fig. 2. Dealing with trust on different evaluation targets using SLA

4   Conclusion and Future Work

A multi-cloud is a collaborative environment where service providers can increase their access to multiple cloud resources and tune their conditions. This collaboration generates the proliferation of data-provisioning services offering to end users heterogeneous SLAs. This facility may generate doubts for users who delegated data management to the cloud and they may want some trust warranties (e.g., completeness of data, resource availability etc.).

This paper aimed at presenting a systematic mapping study about trust in data provisioning environments and especially the cloud. It identified trends and open issues and presented the general lines of a multi-level trust-based data integration solution. In our ongoing work, we intend to develop a solution by focusing on trust in the cloud and also study SLAs in more depth to adapt them and use them to guide trusted data integration.

References

1. Carvalho, D.A.S., Neto, P.A.S., Vargas-Solar, G., Bennani, N., Ghedira, C.: Can data integration quality be enhanced on multi-cloud using SLA? In: Chen, Q., Hameurlain, A., Toumani, F., Wagner, R., Decker, H. (eds.) DEXA 2015. LNCS, vol. 9262, pp. 145–152. Springer, Cham (2015). https://doi.org/10.1007/978-3-319-22852-5_13
2. Petersen, K., Feldt, R., Mujtaba, S., Mattsson, M.: Systematic mapping studies in software engineering. In: Ease, vol. 8, pp. 68–77. ACM, Italy (2008)
3. Zhang, Q., Cheng, L., Boutaba, R.: Cloud computing: state-of-the-art and research challenges. J. Internet Serv. Appl. 1(1), 7–18 (2010)

CSI2: Cloud Server Idleness Identification by Advanced Machine Learning in Theories and Practice

Jun Duan[1(✉)], Guangcheng Li[2], Neeraj Asthana[1], Sai Zeng[1], Ivan Dell'Era[1],
Aman Chanana[1], Chitra Agastya[1], William Pointer[1], and Rong Yan[2]

[1] IBM T. J. Watson Research Center,
1101 Kitchawan Rd, Yorktown Heights, NY 10598, USA
{jun.duan,neeraj.asthana,Aman.Chanana,Chitra.S.Agastya}@ibm.com,
{saizeng,ivd,pointer}@us.ibm.com
[2] IBM China Research Lab, 8 Dongbeiwang Western Rd, Beijing 100193, China
{liguangc,yanrong}@cn.ibm.com

Abstract. Studies show that virtual machines (VMs) in cloud are easily forgotten with non-productive status. This incurs unnecessary cost for cloud tenants and resource waste for cloud providers. As a solution to this problem, we present our Cloud Server Idleness Identification (CSI2) system. The CSI2 system collects data from the servers in cloud, performs analytics against the dataset to identify the idle servers, then provides suggestions to the owners of the idle servers. Once the confirmation from the owners are received, the idle servers are deleted or archived. We not only design and implement the CSI2 system, but also bring it alive into production environment.

How to accurately identify the idleness in cloud is the challenging part of this problem, because there is a trade-off between the cost saving and the user experience. We build a machine learning model to handle this challenge. In addition to that, we also build an advanced tool based on Bayesian optimization (BO) to help us finely tune the hyperparameters of the models. It turns out that our finely tuned models works accurately, successfully handling the aforementioned conflict, and outperforms its predecessors with a F1 score of 0.89.

Keywords: Classification · Machine learning · Cloud idleness · Bayesian optimization

1 Introduction

Recent study [1] shows that more than 30% of servers in enterprise data centers are "comatose", meaning that these servers are not being used for any productive work in their organizations. A number of techniques have been proposed to address the challenge of detecting virtual machines that appear to have low computing resource utilization [2,3] and consolidate them using resource oversubscription [4,5]. However, resource utilization can be distorted by a couple of

© Springer Nature Switzerland AG 2019
S. Yangui et al. (Eds.): ICSOC 2019, LNCS 11895, pp. 243–248, 2019.
https://doi.org/10.1007/978-3-030-33702-5_19

common situations. For example, enterprises invest to make sure their IT infrastructures are secured, highly available, and resilient. In order to do that, a set of IT software/agents are deployed to the target servers to perform IT operations like virus scan, backup, configurable changes, remediation, etc. Without any productive workloads deployed or run on the target servers, those tools can sometimes consume very significant resource and be perceived as "productive". On the opposite side, for scenarios like elasticity to scale in and out the resource, resiliency, high availability, some servers are designed to be in standby modes with very low resource utilization, but those servers might be (incorrectly) perceived as "non-productive" if we only look at resource utilization. In order to correctly classify servers in productive or non-productive usage, we need to understand *the business application related activities*, much beyond the resource consumption.

In order to handle this issue, we present our AI based Cloud Server Idleness Identification (CSI2) system, which smartly distinguish the productive and non-productive servers.

2   System Design

In this section, we introduce the high-level design of the entire CSI2 system.

The CSI2 system was firstly released into production environment on October 26th, 2018. The system works with IBM's internal cloud provisioning platform, iRIS-IMS, which manages multiple geographically distributed data centers globally. The system (1) collects data from the virtual machines on the cloud, (2) accepts end users' inputs regarding the status of their virtual machines, (3) performs analytics based on the collected data and accepted inputs and provides suggestions on the idle virtual machines. Therefore, the CSI2 system is composed of three modules, corresponding to the three functionalities. They are the data collection, the web portal, and the analyzer, respectively. The data collection module regularly monitors the virtual machines, actively collect data which is relevant to the idleness of the machine. The web portal is the interface between

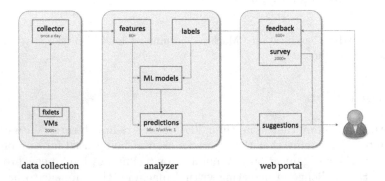

Fig. 1. The overview of the CSI2 system. The CSI2 system is composed of three modules: the data collection, the web portal, and the analyzer.

the CSI2 system and the end users. The analyzer lies at the heart of the CSI2 system. On one hand, the analyzer extracts the features from the data which is gathered by the data collection module. On the other hand, it accepts the feedback from the web portal. Next, the accepted feedback is used to label the extracted features. The three modules of the CSI2 system is illustrated in Fig. 1.

3   Implementation

The features we extracted from the raw data can be roughly classified into three categories. The first category generally provides basic information of the virtual machines, such as CPU time, memory consumption, network throughput, etc. What is unique in the CSI2 system is the other two categories, which provides insights into the running processes and user activities, respectively. We list a set of representative features that belong to these two unique categories in Table 1.

Table 1. Representative features in the CSI2 system

Symbol	Description
Features regarding running processes	
F_%MEM_IP	Memory usage of important processes
F_%MEM_IP_S	Memory usage of important processes over that of the server
F_%CPU_IP	CPU usage of important processes
F_%CPU_IP_S	CPU usage of important processes over that of the server
Features regarding user activities	
F_AVGLAHR	Average Login durations
F_MAXLAHR	Max login durations
#DTLA	Num of daytime login activities
SSH_CONN	SSH connections

In order to train the model, we need to select a subset from the 60+ features that are extracted from the raw data. We use correlation analysis to select a set of features among the 60+ to train our models. In addition to the automatic methods, we also manually checkout the selected feature set and make corrections. For example, we manually exclude the feature "TIMESTAMP" from the selected feature set. Before the CSI2 system is alive, we collect the feedback from the user surveys, and use the feedback to label the features. After that, we use the labeled dataset to train our model.

The metric we use to guide the training is based on the business impact of the CSI2 system. In order to maximize the business impact of the CSI2 system, we need to identify as many as "real" idle virtual machines, i.e. actual idle virtual machines that are also predicted as idle virtual machines. The "real" idle virtual machines are presented in Table 2 as "true negative".

Table 2. The confusion matrix of the machine leaning models

	actual active	actual idle
predicted active	true positive (happy users)	false positive (missed)
predicted idle	false negative (unhappy users)	true negative (identified)

Ideally, we should identify all the actual idle virtual machines, without any actual idle virtual machines been classified as active. This way, we can achieve maximized monetary saving. But in practice, a small fraction will be missed because of misclassification. This portion listed in Table 2 as "false positive".

Similarly, we should classify all actual active virtual machines as active. Otherwise, a small portion of the users will be bothered by suggestions saying that their systems are idle but they are actively in use. But in reality, this small fraction almost always exist because of the imperfection of the models. This fraction is shown in Table 2 as "false negative".

We know there is always a trade-off between the recall and precision of any machine learning model. In other words, the false positives and the false negatives can not be simultaneously minimized. In the CSI2 system, we fight with this trade-off. We reduce the number of missed actual virtual machines for greater business impact with moderate degradation of the user experience.

In addition to the tuning of the models by human expertise, we also make further adjustment of the hyperparameters, using our advanced tuning tool. We have developed a toolkit named AI Performance Advisor, which uses AI techniques, specifically Bayesian Optimization ([6]), to automatically identify optimal parameters set for different workloads including identifying the optimal hyperparameters for AI workloads, the goal of this tool is to find optimal or near optimal tunable parameters setting within predefined constrains like time or iterations. The design of AI performance advisor is quite flexible, it could be used to tune any application, from AI workloads, simple web servers to complex distributed micro-service applications. AI performance advisor takes the system to be optimized as a black box, the only interface between AI performance advisor and the system to be optimized is the evaluation interface: AI performance advisor will configure the suggested tunable parameters sets to the target system and will query the performance metrics of different sets of the tunable parameters, but it does not obtain gradient information or any internals of the system to be tuned.

4   Performance Evaluation

We tuned the models in the analyzer using human expertise first. We then apply our Bayesian optimization tool to finely tune the models, the performance is shown as Fig. 2.

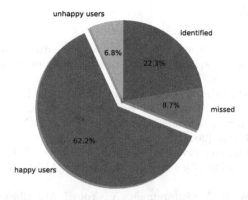

Fig. 2. The performance of the finely tuned CSI2 models, with 0.90 recall, 0.88 precision, and 0.89 F1 score.

We compared the performance with other approaches to identify idleness in cloud environment. For example, graph based approaches [7,8], rule based approaches [11–13], and AI based approaches [9,10]. We pick some of the most advanced approaches as the baseline to compare with the CSI2 system, such as Garbo [8], Pleco [7], and iCSI [9]. It turns out that CSI2 outperforms all these predecessors, with a F1 score of 0.89. Garbo, Pleco, and iCSI have F1 score of 0.68, 0.74, and 0.85, respectively.

The CSI2 system was first released to production on Oct 26th. The first launch identified 400+ idle servers. As of Dec 11th, 120 servers were marked for deletion by server owners which translates to the cost savings between 250 K to 500K. The potential estimated yearly savings is estimated as about 2.2 million US dollars.

5   Conclusions

Virtual machines are easy to be created and easier to be forgotten, resulting in considerable non-productive/idle servers in the cloud. In this paper, we proposed our solution to this problem: the Cloud Server Idleness Identification (CSI2) system. We designed, implemented and made it alive for our infrastructure provisioning platform. Lying at the heart of the CSI2 system is the machine learning model, which is trained by our unique set of features, and then finely tuned by our home made Bayesian optimization tool. Equipped with these models, the CSI2 system successfully handles the conflict between the cost saving and the user experience. That is, it identifies significant amount of idle servers with reduced number of false negatives. From theoretical perspective, the models of the analyzer outperforms its predecessors. From business perspective, the CSI2 system has been running in production environment for a couple of months, bring real-life monetary cost saving everyday for our globally distributed data centers.

References

1. Koomey, J., Taylor, J.: 30 percent of servers are 'comatose'. http://anthesisgroup. com/wp-content/uploads/2015/06/Case-Study_DataSupports30PercentComatose Estimate-FINAL_06032015.pdf
2. Stoess, J., Lang, C., Bellosa, F.: Energy management for hypervisor-based virtual machines. In: 2007 USENIX Annual Technical Conference on Proceedings of the USENIX Annual Technical Conference, ATC 2007, USENIX Association, Berkeley, CA, USA, pp. 1:1–1:14 (2007)
3. Wu, H., et al.: Automatic cloud bursting under fermicloud. In: 2013 International Conference on Parallel and Distributed Systems (ICPADS), pp. 681–686, December 2013
4. Wood, T., Shenoy, P., Venkataramani, A., Yousif, M.: Black-box and gray-box strategies for virtual machine migration. In: Proceedings of the 4th USENIX Conference on Networked Systems Design and Implementation, NSDI 2007, USENIX Association, Berkeley, CA, USA, p. 17 (2007)
5. Breitgand, D., Epstein, A.: Improving consolidation of virtual machines with risk-aware bandwidth oversubscription in compute clouds. In: INFOCOM, 2012 Proceedings IEEE, pp. 2861–2865, March 2012
6. Snoek, J., Larochelle, H., Adams, R.P.: Practical bayesian optimization of machine learning algorithms. In: NIPS (2012)
7. Shen, Z., Young, C.C., Zeng, S., Murthy, K., Bai, K.: Identifying resources for cloud garbage collection. In: 2016 12th International Conference on Network and Service Management (CNSM), pp. 248–252. IEEE, October 2016
8. Cohen, N., Bremler-Barr, A.: Garbo: Graph-based cloud resource cleanup. In: 2015 ACM Symposium on Cloud Computing (SoCC 2015), Kohala Coast, Hawaii, USA, August 2015
9. Kim, I.K., Zeng, S., Young, C., Hwang, J., Humphrey, M.: iCSI: a cloud garbage VM collector for addressing inactive VMs with machine learning. In: 2017 IEEE International Conference on Cloud Engineering (IC2E), pp. 17–28. IEEE, April 2017
10. Kim, I.K., Zeng, S., Young, C., Hwang, J., Humphrey, M.: A supervised learning model for identifying inactive VMs in private cloud data centers. In: Proceedings of the Industrial Track of the 17th International Middleware Conference, p. 2. ACM, December 2016
11. Zhang, B., Al Dhuraibi, Y., Rouvoy, R., Paraiso, F., Seinturier, L.: CloudGC: recycling idle virtual machines in the cloud. In: 2017 IEEE International Conference on Cloud Engineering (IC2E), pp. 105–115. IEEE, April 2017
12. Devoid, S., Desai, N., Hochstein, L.: Poncho: enabling smart administration of full private clouds. In: LISA, pp. 17–26, November 2013
13. Baek, H., Srivastava, A., Van der Merwe, J.: Cloudvmi: virtual machine introspection as a cloud service. In: 2014 IEEE International Conference on Cloud Engineering (IC2E), pp. 153–158. IEEE, March 2014

Services in the Cloud

An Energy Efficient and Interference Aware Virtual Machine Consolidation Algorithm Using Workload Classification

Rachael Shaw[(✉)], Enda Howley, and Enda Barrett

College of Engineering and Informatics, National University of Ireland,
Galway, Ireland
{r.shaw4,ehowley,enda.barrett}@nuigalway.ie

Abstract. Inefficient resource usage is one of the greatest causes of high energy consumption in cloud data centers. Virtual Machine (VM) consolidation is an effective method for improving energy related costs and environmental sustainability for modern data centers. While dynamic VM consolidation can improve energy efficiency, virtualisation technologies cannot guarantee performance isolation between co-located VMs resulting in interference issues. We address the problem by introducing a energy and interference aware VM consolidation algorithm. The proposed algorithm utilizes the predictive capabilities of a Machine Learning (ML) model in an attempt to classify VM workloads to make more informed consolidation decisions. Furthermore, using recent workload data from Microsoft Azure we present a comparative study of two popular classification algorithms and select the model with the best performance to incorporate into our proposed approach. Our empirical results demonstrate how our approach improves energy efficiency by 31% while also reducing service violations by 69%.

Keywords: Energy efficiency · Interference aware · Virtual machine consolidation · Machine Learning · Classification

1 Introduction

Cloud computing offers a pool of elastic resources charged on a pay-as-you-go basis with the capacity to execute diverse workloads including long running background jobs to real-time web applications [1,2]. Energy related costs and environmental sustainability have been identified as major concerns in the operation of data centers today. Research has revealed that by 2020 U.S data centers alone are estimated to consume 140 billion kilowatt-hours yearly, costing 13 billion dollars per year and generating carbon emissions of 150 million metric tons [3].

R. Shaw—This work is supported by the Irish Research Council through the Government of Ireland Postgraduate Scholarship Scheme.

© Springer Nature Switzerland AG 2019
S. Yangui et al. (Eds.): ICSOC 2019, LNCS 11895, pp. 251–266, 2019.
https://doi.org/10.1007/978-3-030-33702-5_20

In particular, research has shown that inefficient resource utilisation is one of the leading causes of high energy consumption in data center deployments [4].

VM consolidation is one approach that can improve resource management and data center efficiency by using live migration to optimize the distribution of VMs across the data center while also satisfying user specified Service Level Agreements (SLA) [7]. However, one limitation of virtualisation technologies is that they do not guarantee performance isolation [10]. Consequently, while energy consumption can be reduced through dynamic VM consolidation algorithms, performance degradation can result from interference effects between co-located VMs. As a result, balancing energy efficiency and the delivery of service guarantees through VM consolidation becomes a more complex issue in multi-tenant environments. Existing approaches need to be adapted to consider the implications of co-located interference effects. While VM consolidation approaches often have different core objectives the majority of VM consolidation algorithms focus on minimizing the number of active hosts in the data center, however, performance interference issues between co-located VMs are not considered [4,8,11]. These approaches are less effective as they do not accurately represent performance degradation caused by resource contention between co-located VMs. Prior to consolidating VMs it would be beneficial to consider the VM's resilience to interference from other co-located workloads to improve the delivery of service guarantees. Other works in the literature propose interference aware consolidation algorithms which focus on the delivery of service guarantees but are not specifically energy driven [12,13].

In this paper, we propose a Predictive Interference and Energy Aware (PIEA) consolidation algorithm to improve both energy efficiency and performance for multi-tenant cloud environments. Leveraging the predictive capabilities of an Artificial Neural Network (ANN) our approach attempts to classify VM workloads into two groups namely delay-insensitive and interactive based on their resource usage features. Our algorithm consolidates delay-insensitive VMs more aggressively, tightly packing them together as they are generally more robust to interference issues [21], while interactive workloads requiring low response time and high performance are consolidated in such a way to reduce direct contention for resources between other similar workloads on the host.

We expect this work to advance the state-of-the-art in three regards:

- Our work focuses on improving the VM consolidation problem by attempting to classify VM workloads while considering both energy efficiency and interference issues between co-located VMs.
- We compare the accuracy of two popular classification algorithms namely an ANN and Support Vector Machine (SVM) and demonstrate their application in classifying VM workloads to resolve the VM consolidation problem. We also propose the PIEA consolidation algorithm and show its ability to achieve improved energy efficiency and performance.
- To the best of our knowledge our work is one of the first to apply ANN and SVM classifiers to the recent workload data released by the Microsoft Azure's

public cloud platform. We also compare our solution to a widely known energy aware consolidation heuristic which has shown to deliver good results [6].

The remainder of this paper is structured as follows: Sect. 2 discusses related work and background material. Section 3 formulates the research problem and the proposed solution. In Sect. 4 we evaluate the accuracy of two popular classification techniques and select an appropriate model to incorporate into our consolidation strategy. Section 5 presents our experimental results. Lastly, Sect. 6 concludes the paper.

2   Related Research and Background

This section discusses related research while also providing the necessary background material for the classification techniques that have been compared in this work.

2.1   Virtual Machine Consolidation

Over the last number of years VM consolidation has gained widespread attention in the literature. Heuristic based methodologies are the most commonly used due to their simplicity and their ability to deliver good results. Lee et al. [4] proposed two task consolidation heuristics which seek to maximize resource utilisation while considering active and idle energy consumption. Verma et al. [5] presented a power and migration cost aware placement controller which aims to dynamically minimize energy consumption and migration costs while maintaining service guarantees. Beloglazov et al. [11] proposed the Power Aware heuristic which allocates VMs to the most power efficient hosts first. Recently, more efforts have also been made to develop consolidation approaches using sophisticated ML algorithms. Farahnakian et al. [8] introduced a predictive VM consolidation approach which employs a K-nearest neighbours forecasting methodology. Nguyen et al. [9] employed Multiple Linear Regression (MLR) to predict over and under-loaded server capacity and demonstrated how it can be integrated with existing consolidation solutions to improve energy consumption. Shaw et al. [15] proposed a predictive anti-correlated VM consolidation algorithm which also considers optimal data transfer times. These works focus on improving resource usage and energy efficiency in the data center, however, they do not consider performance degradation due to interference issues between co-located VMs. Xu et al. [12] introduced i-Aware, a heuristic based approach which focuses on minimizing interference during and after migration has occurred. Verboven et al. [14] proposed an interference aware approach for resource intensive applications. Their approach uses performance prediction and application clustering. Jersak et al. [13] proposed an approach that considers adjustable VM interference thresholds. While these works advocate the importance of managing performance interference issues when consolidating VMs on a host, energy efficiency is not the core objective. Our work proposes a novel algorithm which attempts to improve both energy efficiency and interference issues using predictive modelling to classify workloads for a more holistic approach. Studies which are the most similar to our approach include the work of Sampaio et al. [10] and Moreno et al. [1]. Sampaio et al. proposed an interference and power aware heuristic based solution. Our work differs in two regards. Firstly, our methodology is based on a ANN learning algorithm which is a state-of-the-art technique for many different problems and secondly, we use recent data released from Microsoft Azure's public cloud platform to train our ML models. Moreno et al. also attempts to classify workloads to improve energy consumption and interference. However, our work provides on evaluation on the performance of two popular classification algorithms while also using recent data released from the Microsoft Azure cloud platform to train our algorithms.

2.2 Classification

Classification techniques have been successfully applied to many areas in the ML literature including intrusion detection, image classification and text characterization [16]. ANNs and SVMs are two of the most widely used non-linear classification algorithms known for their predictive accuracy and ability to model complex real world problems [14,17]. Given the complex relationship between cloud workloads and resource usage metrics, these two non-linear algorithms are suitable for our needs. A brief description of these techniques is outlined below.

Artificial Neural Networks are a state-of-the-art learning technique for many different problems including classification, control and online and offline learning [18]. One of the most popular ANN classifiers is a feedforward neural network [17]. The network consists of numerous interconnected computational nodes organized into an input layer, one or more hidden layers and an output layer. During the training process the network receives data through the input layer. These values are fed to the neurons in the hidden layer each of which is characterized by a set of weighted connections. The network calculates the sum of the weighted signals for each neuron u_k as given in Eq. (1).

$$u_k = \sum_{j=1}^{m} w_{kj} x_j. \tag{1}$$

where $\{x_1, x_2, ..., x_m\}$ are the input signals of neuron k and $\{w_{k1}, w_{k2}, ..., w_{km}\}$ are the connection weights. An activation function is applied to the output signal of each neuron which transforms the range of the signal to a value between 0 and 1. The most widely used activation function is the sigmoid function as defined in Eq. (2).

$$\varphi(u_k) = \frac{1}{1 + \exp(-a u_k)}. \tag{2}$$

where a is the slope, u_k is the activation value for neuron k and $exp()$ is the exponential function. Once the signal has been propagated through the network it generates the probability of the input features belonging to class A or class B given that this is a binary classification problem. The output node with the highest probability is selected and is compared to the target output class to calculate the error term δ_k. The popular backpropagation algorithm [18] is used to propagate the error back through the network in order to update the weighted connections.

Support Vector Machines. SVM are a popular alternative model to an ANN. This learning algorithm is capable of modelling complex real world problems with data that has many input features even if only a relatively small data set is available to train the model [14]. Unlike an ANN, SVMs seek to find the optimal hyperplane that maximizes the margin between the two classes using a subset of the training examples H known as the Support Vectors [19]. These data points tend to be the most difficult to classify and have a direct influence on the optimum location of the separation boundary. The optimal hyperplane is one that satisfies the following equation:

$$w * x + b = 0. \tag{3}$$

where w is the weight vector, x are the feature values and b is the bias parameter. The classification of a sample feature vector x_i is denoted below [20]:

$$y_i = sign\left(\sum_{h=1}^{H} \alpha_h y_h s_h x_i + b\right). \tag{4}$$

where α_h is the Lagrange multiplier used to find the optimal hyperplane, y_h is the classification of the support vector h, s_h is defined as the sample vector for support vector h and b is the bias. Kernel functions can be used to generate non-linear SVMs which transforms data into a higher dimensional space, generating a clearer separation boundary between distinct classes. The non-linear classification function can now be defined as [20]:

$$y_i = sign\left(\sum_{h=1}^{H} \alpha_h y_h K(s_h, x_i) + b\right). \tag{5}$$

3   Energy and Interference Aware VM Consolidation

In this work we consider interference issues between co-located VMs as an important aspect of the VM consolidation problem. Balancing the distribution of VM workloads across available hosts in a multi-tenant environment while also seeking improved energy consumption is a challenging issue. Energy efficiency optimization and the delivery of application performance guarantees are conflicting objectives. By consolidating a large number of VMs on to a smaller number of hosts energy wastage can be mitigated, however, performance degradation can also occur due to interference and resource contention between co-located

VMs [10]. To overcome this issue, prior to placing a VM on a host a more plausible consolidation algorithm should consider a VM's resilience to interference effects. For example interactive VMs typically require low response times and high performance while background workloads are generally more robust to such effects [21]. In our work we present a more effective VM consolidation strategy which attempts to classify VM workloads using a state-of-the-art ML approach to foster a more intelligent energy and interference aware approach.

The proposed system model is depicted in Fig. 1. In our system, VMs are initially allocated on to a Physical Machine (PM) based on the requested resources. To reduce energy and service violations it is critical to optimize the distribution of VMs using live migration. In our system architecture the global resource manager is responsible for managing resource allocation and live migration. It consists of three key components: the performance monitor, the trained classifier and the proposed PIEA algorithm which provides decision support for VM consolidation. The performance monitor continuously monitors resource usage on each host and stores this as historical resource usage data. Next the popular Local Regression Minimum Migration Time (LR-MMT) algorithm [11] is used to infer the probability of a host becoming loaded and selects which VMs to migrate and places them on a migration list. The classification model is then used to classify the VM workloads in the migration list using their resource usage features. Based on these classifications the PIEA algorithm makes consolidation decisions considering potential interference issues between co-located VMs.

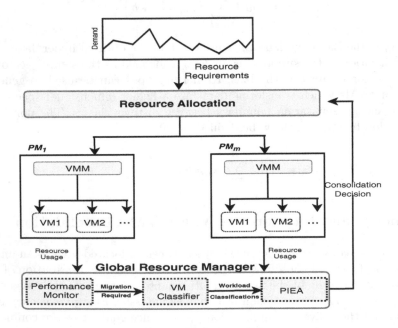

Fig. 1. System model

3.1   Interference Model

The rate at which interference occurs in a virtualised environment largely depends on the number and type of workloads being executed [13]. According to a study by Xu et al. [12] interference effects are highly correlated with the number of VMs running on the host. In particular, they found that interference effects are roughly linear to the number of VMs executing on a given host when comparing CPU and memory intensive applications. As a result, the authors argue that the number of VMs on the host can be used to estimate the expected interference among co-located VMs. In our work we use these findings to generate a simple interference model as proof of concept with the proposed PIEA consolidation algorithm.

In more detail, our work considers heterogeneous workloads which are classified by our ML model as either interactive or delay-insensitive workloads. Given that interactive workloads require high performance and low response times we devise an interference model which results in a exponential rise in the number of Service Level Agreement Violations (SLAV) depending on the number of interactive workloads allocated to the host $PM \in \{pm_1, pm_2, ..., pm_m\}$. Delay-insensitive workloads tend to be more resilient to interference effects. Therefore, we reflect this in our interference model by using a more linear increase in the number of SLAV according to the number of delay-insensitive workloads running on the host. In our performance analysis the level of interference on each host is calculated to estimate the degree of interference among the VMs in the entire data center W_j according to Eq. 6. The estimated interference is used in conjunction with the original SLA violation performance metric computed by CloudSim.

$$W_j = \frac{1}{M} \sum_{j=1}^{M} \left(\sum_{k=1}^{N} v_{kij} \right)^x + \left(\sum_{k=1}^{N} v_{kdj} \right)^x. \tag{6}$$

where M is the total number of active hosts in the data center, N defines the total number of each class of VM, v_{ki} denotes VM workloads classified as interactive, v_{kd} are workloads classified as delay-insensitive, k denotes the VM index, j indicates the host index and x is the exponent value set for each class of VM.

3.2   PIEA Consolidation Algorithm

Our proposed PIEA algorithm below has two objectives. It firstly attempts to allocate VMs to hosts such that interference effects are reduced and secondly it seeks to minimize the amount of PMs needed to execute the workloads in order to improve energy efficiency and the delivery of service guarantees. The system leverages the well known LR-MMT algorithm introduced by Beloglazov et al. [11]. This algorithm manages host overloaded detection and VM selection, two fundamental aspects of dynamic VM resource optimization. A VM migration list is generated by the performance monitor component in our system model as shown in Fig. 1. Using our trained ML model we generate a classification for each VM workload in the migration list depending on the type of resources the VM is using as indicated by the VM's resource usage features, these classifications act as input into our PIEA algorithm.

Algorithm 1: *PIEA Algorithm*

Input: migrationList, hostList & workloadClassifications

foreach Vm_k *in migrationList* **do**

    if $Vm_k \rightarrow$ *"interactive"* **then**

        | interactiveList $\leftarrow Vm_k$

    end

    else

        | delayInsensitiveList $\leftarrow Vm_k$

    end

end

foreach Vm_k *in delayInsensitiveList* **do**

    min $\leftarrow \infty$

    selectedHost $\leftarrow$ *null*

    foreach pm_m *in hostList* **do**

        sum $\leftarrow 0$

        if $pm_m^r > Vm_k^d$ **then**

            //estimate co-location interference on destination PM

            $pm_m^i \leftarrow \left(\sum_{k=1}^{N} v_{ki} \right)^x + \left(\sum_{k=1}^{N} v_{kd} \right)^x$

            if $pm_m^i <= min$ AND $\sum_{k=1}^{N} v_{kd} >= sum$ **then**

                selectedHost $\leftarrow pm_m$

                min $\leftarrow pm_m^i$

                sum $\leftarrow \sum_{k=1}^{N} v_{kd}$

            end

        end

    end

    allocate $Vm_i \rightarrow$ selectedHost

end

foreach Vm_k *in interactiveList* **do**

    min $\leftarrow \infty$

    selectedHost $\leftarrow$ *null*

    foreach pm_m *in hostList* **do**

        sum $\leftarrow \infty$

        if $pm_m^r > Vm_k^d$ AND $pm_m \neq OFF$ **then**

            //estimate co-location interference on destination PM

            $pm_m^i \leftarrow \left(\sum_{k=1}^{N} v_{ki} \right)^x + \left(\sum_{k=1}^{N} v_{kd} \right)^x$

            if $pm_m^i <= min$ AND $\sum_{k=1}^{N} v_{ki} <= sum$ **then**

                selectedHost $\leftarrow pm_m$

                min $\leftarrow pm_m^i$

                sum $\leftarrow \sum_{k=1}^{N} v_{ki}$

            end

        end

    end

    if *selectedHost==null* **then**

        | TURN ON pm_m

        | selectedHost $= pm_m$

    end

    allocate $Vm_i \rightarrow$ selectedHost

end

Our proposed solution firstly sorts the VMs in the migration list using the predicted classification of each workload to make more informed allocation decisions considering the potential interference effects on each host. The min variable is defined to keep track of the host with the least estimated interference and is set to infinity at the start while the sum variable is used to track the number of interactive or delay-insensitive workloads depending on which type of workloads are being consolidated. Next the algorithm allocates the VMs in the delay-insensitive list first as they are less sensitive to allocation decisions. The algorithm first checks that each potential host pm_m has enough resources pm_m^r to execute the demand of Vm_k denoted Vm_k^d. To estimate the degree of potential interference on the host we utilize the core components of Eq. 6. The algorithm's strategy is to allocate each VM executing a delay-insensitive workload to a host that has the least estimated interference denoted $pm_m^i <= min$ and the largest number of delay-insensitive workloads $\sum_{k=1}^{N} v_{kd} >= sum$ as these workloads are less sensitive to interference issues. Essentially the algorithm packs these VM workloads more tightly while also making more efficient use of the available resources. Once all of the delay-insensitive VMs have been allocated the algorithm generates a mapping for all of the VMs in the interactive list on to preferably the available hosts. The algorithm first checks that each potential host pm_m in the host list is currently active and not switched off denoted $pm_m \neq OFF$ and has enough resources pm_m^r to execute the workload of Vm_k denoted as Vm_k^d. By firstly considering active hosts we are optimizing the usage of available resources, preventing valuable resources from being left in an idle state. Next PIEA estimates the degree of interference on the host denoted pm_m^i. Given the high performance requirements of interactive workloads and their sensitivity to interference between competing workloads, our algorithm attempts to find a host that has the least interference $pm_m^i <= min$ and the smallest possible number of interactive workloads denoted $\sum_{k=1}^{N} v_{ki} <= sum$ to reduce direct contention for similar resources. In a situation where none of the active hosts are suitable for allocation a new host is turned on and the VM is allocated.

4   Classification Experimental Details and Results

This section presents the experimental analysis and results of the selected classification models detailed in Sect. 2.2.

4.1   Classification Experimental Setup

Selecting a good network topology for an ANN is important in achieving good performance for any problem. In this work the number of layers and neurons was determined using a parameter sweep. By using 2 layers with 50 neurons each it was found that the network could model more complex non-linear behaviour to yield better performance. We define inputs to the model as the resource usage features belonging to each VM in the training data. The network is configured with two output neurons that corresponds to each class, namely delay-insensitive or interactive. To train the model the backpropagation algorithm with gradient descent and momentum was implemented and the network was trained over 3000 epochs. The momentum term considers the gradient in previous steps when updating the weights to help prevent the algorithm from getting stuck in a local minimum. An ANN can often be sensitive to the initial weights assigned to the network, as a result the model was run 10 times and the average was calculated to ensure reliability. The popular Radial Basis Function (RBF) kernel was used for the SVM. The settings for gamma and c were determined based on the best performance output. The accuracy of both models was evaluated using k-fold cross validation. Table 1 provides a summary of the parameter settings.

Table 1. Summary of experimental parameters

ANN	SVM	Resource usage features
Learning rate α: 0.05	Kernel: RBF	Average CPU
Momentum γ: 0.01	Gamma: 0.01	Max CPU
Training epochs: 3000	C: 1.0	Memory
Number of layers: 2	k-fold: 10	Virtual core hours
Neurons per layer: 50		Subscription ID
k-fold: 10		

4.2 Microsoft Azure Dataset

In this work we use real VM profile data recently released for Microsoft's Azure public cloud platform [21] to train each classifier to identify the type of workload executing on a particular VM. The dataset contains resource usage profiles of over two million VMs running on the Azure platform over 30 consecutive days. To construct the data to evaluate the performance of the selected prediction models we firstly removed instances in the data where the category of the VM was unknown and we selected ten random subscriptions from the dataset. To successfully train a ML classifier class balance is important, imbalanced data occurs when the classes are not represented equally in the data and can result in misleading accuracy. To overcome this problem we under sampled any subscription where a particular class was over represented and implemented a stratified version of k-fold cross validation to preserve the class balance. Overall we obtain 5,816 samples while the average and maximum CPU utilisation, memory usage, virtual core hours and user subscription ID are the input features provided by the dataset.

4.3 Error Metrics

To fully evaluate the performance of our models we examine the overall classification accuracy, precision and recall metrics. The precision metric is a measure of the classifiers exactness while the recall metric is a measure of completeness. These statistics are defined as follows:

$$OverallClassificationAccuracy = \frac{CorrectPredictions}{TotalPredictions} * 100 \qquad (7)$$

$$Precision = \frac{TruePositives}{TruePositives + FalsePositives} \qquad (8)$$

$$Recall = \frac{TruePositives}{TruePositives + FalseNegatives} \qquad (9)$$

4.4   Classification Results

A comparison of the overall accuracy of each of the classification models is presented in Fig. 2. As shown, both models provide good performance for the problem generating an accuracy of between 70–74%. In particular, the ANN performed best overall demonstrating its ability to better model the complex underlying correlations in the data while also showing its capacity to generalize to unseen data. However, to fully evaluate the efficacy of the models we must also examine both the precision and recall metrics to provide more insights into the expected performance of each model. Table 2 provides the results of both of these metrics. As shown, for the ANN the proportion of positive identifications that were correct for the delay-insensitive class was approaching 80%. As indicated by the recall metric, the proportion of actual positives for this class in the entire dataset that were identified correctly was approximately 65%. For the interactive samples the ANN generated a precision score of an estimated 71% while the estimated recall for this class scored 84%. In comparison, the SVM resulted in precision of nearly 90% for delay-insensitive samples, however, the recall metric was relatively poor for this class generating a result of a mere 46%. Conversely, for interactive samples the SVM scored a precision and recall of approximately 64% and 95% respectively. Both of these metrics are important to measure the expected accuracy of the models on all future data, therefore we aim to strike a balance between both. Considering the results of all metrics we select the ANN as the best performer overall, we can generally expect the performance of the ANN to be between 73.44% and 75.16% given a Standard Deviation (SD) of 0.86. Furthermore, in our analysis it was also found that the most significant mistake

Table 2. Test data classification accuracy

Class	Algorithm	Precision	Recall
Delay-insensitive	ANN	0.795	0.646
Interactive	ANN	0.708	0.838
Delay-insensitive	SVM	0.897	0.458
Interactive	SVM	0.643	0.949

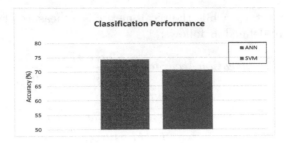

Fig. 2. Overall classification accuracy for ANN and SVM models

incurred by the ANN was that occasionally it classified delay-insensitive work-loads as interactive. However, for our problem this may not have a significant impact as delay-insensitive workloads could potentially require high performance i.e. batch jobs. Therefore, classifying them as interactive could possibly reflect their performance requirements. Based on our empirical evaluation the ANN will be used as the classifier for proposed consolidation approach.

5   Cloud Experimental Analysis

In this section we discuss the experimental analysis and cloud simulation results using the proposed PIEA algorithm.

5.1   Experimental Setup

To evaluate the efficiency of our PIEA algorithm we use the widely used CloudSim toolkit [11]. In CloudSim we model the problem using a data center consisting of 800 physical machines. In particular, the simulator consists of two types of physical hosts modelled as HP ProLiant ML110G4 (Intel Xeon 3075, 2 cores 1860 MHz, 4 GB) and HP ProLiant ML110G5 (Intel Xeon 3075, 2 cores 2660 MHz, 4 GB). Furthermore, we consider four types of VMs consisting of High-CPU Medium Instances (2500 MIPS, 0.85 GB), Extra Large Instances (2000 MIPS, 3.75 GB), Small Instances (1000 MIPS, 1.7 GB) and also Micro Instances (500 MIPS, 613 MB). We compare the performance of the PIEA consolidation algorithm to the PowerAware algorithm proposed by Beloglazov et al. [6]. Although there exists numerous approaches for the VM consolidation problem the most well-known and commonly used benchmark is the PowerAware approach when energy efficiency is one of the core objectives and therefore this benchmark is an important measure in our work. The PowerAware algorithm considers the heterogeneity of cloud resources and efficiently allocates VM instances to hosts by selecting the most energy efficient hosts first.

5.2   Cloud Performance Metrics

The key performance metrics used to evaluate the effectiveness of the proposed algorithm are:

- **Energy Consumption**: In our work the energy consumption metric is computed by CloudSim where power consumption of a host is represented by its CPU utilisation and reported as energy consumption over time (kWh) [11].
- **SLAV**: A service violation is measured as the performance degradation experienced by each VM due to both hosts becoming overloaded, the VM migrations incurred by the cloud system and also the level of interference on each host.

5.3   Simulation Results

The PIEA algorithm was evaluated over a 10 day workload. As shown in Fig. 3, the PIEA algorithm consistently outperforms the PowerAware algorithm over the 10 days. Specifically, it resulted in a significant improvement in energy consumption by 31%.

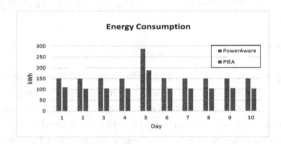

Fig. 3. Energy generated by the PIEA and PowerAware consolidation algorithms

The predictive capabilities of our ANN classifier enables the PIEA algorithm to reason over the execution of heterogeneous workloads. In particular, it attempts to make more efficient consolidation decisions, effectively minimizing the amount of hosts needed to execute the workloads. The algorithm improves energy efficiency by consolidating workloads classified as delay-insensitive more aggressively given their general tolerance to interference issues while interactive

Fig. 4. SLAV incurred by the PIEA and PowerAware consolidation algorithms

workloads where possible are allocated to an active host. As a result, the PIEA algorithm generates improved usage of available resources which is a key factor in causing excessively large energy rates in data centers today.

An important dimension in achieving greater energy efficiency through VM consolidation is managing the tradeoff between energy and performance. As shown in Fig. 4, the PIEA algorithm also generates a significant reduction in the number of SLAV by 69%. This demonstrates the algorithms ability to better strike a balance between energy and performance in order to deliver an approach that successfully reduces energy consumption while also improving the delivery of service guarantees to the users. The ability to classify workloads with some element of precision enables the PIEA algorithm to make more informed consolidation decisions regarding the expected SLAV for co-located VMs. Furthermore, a paired t-test confirmed that the results are also statistically significant. The test resulted in a p-value less that 0.0051 (energy) and a p-value of 0.0001 (SLAV) with a 95% confidence interval. These results indicate the improved efficiency achievable through the implementation of the proposed PIEA algorithm.

6   Conclusion

In this work, we presented PIEA, an interference and energy aware VM consolidation algorithm for multi-tenant cloud environments. Using the more recent Microsoft Azure data, we demonstrate how the predictive capabilities of our ML classifier enable our algorithm to infer the expected level of interference between co-located workloads while also being cognizant of energy consumption for a more rigorous and reliable solution. Our results show an improvement in energy consumption by 31% and SLAV by a significant 69% in comparison to the popular PowerAware consolidation approach.

Acknowledgments. The primary author would like to acknowledge the ongoing financial support provided to her by the Irish Research Council.

References

1. Moreno, I.S., Yang, R., Xu, J., Wo, T.: Improved energy-efficiency in cloud datacenters with interference-aware virtual machine placement. In: 2013 IEEE Eleventh International Symposium on Autonomous Decentralized Systems (ISADS), pp. 1–8. IEEE (2013)
2. Shaw, R., Howley, E., Barrett, E.: Predicting the available bandwidth on intra cloud network links for deadline constrained workflow scheduling in public clouds. In: Maximilien, M., Vallecillo, A., Wang, J., Oriol, M. (eds.) ICSOC 2017. LNCS, vol. 10601, pp. 221–228. Springer, Cham (2017). https://doi.org/10.1007/978-3-319-69035-3_15
3. Whitney, J., Delforge, P.: Scaling up energy efficiency across the data center industry: evaluating key drivers and barriers. Technical report, Natural Resources Defense Council (2014)

4. Lee, Y.C., Zomaya, A.Y.: Energy efficient utilisation of resources in cloud computing systems. J. Supercomput. **60**, 268–280 (2012)
5. Verma, A., Ahuja, P., Neogi, A.: pMapper: power and migration cost aware application placement in virtualized systems. In: Issarny, V., Schantz, R. (eds.) Middleware 2008. LNCS, vol. 5346, pp. 243–264. Springer, Heidelberg (2008). https://doi.org/10.1007/978-3-540-89856-6_13
6. Beloglazov, A., Abawajy, J., Buyya, R.: Energy-aware resource allocation heuristics for efficient management of data centers for cloud computing. Future Gener. Comput. Syst. **28**, 755–768 (2012)
7. Shaw, R., Howley, E., Barrett, E.: An advanced reinforcement learning approach for energy-aware virtual machine consolidation in cloud data centers. In: Proceedings of the 12th International Conference for Internet Technology and Secured Transactions, pp. 61–66. IEEE, December 2017
8. Farahnakian, F., Pahikkala, T., Liljeberg, P., Plosila, J., Hieu, N.T., Tenhunen, H.: Energy-aware VM consolidation in cloud data centers using utilisation prediction model. IEEE Trans. Cloud Comput. **7**, 524–536 (2016)
9. Nguyen, T.H., Di Francesco, M., Yla-Jaaski, A.: Virtual machine consolidation with multiple usage prediction for energy-efficient cloud data centers. IEEE Trans. Serv. Comput. (2017). https://doi.org/10.1109/TSC.2017.2648791
10. Sampaio, A.M., Barbosa, J.G., Prodan, R.: PIASA: a power and interference aware resource management strategy for heterogeneous workloads in cloud data centers. Simul. Model. Pract. Theory **57**, 142–160 (2015)
11. Beloglazov, A., Buyya, R.: Optimal online deterministic algorithms and adaptive heuristics for energy and performance efficient dynamic consolidation of virtual machines in cloud data centers. Concurr. Comput. Pract. Exp. **24**, 1397–1420 (2012)
12. Xu, F., Liu, F., Liu, L., Jin, H., Li, B., Li, B.: iAware: making live migration of virtual machines interference-aware in the cloud. IEEE Trans. Comput. **63**, 3012–3025 (2014)
13. Jersak, L.C., Ferreto, T.: Performance-aware server consolidation with adjustable interference levels. In: Proceedings of the 31st Annual ACM Symposium on Applied Computing, pp. 420–425. ACM, April 2016
14. Verboven, S., Vanmechelen, K., Broeckhove, J.: Black box scheduling for resource intensive virtual machine workloads with interference models. Future Gener. Comput. Syst. **29**(8), 1871–1884 (2013)
15. Shaw, R., Howley, E., Barrett, E.: An energy efficient anti-correlated virtual machine placement algorithm using resource usage predictions. Simul. Model. Pract. Theory (2019). https://doi.org/10.1016/j.simpat.2018.09.019
16. Zhang, J., Figueiredo, R.J.: Application classification through monitoring and learning of resource consumption patterns. In: 20th International Parallel and Distributed Processing Symposium, IPDPS 2006, pp. 10–20. IEEE (2006)
17. Nikravesh, A.Y., Ajila, S.A., Lung, C.H.: Towards an autonomic auto-scaling prediction system for cloud resource provisioning. In: Proceedings of the 10th International Symposium on Software Engineering for Adaptive and Self-Managing Systems, pp. 35–45. IEEE (2015)
18. Mason, K., Duggan, J., Howley, E.: Evolving multi-objective neural networks using differential evolution for dynamic economic emission dispatch. In: Proceedings of the Genetic and Evolutionary Computation Conference Companion, pp. 1287–1294. ACM, July 2017
19. Meyer, D., Leisch, F., Hornik, K.: The support vector machine under test. Neurocomputing **55**(1–2), 169–186 (2003)

20. Dixon, S.J., Brereton, R.G.: Comparison of performance of five common classifiers represented as boundary methods: Euclidean distance to centroids, linear discriminant analysis, quadratic discriminant analysis, learning vector quantization and support vector machines, as dependent on data structure. Chemometr. Intell. Lab. Syst. **95**(1), 1–17 (2009)
21. Cortez, E., Bonde, A., Muzio, A., Russinovich, M., Fontoura, M., Bianchini, R.: Resource central: understanding and predicting workloads for improved resource management in large cloud platforms. In: Proceedings of the 26th Symposium on Operating Systems Principles, pp. 153–167. ACM, October 2017

Thread-Level CPU and Memory Usage Control of Custom Code in Multi-tenant SaaS

Majid Makki[✉], Dimitri Van Landuyt, Bert Lagaisse, and Wouter Joosen

imec-DistriNet, Department of Computer Science, KU Leuven, Leuven, Belgium
{majid.makki,dimitri.vanlanduyt,bert.lagaisse,
wouter.joosen}@cs.kuleuven.be

Abstract. Software-as-a-Service (SaaS) providers commonly support customization of their services to allow them to attract larger tenant bases. The nature of these customizations in practice ranges from anticipated configuration options to sophisticated code extensions. From a SaaS provider viewpoint, the latter category is particularly challenging as it involves executing untrusted tenant custom code in the SaaS production environment. Proper isolation of custom code in turn requires the ability to control the CPU and memory usage of each tenant.

In current practice, OS-level virtualization tools such as hypervisors or containers are predominantly used for this purpose. These techniques, however, constrain the number of tenants that a single node can cost-effectively accommodate.

In this paper, we present a practical solution for thread-level tenant isolation, vis-à-vis CPU and memory usage in presence of tenant-provided custom code. Both Java Runtime Environment (JRE) bytecode and tenant code are instrumented with usage control checkpoints which, based on data gathered using the Java Resource Consumption Management API (JSR-284), ensures that CPU and memory usage of tenants remain within their Service-level Agreements (SLA) limits.

Our experiments show that the tenant accommodation capacity of single node increases 59 times with the proposed solution instead of containers. This scalability improvement comes at the average cost of 0.31 ns performance overhead per control checkpoint.

Keywords: SaaS · Customization · Multi-tenancy · Resource management · Tenant isolation · JRE

1 Introduction

Multi-tenant systems share a single run-time environment among multiple customer organizations (tenants) and consequently require isolation mechanisms to avoid any interference or disturbance between tenants. For instance, tenant isolation mechanisms guarantees that tenant Service Level Agreements (SLA) are respected. In common practice, hypervisors and containers are employed

© Springer Nature Switzerland AG 2019
S. Yangui et al. (Eds.): ICSOC 2019, LNCS 11895, pp. 267–282, 2019.
https://doi.org/10.1007/978-3-030-33702-5_21

which perform tenant isolation at the level of virtual machines and OS processes respectively.

However, as shown in Fig. 1, isolation can also be attained at the higher level of application threads which increases resource utilization. Allocating a separate Virtual Machine (VM) or OS process (cf. [1–4]) to each tenant imposes a constant memory overhead which reduces the number of tenants that a single node can accommodate.

Due to this constant memory overhead, other resources will be underutilized when some tenants are idle or almost inactive. Due to the

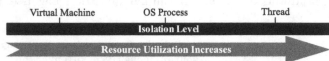

Fig. 1. Effects of enforcing tenant isolation at different levels.

lower per-tenant memory overhead of thread-level tenant isolation, the latter allows accommodating more tenants on a single node and increases resource utilization. Accomplishing tenant isolation at the application level in turn allows for a more cost-efficient deployment: more tenants can be provisioned with less resources.

Software-as-a-Service (SaaS) applications commonly allow tenants to customize the application behavior through custom code extensions (e.g. [5,6]). For instance, in SaaS applications driven by business processes, the code of a certain activity in a workflow may be provided by a tenant instead of the SaaS provider (Business-process-as-a-service, BPaaS). Application platform as a Service (aPaaS) offerings similarly provide application services that can be open to code extension. In contrast to customizations that have been anticipated and developed by the SaaS providers, allowing tenant-provided custom code to be executed creates a number of non-trivial challenges. These code-based customizations are essentially untrusted and tenants may be incentivized to exploit the system, hinder other tenants, etc.

In a SaaS context, existing multi-tenancy approaches [7–10] commonly involve external, black-box measures and techniques to monitor (in terms of metrics such as throughput, requests/second, etc.) and control (e.g. throttling, SLA-aware job scheduling and load balancing) the services delivered to tenants. However, in presence of custom code provided by tenants, these techniques do not suffice. Enforcing tenant isolation at thread-level requires monitoring and controlling the CPU and memory usage of the custom code extensions inside the run-time environment.

In this paper, we present a modified version of the Java Runtime Environment (JRE) which enables running code provided by untrusted tenants in a single JRE instance while CPU and memory usage levels are kept within SLA boundaries. As opposed to experimental Java Virtual Machines (JVM) that target a similar goal [11–15], our JRE modification mechanism can be applied to any JRE used by industrialized JVMs. Our main contribution is, then, providing a portable mechanism for isolating tenants, vis-à-vis CPU and memory usage, at the level of application threads.

Two challenging obstacles have been addressed. The first obstacle is that Java threads are directly managed by the OS kernel and it is not possible to pause/resume them once started using the JRE [16,17]. The second obstacle is that no implementation of the Java Resource Consumption Management API (RCM API specified in JSR-284 [18]; cf. [19]) allows imposing limits on CPU or memory usage of threads. Existing implementations such as Oracle HotSpot JVM are only capable of reporting the CPU and memory usage of each thread.[1]

Our modified JRE is based on the Oracle HotSpot JVM and is extensively based on Java bytecode instrumentation driven by call graph analysis [20], for two main purposes: (i) ensuring that tenants cannot evade usage control checkpoints which enforce SLA compliance, and (ii) forcing threads to sleep or stop when tenant custom code breaks out of the SLA boundaries.

We have validated our implementation using an illustrative batch-processing application and as such demonstrated that the CPU and memory usage levels can be controlled without using containers or VMs. Furthermore, the evaluation results show that the proposed solution increases tenant accommodation capacity with a factor of 59 compared to process-level solution, and only with a marginal average performance overhead of 0.31 ns per usage control checkpoint.

Section 2 formulates the problem at stake in terms of requirements. Section 3 presents the solution. Section 4 reports on the evaluation results. Section 5 discusses practical issues and draws perspectives for future work. Section 6 discusses related work and finally, Sect. 7 concludes the paper.

2   Problem Statement

This section demarcates the problem addressed by this paper as a set of requirements. The functional requirements are marked by F whereas quality requirements are marked by Q:

F1 While executing the code provided by multiple tenant organizations, the CPU and memory usage of tenants should be kept below the limits specified in their SLA.

F2 It is required to allow tenants to use CPU as much as possible within SLA limits.[2]

Q1 The number of tenants that can be accommodated on a single node should be significantly increased compared to OS-level virtualization techniques that implement tenant isolation at the process level.

Q2 It is required to keep the performance overhead imposed by usage control and SLA management within acceptable boundaries.

Section 3 explains how these requirements are fulfilled.

---

[1] Storage and network resources are not dealt with in this paper because the Java RCM API already provides quite straightforward ways to control IO usage.

[2] This is specifically required for CPU because fulfilling **F1** for the latter is feasible by suppressing the usage too much.

3   Thread-Level Resource Usage Control

In order to address **Q1**, a single JRE instance is used for running code belonging to multiple tenants. This entails executing the code of each tenant in separate threads from each other and the main SaaS service. To enact fine-grained control over these threads, the platform support is introduced for preventing excessive memory usage as well as pause, resume and stop operations to throttle CPU usage (cf. **F1**, **F2**). The proposed solution consists of two main parts: (i) principal components in charge of usage monitoring and control presented in Sect. 3.1, and (ii) bytecode instrumentation discussed in Sect. 3.2.

3.1   Principal Components

The Java RCM API [18] provides meters for measuring the usage level of all types of resources, such as network bandwidth and CPU/memory, on a per-thread basis (cf. **F1**). Since the only implementation of this API in Oracle HotSpot JVM is not capable of imposing limits on CPU and memory usage, we have supplemented it to make it suitable for CPU and memory usage control.

The four principal components in charge of resource usage control are shown in Fig. 2. The `Monitoring` component, which uses the Java RCM API, provides two meters, namely `CPUMeter` and `MemoryMeter`, counting CPU cycles per second and memory space in terms of bytes respectively. Both of these meters are responsible for notifying a central `UsageStatusRegistry` when a tenant exceeds its SLA limit (cf. **F1**) and also when the tenant usage level goes back to normal (cf. **F2**).

One instance of each meter is initialized for each tenant, holding the

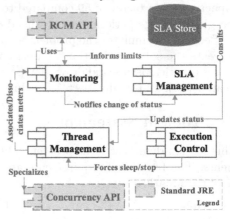

Fig. 2. Usage control components

SLA *limits*, representing the permitted CPU cycles per second and the permitted number of memory bytes, provided by the `SLA Management` component which reads them from the `SLA Store`. Tenant meters are grouped in a `ResourceContext` and the latter is associated to tenant threads. The `Thread Management` component, which is an extension of the Java `Concurrency API`, is responsible for associating meters to `ControlledThread` instances.

For correct and efficient association of the meters to threads, the `Thread Management` component employs a multi-tenant thread pool. The multi-tenant thread pool instantiates and reserves a separate set of (dormant) threads for each tenant and forbids swapping threads across pools. This ensures that each thread is only used for a single tenant. Consequently, associating meters to threads, which incurs a considerable performance overhead, is restricted to the creation time of threads (cf. **Q2**).

The `Execution Control` component is responsible for forcing threads to sleep or stop (cf. **F1**) and, in this regard, implements a `control` method which is summarized in Listing 1.1. As a tenant can be recovered from excessive CPU usage by rescheduling threads, threads are forced to sleep in such cases, for a duration determined in the tenant SLA (lines 5–9). In contrast, excessive memory usage cannot be healed by passing of time. Hence, in that case, the thread will be removed from the `UsageStatusRegistry` and will kill itself by throwing an `OutOfMemoryError` (lines 1–4).

```
if (memoryExcess) {                                            1
    UsageStatusRegistry.removeThread(this);                    2
    throw new OutOfMemoryError(); // kills the thread          3
}                                                              4
while (cpuExcess) {                                            5
    awake = false;                                             6
    sleep(duration);   // throttles the usage                 7
    awake = true;                                              8
}                                                              9
```

Listing 1.1. Thread Control Behavior

It is possible that all threads of a tenant are eventually put into the sleep mode. In that case, the `CPUMeter` of that specific tenant is not updated anymore and updating the corresponding `cpuExcess` flag cannot be triggered by the meter. Therefore, the `Execution Control` component, specifically

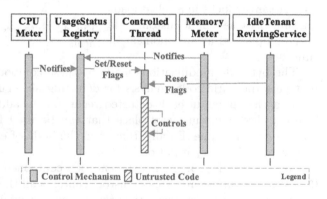

Fig. 3. Object interactions for usage control

its `IdleTenantRevivingService` which is scheduled to run repeatedly at fixed intervals, scans for tenants with all threads in sleep mode and resets their `cpuExcess` flag. Determining whether all threads of a tenant are in sleep mode requires (re)setting a specific flag before sleeping and after wakeup (lines 6 and 8 in Listing 1.1). Figure 3 summarizes the mechanism described above.

We call every invocation of the `control` method a checkpoint. To ensure that tenants cannot evade the control mechanism (cf. **F1**), at least one checkpoint is enforced in each of the following places: (i) every set of methods which can possibly make a recursion and (ii) every iterative structure such as a for-loop. Despite its exhaustive nature, this approach does not degrade performance considerably (cf. **Q2**) because, rather than measuring usage in every checkpoint, the latter basically involves verifying boolean variables which are *asynchronously* set every time each individual meter recognizes a change of status.

Inserting a checkpoint in the aforementioned places is performed using Java bytecode instrumentation which is discussed in the following.

3.2 Bytecode Instrumentation

Checkpoints are not only required in the tenant custom code but also in the JRE and all cloud service classes accessible for tenants. Inserting usage checkpoints, hence, occurs at two stages by two distinct components shown in Fig. 4 namely the `Offline Instrumentor` and the `Tenant Code Instrumentor`. These components are responsible for instrumenting the JRE bytecode alongside the code of the cloud service and tenant custom code respectively.

Since Java does not allow replacing the bytecode of certain JRE classes once they are loaded, instrumenting the JRE bytecode and that of the cloud service takes place *offline*, i.e. even before starting up the shared JRE. The `Tenant Code Instrumentor` kicks in at class loading time because tenant custom code may be uploaded at any moment in time.

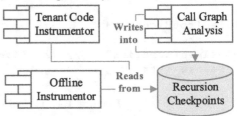

Fig. 4. Bytecode instrumentation components

The bytecode modifications made by these components are identical. They first perform static code analysis for detecting all recursions. Afterwards, they insert a checkpoint in each detected recursion. In addition, the instrumentors insert a checkpoint in every place that can be used for dynamically building recursions at runtime. Finally, they scan the body of each method for inserting a checkpoint in every iteration.

As shown in Fig. 4, the instrumentation components rely on the `Recursion Checkpoints` datastore. This datastore contains all the methods where a checkpoint is required for ensuring that tenants cannot exploit recursions to circumvent the usage control mechanism. To build this datastore, the `Call Graph Analysis` component analyzes a large directed graph, $CG = (M, I)$ where M is the set of all methods and I is the set of all possible invocations as defined in the following:

$$I = \{< m_1, m_2 > | m_1, m_2 \in M \ \& \ invoke(m_1, m_2)\} \tag{1}$$

where $invoke(m_1, m_2)$ is true *iff* m_1 may invoke m_2 at runtime. The possibility of polymorphic method invocations are taken into account as well. All simple cycles in CG are detected and a minimal subset of M is saved into the `Recursion Checkpoints` datastore such that each detected cycle has at least one member in the datastore.

The instrumentation components insert a checkpoint at the beginning of each method stored in `Recursion Checkpoints`. However, that is not sufficient to cover all possible recursions. In addition to the statically-detectable recursions, it is also possible to build recursions *dynamically* using the Reflection API or lambdas. To protect the system against exploitation of the Reflection API, a checkpoint is inserted in the `invoke` method of the `java.lang.reflect.Method`. A lambda expression, when compiled, yields one or more `invokedynamic` byte-code instruction(s). The target method of an `invokedynamic` instruction is determined at runtime. Therefore, a checkpoint is inserted before every instance of this instruction.

For inserting checkpoints in every iterative programming structure (e.g. a for-loop), the instrumentation components scan the body of each method and look for instructions jumping backward as indicators of iterations. Before every backward jump instruction, one checkpoint is inserted.

Circumventing the usage control mechanism requires exploiting repetitive programming instructions, i.e. either recursions or iterations. Our bytecode instrumentation covers all possible recursions (statically-detectable recursions, recursions made by the Reflection API, and those made by lambdas) and all iterations. Therefore, it is ensured that no tenant can evade the usage control mechanism (cf. **F1**).

4   Validation and Evaluation

This section presents the results of validating the proposed mechanism in terms of **F1** and **F2** and the evaluation results for **Q1** and **Q2**. Section 4.1 details the technical setup of the experiment environment and the subsequent sections present the experiments and analyzes the observations and the obtained results for each of the aforementioned requirements.

4.1   Implementation and Technical Setup

We have implemented the above solution on top of the JRE 1.8 shipped with Oracle HotSpot JVM.[3] Our current implementation is limited for use in a single-node setup and evaluated on a Windows 10 (64-bit) machine with Intel Core i7 (3.6 GHz) and 16 GB of memory.

For the experiments, a multi-tenant batch-processing SaaS application is developed that runs batch jobs involving tenant custom code. Software artifacts of each tenant are wrapped in an OSGi bundle [21]. These tenant-provided custom code extensions are instrumented using the mechanism described in Sect. 3.2.

Before each set of experiments reported in the following section, a warmup task is performed by the multi-tenant application to make sure that the JVM bytecode optimizations are performed before main experiments start. For experiments validating/evaluating CPU usage control, the JVM OS process running

---

[3] The source code can be downloaded via http://people.cs.kuleuven.be/~majid. makki/icsoc-2019/main.html.

the prototype SaaS application is given *realtime* priority on *exactly* 4 CPU cores out of 8 to ensure that the impact of other OS processes on the obtained results are kept minimal.

4.2   Validation of F1 for Memory Usage

In this experiment, the code of a tenant, whose SLA specifies a 300 kB memory limit, aims at instantiating the `java.math.BigDecimal` class one million times and keeping the instances in a `LinkedList`. The tenant custom code is allowed to instantiate objects and keep them in memory until it exceeds the 300 kB limit. This functional test shows that the thread running tenant custom code kills itself at that moment by throwing an `OutOfMemoryError` and the multi-tenant application hosting tenant custom code keeps working and serving requests.

4.3   Validation of F1/F2 for CPU Usage

Two specific tenants, whose CPU-related parameters of their SLA are presented in Table 1, are involved in 9 independent experiments each consisting of 10 concurrent jobs per tenant. Each job performs millions of `ADD` operations in a loop and is engineered to have a fixed number of usage checkpoints executed starting at 10 million checkpoints in the first experiment, increased by 10 million each time up to 90 million checkpoints in the last experiment. The length of jobs increase linearly with the number of executed checkpoints in these specific experiments. Therefore, these experiments verify the validity of **F1** and **F2** independent of the job length.

Four parameters are constantly recorded during all experiments: the start time of each job, its end time, its total sleep time, and finally the number of CPU cycles recorded by the `CPUMeter`.[4]

Table 1. CPU parameters in SLA.

Tenant	Limit	Sleep duration	Max threads
Premium	100 MHz	25 ms	4
Standard	50 MHz	50 ms	4

The average CPU usage of each tenant in every experiment is calculated using the following equation:

$$usage_{avg} = (1 - \frac{sleep_{avg}}{execution_{avg}}) \times request_{avg} \tag{2}$$

where $sleep_{avg}$, $execution_{avg}$ and $request_{avg}$ are the average sleep time, the average execution time and the average number of CPU cycles requested from the `CPUMeter` for each tenant in a specific experiment.

Figure 5 shows the average CPU usage of each tenant in each of the 9 experiments separately. It clearly shows that the `Standard` tenant is kept below its 50 MHz limit (depicted as a dotted line in Fig. 5) while the `Premium` tenant is

---

[4] The act of constantly recording these parameters has no impact on the obtained results.

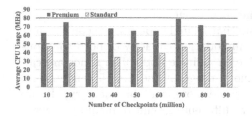

Fig. 5. Average CPU usage

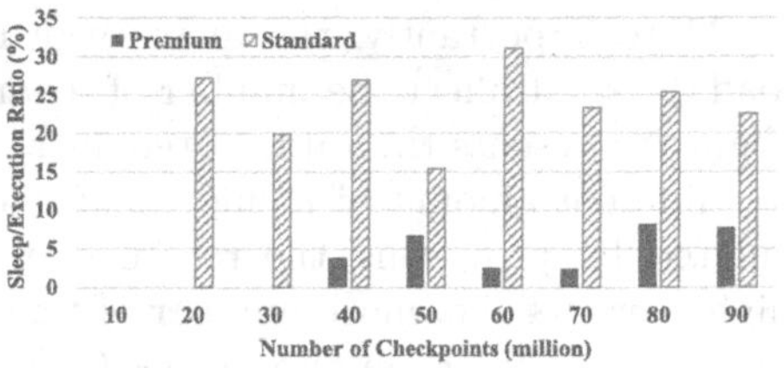

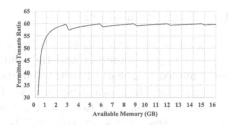

Fig. 6. Sleep ratio

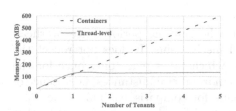

Fig. 7. Load-independent memory usage compared with containers.

Fig. 8. Tenant accommodation capacity compared with containers.

allowed to go up to 80 MHz on average, which is below their SLA limit but sufficient for the submitted tasks. Non-zero sleep ratios depicted in Fig. 6 show in effect that both tenants had tried to exceed their limits at certain time in some experiments. However, the control mechanism has forced them to sleep and kept the *average* CPU usage below the specified limits.

4.4 Evaluation of Q1

The goal is to compare process-level tenant isolation, representative of containers, with the proposed solution in terms of tenant accommodation capacity. A single-tenant variant of the experimental application is created on top of the standard JRE (i.e. no bytecode instrumentation) and executed separately for each tenant. The multi-tenant application is executed once on top of the modified JRE but without any tenant. The memory usage of each OS process is recorded 5 min after startup in absence of any load. For the multi-tenant variant, the OS process memory usage is also recorded 5 min after each tenant taken on-board. The above is performed for 5 distinct but identical tenants.

Figure 7 shows the recorded values for both solutions. Not surprisingly, when tenant isolation is enforced at level of OS processes, the load-independent memory overhead increases linearly with the number of tenants whereas the same factor reaches a nearly constant ceiling quite soon in the thread-level solution. Evidently, the memory usage will increase when load is imposed on the system but that would even more constrain the tenant accommodation capacity of the process-level solution.

More importantly, the increase in memory usage incurred by the imposed load does not affect the number of tenants that a single node can accommodate. Figure 8 presents the ratio of tenant accommodation capacity of both solutions for different amount of memories available on a single node. The ratios are calculated by projecting the recorded memory usage of the first 5 tenants into higher orders (i.e. more number of tenants and more available memory). It can be seen that the ratio approaches 60 when sufficient amount of memory is available (cf. **Q1**).

4.5   Evaluation of Q2

The goal of this evaluation is to measure the runtime performance overhead imposed by the metering and the control mechanisms. It does not reflect the performance overhead of instrumentation which takes place only once for the JRE and once for tenant custom code. The normal circumstances, i.e absence of any excessive usage, is taken as the baseline for comparisons. This is because, otherwise, the CPU sleep time will be involved in one case but not the other hence yielding incomparable results. To ensure that no usage excess will occur, the CPU and memory usage limits are set extremely high in the experiment.

The experiment involves two groups of 10 independent jobs for a single tenant. The jobs, identical across groups, consist of tenant custom code engineered to have exactly 100 million up to 1 billion checkpoints, increased by the factor of 100 million each time. In the first group of executions, our bytecode instrumentation is applied whereas the second group is performed on the standard JRE without instrumenting neither the cloud service code nor tenant custom code, and without any meters involved.

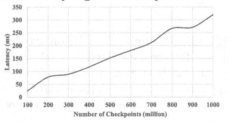

Fig. 9. Performance overhead.

The differences between the execution time of each pair of identical jobs are presented in Fig. 9. Based on the obtained results, the performance overhead of the control mechanism is on average 0.31 ns per checkpoint with standard deviation of 0.03 ns.

5   Discussion

This section elaborates on a number of issues concerning further improvement of the proposed solution as well as its real-world application.

Distribution. Currently, the focus has been on increasing the tenant accommodation capacity on a single node. However, coping with load imposed on the system and realistic cloud deployment will require distributed deployment. Dedicated types of orchestration facilities (e.g. SLA-aware load-balancers or thread schedulers) will be required to ensure that the SLA limits are respected across all nodes (cf. [22,23]).

Supplementary Building Blocks. Beside resource usage control, a thread-level tenant isolation solution requires mechanisms for access control and code restriction facilities (cf. [24]) to avoid problems with **static** members (cf. [17]) and exploitation of the usage control mechanism by tenants.

Flexible and Adaptive Control. The implemented solution imposes a *fixed* and *strict* limit on tenant usage. In practice, it is possible to allow tenants to slightly surpass their SLA limits if sufficient resources are available. Hence, system health should be monitored and more flexible limit enforcement policies control the tenant usage levels. For instance, a *leniency factor* may be used to determine the extent to which each tenant may go beyond their SLA limits (cf. [24]).

In addition, thread sleeping can be adaptive. Instead of a fixed sleep duration, specified in the tenant SLA, the latter can be adjusted at runtime based on previous records of CPU usage. Furthermore, the number of threads forced to sleep when usage excess is observed can be in function of the transgression rate while in the current implementation, all threads belonging to the aggressive tenant are forced to sleep.

Performance Optimization. Our observations shows that a great majority of checkpoints are inserted in *iterations* rather than recursions. Therefore, the overall performance overhead of usage control mechanism can be further reduced by using a local counter in the iterations for intelligently determining how frequently the checkpoint should actually be involved at runtime instead of the current brute-force machinery.

Hybrid Approaches. The proposed solution is not incompatible to other tenant isolation approaches, and in some cases, it could be beneficial to combine different solutions (cf. [25]). For example, a potential tenant accommodation model could involve clustering different groups of tenants (e.g. premium vs. standard tenants) in separate containers and our thread-level solution could be employed to protect tenants within each container. As shown in the case-driven study of Ochei et al. [26], decisions related to tenant isolation are impacted by many complex trade-offs, and depend on many factors such as the application nature, the trust bestowed upon tenants, the nature of the customizations, etc.

Applicability Beyond JRE. Our approach can be implemented in runtime platforms of other languages given that they meet the following conditions: (i) threads or similar structures can be safely paused/resumed, (ii) CPU and memory can be measured on a per-thread basis, (iii) the code of the programming language is compiled into an intermediate language, such as Java bytecode, which can be instrumented before ultimately compiled into machine code.

6   Related Work

This section compares and contrasts our solution with related work.

Performance Isolation. Related work on performance isolation of multi-tenant SaaS applications [7–10,27–29] focuses on aspects of performance isolation between tenants sharing a single run-time environment. The main distinction however is that these approaches involve *known* and *trusted* service logic, whereas the specific problem addressed in this paper starts when tenants implement part of the system functionality by providing their own code which is by nature *untrusted*.

The use of tenant custom code that runs in the SaaS application makes the external metrics commonly used in this context (such as job execution time, throughput or response time) unsuited for isolating tenants performance-wise within SaaS applications (cf. [29]). Other elements of related work also rely on internal metrics such as memory and CPU usage [7,10,27,28]. PerfCloud [30] utilizes system-level metrics to proactively detect performance interference between tenant workloads and shows that such approaches succeed in avoiding costly workload profiling and prediction mechanisms without having any interference on application code.

Java Studies. This work is in continuation of existing work that deals with the limitations of running user code in Java threads. Herzog et al. [16] and Rodero-Merino et al. [17] highlight safe termination of threads and resource control as one of the main obstacles. Work aimed at resource consumption control in the JRE [19,31,32] has led to the JSR-284 specification [18] also known as the Java RCM API. However, neither the specification nor its implementations (e.g. Oracle HotSpot JVM) currently provide any way for imposing limits on CPU and memory usage. The solution presented here involves complex, holistic and cohesive instrumentation of (i) the JRE, (ii) cloud service provider code, and (iii) tenant-provided code to overcome the above shortcomings.

Multi-tenant JVM. Specialized Java Virtual Machines (JVM) have been built for executing the code provided by multiple tenants in a single JVM instance [11–15]. In contrast, instead of developing specialized JVMs, our approach provides a customized yet backwards-compatible JRE, which can as such be used in industrialized JVMs. In MVM [12,14], I-JVM [13] and IBM MT JVM [15], tenant custom code is executed as a separate application. This is not desirable in the context of multi-tenant SaaS applications in which tenant custom code runs as an integrated part of the SaaS application, rather than an independent application. In addition, our approach allows sharing JRE and other libraries and consequently increases scalability.

Despite requiring a separate OS process for each tenant, KaffeOS [11] can still be used for SaaS applications that execute tenant custom code, mainly owing to its hierarchical memory management which supports objects being shared between Java processes. This sharing mechanism however sacrifices application portability: every time an object is to be shared or a shared object is required, a specific `Heap` class is *explicitly* used, and this makes it impossible to port the code to another JVM. This becomes even more problematic when an existing application or platform (e.g. a web-server) is required as a multi-tenant cloud service. Everything should be redesigned according to the new programming model which is fundamentally different from standard Java practices whose memory management is entirely hidden from application developers.

Interpretive Approach. The Activiti workflow engine allows *Secure Scripting* [33] by means of the instruction count callback mechanism provided by the Rhino [34] JavaScript engine. Even though resource usage control is limited to memory,[5] the Java RCM API can be used to support other types of resources. However, this approach is only applicable to interpreted languages because it relies on counting the number of intermediate language instructions before performing a usage control. Our approach, instead, deals with languages whose bytecode are ultimately compiled into native machine code. In that case, there is no interpreter that can count the executed instructions and perform usage control via a callback function. Due to independence of our approach from interpreters, the performance degradation is considerably lower.

7   Conclusion

When it comes to processing service requests, for example in the context of web content, thread-level processing allows for high scalability and resource efficiency. In the context of multi-tenancy however, the limited monitorability and controllability of server threads in terms of their CPU and memory usage impede attaining the desired property of tenant isolation. This is especially problematic in service offerings that can be customized by tenants through custom code. For these reasons, tenant isolation is in practice accomplished by means of containers or virtual machines (VM) in multi-tenant architectures (cf. [35]).

In this paper, which fits into our ongoing research track on application-level tenant isolation in SaaS offerings, we take advantage of Java bytecode instrumentation and the Java RCM API to accomplish CPU and memory usage control at thread-level. By validating our solution in a prototype application, it is shown that the usage level of these two critical resources can be controlled without using containers or VMs. Evaluation results show that the proposed solution increases tenant accommodation capacity with a factor of 59 compared to process-level tenant isolation at the expense of 0.31 ns average performance overhead per usage control checkpoint.

Acknowledgment. This research is partially funded by the Research Fund KU Leuven (project GOA/14/003 - ADDIS) and the strategic basic research (SBO) project DeCoMAdS.

---

[5] The claimed CPU usage control in fact restricts the response time of the untrusted script rather than its CPU usage.

References

1. Gupta, D., Cherkasova, L., Gardner, R., Vahdat, A.: Enforcing performance isolation across virtual machines in Xen. In: van Steen, M., Henning, M. (eds.) Middleware 2006. LNCS, vol. 4290, pp. 342–362. Springer, Heidelberg (2006). https://doi.org/10.1007/11925071_18

2. Somani, G., Chaudhary, S.: Application performance isolation in virtualization. In: IEEE International Conference on Cloud Computing, CLOUD 2009, pp. 41–48. IEEE (2009)

3. Li, Y., Li, W., Jiang, C.: A survey of virtual machine system: current technology and future trends. In: 2010 Third International Symposium on Electronic Commerce and Security (ISECS), pp. 332–336. IEEE (2010)

4. Vaquero, L.M., Rodero-Merino, L., Buyya, R.: Dynamically scaling applications in the cloud. ACM SIGCOMM Comput. Commun. Rev. **41**(1), 45–52 (2011)

5. Weissman, C.D., Bobrowski, S.: The design of the force.com multitenant internet application development platform. In: Proceedings of the 2009 ACM SIGMOD International Conference on Management of Data, pp. 889–896. ACM (2009)

6. Song, H., Chauvel, F., Solberg, A.: Deep customization of multi-tenant SaaS using intrusive microservices. In: 2018 IEEE/ACM 40th International Conference on Software Engineering: New Ideas and Emerging Technologies Results (ICSE-NIER), pp. 97–100. IEEE (2018)

7. Li, X.H., Liu, T.C., Li, Y., Chen, Y.: SPIN: service performance isolation infrastructure in multi-tenancy environment. In: Bouguettaya, A., Krueger, I., Margaria, T. (eds.) ICSOC 2008. LNCS, vol. 5364, pp. 649–663. Springer, Heidelberg (2008). https://doi.org/10.1007/978-3-540-89652-4_58

8. Lin, H., Sun, K., Zhao, S., Han, Y.: Feedback-control-based performance regulation for multi-tenant applications. In: 2009 15th International Conference on Parallel and Distributed Systems (ICPADS), pp. 134–141. IEEE (2009)

9. Leitner, P., Wetzstein, B., Rosenberg, F., Michlmayr, A., Dustdar, S., Leymann, F.: Runtime prediction of service level agreement violations for composite services. In: Dan, A., Gittler, F., Toumani, F. (eds.) ICSOC/ServiceWave -2009. LNCS, vol. 6275, pp. 176–186. Springer, Heidelberg (2010). https://doi.org/10.1007/978-3-642-16132-2_17

10. Wang, W., Huang, X., Qin, X., Zhang, W., Wei, J., Zhong, H.: Application-level CPU consumption estimation: towards performance isolation of multi-tenancy web applications. In: 2012 IEEE 5th International Conference on Cloud computing (CLOUD), pp. 439–446. IEEE (2012)

11. Back, G., Hsieh, W.C., Lepreau, J.: Processes in KaffeOS: isolation, resource management, and sharing in Java. In: Proceedings of the 4th Conference on Symposium on Operating System Design & Implementation-Volume 4, p. 23. USENIX Association (2000)

12. Czajkowski, G., Daynès, L., Titzer, B.L.: A multi-user virtual machine. In: USENIX Annual Technical Conference, General Track, pp. 85–98 (2003)

13. Geoffray, N., Thomas, G., Muller, G., Parrend, P., Frénot, S., Folliot, B.: I-JVM: a Java virtual machine for component isolation in OSGi. In: IEEE/IFIP International Conference on Dependable Systems & Networks, DSN 2009, pp. 544–553. IEEE (2009)

14. Czajkowski, G., Daynàs, L.: Multitasking without compromise: a virtual machine evolution. ACM SIGPLAN Not. **47**(4a), 60–73 (2012)

15. Johnson, G., Dawson, M.: Introduction to Java multitenancy. Technical report (2015)
16. Herzog, A., Shahmehri, N.: Problems running untrusted services as Java threads. In: Nardelli, E., Talamo, M. (eds.) Certification and Security in Inter-Organizational E-Service. IOLCS, vol. 177, pp. 19–32. Springer, Boston (2005). https://doi.org/10.1007/11397427_2
17. Rodero-Merino, L., Vaquero, L.M., Caron, E., Muresan, A., Desprez, F.: Building safe PaaS clouds: a survey on security in multitenant software platforms. Comput. Secur. **31**(1), 96–108 (2012)
18. JCP: JSR 284: Resource Consumption Management API. https://jcp.org/en/jsr/detail?id=284. Accessed 04 Dec 2018
19. Czajkowski, G., Hahn, S., Skinner, G., Soper, P., Bryce, C.: A resource management interface for the Java^{TM} platform. Softw. Pract. Exp. **35**(2), 123–157 (2005)
20. Grove, D., DeFouw, G., Dean, J., Chambers, C.: Call graph construction in object-oriented languages. ACM SIGPLAN Not. **32**(10), 108–124 (1997)
21. OSGi Alliance: OSGi specification (2012). https://osgi.org/download/r4v43/osgi.core-4.3.0.pdf. Accessed 19 Apr 2017
22. Simão, J., Lemos, J., Veiga, L.: A^2-VM: a cooperative Java VM with support for resource-awareness and cluster-wide thread scheduling. In: Meersman, R., et al. (eds.) OTM 2011. LNCS, vol. 7044, pp. 302–320. Springer, Heidelberg (2011). https://doi.org/10.1007/978-3-642-25109-2_20
23. Kim, Y.J., Lee, Y.C., Han, H., Kang, S.: Hierarchical recursive resource sharing for containerized applications. In: Pahl, C., Vukovic, M., Yin, J., Yu, Q. (eds.) ICSOC 2018. LNCS, vol. 11236, pp. 781–796. Springer, Cham (2018). https://doi.org/10.1007/978-3-030-03596-9_56
24. Makki, M., Van Landuyt, D., Joosen, W.: Towards PaaS offering of BPMN 2.0 engines: a proposal for service-level tenant isolation. In: Mann, Z.Á., Stolz, V. (eds.) ESOCC 2017. CCIS, vol. 824, pp. 5–19. Springer, Cham (2018). https://doi.org/10.1007/978-3-319-79090-9_1
25. Truyen, E., Van Landuyt, D., Reniers, V., Rafique, A., Lagaisse, B., Joosen, W.: Towards a container-based architecture for multi-tenant SaaS applications. In: Proceedings of the 15th International Workshop on Adaptive and Reflective Middleware, p. 6. ACM (2016)
26. Ochei, L.C., Bass, J.M., Petrovski, A.: Degrees of tenant isolation for cloud-hosted software services: a cross-case analysis. J. Cloud Comput. **7**, 22 (2018)
27. Zhang, X., Tune, E., Hagmann, R., Jnagal, R., Gokhale, V., Wilkes, J.: CPI 2: CPU performance isolation for shared compute clusters. In: Proceedings of the 8th ACM European Conference on Computer Systems, pp. 379–391. ACM (2013)
28. Krebs, R., Spinner, S., Ahmed, N., Kounev, S.: Resource usage control in multi-tenant applications. In: 2014 14th IEEE/ACM International Symposium on Cluster, Cloud and Grid Computing (CCGrid), pp. 122–131. IEEE (2014)
29. Walraven, S., De Borger, W., Vanbrabant, B., Lagaisse, B., Van Landuyt, D., Joosen, W.: Adaptive performance isolation middleware for multi-tenant SaaS. In: 2015 IEEE/ACM 8th International Conference on Utility and Cloud Computing (UCC), pp. 112–121. IEEE (2015)
30. Lama, P., Wang, S., Zhou, X., Cheng, D.: Performance isolation of data-intensive scale-out applications in a multi-tenant cloud. In: 2018 IEEE International Parallel and Distributed Processing Symposium (IPDPS), pp. 85–94. IEEE (2018)
31. Binder, W., Hulaas, J.G., Villazón, A.: Portable resource control in Java. ACM SIGPLAN Not. **36**, 139–155 (2001)

32. Janik, A., Zieliński, K.: Transparent resource management with Java RM API. In: Alexandrov, V.N., van Albada, G.D., Sloot, P.M.A., Dongarra, J. (eds.) ICCS 2006. LNCS, vol. 3994, pp. 1023–1030. Springer, Heidelberg (2006). https://doi.org/10.1007/11758549_136
33. Activiti. https://www.activiti.org/. Accessed 04 Dec 2018
34. Rhino.   https://developer.mozilla.org/en-US/docs/Mozilla/Projects/Rhino/. Accessed 04 Dec 2018
35. HoseinyFarahabady, M.R., Lee, Y.C., Zomaya, A.Y., Tari, Z.: A QoS-aware resource allocation controller for function as a service (FaaS) platform. In: Maximilien, M., Vallecillo, A., Wang, J., Oriol, M. (eds.) ICSOC 2017. LNCS, vol. 10601, pp. 241–255. Springer, Cham (2017). https://doi.org/10.1007/978-3-319-69035-3_17

Optimized Application Deployment in the Fog

Zoltán Ádám Mann[1]([✉]), Andreas Metzger[1], Johannes Prade[2],
and Robert Seidl[3]

[1] University of Duisburg-Essen, Essen, Germany
zoltan.mann@gmail.com
[2] Nokia, Munich, Germany
[3] Nokia Bell Labs, Munich, Germany

Abstract. Fog computing uses geographically distributed fog nodes
that can supply nearby end devices with low-latency access to cloud-
like compute resources. If the load of a fog node exceeds its capacity,
some non-latency-critical application components may be offloaded to
the cloud. Using commercial cloud offerings for such offloading incurs
financial costs. Optimally deciding which application components to keep
in the fog node and which ones to offload to the cloud is a difficult
combinatorial problem. We introduce an optimization algorithm that (i)
guarantees that the deployment always satisfies capacity constraints, (ii)
achieves near-optimal cloud usage costs, and (iii) is fast enough to be
run online. Experimental results show that our algorithm can optimize
the deployment of hundreds of components in a fraction of a second on
a commodity computer, while leading to only slightly higher costs than
the optimum.

1 Introduction

Fog computing provides a decentralized infrastructure for supporting applications in domains like Internet of Things (IoT), cyber-physical systems, or smart
manufacturing (Industry 4.0) [9,13]. Such applications process data from distributed end devices. Processing these data in the end devices is often not feasible because of the very limited capacity (in terms of CPU, storage, battery) of
the devices. Fog computing uses computational resources called *fog nodes* at the
network edge, which offer higher capacity than end devices. A fog node thus can
host applications that process data from end devices that are in the proximity
of the fog node [1,23]. This facilitates data processing with low latency, since
modern communication technologies (like 4G and 5G) make the transfer of data
from the end devices to nearby fog nodes very fast (e.g., 5G even offers real-
time guarantees). This does not mean that all of the application's components
need to reside in the fog node. Some application components, e.g., ones that are
not latency-critical, may even be offloaded to the cloud instead of fog nodes, to
benefit from the virtually unlimited computational capacity of the cloud [3].

© Springer Nature Switzerland AG 2019
S. Yangui et al. (Eds.): ICSOC 2019, LNCS 11895, pp. 283–298, 2019.
https://doi.org/10.1007/978-3-030-33702-5_22

This paper focuses on optimizing application component deployment between a fog node and the cloud. The fog node, which can be considered a small data center at the network edge, hosts a set of applications [10]. Each application consists of a set of components (e.g., microservices). The fog node offers virtualized, cloud-like resources for hosting the components, e.g., in virtual machines or containers. Although the computational capacity of a fog node is typically larger than that of end devices, it is still limited and much lower than that of the cloud [12]. If the load of the fog node exceeds its capacity, some application components thus may have to be offloaded to the cloud. However, this offloading entails two concerns. On the one hand, using a commercial cloud is associated with financial costs, both for the usage of cloud compute resources and for data transfers into and out of the cloud. On the other hand, for some of the components there may be an *affinity requirement* prescribing the component to remain in the fog node, e.g., because the component is critical in terms of latency or because the component deals with sensitive data that must not be uploaded to the cloud due to data protection reasons [18]. Deciding which components to move to the cloud leads to a complex optimization problem, in which capacity and affinity constraints have to be satisfied while costs stemming from using the cloud are minimized. In addition, optimizing application deployment is not a one-off activity. The deployment should be re-optimized regularly during operation, e.g., when new application is added or an application is removed, the load on an application changes, cloud prices change, etc. After such events, the deployment of all applications may be re-optimized. Components can be migrated between the fog node and the cloud to adapt the deployment in these cases [24]. This requires the optimization algorithm to be fast enough to be used online.

This paper makes the following contributions:

(i) We formalize the problem of optimizing the deployment of application components between a fog node and the cloud.

(ii) We devise a heuristic algorithm (FOGPART) for the problem. The result of the algorithm always satisfies the capacity and affinity requirements, whenever they can be satisfied. FOGPART is a significantly extended version of the Kernighan-Lin algorithm for balanced graph partitioning [11]. FOGPART is a fast heuristic that iteratively improves an existing partition by a sequence of local changes, while also being able to escape local optima.

(iii) We demonstrate the applicability of our algorithm by applying it to the smart manufacturing case study "Factory in a Box".

(iv) We experimentally evaluate the effectiveness of FOGPART in terms of the resulting cloud usage cost and the algorithm's execution time and compare it with an exact algorithm and another heuristic.

The results show that the cost of the deployment found by FOGPART is on average only 2.1% higher than the results of the exact algorithm. At the same time, FOGPART is orders of magnitude faster, taking less than 300 ms on a commodity computer to optimize the deployment of 450 components. FOGPART delivers near-optimal results very quickly, making it applicable to practical use.

2   Problem Formalization

Figure 1 gives a schematic overview of the addressed problem. We are given a set $\mathcal{A}$ of applications to be deployed. An application $A \in \mathcal{A}$ is represented by an undirected graph $A = (V_A, E_A)$, where V_A is the set of components of application A and E_A is the set of connectors among the components. V_D denotes the set of end devices connected to the fog node, and E_D is the set of connectors between end devices and application components. The set of all end devices and components is $V = V_D \cup \bigcup \{V_A : A \in \mathcal{A}\}$. The set of all connectors between end devices and components as well as among components is $E = E_D \cup \bigcup \{E_A : A \in \mathcal{A}\}$.

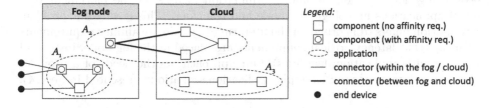

Fig. 1. Schematic example of applications deployed in a fog node and the cloud

For a component $v \in V$, $p(v) \in \mathbb{R}^+$ is the compute capacity required by v. As an example, this can be the number of CPU cores required by v. The predicate $s(v)$ is used to model the affinity requirement. The predicate is true if and only if v must remain in the fog node. If $v \in V_D$, then $p(v) = 0$ and $s(v) =$ true. For a connector $e \in E$, $h(e) \in \mathbb{R}^+$ denotes the amount of data exchanged along e.

$P \in \mathbb{R}^+$ denotes the compute capacity (e.g., number of CPU cores) of the fog node. The cost of renting a compute unit (vCPU) in the cloud is denoted by c_1, the unit cost of data transfer between the fog node and the cloud by c_2.

A *deployment* is a function $d : V \rightarrow \{\text{fog}, \text{cloud}\}$ that maps each component to either the fog node or the cloud. We use $\varrho(d)$ to denote the total compute capacity occupied in the fog node by deployment d: $\varrho(d) = \sum_{v \in V, \ d(v) = \text{fog}} p(v)$. A *valid* deployment must respect the following constraints:

$$\varrho(d) \leq P, \tag{1}$$

$$\forall v \in V : \ s(v) \Rightarrow (d(v) = \text{fog}). \tag{2}$$

Constraint (1) ensures that the total compute power required by the components in the fog node does not exceed the capacity of the fog node. Constraint (2) ensures that all affinity requirements are observed.

Our aim is to find a solution that minimizes the financial cost. For a deployment d, the set of connectors between the fog node and the cloud is defined as $E(d) = \{uv \in E : d(u) \neq d(v)\}$. Then, the cost of deployment d is:

$$\text{cost}(d) = \sum_{v \in V, \ d(v) = \text{cloud}} c_1 \cdot p(v) + \sum_{e \in E(d)} c_2 \cdot h(e), \tag{3}$$

where the first term is the cost of leased cloud resources and the second term is the cost of data transfers between the fog node and the cloud. Hence our aim is to minimize (3) while satisfying (1) and (2).

For a connector between an end device v_1 and a component v_2, $s(v_1) =$ true ensures that v_1 cannot be moved to the cloud. If $d(v_2) =$ cloud, then the connector crosses the boundary between fog and cloud, and thus it contributes to the costs in the second term of (3), otherwise it does not.

The deployment must be adapted in three cases: (i) when a new application is added, (ii) when an application is removed, (iii) when something changes in the deployed applications or in their environment.

Note that, in contrast to approaches aiming at placing one application on several fog nodes [4], our problem formulation focuses on the placement of a set of applications in a single fog node and the cloud. This is why our problem formulation differs from others in the literature (e.g., we use affinity requirements to ensure that latency-critical components are placed in the fog node, instead of working with application deadlines). Our approach fits the needs of a provider of an edge data center (an example application scenario is presented in Sect. 4).

3   The FogPart Algorithm

The FOGPART algorithm we propose to address the above optimization problem works on a model of the system. This means that the algorithm tentatively allocates and moves the components between the fog node and the cloud. Only after the algorithm terminates, the best found configuration is enacted by actually carrying out the necessary allocations and migrations.

When a new application is added, FOGPART first places each new component v as follows: if $s(v) =$ true (i.e., v is subject to an affinity requirement), then v is placed in the fog node, otherwise in the cloud. Afterwards, the algorithm re-optimizes the deployment. When an application is removed, all its components are removed from the deployment, and a re-optimization is carried out. When there is a change in the deployed applications (e.g., in the CPU requirements of some components, the amount of data transfer between components, the affinity requirements of components) or in the environment (e.g., in the unit price of using the cloud or the capacity of the fog node), FOGPART first ensures that the affinity requirement continues to hold by moving any affected component from the cloud to the fog node, and then performs re-optimization.

Re-optimization works the same way in each case. Re-optimization is based on iterative improvement: it starts from a – not necessarily valid – deployment and tries to improve it (making it valid and decreasing its cost) through a series of local changes. In each step, one component is moved either from the fog node to the cloud or vice versa; however, if the current deployment violates the capacity constraint, then only moves from the fog node to the cloud are allowed. The idea of the algorithm is to move the component leading to the highest decrease in cost, captured by the *gain* of the components.

Definition 1. *Let d be a deployment and $v \in V$ a component. Let d' be the deployment obtained from d by moving v. Then, given deployment d, the gain of moving v is defined as*

$$gain(d, v) = \begin{cases} -\infty & \text{if } d \text{ is valid}, d' \text{ is invalid}, \\ cost(d) - cost(d') & \text{otherwise}. \end{cases}$$

The algorithm prefers moves with higher gain values. To escape local optima, the move with highest gain is made even if its gain is negative, i.e., the move increases the cost (except if the gain is $-\infty$). To avoid infinite loops, each component may be moved only once during a re-optimization. When no further move is possible, the deployment with the lowest cost that was encountered during the algorithm is taken as the resulting new deployment.

Algorithm 1. Deployment re-optimization

```
1:  procedure RE-OPTIMIZE(d)
2:      bestDeployment ← d
3:      bestCost ← cost(d)
4:      L ← {v ∈ V : ¬s(v)}
5:      end ← (L = ∅)
6:      while ¬end do
7:          bestGain ← −∞
8:          for v ∈ L do
9:              if ϱ(d) ≤ P or d(v) = fog then
10:                 g ← GAIN(d,v)
11:                 if g > bestGain then
12:                     bestComp ← v
13:                     bestGain ← g
14:                 end if
15:             end if
16:         end for
17:         if bestGain > −∞ then
18:             forced ← (ϱ(d) > P)
19:             flip d(bestComp)
20:             L.remove(bestComp)
21:             if forced or cost(d) < bestCost
    then
22:                 bestDeployment ← d
23:                 bestCost ← cost(d)
24:             end if
25:         end if
26:         end ← (L = ∅ or bestGain = −∞)
27:     end while
28:     d ← bestDeployment
29: end procedure
```

Algorithm 2. Calculation of the gain of moving a component

```
1:  procedure GAIN(d, v)
2:      if d(v) = fog then
3:          r ← −c₁ · p(v)
4:      else if ϱ(d) ≤ P and ϱ(d)+
    p(v) > P then
5:          return −∞
6:      else
7:          r ← c₁ · p(v)
8:      end if
9:      for vw ∈ E do
10:         if d(v) = d(w) then
11:             r ← r − c₂ · h(vw)
12:         else
13:             r ← r + c₂ · h(vw)
14:         end if
15:     end for
16:     return r
17: end procedure
```

The above re-optimization procedure in FOGPART is an extended version of the Kernighan-Lin (KL) algorithm for balanced graph partitioning [11,17].

Variants of the KL algorithm have been successfully applied to different partitioning problems [16,19–21], thanks to the fact that it is a fast heuristic which can escape local optima. Applying the KL algorithm to our optimization problem required several extensions, since the original algorithm supports only edge costs, whereas our problem also contains costs related to vertices, as well as hard constraints on capacity and affinity, which are not supported by the original algorithm.

A more detailed description of the re-optimization procedure is given in Algorithm 1. The algorithm starts by setting "bestDeployment" and "bestCost" to the current deployment respectively its cost (lines 2–3). The list L contains the components that may be moved. In line 4, L is initialized to the set of all components without affinity requirements; the components with affinity requirements are not movable since they must remain in the fog node. In each iteration, one component is moved and it is removed from L (line 20); the procedure ends if L becomes empty, as captured by the Boolean variable "end" (lines 5, 6, 26).

In each iteration, first the component to be moved is determined ("bestComp"). For that purpose, "bestGain" is initialized to $-\infty$ (line 8), and then all movable components are checked (lines 8–16). Line 9 ensures that moving a component from the cloud to the fog node is not considered if the fog node is already overloaded. Lines 10–14 determine the component with the highest gain. If an allowed move is found, then it is performed (line 19) and the corresponding component is removed from L (line 20). If the fog node was overloaded before the move, then the move is forced to be from the fog node to the cloud, as captured by the Boolean variable "forced". In this case, "bestDeployment" and "bestCost" are certainly updated with the changed deployment and its cost, otherwise they are updated only if the changed deployment is better than the best deployment encountered so far in terms of costs (lines 18, 21–24). The loop ends if there are no more movable components ($L = \emptyset$) or there are no valid moves, i.e., there are only moves that would invalidate the deployment ("bestGain" $= -\infty$) (line 26). Finally, the best deployment found is chosen (line 28).

The gain of a component is computed by Algorithm 2, in line with Definition 1. If the component v is currently in the fog node, then moving it to the cloud would increase costs by $c_1 \cdot p(v)$ (lines 2–3). If v is in the cloud, then moving it to the fog node would decrease costs by the same amount (lines 6–7). However, if the move violates the capacity constraint of the fog node, then the move is not allowed, resulting in a gain of $-\infty$ (lines 4–5). In lines 9–15, the connectors of v are investigated. For a connector vw, if v and w are either both in the cloud or both in the fog node, then the move would increase costs by $c_2 \cdot h(vw)$ (lines 10–11); otherwise, it would decrease costs by the same amount (lines 12–13).

4   Case Study

To demonstrate the applicability of our approach and illustrate its operation, we applied it to a case study from the smart manufacturing domain, called "Factory in a Box" (FiaB). FiaB is an innovative factory solution, representing a

Fig. 2. Factory in a Box (FiaB): outside and inside view

Table 1. Characteristics of components in the FiaB case study

Application	Component	Required CPU cores	Affinity Req.
A_1	AM task manager	1	No
	iWh manager	1	No
	Robot control	1	Yes
	Manual assembly SW	2	No
	Order management	2	No
	Supply management	2	No
	Tool management	1	Yes
	Process management	1	Yes
	ERP system	2	No
A_2	FiaB remote management	1	No
	Shop floor management	1	Yes
A_3	Sensor evaluation SW	1	No
	Sensor dashboard	1	No

complete production environment, integrated in a standard 20-feet freight container (see Fig. 2). It can host many different types of production lines, ranging from chemical processes, electronic device manufacturing to consumer goods. It accommodates a heterogeneous internal communication infrastructure, including novel mobile and fixed telecommunication technologies (e.g., private LTE and 5G) to serve various applications in the Industrial IoT environment. In addition to the computing capabilities within the FiaB (which we consider as the fog node), it connects to a cloud infrastructure using a public network.

For managing the production, multiple applications are needed. The characteristics of the application components respectively the connectors are shown in Table 1[1] and Table 2. The unit costs of compute resources and of data trans-

---

[1] Abbreviations: AM = Additive Manufacturing, iWh = inbound Warehouse, VR/AR = virtual reality/augmented reality, ERP = Enterprise Resource Planning.

Table 2. Characteristics of connectors in the FiaB case study

App.	Connector (endpoint1 ↔ endpoint2)	Data transfer [GB/day]
A_1	AR/VR glasses (device) ↔ Manual assembly SW	15
	Tool management ↔ Process management	1
	AM task manager ↔ Tool management	2
	iWh manager ↔ Tool management	0.5
	Robot control ↔ Tool management	2
	AM task manager ↔ Process management	0.1
	Robot control ↔ Process management	0.1
	Manual assembly SW ↔ Process management	1
	ERP system ↔ Order management	1
	Order management ↔ Supply management	0.1
	Order management ↔ Process management	0.1
A_2	Shop floor management ↔ FiaB remote management	5
A_3	Sensor evaluation SW ↔ Sensor dashboard	2.5

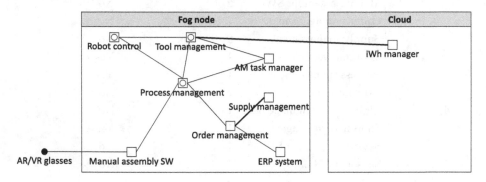

Fig. 3. Deployment of the first application in the FiaB case study

fers to and from the cloud are determined based on Amazon EC2 pricing[2]. The hourly rental fee of a t2.small instance is USD 0.023, leading to a daily fee of USD 0.552, which is used as c_1. The transfer of 1GB of data to or from Amazon EC2 costs USD 0.09, which is used as c_2. The fog node has 12 CPU cores.

Running FogPart to add application A_1, first the components with affinity requirements (Robot control, Tool management, Process management) are put into the fog node and all other components are tentatively put into the cloud. Then, Algorithm 1 is executed to optimize the deployment. Algorithm 1 moves five further components from the cloud to the fog node, until the capacity of the fog node is exhausted, leading to the deployment shown in Fig. 3.

---

[2] https://aws.amazon.com/ec2/pricing/on-demand/.

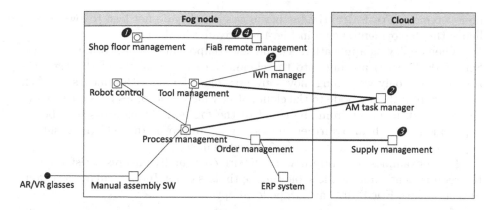

Fig. 4. Deployment of the second application. The numbers show the order in which the components are allocated and moved by FOGPART

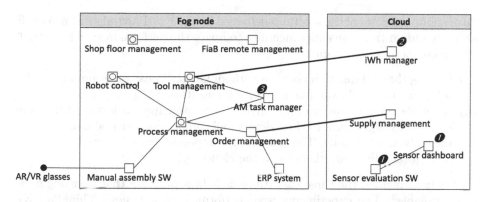

Fig. 5. Deployment of the third application (numbering as in Fig. 4)

When application A_2 is deployed, first its component with an affinity requirement (Shop floor management) is put into the fog node and the other component (FiaB remote management) into the cloud. When re-optimizing the deployment, FOGPART is confronted with an invalid deployment requiring 13 CPU cores in the fog node. Hence, FOGPART first makes a forced move: the AM task manager is moved from the fog node to the cloud. This way, the deployment becomes valid, and it even reaches a local optimum: only moves from the fog node to the cloud are possible, which increase costs. FOGPART makes one of these worsening moves: the Supply management is moved from the fog node to the cloud. As it turns out, this worsening move pays off: it frees up 2 CPU cores in the fog node, so that in the next two steps the FiaB remote management and iWh manager components can be moved to the fog node. The resulting deployment is better than the local optimum found earlier, as the heavy traffic between the Shop floor management and FiaB remote management components does not leave the fog node anymore. FOGPART tries further moves but they do not lead to lower costs, hence the deployment shown in Fig. 4 is activated in the end.

When deploying application A_3, the new components (Sensor evaluation SW, Sensor dashboard) are put into the cloud. Since the capacity of the fog node is exhausted, only worsening moves are possible. The algorithm moves the iWh manager from the fog node to the cloud, after which it becomes possible to move the AM task manager from the cloud to the fog node. This leads to a better deployment, which also further moves cannot improve. In fact, the resulting deployment, which is shown in Fig. 5, is optimal.

These examples illustrate how FOGPART continually ensures satisfaction of the requirements, and at the same time optimizes costs. In particular, the examples show how FOGPART can escape local optima.

5   Experimental Evaluation

To evaluate the costs of the solutions delivered by the FOGPART algorithm as well as its execution time, we experimentally compare the performance of FOGPART to two competing algorithms:

(i) Solving the optimization problem with an integer linear programming (ILP) solver as a typical example of an exact algorithm.
(ii) A simple heuristic based on the first-fit (FF) principle, as a typical example of a greedy algorithm. FF first deploys all components with affinity requirements in the fog node. The remaining components are deployed in the fog node if they fit, and otherwise in the cloud.

We implemented the three algorithms as a Java program that we made publicly available[3]. The experiments were performed on a Lenovo ThinkPad X1 laptop with Intel Core i5-4210U CPU @ 1.70 GHz and 8 GB RAM. The ILP-based algorithm uses the Gurobi Optimizer, version 7.0.2, as an external solver. The ILP solver was executed in single-threaded mode with a timeout of 60 s.

We simulated the following scenario:

– 10 applications are randomly generated with the following parameters:
  • $|V_A| = 30$
  • $p(v)$ is uniformly chosen from $\{1, 2, 3, 4\}$ for each $v \in V_A$
  • $s(v)$ is true with probability 0.1 for each $v \in V_A$
  • (V_A, E_A) is a complete graph
  • $h(e)$ is uniformly chosen from $[0.0, 3.0]$ for each $e \in E_A$
– Starting with $\mathcal{A} = \emptyset$, the applications are added one by one in the first 10 steps. Afterwards, 10 change steps are carried out, and finally the applications are removed one by one. Each change step performs one of the following actions (each with equal probability):
  • For each application, pick 3 random components and either increase or decrease their number of CPU cores by 1.

---

[3] https://sourceforge.net/p/vm-alloc/hybrid-deployment/.

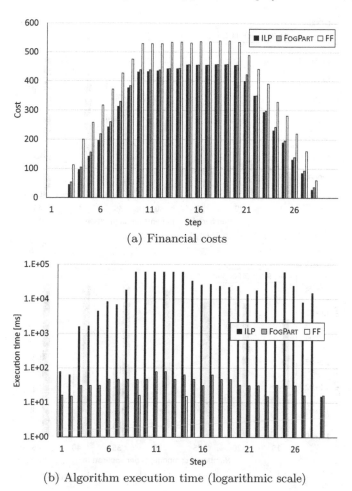

(a) Financial costs

(b) Algorithm execution time (logarithmic scale)

Fig. 6. Results of first adding, then changing, and finally removing 10 applications

- For each application, pick a random component v and let $s(v) := \neg s(v)$.
- For each application, pick 10 random connectors and change their traffic intensity by multiplying with 2 or 0.5.
- Change c_1, the unit cost of compute resources, by either increasing or decreasing it by 10%.
- As before, $c_1 = 0.552$ and $c_2 = 0.09$ (in line with Amazon EC2 pricing)
- $P = 150$

Figure 6a shows the costs achieved by the three algorithms after each algorithm call. As expected, the costs monotonously increase in the first 10 steps and decrease in steps 20–30. In steps 1–2 and 29–30, it is possible to deploy all components in the fog node, leading to 0 costs; this optimal deployment is found by all algorithms. In the other steps, some components must be deployed in the

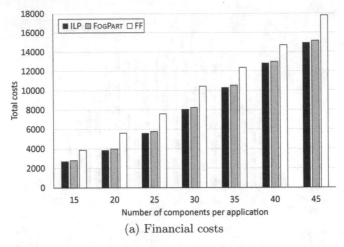

(a) Financial costs

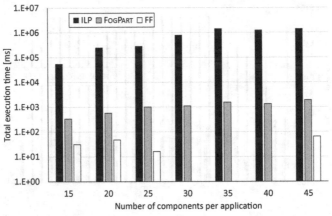

(b) Algorithm execution time (logarithmic scale)

Fig. 7. Impact of increasing the number of components

cloud, leading to non-zero costs. Consistently across all steps 3–28, the results of FOGPART are only slightly higher than those of the ILP-based algorithm, whereas the FF algorithm yields significantly higher costs. The costs achieved by FOGPART are on average 2.19% higher than the costs achieved by the ILP-based algorithm; the costs of FF are 29.32% higher than those of ILP.

Figure 6b shows the execution time of the three algorithms in each step. The time is shown in milliseconds, using logarithmic scale. The execution time of the ILP-based algorithm is consistently significantly higher than the execution time of the two heuristics. The average execution time of the ILP-based algorithm is roughly 26 s, while the average execution time is only about 36 ms for FOGPART and 1 ms for FF. In 8 cases, the execution time of the ILP-based algorithm reaches the timeout threshold of 60 s.

To evaluate scalability, we repeated the same call sequence as above, with varying number of components per application. In Fig. 7a, we report the total costs achieved by the three algorithms aggregated along the whole call sequence of adding, changing, and removing 10 applications. The number of components per application increased from 15 to 45 in increments of 5, thus leading to 150–450 components within a call sequence. Consistently across all application sizes, the cost of the deployments found by FOGPART is only slightly higher than the costs achieved with ILP, whereas the costs achieved by FF are significantly higher. On average, FOGPART leads to 2.1% higher costs than ILP, whereas FF leads to 24.3% higher costs than ILP. Interestingly, as the number of components grows, the relative difference between the algorithms' results decreases. This is because, as the number of components grows, also the number of components with affinity requirements grows, using up an increasing part of the fog node's capacity, and leaving less optimization opportunities for the deployment of the components without affinity requirements. E.g., when each application consists of 45 components, the expected number of CPU cores needed by the components with affinity requirements is 112.5, using up 75% of the capacity of the fog node.

Figure 7b shows the total execution time – aggregated over the whole call sequence – of the three algorithms (note the logarithmic scale of the vertical axis). The execution time of FF is very low (tens of milliseconds for the whole call sequence), that of FOGPART is somewhat higher but still quite low (less than 2 s in each case for the whole call sequence in total), and that of ILP is much higher (more than 20 min for a call sequence when the number of components is over 300). As the number of components grows, the execution time of both FOGPART and ILP tends to grow. However, the growth rate is very different in the two cases. When the number of components grows from 150 to 450 – a threefold increase – the execution time of FOGPART increases by a factor of 5.7, suggesting a moderate polynomial complexity. At the same time, the execution time of ILP grows by a factor of 26, suggesting an exponential execution time, damped down by the timeout of 60 s per run.

6 Related Work

Some approaches have already been proposed in the literature for the optimized deployment of applications in the fog [4]. Mahmud et al. proposed a heuristic to allocate application components in a multi-layer fog system [14]. Taneja and Davy developed a greedy algorithm for placing application modules in the cloud and on fog nodes [27]. Skarlat et al. devised a genetic algorithm for optimizing the deployment of IoT applications on fog nodes [26]. Da Silva et al. considered the deployment of distributed stream processing applications on cloud and edge resources with the aim of minimizing application latency [25]. Cai et al. addressed the deployment of complex event processing applications on edge resources with the aim of minimizing the average application latency [5]. Mouradian et al. use tabu search to minimize the makespan of applications consisting of virtual network functions in the context of mobile fog nodes [22]. However, these approaches suffer from some serious limitations. First, some approaches support only applications with a special structure (cycles of four vertices [14], series-parallel graphs [22,25], or directed acyclic graphs [5]). In contrast, our algorithm works for any application topology. Second, some approaches do not consider the costs of using the cloud at all [5,25], or do not take data transfers between application components into account [26,27], which, however, can lead to significant costs. In contrast, our algorithm explicitly minimizes the costs of using the cloud, including costs for both compute resources in the cloud and data transfer between the fog node and the cloud. Third, some approaches were based on simple greedy algorithms [14,27] that consider only one application at a time and deploy its components sequentially. In contrast, our algorithm optimizes the deployment of all applications together, which increases the probability of finding overall good solutions, and uses special techniques to escape local optima.

Similar problems also arise when optimizing the deployment of applications in hybrid clouds. Several authors investigated the problem of scheduling a workflow using the resources of a hybrid cloud [2]. Chopra et al. proposed an algorithm for minimizing costs while respecting a given deadline [8]. Chang et al. proposed an agent-based mechanism to continually re-optimize the deployment of the jobs of a workflow in a hybrid cloud [7], while Zhu et al. addressed the scheduling of deadline-constrained workflows with stochastic tasks [29]. Another related area is the allocation of massively parallel tasks using the resources of a hybrid cloud. Van den Bossche et al. addressed the allocation of tasks to hybrid clouds taking into account application deadlines and cloud resource costs [28]. Candeia et al. aimed at maximizing profit, taking into account the benefit of finishing a set of compute tasks early and the costs of using cloud resources [6]. Malawski et al. used mixed integer nonlinear programming to allocate tasks to hybrid cloud resources, subject to deadline constraints, minimizing costs [15]. In all these papers, the communication structure between tasks is either constrained to be acyclic, which is an unrealistic assumption for many applications, or not considered at all. In contrast, our approach works with arbitrary communication topologies among the components of an application.

7   Conclusions

This paper addressed the problem of deploying application components on a fog node or in the cloud, such that components which need to be kept close to the end devices are deployed on the fog node, the capacity of the fog node is not overloaded, and the costs of using the cloud for computation and data transfer are minimized. We devised a heuristic for this problem. Our experimental results suggest that the results of our algorithm are close to optimal, while the algorithm is very fast so that it can be used online.

In the future, we aim to extend our approach to handle further constraints (e.g., modeling a more fine-grained control of latency) and optimization objectives (e.g., relating to energy consumption).

Acknowledgments. Research leading to these results received funding from the European Union's Horizon 2020 research and innovation programme under grant agreements no. 731678 (RestAssured) and 731932 (TransformingTransport).

References

1. Abbas, Z., Li, J., Yadav, N., Tariq, I.: Computational task offloading in mobile edge computing using learning automata. In: IEEE ICCC, pp. 57–61 (2018)
2. Alkhanak, E.N., Lee, S.P., Rezaei, R., Parizi, R.M.: Cost optimization approaches for scientific workflow scheduling in cloud and grid computing: a review, classifications, and open issues. J. Syst. Softw. **113**, 1–26 (2016)
3. Bermbach, D., et al.: A research perspective on fog computing. In: Braubach, L., et al. (eds.) ICSOC 2017. LNCS, vol. 10797, pp. 198–210. Springer, Cham (2018). https://doi.org/10.1007/978-3-319-91764-1_16
4. Brogi, A., Forti, S., Guerrero, C., Lera, I.: How to place your apps in the fog - state of the art and open challenges. arXiv preprint, arXiv:1901.05717 (2019)
5. Cai, X., Kuang, H., Hu, H., Song, W., Lü, J.: Response time aware operator placement for complex event processing in edge computing. In: Pahl, C., Vukovic, M., Yin, J., Yu, Q. (eds.) ICSOC 2018. LNCS, vol. 11236, pp. 264–278. Springer, Cham (2018). https://doi.org/10.1007/978-3-030-03596-9_18
6. Candeia, D., Araújo, R., Lopes, R., Brasileiro, F.: Investigating business-driven cloudburst schedulers for e-science bag-of-tasks applications. In: CloudCom, pp. 343–350 (2010)
7. Chang, Y.S., Fan, C.T., Sheu, R.K., Jhu, S.R., Yuan, S.M.: An agent-based workflow scheduling mechanism with deadline constraint on hybrid cloud environment. Int. J. Commun Syst **31**(1), e3401 (2018)
8. Chopra, N., Singh, S.: Deadline and cost based workflow scheduling in hybrid cloud. In: ICACCI, pp. 840–846 (2013)
9. Dastjerdi, A.V., Buyya, R.: Fog computing: helping the Internet of Things realize its potential. Computer **49**(8), 112–116 (2016)
10. Deng, S., Xiang, Z., Yin, J., Taheri, J., Zomaya, A.Y.: Composition-driven IoT service provisioning in distributed edges. IEEE Access **6**, 54258–54269 (2018)
11. Kernighan, B.W., Lin, S.: An efficient heuristic procedure for partitioning graphs. Bell Syst. Techn. J. **49**(2), 291–307 (1970)
12. Lai, P., et al.: Optimal edge user allocation in edge computing with variable sized vector bin packing. In: Pahl, C., Vukovic, M., Yin, J., Yu, Q. (eds.) ICSOC 2018. LNCS, vol. 11236, pp. 230–245. Springer, Cham (2018). https://doi.org/10.1007/978-3-030-03596-9_15
13. Mahmud, R., Kotagiri, R., Buyya, R.: Fog computing: a taxonomy, survey and future directions. In: Di Martino, B., Li, K.-C., Yang, L.T., Esposito, A. (eds) Internet of Everything. IT, pp. 103–130. Springer, Singapore (2018). https://doi.org/10.1007/978-981-10-5861-5_5
14. Mahmud, R., Ramamohanarao, K., Buyya, R.: Latency-aware application module management for fog computing environments. ACM ToIT **19**(1), 9 (2018)
15. Malawski, M., Figiela, K., Nabrzyski, J.: Cost minimization for computational applications on hybrid cloud infrastructures. FGCS **29**(7), 1786–1794 (2013)
16. Mann, Z.Á.: Partitioning algorithms for hardware/software co-design. Ph.D. thesis, Budapest University of Technology and Economics (2004)
17. Mann, Z.Á.: Optimization in Computer Engineering - Theory and Applications. Scientific Research Publishing, Irvine (2011)

18. Mann, Z.Á., Metzger, A.: Optimized cloud deployment of multi-tenant software considering data protection concerns. In: CCGRID, pp. 609–618 (2017)
19. Mann, Z.Á., Orbán, A., Farkas, V.: Evaluating the Kernighan-Lin heuristic for hardware/software partitioning. AMCS **17**(2), 249–267 (2007)
20. Mann, Z.Á., Papp, P.A.: Formula partitioning revisited. In: 5th Pragmatics of SAT Workshop, vol. 27, pp. 41–56. EasyChair Proceedings in Computing (2014)
21. Mann, Z.Á., Papp, P.A.: Guiding SAT solving by formula partitioning. Int. J. Artif. Intell. Tools **26**(4), 1750011 (2017)
22. Mouradian, C., Kianpisheh, S., Abu-Lebdeh, M., Ebrahimnezhad, F., Jahromi, N.T., Glitho, R.H.: Application component placement in NFV-based hybrid cloud/fog systems with mobile fog nodes. IEEE JSAC **37**(5), 1130–1143 (2019)
23. Nan, Y., Li, W., Bao, W., Delicato, F.C., Pires, P.F., Zomaya, A.Y.: A dynamic tradeoff data processing framework for delay-sensitive applications in cloud of things systems. J. Parallel Distrib. Comput. **112**, 53–66 (2018)
24. Ravindra, P., Khochare, A., Reddy, S.P., Sharma, S., Varshney, P., Simmhan, Y.: ECHO: an adaptive Orchestration platform for Hybrid dataflows across Cloud and Edge. In: Maximilien, M., Vallecillo, A., Wang, J., Oriol, M. (eds.) ICSOC 2017. LNCS, vol. 10601, pp. 395–410. Springer, Cham (2017). https://doi.org/10.1007/978-3-319-69035-3_28
25. da Silva Veith, A., de Assunção, M.D., Lefèvre, L.: Latency-aware placement of data stream analytics on edge computing. In: Pahl, C., Vukovic, M., Yin, J., Yu, Q. (eds.) ICSOC 2018. LNCS, vol. 11236, pp. 215–229. Springer, Cham (2018). https://doi.org/10.1007/978-3-030-03596-9_14
26. Skarlat, O., Nardelli, M., Schulte, S., Borkowski, M., Leitner, P.: Optimized IoT service placement in the fog. Service Oriented Comp. Appl. **11**(4), 427–443 (2017)
27. Taneja, M., Davy, A.: Resource aware placement of IoT application modules in fog-cloud computing paradigm. In: IEEE IM, pp. 1222–1228 (2017)
28. Van den Bossche, R., Vanmechelen, K., Broeckhove, J.: Cost-optimal scheduling in hybrid IaaS clouds for deadline constrained workloads. In: IEEE CLOUD, pp. 228–235 (2010)
29. Zhu, J., Li, X., Ruiz, R., Xu, X.: Scheduling stochastic multi-stage jobs to elastic hybrid cloud resources. IEEE TPDS **29**(6), 1401–1415 (2018)

Toward Cost Efficient Cloud Bursting

Amirmohammad Pasdar[1], Young Choon Lee[1(✉)], and Khaled Almi'ani[2]

[1] Macquarie University, Sydney, NSW 2109, Australia
amirmohammad.pasdar@hdr.mq.edu.au, young.lee@mq.edu.au
[2] Al-Hussein Bin Talal University, Ma'an, Jordan
k.almiani@ahu.edu.jo

Abstract. While private clouds are still widely adopted due primarily to privacy and security reasons, they are often less resilient with fluctuating workloads compared to public clouds. Workload surges in private clouds can be dealt with by offloading some workload/jobs to public clouds; this is referred to as cloud bursting. Although the dynamic use of public clouds is claimed to be cost efficient, the actual realization of such cost efficiency is highly dependent on judicious scheduling decisions. In this paper, we present Cost Efficient Cloud Bursting Scheduler (CECBS) as a new scheduling framework that optimizes cost efficiency while preserving privacy by taking advantage of benefits of each of two cloud types. In particular, CECBS schedules jobs taking into account (1) public cloud pricing policy (billing cycle), (2) privacy of data/job and (3) local electricity rates for private clouds. Based on simulation results obtained from real workload traces, CECBS achieves 20% cost savings on average compared with costs of Resource Management Service (RMS) [11].

1 Introduction

Cost efficiency is one of the key benefits of cloud computing. The optimization of cost efficiency is of great practical importance with ever increasing operating expenses including energy prices. Such optimization can be achieved by deploying all ICT solutions to public clouds, such as Amazon Web Services (AWS) [1], Microsoft Azure (MS) [5] and Google Compute Engine (GCE) [3]. However, when it comes to job/data privacy, the use of private clouds is often inevitable. While such use resolves the privacy issue, it brings another issue of less resilient resource provisioning particularly when private clouds encounter workload surges that exceed the resource capacity.

A practical solution for the above stated issues is the mix use of private clouds and public clouds (i.e., hybrid clouds). There have been many works on scheduling in geo-distributed clouds and hybrid clouds [13,15,16,18]. Nevertheless, they tend to neglect the data privacy. In addition, their cost optimization focuses on the minimization of public cloud usage considering different rates of virtual machines (VMs or instances in the AWS terminology), but not billing cycles, e.g., the hour in AWS and the second in GCE.

In this paper, we study the cost efficiency of cloud bursting explicitly taking into account privacy, billing cycles and local electricity rates. To this end, we

© Springer Nature Switzerland AG 2019
S. Yangui et al. (Eds.): ICSOC 2019, LNCS 11895, pp. 299–313, 2019.
https://doi.org/10.1007/978-3-030-33702-5_23

develop **C**ost **E**fficient **C**loud **B**ursting **S**cheduler **(CECBS)** as a new scheduling framework. The overall structure of CECBS is shown in Fig. 1. In particular, CECBS consists of two main components: a hybrid scheduler (Algorithm 1) and a Q-learning based VM manager (Algorithm 5). The former further consists of three scheduling algorithms that deal with privacy-sensitive jobs (Algorithm 2) and regular jobs (Algorithms 3 and 4 for private cloud and public cloud, respectively). The latter Q-learning based VM manager constantly monitors states of VMs in the private cloud. The state information is then used to (1) make scheduling decisions for the private cloud using Algorithms 2 and 3 and (2) activate/deactivate VMs to save energy as CECBS concerns local electricity rates.

For a job, if it is privacy sensitive, it is scheduled to the private cloud. Otherwise, it is scheduled to either cloud based on cost efficiency comparison between private cloud and public cloud. The cost efficiency of private cloud is determined based on primarily local electricity rates (as energy prices are soaring and account for a large portion of operating expenses) while that of public cloud is determined based on its billing cycle (e.g., the hour or second).

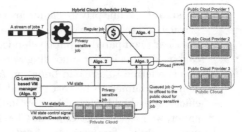

Fig. 1. Structure of CECBS framework.

Based on simulation results obtained from 24 h of real workload traces, CECBS saves costs by 20% compared with costs of Resource Management Service (RMS) [11]. For the private cloud alone, CECBS reduces the private cloud usage cost up to 54%, 55%, and 55% in comparison with RMS with respect to VM monitoring intervals of 30 s, 60 s and 120 s, respectively. It also improves resource utilization up to 31% compared with RMS.

2   Problem Statement

The hybrid cloud consists of a private cloud and a set of M public clouds $(CP = \{CP_1, \cdots, CP_M\})$. A public cloud CP_i consists of k VMs, $CP_i = \{vm_1, \cdots, vm_k\}$. Public cloud CP_i has its own billing cycle BC_{CP_i}. Each BC_{CP_i} may have remaining time that vm_i could be used for "free". There may be a completely new billing cycle $(BC_{CP_i}^{new})$ that can incur charges or an existing billing cycle $(BC_{CP_i}^{active})$ that can be used for free before the end of billing cycle.

The private cloud consists of a number of servers, each of which hosts one or more VMs. The private cloud has varying electricity rates (Ch_τ) with respect to different times of day, i.e., off-peak, shoulder and peak. It may also follow a fixed rate (Ch_f) per a specific period of contract, such as the year. The energy consumption of a server can be calculated based on Thermal Design Power (TDP). We assume servers are equipped with power management that allows them to be put into deep sleep mode on which power consumption is negligible.

Algorithm 1: Hybrid Cloud Scheduler

Data: T

1 **for** $t_i \in T$ **do**
2   **if** t_i *is privacy sensitive* **then**
3 | Privacy-aware scheduling (Algorithm 2)
4   **end**
5   **else**
6   Calculate $ec^{t_i}_{private}$ at Ch_τ with current VM states
7   Calculate $ec^{t_i}_{public}$ based on t_i^{res} considering $ec^{active}_{private}$
8   **if** $ec_{private} \leq ec_{public}$ **then**
9 | Schedule t_i to the private cloud (Algorithm 3)
10   **end**
11   **else**
12 | Schedule t_i to the public cloud (Algorithm 4)
13   **end**
14   **end**
15 **end**

Workloads are considered as a stream of T jobs at time τ. Each job (t_i) within this stream of jobs (T) has certain characteristics, such as a deadline (d_t) and privacy sensitivity (p_t). A job with a privacy concern must be executed on the private cloud. Required resources are expressed in terms of the number of CPU cores $(core_t)$ and the required memory (mem_t).

The problem in our study is how to schedule a stream of jobs which become available at different times to resources within a hybrid cloud environment so that cloud bursting improves the cost efficiency while preserving privacy.

3 Cost Efficient Cloud Bursting Scheduler

In this section, we present CECBS (Fig. 1) with its two main components: Hybrid cloud scheduler and Q-learning based VM manager.

3.1 Hybrid Cloud Scheduler

Hybrid cloud scheduler (Algorithm 1) is the key scheduling component. It always schedules privacy-sensitive jobs to the private cloud (Algorithm 2). In the meantime, it schedules regular jobs, without privacy concerns, based on the cost of execution between private cloud and public cloud (Algorithm 3).

Privacy-Aware Scheduling. Jobs within a workload which arrived at time τ may be processed within the private cloud due their privacy constraints. This is an optimization allocation achieved through the use of Algorithm 2 that assigns privacy concerned jobs *cost efficiently* to the virtual machines within the private cloud while considering the job deadlines.

Algorithm 2: Privacy-aware scheduling

Data: NF($privacy - sensitive$) jobs

Result: PS(Privacy Schedule)

1 Initialize $incapableVMs \leftarrow null$, $|DMatrix| \leftarrow |NF| \times |activeVMs|$,
   $l_{off} \leftarrow null$, $V \leftarrow null$, $flag \leftarrow true$

2 **do**

3   Update $DMatrix$ with $activeVMs$ & its $VMWorkload$

4   Initialize $incapableVMs$

5   **for** $i \leftarrow 0$ **to** $|NF|$ **do**

6   **for** $t_k \in NF \setminus (l_{off} \cup V)$ **do**

7   **for** $vm_j \in activeVMs \setminus incapableVMs$ **do**

8   **if** $i = 0$ and $DMatrix[t_k][vm_j] = -1$ **then**

9                      $DMatrix[t_k][vm_j] \leftarrow Exce(t_k, vm_j)$ - $wdealy$

10   **end**

11   **else**

12                     $DMatrix[t_k][vm_j] \leftarrow Exce(t_k, vm_j) - DMatrix[t_k][vm_j]$

13   **end**

14

15   **end**

16   **end**

17     $[t_{rw}, vm_{cl}] = FindMinValue(DMatrix)$

18   **if** t_{rw} or vm_{cl} is null **then**

19         $flag \leftarrow false$

20         $activeVMs = poll(nonActiveVMs)$

21   break

22   **end**

23   **else**

24   assign t_{rw} to vm_{cl}

25   update $DTMatrix$ & add t_{rw} to V

26   update $VMWorkload$ of vm_{cl}

27   add $[t_{rw}, vm_{cl}]$ to PS

28   update vm_{cl}^{core} and vm_{cl}^{mem}

29   **end**

30   **end**

31 **while** $!flag$ and $nonActiveVMs \neq \emptyset$

32 **if** $|V| \neq |NF|$ **then**

33     $R \leftarrow NF \setminus (l_{off} \cup V)$

34   **for** $t_R \in R$ **do**

35   swap t_r with regular jobs in $activeVMs$ queue

36   **end**

37 **end**

In the beginning, we initialize a matrix ($DMatrix$) which is updated with the current workload of $activeVMs$ at time τ. Each virtual machine also has a queue for keeping track of jobs for execution. We also maintain a list of incapable virtual machines ($incapableVMs$) on which jobs that arrived at time τ would miss their deadlines.

The $DMatrix$ becomes updated by estimating the remaining time of the job ($t_k \in NF$) on the VM ($vm_j \in activeVMs$). These values represent the remaining time when vm_j can finish executing t_k while considering the corresponding job deadline (lines 6–15). Then, the $DMatrix$ is scanned to find the minimum positive value. If there is such a value, the corresponding job and virtual machine will be confirmed and will be referred to t_{rw} and vm_{cl} as the last confirmed assignment (lines 24–28). Otherwise, a deep sleep virtual machine, if available, will be added to the $activeVMs$ list, and the process will be repeated again (lines 18–21). For the newly added machine(s), a value called the wake-up delay ($wdelay$) is maintained. This is the approximate time needed to have the virtual machine ready for serving workloads. In the case of unavailability of any deep sleep machines, active virtual machine queues will be scanned, and the jobs within the queue will be replaced with the privacy-concerned jobs, and the selected ones would be added to a list called the offloading list (l_{off}). The job(s) which would be selected for swapping purposes, would have to comply with the privacy concerned job(s) resource requirements. This list of jobs will be redirected to the public cloud scheduling for execution on public cloud vms.

Regular Job Scheduling. In this section, we present a particle swarm optimization (PSO)-based algorithm to schedule regular jobs to the private cloud (Algorithm 3). PSO is a computational method that improves a candidate solution based on a measure of quality through repetition. Having a population of candidates (or particles) helps the problem to be solved by moving these particles around in the search-space based on the position and velocity of particles. The local and the global best-known positions affect each particle's movement toward the best-known positions in the search space which eventually will lead to moving the swarm toward the best solutions. The representation of a solution (particle P) in the algorithm is based on the structure of jobs and its corresponding virtual machine. This structure has a length which is equal to the number of available jobs t within the stream of jobs T at time τ for execution on the a active virtual machines. For example, if at time τ, q jobs were to become available, the structure would be $\{(t_1, VM_1), \ldots, (t_q, VM_a)\}$.

The primary objective of the PSO scheduler is determining jobs that could be executed within the private cloud based on their resource requirements and user-specified deadlines in a cost-effective manner. This results in considering several factors during the representation of the fitness function. We define a variable called $UsedVm(P)$ which represents how many virtual machines are used within the solution. The fewer the number of used virtual machines, the lower the power consumption. Additionally, a parameter known as $Exec(P)$ checks whether jobs in the particle could be processed within the specified deadline on the designated virtual machine(s). As jobs have specific resource requirements, we use parameter $Res(P)$ to determines the particle (P) which would be satisfied in terms of the required CPU core and memory. Jobs within the particle might be assigned to

---

Algorithm 3: Regular Job Scheduling in the Private Cloud

Data: Private Cloud *activeVMs* List, Private Cloud *nonActiveVMs* List, Task
        List (*t*), Max #generation, and Particle Swarm Optimization Variables

Result: The best schedule within the private cloud

1 Initiate particle swarm optimization generation (*initGen*), *schedule* ← *null*,
  and *flag* ← *true*;

2 Initialize *localBest*, and *globalBest* Particles based on *initGen* ;

3 Evaluate generation via Equation 1;

4 **while** *schedule* = *null and nonActiveVMs* ≠ ∅ *and flag* **do**

5   **while** *#generations not exceeded* **do**

6   Update *localBest* and *globalBest* ;

7   **for** *p* ∈ *initGen* **do**

8   Update *velocity(p)* by Equation 2;

9   Update *location(p)* by Equation 3;

10   Update *fitness(p)* by Equation 1;

11   **end**

12   **end**

13   **if** *schedule* = *null* **then**

14   *activeVms* = *poll(nonActiveVms)* ;

15   **else**

16   *flag* ← *false* ;

17   return the best dynamic schedule;

18   **end**

19 **end**

20 **if** *schedule* = *null* **then**

21   l_{off} ← *t* ;

22   Public Cloud Assignment (l_{off}) ;

23 **end**

---

the same virtual machine. In this case, it is essential that firstly, jobs assigned
to the same virtual machines would have access to their required resources at
the same time. Secondly, it should not cause any delays in the execution of
jobs concurrently. Thus, parameter $Cur(P)$ evaluates the particle against the
criteria above. If none of the mentioned parameters is satisfied, a negative sign
will be applied to mark a non-eligible particle. Moreover, to avoid overloading a
VM, parameter $Wl(P)$ is defined which determines the number of queued jobs
for execution for each of the designated VMs within the particle. It checks the
queued jobs for execution based on the average number of jobs per active VM.
Based on these definitions, the fitness function is defined as:

$$fitness(P) = UsedVm(P) \times Exec(P) \times Res(P) \\ \times Cur(P) \times Wl(P) \tag{1}$$

The particle swarm optimization utilizes the following equations in regard to updating particle velocity and location in which $c1$ and $c2$ are considered learning factors.

$$\begin{aligned}
velocity(P) = {} & velocity(P) + c1 \times rand() \\
& \times (localBest - location(P) \\
& + c2 \times rand() \\
& \times (globalBest - location(P))
\end{aligned} \tag{2}$$

$$location(P) = location(P) + velocity(P) \tag{3}$$

Algorithm 3 tries to schedule jobs which become available at time τ onto private cloud virtual machines through an extended particle swarm algorithm considering minimizing on-premises cost. Since scheduling jobs onto available resources is computationally intractable, optimization approaches could provide a near-optimal solution. The structure of the algorithm is based on the number of available active virtual machines within the private cloud. In case none is found, the algorithm will iterate over deep sleep mode virtual machines ($nonActiveVMs$). If the job(s) cannot be hosted within the private cloud, they will be dispatched to the public cloud.

Privacy-aware scheduling (Algorithm 2) is also used to relocate regular jobs in one or more waiting queues (lines 32–37) when VMs in the private cloud are overloaded and a privacy-sensitive job needs to be scheduled (see the interaction between Algorithms 2 and 3).

Public Cloud Scheduling. To execute jobs offloaded to the public cloud, we propose in this section a cost-efficient approach to select the best virtual machine from the available cloud providers (Algorithm 4). This algorithm takes into consideration the available active cycles BC_{CP}^{active} during the scheduling of the jobs. For each job $t_i \in l_{off}$, if none of $vm \in BC_{CP}^{active}$ suited the job (t_i) requirements in terms of resource requirements and deadline, a new virtual machine from any available cloud provider should be launched. For launching a new virtual machine, it is necessary to check whether which cloud provider and under which billing cycle should the job(s) be offloaded. Therefore, in lines 5–7 of Algorithm 4, the cost of launching a new virtual machine based on the job requirements from cloud providers under different billing cycle policies would be determined (i.e. per second v. per hour). Then, the estimated cost of cloud providers is compared to each other (lines 7–11). Then, if it were more cost-efficient, the job would be dispatched to a new virtual machine from a cloud provider with a per second billing cycle policy. Otherwise, in lines 13–16, a new virtual machine would be launched from a cloud provider with a per hour billing cycle policy, and the job would be assigned to it. In this case, the new billing cycle $BC_{CP_{hour}}^{new}$ would be added to the existing BC_{CP}^{active}, and the corresponding job would be removed from the offloading list (l_{off}).

Algorithm 4: Public Cloud Scheduling

Data: l_{off}, BT_{CP}, and list of public cloud BC_{CP}^{active}
Result: LBC(Launching new Billing Cycles)

1   $S \leftarrow null$
2   **if** $l_{off} \neq \emptyset$ **then**
3   **for** $t_i \in l_{off}$ **do**
4       $t_i^{res} \leftarrow \{mem_{t_i} \& core_{t_i}\}$
5   Estimate the $cost_{CP}^{hour}$ of launching a $BC_{CP_{hour}}^{new}$ for t_i^{res}
6   Estimate the $cost_{CP}^{sec}$ of launching a $BC_{CP_{sec}}^{new}$ for t_i^{res}
7   **if** $cost_{CP}^{sec} \leq cost_{CP}^{hour}$ **then**
8   Launch $BC_{CP_{sec}}^{new}$
9         $S \leftarrow vm_{CP_{sec}}$
10   Remove t_i from l_{off}
11   **end**
12   **else**
13   Launch a $BC_{CP_{hour}}^{new}$ based on t_i^{res}
14   Add $BC_{CP_{hour}}^{new}$ to BC_{CP}^{active}
15         $S \leftarrow vm_{CP_{hour}}$
16   Remove t_i from l_{off}
17   **end**
18   **end**
19 **end**
20 $LBC \leftarrow S$

3.2   Q-Learning Based VM Manager

As idle and active virtual machines consume energy, there should be a mechanism that regularly monitors the private cloud (i.e. either putting virtual machines into deep sleep mode or activating one or more). In this section, we present a Q-Learning-based algorithm for virtual machine management. Q-Learning as a values-based learning algorithm in reinforcement of learning aims at learning a policy (e.g. VM management) to prepare agents (the hybrid scheduler) to take suitable actions under different circumstances. The learning process for VM management could be improved during time as it could make decisions based on the behaviours which had been seen, and choose the proper action. The entire learning process is straightforward which would not add any complexities to the entire framework.

The proposed Q-Learning algorithm is presented in Algorithm 5. In this algorithm, per a defined cycle, it is decided that virtual machines should be kept active or put into deep sleep mode. The decision is made based on either the past behaviours of virtual machines as observed and learned till time τ or an adjustment of the learning process through supervised learning taking into account the virtual machines' workloads at time τ. In this way, the number of active virtual machines for serving workloads can be balanced against incoming workloads.

Algorithm 5: Q-Learning based VM Management

Data: Private cloud $activeVMs$ and $nonActiveVMs$, Q-Learning $qTable$, p_{au}, p_{sp}, virtual machine under-utilized factor f_{uu}, and virtual machine over-utilized factor f_{ou}

Result: Activate, deactivate, or keep the current status virtual machines

1 Determine the current $workload$ of $activeVMs$
2 Initialize $reward$, a random double number rnd, and $pastRewards$
3 **if** $rnd \leq p_{au}$ **then**
4     $pastRewards \leftarrow average(k)$ rewards from $qTable$
5   Sort $pastRewards$ in descending order and return the $index$ of first element
6   **if** $index = 2$ **then**
7        $reward = reward \times cf_{dec}$
8        $decrease(activeVMs)$
9   **else if** $index = 1$ **then**
10       $reward = reward \times cf_{non}$
11   Keep the current $activeVMs$ status
12   **else**
13       $reward = reward \times cf_{inc}$
14       $increase(activeVMs)$
15   **end**
16 **end**
17 **else**
18   **if** $workload \leq f_{uu}$ **then**
19       $reward = reward \times cf_{dec}$
20       $decrease(activeVMs)$
21   **else if** $workload \leq f_{ou}$ and $f_{uu} \leq workload$ **then**
22       $reward = reward \times cf_{non}$
23   Keep the current $activeVMs$ status
24   **else**
25       $reward = reward \times cf_{inc}$
26       $increase(activeVMs)$
27   **end**
28 **end**
29 Update QT using Equation 4

The presented algorithm leverages a combination of the current virtual machines' workload at time τ and k-past Q-Learning observations of virtual machines behaviours with their corresponding probabilities. The former acts as a supervised learning that corrects the learning process with a probability of p_{sp}. In other words, it relies on the current status of VMs in the private cloud to correct the learning process if necessary. The latter relies on some specific past seen behaviours and autonomously manages the status of virtual machines with a probability of p_{au}.

The output action of the Q-Learning will be one of the following in a greedy way: (1) activating a new virtual machine, (2) keeping the current number of active virtual machines, or (3) deactivating one or more virtual machines.

The action will affect the list of active virtual machines $(activeVMs)$ and deep sleep VMs $(nonActiveVMs)$. The corresponding value of the action is recorded in a table called Q-Learning Table (QT). The corresponding reward for each action is multiplied by a coefficient of $(-cf_{inc}, cf_{non}, cf_{dec})$ which represents (increment, none, decrement) that clearly shows increasing active VMs (the negative sign of cf_{inc}) is not in favour of the learning process. In contrast, decreasing the active VMs is aligned with the goal of virtual machine management.

To update each record of corresponding action at time τ, Eq. 4 is used. In this Equation ql_{lr} and ql_{df} are the learning factor and the discount factor, respectively. The learning factor controls to what extent the old information should be overridden with the new obtained information. The discount factor evaluates the importance of future rewards. Function $actionEstimator()$ is an estimation of optimal value in the future which is based on the current virtual machines' workload at time τ.

$$QT[action] = (1 - ql_{lr}) \times QT[action]$$
$$+ ql_{lr} \times reward + ql_{lr} \qquad (4)$$
$$\times ql_{df} \times actionEstimater();$$

4   Evaluation

In this section, we evaluate the performance of CECBS in terms of VM usage and cost in comparison with RMS [11] that dynamically schedules deadline-constrained jobs in hybrid clouds.

4.1   Simulation Setup

Our simulations have been conducted using synthesized workloads based on Facebook workload traces [2] which are historical Hadoop traces on a 600-machine cluster at Facebook. In particular, we have synthesized jobs to be one of three types: short, medium or long. Each job is associated with the length (the number of instructions) which follows a Gaussian distribution for the purpose of execution time estimation. Short, medium, and long jobs are selected based on (mean, variance) values that are (1.2, 0.125), (1.512, 1) and (15.12, 10), respectively. The ratio between three job types is 89:10:1 as reported in [19]. We also make some jobs to be privacy sensitive, i.e., 5–50%.

The private cloud consists of 50 VMs with 4 vCPUs and computing capacity of 2200MIPS[1]. The private cloud is charged based on the electricity rate at the different time of day which is categorized as off-peak, peak, shoulder with the corresponding rate of \$12.08196, \$51.04627, and \$24.44365 kilowatts per hour [7]. The fixed rate for electricity is also considered. Public clouds modeled are AWS, MS Azure and GCE.

---

[1] We use Intel® Xeon ® E5-4603V2 Processor as a model CPU, with a 95 W TDP and the typical usage of 77.19 W [4].

Q-Learning parameters values are f_{uu} of 0.3, f_{ou} of 0.7, both ql_{lr} and ql_{lr} of 0.8, reward coefficients of -1, 0.5, $+1$ for cf_{inc}, cf_{non}, and cf_{dec}, respectively. The VM management is called every 30 s, 60 s, and 120 s. Particle swarm optimization parameters are c_1 and c_2 of 2 and w of 8.

4.2 Results

In this section, we present results when (1) jobs are all scheduled to the private cloud (Fig. 2) and (2) jobs are scheduled to both private and public clouds (Figs. 3, 4 and 5), with respect to primarily VM usage and cost including the number of free billing cycles used in public clouds.

By increasing the number of privacy workload shown in Fig. 2a, the usage of VMs in

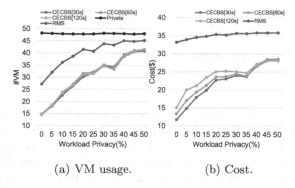

(a) VM usage.   (b) Cost.

Fig. 2. Scheduling using the private cloud alone.

average also increased. Also, taking a look at the VM usage, it is understood from Fig. 2a that VM usage in RMS is high which also can be referred from Fig. 3a. However, it still could not utilize resources for effective execution of jobs within their expected deadlines.

Workload distribution is also shown for CECBS (and its derivatives), and RMS (and its derivatives) in Figs. 3a, b, c, and d, respectively. The workload distribution based on these figures shows that CECBS could effectively respond to the availability of cost-efficient resources under their corresponding price scheme (w.r.t Fig. 4a). The lack of diversity and incurring higher cost lead to CECBS to use more internal resources when it would have to collaborate with Google. In contrast, when CECBS collaborated with AWS and Microsoft, it used more external resources as it was beneficiary to have the workload executed on the public clouds. Therefore, this is not considerable for the usage of Google resources as it is not as much as the other providers for both CECBS and RMS. When the workload privacy percentage increases, the private cloud uses more resources in a cost-efficient way.

Figure 2b (and Fig. 4) illustrates that higher dispatching jobs to the private clouds is not always beneficial in terms of cost. As shown in Fig. 3, with higher privacy rates, CECBS uses lower number of VMs than RMS while the number of jobs executed on the private cloud is much higher than RMS. Moreover, on average and per all privacy workloads, RMS has submitted more jobs than CECBS. But RMS led to having higher private cloud cost due to using almost all the VMs for job execution. Therefore, the actual VM usage of RMS and CECBS shows that RMS could have dealt with jobs within the private cloud effectively if it had managed to use VMs appropriately. Although CECBS did not send off many jobs to the private cloud for privacy workloads under 30%,

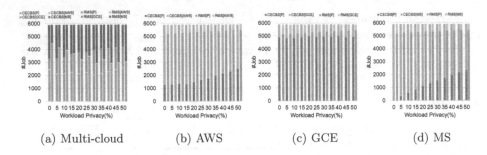

(a) Multi-cloud   (b) AWS   (c) GCE   (d) MS

Fig. 3. Job proportion when CECBS and RMS collaborate with all cloud providers and only one provider, respectively. *P* means private.

for higher privacy workloads, it dispatched more jobs to the private cloud while keeping number of VM usage as low as possible. Taking a look at the VM usage and the private VM cost, shows that the total private cost for RMS would be nearly the same for all privacy workloads regardless of number of jobs sent off to the private cloud. In other words, RMS has kept VMs active but CECBS has aligned its VMs usage based on the workload arrival time.

Figure 4 illustrates the total cost incurred during workload execution under each different approach. CECBS in comparison to its derivatives achieved the lower cost due to the cost comparison across multiple cloud providers. This cost reduction emerges from Hybrid Cloud Scheduler (Algorithm 1), Public cloud scheduling (Algorithm 4) in particular. They firstly determine whether there is a suitable billing cycle to dispatch any workload to, and the cost comparison between the private and public cloud providers to evaluate which cloud environment would minimize the total cost for the workload execution. It is also undeniable the cost of non-active virtual machines (idle) plays an essential role in the total cost of workload execution.

As CECBS and its derivative forms dynamically manage active virtual machines, the required number of them is aligned with the current workload. Usage of active billing cycles as well as the diversity of resources on each cloud provider helped CECBS to be more cost efficient. RMS and its derivatives could not achieve the lowest cost (Fig. 4a and c) in spite of relying more on the private cloud resources. RMS-Google (Fig. 4c) has the highest cost after RMS-AWS as the resource types are not as diverse as the other cloud providers (which is also true for CECBS), and if it was necessary to offload workloads to Google, it might select instances that were not affordable.

It should be mentioned that when CECBS only considers Google for workload bursting, workloads tend to be executed within the private cloud due to the cost-efficiency. That is why CECBS has relatively the lower cost regarding resource usage in comparison to the other CECBS derivatives. Since electricity providers may offer a fixed rate of electricity, CECBS and RMS were also evaluated and generally CECBS achieved the lower cost usage based on a recommended plan [6] shown in Fig. 4b and d. Since this is only a 24 h workload execution on a

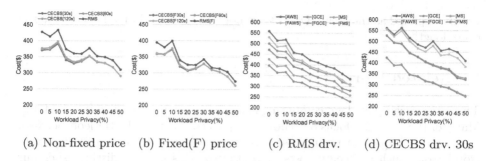

(a) Non-fixed price   (b) Fixed(F) price   (c) RMS drv.   (d) CECBS drv. 30s

Fig. 4. (a) Total cost of CECBS and RMS while the electricity price is not fixed, (b) CECBS and RMS with fixed rate, (c) RMS derivatives, (d) reporting only CECBS drv. 30 s.

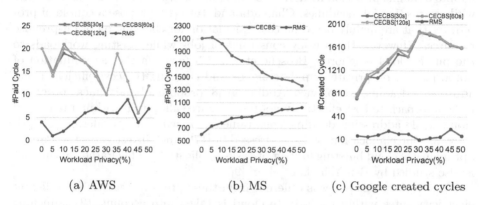

(a) AWS   (b) MS   (c) Google created cycles

Fig. 5. The number of free cycles used by CECBS and RMS. For MS, CECBS per each VM management cycle obtained the same value.

hybrid cloud environment, it is obvious that for a longer period of time RMS would eventually incur high cost of using public cloud resources in comparison to CECBS. This is also true when RMS would collaborate with only one cloud provider.

Figure 5 shows the number cycles that jobs are executed free of charge for CECBS and RMS. Regardless of number of jobs offloaded to the public cloud, RMS has the lowest number of free cycles (i.e., already paid cycles) which is shown in Fig. 5a and b for Amazon and Microsoft, correspondingly. RMS could not re-use the paid cycles and its usage is not as high as CECBS which could be interpreted as jobs sent to public clouds might not be eligible for using the paid cycles. At different VM management cycle time, it is understood the number of free cycle usage is almost the same for CECBS which could be related to the number of jobs dispatched to these providers, and the types of jobs which are dispatched for execution based on the cost comparison. Figure 5c refers to the creation of billing cycles for Google. Since the billing is per second, the creation is only depicted as the created cycles are not eligible as valid paid cycles due the cycle length.

5   Related Work

The cost efficiency of cloud computing has been extensively studied [8–12,14,17]. Many of these studies focus on scheduling jobs considering the tradeoff between performance improvement and cost savings. However, they often neglect private cloud costs, such as energy costs, and privacy; this is what distinguishes our work from these studies.

The work in [11] is probably closest to our work in this paper. Calheiros et. al in [11] propose a resource management system for cloud bursting. This system adopts dynamic provisioning and scheduling of cloud resources to minimize cost while respecting job deadlines. Charrada and Tata [12] propose a couple of procedures that are mainly based on cost calculation for choosing on or off-premise resources. However, the privacy constraint of jobs while bursting workloads to the public cloud is ignored. Bossche et al., [10] focus on the determination of potential cost on private or public clouds and choosing the cost-efficient cloud addressing deadline compliance. Abdi et al. [8] propose a binary linear programming approach to cost-effectively address resource allocation within a federated cloud while addressing deadline-constrained jobs without considering job privacy. Resource allocation is also addressed in [17] which investigates the Pareto-optimality of cloud bursting for bag-of-tasks applications. This Pareto-optimality is also studied by Ben-Yehuda et al. in [9].

Our work in this paper is different from these previous studies: (1) different electricity rates within the private cloud is taken into account, (2) launching and activating new billing cycles of different public cloud providers based on their chagrining policies are explicitly considered, and (3) privacy is explicitly considered.

6   Conclusion

In this paper, we have studied cost efficiency of cloud bursting with the development of CECBS as a new scheduling framework. Due to the nature of hybrid clouds in terms of billing policies and the ongoing cost of a private cloud, it is crucial to cost efficiently deal with workloads. Besides, the privacy of data/jobs should not be overlooked. We have shown this complex scheduling problem with multiple objectives and constraints can be addressed by taking advantage of benefits of both cloud types. Results based on real workload traces have proved our claims.

Acknowledgment. Authors would like to express their deepest appreciation to Ms. Chakaveh Saedi who provided valuable comments for the paper completion.

References

1. Amazon EC2 Pricing. https://aws.amazon.com/ec2/pricing/
2. Facebook Workload Traces. https://github.com/SWIMProjectUCB/SWIM/wiki/Workloads-repository
3. Google Compute Engine. https://cloud.google.com/compute/pricing
4. Intel Xeon E5–4603V2. https://www.zones.com/site/product/index.html?id=102611016&page_name=product_spec
5. Microsoft Azure Pricing. https://azure.microsoft.com/en-au/pricing/
6. Secure Saver. https://www.energyaustralia.com.au/home/electricity-and-gas/understand-electricity-and-gas-plans/secure-saver
7. Energy Australia: Energy price fact sheet NSW business (electricity) (2017). https://secure.energyaustralia.com.au/EnergyPriceFactSheets/Docs/EPFSIE_B_N_BBAS_EA_6_02-01-2017.pdf
8. Abdi, S., PourKarimi, L., Ahmadi, M., Zargari, F.: Cost minimization for deadline-constrained bag-of-tasks applications in federated hybrid clouds. Future Gener. Comput. Syst. **71**(C), 113–128 (2017)
9. Ben-Yehuda, O.A., Schuster, A., Sharov, A., Silberstein, M., Iosup, A.: Expert: pareto-efficient task replication on grids and a cloud. In: 2012 IEEE 26th International Parallel and Distributed Processing Symposium, pp. 167–178 (May 2012)
10. den Bossche, R.V., Vanmechelen, K., Broeckhove, J.: Cost-optimal scheduling in hybrid IaaS clouds for deadline constrained workloads. In: 2010 IEEE 3rd International Conference on Cloud Computing, pp. 228–235, July 2010
11. Calheiros, R.N., Buyya, R.: Cost-effective provisioning and scheduling of deadline-constrained applications in hybrid clouds. In: Wang, X.S., Cruz, I., Delis, A., Huang, G. (eds.) WISE 2012. LNCS, vol. 7651, pp. 171–184. Springer, Heidelberg (2012). https://doi.org/10.1007/978-3-642-35063-4_13
12. Charrada, F.B., Tata, S.: An efficient algorithm for the bursting of service-based applications in hybrid clouds. IEEE Trans. Serv. Comput. **9**(3), 357–367 (2016)
13. Chen, L., Liu, S., Li, B., Li, B.: Scheduling jobs across geo-distributed datacenters with max-min fairness. IEEE Trans. Netw. Sci. Eng. **6**, 1 (2018)
14. Chen, Y., Sion, R.: To cloud or not to cloud?: Musings on costs and viability. In: Proceedings of the 2nd ACM Symposium on Cloud Computing, SOCC 2011, pp. 29:1–29:7. ACM, New York, NY, USA (2011)
15. Clemente-Castello, F.J., Nicolae, B., Rafique, M.M., Mayo, R., Fernandez, J.C.: Evaluation of data locality strategies for hybrid cloud bursting of iterative MapReduce. In: 2017 17th IEEE/ACM International Symposium on Cluster, Cloud and Grid Computing (CCGRID), pp. 181–185, May 2017
16. Clemente-Castelló, F.J., Mayo, R., Fernández, J.C.: Cost model and analysis of iterative MapReduce applications for hybrid cloud bursting. In: IEEE/ACM International Symposium Cluster, Cloud and Grid Computing (CCGRID), pp. 858–864, May 2017
17. Farahabady, M.R.H., Lee, Y.C., Zomaya, A.Y.: Pareto-optimal cloud bursting. IEEE TPDS **25**(10), 2670–2682 (2014)
18. Hoseinyfarahabady, M.R., Samani, H.R.D., Leslie, L.M., Lee, Y.C., Zomaya, A.Y.: Handling uncertainty: pareto-efficient BoT scheduling on hybrid clouds. In: 2013 42nd International Conference on Parallel Processing, pp. 419–428, October 2013
19. Reiss, C., Tumanov, A., Ganger, G.R., Katz, R.H., Kozuch, M.A.: Heterogeneity and dynamicity of clouds at scale: Google trace analysis. In: Proceedings of the Third ACM Symposium on Cloud Computing, SoCC 2012, pp. 7:1–7:13 (2012)

Optimized Renewable Energy
Use in Green Cloud Data Centers

Minxian Xu[1,2], Adel N. Toosi[2(✉)], Behrooz Bahrani[3], Reza Razzaghi[3],
and Martin Singh[4]

[1] Shenzhen Institutes of Advanced Technology, Chinese Academy of Sciences,
Shenzhen 518055, China
[2] Faculty of Information Technology, Monash University,
Clayton, VIC 3800, Australia
{minxian.xu,adel.n.toosi}@monash.edu
[3] Department of Electrical and Computer Systems Engineering, Monash University,
Clayton, VIC 3800, Australia
{behrooz.bahrani,reza.razzaghi}@monash.edu
[4] School of Earth, Atmosphere and Environment, Monash University,
Clayton, VIC 3800, Australia
martin.singh@monash.edu

Abstract. The huge energy consumption of cloud data centers not only increases costs but also carbon emissions associated with such data centers. Powering data centers with renewable or green sources of energy can reduce brown energy use and consequently carbon emissions. However, powering data centers with these energy sources is challenging, as they are variable and not available at all times. In this work, we formulate the microservices management problem as finite Markov Decision Processes (MDP) to optimise renewable energy use. By dynamically switching off non-mandatory microservices and scheduling battery usage, upon the user's preference, our proposed method makes a trade-off between the workload execution and brown energy consumption. We evaluate our proposed method using traces derived from two real workloads and real-world solar data. Simulated experiments show that, compared with baseline algorithms, our proposed approach performs up to 30% more efficiently in balancing the brown energy usage and workload execution.

1 Introduction

The adoption of cloud computing has been rapid; it has been found that 70% of organizations have at least one application deployed in clouds [1]. These applications are hosted in cloud data centers which allow users to access them via the Internet. Due to the rapid growth of cloud data centers, it is anticipated that

---

Minxian Xu was with the Faculty of Information Technology, Monash University; he is now with Shenzhen Institutes of Advanced Technology, Chinese Academy of Sciences, China. A major part of this work was done while the author was at the Monash University.

© Springer Nature Switzerland AG 2019
S. Yangui et al. (Eds.): ICSOC 2019, LNCS 11895, pp. 314–330, 2019.
https://doi.org/10.1007/978-3-030-33702-5_24

data centers will consume significant worldwide generated electricity [1]. This huge energy consumption has an immense impact on the environment through greenhouse gas emissions. Thus, improving the energy efficiency of the cloud data center has attracted significant attention from researchers and the IT industry.

To ensure the sustainability of clouds, the carbon footprint of data centers must be reduced. Apart from reducing the total energy consumption, powering data centers with renewable (green) energy sources like wind or solar significantly reduces the carbon emissions associated with data centers. However, the limitation of renewable energy is that it is not as reliable as the grid power, and it is stochastic and intermittent in its behaviour.

Microservices are small, autonomous services that are rapidly becoming the norm for building large-scale applications in cloud data centers. With their isolation and light-weight features, microservices can be dynamically switched on/off to improve resource usage of application. This allows service providers to execute optional microservices (e.g., an analytics engine for E-commerce website) to better match the workload with the energy supply. To this end, one must develop algorithms to switch microservices on/off so that the overall executed number of microservices is maximized while minimizing the use of non-green power. In this work, we develop a method to manage resources at the microservice level to match the energy demand with the renewable energy supply of a data center.

Currently, most energy efficient scheduling algorithms for cloud data centers are heuristic-based, e.g., [2,6,7]. Heuristics are designed to provide acceptable results in a reasonable time frame. However, the entire solution space is not searched in heuristic approaches and their performance is not guaranteed. In practice, both future workloads and the availability of green energy are non-deterministic, and must be modelled probabilistically. Therefore, we consider using Markov Decision Processes (MDP) to model the stochastic nature of workloads and green energy availability in green cloud data centers. In this work, we assume that the data center is powered by an on-site renewable energy system (e.g., a photovoltaic solar power system) and the residual green energy can be stored in batteries for near future use. When battery storage is used, a challenging question to address is "when and in what capacity should batteries be discharged to maximize the overall executed number of microservices?"

We aim to find the optimised policy that maximizes the number of executed microservices while minimizing brown energy (energy produced from polluting sources) use. The policy contains actions that select how many microservices are to be switched off and whether and in what capacity the battery power is consumed in each time slot in accordance with the system administrator's preference for environmental friendliness. The key **contributions** are as follows:

- We model the green-aware microservices management problem as a *finite horizon Markov Decision Process* problem with the objective to minimize the usage of brown energy while maximizing the number of microservices deployed. In our model, we consider renewable energy (green), grid electricity (brown) and battery to power the system.

– We propose an algorithm based on MDP to dynamically switch off microservices and schedule battery usage to achieve the optimised results.
– We propose a tuning parameter which allows the system administrator to make a trade-off between the workload execution and brown energy use.
– We conduct simulation-based experiments using real data derived from workload traces and renewable energy availability. The results show that our proposed approach significantly reduces brown energy usage while deploying more microservices compared with baselines.

2 Related Work

Green cloud data centers powered by renewable energy is becoming an important topic in operating cloud data centers. To the best of our knowledge, our work is the first one to apply MDP to optimise the renewable energy use in cloud data centers. We now discuss the related work. Table 1 also shows the comparison of the related work based on key approaches, energy sources and objectives.

Markov Decision Process in Cloud Computing Environment. To model the probabilistic features of cloud computing environments and make resource management decisions, MDP has been applied in some research. Xu et al. [13] applied approximate MDP to schedule application components in cloud data centers to improve the trade-offs between the energy consumption and discount offered to users. Terefe et al. [11] adopted an MDP-based multi-site offloading algorithm for mobile cloud computing, which aims to achieve the energy-efficient objective of mobile devices. Han et al. [5] proposed a VM migration approach based on MDP to reduce data center energy consumption and resource shortage. Shen et al. [10] proposed an MDP-based approach to balance the VM loads on physical machines, which can achieve lower SLA violations and better load balancing effects than baselines.

Our work differs significantly from these MDP-based efforts in several perspectives: (1) none of them applied MDP to model the probabilistic feature of workloads and renewable energy together; (2) none of them put the efforts on optimising the use of renewable energy; and (3) none of them considered the actions on microservices and battery.

Renewable Energy Use in Data Centers. Renewable energy has been used to power data centers to reduce their carbon footprint. Zhang et al. [15] proposed a middleware system to dynamically dispatch requests to maximize the percentage of renewable energy used to power a network of distributed data centers while satisfying the desired cost/budget of the service provider. They applied a requests dispatching algorithm based on linear-fractional programming. In contrast, our approach is based MDP and considers the actions for battery to further maximize the renewable energy use.

Giori et al. [4] proposed a prototype green data center called *Parasol*, which is powered by solar panels, battery and grid power. They used linear programming to manage workloads and select sources of energy. In contrast, our approach does

Table 1. Comparison of related work

Approach	Approach			Energy sources			Objective		
	Linear programming	Prediction	MDP	Brown	Green	Battery	Energy-aware	Green-aware	QoS-aware
Xu et al. [13]			✓	✓			✓		✓
Terefe et al. [11]			✓				✓		✓
Han et al. [5]			✓	✓			✓		✓
Shen et al. [10]			✓						✓
Zhang e al. [15]	✓			✓	✓			✓	✓
Giori et al. [4]	✓	✓		✓	✓	✓		✓	✓
Liu et al. [8]		✓		✓	✓			✓	✓
Our approach			✓	✓	✓	✓		✓	✓

not need a prediction model to predict future renewable energy availability and workloads as *Parasol* does. We model workloads and renewable energy based on probabilistic model and introduce a tuning parameter (dimmer) to balance the trade-offs between the workload execution and brown energy use.

Liu et al. [8] used a holistic approach by considering renewable energy supply, electricity pricing and cooling costs to improve the sustainability of data centers. Our work differs from this one as our objective is maximising the use of renewable energy. Toosi et al. [12] proposed an approach to redirect virtual machine requests to other data centers with available renewable energy. They introduced two online deterministic algorithms for maximizing renewable energy usage. In contrast, we apply the MDP approach for a single data center and manage the actions for microservices and battery rather than virtual machines.

3 System Modeling and Problem Statement

Figure 1 shows the schematic view of the proposed system. We consider a data center that consists of multiple physical machines (servers). To power the data center, several energy sources are considered, including brown energy generated by coal-based facilities, green energy generated by solar panels and batteries that can store the surplus green energy. Applications constructed via self-contained microservices deployed on physical machines to provide services for the end users. Many applications including web applications often have microservices that fit

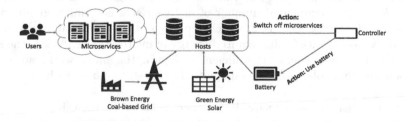

Fig. 1. Schematic view of the system.

into the **brownout** [14] feature, which can be regarded as non-mandatory components that can be dynamically activated/deactivated as need arises. For example, microservices handling the recommendation engines for a shopping website, or microservices running ad selection algorithms and optimization. Our approach only targets microservices having brownout feature and all other microservices remain untouched in the system.

3.1   States

We consider the discrete time **finite-state** MDP, and we aim to find an optimal policy (state to action mapping) to achieve best results for a single day. We discretize the time horizon into identically sized slots, i.e., each day is divided into 24 h time slots. A finer grain time slot can be used in our model. However, since weather data is often available in hourly basis[1] and service are billed per hour in well-known cloud providers such as AWS[2], here, we focus on hourly time slots throughout the day (solar cycle).

The system state $S(t)$ at time-slot t includes the status of (1) demanded microservices, (2) available renewable energy, and (3) level of battery state of charge (SoC). The state space of active microservices at time t is given as $W(t) \leq \bar{W} \in \mathbb{Z}^+$, where $\mathbb{Z}^+$ is the set of non-negative integers and $\bar{W}$ is the maximum number of microservices the system can accommodate. The number of active microservices represents the intensity of workloads, that is, more active microservices are required when workload is high. Availability of renewable energy at time t is represented by a discrete random value $G(t) \leq \bar{G} \in \mathbb{Z}^+$. $G(t)$ represents the level of electricity generated by the renewable power system and $\bar{G}$ is the maximum level of renewable power can be generated in the system. Similarly, $B(t) \leq \bar{B} \in \mathbb{Z}^+$ is a discrete value denoting the battery level SoC, where $\bar{B}$ is the maximum charge level that battery can hold. Therefore, the state of the system at time t, $S(t)$, is denoted by:

$$S(t) \stackrel{\Delta}{=} [W(t), G(t), B(t)] \in \mathbb{S}, \tag{1}$$

where $\mathbb{S}$ stands for all possible states.

Figure 2a shows an example of states in our MDP-based modeling. In this example, we have four time intervals at different states. We assume one unit microservice(s) consumes one unit green energy or battery. Microservices are presumed to be grouped in a way that each group roughly consume one unit of energy. At $T0$, the demanded number of microservices is 6 units, green energy level is 3 and battery level is 2, which represents the state that green energy and battery cannot satisfy the required energy of microservices. At $T1$, the state represents that green energy is sufficient to handle the entire workload, e.g. at the noontime that solar power is adequate. In this state, no extra brown energy

---

[1] http://www.bom.gov.au/climate/data-services/solar-information.shtml.
[2] https://aws.amazon.com/premiumsupport/knowledge-center/ec2-instance-hour-billing/.

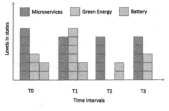

(a) Possible states.

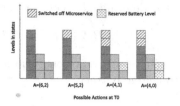

(b) Possible actions.

Fig. 2. Example of states and actions in the system

is required. At $T2$, the state represents the situation where no green energy is available. The number of microservices is 5, green energy level is 0 and battery level is 2. At $T3$, the state represents the condition where battery is empty, so the battery level is 0.

3.2 Actions

At the beginning of each time-slot, the system determines the control action to switch off some microservices and to decide the allowed battery discharge. The next state $S(t + 1)$ depends on the current state $S(t)$ and the decision maker's action A. Our model must decide to perform the best possible action in each state. Actions are denoted as $A = (a, b)$, where a is the number of executed microservices and b denotes the maximum battery level allowed to be consumed to execute microservices. The actions change the states from one to another and achieve different rewards. The goal is to calculate the optimal policy, which is a mapping from states to actions such that the reward is maximized. The reward function will be discussed in the next subsection.

Figure 2b demonstrates a set of sample possible actions corresponding to the Fig. 2a state at $T0$. In $T0$, green energy and battery cannot fully satisfy the number of microservices. One may choose to run all 6 units of microservices using one unit of brown energy plus the entire battery charge, i.e., $A = (6, 2)$. Note that green power is always being used to the maximum a head of other sources, i.e. grid and battery. Another possible action executes only 5 out of 6 microservices and uses the entire battery storage levels so that no extra brown energy is required, i.e., $A = (5, 2)$. To reserve battery level charge for the next time slot, a possible action is to execute only 4 microservices and use one or none of the battery levels, i.e., $A = (4, 1)$ and $A = (4, 0)$.

The demanded workload and available green energy level at $S(t + 1)$ are independent of the state $S(t)$ and are determined stochastically according to the time. However, battery level at $S(t + 1)$ depends on $S(t)$ and action A. If there is extra green energy in the last state, it will be used to charge battery in the next state. For $S(t) = [W(t), G(t), B(t)]$, the number of microservices that can be executed is $0 \leq a \leq W(t)$ and the battery level that can be consumed is $0 \leq b \leq min(B(t), [a - G(t)]^+)$, where $[x]^+ = max[0, x]$. Thus, the battery level at $t + 1$ is determined according the following equation:

$$B(t+1) = min(\bar{B}, B(t) - b + [G(t) - a]^+),\qquad(2)$$

where $[G(t) - a]^+$ represents the level of not consumed green energy at t and used to charge battery.

3.3 Reward Function

At each time slot, the process is in a state $S(t)$, and we choose a possible action A. The process randomly moves to the next state $S(t+1)$ at the next time slot, and gives the corresponding reward $R(S(t), A)$. Our model intends to optimise two contradictory objectives: *minimizing brown energy consumption* and *maximizing the number of microservices executed*. Note that we target optional microservices with an interactive nature in our model that they cannot be delayed to be executed in the future. For example, current end users of a shopping website do not receive suggestions for items if the recommendation service is switched off. We introduce λ_r parameter to balance the trade-off between the number of microservices and brown energy usage. λ_r can be set by the system administrators to satisfy their cost and QoS requirements. Thus, we define the reward function $R(.)$ as:

$$R(.) = -\lambda_r \times [a - G(t) - b]^+ + (1 - \lambda_r) \times a.\qquad(3)$$

The first part $[a - G(t) - b]^+$ represents the brown energy usage and the second part, a, shows the number of executed microservices at time slot t. When $\lambda_r = 1$, the reward function only considers the brown energy usage. When $\lambda_r = 0$, the reward function is $R(.) = a$, that is, the reward function only considers the executed microservices. When λ_r is between 0 and 1, the reward function makes a balance between the number of executed microservices and brown energy consumption. The impact of λ_r will be evaluated in Sect. 5.4.

3.4 Transition Probabilities

The probability that the MDP moves into $S(t + 1)$ is influenced by the chosen action A. We assume that the decision maker has access to a long-time history of workloads demand and renewable power generation to compute probabilities. Thus, for each time slot, the probability of receiving the specific level of workload (the number of demanded microservices), $W(t)$, is known in advance and is denoted by $P(W(t))$. In Sect. 5.1, we explain how these probabilities are computed. The probability that the specific level of green power is generated at time slot t is denoted by $P(G(t))$. These values are also known to the decision maker in advance and are computed according to the history of renewable power generation. By knowing $W(t)$ and $G(t)$ and action $A = (a, b)$, we can compute the battery level SoC at $t + 1$. Therefore, the transition probability from $S(t)$ to $S(t + 1)$ with a given action A is computed as:

$$P_A(S(t), S(t+1)) = P(W(t+1)) \times P(G(t+1)).\qquad(4)$$

3.5   Optimal Policy

The optimal policy π^* describes the best action for each state in MDP which maximizes the expected reward in observation period, e.g. 24 h. The equation for the optimal policy is shown as follows:

$$V^{\pi^*}(S(t)) = \max_A \{R(S(t), A) + \sum_{S(t+1)} P_A(S(t), S(t+1)) \times V^{\pi^*}(S(t+1))\}, \quad (5)$$

where $V(S(t))$ is the expected reward obtained in the observation period, i.e., from the current time to the last time slot. In Eq. (5), the maximum reward that can be obtained at state $S(t)$ is computed by optimally choosing action A that maximizes the reward over all possible, next states $S(t+1)$. The above analysis converts our model to a dynamic programming problem.

4   MDP-Based Green-Aware Algorithm

Algorithm 1 shows the pseudocodes of our MDP-based green-aware algorithm.

Initializing System Information: At the beginning time interval, the algorithm uses the information to initialize system, including, the observation period, e.g. 24 h, the maximum number of levels for workloads, green energy and battery capacity (line 1).

Finding Reachable States and Possible Actions: Based on the probabilities of all states, only states with probability larger than 0 are considered as reachable. Meanwhile, based on the predefined maximum levels of workloads and green energy, possible actions can be found (lines 2–16).

Algorithm 1. MDP-based Green-aware algorithm

Input: System state, transition probabilities, observation time periods.
Output: Control actions
1: Initializing observation period T, the maximum levels of workloads $\bar{W}$ and green energy $\bar{G}$, battery capacity $\bar{B}$
2: **for** t from 0 to T **do**
3:    **for** $W(t)$ from 0 to $\bar{W}$ **do**
4:       **for** $G(t)$ from 0 to $\bar{G}$ **do**
5:          $P(S(t)) = P(W(t)) \times P(G(t))$
6:          **for** $B(t)$ from 0 to $\bar{B}$ **do**
7:             **if** $Pr[S(t)] > 0$ **then**
8:                Adding $S(t)$ into reachable states $\mathbb{S}$
9:             **end if**
10:          **end for**
11:       end for
12:    **end for**
13: **end for**
14: **for** all reachable states in $\mathbb{S}$ **do**
15:    Adding action $A(a, b)$ into possible actions $A(S(t))$ for $S(t)$, $\forall\, 0 \leq a \leq W(t)$, $\forall\, 0 \leq b \leq min(B(t), [a - G]^+)$
16: **end for**
17: Updating transition probabilities $P_A(S(t), S(t+1))$ from $S(t)$ to $S(t+1)$
18: Updating the reward function $R(.)$ from $S(t)$ to $S(t+1)$
19: Calculating the optimal expected reward by algorithm 2 to find the $V^{\pi^*}(S(t))$
20: Deciding the control actions based on $V^{\pi^*}(S(t))$.
21: **return** best actions for states

Updating Transition Probabilities of States: Fetching the probabilities of different levels of workloads and availability of green energy (line 17).

Updating the Reward of States: Based on the different levels of workloads, green energy and consumed battery, the reward of each state is updated according to Eq. (3) (line 18).

Calculating the Utility Function: Using Algorithm 2, Algorithm 1 calculates the optimal expected reward value of reachable states (line 19).

Deciding the Actions: According to the optimised expected reward value that can be achieved, algorithm selects the action which maximizes the objective function for each state according to Eq. (5).

Algorithm 2 shows how to calculate the optimal expected reward by iterating over actions. The algorithm is based on value iteration to maximize the reward value, which represents the best control policy. With the inputs of reachable states and corresponding possible actions, the algorithm iterates over time periods 0 to T. The expected reward of a state is calculated in line 6. Then the algorithm iteratively updates the best reward value by going through all the reachable states and possible actions. In each iteration, the optimal expected reward value $V^{\pi*}(S(t))$ with optimal policy $\pi*$ is updated based on the expected reward in the previous state. After obtaining the optimal reward value, we can find the optimal control action.

Complexity Analysis: In our algorithm, for each state at a specific time interval, only the best action to reach the state is kept, which means the other actions are eliminated. Thus, the solutions space is $\Theta(\Lambda \times \Gamma \times \Delta)$ which is in polynomial complexity, where Λ, Γ, and Δ are the maximum level for the number of active microservices, green energy and battery, respectively.

Algorithm 2. The optimal expected reward value for all the states

---

Input: reachable states $S(t) \in \mathbb{S}$, possible actions $A(S(t))$ and estimated transition probabilities at
  time interval t as $P_A(S(t), S(t+1))$
Output: The optimal expected reward value
1: $t = 0$, $V(S(0)) = 0$, $\forall S(0) \in \mathbb{S}(0)$
2: **for** t from 0 to $T - 1$ **do**
3:    $t = t + 1$
4:    $V^{\pi*}(S(t)) = -\infty$
5:    **for** $S(t) \in \mathbb{S}(t)$ **do**
6:        $V(S(t)) = \max_A \{R(S(t), A) + \sum_{S(t+1)} P_A(S(t), S(t+1)) \times V(S(t+1))\}$
7:        **if** $V(S(t)) > V^{\pi*}(S(t))$ **then**
8:            $V^{\pi*}(S(t)) = V(S(t))$
9:        **end if**
10:    **end for**
11: **end for**
12: **return** $V^{\pi*}(S(t))$ as optimal expect reward value

---

5 Performance Evaluations

In the following, we evaluate the performance of our proposed MDP-based app-roach. We use two workloads derived from realistic traces along with the histor-ical solar data from the Australian Government Bureau of Meteorology[3].

5.1 Workload Traces

We use two realistic workload traces derived from Wikipedia[4] and Nectar[5] in our experiments. To convert workloads to fit into the states, we divide workloads into a set of levels with a specific range.

We use one-month Wikipedia data traces that contain 10% of all user requests issued to the Wikipedia website during this period. The total number of requests per hour ranges from 4 to 14 millions as shown in Fig. 3(a). The figure shows that the Wikipedia trace follows a typical pattern with the top and bottom number of requests during the day and night time, respectively. We divide the number of requests per hour into 10 levels, each representing a workload level in MDP. Each level is associated with a request rate range, of which the midpoint is used as the representative value for the corresponding level. For instance, the representative value for level 0 is 670 thousand and covers the range of 0 to 1340 thousand requests per hour. Figure 3(b) depicts the workload level conversion for the Wikipedia traces. It can be observed that the data still follows the pattern in Fig. 3(a), while the total workload levels are reduced to 10. Note that, in our experiment, we shifted Wikipedia data traces timing in a way that its user base would be in Australia at the same place as we consider the renewable power generation. Therefore, the peaks of workload coincides with the peaks of renewable power generation for the Wikipedia workload.

The Nectar Cloud platform provides the scalable computing infrastructure to Australian researchers and contains the traces of requests submitted for instan-tiating VM instances. Different from the Wikipedia trace, Nectar does not have a clear diurnal pattern and requests have start time, end time and five different VM types with the different number of vCPUs (virtual CPUs), e.g. small type has 1 vCPU and medium type has 2 vCPUs. We calculate the cumulative vCPU demand from users during 30 days as shown in Fig. 3(c), in which the demanded resource ranges from 500 to 2600 vCPUs. In Nectar traces, we cannot see an apparent pattern like that of Wikipedia. Similar to Wikipedia traces, we convert the vCPU resource consumption into 10 levels (Fig. 3(d)). For instance, level 0 represents values from 0 to 286 vCPUs.

5.2 Workload Level Probabilities

The probability $P(W(t))$ shows the likelihood that workload demand falls into a certain level in time slot t. In order to compute $P(W(t))$, we use existing

[3] http://www.bom.gov.au/climate/data-services/solar-information.shtml.

[4] http://www.wikibench.eu/wiki/2007-10/.

[5] https://nectar.org.au/research-cloud/.

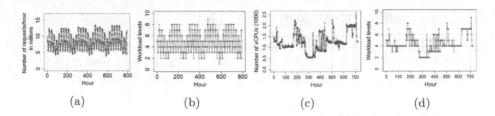

Fig. 3. (a) Original Wikipedia workloads. (b) Converted workload levels. (c) Original Nectar workloads. (d) Converted workload levels.

historical data based on a weekly cycle. Therefore, we keep different values of $P(W(t))$ for different hours and different days of a week. In order to compute $P(W(t))$ for a given time slot of a weekday (e.g., Monday, 8:00 to 9:00 am), we count the number of times that the historical workload hits a certain level (e.g., level 5) in the existing traces. Then the number is divided by the total number in all levels in time slot t to obtain the probability. This way, we create seven probability matrices (each for one day of a week) that contains 10 rows and 24 columns. Each cell shows the probability of receiving a certain level of workload at the specific time slot. The history data we used for the probability computation for Wikipedia is from September 19 to October 19, 2007 and for the Nectar is from December 1 to December 30, 2013.

5.3   Solar Power Levels

In order to make the solar data incorporated into our model, we use the hourly satellite data for the solar irradiation falling on a horizontal surface collected by the Australian Bureau of Meteorology. The trace has more than 30 years of hourly global horizontal solar irradiance (GHI) across Australia. We assume that the solar system fully converts hourly GHI value to power. Figure 4 shows the historical (original) and converted one-month solar irradiance data in Jan 2017 for the gridded data that covers Clayton campus at Monash University. In the historical data, the maximum value of GHI is $1108\,\mathrm{W/m}^2$ and the minimum value is zero. We also map GHI data into 10 levels of power, where the minimum solar level is 0 and the maximum solar level is 9.

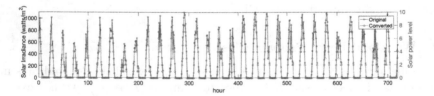

Fig. 4. Historical and converted solar irradiance.

To compute the likelihood of green power generation at a specific level $P(G(t))$, we use historical data at the same hour from the previous years. For example, if we want to calculate the probability of renewable power generation at level 2 at hour 11:00 am on the 1st of January, 2018, we look at the historical data at 11:00 am on the 1st of January from 1990 to 2017. Then, the probability that green power generation reaching level 2 is calculated based on the sample data.

Table 2. Impact of λ_r on the number of microservices and brown energy usage.

λ_r	0	0.25	0.5	0.75	1
Average number of microservices	4.26	4.26	2.47	2.47	0
Average brown energy usage	3.26	2.4	0.60	0.60	0

5.4 Evaluations with Different λ_r Values

To evaluate the impact of different λ_r values on the number of executed microservices and average energy consumption, we vary λ_r from 0 to 1 in the reward function as noted in Eq. (3) for the Wikipedia workload. The results are shown in Table 2. As we expect, the larger λ_r value, the fewer average number of microservices are executed and less brown energy is consumed. When $\lambda_r = 0$, the approach runs the maximum average number of 4.2 microservices and consume 3.3 units of brown energy. When $\lambda_r = 0.5$, the average number of microservices is reduced to 2.5 and the brown energy usage is decreased to 0.6. When $\lambda_r = 1$, no microservice is executed and no brown energy is consumed. We choose $\lambda_r = 0.5$ to balance the trade-off in the rest of experiments. In practice, the service administrators can set λ_r to fit into their preferences.

5.5 Baseline Algorithms

We use the following state-of-the-art heuristic algorithms as baselines:

DMWB (Demanded Microservices Without Battery): The algorithm executes the demanded number of microservices as it is received by the system, but does not use the battery.

SLW (Sliding Window): This sliding window algorithm [9] uses the recent historical actions to make an action. We set the sliding window size as 3 and the current action is the average number of microservices in the last 3 time intervals. SLW uses the maximum available battery capacity to power system whenever green energy is not sufficient.

BF (Best Fit): This algorithm is a representative energy management algorithm derived from [3]. It chooses the action that executes the maximum number of microservices with the least brown energy usage. The full battery capacity is consumed whenever green energy is insufficient.

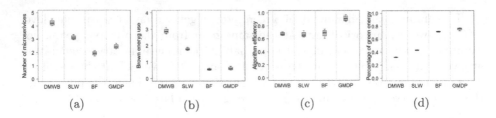

Fig. 5. Performance comparison of algorithms using Wikipedia workload.

We investigate the following metrics to evaluate system performance:

Number of Microservices: As one of the main objectives is to maximize the number of executed microservices, this metric measures the number of microservices on average over all hours.

Brown Energy Usage: Another main objective is to reduce brown energy consumption. This metric represents the average amount of brown energy usage over all hours. This metric can be read as the carbon footprint as well.

Algorithm Efficiency: The algorithm efficiency is represented as the optimization objective that considers both the brown energy usage and the number of active microservices simultaneously. The combined two objectives are derived from Eq. (3) as: $\frac{1}{T} \times \{\lambda \times \sum_{t=0}^{t=T} [a(t) - G(t) - b(t)]^+ + (1 - \lambda) \times \sum_{t=0}^{t=T} a(t)\}$, where $a(t)$ is the number of active microservices, $b(t)$ is the battery discharge at time interval t, and T is the 72-h observation period.

Percentage of Green Energy Usage: We also evaluate the percentage of green energy consumed out of the total energy usage on average over all hours.

5.6 Experimental Results

Figure 5 shows the performance comparison under the Wikipedia workload for three baseline algorithms and our proposed Green-Aware MDP-based algorithm (GMDP) over 3 days. The evaluated Wikipedia workloads start from October 20 to 22, 2007 and the evaluated Nectar workloads are from January 1 to 3, 2014. To avoid the seasonal variance of solar irradiance, we repeat our experiments with the solar data in the first three days in January, April, July and October 2017 respectively under the same Wikipedia workloads. From Fig. 5(a) and (b), DMWB represents the baseline that executes the demanded number of microservices as received, which executes 4.234 with 95% Confidence Interval (CI) (3.882, 4.586) microservices and 2.88 with 95% CI: (2.609, 3.153) brown energy usage. The SLW algorithm lowers the number of microservices and brown energy usage to 3.115 with 95% CI: (2.846, 3.384) and 1.781 with 95% CI: (1.649, 1.912) respectively. The BF algorithm supports the minimum number of microservices as 1.922 with 95% CI: (1.645, 2.199) and consumes the minimum brown energy as 0.544 with 95% CI: (0.432, 0655). Our proposed GMDP runs 27% more microservices than BF as 2.436 with 95% CI: (2.137, 2.736) and its brown energy usage is

0.60 with 95% CI: (0.449, 0.756), which is only 0.6 more than BF. Figure 5(c) and
(d) depict the comparison of efficiency and percentage of green energy usage for
algorithms. While GMDP reduces the number of microservices, it achieves the
highest efficiency and percentage of green energy usage, which means GMDP can
run the maximum number of microservices with the least brown energy usage.

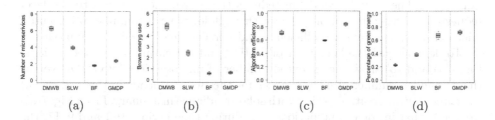

(a)   (b)   (c)   (d)

Fig. 6. Performance comparison of algorithms using Nectar workload.

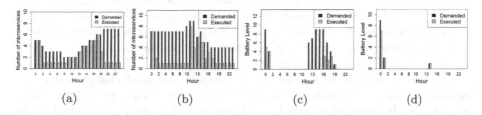

(a)   (b)   (c)   (d)

Fig. 7. Actions corresponding to demanded workloads for (a) Wikipedia and (b) Nectar. Battery actions corresponding to available battery (c) Wikipedia and (d) Nectar.

Figure 6 depicts the comparison based on the Nectar workload. In Fig. 6(a)
and (b), we can observe that the DMWB executes the maximum number of
microservices as 6.253 with 95% CI: (5.833, 6.673) and the corresponding brown
energy is 4.836 with 95% CI: (4.344, 5.329). SLW reduces the number of microservices to 3.919 with 95% CI: (3.585, 4.254) and brown energy usage to 2.425 with
95% CI: (2.064, 2.787). BF achieves the least number of 1.773 with 95% CI:
(1.589, 1.958) microservices and minimum brown energy usage of 0.583 with
95% CI: (0.386, 0.782). GMDP increases microservices and brown energy usage
to 2.34 with 95% CI: (2.083, 2.598) and 0.658 with 95% CI: (0.475, 0.841), respectively. Compared with BF, GMDP executes 31% more microservices with only
12% more brown energy use. GMDP has the highest efficiency and the largest
percentage of green energy usage as shown in Fig. 6(c) and (d).

As a conclusion, we can say that GMDP achieves the best trade-off between
the number of executed microservices and brown energy use, highest efficiency
and the maximum percentage of green energy use. The DMWB algorithm executes the demanded number of microservices as received, however, its actions are

not optimised according to the availability of green energy and battery status of charge. The SLW algorithm takes the advantage of the recent actions. However, the percentage of green energy usage is not maximized. BF finds the best action at the current time period, however, the average value in the long term is not optimal. The GMDP algorithm avoids the limitations of baseline algorithms by reacting to the number of demanded microservices and searching a larger solution space. The GMDP algorithm reduces the brown energy usage to the level requested by the system administrator through lowering the number of executed microservices, and improves efficiency and percentage of green energy usage.

To demonstrate the behaviour of GMDP and the nature of selected actions, Fig. 7(a) and (b) show the executed number of microservices by GMDP versus the demanded number of microservices for the two workloads in the first day of the three-day observation period with solar irradiance in January. From Fig. 7(a), we notice that in some time periods, e.g. during time periods 0–1 and 9–17, the number of demanded microservices is the same as the executed microservices for the Wikipedia workload. This happens when the energy drawn from green sources and battery are sufficient to handle the entire workload. However, when the green energy and battery charge are not sufficient, e.g. during time periods 2–8, the executed microservices controlled by actions and are less than the demanded ones. Figure 7(b) shows similar behaviors for the Nectar workload. GMDP executes more microservices during the time period that green energy or battery charge are sufficient and efficiently reduces the executed microservices with the limitation in green energy according to the administrator preference (λ_r).

Figure 7(c) and (d) shows the sample battery status of charge and corresponding actions in the first day of our three-day observation period with solar irradiance in January for Wikipedia and Nectar workloads respectively. For the Wikipedia workload, we can notice that the initial battery is consumed in time periods 0 and 1., e.g. battery is discharged for 5 and 4 units respectively. The battery is not recharged until the time period 12, when the green energy is enough and can be charged into battery. Then the battery level is decreased to 0 during time periods 16 to 19, and there is no action for the battery in the time periods 20–23. The battery actions for Nectar workloads are much simpler compared with Wikipedia workloads. The battery is consumed in time period 0 and 1, and only recharged 1 unit at time period 14. This is because the Nectar workloads during time periods 0 to 13 are higher than Wikipedia workloads. Thus the green energy is consumed completely, and the battery has no chance to get recharged.

6   Conclusions and Future Work

We modeled the green-aware microservices management problem as a finite Markov Decision Process to reduce brown energy usage while provisioning resources for microservices. In our model, we consider brown energy, green energy (solar power) and a chargeable battery as the energy sources to power the data centers. To optimise system performance, our proposed MDP-based approach called GMDP controls system actions and decides the number of microservices that must be executed out of the incoming workload and how much battery must be consumed in each time slot. We used real traces derived from Wikipedia and Nectar and Solar irradiance data from the Australian government Bureau of Meteorology to evaluate our system performance. Experimental results show that the proposed approach can efficiently balance the trade-off between the number of microservices and brown energy usage. In future, we plan to design and develop a prototype system incorporating the proposed algorithm. We will extend our model to consider more complex scenarios including battery self-discharge, variable grid electricity prices, and net metering. We will use a reinforcement learning approach to solve Markov decision processes.

Acknowledgments. This work is partially supported by Monash Infrastructure Research Seed Fund Grant and FIT Early Career Researcher Seed Grant.

References

1. Buyya, R., Srirama, S.N., et al.: A manifesto for future generation cloud computing: research directions for the next decade. ACM Comput. Surv. **51**(5), 105:1–105:38 (2018)
2. Cianfrani, A., Eramo, V., Listanti, M., Polverini, M., Vasilakos, A.V.: An OSPF-integrated routing strategy for QoS-aware energy saving in IP backbone networks. IEEE Trans. Netw. Service Manag. **9**(3), 254–267 (2012)
3. Farahnakian, F., Pahikkala, T., Liljeberg, P., Plosila, J., Hieu, N.T., Tenhunen, H.: Energy-aware VM consolidation in cloud data centers using utilization prediction model. IEEE Trans. Cloud Comput. **7**(2), 524–536 (2019). https://doi.org/10.1109/TCC.2016.2617374
4. Goiri, Í., Katsak, W., Le, K., Nguyen, T.D., Bianchini, R.: Parasol and GreenSwitch: managing datacenters powered by renewable energy. In: ACM SIGARCH Computer Architecture News, vol. 41, pp. 51–64. ACM (2013)
5. Han, Z., Tan, H., Chen, G., Wang, R., Chen, Y., Lau, F.C.M.: Dynamic virtual machine management via approximate Markov decision process. In: Proceedings of the 35th Annual IEEE International Conference on Computer Communications (INFOCOM), pp. 1–9 (2016)
6. Jiang, D., Xu, Z., Liu, J., Zhao, W.: An optimization-based robust routing algorithm to energy-efficient networks for cloud computing. Telecommun. Syst. **63**(1), 89–98 (2016)
7. Liu, H., et al.: Thermal-aware and DVFS-enabled big data task scheduling for data centers. IEEE Trans. Big Data **4**(2), 177–190 (2018)
8. Liu, Z., et al.: Renewable and cooling aware workload management for sustainable data centers. In: ACM SIGMETRICS Performance Evaluation Review, vol. 40, pp. 175–186. ACM (2012)
9. Shaw, R., Howley, E., Barrett, E.: A predictive anti-correlated virtual machine placement algorithm for green cloud computing. In: 2018 IEEE/ACM 11th International Conference on Utility and Cloud Computing, pp. 267–276. IEEE (2018)
10. Shen, H., Chen, L.: Distributed autonomous virtual resource management in datacenters using finite-Markov decision process. IEEE/ACM Trans. Netw. **25**(6), 3836–3849 (2017)

11. Terefe, M.B., Lee, H., Heo, N., Fox, G.C., Oh, S.: Energy-efficient multisite offloading policy using Markov decision process for mobile cloud computing. Pervasive Mob. Comput. **27**, 75–89 (2016)
12. Toosi, A.N., Qu, C., de Assunção, M.D., Buyya, R.: Renewable-aware geographical load balancing of web applications for sustainable data centers. J. Netw. Comput. Appl. **83**, 155–168 (2017)
13. Xu, M., Buyya, R.: Energy efficient scheduling of application components via brownout and approximate Markov decision process. In: Maximilien, M., Vallecillo, A., Wang, J., Oriol, M. (eds.) ICSOC 2017. LNCS, vol. 10601, pp. 206–220. Springer, Cham (2017). https://doi.org/10.1007/978-3-319-69035-3_14
14. Xu, M., Buyya, R.: Brownout approach for adaptive management of resources and applications in cloud computing systems: a taxonomy and future directions. ACM Comput. Surv. **52**(1), 8:1–82:7 (2019)
15. Zhang, Y., Wang, Y., Wang, X.: GreenWare: greening cloud-scale data centers to maximize the use of renewable energy. In: Kon, F., Kermarrec, A.-M. (eds.) Middleware 2011. LNCS, vol. 7049, pp. 143–164. Springer, Heidelberg (2011). https://doi.org/10.1007/978-3-642-25821-3_8

Operating Enterprise AI as a Service

Fabio Casati(✉), Kannan Govindarajan, Baskar Jayaraman,
Aniruddha Thakur, Sriram Palapudi, Firat Karakusoglu, and Debu Chatterjee

ServiceNow™, Inc., Santa Clara, CA 95054, USA
fabio.casati@servicenow.com

Abstract. This paper discusses the challenges in providing AI functionality "as a Service" (AIaaS) in enterprise contexts, and proposes solutions to some of these challenges. The solutions are based on our experience in designing, deploying, and testing AI services with a number of customers of ServiceNow, an Application Platform as a Service that enables digital workflows and simplifies the complexity of work in a single cloud platform. Some of the underlying ideas were developed when many of the authors were part of DxContinuum inc, a machine learning (ML) startup that ServiceNow bought in 2017 with the express purpose of embedding ML in the ServiceNow platform. The widespread adoption of ServiceNow by the majority of large corporations has given us the opportunity to interact with customers in different markets and to appreciate the needs, fears and barriers towards adopting AIaaS and to design solutions that respond to such barriers. In this paper we share the lessons we learned from these interactions and present the resulting framework and architecture we adopted, which aims at addressing fundamental concerns that are sometimes conflicting with each other, from automation to security, performance, effectiveness, ease of adoption, and efficient use of resources. Finally, we discuss the research challenges that lie ahead in this space.

Keywords: Machine learning · Cloud computing · PaaS

1 Introduction and Motivations

Machine learning (ML)[1] is becoming widespread and used in everyday consumer applications, from face recognition on our phones to shopping recommendations, smart dieting and fitness. It is increasingly adopted not only by big players with deep machine learning competencies, but also by small startups and individual developers with limited ML skills. Some of the reasons for the recent ML success include:

---

[1] In this paper, we use the machine learning (ML) and artificial intelligence (AI) somewhat interchangeably because the distinction is not significant for the purposes of this paper.

© Springer Nature Switzerland AG 2019
S. Yangui et al. (Eds.): ICSOC 2019, LNCS 11895, pp. 331–344, 2019.
https://doi.org/10.1007/978-3-030-33702-5_25

1. Ubiquity of Data: The volume, variety and velocity of data being collected and available for analysis has exploded. A small number of platforms control an enormous amount of data on consumer behavior, and use ML to effectively increase engagement on their platforms. Enterprises are also generating a lot of data about their operations that can be leveraged to improve business outcomes.
2. Ubiquity of Compute: The advent of cheap computing and of computing on demand has significantly lowered the barriers to throwing significant computing resources at ML problems.
3. New representations and algorithms: ML algorithms themselves have improved with highly scalable/parallel versions of various classic algorithms. In addition, newer representation techniques for unstructured text, audio and images using deep neural networks have revolutionized traditionally difficult tasks.

This has led to applications that were the realm of "science fiction" to be now realized and deployed, from self-driving cars to automated conversational agents.

However, ML adoption within the enterprise (to automate or assist enterprise processes such as those driving supply chain management, HR, sales, marketing, IT service and operations management and the like) is still limited. According to recent surveys, only 26% of the companies have integrated AI into their processes and day-to-day operations, *even in the most "digitized" organizations*. While there are pilots running in all areas[2], only 18% of companies have ML embedded in more than one functions or business unit [18][3]. The challenge most companies face - besides lack of digitization - is the shortage of AI talent, the prohibitive cost of adopting ML/AI at scale starting with inadequate IT infrastructure, and the lack of a clear company strategy within the organization [18].

Cloud services provide the opportunity to solve, or at least mitigate, some of the aspects related to skills and infrastructure. Google, Amazon, Microsoft and many other vendors provide ML services that can be invoked via API and can scale with a few clicks, and offer both pre-trained models as well as services to train a model over our own data. Indeed, it seems that as part of the enterprise IT infrastructure moves to the cloud or embraces the "as a service" approach (for both private and public clouds), ML will follow the same path.

However, doing so presents its own challenges that go well beyond developing "good" ML algorithms. This paper discusses these challenges based on years of experience of operating low-code/no-code ML services with automated devops at scale to businesses around the world, including the majority of Fortune 500 companies. We also present how we approached these challenges, focusing specifically on how to define and operate an automated, scalable and secure ML service. Despite the progress, there are important research questions that are

---

[2] See, e.g., https://emerj.com/ai-executive-guides/enterprise-adoption-of-artificial-intelligence/.

[3] The survey was run across regions and industries in the US, reaching over 2000 companies.

far from being solved, and in the discussion section we will outline what we experienced as some of the key challenges lying ahead.

2 Related Work

With cloud and AI being emerging trends [3,10], many solutions that offer AI as a service have appeared. We divide such solutions in three main classes:

- *Inference* as a service: the cloud service provider offers pre-trained models that can be used via APIs. For example, nearly every big player in the IT space provides models to detect content in images or extract features from text snippets.
- *Training* as a service: here the cloud provider offers algorithms (and supporting infrastructure), but users can also train the model on their data or to focus on detecting specific classes. Depending on the level of flexibility provided (or desired by users), these can range from fixed, predefined algorithms to fully customizable or even programmable ones, or to providing Auto-ML functionality where "good" parameters and hyper-parameters of the algorithms are learned automatically based on the training data.
- *Embedded AI solution* as a service. AI training and prediction are still cloud services, but they are integrated with the enterprise business process management system (BPMS). This means that AI abstractions are made available from within the BPMS platform and can be leveraged to assist in process execution with little or no ad hoc coding and from within the user interface users are already familiar with. Servicenow and Salesforce are example of companies that offer such functionality in various ways. This approach has many variants depending on what AI is embedded into. For example, relational DBMS providers may think of providing out of the box functionality to predict cell values in tuples, possibly implemented via DB triggers that populate specific cell values upon insertion or updates to records.

Many research contributions exist in all of the above solution types. For example, Ribeiro and colleagues [12] provide a service component architecture for providing ML as a service, aimed at scalability and also at flexibility in terms of accommodating a variety of ML models.

As another example, Rafiki provides a cloud architecture that allows clients to perform model training and inference [17]. The approach performs automated and distributed hyper-parameter tuning and semi-automates model selection, thereby relieving the user from having competences in these areas. Rafiki also manages the trade-off between accuracy and response time during inference, as higher accuracy, often achieved via ensemble models, may require increased prediction time as it needs to wait for all models to complete their work.

Ease.ml addresses the problem of multi-tenant resource management for providing ML services [9]. Specifically, the work focuses on automatic selection of the ML model to be adopted for each user with the goal of maximizing average accuracy across users. The main contribution of the work is an algorithm for multi-tenant, cost-aware model selection based on first estimating the potential accuracy improvement for each user based on the best model to run for them, and on then picking the user with highest potential improvement. Experiments show significant improvement with respect to baselines and state of the art systems.

These contributions solve problems that are related but orthogonal to what we tackle here. Our focus is on providing an operational environment for ML so that non ML experts can develop solutions that incorporate intelligence into their processes without having to worry about operational aspects and while satisfying performance, security and other enterprise-level non-functional requirements. While these requirements may restrict the freedom in terms of modeling techniques available, in our experience, the benefits of automatic operationalization outweigh a few additional points of improved accuracy that extended experimenting with ad hoc solutions may bring. Indeed, it is no secret that many ML models that are developed do not make it into production because the engineering and deployment are too complex and what actually goes into production are simpler models where the vast majority of the benefit is gained [1].

Recent research aimed at addressing the problem of data (and model) confidentiality. *MLcapsule* [8] tackles the problem by conceiving a AIaaS approach where the model is downloaded and run on the client side, while however maintaining the model secret. The client in turns maintains the data secret as the data never leaves the client. The assumption here is that the model is pretrained and the main focus on the paper is in avoiding model stealing and reverse engineering.

On the *embedding* side, ML algorithms and architectures have been proposed to extend databases and workflows with intelligent capabilities. For example, embedding AI into databases can be seen as promising in terms of allowing a generic way to predict an attribute of a record based on the values of other attributes for the same record. This can for example be implemented via user-defined functions (UDFs) in SQL, but as observed in [17] it would require implementing various ML models in UDFs as well as careful tuning to optimize performances and prediction accuracy.

One of the largest category of embedded models are those in the context of workflow management, and specifically in process mining and Robotic Process Automation (RPA). Process mining - and more generally, the notion of applying ML to process management, is a topic that has received a lot of attention in the last two decades. The large majority of the efforts focused again on the algorithm side, with the bulk of the work aimed at extracting process model from traces (e.g., [2,11,19]), clustering execution traces, detecting outliers [15,16], as well as predicting paths and execution times [5,7]. RPA leverages the results of process mining in many ways, including identifying promising opportunities for RPA adoption [6]. Companies providing process mining and RPA capabilities do offer cloud services and address integration with the BPMS. For example, companies such as Celonis or TimelinePI can connect to enterprise data stores and application platforms (such as ServiceNow) and process execution traces, offering a scalable cloud-based analytic system to make sense of the data from a process perspective. On-premises solutions are also available. RPA systems also provide cloud-based solutions, sometimes marketed as "automation as a service", as well as enable in-house deployments[4].

The challenges we tackle in this paper are related but we focus on abstractions of ML functionality and on secure, integrated and scalable deployment within the same data center of the BPMS.

3 Background: Enterprise Business Process Management

We present our concepts and architecture in the context of a digitized enterprise where various processes are supported or automated via systems such as Salesforce, Jira, SAP or ServiceNow. As an example, ServiceNow[5] is an application platform as a service that offers functionality for modeling and running workflows, and provides built-in capabilities for typical workflows, tasks, data models and UIs in areas such as IT service management, IT operations management, customer service and HR. The value proposition of such platforms derive therefore not only from the application development features (e.g., the workflow model designer, the workflow engine, the UI form designer, etc.), but also from the built-in modules, from the ecosystem of plugins and extensions (much like an app store for enterprise applications), from the ability to define and enforce access to applications and data, and from the secure, scalable, efficient management of applications and data.

Application platforms such as ServiceNow are interesting from an AI perspective for two reasons: First, they collect data that can be used by ML algorithms to support the process. For example, they store data about how problems or incidents are assigned to specific customer support agents or to a given level of priority, or on how incidents are resolved. Second, they provide a uniform way to define applications and workflows, extending the ones available out of the box. This means that the same platform can run a variety of user-defined applications and that the platform is aware of the UI forms, workflows and data models that are part of an application. This provides an opportunity for integrating ML capabilities into the platform: if we find a way to do so that is (i) secure and effective from cloud management perspective and that (ii) offers ML abstractions that make it easy for customers to leverage the intelligent features, then we can inject ML into many processes, not just one, and with relatively limited effort, skills required, and by leveraging the same information security, scalability, and service level offered by the cloud BPMS

---

[4] See for example https://docs.uipath.com/orchestrator/docs/about-physical-deployment for RPA architectures on UIPath.

[5] https://developer.servicenow.com.

4   AI as an Embedded Enterprise Service

4.1   Challenges

Capturing the opportunity offered by enterprise BPMS from an AI perspective presents several challenges, especially if we want to provide the same convenience that cloud services provide, with a low total cost of ownership so that the services can be affordable and sustainable.

(a) Enterprise data is often the property of the enterprise, even if it is hosted in a public cloud or service provider's infrastructure, and consequently has very strict access requirements. In addition, for machine learning to be effective in making complex decisions inside enterprise applications, they have to be well integrated with them. This is not just about exposing a model through a REST API, but it involves encapsulating and aligning the pipeline for training and prediction that goes from the data as it exists in the application's database to the form required for training and inference. Once the inference is done, ML platforms should provide a variety of mechanisms for utilizing the output of the inference, given that it is a probabilistic outcome and not a deterministic one.

(b) The pre-trained models that work well in the consumer context may not be as effective in the enterprise context. For example, if we want to use Natural Language Processing for analyzing chatbot or email interactions between a customer service representative and a customer to determine what the problem is, we may not be able to use commonly available word embeddings in all situations, for several reasons:

   – A word like *London* or *Madrid* denotes a location, but in specific contexts (such as ServiceNow), it denotes product releases[6]. *Louise* can be the name of a person or a lake, but it can also be the name of a conference room in an organization. Pre-trained word embeddings will skew the weights to what is reasonable in the "wild wild west", but in different enterprises the neighborhood of "Madrid" or "Louise" will be very different.
   – More sophisticated pre-trained models such as models for dependency parsing are also trained on public corpora and may not have the precision needed to be effective in enterprise settings. In most cases they would require at least some pre- and post-processing of text to bring them into a form that will parse with the necessary precision.

(c) Expecting the average developers and product managers in IT departments of enterprises or software companies to be familiar with such technologies - and their many nuances - to make use of them is too high a hurdle for adoption to happen effectively. Therefore we have to enable effective low-code/no-code ML solution development, which in turn implies exposing ML abstractions that can be easily integrated into enterprise processes and that strike the right balance between generality, ease of use, and effectiveness.

---

[6] ServiceNow releases are named from cities around the world.

(d) The whole as-a-Service movement, especially the Software-as-a-Service movement, has changed the economics of software. As mentioned earlier, platforms like ServiceNow and Salesforce enable developers to develop fairly sophisticated applications and not have to worry about deploying them because the platform provides that for free. In order to extend that to machine learning capabilities available within the platform, the process of deploying machine learning solutions has to be automated so that the developer can focus on specifying what they want to train, and utilize the results of inference in the application environment itself. Without this automation and uniformity, the cost of operating the ML solution can materially increase. Indeed, developing and deploying complete ML solutions is much more complex than just creating models [14]. While some ML workloads perform significantly better on special purpose hardware, uniformity in the upper layers of the software stack can materially reduce the cost of ongoing operations.

(e) *Testability* and *explainability* are other big challenges that have to be overcome for ML to be incorporated into enterprise applications. Since ML computations are inherently probabilistic, it is often difficult to test ML solutions using traditional testing methods that compare actual results with expected results and test for equality [13]. In addition, ML-based decisioning in the enterprise requires explainability and justification for predictions, often to increase confidence before adoption or for legal reasons. For example, in some restricted/regulated markets enterprises have to show that ML models they use do not have bias (and using pre-trained models from a the consumer context can allow bias to creep in complex ML solutions [4]).

(f) Cloud BPMS vendors carefully architect their solutions to have a footprint that makes scaling them manageable in terms of computing resources and costs. ML is resource-intensive both in terms of compute and storage, and keeping the resource consumption low is essential to scale to thousands of concurrent instances requesting to compute predictions.

(g) Finally, the ML infrastructure has to deliver the necessary security and confidentiality guarantees on the data, the generated models, and the inferences made by ML.

All of these issues contribute to the central problem we aim at, that of lowering the barrier to adoption of effective AI within the enterprise processes. This barrier does not come only from whether a solution is feasible, useful, secure and cost-effective for a company: it also comes from how "hard" it is for the average company to explore such solutions from a technical, architectural, legal perspective, just to name a few. Each of these perspectives will require preparation, discussions, iterations, and possibly eventual approvals, and will invariably involve change. Therefore, they require time, resources, as well as persistent, committed "champions".

We argue therefore that creating a solution that has the desirable properties is only a necessary step towards adoption. We also claim that for the same reasons creating a separate, autonomous cloud platform for AI services would not only create an additional burden for the customer (and raise issues about if and how data, models and inferences are kept secure across clouds as well as to how performance and effectiveness are managed), but would also raise the barrier to adoption in terms of having to go through the due diligence for adopting such architecture.

4.2   AI as a Service

The discussion above emphasizes that the architecture of embedded AI may differ from typical "aaS" approach. As an example, Fig. 1 shows how AIaaS would be used in a typical setting.

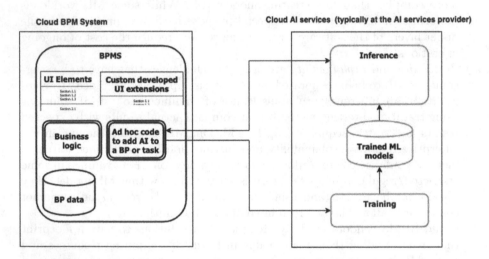

Fig. 1. A common architecture for leveraging AIaaS in enterprise business processes (Color figure online)

A BPMS supports workflow definition and execution, while a separate cloud service is available for training and inference. When the enterprise wants to exploit ML in a process, it leverages the internal team of data scientists to identify where it is promising and possible to do so. For example, it identifies that classifying incoming requests by topic is feasible because of the nature and amount of the available data.

Next, ad hoc code is written and tested by internal developers to identify the source data to be used for training, extract it and package it for delivery to the cloud training service (this is shown in blue in the Figure). A specific ML model also needs to be selected and possibly configured, depending on the flexibility allowed by the cloud AI service and desired by the enterprise.

The enterprise also needs to decide how to store the trained model, e.g., whether it is stored by the AI service provider (convenient, but may not meet security requirements) or internally, and if internally, how and where, weather it should be encrypted and if so what the encryption, decryption and usage workflow looks like.

For inference, additional development is needed to be able to obtain input data, transfer it to the cloud inference engine (possibly along with the model, if it was stored internally), obtain the prediction and apply it to the process. This is very laborious, requires ML skills, and presents performance and security challenges (for example, transferring the model for each prediction is likely unrealistic, having it stored at the AI service provider may or may not be acceptable by the enterprise). Furthermore, specific UI (again shown in blue in the Figure) also needs to be designed, developed, tested and deployed so that the enterprise process worker can leverage the result of the prediction, and be aware of "metadata" such as the confidence level for the prediction. Code for periodically retraining the model with fresh data (or simply with more data) must also be in place.

While all this is feasible and presents many advantages (such as ample choice of ML algorithms, arbitrary scalability) it requires skills, design and development work, security engineering and very likely many levels of approvals and establishment of contractual relationships to use services and data centers for a new company - the AIaaS provider. None of these issues is a show-stopper, but is likely to significantly delay and raise the barrier for leveraging AI into enterprise processes.

4.3   Embedded ML as a BPMS Service

The objective and value we are pursuing (Fig. 2) is to transition to a framework where ML sits on top of the BPMS platform, tightly integrated with it and enabling low code or no code deployment of ML solutions. The price to pay is that the range of solutions that are possible are those supported by the ML platform, and going outside the platform would imply the need of addressing all the challenges discussed earlier, something often unrealistic in many enterprise contexts.

Figure 3 shows how the "as a service" scenario changes with the embedded architecture we propose. The approach here from an architectural perspective is that the ML services, while being separate cloud services, are deployed and operated along with the BPMS, typically within the same data center and offered as additional services within the same contractual framework with the enterprise. The ML workflow in this case proceeds as follows (we will only describe it briefly in the following, but the interested reader can activate cloud instances of ServiceNow and install the ML functionality for free at http://developer.servicenow. com).

1. The user decides to add ML functionality to a process. For example, it wishes to use ML to automatically categorize incidents, so that they can be then assigned and routed through the incident management process. To do so, users simply state that they want to apply a *classification template* to a BPMS object (in this case, *Incident*). Figure 4 shows part of such a template

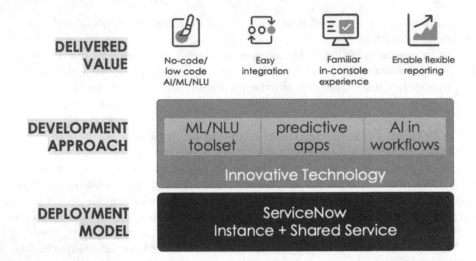

Fig. 2. Integrated ML solutions enable familiar interfaces and low/no code deployments.

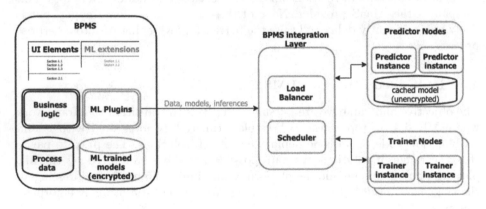

Fig. 3. Integrating cloud AI/ML services with enterprise BPMSs

in ServiceNow. The details are not important at this stage, what matters is that (i) the template has the same UX interaction paradigm as all other applications in the platform, (ii) it is aware of the ServiceNow data model and applications, and as such (iii) the classification task can be defined literally with a few clicks. Users have the options of filtering data and features of interest if they so wish. Users can also set specific prediction and recall thresholds to restrict the automated solution to be applied only above certain levels of confidence and accuracy in the results.

2. Upon definition, when the user applies the template to Incidents, the ML plugin in ServiceNow contacts a scheduler informing it of the need to develop a classification model.

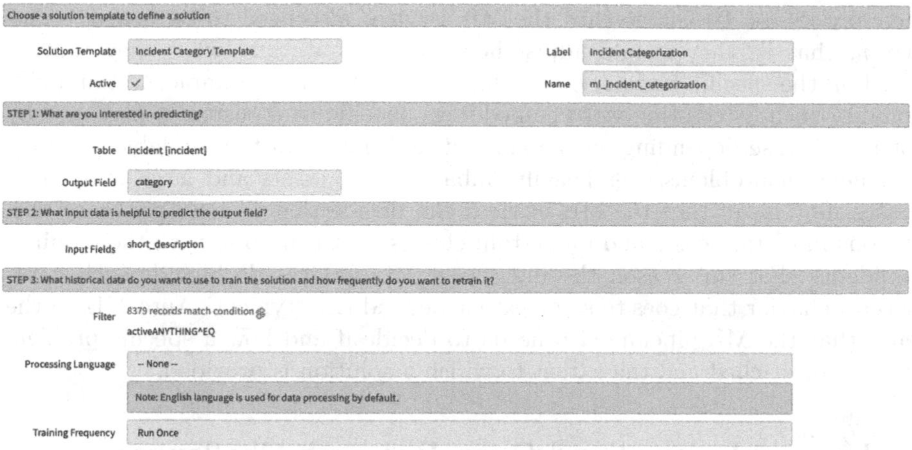

Fig. 4. Template for defining incident classification

3. A set of machines devoted to training run a set of trainer instances. These instances periodically contact the scheduler once they are available to fetch new work to be done. If there is work, the trainers contact the BPMS to fetch the data, build the model, discard the training data, and send the model back to the BPMS.
4. The BPMS encrypt and stores the model, to be then used for prediction.

At prediction time, the following workflow is run:

1. When a new item to be classified is created (in our example, as a new incident comes in), the ML plugin executes a rule that invokes the prediction server.
2. Invocations go through the load balancer, that besides managing the load among instances of the predictor, it supports stickiness, that is, routes requests over a short time span to the same predictor instance.
3. If the predictor instance has the classification model cached, it uses it to make the inference. If not, it checks if it is available (encrypted) on disk. If so, it decrypts it (the key is always passed by the BPMS and not stored) and loads it in cache. If the model is not available locally, it sends a request to the BPMS to fetch it.
4. Periodically, the database at the predictor side is cleaned to remove rarely used models.

The whole infrastructure is set up to be secure and, also importantly, to ensure that it can run smoothly even in the presence of large number of requests. For this reason, each predictor and trainer instance is constrained to a fixed maximum memory usage and the same is true for the model size.

The end benefit is that users with little or no data science and ML competences and no coding skills can get going with an ML solution embedded into their processes. To enable this, the ML services also need to be heavily *data-driven*, that is, they should adjust how they operate and what they provide based on the specific customer data that is available. For example, certain functionality such as creating word embeddings specific to a customer may or may not make sense depending on the amount and nature of the available data; or, classification problems over heavily unbalanced datasets and large number of classes may mean that the ML services can decide that it will only make predictions in certain cases and for certain classes as it can do so with the required confidence. For this reason the integrated ML services do include such data-driven behavior that goes to some extent beyond the "typical" Auto-ML, in the sense that the ML pipeline also needs to decide if and how a specific problem can be approached and the extent to which a solution is provided.

5   Lessons Learned and Open Research Challenges

The concepts and architecture described here have proven to be successful in a large number of use cases and customer engagement across the globe. However, there are abundant opportunities for research in this space as the number of unsolved problems remain high.

A key challenge is identifying which ML abstractions should be exposed to *strike the right balance between generality and efficacy*. We want to avoid creating and maintaining separate algorithms and ML workflows for different specific problems, but on the other hand we need solution to be effective for such problems, and sometimes general solutions lack such effectiveness. The current version of the platform provides functionality such as classification, clustering and similarity, but the challenge here is to identify classes of problems that are sufficiently large to warrant their own, specific ML solution. These for example may involve process-aware ML, algorithms for replacing forms in process steps with a chatbot-like interfaces, or methods for assisting users in ensuring the quality of the information they provide (e.g., ensuring that when a defect or incident is reported, there is enough information to understand, replicate and diagnose the problem).

A related concern is how to expose and explain the results of ML in the tool and how this is made part of a successful user experience. This issue also includes how to explain, when needed, the result of the ML algorithms, particularly in terms of confidence and how to configure behaviors based on such confidence (e.g., automate classification for some classes if confidence is high, provide suggestions in other cases in more or less explicit ways).

A second set of challenges revolves around how to identify opportunities for injecting ML (in which workflows, at what stage and for what), as well as semi-automatically defining an appropriate training datasets/featureset. Today to some extent users still need to identify attributes of interests "by hand", and the system provides support in terms of (i) performing the data extraction as needed, and (ii) alerting if data is insufficient. However, in general we can imagine to automate the process by having the ML plugins automatically scan data and decide which features are relevant, or simply "dump" all possible features into a deep learning model, perhaps tuned via auto-ML. The challenge here is that if we do this frequently we overload both the BPMS node and the ML service node, and the goal of keeping a low TCO is compromised.

Finally, interesting challenges remain on the UX side, related to how to help users become familiar with how to apply ML for their problems and processes, how to understand the value and potential of ML, and how to gauge the accuracy (or lack thereof) of ML solution in general as well as of individual predictions or recommendations.

If we can solve these three open problems we can take a big leap forward in addressing the issue mentioned in the introduction - the very low adoption of ML within enterprise processes.

References

1. Amatriain, X., Basilico, J.: Netflix recommendations: Beyond the 5 stars. https://medium.com/netflix-techblog/netflix-recommendations-beyond-the-5-stars-part-1-55838468f429a (2012)
2. Augusto, A., et al.: Automated discovery of process models from event logs: review and benchmark. IEEE Trans. Knowl. Data Eng. **PP**, May 2017. https://doi.org/10.1109/TKDE.2018.2841877
3. Bouguettaya, A., et al.: A service computing manifesto: the next 10 years. Commun. ACM **60**, 64–72 (2017). https://doi.org/10.1145/2983528
4. Brunet, M., Alkalay-Houlihan, C., Anderson, A., Zemel, R.S.: Understanding the origins of bias in word embeddings. CoRR abs/1810.03611 (2018). http://arxiv.org/abs/1810.03611
5. Di Francescomarino, C., Ghidini, C., Maggi, F., Milani, F.: Predictive process monitoring methods: which one suits me best?, April 2018
6. Geyer-Klingeberg, J., Nakladal, J., Baldauf, F., Veit, F.: Process mining and robotic process automation: a perfect match, July 2018
7. Grigori, D., Casati, F., Castellanos, M., Dayal, U., Sayal, M., Shan, M.C.: Business process intelligence. Comput. Ind. **53**(3), 321–343 (2004). https://doi.org/10.1016/j.compind.2003.10.007
8. Hanzlik, L., et al.: MLCapsule: guarded offline deployment of machine learning as a service. Technical report, September 2018. https://arxiv.org/abs/1808.00590
9. Li, T., Zhong, J., Liu, J., Wu, W., Zhang, C.: Ease.ml: Towards multi-tenant resource sharing for machine learning workloads, September 2017
10. Mistry, S., Bouguettaya, A., Dong, H.: Economic Models for Managing Cloud Services. Springer, Cham (2018). https://doi.org/10.1007/978-3-319-73876-5
11. Osman, C., Ghiran, A.M.: Extracting customer traces from CRMS: from software to process models. Procedia Manufact. **32**, 619–626 (2019). https://doi.org/10.1016/j.promfg.2019.02.261
12. Ribeiro, M., Grolinger, K., Capretz, M.: MLaaS: machine learning as a service, December 2015. https://doi.org/10.1109/ICMLA.2015.152
13. Sampson, A., Panchekha, P., Mytkowicz, T., McKinley, K.S., Grossman, D., Ceze, L.: Expressing and verifying probabilistic assertions. In: Programming Language Design and Implementation (PLDI), June 2014. https://www.microsoft.com/en-us/research/publication/expressing-and-verifying-probabilistic-assertions/

14. Sculley, D., et al.: Hidden technical debt in machine learning systems. In: Cortes, C., Lawrence, N.D., Lee, D.D., Sugiyama, M., Garnett, R. (eds.) Advances in Neural Information Processing Systems, vol. 28, pp. 2503–2511. Curran Associates, Inc. (2015). http://papers.nips.cc/paper/5656-hidden-technical-debt-in-machine-learning-systems.pdf
15. Seeliger, A., Nolle, T., Mühlhäuser, M.: Finding structure in the unstructured: hybrid feature set clustering for process discovery. In: Weske, M., Montali, M., Weber, I., vom Brocke, J. (eds.) BPM 2018. LNCS, vol. 11080, pp. 288–304. Springer, Cham (2018). https://doi.org/10.1007/978-3-319-98648-7_17
16. Seeliger, A., Sánchez Guinea, A., Nolle, T., Mühlhäuser, M.: ProcessExplorer: intelligent process mining guidance. In: Hildebrandt, T., van Dongen, B., Röglinger, M., Mendling, J. (eds.) BPM 2019. LNCS, vol. 11675. Springer, Cham (2019). https://doi.org/10.1007/978-3-030-26619-6_15
17. Wang, W., et al.: Rafiki: machine learning as an analytics service system. Proc. VLDB Endowm. **12**, 128–140 (2018). https://doi.org/10.14778/3282495.3282499
18. Webb, N.: Notes from the AI frontier: AI adoption advances, but foundational barriers remain (2018)
19. Yang, S., Li, J., Tang, X., Chen, S., Marsic, I., Burd, R.: Process mining for trauma resuscitation, vol. 18, August 2017

Towards Automated Patch Management
in a Hybrid Cloud

Ubaid Ullah Hafeez[1][✉], Alexei Karve[2][✉], Braulio Dumba[2][✉],
Anshul Gandhi[1][✉], and Sai Zeng[2][✉]

[1] PACE Lab @ Stony Brook University, Stony Brook, NY 11794, USA
{uhafeez,anshul}@cs.stonybrook.edu
[2] IBM Thomas J. Watson Research Center, Yorktown Heights, NY 10598, USA
karve@us.ibm.com, Braulio.Dumba@ibm.com, saizeng@us.ibm.com

Abstract. Software patching is routinely employed for enterprise online
applications to guard against ever-increasing security risks and to keep up
with customer requirements. However, in a hybrid cloud setting, where
an application deployment can span across diverse cloud environments,
patching becomes challenging, especially since application components
may be deployed as containers or VMs or bare-metal machines. Further,
application tiers may have dependencies, which need to be respected.
Worse, to minimize application downtime, selected patches need to be
applied in a finite time period. This paper presents an automated patching strategy for hybrid-cloud—deployed applications that leverages a
greedy algorithm design to optimally patch applications. Our implementation and evaluation results highlight the efficacy of our strategy and
its superiority over alternative patching strategies.

1 Introduction

Online enterprise applications today are often deployed in a hybrid cloud—a
computing environment that combines the benefits of public and private clouds
by sharing data and application deployment between them. A hybrid cloud is
cost-effective and elastic as the public cloud portion of the application follows a
pay-as-you-go model. On the other hand, the private cloud portion can be kept
behind a firewall, on compliant machines, to ensure data security and privacy.

To avoid security breaches and keep the application updated according to customer requirements, most online applications employ software patching. Applying a security patch as soon as it is available can prevent 57% of the security
breaches [2]. In addition to security patches, application update patches are also
important. For example, an online application launched a time ticker sidebar
which was regarded as "spambar" by users and decreased the popularity of the
application among desktop users; this sidebar was taken down shortly to avoid
any further customer disappointment [6]. Thus, timely patching is one of the key
requirements for secure and performant functioning of online applications [2].

Patch management of applications deployed in a hybrid cloud environment
is complicated and tedious. Applications in hybrid cloud often span multiple

© Springer Nature Switzerland AG 2019
S. Yangui et al. (Eds.): ICSOC 2019, LNCS 11895, pp. 345–350, 2019.
https://doi.org/10.1007/978-3-030-33702-5_26

components, also referred to as services or tiers. There may be numerous pending patches, with different priorities, including those that are critical. Typically, there is only a limited time period, referred to as *maintenance window*, during which the application can be brought down and patched in an offline manner. Also, while patching, application components should be turned off in a specific order to avoid violating dependencies and to prevent the application from crashing. This makes manual patching for different tiers across different types of clouds and deployment types expensive (and possibly infeasible) and prone to human error. Clearly, an automated patch management system would be invaluable for applications deployed in a hybrid cloud.

There are some existing application management tools, e.g., Puppet [12], RCP [11] which are used for automating application patching. However, these tools do not allow application owners to limit downtime for patching by specifying a maintenance window. Enterprise applications cannot be taken offline for arbitrarily long time periods, making existing tools ineffective for automated patching of enterprise applications. There is another prior work on patching which focus on applications deployed in just a single cloud [10]. While there are some works that discuss patch management in a hybrid cloud [8], they assume that all components of the application have replicas and can be patched online.

This paper presents Hybrid Cloud Patch Manager (HCPM), a framework for automated patch management for applications deployed in a hybrid cloud. HCPM applies the optimal subset of patches in any given maintenance window and patches tiers that can be patched online whenever possible. For patch selection in a given window, HCPM employs PatchSelect, a greedy yet optimal algorithm. While patching, HCPM takes application dependencies into account, by constructing a dependency graph, thus ensuring that the application is always healthy and does not crash. Experiments confirm that HCPM effectively patches hybrid-cloud–deployed multi-tier applications within the given offline window. We further evaluate HCPM using simulations, and compare against other patching strategies, for a complex, 11-tier application. Our results, in various patching scenarios, show that HCPM outperforms other strategies by 2–29%, on average, and by as much as 2×. To make HCPM easily deployable in practice, we implement it as a plug-in that can be integrated with existing applications.

To the best of our knowledge, this is the first work on automated patch management for enterprise applications, deployed across containers and VMs in a hybrid cloud, that considers the length of the maintenance window and dependencies across application tiers.

2   Automated Patch Management

HCPM automates patch management for applications deployed in a hybrid cloud and ensures that critical patches are applied as early as possible while complying with application dependencies. HCPM's architecture is shown in Fig. 1(a). HCPM consists of a *DependencyMapper*, a *PatchMonitor*, a few *PatchAgents* and a *PatchManager*. The *PatchMonitor* and *DependencyMapper* provide inputs to *PatchManager* to enable automated patching, whenever feasible.

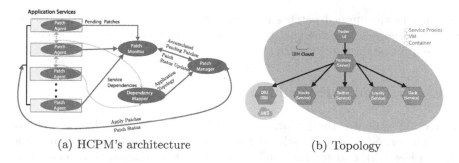

(a) HCPM's architecture   (b) Topology

Fig. 1. Stock-trader application deployment in our hybrid cloud environment. The direction of the edges represents the dependence relationship between each component of the application: *trader* → *portfolio* → *Db2*; *Stocks*; *Twitter*; *Slack*; *Loyalty*.

The *PatchAgent* (per-cloud or per-tier) monitors the state of the application and OS patches for each node, and maintains a list of pending patches along with their importance. Whenever there is a new pending patch, the *PatchAgent* communicates this list to the *PatchMonitor*. The *PatchMonitor* aggregates pending patches, along with their importance scores, across all *PatchAgents*. When required, *PatchMonitor* communicates the pending patches to *PatchManager*.

The *DependencyMapper* constructs the dependency graph of the application using tools for automatic discovery as well as direct input from the application. *DependencyMapper* keeps updating the topology in real time as it discovers more information about the application. The *PatchManager* communicates with *DependencyMapper* and *PatchMonitor* to perform the actual patching.

For selection of offline patches, *PatchManager* employs our PatchSelect algorithm. For a given maintenance window of size, say, W minutes, PatchSelect finds optimal subset of patches for each tier separately as multiple tiers can be patched simultaneously in the offline window. For a given tier, let the estimated time to reboot its node be R and that to reboot all its dependent tiers be R'; then, we have $W_{actual} = W - R - R'$ minutes left to apply patches to the tier. PatchSelect partitions all patches according to their importance level and then sorts the patches, for each level, in ascending order of their patching time. Starting from the most important level (level $i = 1$), PatchSelect greedily selects as many patches as possible, in sorted order, such that the sum of their patching time is less than W_{actual}. If the time to apply patches of level $i = 1$ is $W_1 < W_{actual}$, and either all patches of level $i = 1$ have been applied or no more patches of level $i = 1$ can be applied without exceeding W_{actual}, then the algorithm proceeds similarly to the next priority levels, in order, with remaining time $W_{actual} = W_{actual} - W_1$. Given an application with S tiers and N number of pending patches, the time complexity of PatchSelect is $\mathcal{O}(S^2 + N \log(N))$.

To minimize the time for applying patching, *PatchManager* is implemented as a multi-process agent which brings down tiers in order of dependencies and starts applying patches to offline tiers simultaneously. Once the patching of a subset of patches is successful, *PatchManager* informs *PatchMonitor*, which in turn removes the applied patches from the pending list. If some of the patches fail, *PatchManager* logs the specific cause of failure and reverts the patches so that the application stays healthy.

3   Experimental Evaluation

This section evaluates the performance of HCPM for stock-trader [5], a multi-tier microservice-based application deployed in our hybrid cloud environment as shown in Fig. 1(b). Our hybrid cloud environment is composed of a 2-core, 8 GB memory VM on AWS public cloud, and 4 4-core, 16 GB memory VMs on our private cloud. All VMs on our private cloud are connected as a cluster using the open-source ICP—a Kubernetes-based private cloud. To simulate real workload of multiple users (create new portfolios, buying stocks, etc.), we use jmeter [4].

HCPM Deployment: We implement HCPM as follows: the *PatchAgent* module is implemented using the publicly available Vulnerability Advisor (VA) [3] and BigFix [1]. We use REST APIs of VA and BigFix to communicate with *PatchManager*. The *PatchMonitor* and *PatchManager* are implemented in Python. The *DependencyMapper* module is implemented using WeaveScope [7].

Evaluation: In our deployment of HCPM, the *PatchAgent* module periodically scans for services that are missing critical security patches. HCPM extracts the dependency (see Fig. 1(b)) among the components of the stock-trader using its *DependencyMapper* module. Then, it uses the PatchSelect algorithm to find and apply the optimal subset of patches from the list of pending patches (see Table 1) for the given maintenance window, which is set to 2 min, and restarts the containers within the maintenance window. While restarting, HCPM makes sure that dependency constraints are not violated. Given a short maintenance window of 2 min, HCPM identifies that the patches for the Db2 VM cannot be applied, and these are thus omitted by PatchSelect; the remaining patches are applied in 54 s.

Table 1. Pending packages for the images of stock-trader.

Tier	Pending vulnerable packages
Portfolio	libgcrypt20, procps, gpgv, libssl1.0.0, gnupg, libprocps4
Trader	gnupg, libgcrypt20, libssl1.0.0, libprocps4, gpgv, procps
Db2	java (RHSA-2018:0349-01), wget (RHSA-2018:3052)

4   Simulation Results

For simulations (written in Python), we consider a large, multi-tier data streaming application, as in VScope [9], which has 11 tiers. We use details of pending

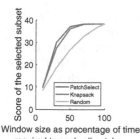
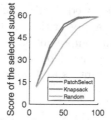
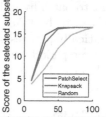

(a) Uniformly distributed patch importance levels i.e. 33% hi, 33% med., 33% low.

(b) Skewed distribution of patch importance levels i.e. 50% hi, 30% med., 20% low.

(c) Empirically distributed patch importance levels i.e. 12% hi, 48% med., 40% low.

Fig. 2. Simulation results showing the performance of PatchSelect, knapsack, and random patch selection under different patch importance levels.

patches based on the statistics of OS patches from last year [3]. To assign importance scores to patches, we consider three different scenarios using scores of 1 (high), 2 (med), and 3 (low) as shown in Fig. 2.

Figure 2 compares the performance of PatchSelect with two other strategies i.e. *Knapsack*, which models patch selection as a knapsack problem and uses a dynamic programming algorithm and *Random*, which is a simple strategy of randomly selecting patches until the maintenance window is exhausted. In Fig. 2, we use geometric scores when computing the accumulated score for a subset because typically, it is more important to apply a *single* high priority patch as compared to numerous low priority patches. Let N be the total number of pending patches. Consider a subset s with m_i number of patches of importance i, for $i \in \mathbb{Z}^+$. We define the accumulated geometric score for a subset s as:

$$score(s) = \sum_{i \geq 1} \sum_{j=1}^{m_i} \frac{1}{N^i} = \sum_{i \geq 1} \frac{m_i}{N^i} \qquad (1)$$

In all three scenarios in Fig. 2, PatchSelect improve the performance over random by about 18–29%, on average, with a maximum improvement of 53–101%. Against knapsack, we improve performance by about 2–3%, on average, with a maximum improvement of 6–13%. While the knapsack score is often close to that of PatchSelect, we find that the running time of knapsack is about 100× that of PatchSelect in almost all cases.

5   Conclusion

The emergence of hybrid cloud computing has made it easier for businesses to leverage the elasticity of economical public clouds while safeguarding sensitive data in their private clusters. However, this distributed deployment makes it difficult to patch hybrid-cloud–deployed applications, especially when the application has to be taken down to apply critical patches. Our solution, HCPM, automatically patches application components across clouds within the allotted offline time period while respecting tier dependencies. Importantly, HCPM does so while providing optimality guarantees and bounds on running time.

References

1. BigFix. https://www.ibm.com/security/endpoint-security/bigfix
2. How to shut the window of (unpatched) opportunity. https://www.welivesecurity.com/2018/04/19/patching-shut-window-unpatched
3. IBM Vulnerability Advisor. https://github.com/IBM-Bluemix-Docs/va
4. Jmeter. https://jmeter.apache.org
5. Stock-trader application. https://github.com/IBMStockTrader
6. Time's up for the Ticker? Facebook appears to axe feed for tracking your friends' activity. https://techcrunch.com/2017/12/10/times-up-for-facebook-ticker/
7. Weavescope. https://github.com/weaveworks/scope
8. Hopmann, A., et al.: High availability of machines during patching
9. Wang, C., et al.: VScope: middleware for troubleshooting time-sensitive data center applications. In: Narasimhan, P., Triantafillou, P. (eds.) Middleware 2012. LNCS, vol. 7662, pp. 121–141. Springer, Heidelberg (2012). https://doi.org/10.1007/978-3-642-35170-9_7
10. Dake, S.C.: Containerized upgrade in operating system level virtualization
11. Kloeckner, K., et al.: Building a cognitive platform for the managed it services lifecycle. IBM J. Res. Dev. **62**(1), 8–11 (2018)
12. Plummer, S., Warden, D.: Puppet: introduction, implementation & the inevitable refactoring. In: Proceedings of the 2016 ACM SIGUCCS Annual Conference (2016)

Services on the Internet of Things

QCF: QoS-Aware Communication Framework for Real-Time IoT Services

Omid Tavallaie[1(✉)], Javid Taheri[2], and Albert Y. Zomaya[1]

[1] School of Computer Science, The University of Sydney, Sydney, Australia
{omid.tavallaie,albert.zomaya}@sydney.edu.au
[2] Department of Computer Science, Karlstad University, Karlstad, Sweden
Javid.taheri@kau.se

Abstract. Routing Protocol for Low-power Lossy Networks (RPL) is designed by Internet Engineering Task Force (IETF) as the de facto routing standard for Internet of Things (IoT). Supporting mobility and providing Quality of Service (QoS) in the timeliness domain were not addressed in the IETF standard. RPL performs poorly when it comes to satisfying QoS constraints and adaptability to changes in the network topology. In this paper, we address this formidable problem by proposing QCF, a QoS-aware Communication Framework for real-time IoT services. Our proposed framework provides a lightweight practical approach to support timeliness requirements, and node mobility. It applies fuzzy logic to balance energy resources and traffic loads in the network. QCF estimates node mobility and the one-hop delay by using two novel methods. It employs two-hop neighbor information to enhance the parent selection process, and estimates the remaining time to the packet's deadline without using synchronized clocks. We integrate QCF into the Contiki operating system and implement it on Zolerita IoT motes. Emulation results show that QCF improves the deadline delivery ratio by up to 67% and reduces the end-to-end delay by up to 63%.

Keywords: Internet of Things (IoT) · Quality of Service (QoS) · Service-oriented networking · Real-time services

1 Introduction

Routing Protocol for Low-power Lossy Networks (RPL) was designed by Internet Engineering Task Force (IETF) as an IPv6 routing standard for Low-power and Lossy Network (LLN) applications of Internet of Things (IoT). LLNs consist of embedded devices with limited power, memory and processing resources interconnected by lossy links. These networks can be used in a wide variety of applications including home and building automation [1], industrial control [2] and smart grids [3]. Due to inherent characteristics of LLNs, routing and connecting resource constrained LLN devices to the Internet are challenging issues. LLN nodes are usually interconnected by lossy unstable links support low data

© Springer Nature Switzerland AG 2019
S. Yangui et al. (Eds.): ICSOC 2019, LNCS 11895, pp. 353–368, 2019.
https://doi.org/10.1007/978-3-030-33702-5_27

rates. Topology of the network is dynamically changed due to the node failure and mobility. Furthermore, multi-hop transmission over short range wireless links is used for forwarding data through the network [4].

Based on the characteristics of LLNs, specified in [1,2], RPL is defined in RFC 6550 [5] as an IPv6 distance vector routing protocol that creates a Directed Acyclic Graph (DAG) topology in the network. In this topology, all resource-limited IoT devices send their data to root nodes, border routers that connect LLNs to the Internet and cloud servers. Based on a predefined Objective Function (OF), IoT devices estimate their logical distances to root nodes to select a path for forwarding packets. An OF indicates how routing metrics can be used for selecting the preferred parent from a set of one-hop neighbors. While IETF proposed two OFs by considering the Expected Transmission Count (ETX) and the hop count in [6,7], many implementation details are left open. For example, combining different metrics and converting them to an OF is not addressed in RPL, and it is still an open research topic [8]. Meeting different Quality of Service (QoS) constraints exposes hard trade-offs among routing metrics, which is known as a NP-complete optimal path problem [9].

In real-time IoT services, data must be delivered to root nodes before a deadline. Therefore, only routes that can guarantee timely end-to-end delivery, must be selected for forwarding packets [10]. In these services, the performance of the routing operation is evaluated based on the end-to-end delay, the energy consumption, and the ratio of packets can be delivered to root nodes before their deadlines. Various factors impact each of these metrics that usually have different priorities for nodes and packets. For example, for nodes which are close to the roots, energy balancing has the highest priority as node failure may lead to the disconnected network. To design an effective routing that can meet timeliness requirements, not only must a good trade-off be made among given metrics, but also criteria that impact each of these metrics must be detected and considered in the parent selection process.

In this paper, we propose a QoS-aware Communication Framework (QCF) that can be integrated into RPL to provide QoS guarantee of timeliness in soft real-time IoT services. QCF supports node mobility and considers packets' deadlines in the routing operation. Our contribution in this paper is summarized as follows:

- We design a flexible communication framework, namely QCF, to (a) work with any user-defined OF, (b) provide an efficient QoS support in the timeliness domain, (c) balance the energy consumption and traffic loads in the network, and (d) provide adaptability to time-varying network topology by estimating node mobility.
- Our proposed framework does not use costly synchronization techniques or global clocks to meet timeliness requirements.
- We apply fuzzy logic to make robust decisions and decrease the complexity of the parent selection process.
- While most of the proposed mobility-aware IoT solutions can be applied only on GPS-enabled nodes, our framework can estimate node mobility by

monitoring the neighbor table in a lightweight method. This feature makes QCF applicable for a wide range of IoT motes with different hardwares.

– We implement QCF on Contiki OS (open source operating system for IoT) [11] and Zolerita IoT motes [12]. It can be easily integrated into the IoT protocol stack to be used as a service-oriented middleware for real-time services.

To elaborate our work in this paper, we organize the following sections. Section 2 provides an overview of RPL; Sect. 3 details our proposed framework. Section 4 is to evaluate the performance of QCF. Section 5 discusses related work. Finally, Sect. 6 concludes this paper. Table 1 summarizes most of symbols used in this work.

2   RPL Overview

Constructing topology is performed in RPL based on the OF that defines how routing metrics can be used for the rank calculation. A node's rank shows its

Table 1. Main symbols used in this paper

Symbol	Definition
G	The topology graph of the network
V	The set of all nodes
S	The set of all IoT nodes
R	The set of all root nodes
$\mathcal{E}$	The set of all links
$Rank_i$	The rank of node i in the DAG topology
$Cost_{i,j}$	The cost of using the wireless link between nodes i and j
CS_i	The candidate set of node i
NS_i	The neighbor set of node i
PS_i	The parent set of node i
D_j^i	The computed one-hop delay metric for node j, in node i
P_i	The parent of node i in the DAG topology
W_j^i	The computed weight for node j, in node i
E_j	The residual energy of node j
E_j^i	The computed energy metric for node j, in node i
Q_j	The queue length of node j
Q_j^i	The computed queue metric for node j, in node i
N_j^i	The computed node metric for node j, in node i
QoS_j^i	The computed QoS metric for node j, in node i
M_i	The mobility metric of node i
$TwoHopD_j^i$	The computed two-hop delay metric for node j, in node i

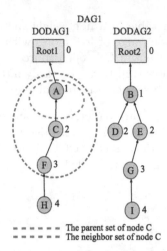

Fig. 1. An example of a DAG topology.

logical distance from a root node in the DAG topology. Ranks are increased in the direction from root nodes to leaf nodes. In the DAG topology, all edges are directed toward and terminate at DAG roots in a way that no cycle exists. Each DAG consists of at least one Destination Oriented Directed Acyclic Graph (DODAG). A DODAG has only one root node so that each IoT node in a DAG can belong to only one DODAG. In addition, all DODAGs in the same RPL instance use the same OF. Figure 1 shows a DAG consists of two DODAGs in a network of nine IoT nodes and two root nodes. Hop-count was considered as the OF for this network.

For a DAG $G = (V, \mathcal{E})$ consists of n DODAGs $G_i = (V_i, \mathcal{E}_i)$, the sets of all nodes and all possible wireless links can be seen as

$$V = \bigcup_{i=1}^{n} V_i, \qquad \mathcal{E} = \bigcup_{i=1}^{n} \mathcal{E}_i. \tag{1}$$

All nodes can be categorized into two classes of roots and IoT nodes. Thus, the set of all nodes in DAG G can be defined as

$$V = (S \cup R), \tag{2}$$

where S and R are sets of IoT nodes and roots respectively. Since each node of a DAG belongs to one DODAG, S and R can be defined as

$$S = \bigcup_{i=1}^{n} S_i, \qquad R = \bigcup_{i=1}^{n} R_i. \tag{3}$$

$\forall i \leqslant n, |R_i| = 1$ reflects that each DODAG consists of only one root node. Building a DAG starts from root nodes by broadcasting DODAG Information

Object (DIO) messages to one-hop neighbors. DIO is an ICMPv6 message that contains the node rank and information about the DODAG. By receiving a DIO message, the receiver adds one-hop neighbors with lower ranks to its parent set. After selecting the preferred parent from the parent set, each node i with the parent P_i updates its rank by

$$Rank_i = Rank_{P_i} + Cost_{i,P_i}, \tag{4}$$

where $Cost_{i,P_i}$ is the cost of using the wireless link (i, P_i) that connects node i to its parent P_i. In Fig. 1, this cost is considered as one unit for all links between one hop neighbors. When a node updates its rank, it broadcasts a DIO message contains the new rank to inform its one-hop neighbors of the change in the DODAG topology. In order to avoid loops, nodes with higher ranks cannot be selected as parents. Nodes' ranks are decreased toward the roots that have the minimum rank in the network topology.

3   QCF: QoS-Aware Communication Framework

In this section, we present our framework and explain its modules. QCF considers node and link metrics in selecting the preferred parent as the next hop. It employs information of two-hop neighbors for calculating energy, queue and delay metrics. Moreover, our framework updates the remaining time to the packet's deadline in each hop by estimating the one-hop delay.

3.1   Creating the Parent Set

A node can select only neighbors with lower ranks as its parents. The candidate set of node i is defined as

$$CS_i = \{j | j \in NS_i, Rank_j < Rank_i\}, \tag{5}$$

where NS_i is the neighbor set of node i. This set contains all nodes placed in the radio range of node i. For on-time delivery of packet p, the estimated one-hop delay of a neighbor must be less than the packet's deadline. Hence, the parent set of node i is defined according to

$$PS_i = \{j | j \in CS_i, D_j^i < Deadline_p^i\}, \tag{6}$$

where D_j^i is the estimated delay for forwarding a packet from node i to node j. To choose the preferred parent as the next hop in the DAG topology, node i computes both node and delay metrics for each neighbor, and then combines them to a QoS metric. As a result, for all nodes $j \in PS_i$, a weight is computed by node i. Finally, the neighbor with the maximum weight is selected as the next hop, i.e.

$$P_i = \arg \max_{j \in PS_i} W_j^i. \tag{7}$$

It is important to note that ranks are calculated based on the OF which is independent from QCF.

3.2 Node Metric

In QCF, the node metric is computed based on two-hop neighbor information. This solution is implemented without increasing the number of control packets, mainly because each node not only broadcasts its residual energy and its queue length, but also sends information of its parent within the option field of DIO messages. As shown in [13], the performance of the network can be improved by using multi-hop information, although this may reduce the network life-time for increasing the control packet overhead. In our proposed framework, we do not increase the number of DIO messages for sending QCF's control information, yet still, we can make better decisions for selecting the next hop. We consider different priorities for the information of two hops. This is based on the fact that energy consumption and congestion are severely increased for the nodes that are close to the root node. To address this issue, node i computes the energy metric for node $j \in PS_i$ by

$$E_j^i = \lambda E_j + \gamma E_{p_j}, \tag{8}$$

where E_j and E_{p_j} indicate the residual energies for nodes j and P_j respectively. Node i receives this information in DIO messages, and computes E_j^i. λ and γ are used to prioritize nodes based on their logical distances to the root. We consider higher priorities for parent nodes as they are always closer to the root node ($\lambda < \gamma$). The values of λ and γ are determined by the following conditions:

$$\lambda + \gamma = 1, \quad \lambda = \frac{Rank_{P_j}}{Rank_{P_j} + Rank_j}, \tag{9}$$

thus

$$\gamma = \frac{Rank_j}{Rank_{P_j} + Rank_j}. \tag{10}$$

For example, $\gamma = 0.66$ ($\lambda = 0.33$) when $Rank_j = 2$ and $Rank_{P_j} = 1$. In the RPL standard, ranks are increased in the direction from roots toward the leaf nodes. By increasing the logical distance from the root node, both $Rank_j$ and $Rank_{P_j}$ are increased that results in reducing the difference between λ and γ.

By using the same approach, node i computes the queue metric for node j according to

$$Q_j^i = \lambda Q_j + \gamma Q_{P_j}, \tag{11}$$

where Q_j is the number of packets are stored in the queue of node j. Exponential Weighted Moving Average (EWMA) is applied to smooth the queue metric and make it resilient against sudden changes as

$$Q_j(t) = \alpha Q_j(t-1) + (1-\alpha)q_j(t), \tag{12}$$

where $q_j(t)$ is the queue length of node j at time t, $Q_j(t-1)$ is the weighted average queue length of node j at time $t-1$, and $0 < \alpha < 1$ is the smooth factor.

To combine Q_j^i with E_j^i and convert them into the node metric, we use a fuzzy system with three membership functions for each metric. Figure 2(a)

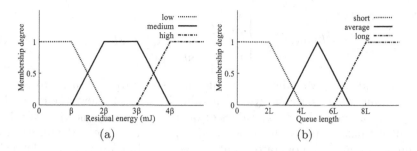

Fig. 2. Membership functions for (a) the energy metric, (b) the queue metric.

shows the trapezoidal membership functions that we use for the energy metric. These functions are defined as

$$
low(E_j^i) = \begin{cases} 1 & E_j^i \leq \beta \\ \frac{E_j^i - 2\beta}{\beta - 2\beta} & \beta < E_j^i < 2\beta \\ 0 & 2\beta \leq E_j^i \end{cases} , \tag{13}
$$

$$
medium(E_j^i) = \begin{cases} 0 & E_j^i \leq \beta \\ \frac{E_j^i - \beta}{2\beta - \beta} & \beta < E_j^i < 2\beta \\ 1 & 2\beta \leq E_j^i \leq 3\beta \\ \frac{E_j^i - 4\beta}{3\beta - 4\beta} & 3\beta < E_j^i < 4\beta \\ 0 & 4\beta \leq E_j^i \end{cases} , \tag{14}
$$

$$
high(E_j^i) = \begin{cases} 0 & E_j^i \leq 3\beta \\ \frac{E_j^i - 3\beta}{4\beta - 3\beta} & 3\beta < E_j^i < 4\beta \\ 1 & 4\beta \leq E_j^i \end{cases} , \tag{15}
$$

where β is one fifth of the node's initial energy. Each membership function generates a value that shows the membership degree of the residual energy to a fuzzy set. Likewise, we use 3 membership functions for the queue metric according to Eqs. (16), (17), and (18). Figure 2(b) shows these membership functions where L is set as one tenth of the maximum queue size.

$$
short(Q_j^i) = \begin{cases} 1 & Q_j^i \leq 2L \\ \frac{Q_j^i - 4L}{2L - 4L} & 2L < Q_j^i < 4L \\ 0 & 4L \leq Q_j^i \end{cases} , \tag{16}
$$

$$
average(Q_j^i) = \begin{cases} 0 & Q_j^i \leq 3L \\ \frac{Q_j^i - 3L}{5L - 3L} & 3L < Q_j^i < 5L \\ 1 & Q_j^i = 5L \\ \frac{Q_j^i - 7L}{5L - 7L} & 5L < Q_j^i < 7L \\ 0 & 7L \leq Q_j^i \end{cases} , \tag{17}
$$

$$long(Q_j^i) = \begin{cases} 0 & Q_j^i \leq 6L \\ \frac{Q_j^i - 6L}{8L - 6L} & 6L < Q_j^i < 8L \\ 1 & 8l \leq Q_j^i \end{cases} \cdot \tag{18}$$

In the next step, Mamdani fuzzy inference system [14] is used to combine fuzzified input values to the fuzzy output value n_j^i. Table 2 shows the rules which are applied for combining fuzzy values of queue and energy metrics. We define three output fuzzy sets for the node metric: *good*, *moderate* and *bad*. By using maximum and minimum operators, output membership functions are defined as

$$good(n_j^i) = Max \begin{pmatrix} Min(medium(E_j^i), short(Q_j^i)), \\ Min(high(E_j^i), average(Q_j^i)), \\ Min(high(E_j^i), short(Q_j^i)) \end{pmatrix}, \tag{19}$$

$$moderate(n_j^i) = Max \begin{pmatrix} Min(low(E_j^i), short(Q_j^i)), \\ Min(medium(E_j^i), average(Q_j^i)), \\ Min(high(E_j^i), long(Q_j^i)) \end{pmatrix}, \tag{20}$$

$$bad(n_j^i) = Max \begin{pmatrix} Min(low(E_j^i), long(Q_j^i)), \\ Min(medium(E_j^i), long(Q_j^i)), \\ Min(low(E_j^i), average(Q_j^i)) \end{pmatrix}. \tag{21}$$

Finally, in the defuzzification step, we generate a crisp value for the node metric from the outputs of three membership functions. Centroid defuzzification is used for generating the crisp output N_j^i that ranges from 0 to 100. Figure 3 shows output membership functions are used in the defuzzification process.

Table 2. Rules for combining energy and queue length metrics

Energy/Queue	Short	Average	Long
Low	Moderate	Bad	Bad
Medium	Good	Moderate	Bad
High	Good	Good	Moderate

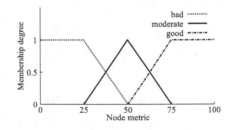

Fig. 3. Output membership functions used in the defuzzification process.

3.3 Delay Metric

In QCF, each node estimates the one-hop delay to the next hop when it receives an Acknowledgement (ACK) packet. Before sending the packet p to the next hop, the sender (node i) saves its local time $Send_p^i$ in a delay table which has two columns $PacketID$, and $SendTime$. When node i receives the ACK packet at time $RecvACK_p^i$, it estimates the one-hop delay to its next hop (node j) as

$$D_j^i = (RecvACK_p^i - Send_p^i) - TransD_{j,i}(ACK) - PropD_{j,i}(ACK), \quad (22)$$

where $PropD_{j,i}(ACK)$ is the propagation delay for sending the ACK packet from node j to node i. The propagation delay depends on the distance between two nodes and the propagation speed of the wireless medium, that is equal to, or a little less than the speed of light [15]. We consider a constant value for the propagation delay in computing the delay metric, as it is less than 1 ms in our experiments. $TransD_{j,i}(ACK)$ is the transmission time of the ACK packet that depends on the size of the packet and the channel capacity between nodes j and i ($c_{j,i}$). In order to estimate this delay, the receiver sends its transmission rate to the sender in the ACK packet. Thus, node i can compute $TransD_{j,i}(ACK)$ by

$$TransD_{j,i}(ACK) = \frac{PacketSize(Ack)}{c_{j,i}}. \quad (23)$$

To improve the delay estimation process, we employ the two-hop neighbor information in QCF. This idea can provide a better insight to select the next hop in the path that results in decreasing the end-to-end delay from the source node to the root. The two-hop delay metric for selecting node j as the parent of node i is defined as

$$TwoHopD_j^i = \lambda D_j^i + \gamma D_{P_j}^j. \quad (24)$$

We differentiate two hop neighbors based on their logical distances to the root node, as we applied it for energy and queue metrics. Based on this, higher priorities are always considered for parent nodes in the routing operation.

3.4 QoS Metric

In order to define the joint QoS metric, node and delay metrics are normalized by

$$QoS_j^i = (1 - \delta_p^i)(1 - \frac{TwohopD_j^i}{\max\limits_{k \in PS_i} TwoHopD_k^i}) + \delta_p^i \frac{N_j^i}{\max\limits_{k \in PS_i} N_k^i}, \quad (25)$$

$$\delta_p^i = \frac{Deadline_p^i}{Deadline_p}, \quad (26)$$

where δ_p^i is a trade-off parameter between node and delay metrics. δ_p^i is defined by Eq. (26) based on the fact that by decreasing the remaining time to the deadline of a packet, the priority of the delay metric should be increased. In Eq. (26), $Deadline_p^i$ and $Deadline_p$ show the current updated deadline (when the packet is processed at node i) and the initial deadline of packet p respectively.

3.5   Mobility Metric

For IoT nodes without GPS modules, mobility can be estimated based on the changes in the set of one-hop neighbors. We use this idea to define the mobility metric. We noticed that changes in the number of rows of the neighbor table cannot be detected when mobile nodes move in a network with the uniform node distribution, while insert and delete operations are performed on the neighbor table for adding or removing neighbors. We monitor the neighbor table during n time slots to deal with stop times in mobility models. Node j computes its mobility metric by

$$M_j = \frac{\sum_{k=0}^{n-1} Min(\frac{\omega_j(t-k)}{Max(\phi_j(t-k),1)}, 1)}{n}, \tag{27}$$

where $\phi_j(t)$ and $\omega_j(t)$ are the number of rows (neighbors), and the number of insert/delete commands that are applied at time slot t on the neighbor table of node j. This metric is computed and sent to one-hop neighbors in DIO packets. $0 \le M_j \le 1$ and more mobility a node has, the higher would be its mobility metric. As a result, $M_j = 0$ reflects no mobility that does not have any impact on the final weight of node j, as it is computed by

$$W_j^i = QoS_j^i \times (1 - M_j). \tag{28}$$

Algorithm 1. QCF operation for forwarding packet p in node i

---

1 $PS_i \leftarrow \emptyset$, $MaxNodeMetric \leftarrow -1$, $MaxDelay \leftarrow -1$
2 **for** *each node* $j \in NS_i$ **do**
3 | **if** $Rank_j < Rank_i$ **then**
4 | | **if** $D_j^i < Deadline_p^i$ **then**
5 | | | $PS_i \leftarrow PS_i \cup \{j\}$
6 | | | **if** $MaxDelay < TwoHopD_j^i$ **then**
7 | | | | $MaxDelay \leftarrow TwoHopD_j^i$
8 | | | **end**
9 | | | **if** $MaxNodeMetric < N_j^i$ **then**
10 | | | | $MaxNodeMetric \leftarrow N_j^i$
11 | | | **end**
12 | | **end**
13 | **end**
14 **end**
15 **if** $PS_i = \emptyset$ **then**
16 | Drop Packet p
17 **else**
18 | $MaxWeight \leftarrow -1$
19 | Compute δ_p^i by Eq. (26)
20 | **for** *each node* $k \in PS_i$ **do**
21 | | Compute QoS_k^i by Eq. (25)
22 | | Compute W_k^i by Eq. (28)
23 | | **if** $MaxWeight < W_k^i$ **then**
24 | | | $MaxWeight \leftarrow W_k^i$
25 | | | $P_i \leftarrow k$
26 | | **end**
27 | **end**
28 | Forward packet p to node P_i
29 **end**

Node i computes this weight for all nodes in its parent set ($\forall j \in PS(i)$). Finally, the neighbor with the maximum weight is selected as the preferred parent. Algorithm 1 shows how QCF operates in node i for forwarding packet p. In this algorithm, $MaxDelay$, and $MaxNodeMetric$ are the maximum values of two-hop delays and node metrics for neighbors with estimated one-hop delay less than the packet's deadline. These values are used for computing the QoS metric in Eq. (25). It should be noted that, Algorithm 1 does not compute the metrics that are independent from the packet's deadline. These metrics are computed only when nodes receive DIO or ACK packets.

3.6   Updating the Packet's Deadline in Each Hop

In delay sensitive IoT applications such as health care monitoring, the performance of a system is measured based on the number of packets can be delivered to the roots before their deadlines. In these applications, sending packets without considering their deadlines not only wastes bandwidth and energy resources, but also increases the average end-to-end delay in the network. By calculating the elapsed time and updating the packet's deadline in each hop, only neighbors with one-hop delays less than the packet's deadline, can be selected as the next hop. In addition, packets with expired deadlines are detected and dropped for saving network resources. However, synchronizing IoT nodes in LLN is challenging due to limited energy resources and lossy communications. In QCF, we update deadlines of packets in each hop without using synchronization; by applying a cross layer solution in the MAC and network layers. To this end, we compute the following four delays for each neighbor:

- **Processing delay**: the time interval between receiving a packet at the MAC layer, to completion of routing operations and directing the packet to the queue. This delay includes the required time for different operations such as checking bit level errors, and examining the header of the packet.
- **Queuing delay**: the waiting time of a packet in the queue before transmission. This delay includes channel access time for finding the channel idle, and also the waiting time for re-sending collided packets.
- **Transmission delay**: the time required for pushing all the bits of a packet into the link and transmitting them to the receiver. This delay depends on the packet size and the transmission rate of the wireless link.
- **Propagation delay**: the time required for propagating one bit from the sender to the receiver. It depends on the distance between two neighbors and the propagation speed of the wireless link.

For updating the deadline of a packet, QCF does not send any additional control messages, instead, we use only four bytes to store the current deadline of a packet on its header. By receiving the last bit of the packet p in node i, QCF saves the local receive time $Recv_p^i$, and calculates the sum of the processing delay ($ProcD_p^i$) and the queuing delay ($QueD_p^i$) just before forwarding the packet at time $Forward_p^i$ as

$$ProcD_p^i + QueD_p^i = Forward_p^i - Recv_p^i. \tag{29}$$

Transmission delay for sending the packet p from node i to node j can be computed by Eq. (23), as we explained in Sect. 3.3. Hence, the total elapsed time of packet p in node i is computed as

$$Elapse_p^i = (Forward_p^i - Recv_p^i) + TransD_{i,j}(p) + PropD_{i,j}(p). \tag{30}$$

Node i subtracts $Elapse_p^i$ from the current deadline ($Deadline_p^i$) just before transmitting the packet to node j. Thus, node j receives the packet p with the deadline ($Deadline_p^j$) updated in node i just before the transmission by

$$Deadline_p^j = Deadline_p^i - Elapse_p^i. \tag{31}$$

By using this approach, nodes can drop packets that have deadlines shorter than estimated one-hop delays of parents. This leads to saving network resources and decreasing the average end-to-end delay.

4   Performance Evaluation

We integrated QCF into the Contiki OS and evaluated its performance in Cooja (Contiki network emulator). Also, we implemented our framework on Zolerita IoT motes (Fig. 4) to take advantage of the unique characteristic of Cooja that allows us to generate the exact binary codes that could be run on real motes as well. Memory limitation of Zolerita motes was considered in the implementations; the size of generated binary codes is less than 32 KB in all experiments. In our emulation scenarios, 2 roots and 50 IoT nodes are distributed in an area with the size 200 m-by-200 m, while root nodes are placed in the top area of the terrain. We used 2 scenarios for each experiment: (1) without any mobile nodes, (2) using random waypoint mobility model in 10% of nodes. In addition, we have evaluated the performance of QCF for different timeliness requirements and traffic loads. IEEE 802.15.4 is used as the MAC layer; transmission and interference ranges are adjusted to 50 m and 100 m respectively.

Figure 5(a) shows the ratio of the packets are delivered to the roots before their deadlines. In all cases, QCF enhances Deadline Delivery Ratio (DDR) of RPL by at least 25%. In addition to considering the queue length, QCF updates deadlines of packets at each hop, and selects only parents with the estimated

Fig. 4. Zolerita IoT motes used in emulations.

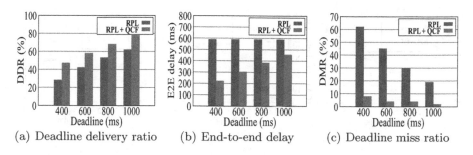

Fig. 5. Performance of QCF in a static network under varied deadline.

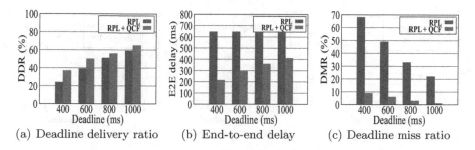

Fig. 6. Performance of QCF in a mobile network under varied deadline.

one-hop delay less than the packet's deadline. This results in dropping packets with expired deadlines and decreasing the average end-to-end delay, as shown in Fig. 5(b). RPL has the same end-to-end delay in all experiments as it does not have any mechanism to update and consider the packet's deadline in the parent selection process. QCF decreases the end-to-end delay of RPL by 63% when the deadline is 400 ms. Figure 5(c) presents the performance of QCF for Deadline Miss Ratio (DMR), the percentage of delivered packets that missed their deadlines. By decreasing the remaining time to the deadline, QCF increases the priority of the two-hop delay metric in Eq. (25) for computing the QoS metric. This leads to selecting parents with shorter two-hop delays. Also, by updating the packet's deadline, QCF drops packets with expired deadlines at each hop. As a result, QCF has DMR less than 10% in all experiments, while the DMR of RPL is increased from 19% to 62%, when the packet's deadline is decreased from 1000 ms to 400 ms.

Figure 6 shows the performance of QCF in a network with mobile nodes. As Fig. 6(a) and (b) present, QCF can enhance the performance of RPL by considering node mobility in selecting the preferred parent. Based on Eq. (28), neighbors with high mobility have less chance to be selected as the next-hop. This leads to avoid retransmissions of packets that cannot be delivered to mobile parents. Similar to experiments in the static network, QCF has deadline miss ratio less than 10%, while up to 68% of packets delivered by RPL missed their

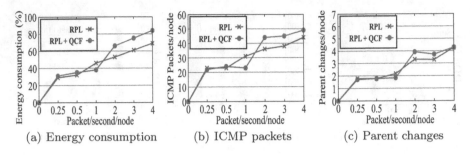

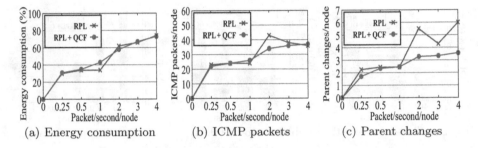

Fig. 7. Performance of QCF under different traffic loads in a static network.

Fig. 8. Performance of QCF under different traffic loads in a mobile network.

deadlines, as shown in Fig. 6(c). This increases the energy consumption and the end-to-end delay, that makes RPL inefficient in delay-constrained applications.

Figure 7(a) presents the average energy consumption per node in a static network. For traffic loads with data rates less than 1 packet per second, both methods have roughly the same energy consumption. QCF increases the energy consumption of RPL when the packet generation rate is higher than 1 packet per second. This is because QCF changes the preferred parent more frequently to balance the loads of parent nodes, as it considers the queue length in the parent selection process. This results in broadcasting DIO packets to inform one-hop neighbors of the change in the DAG topology. As shown in Fig. 7(b), and (c), QCF increases the average number of ICMP packets and the average number of parent changes of RPL when the packet generation rate is higher than 1 packet per second, similar to Fig. 7(a).

Figure 8 shows the performance of QCF in a mobile network. By estimating mobility of neighbor nodes, QCF decreases ICMP packets overhead and the average number of parent changes by up to 21% and 41% respectively.

5   Related Work

The load balancing problem of RPL has been investigated in various articles [8, 16–18]. The combination of ETX and the queue length was used in QU-RPL [8] for improving the load balancing and the delivery ratio. This protocol considers higher priorities for parent nodes and computes the final rank of each node based on the number of hops, ETX and the queue length. Compatibility of QU-RPL with RPL was not discussed by authors. In [16], authors proposed a backward compatible extension of RPL (BRPL) for high-throughput IoT networks. BRPL supports mobility and tries to switch smoothly between back-pressure routing and RPL. It creates the DAG topology based on the queue backlog and the OF provided by the user. BRPL is fully compatible with RPL, it tries to eliminate traffic congestions by utilizing network resources.

A minimum degree spanning tree is built in MD-RPL [17] to maximize the lifetime of IoT nodes. MD-RPL modifies the original tree formed by RPL to decrease the degree of the tree and enhance load balancing. MD-RPL forms the minimum tree based on the number of hops. To decrease the overhead of control packets, MD-RPL's control packets are encapsulated in the original packets of RPL. The number of children in the DAG topology was used in LB-OF [18] for increasing the network life-time. LB-OF employs the combination of ETX and the number of children to calculate the rank of each node. It tries to decrease the congestion by considering higher priorities for parents with less children. In nodes that are close to the root and have one child, LB-OF cannot detect the congestion as it does not use the queue length in the parent selection process.

[19, 20] discussed the energy-efficiency of RPL in different IoT applications. Authors in [19] designed Smart Energy Efficient Objective Function (SEEOF) for IoT based smart metering applications. SEEOF was designed based on the energy and the link quality metrics. It defines a new energy metric by combining the drain rate and the residual energy for selecting the preferred parent. The drain rate metric of SEEOF depends on the quality of the path and the number of children. An energy efficient region based RPL protocol (ER-RPL) was proposed in [20] for LLNs. ER-RPL tries to reduce energy consumption in the network by participating only a subset of nodes in the routing operation. It exploits the region feature of IoT applications. A self-regioning algorithm is used in ER-RPL to help nodes find their region codes, while ETX is employed as the reliability metric. ER-RPL can be applied for supporting P2P traffic patterns in LLNs.

6 Conclusion

In this paper, we proposed QCF, a new QoS-aware communication framework for real-time IoT services. QCF considers link and node metrics in the routing operation and employs fuzzy logic to improve the parent selection process. Our proposed framework updates the packet's deadline at each hop by using a novel method that does not require any coordination between IoT nodes. By estimating the node mobility in a lightweight approach, QCF provides adaptability to changes in the network topology. To evaluate the performance of our proposed framework, we integrated QCF into the Contiki OS, and implemented it on Zolerita IoT motes. Emulation results showed that QCF significantly improves QoS in terms of the deadline delivery ratio and the end-to-end delay.

References

1. Martocci, J., De Mil, P., Riou, N., Vermeylen, W.: Building automation routing requirements in low-power and lossy networks. IETF RFC 5867 (2010)
2. Pister, K., Thubert, P., Dwars, S., Phinney, T.: Industrial routing requirements in low-power and lossy networks. IETF RFC 5673 (2009)
3. Spano, E., Niccolini, L., De Pascoli, S., Iannacconeluca, G.: Last-meter smart grid embedded in an Internet-of-Things platform. IEEE Trans. Smart Grid. **6**(1), 468–476 (2015)
4. Liu, X., Sheng, Z., Yin, C., Ali, F., Roggen, D.: Performance analysis of routing protocol for low power and lossy networks (RPL) in large scale networks. IEEE Internet Things J. **4**(6), 2172–2185 (2017)
5. Winter, T., et al.: RPL: IPv6 routing protocol for low-power and lossy networks. IETF RFC 6550 (2012)
6. Thubert, P.: Objective function zero for the routing protocol for low-power and lossy networks (RPL). IETF RFC 6552 (2012)
7. Vasseur, J.P., Kim, M., Pister, K., Dejean, N., Barthel, D.: Routing metrics used for path calculation in low-power and lossy networks. IETF RFC 6551 (2012)
8. Kim, H.-S., Kim, H., Paek, J., Bahk, S.: Load balancing under heavy traffic in RPL routing protocol for low power and lossy networks. IEEE Trans. Mobile Comput. **16**(4), 964–979 (2017)
9. Kamgueu, P.O., Nataf, E., Ndie Djotio, T.: On design and deployment of fuzzy-based metric for routing in low-power and lossy networks. In: LCN Workshops 2015, pp. 789–795. IEEE (2015)
10. Qiu, T., Lv, Y., Xia, F., Chen, N., Wan, J., Tolba, A.: ERGID: an efficient routing protocol for emergency response Internet of Things. J. Netw. Comput. Appl. **72**, 104–112 (2016)
11. Contiki operating system. http://www.contiki-os.org/
12. Zolerita. https://zolertia.io/
13. Li, Y., Chen, C.S., Song, Y.-Q., Wang, Z., Sun, Y.: Enhancing real-time delivery in wireless sensor networks with two-hop information. IEEE Trans. Ind. Inform. **5**(2), 113–122 (2009)
14. Mamdani, E.H., Assilian, S.: An experiment in linguistic synthesis with a fuzzy logic controller. Int. J. Man Mach. Stud. **7**(1), 1–13 (1975)
15. Kurose, J., Ross, K.: Computer Networking: A Top-Down Approach, 6th edn. Addison Wesley, Boston (2013)
16. Tahir, Y., Yang, S., McCann, J.: BRPL: backpressure RPL for high-throughput and mobile IoTs. Trans. Mobile Comput. **17**(1), 29–43 (2018)
17. Mamdouh, M., Elsayed, K., Khattab, A.: RPL load balancing via minimum degree spanning tree. In: WiMob 2016, pp. 1–8. IEEE (2016)
18. Qasem, M., Al-Dubai, A., Romdhani, I., Ghaleb, B., Gharibi, W.: A new efficient objective function for routing in Internet of Things paradigm. In: CSCN 2016, pp. 1–6. IEEE (2016)
19. Shakya, N.M., Mani, M., Crespi, N.: SEEOF: smart energy efficient objective function: adapting RPL objective function to enable an IPv6 meshed topology solution for battery operated smart meters. In: Global Internet of Things Summit (GIoTS), pp. 1–6. IEEE (2017)
20. Zhao, M., Ho, I.W., Chong, P.H.J.: An energy-efficient region-based RPL routing protocol for low-power and lossy networks. IEEE Internet Things J. **3**(6), 1319–1333 (2016)

Constraint-Aware Drone-as-a-Service Composition

Babar Shahzaad$^{(\boxtimes)}$, Athman Bouguettaya, Sajib Mistry,
and Azadeh Ghari Neiat

The University of Sydney, Sydney, NSW 2000, Australia
{babar.shahzaad,athman.bouguettaya,sajib.mistry,
azadeh.gharineiat}@sydney.edu.au

Abstract. We propose a novel Drone-as-a-Service (DaaS) composition framework considering the recharging constraints and the stochastic arrival of drone services. We develop a service model and a quality model for drone delivery services. A skyline approach is proposed that selects the optimal set of candidate drone services to reduce the search space. We propose a heuristic-based multi-armed bandit approach to compose drone services minimizing delivery time and cost. Experimental results prove the efficiency of the proposed approach.

Keywords: DaaS · Service selection · Service composition ·
Recharging constraint · Lookahead heuristic

1 Introduction

Drones are aircraft that have no onboard human pilot. A plethora of new opportunities and applications have been created using drones in diverse sectors such as shipping, shopping, security, and surveillance [5]. Different types of drones offer several services including inspection, sensing, and delivery [21]. The drone-based delivery service is a fast-growing industry that includes large commercial organizations such as Amazon, DHL, and Google [2].

A *Drone-as-a-Service* (DaaS) consists of both *functional* and *non-functional* or *Quality of Service* (QoS) properties [20]. The functional properties state that a drone can deliver a package from a source to a destination following a skyway network. A skyway network is a set of skyway segments following the line-of-sight drone flying regulations [8]. Each line segment between two particular nodes is a skyway segment. The non-functional properties of a DaaS include flight range, battery capacity, endurance, and payload.

Given a skyway network, *our objective is to compose the optimal set of DaaS services that deliver the package from a source to a destination with the minimum delivery time*. We assume that the DaaS services will be instantiated with the same drone, i.e., there will be no *handover* of packages among different drones. We identify the following key challenges in a DaaS composition:

- *Limited flight range*: A flight range of a drone is influenced by the limited battery capacity, the speed, and the weather conditions [9]. A limited flight range may affect the delivery time and profitability of the business.

© Springer Nature Switzerland AG 2019
S. Yangui et al. (Eds.): ICSOC 2019, LNCS 11895, pp. 369–382, 2019.
https://doi.org/10.1007/978-3-030-33702-5_28

– *Recharging requirements*: The power consumption of a drone depends on the *payload weight*, the *drone speed*, and the *wind speed*. The power consumption increases as the weight of payload increases. As a result, drones need recharging to serve a wider service area. The maximum service area of drones with full capacity charge ranges from 3 to 33 km [10]. In some cases, *multiple times of recharging* may be required to support persistent drone delivery in the long-distance areas.
– *Constraints on recharging pads at the stations*: The number of recharging pads at a station (an intermediate node in the skyway network) is usually *finite* [10]. The availability of recharging pads may not be guaranteed.
– *Dynamic DaaS services*: Multiple DaaS services which are *instantiated* by different drones may operate in the same skyway network at the same time. As a result, a *congestion* may occur at the network. The congestion is defined as the total waiting time of a drone for the availability of a recharging pad at a certain recharging station [10]. The arrival of the drone services at a recharging station is usually stochastic in nature [24].

We focus on the composition of DaaS services considering the *recharging constraints* and *stochastic arrival of other drone services*. *To the best of our knowledge, existing approaches do not focus on the constraint-aware compositions.* Current research mainly focuses on the route planning for drones by formulating the problem as vehicle routing problem (VRP) [9] and travelling salesman problem (TSP) [11]. A single drone routing problem is studied with the objective of minimizing total fuel consumption in [23]. The proposed approach generates delivery routes for only a single drone with a fixed number of stations. A *multi-objective* optimization approach is proposed for using a swarm of drones for delivery purposes without considering the payload effects on energy consumption in [18]. An energy consumption model is proposed for maximizing profitability and minimizing the overall delivery time in [16]. This approach does not consider the effect of the flight range with dynamic payloads.

We propose a constraint-aware DaaS composition framework that selects an optimal drone service from multiple candidate services. We consider the recharging constraints and influence of one drone's recharging time on others at each node. *We transform the composition problem into a multi-objective optimization problem, i.e., minimizing the delivery time and cost.* For simplicity, we assume that the available drone services are *deterministic*, i.e., we know a priori about the payload, speed, battery capacity, flight range, and battery consumption rate of each drone. We also assume that the service environment is *deterministic*, i.e., we have complete knowledge about available charging pads and the trajectory of other drone services. The deterministic model is used to estimate the arrival time, recharging time, and waiting time of each drone at a specific node. We also estimate the overall *travel time* and *delivery cost* for each drone to its respective destination using the service statistics. Finally, we solve the optimization problem using the *multi-armed bandit tree exploration* approach [7]. We summarize the main contributions of this paper as follows:

• A new service model and a quality model for drone delivery services.

- Formulation of the DaaS composition as a multi-armed bandit tree exploration problem.
- A new composability model for drone delivery services.
- A new heuristic-based optimal drone service composition algorithm.
- A simulation-based evaluation with a real-world dataset to show the efficiency of the proposed model in comparison to the baseline approach.

2 Motivating Scenario

We consider drone-based package delivery with recharging constraints as a motivating scenario. Figure 1 presents the skyway network for drone delivery with recharging stations. We construct a skyway network which follows drone regulations such as visual line-of-sight (LOS) and no-fly zones [26]. The skyway network is divided into line segments. Each line segment is limited by two nodes. Each node is either a *recharging station*, a *delivery target*, or *both*. A fixed number of recharging pads are available at each node where any drone can recharge.

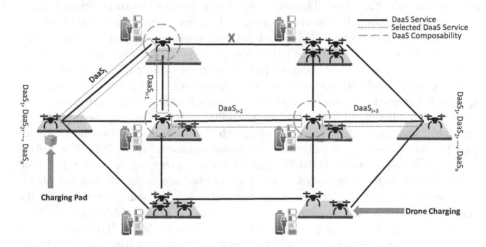

Fig. 1. Skyway network for drone delivery

We abstract each skyway segment as a drone service. Each drone service has specific QoS attributes such as battery capacity, payload capacity, speed, and flight range. We assume that the QoS attributes of a drone service are deterministic. Drones have limited battery and payload capacities and flight ranges. It is possible that a single drone service may not deliver the package from source to destination. Therefore, multiple recharging may be required for long-distance drone delivery services. We formulate this problem as composition of several drone services at intermediate nodes to deliver packages.

We need to select an optimal set of candidate drone services at the source node for each delivery demand. We assume that the same drone delivers the package from a source to a destination. We have the recharging constraints at each node because of the limited number of recharging pads. Given a set of delivery demands, our target is to select and compose optimal drone services to meet the user's requirements. An optimal drone service composition avoids congestion at any node and minimizes delivery time and cost. We focus on the composition of optimal drone services considering the recharging constraints, delivery time, and cost.

3   Related Work

Several studies address the routing problems for delivery by drones. Most of these previous studies focus on last-mile delivery by drones with a combination of ground vehicles. The hybrid ground vehicle and drone model was first studied by [13]. Two new approaches are introduced for drone-assisted parcel delivery problems. In the first approach, while a ground vehicle is serving a customer, a drone is dispatched from the ground vehicle to serve another customer. The drone returns back to meet with the ground vehicle in a rendezvous location after serving the customer. The objective is to minimize the total delivery time. In the second approach, ground vehicles and drones operate separately. In this case, while ground vehicles are routed between customers, drones operate from the depot to perform dedicated deliveries. *It is concluded that the flight range of a drone is a function of its speed* [13]. The speed of a drone has a significant impact on drone delivery operations due to the impact on its range. The proposed approach is tested only on small-sized instances with 10 to 20 customers. This work is extended by [17] to enhance the efficiency of the proposed model. A simulated annealing meta-heuristic approach is proposed to solve the problem. The proposed solution is tested for customer instances up to 200. *The hybrid approach is not suitable for deliveries in remote areas where either the road infrastructure is very congested or there is no road access for ground vehicles.*

Comparatively fewer studies have focused solely on using drones to make deliveries. A single drone routing problem is studied in [23]. Multiple refuelling depots are considered and the drone can refuel at any depot. The objective of this problem is to minimize the total fuel consumption for visiting all the delivery targets. *It is assumed that drone will never run out of fuel during the journey to a target.* An MILP formulation is proposed to model the problem which is solved using an approximation algorithm. The proposed approach is tested for 6 depots and 25 targets only. *Temporal logic constraints are not considered in the proposed model.* The proposed approach can generate delivery routes for only a single drone with a fixed number of stations which limits its potential applicability to problems in the real world.

A multi-objective optimization approach is proposed for delivery by a swarm of drones in [18]. Several constraints have been taken into consideration for delivering items to target locations. A Genetic Algorithm (GA) is proposed to solve the problem. The proposed approach is limited to visiting only one customer per trip. Moreover, *the energy consumption and the effects of payloads are not modelled in the proposed approach.* An energy consumption model for drones has been proposed to automate the delivery by drone in [6]. It is assumed that drones can deliver multiple packages within a specified service area. The impact of parcel payloads and flight ranges related to battery capacities are analysed to optimize the drone fleet size. It is concluded that increasing battery capacity and flight range of a drone can reduce the overall delivery costs.

An economic analysis is performed on drone utilization for delivery businesses in [16]. It is identified that energy efficiency and battery aging are the major sources of expense. *The proposed scheme does not consider the optimization and planning of end-to-end drone deliveries.* In [22], a scheduling model is developed for persistent drone delivery services. The fundamental characteristics of drone deliveries are mainly focused such as payload capacity, limited flight time, and the effect of payload on flight ability. There are multiple service stations for drones to replenish their batteries during the delivery operation. The problem is formulated as a Mixed Integer Linear Programming (MILP) model and a heuristic approach is developed to address the computational issues in large-scale problems. *The proposed model does not consider recharging constraints at each service station and its influence on other drones.*

The service paradigm is leveraged to model different transport service for multi-modal travel purposes in [14,15]. A service composition framework is proposed for composing spatio-temporal line segment services. In our previous paper, we propose the service model of a DaaS [20]. Services are composed based on their QoS parameters. The battery capacities and recharging constraints are not considered in the proposed model. *To the best of our knowledge, this paper is the first attempt to model the recharging constraints of drone delivery services and constraint-aware composition of drone delivery services.*

4 Multi-armed Bandit Formulation of DaaS Composition

Given a set of n drones $D = \{d_1, d_2, \ldots, d_n\}$ and a set of m delivery targets $T = \{t1, t2, \ldots, tm\}$, we formulate the problem as an undirected graph $G = (V, E)$, where V is a set of vertices representing the targets and E is a set of edges representing skyway segment services joining any two vertices. Each delivery target is assumed to be a charging station. We assume that each node has a *limited number of charging pads*. We also assume that there are no self-loops in the edges. B represents the battery capacities of all the drones. b_{ij} is the battery consumed in traveling from vertex i to j. c_{ij} represents the cost to travel from vertex i to j. We also assume that battery consumption of the drone is *linear* with respect to payload and distance travelled by the drone. The delivery cost is directly proportional to the battery consumption of the drone. It is symmetric for delivery time and cost from i to j and j to i. To avoid any failure in delivery, we assume that drones never run out of battery while traveling from i to j. Drones have different payload, battery capacities, and flight ranges. There is a constraint that each delivery is done by the same drone from source to destination, i.e., no *handover* are allowed on intermediate nodes. We also assume that drones are charged to their capacities at their respective source nodes.

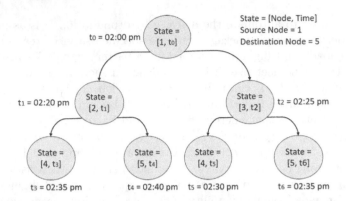

Fig. 2. An example of a state tree

We formulate the DaaS composition as the multi-armed bandit tree exploration [7] problem. The multi-armed bandit problem has extensively been studied in the literature. ϵ-Greedy algorithm, optimistic exploration, and Thompson Sampling are the most used approaches for multi-armed bandit problems [19]. Most of the bandit algorithms based on Upper Confidence Bounds (UCB) are applied to tree search. In multi-armed bandits, an arm represents a choice or an action which is initially unknown to the player. The target is to maximize the reward by selecting optimal arms. This approach is suitable for both deterministic and non-deterministic types of problems. If the arms are known a priori, the arm with the highest reward would be selected. In case of unknown arm distribution, each arm is pulled several times to get more information about the arms, which is regarded as exploration.

We consider a finite set of actions which can be taken by drone at each node while traveling to the destination. A drone can either *wait, recharge,* or *travel* from one node to another. The waiting and recharging times also affect the overall delivery time and cost of drone services. These actions can generate a large set of possible states. We represent these states in the form of a *multi-armed bandit search tree. The objective is to take the optimal actions which favour the optimal states to reach the destination faster at a lower cost.* At each node, the selection of the right arm (action/choice) is of paramount importance. Figure 2 presents an example of a temporal state tree. Each state is a combination of a node identity and timestamp. For the sake of simplicity, we consider that the states are known beforehand. In case of immediate optimal state selection, the selected state may lead to a non-optimal state. The more information about the neighbour and the next states guides more efficiently about the selection of optimal states.

5   Candidate Drone Service Selection Using Skyline

The selection of the candidate drone services from a set of available drone services is the first step to begin the composition. The service selection problem based on functional features has been investigated in [4, 25]. We focus solely on QoS

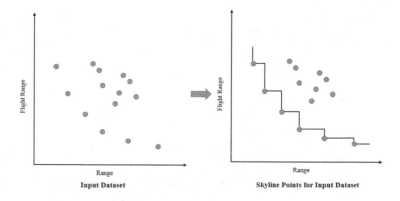

Fig. 3. Skyline for the drone selection

properties for the selection of functionally equivalent drone services [12, 27]. We use the drone's payload capacity to filter out those drones which are not able to carry the delivery package. We then use *skyline* [3, 28] to select the *non-dominated* drone services based on the best QoS features for each drone service.

Without loss of generality, we assume that the cost for each drone service is same for simplicity. We use the following three QoS parameters to compute the skyline: (1) *flight duration* without recharging (in minutes), (2) *flight range*: how far a drone can travel (in kilometers) without recharging, and (3) recharging time from 0 to 100% (in minutes).

Given a set of drone services, $DaaS = \{DaaS_1, DaaS_2, \ldots, DaaS_n\}$, and a set of QoS parameters $Q = \{q_1, q_2, \ldots, q_m\}$, we say that $DaaS_i$ dominates $DaaS_j$ (denoted as $DaaS_i \succeq DaaS_j$) when $DaaS_i$ is equal or better to $DaaS_j$ on all quality parameters and strictly better at least on one quality attribute. In the mathematical form, we represent the relation as Pareto dominance relation. A drone service $DaaS_i \succeq DaaS$ is Pareto dominant to another drone service $DaaS_j$ if for all QoS parameters q_a of Q, $a \in \{1, 2, \ldots, m\}$

$$\begin{cases} q_a(DaaS_i) \succeq q_a(DaaS_j), & \text{if } q_a \text{ is positive QoS parameter.} \\ q_a(DaaS_i) \preceq q_a(DaaS_j), & \text{if } q_a \text{ is negative QoS parameter.} \end{cases} \tag{1}$$

and for at least one QoS parameter $q_b \in Q$, $b \in \{1, 2, \ldots, m\}$

$$\begin{cases} q_b(DaaS_i) \succ q_b(DaaS_j), & \text{if } q_b \text{ is positive QoS parameter.} \\ q_b(DaaS_i) \prec q_b(DaaS_j), & \text{if } q_b \text{ is negative QoS parameter.} \end{cases} \tag{2}$$

where the travel distance is a positive quality parameter and range and recharging time are negative quality parameters. Here range represents the time taken by a drone to cover a certain distance. Figure 3 presents a 2-dimensional representation of skyline for selecting a set of candidate services from the dataset.

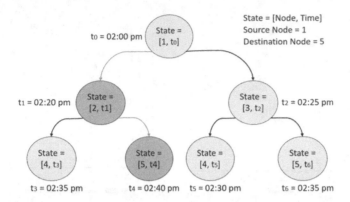

Fig. 4. State selection without lookahead

6   DaaS Composition Using Lookahead Tree Exploration

A single drone service may not deliver packages to long-distance areas. The selection and composition of optimal drone services from a large number of candidate services is a challenging task. The uncertainty is the main issue in a DaaS composition. In many cases, an immediate optimal service may lead to a non-optimal service. For example, we have a skyway network where node 1 is the source node and node 5 is the destination node. Here we find a temporal optimal neighbour leading to a non-optimal state. Temporal optimal means taking towards destination faster. As shown in Fig. 2, the service of state $[2, t_1]$ is optimal but the overall delivery time is more compared to state $[3, t_2]$. This uncertainty can cause long delays for drones to deliver packages. It is time inefficient to look for all possible service compositions or tree explorations to find the best composition. The time complexity for such problems is exponential. Hence, we need a heuristic-based solution to find the optimal composition of drone services.

We propose a lookahead heuristic-based solution to the multi-armed bandit tree exploration problem. The selection of optimal actions in a DaaS composition is performed by looking ahead of immediate available services. We consider the current waiting time, expected waiting time, and flight time to the destination for selection of optimal drone services. Here lookahead means looking at the states next to the neighbour states. Figures 4 and 5 illustrate the difference between without lookahead and with one lookahead based service (state) selection. Without lookahead considers only the neighbour optimal state which leads to an overall non-optimal solution. Using lookahead heuristic provides more information to select the overall optimal state.

6.1   DaaS Multi-armed Bandit Tree Lookahead

In the proposed approach, lookahead means considering the possible states next to the neighbour states while making a decision. Tree exploration works like a depth-first search approach. But we select only one service at a time by looking

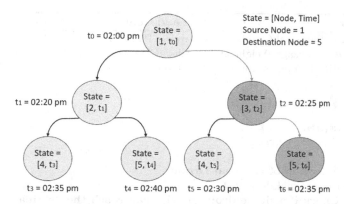

Fig. 5. State selection with one lookahead

ahead of neighbour states. We propose a novel heuristic-based algorithm for drone service selection and composition. The details of the proposed approach are given in Algorithm 1. In Algorithm 1, the output is an optimal drone service composition from source to destination for the input of skyway segment spatio-temporal graph G, the set of recharging pads RP, the set of drones D, the source src, the destination dst, the weight of the package w, the number of lookaheads $lookahead$, and the start time of the service $sTime$. In lines 1–3, we create empty lists for the optimal drone service composition plan, a temporary $DaaS$ variable, and an optimal drone to be selected d_{sel}. We define a set of state space, a set of action space, and a temporary variable n in lines 4–6. We divide the proposed algorithm into three steps. In the first step, we select an optimal drone from a set of available drones given the weight of the package. In the second step, we determine either a single drone service can fulfill the user's requirements or not. We select an optimal state representing a drone service leading to the desired destination in line 9. As we stated earlier that we assume the drones are charged to their capacities at the respective source locations. In the case of a single drone service, a drone does not need to be recharged. Here optimal state represents the minimum delivery time to the destination.

In the third step, we compose the optimal drone services because a single drone service cannot deliver the package from source to the destination. In line 13–17, we select optimal states from the set of state space based on the given lookahead. At each step, we have a finite set of actions. Either we can wait, recharge, or transit from one state to the next state. Each new state depends upon the action taken in current state, i.e., $X_{i+1} = f(X_i, A_j)$ where X_{i+1}, X_i, and A_j represent the next state, current state, and action taken in current state. Each action in the current state should be close to the optimal. The selection of an optimal state depends on the current waiting time, expected waiting time on the next state(s), and expected flight time to the destination. This highly depends on the availability of recharging pads on the subsequent nodes. In many cases, a greedy approach without lookahead may lead to non-optimal states.

Algorithm 1. Drone Service Selection and Composition Algorithm

---

Input: Spatio-Temporal Graph G, Recharging Pads RP, Drones D, Source src, Destination dst, Package Weight w, Lookahead $lookahead$, Start Time $sTime$

Output: Optimal Composition Plan Opt_Comp

 1: $Opt\_Comp \leftarrow \phi$
 2: $DaaS \leftarrow \phi$
 3: $d_{sel} \leftarrow \phi$
 4: $X = \{x_0, x_1, x_2, \ldots, x_n\}$
 5: $A = \{wait, recharge, travel\}$
 6: $n = 0$
   Step 1. Selection of Optimal Drone
 7:   $d_{sel} = $ select_optimal_drone (D, w)
   Step 2. Check if a single drone service can reach the destination or not
 8: **if** $Dist_{src,dst} \leq Range_{d_{sel}} * Speed_{d_{sel}}$ **then**
 9:    $x = $ select_optimal_state $(X, A, lookahead)$
10:    $Opt\_Comp \leftarrow x$
11:    **return** Opt_Comp
   Step 3. If a single drone service cannot deliver to destination
12: **else**
13:    **while** $X_i \neq dst$ **do**
14:       $x = $ select_optimal_state $(X, A, lookahead)$
15:       $DaaS_n \leftarrow x$
16:       $n = n + 1$
17:    **end while**
18:    $Opt\_Comp \leftarrow DaaS$
19: **end if**
20: **return** Opt_Comp

In such cases, we select optimal states by looking ahead of immediate states. This approach is a bit computational time expensive but the overall results are near-optimal to the exact solution of the problem. We use two types of lookahead approaches (1) Fix (2) Adaptive. The adaptive lookahead depends on the size of the number of nodes in the graph and distance to destination.

7 Experiments and Results

In this section, we present the performance evaluation of the proposed approach. We conducted a set of experiments to assess the performance of the proposed approach. We compared the proposed approach with a baseline (i.e., Brute-Force) approach and a without lookahead approach in terms of execution time and delivery time. We conducted all the experiments on an Intel Core i7 processor (3.20 GHz and 16.0 GB RAM) under Windows 10. We implemented all the algorithms in Python.

7.1 Baseline Approach

We use Brute-Force as a baseline approach to finding an optimal composition of services. It finds all the possible compositions of drone services from a given source to destination. We then select an optimal composition based on the QoS parameters of drone services. Finding all possible compositions of drone services is time exponential. This reduces the performance of Brute-Force approach to find optimal DaaS composition.

Table 1. Dataset description

Attribute	Value
No. of Drones	15
No. of Nodes in Skyway Network	2500
No. of Services	1250
Payload Capacity	1–4 (kg)

7.2   Experimental Setup

We evaluated the proposed approach using a synthesized dataset for different types of drones and a publicly available drone dataset for flight data [1]. The Brute-force approach performs the exhaustive operation and takes exponential time. The baseline approach exhausted for more than 100 nodes. For this reason, the number of nodes varies from 10–100 for all approaches and 500–2500 for without lookahead and proposed lookahead heuristic-based approaches. We conducted the experiments for 10% times the total number of nodes and computed the average results. For example, we run the experiment 250 times for 2500 nodes. We selected a random source and destination for each experiment.

7.3   Results and Discussion

The baseline approach finds all the possible compositions from a given source to a destination and selects an optimal composition for each experiment. The proposed approach performs composition of selective services based on certain parameters to reach the destination faster.

Average Execution Time. The time complexity of the baseline approach is exponential. The computational time for service composition using Brute-Force approach is very high in comparison to without lookahead and proposed lookahead heuristic-based approaches. The difference in average execution time for Brute-Force, without lookahead, and proposed heuristic-based approaches is shown in Fig. 6. As expected, the average execution time for the increasing number of nodes is much higher for the baseline approach than the proposed approach. Depending upon the number of lookaheads, the computation time varies for composing drone services. The higher the number of lookaheads we have, the more computational time is required to compose drone services. As shown in Fig. 7, the average execution time of our proposed approach with a lower number of lookaheads is closer to without lookahead based composition approach.

Delivery Time. The delivery time for drone services is highly uncertain when a single drone service cannot fulfill the user's requirements. At each station, the number of recharging pads are limited which can be occupied by other drones for long time periods. In this context, the delivery time of a drone service includes the flight time, recharging time, and waiting time. The selection of a *right* drone service is of paramount importance as it ensures the availability of recharging pads ahead of time minimizing the overall delivery time. The performance of the proposed approach varies for a varying number of lookaheads. The increasing number of lookaheads requires more computational time for finding an optimal solution. As shown in Fig. 8, the proposed lookahead heuristic-based approach finds a near-optimal solution compared to Brute-Force approach. However, the time complexity of the proposed approach is much better than the baseline approach. The delivery time for large networks is shown in Fig. 9 considering without lookahead and lookahead-based proposed approaches.

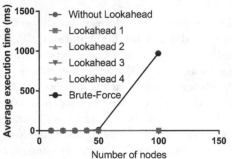

Fig. 6. Execution time (10–100 nodes)   **Fig. 7.** Execution time (500–2500 nodes)

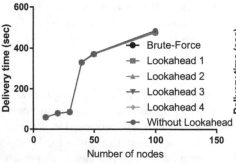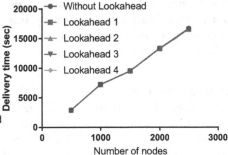

Fig. 8. Delivery time (10–100 nodes)   **Fig. 9.** Delivery time (500–2500 nodes)

8 Conclusion

We propose a constraint-aware DaaS composition framework for drone-based delivery services. We propose a skyline approach to select optimal candidate drone services. A heuristic-based service composition using multi-armed bandit approach is proposed for composing the drone services. We conduct several experiments to illustrate the performance of the proposed approach in comparison to Brute-Force approach. Experimental results show that our proposed approach overall performs better than the Brute-Force approach. In future work, we will focus on dynamic QoS parameters, environmental uncertainties such as weather conditions, and the multi-source multi-destination drone delivery services.

Acknowledgment. This research was partly made possible by NPRP 9-224-1-049 grant from the Qatar National Research Fund (a member of The Qatar Foundation) and DP160103595 and LE180100158 grants from Australian Research Council. The statements made herein are solely the responsibility of the authors.

References

1. Drone swarms. https://figshare.com/articles/Flight_logs_of_drone_swarms/6843977
2. Bamburry, D.: Drones: designed for product delivery. Des. Manage. Rev. **26**(1), 40–48 (2015)
3. Borzsony, S., Kossmann, D., Stocker, K.: The skyline operator. In: Proceedings 17th International Conference on Data Engineering, pp. 421–430 (2001)
4. Bouguettaya, A., et al.: End-to-end service support for mashups. IEEE Trans. Serv. Comput. **3**(3), 250–263 (2010)
5. Chmaj, G., Selvaraj, H.: Distributed processing applications for UAV/drones: a survey. In: Selvaraj, H., Zydek, D., Chmaj, G. (eds.) Progress in Systems Engineering. AISC, vol. 366, pp. 449–454. Springer, Cham (2015). https://doi.org/10.1007/978-3-319-08422-0_66
6. Choi, Y., Schonfeld, P.M.: Optimization of multi-package drone deliveries considering battery capacity. Technical report (2017)
7. Coquelin, P.A., Munos, R.: Bandit algorithms for tree search. In: Proceedings of the Twenty-Third Conference on Uncertainty in Artificial Intelligence, UAI 2007, pp. 67–74 (2007)
8. Corbett, M.J., Xie, F., Levinson, D.: Evolution of the second-story city: the Minneapolis skyway system. Environ. Plann. B Plann. Des. **36**(4), 711–724 (2009)
9. Dorling, K., Heinrichs, J., Messier, G.G., Magierowski, S.: Vehicle routing problems for drone delivery. Trans. Syst. Man Cybern. **47**(1), 70–85 (2017)
10. Kim, J., Kim, S., Jeong, J., Kim, H., Park, J., Kim, T.: CBDN: cloud-based drone navigation for efficient battery charging in drone networks. Trans. Intell. Transp. Syst. 1–18 (2018)
11. Kim, S., Moon, I.: Traveling salesman problem with a drone station. IEEE Trans. Syst. Man Cybern. Syst. **49**(1), 42–52 (2019)
12. Liu, X., Bouguettaya, A., Wu, J., Zhou, L.: Ev-LCS: a system for the evolution of long-term composed services. IEEE Trans. Serv. Comput. **6**(1), 102–115 (2013)

13. Murray, C.C., Chu, A.G.: The flying sidekick traveling salesman problem: optimization of drone-assisted parcel delivery. Transp. Res. Part C Emerg. Tech. **54**, 86–109 (2015)

14. Neiat, A.G., Bouguettaya, A., Sellis, T., Mistry, S.: Crowdsourced coverage as a service: two-level composition of sensor cloud services. Trans. Knowl. Data Eng. **29**(7), 1384–1397 (2017)

15. Neiat, A.G., Bouguettaya, A., Sellis, T., Ye, Z.: Spatio-temporal composition of sensor cloud services. In: ICWS, pp. 241–248 (2014)

16. Park, S., Zhang, L., Chakraborty, S.: Design space exploration of drone infrastructure for large-scale delivery services. In: 2016 IEEE/ACM International Conference on Computer-Aided Design (ICCAD), New York, NY, USA, pp. 1–7 (2016)

17. Ponza, A.: Optimization of drone-assisted parcel delivery. Master's thesis, Università Degli Studi Di Padova, Padova, Italy (2016)

18. San, K.T., Lee, E.Y., Chang, Y.S.: The delivery assignment solution for swarms of UAVs dealing with multi-dimensional chromosome representation of genetic algorithm. In: 2016 IEEE 7th Annual Ubiquitous Computing, Electronics Mobile Communication Conference (UEMCON), pp. 1–7 (2016)

19. Scott, S.L.: Multi-armed bandit experiments in the online service economy. Appl. Stochast. Mod. Bus. Ind. **31**, 37–49 (2015)

20. Shahzaad, B., Bouguettaya, A., Mistry, S., Neiat, A.G.: Composing drone-as-a-service (DAAS) for delivery. In: 26th IEEE International Conference on Web Services (ICWS), Milan, Italy (2019)

21. Shakhatreh, H., et al.: Unmanned aerial vehicles: a survey on civil applications and key research challenges. CoRR abs/1805.00881 (2018)

22. Song, B.D., Park, K., Kim, J.: Persistent UAV delivery logistics: MILP formulation and efficient heuristic. CAIE **120**, 418–428 (2018)

23. Sundar, K., Rathinam, S.: Algorithms for routing an unmanned aerial vehicle in the presence of refueling depots. IEEE Trans. Autom. Sci. Eng. **11**(1), 287–294 (2014)

24. Venkatachalam, S., Sundar, K., Rathinam, S.: Two-stage stochastic programming model for routing multiple drones with fuel constraints. arXiv preprint arXiv:1711.04936 (2017)

25. Wang, H., Shi, Y., Zhou, X., Zhou, Q., Shao, S., Bouguettaya, A.: Web service classification using support vector machine. In: 2010 22nd IEEE International Conference on Tools with Artificial Intelligence, vol. 1, pp. 3–6 (2010)

26. West, G.: Drone on. Foreign Aff. **94**, 90 (2015)

27. Ye, Z., Bouguettaya, A., Zhou, X.: QoS-aware cloud service composition based on economic models. In: Liu, C., Ludwig, H., Toumani, F., Yu, Q. (eds.) ICSOC 2012. LNCS, vol. 7636, pp. 111–126. Springer, Heidelberg (2012). https://doi.org/10.1007/978-3-642-34321-6_8

28. Yu, Q., Bouguettaya, A.: Computing service skylines over sets of services. In: 2010 IEEE International Conference on Web Services, pp. 481–488 (2010)

An Adaptive Monitoring Service Exploiting Data Correlations in Fog Computing

Monica Vitali$^{(\boxtimes)}$, Xuesong Peng, and Barbara Pernici

Politecnico di Milano, Piazza Leonardo da Vinci 32, 20133 Milan, Italy
{monica.vitali,xuesong.peng,barbara.pernici}@polimi.it

Abstract. In smart environments, a big amount of information is generated by sensors and monitoring devices. Moving data from the edge where they are generated to the cloud might introduce delays with the growth of data volume. We propose an adaptive monitoring service, able to dynamically reduce the amount of data moved in a fog environment, exploiting the dependencies among the monitored variables dynamically assessed through correlation analysis. The adaptive monitoring service enables the identification of dependent variables that can be transmitted at a highly reduced rate and the training of prediction models that allow deriving the values of dependent variables from other correlated variables. The approach is demonstrated in a smart city scenario.

1 Introduction

Monitoring Data are generated by sensors used to monitor an environment of interest, that are intended to be utilized by different applications deployed across edge/IoT, fog, and cloud layers. In a smart city, data collected from scattered, different places, converge into a unified monitoring data service used by different applications. The volume of data collected by IoT and sensors makes it time consuming to move all data from the edge where they are generated to the cloud for analysis, likely introducing critical delays. It is important to reduce the size of the data to be moved in order to make this task more agile [1]. As described in Sect. 2, existing approaches focus on the definition of possibly adaptive sampling rates for each variable. As illustrated in [2,3], variables collected by a monitoring system may be not independent. In this paper, we propose a service oriented approach to reduce the data volume by exploiting hidden relations among data, distinguishing between regressor variables and dependent variables, for which it is possible to significantly reduce the volume of transmitted data. The paper is organized as follows. Section 2 analyzes the state of the art. Section 3 describes the overall approach and Sect. 4 illustrates the monitoring reduction service. In Sect. 5 we apply the framework to a smart city scenario.

© Springer Nature Switzerland AG 2019
S. Yangui et al. (Eds.): ICSOC 2019, LNCS 11895, pp. 383–389, 2019.
https://doi.org/10.1007/978-3-030-33702-5_29

2   State of the Art

Data reduction in Big Data systems generally reduces either data storage, in-network data transmissions, or data redundancy [4]. The reduction methods include compressing raw data, decreasing the data sampling rate, and reducing the overall data according to the network topology. The work of [5] proposes a knowledge-driven data sharing framework in IoT-based Big Data systems, transmitting knowledge patterns instead of raw data. In our approach we propose to dynamically derive the relationships among variables, based on the actual data, rather than on predefined knowledge patterns. The problem of adaptive monitoring has been widely discussed in the literature [6]. The authors review monitoring tools and techniques for Fog Computing, and consider the reduction in the amount of network traffic as one of the challenges in current monitoring systems. A solution is proposed in [7], where a lightweight adaptive monitoring framework suitable for IoT devices is proposed. The authors reduce the data volume considering an adaptive sampling and (ii) an adaptive filtering. Similarly to [8], the focus is on the adjustment and reduction of single signals generated by sensors, without considering the possible dependencies existing between them.

Smart cities and smart homes are typical applications of the fog computing technology. In [9,10], architectures for optimizing near real-time services for prediction analytics are discussed. In order to show the performance of our approach, we applied the AMS to a real dataset representing a smart city scenario.

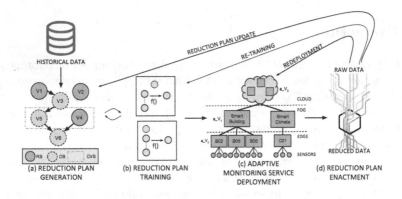

Fig. 1. Adaptive monitoring service

3   Adaptive Monitoring Service

The proposed Adaptive Monitoring Service (Fig. 1) has the goal to reduce monitoring data deriving and exploiting correlations among monitored variables (i.e., sensor-generated data). The first step is the *Reduction Plan Generation (a)*, where historical data are analyzed to discover relations among variables and to generate a Reduction Plan, which indicates the variables that must be collected (regressor variables - RV) and the ones (dependent variables - DV) that can be reconstructed from the values of the collected ones. Each variable can therefore be monitored in three different modalities: (i) *EMPTY* means no data are transmitted; (ii) *NORMAL* means all the produced data are transmitted; and (iii) *REDUCED* means a highly reduced down-sampled set of data is transmitted, used only for validation purposes. To derive the prediction models, i.e. functions to reconstruct dependent variables from regressor variables, a *Reduction Plan Training (b)* phase is performed. An *Adaptive Monitoring Service Deployment (c)* phase decides how to deploy the services that are needed to enact the Reduction Plan on a fog hierarchical infrastructure, trying to reduce the overall volume of data traveling from the edge of the network to the cloud. The optimization of this step will be analysed in future work. The *Reduction Plan Enactment (d)* transforms the raw data produced by sensors into a reduced dataset. Monitoring can be enhanced considering the variability of the environment [8]. During the collection of reduced data, several events might occur that require adjustments. Therefore, the AMS execution requires a continuous validation phase, where data of dependent variables are collected at a highly reduced frequency only to verify the validity of the prediction functions. Minor events might require a refinement of the prediction models (re-training). However, since the observed environment is dynamic and relations among variables might change, the derivation of a new Reduction Plan might also be needed in some cases.

4   Monitoring Data Reduction

Dependencies between variables are represented through a Direct Acyclic Graph (DAG), derived from the *correlation matrix*, i.e., the matrix obtained by computing the correlation between each pair of variables collected by the monitoring system, orienting the edges by discovering causal relations, using the technique described in [2]. The approach discovers relations between variables by computing the Pearson correlation coefficient between each couple of variables, applying a threshold to filter weak correlations, and deriving causal dependencies through a heuristic search algorithm. Once dependencies are detected, prediction can be provided by building a regression formula able to properly combine all the concurring variables to reconstruct a missing signal. In this way, some of the data produced by sensors can be omitted and reconstructed after the transmission if needed, thus reducing the volume of the data to move.

Before going into the details, we introduce some terminology. We denote the set of all monitoring variables as U, which is split into two sets: (i) *Regressor Variable Set* (RS), composed of all the variables that cannot be derived from other information (independent variables); (ii) *Dependent Variable Set* (DS), composed of variables derivable from other monitored information. According to this, $U = RS \bigcup DS$. Each variable in DS depends on the value of other variables - referred to as *Correlated Variables Set* (CVS) - and can be reconstructed using a **regression function**. Variables in CVS can be both regressor variables $rv \in RS$ and dependent variables $dv \in DS$. In Fig. 1(a) we show an example with six variables and their dependencies. Variable v_6 is depending both on v_4 and v_5, therefore the CVS for v_6 is $\{v_4, v_5\}$. In the figure, we also see that v_4 is a regressor variable while $v5$ is a dependent variable, depending on $v3$. So in this case we have $RS = \{v_1, v_2, v_4\}$ and $DS = \{v_3, v_5, v_6\}$. The correlated variable sets are $cvs(v_3) = \{v1\}$, $cvs(v_5) = \{v_3\}$, $cvs(v_6) = \{v_4, v_5\}$.

As described in [2], the dependencies between monitoring variables are not static (e.g., a sensor might stop working for a period of time, an existing sensor might be moved from a location to another, a new sensor might be installed). The CVS used to predict a variable in DS can change accordingly. Thus, we model an element of CVS as a variable $cvs_{t,k} \subseteq U$ dependent on timestamp t. In the reduced monitoring data, variables in RS keep all raw samples, since they cannot be derived from other variables. Variables in DS, instead, are collected at a reduced sampling rate. Samples are used for continuously validating the reliability of the prediction.

The **Reduction Plan** is the key element of the AMS and the basis for the service to enact data reduction. It gives information on which variables to reduce and on how to reconstruct their value from their correlate variables. It consists of the following parts: (i) *RS/DS partition*: the set of variables U is partitioned into the two subsets RS and DS. The partition at timestamp t is denoted as $< RS_t, DS_t >$; (ii) *CVS*: for each variable in DS the set of correlated variables $cvs_{t,k}$ is used to train the prediction function of $dv_k \in DS$ at time t; (iii) *Prediction parameters*: the prediction parameters describe the quantitative relation between a variable dv_k and its correlated variables $cvs_{t,k}$. A reduction plan is represented as a labeled-DAG (LDAG), sub-graph of the DAG of the dependencies. An edge from v_i to v_j indicates that v_j is reduced and rebuilt starting from the values of v_i. Since the reduction plan can evolve, we denote the reduction plan used at time t as $LDAG_t$ (Eq. 1):

$$LDAG_t = [Nodes_t, Edges_t, Labels_t] \tag{1}$$

Given the Reduction Plan, for each dv_k, the service provides the parameters of the model for enacting the prediction. To capture the correlations between variables collected by the monitoring system, a regression analysis is performed on a training dataset. In this paper we have applied Linear Regression as the regression method, due to its low complexity and reduced execution time given the need to build the model on edge and fog devices with limited resources and to quickly rebuild the model when needed. We assume the CVS of $v_k \in DS$ contains N variables $X = \{x_1, x_2, \cdots, x_N\}$ and the training dataset comprises samples of P timestamps. The linear regression method assumes that the relationships between X and $f_{t,k}$ are linear, as depicted in Eq. 2 at timestamp t:

$$f_{t,k}(X) = \beta_0 1 + \beta_1 x_{t,1} + \cdots + \beta_n x_{t,N} + \epsilon_t \tag{2}$$

In this work, we adopt the Ordinary Least Squares (OLS) method [11] to estimate the parameters values β, as described in [12]. This approach is only used as a proof of concept and alternative methods can be adopted. As an example, we are also investigating alternative solutions such as neural networks.

5   Validation

We applied the AMS to the REFIT Smart Home dataset[1], which includes sensor measurements of smart buildings and climate data recorded at a nearby weather station. Each building is connected to an edge device, collecting the information before sending them to be stored in the cloud.

We used the data collected in 80 days, from 2014-02-05 to 2014-05-05 at a fixed sampling interval of 30 min. We used 14 days of data to train the Reduction Plan, then we tested the performance of data reduction with the data left (59 days). Applying the proposed methodology, we found 31 regressor variables rv and 43 dependent variables dv to be predicted. For 17 of these dvs, the AMS reduces the sensor data of more than 40% while maintaining a reasonable accuracy. Table 1 shows a subset of the selected reductions, focusing on buildings $B05$ and $B06$. The first column represents the DS discovered while column 2 represents the CVS for each dv. The correlation value of the relation is shown in column 3. As it can be observed, strong relations are discovered between variables of the same kind in the same building, and most of all between temperatures of different rooms. The reduction ratio for the whole dataset of 74 variables in 59 days is 15.95%. This is a good achievement considering also that 31 variables are not reduced and that a portion of the 43 dvs are collected as raw data during the validation and re-training phases. The average reduction ratio considering only the 43 dvs is 27%.

Table 1. Reduction performance scoring of B05 and B06 variables

DV	CVS	Corr.
B06_HW1_Temp	B06_S1_Temp	0.88
B05_LR1_Temp	B05_K1_Temp	0.86
B06_BR1_Temp	B06_K1_Temp	0.85
B05_BR2_Temp	B05_S1_Temp	0.89
B05_BR3_Temp	B05_BR2_Temp B05_S2_Temp	0.96
B05_BR1_Temp	B05_S1_Temp	0.85
B06_BT2_Temp	B06_BR3_Temp	0.89
B06_BT3_Temp	B06_LR1_Temp B06_BR1_Temp	0.90
B06_LD1_Temp	B06_BT3_Temp	0.80
B05_BR4_Temp	B05_BR1_Temp B05_BR3_Temp	0.98
B06_K1_Temp	B06_LR1_Temp B06_S1_Temp	0.88

---

[1] https://lboro.figshare.com/articles/REFIT_Smart_Home_dataset/2070091.

6   Concluding Remarks

The Adaptive Monitoring Service proposed in this paper aims to identify a new systematic reduction of sensor data transmitted in a fog architecture. The relationships among the variables are exploited to reduce the data flow between the layers of a fog environment. The implications on service deployment have been discussed and an example based on a smart city scenario has been presented.

In future work we are going to refine the proposed methodology by focusing on the service deployment. We aim to propose an optimised deployment strategy considering the heterogeneity of the monitoring services and of the nodes in which they can be executed. We will also introduce latency for evaluating the effectiveness of the reduction plans when dealing with high data volumes.

Acknowledgments. This work is supported by European Commission H2020 Programme through the DITAS (Data-intensive applications Improvement by moving daTA and computation in mixed cloud/fog environmentS) Project no. 731945.

References

1. Plebani, P., et al.: Information logistics and fog computing: the DITAS approach. In: Proceedings of CAiSE Forum 2017, Essen, Germany, 12–16 June 2017, pp. 129–136 (2017)
2. Vitali, M., Pernici, B., O'Reilly, U.-M.: Learning a goal-oriented model for energy efficient adaptive applications in data centers. Inf. Sci. **319**, 152–170 (2015)
3. Carvalho, C.G., Gomes, D.G., Agoulmine, N., de Souza, J.N.: Improving prediction accuracy for WSN data reduction by applying multivariate spatio-temporal correlation. Sensors **11**(11), 10010–10037 (2011)
4. Rehman, M.H.U., Liew, C.S., Abbas, A., Jayaraman, P.P., Wah, T.Y., Khan, S.U.: Big data reduction methods: a survey. Data Sci. Eng. **1**(4), 265–284 (2016)
5. Rehman, M.H.U., Chang, V., Batool, A., Wah, T.Y.: Big data reduction framework for value creation in sustainable enterprises. Int J. Inf. Manage **36**(6), 917–928 (2016)
6. Taherizadeh, S., Jones, A.C., Taylor, I., Zhao, Z., Stankovski, V.: Monitoring self-adaptive applications within edge computing frameworks: a state-of-the-art review. J. Syst. Softw. **136**, 19–38 (2018)
7. Trihinas, D., Pallis, G., Dikaiakos, M.: Low-cost adaptive monitoring techniques for the internet of things. In: IEEE Transactions on Services Computing (2018)
8. Andreolini, M., Colajanni, M., Pietri, M., Tosi, S.: Adaptive, scalable and reliable monitoring of big data on clouds. J. Parallel Distrib. Comput. **79–80**, 67–79 (2015). https://doi.org/10.1016/j.jpdc.2014.08.007
9. Yassine, A., Singh, S., Hossain, M.S., Muhammad, G.: IoT big data analytics for smart homes with fog and cloud computing. Future Gener. Comput. Syst. **91**, 563–573 (2019)
10. Aazam, M., Zeadally, S., Harras, K.A.: Fog computing architecture, evaluation, and future research directions. IEEE Commun. Mag. **56**(5), 46–52 (2018)
11. Hayashi, F.: Econometrics, vol. 1, pp. 60–69. Princeton University Press, Princeton (2000)

12. Peng, X., Pernici, B.: Correlation-model-based reduction of monitoring data in data centers. In: Proceedings of the 5th International Conference on Smart Cities and Green ICT Systems, SMARTGREENS 2016, Rome, Italy, 23–25 April 2016, pp. 395–405 (2016)

The Circuit Breaker Pattern Targeted to Future IoT Applications

Gibeon Aquino[1]([☒])[ID], Rafael Queiroz[1][ID], Geoff Merrett[2][ID], and Bashir Al-Hashimi[2]

[1] Department of Informatics and Applied Mathematics, UFRN, Natal, Brazil
gibeon@dimap.ufrn.br, rafaelqueiroz@ufrn.edu.br
[2] School of Electronics and Computer Science, University of Southampton, Southampton, UK
{gvm,bmah}@ecs.soton.ac.uk

Abstract. In the context of the Internet of Things (IoT), there is a growing trend towards increasing the integration and collaboration between IoT systems to create relevant end-to-end solutions. Accordingly, addressing dependability in the future IoT applications will surely be more challenging. In this work, we examine a popular microservices pattern known as Circuit Breaker (CB). This pattern aims at preventing failure from cascading to dependent services. In the context of IoT, it can be used as an intermediary in the communication between critical IoT nodes to increase the dependability of the whole. Notwithstanding, some particularities present in IoT must be considered to allow this pattern to yield similar benefits. Therefore, we compile several aspects concerning the design and implementation of the CB tailored to IoT applications as a taxonomy. Also, we conduct an experimental validation to compare the benefits of the CB in a prototype of a traffic light system.

Keywords: Circuit Breaker · Internet of Things · Microservices architecture · Dependability · Software architecture

1 Introduction

There is a growing trend towards increasing the integration and collaboration between IoT systems to create relevant end-to-end solutions [2]. Under the collaborative perspective, they form a cluster of systems cooperating to solve harder problems. This phenomenon is known as System of Systems (SoS) [1], and it is well applicable to a significant part of existing IoT systems [4]. Indeed, this kind of IoT solutions has been advancing very fast and, shortly, they might represent most of the IoT deployments. The concern is that designing, implementing, and operating IoT applications acting as SoSs is even more complex and introduces new challenges. Therefore, advanced development strategies are required to address dependability in these applications adequately [6].

Meanwhile, Microservices Architecture (MSA) has been increasingly lauded as a successful approach to achieving dependability in information systems. There is also a growing position in favor of applying MSA to in IoT [3,7]. Accordingly, IoT applications could adopt several of the MSA development strategies

© Springer Nature Switzerland AG 2019
S. Yangui et al. (Eds.): ICSOC 2019, LNCS 11895, pp. 390–396, 2019.
https://doi.org/10.1007/978-3-030-33702-5_30

to reap similar benefits. Among the MSA strategies, the Circuit Breaker (CB) is a prevalent pattern to deal with the resilience of distributed services. It works by preventing the failure propagation to dependent services. For IoT systems, it can be used as an intermediary in the communication between critical IoT nodes in order to increase the dependability of the whole solution.

This work seeks to explore the options of designing and implementing the CB in IoT solutions. Although many IoT devices have high computing capabilities (e.g., smartphones, home voice assistants), a significant part has limited capabilities (e.g., memory, processing power, energy availability, connectivity), dedicated systems, and non-preemptive execution [5,8]. Therefore, the CB in IoT applications must address these constraints properly. For this reason, we investigate several CB possibilities target to IoT and organize them as a taxonomy. Moreover, to examine the applicability and trade-offs, we conduct an experimental study using a prototyped IoT application. This prototype simulates a solution of smart traffic lights based on the collaboration of multiple nodes.

2   Circuit Breaker Narrowed to IoT Systems

The CB is a simple and effective pattern for fault tolerance. In the interaction between different microservices, it assumes the responsibility of detecting failures and preventing its propagation. The use of CB brings several benefits directly related to availability and reliability, such as: (a) It prevents to perform the action that is doomed to fail; (b) It allows handling the error quickly and gracefully; (c) The callers do not have to cope with the failure themselves; (d) Custom fallback plans can be used; (e) All callers are spared from calling the crashed service; (f) It can also spare the service from being overwhelmed by large numbers of requests (e.g., it can implement a local cache).

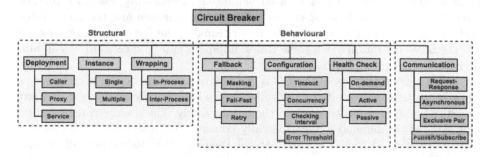

Fig. 1. A taxonomy for the design of the Circuit Breaker targeted to IoT applications.

Although the CB is a simple pattern, there are several issues to take into account when implementing it. For the best of our knowledge, the literature about it is usually focused on information systems and fail to address specific needs required by IoT. For this reason, we sought to compile the main aspects, and possibilities regarding the CB tailored to IoT and organized them as a taxonomy (Fig. 1). It defines three main groups, according to their influence on the CB design. The Structural comprises the options which affect the structure in terms of implementation and execution. The Behavioural includes those related to the behavior at run-time. The last is related to communication.

2.1   Structural

A critical decision to be made in IoT scenarios is the deployment location where the CB will execute, i.e., in which physical node it will be hosted. Because every message must pass through it, its availability, security, and performance have to fit the application needs. In IoT applications, these aspects include the reliability and the capacity of the hardware, the deployment location, the energy supply, the connectivity, and also the other process/services competing in the same node. In essence, it can execute in the caller, service, or as an additional node.

The management of CB instances is another critical decision. Simple solutions can adopt a single instance option running in the caller, service, or proxy. However, in some applications, redundancy strategies involving the use of multiple instances should be considered also to improve its availability. Also, the way how the instances interact with the caller or the service (wrapping) may also be taken into consideration. It can share the same process (In-process), or it can run in a separate process (Inter-process).

2.2   Behavioural

Several options exist, but they can be grouped in the following categories: Masking, Fail-fast, and Retry. While the masking strategy seeks to hide the failure to the caller, the fail-fast allows to notice it as fast as possible. The most common masking strategies are: return a default value; return the last valid result (e.g., from a cache); or return a calculated value (e.g., forecasting based on historical data). Among the fail-fast strategies, the most common are: return an error code; return the original error to the caller. Finally, the Retry strategy seeks to try the failed operation again some times, hoping it can be successful. It can also retry in a surrogate service.

A fundamental ability of the CB is the failure detection on the target service in order to trip the circuit. In the same way, when the circuit is open, it must monitor the service health to close the circuit safely. The main strategies to do this are: (a) On-demand – it periodically transits to the state of half-open and seize a real request to test the service; (b) Passive – it waits for periodic health signals from the service (e.g., heartbeats, keepalives) to confirm if the service is available or unavailable; (c) Active – it regularly checks the service health independently of the caller requests.

Finally, several parameters should be adjusted appropriately, considering the application needs, to attain the CB benefits. One of them is the *timeout*, which is used to establish a limit of how long the CB should wait before assuming an omission failure. The *concurrency* configuration includes parameters such as the maximum of concurrent requests, requests queue size, and maximum throughput. The *checking interval* establishes the frequency of health checking.

To differ intermittent and permanent failures, the CB uses the *error threshold* which indicates the limit of failures it can tolerate.

2.3 Communication

IoT solutions are strongly based on communication between things. Currently, a vast number of communication protocols and technologies coexist. As an intermediary, the CB must follow the same communication model adopted by the peers. Despite the several options, we can abstractly classify them in four models.

The Request-response is the model which the caller sends requests, and the service responds. This model is usually synchronous, as the caller has to wait for the response to continue its task. It is also stateless as no information about the caller is kept between requests. Even in IoT systems, RESTful HTTP solutions are commonly found [3]. However, for constrained devices and networks, other REST derivatives options are frequently mentioned, e.g., the Devices Profile for Web Services (DPWS) and the Constrained Application Protocol (CoAP).

The Asynchronous messaging allows the systems to send messages to each other asynchronously. Commons examples of this model in IoT are WebSocket protocol and Reactive Streams. One variation of that model is the Publish-Subscribe. In this model, the sender of a message (publisher) does not send it directly to the receiver (subscriber). Alternatively, they use an intermediate (i.e., message broker) to asynchronously delivered the messages. One of the most common examples of this model in IoT solutions is the MQTT (Message Queuing Telemetry Transport). Finally, Exclusive-Pair is a simple model and considered a low-level option. It is a bidirectional and fully duplex communication model which uses a persistent connection between a pair of elements.

3 Experimental Study

To demonstrate the suitability of the CB to address the dependability, we developed a prototype[1] that simulates a collaborative traffic light system. It is composed of several micro-controllers, each one placed in a traffic junction to control a traffic light group. Each runs an instance of a Traffic Junction System (TJS) and are wirelessly interconnected. The TJS performs a periodic task of monitoring the traffic density on the roads its controls and also requests data from adjacent TJSs to make a more accurate decision. In this study, we sought to evaluate the consequences of intermittent nodes for the whole solution.

This scenario aims to demonstrate the SoS paradigm applied to IoT. A critical issue in such systems is that failures in one part can induce the dependent systems to fail too, potentially triggering the cascading effect. In order to examine this issue, we ran five TJS instances (TJ0...TJ4) and simulated omission failures in two of them according to the following configuration (*node, start, duration*): {*(TJ1, 30 s, 30 s), (TJ1, 90 s, 10 s), (TJ3, 40 s, 20 s)*}. This kind of

---

[1] https://github.com/labcomu/smart-traffic-prototype.

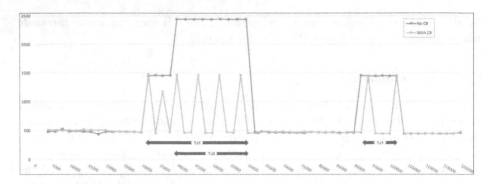

Fig. 2. Task time over the experiment execution.

failure happens when the service omits to respond to a request. The duration of the experiment was 120 s, with task periods of 2 s. For the physical nodes, we used Raspberry Pi 3 Model B, interconnected in a network of 100 Mbps. Concerning the CB design structural decisions, we adopted the following strategies: caller deployment, single instance, and in-process wrapping. Such choices aimed to create a configuration suitable to the typical constraint of traffic junction infrastructures. Concerning the behavior, we implemented the fail-fast strategy, on-demand health checking, and configuration parameters of $\{timeout = 1\,s,$ $error\ threshold = 1,\ no\ concurrency\}$. These choices sought to achieve more accurately the requirements of the TJS.

3.1 Experimental Results

In our study, we extended the traditional availability measurement by introducing the metric *availability to collaborate* (AC). It is defined as the fraction of time the TJS is active responding requests from its peers. As the solution's key point is the collaboration ability, the time it is available to provide information to the adjacent nodes is a relevant quality attribute. Table 1 shows that the AC increased with the use of the CB. It means the solution with CB allowed the TJS to dedicate more time collaborating with its peers and consequently improving the accuracy of its decision.

Table 1. Results of the experiment execution collected on the TJ0 node.

	No CB	With CB		No CB	With CB
Executed Tasks	60	60	Task time (mean)	929 ms	600 ms
Complete Tasks	41	41	Task time (std)	737 ms	329 ms
Partial Tasks	10	19	Availability to	53.6%	70.0%
Aborted Tasks	9	0	collaborate		

This effect is influenced by the decrease of the *Task time*, which is the time to the TJS completes one task. Accordingly, the use of the CB improved the performance and also the stability. Without the CB, the task time becomes very high during the failures (Fig. 2). Because the TJS needs to wait for the adjacent nodes response to complete its task, its performance is strongly affected if some of the peers last to respond.

Finally, we also evaluated the completion of the tasks (Table 1). The tasks were classified as follows: *Complete* – executed considering all peers response and completed before the task cycle expires; *Partial* – completed before the task cycle expires, but could not use information from all peers; *Aborted* – did not complete before the task cycle expires. The results showed a complete reduction in the aborted tasks with the CB. It means the TJS was able to make more accurate decisions.

4 Conclusions

This paper sought to examine the circuit breaker pattern in the context of IoT. We seized the growing belief that some MSA practices are promising to IoT, particularly considering the expected complexity of future applications. Our main contribution was the definition of a taxonomy, based on the compilation of several aspects concerning the design and implementation of the CB tailored to IoT applications. Also, we conducted an experimental validation to compare the benefits of this pattern in a prototype of a traffic light system. The results showed several advantages for this specific application. In particular, it demonstrated the CB ability to improve performance, availability, and accuracy significantly.

Acknowledgments. This research was partially funded by CAPES - Finance Code 001, INES 2.0, CNPq grant 465614/2014-0, FACEPE grant APQ-0399-1.03/17, and CAPES grant 88887.136410/2017-00.

References

1. Ackoff, R.L.: Towards a system of systems concepts. Manag. Sci. **17**(11), 661–671 (1971)
2. Bello, O., Zeadally, S.: Intelligent device-to-device communication in the Internet of Things. IEEE Syst. J. **10**(3), 1172–1182 (2016)
3. Butzin, B., Golatowski, F., Timmermann, D.: Microservices approach for the internet of things. In: 21st International Conference on Emerging Technologies and Factory Automation (ETFA), pp. 1–6. IEEE (2016)
4. Delicato, F.C., Pires, P.F., Batista, T., Cavalcante, E., Costa, B., Barros, T.: Towards an IoT ecosystem. In: Proceedings of the First International Workshop on Software Engineering for Systems-of-Systems, pp. 25–28. ACM (2013)
5. Hahm, O., Baccelli, E., Petersen, H., Tsiftes, N.: Operating systems for low-end devices in the Internet of Things: a survey. IEEE Internet of Things J. **3**(5), 720–734 (2016)

6. Hammoudi, S., Aliouat, Z., Harous, S.: Challenges and research directions for Internet of Things. Telecommun. Syst. **67**(2), 367–385 (2018)
7. Santana, C., Alencar, B., Prazeres, C.: Microservices: a mapping study for internet of things solutions. In: 2018 IEEE 17th International Symposium on Network Computing and Applications (NCA), pp. 1–4. IEEE (2018)
8. Zikria, Y.B., Yu, H., Afzal, M.K., Rehmani, M.H., Hahm, O.: Internet of Things (IoT): operating system, applications and protocols design, and validation techniques. Future Gener. Comput. Syst. **88**, 699–706 (2018)

Services in Organizations, Business and Society

A Catalogue of Inter-parameter Dependencies in RESTful Web APIs

Alberto Martin-Lopez$^{(\boxtimes)}$, Sergio Segura, and Antonio Ruiz-Cortés

Department of Computer Languages and Systems,
Universidad de Sevilla, Seville, Spain
{amarlop,sergiosegura,aruiz}@us.es

Abstract. Web services often impose dependency constraints that restrict the way in which two or more input parameters can be combined to form valid calls to the service. Unfortunately, current specification languages for web services like the OpenAPI Specification provide no support for the formal description of such dependencies, which makes it hardly possible to automatically discover and interact with services without human intervention. Researchers and practitioners are openly requesting support for modelling and validating dependencies among input parameters in web APIs, but this is not possible unless we share a deep understanding of how dependencies emerge in practice—the aim of this work. In this paper, we present a thorough study on the presence of dependency constraints among input parameters in web APIs in industry. The study is based on a review of more than 2.5K operations from 40 real-world RESTful APIs from multiple application domains. Overall, our findings show that input dependencies are the norm, rather than the exception, with 85% of the reviewed APIs having some kind of dependency among their input parameters. As the main outcome of our study, we present a catalogue of seven types of dependencies consistently found in RESTful web APIs.

Keywords: Web services · Constraints · Parameter dependencies

1 Introduction

Web Application Programming Interfaces (APIs) allow systems to interact with each other over the network, typically using web services [10,17]. Web APIs are rapidly proliferating as the cornerstone for software integration enabling new consumption models such as mobile, social, Internet of Things (IoT), or cloud applications. Popular API directories such as ProgrammableWeb [14] and RapidAPI [16] currently index over 21K and 8K web APIs, respectively, from multiple domains such as shopping, finances, social networks, or telephony.

Modern web APIs typically adhere to the REpresentational State Transfer (REST) architectural style, being referred to as RESTful web APIs [7]. *RESTful web APIs* are decomposed into multiple web services, where each service

© Springer Nature Switzerland AG 2019
S. Yangui et al. (Eds.): ICSOC 2019, LNCS 11895, pp. 399–414, 2019.
https://doi.org/10.1007/978-3-030-33702-5_31

implements one or more create, read, update, or delete (CRUD) operations over a resource (e.g. a tweet in the Twitter API), typically through HTTP interactions. RESTful APIs are commonly described using languages such as the OpenAPI Specification (OAS) [13], originally created as a part of the Swagger tool suite [19], or the RESTful API Modeling Language (RAML) [15]. These languages are designed to provide a structured description of a RESTful web API that allows both humans and computers to discover and understand the capabilities of a service without requiring access to the source code or additional documentation. Once an API is described in an OAS document, for example, the specification can be used to generate documentation, code (clients and servers), or even basic automated test cases [19]. In what follows, we will use the terms RESTful web API, web API, or simply API interchangeably.

Web services often impose dependency constraints that restrict the way in which two or more input parameters can be combined to form valid calls to the service, we call these *inter-parameter dependencies* (or simply *dependencies* henceforth). For instance, it is common that the inclusion of a parameter requires or excludes—and therefore depends on—the use of some other parameter or group of parameters. As an example, the documentation of the YouTube Data API states that when using the parameter `videoDefinition` (e.g. to search videos in high definition) the `type` parameter must be set to 'video', otherwise a HTTP 400 code (bad request) is returned. Similarly, the documentation of the cryptocurrency API Coinbase explains that, when placing a buy order, one, and only one of the parameters `total` or `amount` must be provided.

Current specification languages for RESTful web APIs such as OAS and RAML provide little or no support at all for describing dependencies among input parameters. Instead, they just encourage to describe such dependencies as a part of the description of the parameters in natural language, which may result in ambiguous or incomplete descriptions. For example, the Swagger documentation states[1] *"OpenAPI 3.0 does not support parameter dependencies and mutually exclusive parameters. (...) What you can do is document the restrictions in the parameter description and define the logic in the 400 Bad Request response"*. The lack of support for dependencies means a strong limitation for current specification languages, since without a formal description of such constraints is hardly possible to interact with the services without human intervention. For example, it would be extremely difficult, possibly infeasible, to automatically generate test cases for the APIs of YouTube or Coinbase without an explicit and machine-readable definition of the dependencies mentioned above. The interest of industry in having support for these types of dependencies is reflected in an open feature request in OAS entitled "Support interdependencies between query parameters", created on June 2015 with the message shown below. At the time of writing this paper, the request has received over 180 votes, and it has received 43 comments from 25 participants[2].

---

[1] https://swagger.io/docs/specification/describing-parameters/.

[2] https://github.com/OAI/OpenAPI-Specification/issues/256.

*"It would be great to be able to specify interdependencies between query param-
eters. In my app, some query parameters become "required" only when some
other query parameter is present. And when conditionally required parameters
are missing when the conditions are met, the API fails. Of course I can have the
API reply back that some required parameter is missing, but it would be great to
have that built into Swagger."*

This feature request has fostered an interesting discussion where the participants have proposed different ways of extending OAS to support dependencies
among input parameters. However, each approach aims to address a particular
type of dependency and thus show a very limited scope. Addressing the problem
of modelling and validating input constraints in web APIs should necessarily
start by understanding how dependencies emerge in practice. Some previous
papers have addressed this challenge, as a part of other contributions, but they
have studied just a few popular APIs and so they have only scratched the surface [12,21] (c.f. Sect. 5). A systematic and large-scale analysis of the state of
practice is needed in order to answer key questions such as how often dependencies appear in practice or what types of input constraints are found in real-world
web APIs. This is the goal of our work.

In this paper, we present a thorough study on the presence of inter-parameter
dependencies in industrial web APIs. Our study is based on an exhaustive
review of 40 RESTful APIs from multiple application domains carefully selected
from the API repository of ProgrammableWeb [14]. All APIs were carefully
reviewed and classified following a systematic and structured method. Among
other results, we found that 85% of the APIs (34 out of 40) had some kind of
dependency among their input parameters. More specifically, we identified 633
dependencies in 9.7% of the operations analysed (248 out of 2,557). The identified constraints are classified into a catalogue of seven types of inter-parameter
dependencies in RESTful web APIs. This catalogue will hopefully serve as a
starting point for future approaches on modelling and analysis of input dependencies in web APIs.

This paper is structured as follows: Sect. 2 describes the review method followed. Section 3 presents the results of our study. Section 4 describes some potential threats to validity and how they were mitigated. Related work is discussed in
Sect. 5. Finally, Sect. 6 draws the conclusions and presents future lines of research.

2   Review Method

In what follows, we present the research questions that motivate this study as
well as the process followed for the collection and analysis of the data.

2.1   Research Questions

The aim of this paper is to answer the following research questions (RQs):

RQ1: How common are inter-parameter dependencies in web APIs?
We aim to provide an in-depth view of how frequently dependencies appear in

practice, trying to find out whether their presence is correlated to certain characteristics or application domains. Once we confirm the presence of dependencies,
we will try to understand how they look like answering the following question.

**RQ2: What types of inter-parameter dependencies are found in web
APIs?** We wish to provide a catalogue of the types of dependencies among
input parameters most commonly found in real-world APIs, which can serve as
a starting point for future proposals for their modelling and analysis.

2.2   Subject APIs and Search Strategy

The search for real-world APIs was carried out in ProgrammableWeb [14], a
popular and frequently updated online repository with about 21K APIs and
8K mashups at the time of writing this paper. We followed a systematic approach for the selection of a subset of highly-used yet diverse APIs, as follows.
First, we selected the top 10 most popular APIs in the repository overall. Then,
we selected the 3 top-ranked APIs from the top 10 most popular categories in
ProgrammableWeb, i.e. those with a larger number of indexed APIs. APIs on
each category are ordered according to the number of registered applications
consuming them (mashups). We focused on RESTful APIs only, as the de-facto
standard for web APIs. In particular, we selected APIs reaching level 1 or higher
in the Richardson Maturity Model [17], which ensured a minimal adherence to
the REST architectural style, e.g. using the notion of resources. APIs not following the key REST principles and those with poor or no available documentation
were discarded, selecting the next one in the list. Some of the selected APIs were
found in different categories and were included just once, ignoring duplicates.
Table 1 depicts the list of subject APIs analysed in our study, 40 in total. For
each API, the table shows its name, category, number of mashups, number of
operations and percentage of operations containing parameter dependencies. For
the sake of readability, similar categories have been merged into a single one.

Figure 1 shows the classification of subject APIs by category and size. As
illustrated, the subject APIs are evenly distributed among 10 different categories
such as communication, social and mapping. Regarding the size, the majority of
reviewed APIs (75%) provide between 1 and 50 operations, with the largest APIs
having up to 305 (DocuSign eSignature) and 492 (Github) operations. Overall,
the selected APIs represent a large, diverse, and realistic dataset.

2.3   Data Collection and Analysis

We carefully analysed the information available in the official website of the 40
subject APIs to answer our research questions. For each API, we collected the
name, link to the documentation, API version, category, number of mashups
and followers registered in ProgrammableWeb, and total number of operations.
Additionally, for each operation with dependencies, we collected the number
and type of input parameters, type of CRUD operation and inter-parameter
dependencies.

Table 1. List of subject APIs

Name	Category	Mashups	Operations	%Op. with dep.
Google Maps Places	Mapping	2,579	7	57.1
Twitter Search Tweets	Social	829	3	100
Youtube	Media	707	50	34.0
Flickr	Media	635	222	13.1
Twilio SMS	Communication	361	31	6.5
Last.fm	Media	246	58	31.0
Microsoft Bing Maps	Mapping	175	51	21.6
Google App Engine Admin	Development	124	38	0.0
Foursquare	Social	113	40	40.0
DocuSign eSignature	Other	98	305	4.6
Amazon S3	Storage	95	94	16.0
GeoNames	Reference	90	41	24.4
Bing Web Search	Search	67	1	100
Yelp Fusion	Reference	61	12	41.7
Indeed	Search	48	2	0.0
Paypal Invoicing	Financial	39	21	23.8
Google Custom Search	Search	39	2	0.0
Google Geocoding	Mapping	36	1	100
SoundCloud	Media	34	49	2.0
Oodle	Other	34	1	100
NationBuilder	Social	33	107	5.6
Tumblr	Social	26	25	20.0
OpenStreetMap	Mapping	23	39	5.1
iTunes	Media	22	1	100
Google Fusion Tables	Development	20	33	9.1
Tropo	Communication	19	25	8.0
Heroku	Development	18	262	0.0
MapLarge	Mapping	14	31	0.0
Google Drive	Storage	13	39	10.3
CrunchBase	Reference	11	23	8.7
Github	Development	11	492	2.8
Nexmo SMS	Communication	10	3	33.3
Stripe	Financial	8	220	7.7
Kiva	Financial	8	32	0.0
AT&T In-App Messaging	Communication	7	11	9.1
PicPlz	Media	5	18	61.1
Coinbase	Financial	3	43	7.0
Pryv	Other	1	25	16.0
QuickBooks Payments	Financial	1	20	20.0
Forte (Payments Gateway)	Financial	1	79	19.0

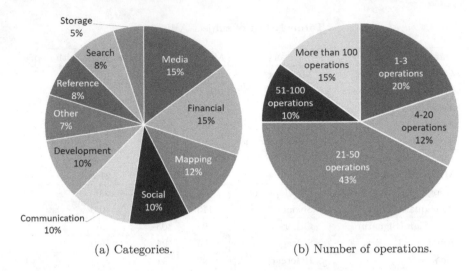

(a) Categories.   (b) Number of operations.

Fig. 1. Classification of subject APIs by category and size.

Dependencies were identified in two steps. First, we recorded all the dependencies among input parameters found in the documentation of the subject APIs. It is worth mentioning that every dependency can be represented in multiple ways, e.g. in conjunctive normal form. At this point, we strove to represent them as they were described in the documentation of the API. This allowed us, for example, to record the *arity* of each dependency, i.e. number of parameters involved in each constraint. In a second step, we studied the shape of all the dependencies and managed to group them into seven general dependency types (c.f. Sect. 3.2). Additionally, we used an online text analysis tool [20] to identify the linguistic patterns most frequently used for the description of each type of dependency. The documentation collected from each API was reviewed by at least two different authors to reduce misunderstanding or missing information. The complete dataset used in our study, including all the data collected from each API, is publicly available in a machine-processable format [5].

3   Results

In this section, we describe the results and how they answer the research questions. Firstly, we present how frequently inter-parameter dependencies appear in practice and whether their presence is correlated to certain API characteristics. Secondly, we detail the different types of dependencies found in the subject APIs.

3.1   Presence of Inter-parameter Dependencies

This section aims to provide an answer to RQ1 by studying how common inter-parameter dependencies are in web APIs and where they are typically found.

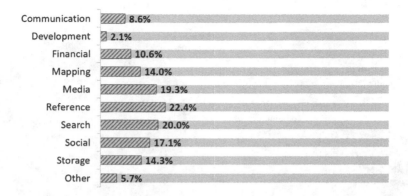

Fig. 2. Percentage of operations with dependencies per category.

We identified 633 total dependencies among input parameters in 85% of the APIs under study (34 out of 40). Specifically, we found dependencies in 9.7% of the operations analysed (248 out of 2,557). The percentage of operations with dependencies of each API is shown in the last column of Table 1. This percentage ranged from less than 5%, in APIs such as Soundcloud and Github, to 100%, in APIs such as Bing Web Search and Twitter Search Tweets. Figure 2 depicts a bar graph with the percentage of operations with dependencies on each category. As illustrated, we found dependencies in all the categories under study, with the percentage of operations with dependencies ranging between 2.1% in the category *development* and 22.4% in the category *reference*. This suggests that the presence of dependencies in real-world APIs is very common, independently of their application domain.

Figure 3a shows the distribution of dependencies by the number of parameters of the operation. Overall, we found that operations with dependencies had between 2 and 221 parameters, 20.1 on average (standard deviation = 21.0, median = 13). Moreover, most of these operations were read operations (61%), followed by create (26%), update (13%) and delete operations (less than 1%). Figure 3b depicts the distribution of dependencies by their arity. The largest portion of dependencies were binary (86%), followed by those involving three (10%) or more parameters (4%). In total, arity ranged between 2 and 10, with dependencies involving 2.2 parameters on average (standard deviation = 0.6, median = 2). Furthermore, the dependencies mostly involved query parameters (65%), followed by body (34%), header (3%) and path parameters (1%). Interestingly, we found 22 dependencies that involved more than one type of parameter. For example, the Bing Web Search API documentation states that, in order to obtain results in a given language, either the `Accept-Language` header or the `setLang` query parameter must be specified, but not both.

Finally, we investigated whether some of the data could be used as effective predictors for the amount of dependencies in a web API. To that end, we studied some potential correlations among the collected data using the R statistical environment in two steps. First, we checked the normality of the data using the

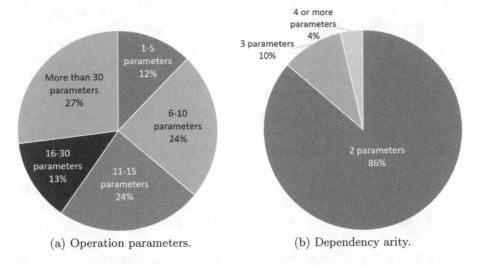

(a) Operation parameters.   (b) Dependency arity.

Fig. 3. Classification of dependencies by the number of parameters in the operation and their arity.

Shapiro-Wilk test concluding that the data do not follow a normal distribution. Second, we used the Spearman's rank order coefficient to assess the relationship between the variables. In particular, we tried to answer the following questions:

- *Are APIs with many operations likely to have a higher percentage of operations with dependencies?* No, quite the opposite. Spearman coefficient reveals a moderate negative correlation ($\rho = -0.45$, p-value $= 0.003$), which indicates that as the number of operations increases, the percentage of operations with dependencies decreases, and vice versa. In other words, the percentage of operations with dependencies tends to be higher in APIs with fewer operations. This may be explained by the fact that APIs with few operations often suffer from low cohesion, with a few operations trying to do too many things through the use of a wide set of parameters and dependencies. Conversely, APIs with many operations avoid some dependencies by distributing the functionality across different related operations
- *Are operations with many parameters likely to have more dependencies?* Yes. Spearman coefficient reveals a moderate positive correlation ($\rho = 0.49$, p-value $= 2.2 \times 10^{-16}$), which means that the number of dependencies in an operation typically increases with the number of input parameters. We found an exception, however, in those operations receiving complex objects as input, where the percentage of object properties with dependencies is usually very low, e.g. a PayPal invoice is composed of 112 JSON properties with just 2 dependencies among them. We repeated the correlation study excluding input objects and obtained a Spearman coefficient of 0.67 (p-value $= 2.2 \times 10^{-16}$), which reflects a stronger positive correlation between the number of parameters of an operation and the number of dependencies.

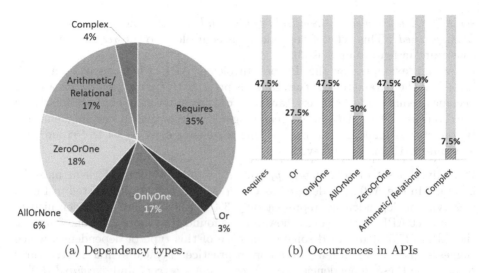

(a) Dependency types.   (b) Occurrences in APIs

Fig. 4. Distribution of dependencies by type and percentage of APIs.

3.2 Catalogue of Inter-parameter Dependencies

In this section, we answer RQ2 by classifying the inter-parameter dependencies identified into seven general types. We took inspiration in the constraints used to model dependencies in feature models, in the context of software product lines, where the authors have wide expertise [3], although we propose more intuitive and self-explanatory names in our work.

Before going in depth into each type of dependency, a number of considerations must be taken into account. First, for the sake of simplicity, dependencies are described using single parameters. However, all dependencies can be generalized to consider groups of parameters using conjunctive and disjunctive connectors. Second, dependencies can affect not only the presence or absence of parameters, but also the values that they can take. In what follows, when making reference to a parameter *being present* or *being absent*, it could also mean a parameter *taking* or *not taking a given value*, respectively. Finally, when introducing each dependency type we will make reference to Fig. 4, which shows the distribution of dependencies by type (Fig. 4a) and the percentage of subject APIs including occurrences of each dependency type (Fig. 4b). Next, we describe the seven types of dependencies found in our study, including examples.

Requires. The presence of a parameter p_1 in an API call requires the presence of another parameter p_2, denoted as $p_1 \rightarrow p_2$. As previously mentioned, p_1 and p_2 can be generalized to groups of parameters and parameters' assignments, e.g. $a \wedge b = x \rightarrow c \vee d$. Based on our results, this is the most common type of dependency in web APIs, representing 35% of all the dependencies identified in our study (Fig. 4a), and being present in 47.5% of the subject APIs (Fig. 4b). The syntactical analysis of API documentations revealed that the most frequently used linguistic patterns to describe this type of dependencies are *"you must also* set *X*", "*X must also be specified*", "*only valid if X is*" and "*[yes,/required] if X is specified*". This type of dependency is equivalent to the *requires* cross-tree constraint in feature models [3].

As an example, in the Paypal Invoicing API, when creating a draft invoice, if the parameter `custom.label` is present, then `custom.custom_amount` becomes required, i.e. `custom.label` → `custom.custom_amount`. Similarly, in the YouTube Data API, when searching for videos with a certain definition (parameter `videoDefinition`), the `type` parameter must be set to '`video`', i.e. `videoDefinition` → `type=video`.

Or. Given a set of parameters $p_1, p_2, \ldots, p_n$, one or more of them must be included in the API call, denoted as $Or(p_1, p_2, \ldots, p_n)$. As illustrated in Fig. 4, this type of dependencies represent only 3% of the dependencies identified in the subject APIs. Interestingly, however, we found that more than one fourth of the APIs (27.5%) included some occurrence of this type of dependency, which suggests that its use is fairly common in practice. Typical syntactic structures to describe these dependencies are "*X or Y must be set*" and "*required if X is not provided*". This type of dependency is equivalent to the *or* relationship in feature models [3].

As an example, when setting the information of a photo in the Flickr API, at least one of the parameters `title` or `description` must be provided, i.e. $Or(\texttt{title}, \texttt{description})$. Similarly, in the DocuSign eSignature API, at least one of the parameters `from_date`, `envelope_ids` or `transaction_ids` must be submitted in the API call when retrieving the status of several envelopes, i.e. $Or(\texttt{from\_date}, \texttt{envelope\_ids}, \texttt{transaction\_ids})$.

OnlyOne. Given a set of parameters $p_1, p_2, \ldots, p_n$, one, and only one of them must be included in the API call, denoted as $OnlyOne(p_1, p_2, \ldots, p_n)$. As observed in Fig. 4, this group of dependencies represent 17% of all the dependencies identified, and they appear in almost half of the APIs under study (47.5%). Among others, we found that this type of dependency is very common in APIs from the category *media*, where a resource can be identified in multiple ways, e.g. a song can be identified by its name or by its ID, and only one value must be typically provided. Common syntactic structures for describing this type of dependencies are "*specify one of the following*", "*only one of X or Y can be specified*", "*use either X or Y*", "*required unless X*" and "*required if X is not provided*". This type of dependency is equivalent to the *alternative* constraint in feature models [3].

For example, in the Twilio SMS API, when retrieving the messages of a particular account, either the parameter `MessagingServiceSid` or the parameter `From` must be included, but not both at the same time, i.e. $OnlyOne(\texttt{Messaging-ServiceSid}, \texttt{From})$. Similarly, when deleting a picture in the PicPlz API, only one of the parameters `id`, `longurl_id` or `shorturl_id` must be submitted in the API call, i.e. $OnlyOne(\texttt{id}, \texttt{longurl\_id}, \texttt{shorturl\_id})$.

AllOrNone. Given a set of parameters $p_1, p_2, \ldots, p_n$, either all of them are provided or none of them, denoted as $AllOrNone(p_1, p_2, \ldots, p_n)$. Very similarly

relatedToVideoId	string The relatedToVideoId parameter retrieves a list of videos that are related to the video that the parameter value identifies. The parameter value must be set to a YouTube video ID and, if you are using this parameter, the type parameter must be set to video. Note that if the relatedToVideoId parameter is set, the only other supported parameters are part, maxResults, pageToken, regionCode, relevanceLanguage, safeSearch, type (which must be set to video), and fields.

Fig. 5. Description of a parameter in the YouTube API that implies multiple *ZeroOrOne* dependencies.

to the *Or* dependency type, only 6% of the dependencies found belong to this category, nonetheless, they are present in about one third of the APIs under study (30%). These dependencies are typically described with structures such as *"can only be used in conjunction with"*, *"required if X is provided"* and *"(in conjunction) with X, (...)"*.

In the GitHub API, for example, the operation to obtain information about a user accepts two optional parameters, subject_type and subject_id, and they must be used together, i.e. *AllOrNone*(subject_type, subject_id). In the payments API Stripe, when creating a Stock Keeping Unit (a specific version of a product, used to manage the inventory of a store), if inventory.type is set to 'finite', then inventory.quantity must be present, and vice versa, i.e. *AllOrNone*(inventory.type=finite, inventory.quantity).

ZeroOrOne. Given a set of parameters $p_1, p_2, \ldots, p_n$, zero or one can be present in the API call, denoted as $ZeroOrOne(p_1, p_2, \ldots, p_n)$. Figure 4 reveals that this type of dependency is common both in terms of the number of occurrences (18% of the total) and the number of APIs including it (47.5%). Commonly used linguistic patterns for describing this type of dependency are *"not supported for use in conjunction with"*, *"cannot be combined with"*, *"if X is set, the only other supported parameters are"* and *"mutually exclusive with X"*.

Interestingly, about one third of the occurrences of this dependency type were found in YouTube, where filtering by a video ID in the search operation restricts the allowed parameters it can be combined with to only 8, as shown in Fig. 5. Since the operation accepts other 22 optional parameters, they are related to the video ID parameter by means of *ZeroOrOne* dependencies, e.g. *ZeroOrOne*(relatedToVideoId, topicId). Other examples of this dependency type include those where the use of a parameter restricts the allowed values of another parameter, like in the Google Maps API: when searching for places nearby, if radius is present, then rankby cannot be set to 'distance', i.e. *ZeroOrOne*(radius, rankby=distance).

Arithmetic/Relational. Given a set of parameters $p_1, p_2, \ldots, p_n$, they are related by means of arithmetic and/or relational constraints, e.g. $p_1 + p_2 > p_3$. As shown in Fig. 4, this type of dependency is the most recurrent across the

Value	Description
browse	Find venues within a given area. Unlike the `checkin intent`, browse searches an entire region instead of only finding venues closest to a point. A region to search can be defined by including either the `ll` and `radius` parameters, or the `sw` and `ne`. The region will be circular if you include the ll and radius parameters, or a bounding box if you include the sw and ne parameters.

Fig. 6. Complex dependency present in the GET /venues/search operation of the Foursquare API.

subject APIs, being present in half of them. Moreover, 17% of the dependencies found are of this type. These dependencies are typically implicit by the meaning of the parameters. For example, in a hotel booking, the checkout date should be later than the checkin date.

As an example, in the GeoNames API, when retrieving information about cities, the north parameter must be greater than the south parameter for the API to return meaningful results, i.e. north > south (north, east, south and west are the coordinates of a bounding box conforming the search area). In the payments API Forte, when creating a merchant application, this can be owned by several businesses, in which case the sum of the percentages cannot be greater than 100, i.e. owner.percentage + owner2.percentage + owner3.percentage + owner4.percentage <= 100.

Complex. These dependencies involve two or more of the types of constraints previously presented. Based on our results, they are typically formed by a combination of *Requires* and *OnlyOne* dependencies. As illustrated in Fig. 4, we found 4% of complex dependencies, being present in 7.5% of the subject APIs.

For example, in the Tumblr API, when creating a new post, if the type parameter is set to 'video', then either embed or data must be specified, but not both, i.e. type=video → $OnlyOne$(embed, data). Figure 6 shows an extract of the documentation of the search operation in the Foursquare API. As illustrated, if intent is set to 'browse', then either ll and radius are present or sw and ne are present, i.e. intent=browse → $OnlyOne((ll \wedge radius), (sw \wedge ne))$.

4   Threats to Validity

The factors that could have influenced our study and how these were mitigated are summarised in the following internal and external validity threats.

Internal Validity. This concerns any factor that might introduce bias. The main source of bias is the subjective and manual review process conducted for identifying dependencies among input parameters in the online documentation of the subject APIs. It is possible that we missed some dependencies or that we misclassified some of them. To mitigate this threat, the documentation of each API was carefully checked several times recording all the relevant data for its later analysis, and also to enable replicability. This was an extremely time-consuming process, but it was somehow alleviated by the familiarity of the authors with web APIs—all the authors have years of experience in the development of service-oriented systems for teaching, research and industrial purposes. The impact of possible mistakes was also minimised by the large number of APIs reviewed (40 APIs and 2,557 operations), which makes us remain confident of the overall accuracy of the results.

External Validity. Threats to external validity relate to the degree to which we can generalise from the experiments. Our study is based on a subset of RESTful web APIs, and thus our results could not generalise to other APIs. To minimise this threat, we systematically selected a large set of real-world APIs from multiple application domains. This set includes some of the most popular APIs in the world with millions of users worldwide.

5 Related Work

Two related papers have addressed the issue of parameter dependencies in contemporary web APIs. Wu et al. [21] presented an approach for the automated inference of parameter dependencies in web services. As a part of their work, they studied four popular RESTful web APIs and classified the dependencies found into six types, four of which are specific instances of the *Requires* dependency presented in our work. Oostvogels et al. [12] proposed a Domain-Specific Language (DSL) for the description of inter-parameter constraints in OAS. They first classified the dependencies typically found in web services into three types: *exclusive* (called *OnlyOne* in our work), *dependent* (*Requires* in our work), and *group constraints* (*AllOrNone* in our paper). Then, they looked for instances of those types of dependencies in the documentation of six popular APIs by searching for specific keywords such as "either" or "one of". Compared to theirs, our work presents a much larger and systematic study: we have manually reviewed 40 APIs from different domains, whereas they have jointly studied 7 "popular" APIs. As a result, the conclusions drawn from our investigation differ sharply from those derived from their papers. Among other differences, we identified a richer set of dependencies (e.g. Oostvogels et al. [12] identified three out of the seven types of dependencies found in our work), and collected a much larger amount of data (e.g. Oostvogels et al. [12] found 19 dependencies in YouTube while we found 82). Consequently, the general trends observed in our paper also differ, e.g. Wu et al. [21] found that an average of 21.9% of service operations had dependency constraints, while in our study that percentage is 9.7%. As a further difference, our work comprises a much more thorough analysis of dependencies including aspects such as their arity, frequently used linguistic patterns and correlations. Overall, however, the three papers complement each other and support the need for supporting inter-parameter dependencies in web APIs.

Several authors have addressed the problem of input dependencies in web services using the Web Services Description Language (WSDL). Xu et al. [22] analysed multiple service specifications to extract different types of constraints that enable syntax, workflow and semantic testing. One type of constraint they were able to infer is inter-parameter dependencies, but no details were given regarding their type and number of occurrences. Cacciagrano et al. [4] identified three types of constraints present in input parameters that hinder the automated invocation of services, one of them being inter-parameter dependencies (e.g. the value of a parameter being conditioned to the value of some other), and proposed an XML-based framework for their formalisation. Gao et al. [9] integrated information about parameters, error messages and testing results to infer data preconditions on web APIs that sometimes are not correctly specified in their documentation. They studied two web services and identified constraints involving one parameter (e.g. an integer that must be lower than certain value) or several parameters (e.g. two parameters that cannot be used together). Compared to them, our work is the first systematic and large-scale study of input constraints in modern web APIs, including a catalogue of the types of constraints most commonly found in practice.

Finally, our work is related to testing approaches for web services where dependency management is a key point to generate valid test cases. Recent contributions on testing of RESTful services [1,2,6,18] have succeeded to automatically generate test cases to some extent, however, none of them support the automated management of dependencies among input parameters. What is more, checking the existence of inter-parameter dependencies could be considered a black-box test coverage criterion to fulfil when testing RESTful APIs [11]. This would, in turn, enable the automatic generation of more thorough test suites. This paper takes a step further to address these challenges.

6   Conclusions and Future Work

In this paper, we reviewed the state of practice on the existence of inter-parameter dependencies in RESTful web APIs. To the best of our knowledge, this is the first systematic study on the topic, and the largest one, with 40 real-world APIs and more than 2.5K operations reviewed. Our results show that dependencies are extremely common and pervasive—they appear in 85% of the APIs under study across all application domains and types of operations. The collected data helped us to characterise dependencies identifying their most common shape—dependencies in read operations involving two query parameters—, but also exceptional cases such as dependencies involving up to 10 parameters and dependencies among different types of parameters, e.g. header and body parameters. We also identified some correlations pointing at the number of operations and the number of parameters as helpful estimators of the amount of dependencies in a web API. As the main result of our study, we present a catalogue of seven types of inter-parameter dependencies consistently found in all the subject APIs. We trust that the results of this study will provide the basis for future research contributions on modelling and analysis of input constraints in web APIs, enabling a more precise description of their capabilities and opening a new range of possibilities in terms of automation in areas such as code generation and testing.

Several challenges remain for future work. On the one hand, it would be desirable to perform an empirical study assessing the validity of the conclusions drawn from our investigation. On the other hand, the results of our study set the ground for approaches for modelling dependencies among input parameters in web APIs. Such proposals should ultimately reach industrial standards, as in the case of tools such as SLA4OAI [8], an OAS extension to model and manage Service Level Agreements (SLAs) in APIs. Our work enables the creation of multiple tools of this kind, namely: a DSL for the description of dependencies; a documentation analyser for the automatic inference of inter-parameter dependencies based on the linguistic patterns found; a tool for the automatic detection of dependencies at *run-time*; and a dependency analyser for the discovery of inconsistencies between multiple dependency constraints, e.g. a *dead* parameter that can never be selected.

Acknowledgements. This work has been partially supported by the European Commission (FEDER) and Spanish Government under projects BELI (TIN2015-70560-R) and HORATIO (RTI2018-101204-B-C21), and the FPU scholarship program, granted by the Spanish Ministry of Education and Vocational Training (FPU17/04077). We would also like to thank Enrique Barba Roque and Julián Gómez Rodríguez for their help in analysing the documentation of some of the APIs considered for this study.

References

1. Arcuri, A.: RESTful API automated test case generation with EvoMaster. ACM Trans. Softw. Eng. Methodol. **28**(1), 3 (2019)
2. Atlidakis, V., Godefroid, P., Polishchuk, M.: REST-ler: automatic intelligent REST API Fuzzing. Technical report, April 2018
3. Benavides, D., Segura, S., Ruiz-Cortés, A.: Automated analysis of feature models 20 years later: a literature review. Inf. Syst. **35**(6), 615–636 (2010)
4. Cacciagrano, D., Corradini, F., Culmone, R., Vito, L.: Dynamic constraint-based invocation of web services. In: 3rd International Workshop on Web Services and Formal Methods, pp. 138–147 (2006)
5. Inter-Parameter Dependencies in RESTful APIs [Dataset] (2019). https://bit.ly/2wvv1m1
6. Ed-douibi, H., Izquierdo, J.L.C., Cabot, J.: Automatic generation of test cases for REST APIs: a specification-based approach. In: IEEE 22nd International Enterprise Distributed Object Computing Conference, pp. 181–190 (2018)
7. Fielding, R.T.: Architectural styles and the design of network-based software architectures. Ph.D. thesis (2000)
8. Gamez-Diaz, A., Fernandez, P., Ruiz-Cortés, A.: Automating SLA-Driven API development with SLA4OAI. In: 17th International Conference on Service-Oriented Computing (2019)
9. Gao, C., Wei, J., Zhong, H., Huang, T.: Inferring data contract for web-based API. In: IEEE International Conference on Web Services, pp. 65–72 (2014)
10. Jacobson, D., Brail, G., Woods, D.: APIs: A Strategy Guide. O'Reilly Media, Inc., Sebastopol (2011)
11. Martin-Lopez, A., Segura, S., Ruiz-Cortés, A.: Test coverage criteria for RESTful Web APIs. In: Proceedings of the 10th ACM SIGSOFT International Workshop on Automating TEST Case Design, Selection, and Evaluation (A-TEST 2019) (2019)

12. Oostvogels, N., De Koster, J., De Meuter, W.: Inter-parameter constraints in contemporary web APIs. In: Cabot, J., De Virgilio, R., Torlone, R. (eds.) ICWE 2017. LNCS, vol. 10360, pp. 323–335. Springer, Cham (2017). https://doi.org/10.1007/978-3-319-60131-1_18
13. OpenAPI Specification. https://github.com/OAI/OpenAPI-Specification. Accessed March 2019
14. ProgrammableWeb API Directory. http://www.programmableweb.com/. Accessed March 2019
15. RESTful API Modeling Language (RAML). http://raml.org/. Accessed March 2019
16. RapidAPI API Directory. https://rapidapi.com. Accessed March 2019
17. Richardson, L., Amundsen, M., Ruby, S.: RESTful Web APIs. O'Reilly Media, Inc., Sebastopol (2013)
18. Segura, S., Parejo, J.A., Troya, J., Ruiz-Cortés, A.: Metamorphic testing of RESTful web APIs. IEEE Trans. Softw. Eng. **44**(11), 1083–1099 (2018)
19. Swagger. http://swagger.io/. Accessed March 2019
20. Text Analyzer - Text analysis Tool. https://www.online-utility.org/text/analyzer.jsp. Accessed April 2019
21. Wu, Q., Wu, L., Liang, G., Wang, Q., Xie, T., Mei, H.: Inferring dependency constraints on parameters for web services. In: Proceedings of the 22nd International Conference on World Wide Web, pp. 1421–1432 (2013)
22. Xu, L., Yuan, Q., Wu, J., Liu, C.: Ontology-based web service robustness test generation. In: IEEE International Symposium on Web Systems Evolution, pp. 59–68 (2009)

Simplification of Complex Process Models by Abstracting Infrequent Behaviour

David Chapela-Campa[✉], Manuel Mucientes, and Manuel Lama

Centro Singular de Investigación en Tecnoloxías Intelixentes (CiTIUS),
Universidade de Santiago de Compostela, Santiago de Compostela, Spain
{david.chapela,manuel.mucientes,manuel.lama}@usc.es

Abstract. Several simplification techniques have been proposed in process mining to improve the interpretability of complex processes, such as the structural simplification of the model or the simplification of the log. However, obtaining a comprehensible model explaining the behaviour of unstructured large processes is still an open challenge. In this paper, we present WoSimp, a novel algorithm to simplify processes by abstracting the infrequent behaviour from the logs, allowing to discover a simpler process model. This algorithm has been validated with more than 10 complex real processes, most of them from Business Process Management Challenges. Experiments show that WoSimp simplifies the process log and allows to discover a better process model than the state of the art techniques.

Keywords: Event abstraction · Model simplification · Log simplification · Process mining

1 Introduction

During the past years process mining has emerged as a discipline focusing on techniques to discover, monitor and enhance real processes [1]. One of the key areas of process mining is process discovery, whose objective is to generate a process model describing the behaviour of the event log of a process. Once a model is discovered, the analysis and enhancement of the process can be performed to detect possible improvements. However, in scenarios where the quality of the discovered process model is far too low —e.g. spaghetti models—, this analysis and enhancement become more difficult.

With the entrance of process mining in the *Big Data* era, these complex and incomprehensible processes have become more and more common. Different simplification techniques have been developed with the objective of obtaining an understandable process model, in order to be able to analyze and enhance the real process behind it. The first proposals focused on a structural simplification of the process model using only the information of the model itself [2]. But they quickly evolved to simplify the process model using also the information from the event log [3,4]. The drawback of these structural simplification techniques

© Springer Nature Switzerland AG 2019
S. Yangui et al. (Eds.): ICSOC 2019, LNCS 11895, pp. 415–430, 2019.
https://doi.org/10.1007/978-3-030-33702-5_32

is that, to maintain the fitness, they may produce unstructured models that deteriorate the understandability of the process.

Other approaches first simplify the log, and then discover an understandable process model. Some of these techniques search for outliers in the log traces, removing them with the aim of retaining the frequent behaviour of the process. In [5] this outlier identification is performed by using the probability of occurrence of each event conditioned by both its k predecessors and its k successors —e.g. how probable is that a follows, or is followed by, the sequence $\langle b, c \rangle$. One drawback of this technique is that, due to the use of sequential conditional probability, parallel relations are not considered. There are also approaches, like [6], that entirely remove activites from the log based on their contribution to the chaotic structure of the process. One drawback of this technique is that the decision of removing an activity depends on its relations with all the other activities, making the approach unscalable when the number of activities grows. Furthermore, the removal of activities from the log can produce the loss of important information if the activity is chaotic in some scenarios, but not in others.

An approach overcoming some of the previous drawbacks is the abstraction of subparts —subprocesses— of the process. This procedure replaces subprocesses with new activities, either in the log or structurally in the model. In [7] the authors propose a supervised method to abstract in the log behavioural activity patterns that capture domain knowledge. Given a set of activity patterns, they compose an abstraction model and align the behaviour of this abstraction model with the original log, creating an abstracted event log. The need of expert domain knowledge is solved in [8], where an unsupervised version of this method is proposed. This technique uses frequent local process models [9] as the activity patterns to abstract. The drawback of this technique is the significant penalization in its quality due to the abstraction of frequent subprocesses —the removal of frequently executed behaviour penalizes the fitness, and the addition of activities not recorded in the log the precision. This abstraction does not help to discover a significantly better process model in terms of F-score, not even undoing the parts of the abstraction after the discovery, as shown in their experimentation.

Figure 1 shows a motivational example, where an ideal abstraction of the infrequent behaviour is performed allowing to focus in the frequent one. In this case, the frequent behaviour is related to the paths through DENIED-CANCELED and through ACCEPTED-SUCCESS. The removal of the other —infrequent— traces would cause a lost of all the behaviour in each trace, not only in the infrequent one. For instance, the behaviour previous to PAY in these infrequent traces might be important in an analysis phase. Table 1c and Fig. 1d show an abstraction where the infrequent behaviour of the paths going through the loop is encapsulated in one activity, ERROR AND RETRY, letting the rest untouched.

In this paper, we present WoSimp, a novel algorithm to simplify processes by abstracting the infrequent behaviour from the log and maintaining the more frequent one, allowing to discover a simpler process model. The main novelty of our approach is that it detects the frequent behaviour of the process in a first

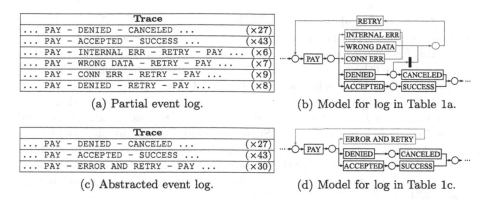

Trace	
... PAY - DENIED - CANCELED ...	(×27)
... PAY - ACCEPTED - SUCCESS ...	(×43)
... PAY - INTERNAL ERR - RETRY - PAY ...	(×6)
... PAY - WRONG DATA - RETRY - PAY ...	(×7)
... PAY - CONN ERR - RETRY - PAY ...	(×9)
... PAY - DENIED - RETRY - PAY ...	(×8)

(a) Partial event log.

(b) Model for log in Table 1a.

Trace	
... PAY - DENIED - CANCELED ...	(×27)
... PAY - ACCEPTED - SUCCESS ...	(×43)
... PAY - ERROR AND RETRY - PAY ...	(×30)

(c) Abstracted event log.

(d) Model for log in Table 1c.

Fig. 1. Motivational example for the algorithm presented in this paper.

phase —using the frequent patterns extracted by WoMine [10]— and abstracts the infrequent behaviour in a second phase. The use of WoMine to detect frequent behaviour allows our technique to retain not only frequent activities, but frequent subprocesses, abstracting the infrequent behaviour which obfuscates the understanding of the overall process. The algorithm has been validated with a set of 11 complex real process logs, 10 of them from Business Process Management Challenges, and one from the health domain. Experiments show that WoSimp simplifies the process log allowing to discover better process models than the state of the art techniques.

2   Preliminaries

In this paper, we represent process models with place/transition Petri nets [11] (P/T Petri net) due to its higher comprehensibility, and the easiness to explain the executed behaviour. A P/T Petri net (Definition 1) is a directed bipartite graph composed by two kinds of nodes: places and transitions —circles and boxes, respectively—, and where arcs connect two nodes of different type, as can be seen in Fig. 2a. Being A the set of activities of a process, each transition in a Petri net modeling its behaviour is identified by a label corresponding to the activity it represents. We assume that the transition labels are unique, i.e. there are no repeated activities in the net. An exception is made for silent transitions, which are unlabeled. Silent transitions are only executed for routing purposes and do not correspond to any activity of the process.

Definition 1 (Petri net). A Petri net is a tuple $M = (P, T, F)$, where

- P is a finite set of places;
- T is a finite set of transitions;
- $P \cap T = \emptyset$; and
- $F \subseteq (P \times T) \cup (T \times P)$ is a set of directed arcs.

We denote as $\bullet t$ and $t\bullet$ the input and output places of $t \in T$ (according to F). The state of a Petri net is defined by the marking function $m : P \nrightarrow A$. m is a partial function returning, for each place $p \in P$, the label of a transition —representing a token— or $\emptyset$ if there are no tokens in that place. The label of a token corresponds with the transition which has produced it. Therefore, a transition t is said to be *enabled* if $\forall p \in \bullet t$, $m(p) \neq \emptyset$. The execution of an enabled transition t consumes a token in each $p \in \bullet t$, and produces another token with its label in each $p \in t\bullet$. Silent transitions maintain the label of the consumed tokens in those it produces. The difference with a usual marking is that the tokens carry the label of their producing transition. This allows to know, when a transition is executed, which visible transitions have produced the tokens it consumed.

Definition 2 (Event, Trace and Event Log). An event ε corresponds to the execution of the activity $\alpha \in A$ in a particular instant. A trace is a list (sequence) $\tau = \langle \varepsilon_1, ..., \varepsilon_n \rangle$ of events ε_i occurring at a time index i relative to the other events in τ. Each trace corresponds to an execution of the process, i.e., a process instance. An event log $L = [\tau_1, ..., \tau_m]$ is a multiset of traces τ_i.

In this paper, to ease the comprehension, an event is represented only with the label of the executed activity, but usually events store more information as timestamps, resources, etc. Nevertheless, it is important to distinguish between an activity —an action from a process that can be modeled with a single transition in the Petri net— and an event —a single execution of an activity. The replacement of an activity implies the replacement of all its events and the transition in the Petri net, but the replacement of an event only implies the replacement of that single execution.

Definition 3 (Behavioural Event). A behavioural event is a tuple $\beta = (\mathcal{B}^\beta, \alpha)$ where:

- $\alpha \in A$ is the activity which execution is recorded in the behavioural event; and
- $\mathcal{B}^\beta$ is the set of behavioural events which have produced the tokens consumed by the execution of α.

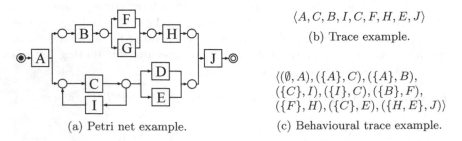

$\langle A, C, B, I, C, F, H, E, J \rangle$

(b) Trace example.

$\langle (\emptyset, A), (\{A\}, C), (\{A\}, B),$
$(\{C\}, I), (\{I\}, C), (\{B\}, F),$
$(\{F\}, H), (\{C\}, E), (\{H, E\}, J) \rangle$

(a) Petri net example.

(c) Behavioural trace example.

Fig. 2. Example of a Petri net, a trace, and the corresponding behavioural trace obtained by replaying the trace in the Petri net. For the sake of simplicity, in each behavioural event, $\mathcal{B}^\beta$ is represented as a set of activities instead of behavioural events.

Similar to an event, a behavioural event can store more information like timestamps, resources, etc. Moreover, a behavioural event also stores its causal inputs, i.e., the previous behavioural events which produced the tokens it consumed. An example can be seen in Fig. 2c, where 9 behavioural events are shown. For instance, the last behavioural event, $(\{H, E\}, J)$, records the execution of J, consuming the tokens generated by the executions of H and E.

Definition 4 (Behavioural Trace). Let M be the Petri net of a process, and $\tau = \langle \varepsilon_1, ..., \varepsilon_n \rangle$ a trace of the same process. The corresponding behavioural trace of τ w.r.t. M is the sequence $\pi = \langle \beta_1, ..., \beta_n \rangle$ of behavioural events. π is the result of a replay of all $\varepsilon_i \in \tau$ in M, extending each ε_i by adding the behavioural events corresponding to the execution of each $\alpha' \in m_i(p)$ for all $p \in \bullet\alpha$, being α the activity executed in ε_i —i.e., the behavioural events producing the tokens consumed by ε_i.

Figure 2c shows the behavioural trace obtained by replaying the trace in Fig. 2b in the Petri net of Fig. 2a.

Definition 5 (Behavioural Log). We define a behavioural event log, or behavioural log, as a multiset $L^\pi = [\pi_1, ..., \pi_m]$ of behavioural traces π_i.

Definition 6 (Abstraction). Given a behavioural trace π, and being A_π the set of activities executed in π. We define an abstraction in π as $\lambda = (\varepsilon^{abs}, \mathcal{B}, A_I, A_O)$ where:

- ε^{abs} is an event representing the execution of an abstracted activity;
- $\mathcal{B}$ is a set of behavioural events from π to be replaced with ε^{abs};
- $A_I \subset A_\pi$ is a set of activities of the events causing the execution of any event in $\mathcal{B}$; and
- $A_O \subset A_\pi$ is a set of activities of the events in π whose execution is caused by events in $\mathcal{B}$,

such that:

- $\mathcal{B}_I = \{\beta' \mid \beta' \in \mathcal{B}^\beta \wedge \beta \in \mathcal{B}\}$;
- $A_I = \{\beta.activity \mid \beta \in \mathcal{B}_I \setminus \mathcal{B}\}$;
- $\mathcal{B}_O = \{\beta' \mid \beta' \in \pi \wedge \beta \in \mathcal{B}^{\beta'} \wedge \beta \in \mathcal{B}\}$; and
- $A_O = \{\beta.activity \mid \beta \in \mathcal{B}_O \setminus \mathcal{B}\}$.

For instance, being π the trace depicted in Fig. 2c, an abstraction could be formed by a new activity Abs as ε^{abs}; $(\{A\}, D)$, $(\{B\}, F)$ and $(\{F\}, H)$ as $\mathcal{B}$; being A the only activity in A_O; and J the only activity in A_I. After the abstraction process, ε^{abs} would replace the behavioural events of $\mathcal{B}$. Related to Definition 6, we use the term *empty abstraction*, represented by $\lambda^\emptyset = (\mathcal{B}, A_I, A_O)$, to define an abstraction without assigned event, and the term *anti-abstraction*, represented by $\bar{\lambda}$, to define the set of behavioural events of a behavioural trace to keep in the abstracted log, i.e., those events not to be abstracted.

3 WoSimp Algorithm

In this section we present WoSimp (Algorithm 1), an algorithm to abstract the infrequent behaviour of a log. The execution of a discovery algorithm over that abstracted log allows to obtain a more precise and simpler process model, keeping a good fitness. Our proposal takes as input an event log, a process model and a frequency threshold, and returns the event log with the abstraction of the infrequent behaviour. The first step of WoSimp is to identify the frequent behaviour to be kept in the log. For this purpose WoMine [10] is used (Algorithm 1: 2), extracting from the process model a set of behavioural patterns executed in a percentage of the traces of the log frequent w.r.t. the defined threshold. Later, the behavioural log with the causal relations of each event is obtained using the given log and the model (Algorithm 1: 3). Then, the algorithm builds the abstractions of the behaviour not covered by the frequent patterns (Algorithm 1: 4). Finally, the log is abstracted with function `abstractLog` (Algorithm 1: 5): each behavioural trace is converted to a trace —removing the behavioural information—, abstracting those behavioural events defined in the abstractions.

Algorithm 1. WoSimp algorithm.

Input: An event log $L = [\tau_1, ..., \tau_m]$ of traces, a process model M, and a threshold t.

Output: An event log $L' = [\tau'_1, ..., \tau'_m]$ with the infrequent behaviour of L abstracted into new activities.

1   **Algorithm** `WoSimp`(L, M, t)
2 | $P \leftarrow$ `getFrequentPatterns`(L, M, t) `// using algorithm in [10]`
3 | $L^\pi \leftarrow$ obtain the behavioural log of L and M `// Definition 5`
4 | $\Lambda \leftarrow$ `buildAbstractions`(L^π, P)
5 | $L' \leftarrow$ `abstractLog`(L^π, Λ)
6 | **return** L'
7   **Function** `buildAbstractions`(L^π, P)
8 | $\Lambda^\emptyset \leftarrow \emptyset$
9 | **forall** $\pi \in L^\pi$ **do**
10 | | $\bar{\lambda} \leftarrow \{\beta \mid \beta \in \pi \wedge \beta \in p.executedEvents[\pi] \wedge p \in P\}$
11 | | $\Lambda^\emptyset_\pi \leftarrow$ `obtainEmptyAbstractions`(π, $\bar{\lambda}$) `// Alg. 2`
12 | | $\Lambda^\emptyset \leftarrow \Lambda^\emptyset \cup \Lambda^\emptyset_\pi$
13 | **end**
14 | $\Lambda \leftarrow$ `assignAbstractedEvents`($\Lambda^\emptyset$) `// Alg. 3`
15 | **return** Λ
16   **Function** `abstractLog`(L^π, Λ)
17 | $L' \leftarrow L^\pi$
18 | **forall** $\lambda \in \Lambda$ **do**
19 | | replace $\lambda.\mathcal{B}$ with $\lambda.\varepsilon^{abs}$ and insert it in L'
20 | **end**
21 | **return** L'

A naive example can be seen in Fig. 1 where, with a threshold of 25%, the frequent patterns obtained by WoMine cover the behaviour going through DENIED - CANCELED and through ACCEPTED - SUCCESS. These patterns allow to abstract the sequences starting in INTERNAL ERR, WRONG DATA, CONN ERR and DENIED, and going through RETRY. The abstraction technique encapsulates all these behaviour in one abstraction —named ERROR AND RETRY in Table 1c—, allowing to discover the process as shown in Fig. 1d.

The technique designed to build the abstractions is composed by two phases. The first phase (Algorithm 1: 9–13) is an horizontal analysis, i.e. one trace at a time, creating the groups of behavioural events to abstract. For each trace, the behavioural events belonging to an execution of a frequent pattern are collected in their anti-abstraction (Algorithm 1: 10). Then, function obtainEmptyAbstractions groups the behavioural events to be abstracted creating the empty abstractions —abstractions without an abstracted event assigned— corresponding to that trace (c.f. Sect. 3.1). In the second phase (Algorithm 1: 14), a vertical analysis going over the log is performed to create the

---

Algorithm 2. Get empty abstractions of a behavioural trace (Algorithm 1: 11).

Input: A behavioural trace π and its anti-abstraction $\bar{\lambda}$.
Output: A set $\Lambda^{\emptyset}$ with the empty abstractions of the behavioural trace π.

```
1  Algorithm obtainEmptyAbstractions(π, λ̄)
2  │   B_infreq ← {β | β ∈ π ∧ β ∉ λ̄}
3  │   B_connected ← groupConnectedEvents(B_infreq) // set of sets of β
4  │   Λ^∅ ← ∅
5  │   forall B ∈ B_connected do
6  │   │   λ^∅ ← obtainEmptyAbstraction(π, B)
7  │   │   Λ^∅ ← Λ^∅ ∪ {λ^∅}
8  │   end
9  │   return Λ^∅
10 Function groupConnectedEvents(B_infreq)
11 │   B_connected ← ∅ // set of sets of β
12 │   forall β ∈ B_infreq do
13 │   │   if β ∉ ∪B_connected then
14 │   │   │   B' ← {β} ∪ {β' | β' ∈ B_infreq ∧ (β' → β ∨ β → β')}
15 │   │   │   B_connected ← B_connected ∪ {B'}
16 │   │   end
17 │   end
18 │   return B_connected
19 Function obtainEmptyAbstraction(π, B)
20 │   A_I ← {β'.activity | β' ∈ (B^β \ B) ∧ β ∈ B}
21 │   A_O ← {β'.activity | β' ∈ (π \ B) ∧ β ∈ B^{β'} ∧ β ∈ B}
22 │   λ^∅ ← (B, A_I, A_O)
23 │   return λ^∅
```

abstractions by assigning an abstracted event with the same activity to the empty abstractions with identical contextual behaviour (c.f. Sect. 3.2). Finally, with all the information of the abstractions, function `abstractLog` abstracts the original behavioural log replacing the behavioural events of each abstraction with the corresponding abstracted event (Algorithm 1: 16).

3.1 Create Abstractions of Infrequent Behaviour from a Trace

The objective of the first phase is to create the empty abstractions with the infrequent behaviour in each trace by grouping the corresponding behavioural events. Algorithm 2 shows this abstraction process over a trace. First, the behavioural events to abstract are collected, i.e., those not present in the anti-abstraction (Algorithm 2: 2). Then, these behavioural events are grouped, where each group contains those connected between them (Algorithm 2: 3). Afterwards, an empty abstraction is created for each group (Algorithm 2: 5–8). Function `obtainEmptyAbstraction` creates this empty abstraction with (i) the set of behavioural events to abstract; (ii) the inputs of this group, i.e., for each behavioural event from the group, the activities of its input behavioural events not contained in the abstraction group (Algorithm 2: 20); and (iii) the outputs of this group, i.e., the activities of the behavioural events of the trace having as inputs any of the behavioural events in the group (Algorithm 2: 21).

As an example, the process model and the two traces from Fig. 3 are going to be used. Assuming a balanced distribution in the selections, and a threshold for the patterns of 70%, WoMine recovers as frequent patterns the initial AND-split (A, B and C) and the final AND-join without the loop (K, O and N). Table 1 shows the results of the main steps of the first phase over the two traces of Fig. 3. To create the groups with the connected behavioural events not present in the anti-abstractions —those unmarked in the trace description— the algorithm performs a forward iteration over them adding each behavioural event to the set where its inputs are. The results can be seen in the $\mathcal{B}_{connected}$ elements. Then, an empty abstraction is created for each group (e.g. $\lambda_1^\emptyset$) with the behavioural events

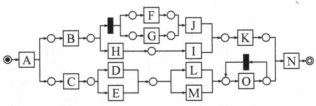

(a) Petri net of a process to abstract.

$\langle A, B, F, C, D, G, L, J, O, K, N \rangle$ $\langle A, C, E, B, H, L, I, O, O, K, O, N \rangle$

(b) Trace example.   (c) Trace example.

Fig. 3. Petri net and two traces to exemplify the abstraction process.

Table 1. Key elements obtained in the first phase of the algorithm for the traces in Fig. 3 —events with a hat in each trace are those belonging to the anti-abstraction. π: the corresponding behavioural trace. $\mathcal{B}_{connected}$: the groups of behavioural events to abstract —to ease the visualization the behavioural events from each $\mathcal{B}_{connected}$ are shown as simple events. $\Lambda^{\emptyset}$: the empty abstractions created from these groups.

$\tau_1 = \langle \hat{A}, \hat{B}, F, \hat{C}, D, G, L, J, \hat{O}, \hat{K}, \hat{N} \rangle$	
π_1	$\langle (\emptyset, A), (\{A\}, B), (\{B\}, F), (\{A\}, C), (\{C\}, D), (\{B\}, G), (\{D\}, L), (\{F, G\}, J),$ $(\{L\}, O), (\{J\}, K), (\{O, K\}, N) \rangle$
$\mathcal{B}_{connected}$	$\{F, G, J\}$ and $\{D, L\}$
$\Lambda^{\emptyset}$	$\lambda_1^{\emptyset} = (\{F, G, J\}, \{B\}, \{K\})$ $\lambda_2^{\emptyset} = (\{D, L\}, \{C\}, \{O\})$
$\tau_2 = \langle \hat{A}, \hat{C}, E, \hat{B}, H, L, I, O, O, \hat{K}, \hat{O}, \hat{N} \rangle$	
π_2	$\langle (\emptyset, A), (\{A\}, C), (\{C\}, E), (\{A\}, B), (\{B\}, H), (\{E\}, L), (\{H\}, I), (\{L\}, O), (\{O\}, O),$ $(\{I\}, K), (\{O\}, O), (\{K, O\}, N) \rangle$
$\mathcal{B}_{connected}$	$\{E, L, O, O\}$ and $\{H, I\}$
$\Lambda^{\emptyset}$	$\lambda_3^{\emptyset} = (\{E, L, O, O\}, \{C\}, \{O\})$ $\lambda_4^{\emptyset} = (\{H, I\}, \{B\}, \{K\})$

of the group (e.g. $\{F, G, J\}$), the input activities of these behavioural events (e.g. $\{B\}$), and the activities of the behavioural events from π whose inputs are in the group (e.g. $\{K\}$). For instance, the input activity for $\lambda_1^{\emptyset}$ is only B because is the firing behavioural event of F and G, and the firing behavioural events of J are inside the group. For the output activities, the behavioural events of π_1 are inspected, searching for those whose firing behavioural events are in the group, i.e., K.

3.2 Activity Assignment to Each Abstraction

Once each trace has its infrequent behaviour grouped in the different empty abstractions, the second phase starts (Algorithm 3). In this phase, all the empty abstractions of the log are compared to assign an event with the same activity to those with identical contextual behaviour —coming from the same activities or going to the same activities in the model. For this, the empty abstractions are first grouped by their input activities (Algorithm 3: 3–8). Then, these groups are merged by their output activities, i.e., the groups sharing the output activities of all their empty abstractions are merged (Algorithm 3: 10–15). Finally, an activity is created for each group of empty abstractions and assigned to each of them (Algorithm 3: 17–23).

Continuing with the example in Table 1, the second phase groups all the empty abstractions first by their input activities obtaining two groups: $\{\lambda_1, \lambda_4\}$ and $\{\lambda_2, \lambda_3\}$. The grouping by their outputs does not merge any group because the output activities of the empty abstractions in the first group are $\{K\}$, and the output activites of the second group are $\{O\}$. Once the empty abstractions are grouped, the assignation of artificial activities is performed. An event with the activity Abs_1 is assigned to the empty abstractions $\lambda_1^{\emptyset}$ and $\lambda_4^{\emptyset}$, and other

---

Algorithm 3. Assign an event with an abstracted activity to each empty abstraction (Algorithm 1: 14).

Input: A set $\Lambda^\emptyset$ of empty abstractions.
Output: The set Λ of abstractions with the events of the abstracted activities.

```
1  Algorithm assignAbstractedEvents(Λ∅)
2      Λ∅_I ← ∅ // set of sets of λ∅ with identical inputs
3      forall λ∅ ∈ Λ∅ do
4          if (λ∅ ∉ ∪Λ∅_I) then
5              Λ̃∅ ← {λ̃∅ | λ̃∅ ∈ Λ∅ ∧ λ̃∅.A_I = λ∅.A_I}
6              Λ∅_I ← Λ∅_I ∪ {Λ̃∅}
7          end
8      end
9      Λ∅_O ← ∅ // set of those sets in Λ∅_I with identical outputs
10     forall Λ∅_i ∈ Λ∅_I do
11         if (Λ∅_i ⊄ ∪Λ∅_O) then
12             Λ̃∅ ← sets in Λ∅_I with identical output activities than Λ∅_i
13             Λ∅_O ← Λ∅_O ∪ {Λ̃∅}
14         end
15     end
16     Λ ← ∅ // set with the abstractions with events assigned
17     forall Λ∅_o ∈ Λ∅_O do
18         α ← create new activity
19         forall λ∅ ∈ Λ∅_o do
20             λ ← λ∅ with α as activity of λ.ε^abs
21             Λ ← Λ ∪ {λ}
22         end
23     end
24     return Λ
```

---

event with activity Abs_2 to $\lambda_2^\emptyset$ and $\lambda_3^\emptyset$, obtaining the corresponding abstractions. With the second phase finished the abstraction process in the log is performed, producing the traces of Fig. 4. With this abstracted log, it is possible to mine the model shown in Fig. 4c.

4   Experimentation

In this section we evaluate the performance of WoSimp. These experiments have been executed in a computer with an Intel Core i7-2600 and 16 GB of RAM[1].

---

[1] The algorithm, datasets and results can be downloaded from http://tec.citius.usc. es/processmining/WoSimp/.

$\langle A, B, Abs_1, C, Abs_2, O, K, N \rangle$

(a) Abstracted trace of Fig. 3b.

$\langle A, C, Abs_2, B, Abs_1, K, O, N \rangle$

(b) Abstracted trace of Fig. 3c.

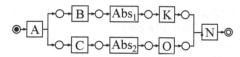

(c) Abstracted Petri net for the process in Fig. 3a.

Fig. 4. Result of the abstraction process of Fig. 3.

4.1 Datasets

For the experimentation a real log from the health domain —sepsis cases from a hospital [12]— and multiple Business Process Challenge logs [13–16] have been used. The characteristics of these logs are presented in Table 2.

Although the abstraction of infrequent behaviour is usually useful to visualize what is happening in the process, there are some scenarios where the penalization it causes in terms of quality metrics makes it worse than other simplification techniques. Two log features are the most relevant to describe in which scenarios the abstraction of infrequent behaviour might produce a better process model.

Table 2. Characteristics of the logs used in the experimentation: number of traces (#Traces); number of events (#Events); number of activities (#Activities); number of variants —traces with the same activity sequence— (Variants), and the percentage of the log covered by the three variants with more traces. All the logs have been modified by adding both single start and end activities to each trace. All event names have been combined with its lifecycle to discern between different phases of the same activity (START, COMPLETE, etc.).

	#Traces	#Events	#Activities	Variants			
				#	% 1st	% 2nd	% 3rd
BPIC11	1143	152577	626	981	3.59%	1.49%	1.40%
BPIC12-financial	13087	288374	38	4366	26.20%	14.30%	2.07%
BPIC13-clo	1487	9634	9	327	32.62%	8.68%	7.40%
BPIC13-inc	7554	80641	15	2278	23.15%	6.94%	4.66%
BPIC13-op	819	3989	7	182	21.49%	15.02%	6.72%
BPIC15_1	1199	54615	400	1170	0.67%	0.50%	0.33%
BPIC15_2	832	46018	412	828	0.24%	0.24%	0.24%
BPIC15_3	1409	62499	385	1349	1.06%	0.85%	0.71%
BPIC15_4	1053	49399	358	1049	0.28%	0.19%	0.19%
BPIC15_5	1156	61395	391	1153	0.17%	0.17%	0.17%
Sepsis-cases	1050	17314	18	846	3.33%	2.29%	2.10%

One of these features is the number of activities. The penalization due to the inclusion of abstracted activities —not present in the log— is too high when the number of activities is low —e.g. BPIC13-clo and BPIC13-op. The other feature is the percentage of the log covered by the most frequent activity sequences — variants. In logs where few variants cover a high percentage of the log traces, the discovery of a model with those variants may already lead to a better and simpler process model. Regarding this feature, note that logs from BPIC12 and BPIC13 contain more than a third of the traces in three variants.

4.2   Results

We have compared our approach with two state of the art techniques: *Matrix Filter*[2] [5], and *Activity Filter*[3] [6]. We have also considered a naive simplification technique such as the removal of the variants with lower percentage of coverage —henceforth referred to as *Repetitions*.

We have run these techniques in each log with 9 simplification thresholds, from 10% to 90% with a step of 10. In *Repetitions* this threshold means the minimum percentage of traces covered with the most frequent variants to be maintained, in *Activity Filter* it refers to the percentage of activities of the log to be maintained[4], and in *Matrix Filter* it means the threshold to consider an event as outlier. For each simplified log, 5 process models have been discovered: one with the Inductive Miner [18], and 4 with the Inductive Miner Infrequent [19] (thresholds 10%, 20%, 30% and 40%). Finally, to check the simplification level of these techniques and how good are the process models they obtain, we have measured the fitness —Alignment-based fitness [20]—, precision —Negative Event Precision [21]— and simplicity —Weighted P/T average arc degree [22]— of each simplified model.

We aim to obtain a simple process model allowing to understand the frequent behaviour happening in the process while both fitness and precision are maintained at desirable levels —a model with an extremely low precision allows too many behaviour not recorded in the log, obfuscating the real behaviour. For this reason, both metrics have been summarized in the F-score, penalizing low values in any of them. Regarding simplicity, we have transformed it into a metric with values in $[0, 1]$, where a greater value is better —as the F-score. We use the percentage of simplification w.r.t. the simplicity of the discovered model with the original log ($S_p = 1 - \frac{min(S_{raw}, S_s)}{S_{raw}}$). Being S_p the percentage of simplification, S_{raw} and S_s the simplicity of the models mined with the original log, and with the simplified log, respectively.

Figure 5 shows the F-score and S_p of the models discovered with two simplified logs as inputs. Figure 5a shows a clear overcoming of WoSimp over the other

---

[2] Using plugin *Matrix Filter* in ProM with Mean as the Threshold adjusting Method.

[3] Using the plugin *Activity Filter: Indirect Entropy optimized with Greedy Search* in ProM [17].

[4] *Activity Filter* takes more than 24 h to converge in datasets with more than 300 activities, thus, no results of this technique are shown in those datasets.

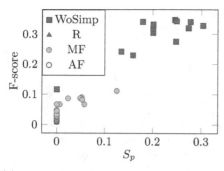
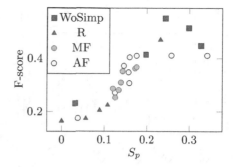

(a) S_p vs. F-score of the models discovered by the IM with the simplified logs of BPIC15_1.

(b) S_p vs. F-score of the models discovered by the IMf with the simplified logs of sepsis cases.

Fig. 5. Scatter plots of S_p against F-score for the models mined with the simplified logs for each technique (R stands for *Repetitions*, MF for *Matrix Filter* and AF for *Activity Filter*).

techniques: for high values of S_p, it obtains models with higher values of F-score. However, there are cases, such as the ones depicted in Fig. 5b, where not all the models from other techniques are overcome by a model obtained with WoSimp. For this reason, to make a fairer comparison between the different techniques, we have used the area covered by the dominant points.

Figure 6 shows for each dataset the area covered by the dominant points of the models obtained with both the Inductive Miner (top) and Inductive Miner Infrequent (bottom), having the logs simplified with each technique as inputs. As it was commented in Sect. 4.1, for datasets with few activities (BPIC13-op and BPIC13-clo), the addition of abstracted unmapped activities is not worth due to its penalization. Furthermore, due to the high quantity of behaviour covered by the more frequent variants, the results of WoSimp in these datasets are overcome by all the approaches, being *Repetitions* the best option. In other datasets where the number of activities is higher, but the more frequent variants still cover more than a third of the log traces (BIC13-inc and BPIC12-fin), WoSimp is only overcome by *Repetitions*. The result in BPIC11 is a particular case. Here, the 10% of more repeated traces contain enough common behaviour to compensate the penalization that WoSimp receives for adding abstracted unmapped activities. Nevertheless, this only happens using the IM, and WoSimp allows IMf to discover better process models than all other techniques.

As commented in Sect. 4.1, in datasets where the trace variability is high (BPIC15_1, BPIC15_2, BPIC15_3, BPIC15_4, BPIC15_5 and sepsis cases) and a naive technique as *Repetitions* is not useful, and WoSimp outperforms the state of the art techniques as Fig. 6 shows. Note that, if the variability in traces is high, the abstraction of WoSimp is the best option for logs with both high (BPIC15) and low (sepsis-cases) number of activities.

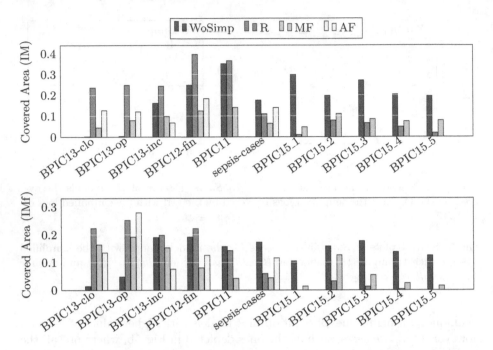

Fig. 6. Area covered by the dominant points (S_p vs. F-score) for the models discovered —IM (top), IMf (bottom)— with the simplified logs of each technique, for each dataset.

5 Conclusions

We have presented WoSimp, a novel algorithm to simplify process logs abstracting the infrequent behaviour, allowing to discover a simpler process model. The proposal is able to detect, using WoMine, the infrequent behaviour which obfuscates a process and abstract it allowing to discover a simpler and comprehensible process model. We have compared WoSimp with the state of the art approaches showing that WoSimp outperforms the state of the art in complex processes.

Acknowledgments. This research was funded by the Spanish Ministry of Economy and Competitiveness under grant TIN2017-84796-C2-1-R, and the Galician Ministry of Education, Culture and Universities under grant ED431G/08. These grants are co-funded by the European Regional Development Fund (ERDF/FEDER program). D. Chapela-Campa is supported by the Spanish Ministry of Education, under the FPU national plan (FPU16/04428).

References

1. van der Aalst, W.M.P.: Process Mining - Data Science in Action, 2nd edn. Springer, Heidelberg (2016). https://doi.org/10.1007/978-3-662-49851-4
2. Polyvyanyy, A., García-Bañuelos, L., Dumas, M.: Structuring acyclic process models. Inf. Syst. **37**(6), 518–538 (2012)
3. Fahland, D., van der Aalst, W.M.P.: Simplifying discovered process models in a controlled manner. Inf. Syst. **38**(4), 585–605 (2013)
4. de San Pedro, J., Carmona, J., Cortadella, J.: Log-based simplification of process models. In: Motahari-Nezhad, H.R., Recker, J., Weidlich, M. (eds.) BPM 2015. LNCS, vol. 9253, pp. 457–474. Springer, Cham (2015). https://doi.org/10.1007/978-3-319-23063-4_30
5. Sani, M.F., van Zelst, S.J., van der Aalst, W.M.P.: Improving process discovery results by filtering outliers using conditional behavioural probabilities. In: Teniente, E., Weidlich, M. (eds.) BPM 2017. LNBIP, vol. 308, pp. 216–229. Springer, Cham (2018). https://doi.org/10.1007/978-3-319-74030-0_16
6. Tax, N., Sidorova, N., van der Aalst, W.M.P.: Discovering more precise process models from event logs by filtering out chaotic activities. J. Intell. Inf. Syst. **52**(1), 107–139 (2019)
7. Mannhardt, F., de Leoni, M., Reijers, H.A., van der Aalst, W.M.P., Toussaint, P.J.: From low-level events to activities - a pattern-based approach. In: La Rosa, M., Loos, P., Pastor, O. (eds.) BPM 2016. LNCS, vol. 9850, pp. 125–141. Springer, Cham (2016). https://doi.org/10.1007/978-3-319-45348-4_8
8. Mannhardt, F., Tax, N.: Unsupervised event abstraction using pattern abstraction and local process models. In: Gulden, J., Nurcan, S., et al. (eds.) BPMDS 2017. CEUR Workshop Proceedings, vol. 1859, pp. 55–63. CEUR-WS.org (2017)
9. Tax, N., Sidorova, N., Haakma, R., van der Aalst, W.M.P.: Mining local process models. CoRR abs/1606.06066 (2016)
10. Chapela-Campa, D., Mucientes, M., Lama, M.: Mining frequent patterns in process models. Inf. Sci. **472**, 235–257 (2019)
11. Desel, J., Reisig, W.: Place/transition Petri Nets. In: Reisig, W., Rozenberg, G. (eds.) ACPN 1996. LNCS, vol. 1491, pp. 122–173. Springer, Heidelberg (1998). https://doi.org/10.1007/3-540-65306-6_15
12. Mannhardt, F. (Felix): Sepsis cases - event log (2016)
13. Van Dongen, B.: Real-life event logs - hospital log (2011)
14. Van Dongen, B.: BPI Challenge 2012 (2012)
15. Steeman, W.: BPI Challenge 2013 (2013)
16. Van Dongen, B.: BPI Challenge 2015 (2015)
17. van Dongen, B.F., de Medeiros, A.K.A., Verbeek, H.M.W., Weijters, A.J.M.M., van der Aalst, W.M.P.: The ProM framework: a new era in process mining tool support. In: Ciardo, G., Darondeau, P. (eds.) ICATPN 2005. LNCS, vol. 3536, pp. 444–454. Springer, Heidelberg (2005). https://doi.org/10.1007/11494744_25
18. Leemans, S.J.J., Fahland, D., van der Aalst, W.M.P.: Discovering block-structured process models from event logs - a constructive approach. In: Colom, J.-M., Desel, J. (eds.) PETRI NETS 2013. LNCS, vol. 7927, pp. 311–329. Springer, Heidelberg (2013). https://doi.org/10.1007/978-3-642-38697-8_17

19. Leemans, S.J.J., Fahland, D., van der Aalst, W.M.P.: Discovering block-structured process models from event logs containing infrequent behaviour. In: Lohmann, N., Song, M., Wohed, P. (eds.) BPM 2013. LNBIP, vol. 171, pp. 66–78. Springer, Cham (2014). https://doi.org/10.1007/978-3-319-06257-0_6

20. Adriansyah, A., van Dongen, B.F., van der Aalst, W.M.P.: Conformance checking using cost-based fitness analysis. In: EDOC 2011, pp. 55–64. IEEE Computer Society (2011)

21. vanden Broucke, S.K.L.M., Weerdt, J.D., Vanthienen, J., Baesens, B.: Determining process model precision and generalization with weighted artificial negative events. IEEE Trans. Knowl. Data Eng. **26**(8), 1877–1889 (2014)

22. vanden Broucke, S.K.L.M., Weerdt, J.D., Vanthienen, J., Baesens, B.: A comprehensive benchmarking framework (CoBeFra) for conformance analysis between procedural process models and event logs in ProM. In: IEEE Symposium on Computational Intelligence and Data Mining, CIDM 2013, pp. 254–261. IEEE (2013)

Improving IT Support by Enhancing Incident Management Process with Multi-modal Analysis

Atri Mandal[1]([✉]), Shivali Agarwal[1], Nikhil Malhotra[2], Giriprasad Sridhara[1], Anupama Ray[1], and Daivik Swarup[1]

[1] IBM Research AI, Bengaluru, India
{atri.mandal,shivaaga,girisrid,anupamar,dvenkata}@in.ibm.com
[2] IBM Global Technology Services, Bengaluru, India
nikhimal@in.ibm.com

Abstract. IT support services industry is going through a major transformation with AI becoming commonplace. There has been a lot of effort in the direction of automation at every human touchpoint in the IT support processes. Incident management is one such process which has been a beacon process for AI based automation. The vision is to automate the process from the time an incident/ticket arrives till it is resolved and closed. While text is the primary mode of communicating the incidents, there has been a growing trend of using alternate modalities like image to communicate the problem. A large fraction of IT support tickets today contain attached image data in the form of screenshots, log messages, invoices and so on. These attachments help in better explanation of the problem which aids in faster resolution. Anybody who aspires to provide AI based IT support, it is essential to build systems which can handle multi-modal content.

In this paper we present how incident management in IT support domain can be made much more effective using multi-modal analysis. The information extracted from different modalities are correlated to enrich the information in the ticket and used for better ticket routing and resolution. We evaluate our system using about 25000 real tickets containing attachments from selected problem areas. Our results demonstrate significant improvements in both routing and resolution with the use of multi-modal ticket analysis compared to only text based analysis.

Keywords: Service delivery · Incident management · Multimodal analysis · Image understanding · Automated routing and resolution

1 Introduction

Incident management process in modern IT service delivery is undergoing a massive transformation with an ever increasing focus on automation of tasks that require human cognizance. Two such key tasks are that of *ticket assignment* and

© Springer Nature Switzerland AG 2019
S. Yangui et al. (Eds.): ICSOC 2019, LNCS 11895, pp. 431–446, 2019.
https://doi.org/10.1007/978-3-030-33702-5_33

resolution as they require considerable amount of manual labour. There are quite a few recent instances in the service industry where assignment/resolution has been automated using analysis of structured and unstructured text content. All these systems generally work for text content only. However, a lot of these tickets have attachments of pictures, screenshots, logs etc. which not only help in giving a visual representation of the problem but also provide necessary context information. For example, an end user needing troubleshooting assistance for a software application (e.g. out of memory issue) will take a screenshot capturing the error message (and error code, if any) and the running application(s) along with CPU/memory usage statistics. Resolution of tickets without considering such important details may not only result in an unsatisfactory resolution, but can also mislead or confuse the user, leading to poor customer experience and multiple escalations. Also in a lot of cases textual information may be completely absent from the ticket and the troubleshooting agent has to infer the problem only from the attachments. In all these scenarios, it is important to address the fundamental problem of understanding the screenshot images, extract the relevant information and generate problem descriptions which can then be utilized in the automation pipeline.

There are a quite a few challenges in extracting information from screenshot images and using them in a proper way to arrive at a resolution. Some of these challenges are: (i) Lack of labeled training data with images/videos annotated for the boxes with important information or labels in the form of actual content of images (text groundtruth). To the best of our knowledge there is no such annotated dataset available for IT support domain with labeled images. Thus, deep learning models, which require a lot of training data cannot be trained on this domain with multimodal data. (ii) Presence of overlapping windows often occludes the text content which might be relevant for better assignment or resolution. Thus conventional image processing algorithms like contour detection [12] or canny edge detection [5] do not work well only by themselves and fail to understand the internal structure or content in the windows (as shown in Fig. 1). (iii) To obtain the embedded text in the image we can use Optical Character Recognition [16]. However the image may have a lot of noisy text which are not related to the problem (e.g. icon labels, menu items, code, console commands etc.) and so the complete text obtained from OCR may not be useful. (iv) The correlation between ticket text and textual content extracted from the image is also challenging as domain knowledge plays a very important part in this correlation and content understanding.

In this paper, we discuss an end-to-end system which can analyze image content in tickets, understand the nature of the problem indicated in the image and automatically suggest a resolution. In this paper we focus on a specific type of attachment, viz. screenshots, as this is the most common type of attachment, requiring human supervision, found in IT support tickets. The key contributions of our paper are described below:

(i) A high-precision hybrid object detection engine which uses a combination of traditional image processing algorithms as well as deep learning based

Fig. 1. (a) Canny-edge detects spurious boxes (b) Contour detection detects objects in background

image classification. The main purpose of the detection engine is to identify if an application window (e.g. error message box, terminal, explorer window etc.) is present and if so, the type of the application window.

(ii) A ticket enrichment module which uses OCR and NLP based techniques to extract relevant pieces of information from the application window(s) detected in the image and uses this extra information to enrich the ticket data for better classification.

(iii) A scalable routing and resolution recommendation framework, having an intelligent decision making mechanism based on its confidence on multiple predicted fields.

Using our system we were able to demonstrate significant improvements in both ticket assignment and ticket resolution accuracy compared to only text based analysis. The automation achieved by our system can result in an estimated saving of 200000 man hours per annum for a helpdesk account receiving 100000 tickets a month.

The rest of the paper is organized as follows. Section 2 discusses some of the related work in the area. Section 3 gives an overview of the system architecture used. In Sect. 5 we present our experimental results while we conclude in Sect. 6.

2   Related Work

Incident management process has been discussed in literature with a focus on ticket categorization/problem determination, ticket dispatch/resolver group prediction, resolver group formation and resolution recommendation. Many systems proposed in the past provide a solution for automated problem determination and resolution e.g. [1,6] talk about auto-remediation by first categorizing the ticket into a problem category and then recommending a solution for the problem category identified. They have used text based classification. The system in [21] proposes resolution recommendation for event tickets using an approach which utilizes both the event and resolution information in historical tickets via topic-level feature extraction. The work in [22] also proposes a solution for automated ticket resolution using a deep neural network ranking model trained on problem text and resolution summary of historical tickets. ReACT system [3] performs an involved natural language processing to help create resolution sequences for ticket categories in a semi-automated way. However all the above mentioned systems analyze only the text part of the ticket. Analysis of images have not been dealt with in these systems.

In another body of work, there is a focus on the ticket dispatch and resolver group aspects. SmartDispatch [2] provides a solution for automated ticket dispatch using Support Vector Machines and discriminative keyword approach. Historical data on agents and their current workloads is used for ticket dispatch in [4]. More recently, the system in [14] uses a combination of rule engine and ensemble classifier to achieve very high accuracy in resolver group prediction. However none of these works analyze the screenshots and attachments that often contain vital information.

There are also systems which have looked solely at the problem of mining information from images. However most of the literature deals with mining, extracting or summarizing information from natural images which cannot be used directly due to the challenges stated in Sect. 1. There is very little work done in the past which focuses on extracting information from technical screenshots. Anand et al. [17] is one such paper. However, it only mines the screenshots to broadly classify the application and does not deal with occlusion and text correlation. Senthil et al. [15] proposes a Question-Answering (QA) system for ticket resolution where they look at image screenshots containing error. However the system has looked at specific types of errors (SAP) and rely solely on OCR to retrieve errors from images. These systems also do not handle occlusion and text inferences.

We have not come across any work that performs multi-modal(text+image) analysis on ticket data addressing the challenges of occlusion, text enrichment and correlation like we have done in this paper. Our proposed approach is generic enough to be applied to chatbots and QA systems.

3   Multi-modal Analysis in Incident Management

The traditional lifecycle of incident management has undergone massive changes in recent times due to the infusion of agent assist capabilities. The motivation is to (i) automate ticket assignment and resolution with high accuracy whenever possible and (ii) reduce the time taken to resolve in case of manual resolution. These objectives are primarily achieved through two functional modules viz. Ticket Enrichment and Resolution Recommendation. The incident management lifecycle with agent assist capabilities is depicted in Fig. 2. The ticket enrichment module uses models trained on historical data to enrich ticket data with knowledge inferred from the ticket data. The resolution recommendation module leverages the enriched ticket information to predict the most accurate resolution with high confidence. Once the ticket is augmented with inferred knowledge on resolution and problem category, it is stored in the system and the agents can leverage it for speedy resolution.

We now explain how the ticket enrichment is done using multi-modal analysis, that is, combined analysis of text and image present in the ticket. We also explain

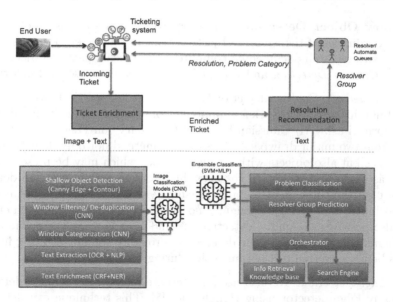

Fig. 2. System architecture

the proposed multi-step process for resolution recommendation which can choose the source of resolution based on the confidence on its own knowledge.

3.1   Ticket Enrichment

Often users are unaware of the exact problem or do not know what all details might be important for solving the problem and end up not specifying relevant information. For example, in a lot of IT support tickets the name of the operating system, application, version and other important contextual information are omitted. Without these information it may be difficult to drill down to the exact problem category and resolver group. Thus, we augment the text data with context information and insights obtained from the image data to create a better ticket which helps in improving the prediction of resolver group and problem category leading to faster ticket resolution. The different stages of the ticket enrichment pipeline are described in detail below.

Image Understanding: The image understanding part analyzes the attachment image and extracts artifacts which are used for understanding the image properties. The most important information in a screenshot is usually contained within one of the application windows. Therefore, one of the key functionalities of our system is to detect an application window. We also classify the detected window based on its type e.g. browser/IDE, console or dialog/message box. We now describe the image understanding steps below.

i. Shallow Object Detection: The objective of this stage is to detect the precise coordinates of the window objects present in the screenshots. We experimented with two well documented computer vision techniques for object detection viz. *Contour Detection* and *Canny Edge detection* as described below.

Contour Detection: Contour detection [12] is used to detect objects with both linear and non-linear contours. Before applying contour detection the input image is transformed using (i) Gaussian blur and (ii) binary conversion. This method suffers from two major drawbacks. Firstly, this method not only detects rectangular boxes but also objects with irregular shapes which may be present in the picture as illustrated in Fig. 1. To solve this problem we use a shape detector to detect relevant objects of rectangular shape. But this still does not exclude the possibility of detecting rectangular non-window objects, so we often end up with false positives. Secondly, detection of window fails when the colors of the background and the object to be detected are roughly similar resulting in both objects being converted to the same color during binarization.

Canny Edge Detection: We also use an alternate method for window detection viz. Canny Edge detector using Hough lines [8]. This technique can detect all horizontal and vertical lines in a picture and as such can be used to detect regular geometrical shapes e.g. triangles or rectangles. Before applying canny edge detector we convert the image to grayscale. The detected lines are clustered based on their coordinates to detect rectangular shapes. However canny edge detection fails when windows do not have clear demarcating lines. Also in some cases canny edge detection ends up mining spurious boxes as shown in Fig. 1.

To increase the accuracy of shallow detection we use an ensemble of both techniques. However, even with the ensemble the precision is low as none of the shallow detection methods look at the internal structure of the window. To reduce false positives and improve precision we use a filtering step as described below.

ii. Window Filtering/Deduplication: We use different filtering technologies to remove spurious and duplicate windows detected in the previous step. We first use a size based filter to remove all windows which are smaller than a threshold. This removes GUI artifacts like radio buttons, alert/minimize/cancel icons etc. We then use a CNN based binary image classifier on the filtered boxes to classify whether the box is an actual application window or not. We use a CNN based binary classification model, which is trained using screen shots of end-user problems downloaded from the net and also on synthetically generated windows. For feature extraction we use ResNet50 model [10] pre-trained with ImageNet weights. We prefer using ResNet50 architecture over VGG19 [18] as it uses skip connections to handle the problem of vanishing gradients. For classification we added two fully connected layers. The classifier layer was fine tuned during training and feature extractor layer was frozen. Our model is able to indicate presence/absence of application window with an accuracy of about 95%.

Finally we apply a de-duplication step to remove duplicate windows. Since both shallow detection techniques are applied independently and in parallel there is the possibility of detecting the same window twice. Duplicate windows can be detected based on the coordinates of the enclosing rectangle and calculating the area of overlap using IOU metric.

iii. Deep Learning Based Window Categorization. In this stage of the pipeline we try to categorize the detected windows as well as identify certain window properties for deeper understanding of the image. Previously there has been work on identifying application name and other properties from text part of the image [15]. However in the case where one or more application windows are overlapped the text in the background window will be occluded and may not be useful for extraction. We take the help of deep learning to try and identify these properties upfront.

We make use of two separate classifiers for this step. The first classifier is used for classification of windows into specific categories to identify the application type. We support only a few selected applications as of now but our classifier can be easily extended to support more applications. The second classifier is used to determine the OS (Windows, Linux, Mac). We used 1 CNN block having a convolution layer followed by ReLU activation, max-pooling and batch normalization for feature extraction followed by two fully-connected (FC) layers for classification.

Text Extraction from Images: Once the window categorization and segmentation phase is over, text is detected and recognized using Tesseract OCR [16] from the detected application windows. Since we are dealing with screenshots, the resolution of the image was not an issue. Due to challenges of overlapping windows/boxes or errors in window detection, the text extraction is not accurate. We use two different types of post-processing on the recognized text. Firstly we use a dictionary based post-processing step (using edit-distance) to correct spellings errors for application names or title boxes. For longer text (e.g. dialog box, console logs etc) we use a word-level language model trained on a very large data of logs and error messages from stack-overflow. This language model not only helps us improve word error rates but also predicts words in occluded windows. We observed in our results that if the text is occluded by a line, we were able to recover it but if the box suffers from a higher overlap the text does not get fully recovered even by the language model.

Ticket Text Enrichment: In this step, we enrich the ticket text with information extracted from the image. However we cannot directly use all the text extracted from the image for ticket enrichment. In order to extract key terms and entities we use a Conditional Random Fields (CRF) based Named Entity Recognition (NER) system [9] on both ticket text as well as all text extracted from images. This extractive system gives us terms such as name of operating system(OS), application/product name, components being mentioned, version numbers, error codes, error messages and other entities such as symptoms or important mentions from log screenshots. For OS name, application name and components, domain specific dictionaries are used and for version and error codes we use regular expression based extraction. For the other attributes such as symptom, activity, action and advise we use deep parsing and understanding [9]. We then correlate these entities with the information obtained from the image to retain only the most relevant parts of the image information. The resulting text is then inserted into the ticket using slot-based templates for ticket completion. The slot templates can differ based on the resolver group. The examples below illustrate the technique of slot-filling for ticket enrichment. The enriched parts of the email are enclosed within square braces and the slot names are mentioned in angular braces along with the corresponding values.

Example1: "Dear sir, My postpaid mobile [**<mobile-no>** = **xxx3224**] having relationship number [**<customer-no>** = **xxx**], billing plan [**<billing-plan>** = **infinityxxx**] has been overcharged with international roaming services [**<pack-details>** = **international roaming XXX nrc**] for the billing period [**<period>** = **08-jan-2019 to 07-feb-2019**] which was not activated by me. You can clearly find the same in the screen shot of bill details sent. Please refund me the overcharged charges asap. Regards, xxx xxx mobile -- xxx3224"

Example2: "I am getting an error [**<errmsg>** = **An error occurred during the installation of assembly component HRESULT: 0x800736FD**] with error code [**< errcode>** = **Error 1935**], while installing [**<appname>** = **Crystal Reports Runtime Engine**] for .Net on [**<os>** = **Windows**] [**<osver>** = **10**]. Please see attached screenshot"

3.2   Resolution Recommendation System

For resolution of tickets we use a recommendation engine which reads the tickets enhanced with information from the ticket enrichment module, understands the user intent and uses it to suggest the most relevant resolver group and resolution(s). The recommendation system is trained using a corpus of historical tickets T which is divided into two parts viz. T_H (*short head*) and T_L (*long tail*). T_H contains the most frequently occurring problem categories having a well known resolution and typically accounts for 75–80% of the tickets. T_L constitutes the rarely occurring problem categories for which a well curated resolution may or may not be present in our training corpus. The division of tickets is done according to the following equation:

$$T = T_H + T_L \tag{1}$$

$$T_H = \bigcup_{p_i \in P_H} T_{p_i} \tag{2}$$

where P_H is the set of problem categories in short head and T_{p_i} is the set of tickets belonging to the problem category p_i. It's important to note that problem category may be a composite field in the ticketing system. In this case we concatenate the constituent sub-field labels to obtain the unique problem category for training.

To select P_H we plot a histogram of frequencies for problem category and select the ones which are above a configured threshold. We also do some post processing to filter out those categories which do not have well defined resolutions. We use separate strategies for resolving the *short head* and the *long tail* tickets as described below.

Ticket Classification: The objective of ticket classification is to predict the resolver group and the problem category. We train an ensemble classifier using only the data in T_H. This reduces noise in training data and also eliminates class imbalance problem [13]. For the ensemble classifier we use simple classification models viz. Linear SVM (ovr) and MLP (feed forward neural nets) for easy deployability and retraining [13]. We plotted the accuracy and coverage of the selected classifiers against different confidence thresholds and selected the optimal threshold value to ensure that both classifiers in the ensemble operate at least at human level efficiency [13].

Ticket Resolution: To obtain a resolution at runtime we first use our ensemble classifiers to predict the resolver group and problem category. If both these fields are predicted with high confidence at runtime it means that the problem category belongs to the short head. In this case we return a resolution directly using a simple database lookup. If the confidence score for the resolver-group or the problem category is low then we resort to our long tail approach which queries the knowledge corpus ingested through an information retrieval infrastructure (e.g. Watson Discovery). We observe that while we have a resolution available for most frequent short head queries, we may not have them for infrequent or unseen queries. To handle this case, we use a web search and combine the retrieved resolutions with web search results using the enriched ticket description as query. We re-rank the combined results and present the top N results to the user. For this, we use a federated search algorithm.

We build a resource representation for ticket content and web resources by sampling tickets and related web search documents respectively. For each, we compute the unigram distribution of terms. Using this unigram language model, we compute the relevance score for tickets as well as for resources from web. We then use the CORI result merging algorithm [20] to merge the results using the relevance scores to obtain the final ranked list as shown in Eq. 3, where d is the normalized score given by the search engine and c is the relevance score computed by the language model.

$$result\_score = \frac{d + 0.4 \times c \times d}{1.4} \tag{3}$$

The different steps in the resolution process is orchestrated by the **orchestrator** which is the key computational module of the recommendation system. The complete ticket resolution process is explained in detail in Algorithm 1.

4 Dataset Details and Experiment Setup

4.1 IT Support Ticket Data

Our evaluation is based on a ticketing dataset having a corpus of 712320 support tickets from 428 resolver groups and spanning 3728 distinct problem categories as shown in Table 1. Out of this corpus 159344 tickets (approx. 22.37%) had attachments. However for this paper we limited our scope to a small subset of this dataset mainly because the image understanding part of our system currently does not handle all possible type of applications. To select our experimental dataset we chose 10 resolver groups with the maximum amount of screenshot attachments. Out of these resolver groups we chose the most frequently occurring 33 problem categories for our short head training dataset. The remaining tickets accounting for 219 problem categories constitutes the long tail. The total number of multimodal tickets in our curated dataset is 25000.

Algorithm 1: Ticket Resolution Algorithm

Input   : Enriched ticket text
Output: result = [resolv_grp,
           prob_category, resolution]

1 **Function**
  ticket-assignment-resolution(
  Enriched-Email-Text):

2 final_result = [None, [], []]

3 classification =
   InvokeCombinedClassifier(
   Enriched-Email-Text)

4 **if** *(classification.conf_resolv_grp >*
   CONF_RESOLV_CUTOFF) and
   (classification.conf_prob_category
   > CONF_PROB_CUTOFF) **then**
   /* short head - directly
      lookup resolution result */

5   resolution = lookup(resolutionDB,
    classification.prob_category)

6   final_result =
    [classification.resolv_grp,
    classification.prob_category,
    resolution]

7 **else**
   /* invoke long tail strategy
      */

8   filter_fields = []

9   **if** *classification.conf_resolv_grp*
    > CONF_RESOLV_CUTOFF
    then

10   filter_fields += resolv_grp

11   final_resolv_grp =
     classification.resolv_grp

1

12 **else**
   /* Assign ticket to manual
      queue   */

13 final_resolv_grp = None

14 **for** *each subfield in*
   PROBLEM_CATEGORY_FIELD
   do

15 result =
    InvokeProblemClassifier(subfield,
    Enriched-Email-Text)

16 **if** *result.conf_subfield >*
    CONF_SUBFIELD_CUTOFF
    then

17   filter_fields += subfield

   /* invoke Information
      Retrieval and web search in
      parallel and combine/rerank
      results   */

18 searchRes = InvokeSearch(
    filter=filter_fields,
    text=Enriched-Email-Text)

19 webSearchRes = InvokeWebSearch(
    Enriched-Email-Text)

20 fedSearchRes =
    InvokeFederatedSearch(
    Enriched-Email-text, searchRes,
    webSearchRes)

21 final_result = [final_resolv_grp,
    fedSearchRes.prob_category,
    fedSearchRes.resolution]

22 **return** final_result

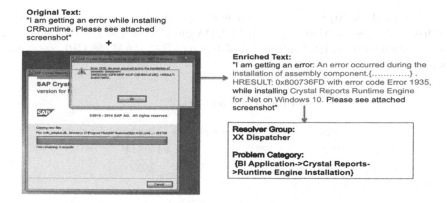

Fig. 3. Illustrative example

4.2   Image Data

Collection: The image data for our training is mainly obtained from the attachments in the ticketing dataset. However to increase the volume for training as well as to get more variety in training data we also scraped relevant images from the web (Google Images). We used a search filter to download images for only selected applications. Apart from this we also generated synthetic screenshot images using a python library (pySimpleGUI). Using this library we can easily control image parameters like size and coordinates of the generated window, text content, size and count of radio buttons etc.

Augmentation: To enhance the size of our training set we used both offline and online image augmentation. We perform the following transformations on each image to generate new images offline, viz. changing brightness and contrast levels, conversion to grayscale and resizing. Apart from these transformations we also use Keras augmentation API for further augmentation of the images during the training process.

Annotation: Annotation of image data is a laborious process as it involves manual annotation of bounding boxes for windows as well as embedded image text. For both these types of annotation we used automation.

For bounding box annotation we used shallow object detection technique described in 3.1. This method of annotation works on most images. However whenever images contain windows with high degree of overlap and confusing images in the background the annotation may not be entirely correct. In these cases we do a manual inspection and annotation.

For getting ground truth data on image text we primarily use synthetically generated screenshots with pre-defined text content. In this case both the window and the text are generated by our script and no manual annotation is necessary. For real screenshots, we first perform OCR on the image and then manually correct the extracted text to generate groundtruth.

Experimental Setup: For our deep learning based experiments we used a NVIDIA Tesla K80 GPU cluster with 4 CUDA-enabled nodes. For the remaining experiments we used a IBM softlayer VM having 256G RAM, 56 CPU cores and 100G HDD.

Table 1. Dataset details

	Total tickets	Problem categories	Multimodal tickets
Overall	712230	3728	159344
Selected	42882	252	25000

Table 2. Accuracy of shallow object detection

Method	1-Window(P,R)	2-windows(P,R)	3-windows(P,R)
Contour	70%,76%	62%,78%	57%,68%
Canny edge	43%,82%	53%,80%	48%,64%
Ensemble+Filter	90%,89%	90%,86%	92%,72%

Table 3. Accuracy of image classification

Method	Window filtering	Operating system	Application category
VGG19	92.3%	91.5%	85.7%
ResNet50	94.9%	94.1%	90.8%

Table 4. Dataset accuracy

	Text only	Multimodal
Assignment(acc/cov)	86.1%,89.3%	88.6%,96.5%
Resolution	74.7%	82.4%

5   Evaluation

Figure 3 illustrates the working of our pipeline with a real example. The bounding boxes detected by our system are indicated in green while those which are filtered out after detection are indicated in red. Interestingly shallow object detection detects the green sliding status bar which is eventually filtered by our deep learning based window filtering technique. Our system is not only able to detect the error message box correctly but also the box in background which has relevant context information. We highlight some of the important context information picked up by our system. Combining the information in the detected windows the system is able to suggest the most relevant troubleshooting page for the error. Evaluation of the different functional stages of our multimodal analysis pipeline is presented below.

Detection of Windows: To detect window objects we first experimented with DL based object detection. However we observed that training the object detection algorithm using traditional image datasets like MSCOCO [11] and ImageNet [7] does not result in high accuracy. One of the reasons is that deep learning based methods usually need a large number of training samples and it is difficult to obtain such a large corpus to train. Also the objects in these datasets correspond to natural images with widely different features than those available in screenshots.

As far as shallow object detection is concerned both canny edge detection and contour detection suffer from the problem of high recall/low precision. This is because both these methods detect objects without understanding the internal structure resulting in false positives. However a combination of the techniques improves both precision and recall significantly as shown in Table 2.

Image Classification: For our DL based image classification models we experimented with various hyper-parameters like learning rate(LR), filters, filter size, number of neurons etc. We found LR to be the topmost contributor in accuracy. We ran LR range test and plotted the accuracy versus LR, noting the LR value when the accuracy starts to increase and when the accuracy becomes ragged [19]. Our results in Table 3 indicate very high accuracy (more than 90%) for image classification with ResNet50. Since the images have large inter-class variance and small intra-class variance we also experimented with shallow CNNs and VGG19. However, with limited amount of training data ResNet50 (with pre-trained weights) proved to be a better choice than its shallow counterparts. The result means our system can identify the application type and OS accurately in more than 90% of the cases even when window text is occluded.

Text Extraction: We evaluated the correctness of our text extraction technique using mainly synthetic images to avoid manual annotation. Synthetic images with pre-defined text content were generated using OpenCV python libraries and the generated text was compared with that obtained from OCR. We used two different OCR techniques for our evaluation viz. Watson Visual Recognition and Tesseract, out of which Tesseract performed better. Our OCR technique was observed to have more than 95% accuracy (character level). However we also manually corroborated the results with real data for a few images.

Routing/Resolution: To evaluate the accuracy of resolution we look at the classification results for resolver group and problem category. As routing is a key step in the resolution of the ticket we have to ensure that routing of the ticket is improved by our multimodal analysis technique.

Also, the most important step in obtaining the resolution strategy is to understand the correct problem category of the ticket as in most cases, the problem category has a one-to-one mapping with the resolution strategy. Even if that is not the case, identifying the correct problem category is a key step in automated resolution as it narrows down the scope of the search. As such we estimate the accuracy of resolution with the accuracy achieved in predicting the problem category in both the short head and long tail cases. The results are shown in Table 4. For our dataset the *problem category* is a composite field constituting three sub-fields. We consider the identified problem category to be accurate if and only if all the three sub-fields were identified correctly. Using this metric we achieved an overall accuracy of 82.4% with multimodal, an improvement of about 8% over text based analysis. In fact, for some problem categories belonging to the long tail the observed improvement was more than 50% proving that multimodal analysis is helpful in automated resolution of tickets. Prediction accuracy of resolver group also improves by about 2.5% but more importantly the automation coverage increases by more than 7% as more tickets are predicted with higher confidence. Considering that these improvements are over and above an already deployed system (using text-based analysis), the numbers are significant.

5.1 Impact to Incident Management Process

We calculate the impact to the incident management process based on two aspects viz. Routing and Resolution. For our dataset the incoming rate of tickets is approximately 100,000 per month. We assume that a human agent takes about 3 min to read and assign each ticket and 10 min to actually resolve the ticket. On the basis of the above assumptions the net savings for an account can be calculated as:

$$S_{assign} = N \times T_{cov} \times 3 \qquad (4)$$

$$S_{resolve} = N \times R_{cov} \times 10 \qquad (5)$$

where N is the total number of tickets per annum, T_{cov} is the coverage for automated routing, R_{cov} is the coverage for automated resolution, S_{assign} is the net savings from routing and $S_{resolve}$ is the net savings from resolution. This gives a total saving of about 194,000 man hours per annum assuming $T_{cov} = 90\%$ and $R_{cov} = 80\%$

6   Conclusion and Future Work

In this paper we have presented an end-to-end system which can analyze image content in ticket attachments, enrich ticket text and automatically suggest a resolution. As of now we have limited our scope to analyzing only images with screenshots. In reality there may be many different types of attachments with varying properties and user intent. Some of these images may require deep understanding of the layout or semantic structure of the image. For example, sales related support issues may require processing of invoices containing tables, bar charts etc having a specific layout. Without understanding the layout we cannot analyze the document for troubleshooting. In the future we will look at advanced computer vision techniques to understand and analyze such types of attachments.

References

1. Agarwal, S., Aggarwal, V., Akula, A.R., Dasgupta, G.B., Sridhara, G.: Automatic problem extraction and analysis from unstructured text in IT tickets. IBM J. Res. Dev. **61**(1), 4:41–4:52 (2017)
2. Agarwal, S., Sindhgatta, R., Sengupta, B.: SmartDispatch: enabling efficient ticket dispatch in an IT service environment. In: 18th ACM SIGKDD (2012)
3. Aggarwal, V., Agarwal, S., Dasgupta, G.B., Sridhara, G., Vijay, E.: ReAct: a system for recommending actions for rapid resolution of IT service incidents. In: IEEE International Conference on Services Computing, SCC 2016 (2016)
4. Botezatu, M.M., Bogojeska, J., Giurgiu, I., Voelzer, H., Wiesmann, D.: Multi-view incident ticket clustering for optimal ticket dispatching. In: 21st ACM SIGKDD International Conference on Knowledge Discovery and Data Mining, KDD 2015, pp. 1711–1720 (2015)
5. Canny, J.: A computational approach to edge detection. IEEE Trans. Pattern Anal. Mach. Intell. **8**(6), 679–698 (1986)
6. Dasgupta, G.B., Nayak, T.K., Akula, A.R., Agarwal, S., Nadgowda, S.J.: Towards auto-remediation in services delivery: context-based classification of noisy and unstructured tickets. In: Franch, X., Ghose, A.K., Lewis, G.A., Bhiri, S. (eds.) ICSOC 2014. LNCS, vol. 8831, pp. 478–485. Springer, Heidelberg (2014). https://doi.org/10.1007/978-3-662-45391-9_39
7. Deng, J., Dong, W., Socher, R., Li, L.J., Li, K., Fei-Fei, L.: ImageNet: a large-scale hierarchical image database. In: CVPR09 (2009)
8. Duda, R.O., Hart, P.E.: Use of the hough transformation to detect lines and curves in pictures. Commun. ACM **15**(1), 11–15 (1972)
9. Gupta, A., Ray, A., Dasgupta, G., Singh, G., Aggarwal, P., Mohapatra, P.: Semantic parsing for technical support questions. In: COLING, Santa Fe, New Mexico, USA, August 2018
10. He, K., Zhang, X., Ren, S., Sun, J.: Deep residual learning for image recognition. In: 2016 IEEE Conference on Computer Vision and Pattern Recognition (CVPR) (2016)
11. Lin, T.-Y., et al.: Microsoft COCO: common objects in context. In: Fleet, D., Pajdla, T., Schiele, B., Tuytelaars, T. (eds.) ECCV 2014. LNCS, vol. 8693, pp. 740–755. Springer, Cham (2014). https://doi.org/10.1007/978-3-319-10602-1_48
12. Maire, M.R.: Contour detection and image segmentation. Ph.D. thesis (2009)
13. Mandal, A., Malhotra, N., Agarwal, S., Ray, A., Sridhara, G.: Cognitive system to achieve human-level accuracy in automated assignment of helpdesk email tickets. ArXiv e-prints, August 2018
14. Mandal, A., Malhotra, N., Agarwal, S., Ray, A., Sridhara, G.: Cognitive system to achieve human-level accuracy in automated assignment of helpdesk email tickets. In: Pahl, C., Vukovic, M., Yin, J., Yu, Q. (eds.) ICSOC 2018. LNCS, vol. 11236, pp. 332–341. Springer, Cham (2018). https://doi.org/10.1007/978-3-030-03596-9_23
15. Mani, S., et al.: Hi, how can I help you? automating enterprise IT support help desks CoRR abs/1711.02012 (2017). http://arxiv.org/abs/1711.02012
16. Mori, S., Nishida, H., Yamada, H.: Optical Character Recognition. Wiley, New York (1999)
17. Sampat, A., Haskell, A.: CNN for task classification using computer screenshots for integration into dynamic calendar/task management systems. http://cs231n.stanford.edu/reports/2015/pdfs/anand_avery_final.pdf

18. Simonyan, K., Zisserman, A.: Very deep convolutional networks for large-scale image recognition. In: International Conference on Learning Representations (2015)
19. Smith, L.: Cyclical Learning Rates for Training Neural Networks, pp. 464–472, March 2017
20. Xu, J., Callan, J.: Effective retrieval with distributed collections. In: Proceedings of the 21st Annual International ACM SIGIR Conference on Research and Development in Information Retrieval, SIGIR 1998, pp. 112–120. ACM (1998)
21. Zhou, W., Tang, L., Zeng, C., Li, T., Shwartz, L., Ya. Grabarnik, G.: Resolution recommendation for event tickets in service management. IEEE Trans. Netw. Serv. Manage. **13**(4), 954–967 (2016)
22. Zhou, W., et al.: Star: a system for ticket analysis and resolution. In: Proceedings of the 23rd ACM SIGKDD International Conference on Knowledge Discovery and Data Mining, KDD 2017, pp. 2181–2190 (2017)

A Recommendation of Crowdsourcing Workers Based on Multi-community Collaboration

Zhifang Liao[1], Xin Xu[1], Peng Lan[1], Jun Long[1(✉)], and Yan Zhang[2]

[1] Department of Software Engineering, School of Computer Science and Engineering, Central South University, Changsha, China
{zfliao,jlong}@csu.edu.cn, xuxin_1996@126.com,
lanpeng5@qq.com
[2] Glasgow Caledonian University, Glasgow, UK
yan.zhang@gcu.ac.uk

Abstract. Currently there are problems such as fuzzy workers' characteristics and complex human relations existing on many crowdsourcing platforms, which lead to the difficulty in the recommendation of workers to complete tasks on crowdsourcing platforms. Aiming at worker recommendations in categorical tasks on crowdsourcing platforms, this paper proposes a recommendation considering workers' multi-community characteristics. It takes factors such as worker's reputation, preference and activity into consideration. Finally, based on the characteristics of community intersections, it recommends Top-N workers. The results show the recommendations generated by the algorithm proposed in this paper performs the best comprehensively.

Keywords: Crowdsourcing · Recommendation · Community discovery

1 Introduction

Crowdsourcing is an open call for online workers and a distributed problem-solving mechanism. Through the combination of computers and unknown online workers, it has completed tasks which cannot be completed by computers only [1]. The concept of crowdsourcing was put forward by Jeff Howe in June, 2006 [2]. Its major participators include Requester and Worker, connected by Human Intelligence Tasks (HIT).

At present, there are many methods for the crowdsourcing recommendation, such as the Recommendation based on collaborative filtering, the Recommendation based on the content of tasks, etc. However, most recommendations proposed by the existing literature are based on workers' skills [3], and some other recommendations only considered workers' interests, preferences or task characteristics [4, 5].

In view of the problems above, the paper proposes a recommendation of crowd workers based on multi-community collaboration in the categorical tasks.

The main contributions of this paper are as follows:

1. The first attempt to explore the multi-community characteristics among workers.
2. A Recommendation of workers that comprehensively considers workers' ability, activity, preference and community properties.

© Springer Nature Switzerland AG 2019
S. Yangui et al. (Eds.): ICSOC 2019, LNCS 11895, pp. 447–451, 2019.
https://doi.org/10.1007/978-3-030-33702-5_34

The rest of this paper is organized as follows. Section 2 discusses the related works. Section 3 introduces the recommendation of workers based on multi-community characteristics. Section 4 elaborates on experiments and results analysis. Section 5 draws the conclusion and shows the future work.

2 Related Work

The concept of crowdsourcing has undergone more than ten years since it was put forward. People have conducted a plenty of researches and studies that mainly focused on the task selection, result inference [7, 12], workers' behavior analysis [6] and so on.

To date, studies on task recommendation are mainly based on traditional recommendations, including the content-based recommendation [8], collaborative filtering (CF) [9], and a hybrid of the two. Zhang et al. proposed a task recommendation based on 2-tuple fuzzy linguistic method [10], the platform recommends tasks to workers who are willing to accept them and capable to complete them. Sun et al. used the negative exponential learning curve model [3] to simulate the skill improvement of developers and then recommend developers through the predictions of the learning curve. For a worker's performance in different types of HITs, combined with similarity metric and trust subnet extraction algorithm, Ye et al. [11] put forward a new worker recommendation based on trust-aware model.

Based on previous work, this paper proposes a Recommendation of workers Based on Multi-community Collaboration (RBMC). The RBMC not only considers the workers' attributes used in traditional recommendations, but also considers workers' other personal characteristics and their characteristics shown in the communities.

3 Recommendation Process

3.1 Constructing the Worker Community Model

The core of the RBMC algorithm lies in discovering the latent characteristics of reputation, activity and preference, and classifying workers into different communities.

Constructing the Worker Ability Matrix. For the multi-class crowdsourcing tasks, Bayesian Network [12] model reasonably describes the dependence between classes, which brings out the good performance. Therefore, the Bayesian Network is chosen to do the aggregation of tags after the classification.

Consider that there are K workers classifying N objects into J possible classes. The row vector $\pi_j^{(k)} = \left\{ \pi_{j,1}^{(k)}, \pi_{j,2}^{(k)}, \ldots, \pi_{j,J}^{(k)} \mid \sum_{l=1}^{J} \pi_{j,l}^{(k)} = 1 \right\}$ of the confusion matrix derives from the Dirichlet distribution. Therefore, each worker w_i has a confusion matrix $\pi^{(k)}$ of size $J \times J$. Hence, the original model of the group of workers can be expressed as $\theta = \{\pi; \varphi\} = \left\{ \pi^1, \pi^2, \ldots, \pi^K; \varphi_1, \ldots, \varphi_K \right\}$, where φ_i is the corresponding parameter of the worker's tag in Dirichlet distribution.

The Evaluation of Workers' Reputation. Calculating the Kappa coefficient k of workers' confusion matrix π^i, and use it as a worker's reputation Rpt_i. Based on the Gaussian distribution features of the worker, we use T-check to work out the confidence interval when the confidence degree is 95% and classify workers into clusters in turn.

$$
CBRi = \begin{cases}
0 & , \quad Rpt_i < 0.5 \\
avg\left(\sum_{i \in L_2}^{m_{low}} Rpt_i\right) & , \quad 0.5 \le Rpt_i < \overline{Rpt} - \frac{S_{RP}}{\sqrt{n}} t_{\frac{z}{2}}(n-1) \\
avg\left(\sum_{i \in L_3}^{m_{nor}} Rpt_i\right) & , \quad \overline{Rpt} - \frac{S_{RP}}{\sqrt{n}} t_{\frac{z}{2}}(n-1) \le Rpt_i < \overline{Rpt} + \frac{S_{RP}}{\sqrt{n}} t_{\frac{z}{2}}(n-1) \\
avg\left(\sum_{i \in L_4}^{m_{high}} Rpt_i\right) & , \quad \overline{Rpt} + \frac{S_{RP}}{\sqrt{n}} t_{\frac{z}{2}}(n-1) \le Rpt_i
\end{cases}
\tag{1}
$$

where $\overline{Rpt}$ indicates the average reputation value of workers, and S_{Rp} stands for the standard deviation of distribution.

According to the distribution, the workers are divided into four cluster: malicious passing, normal, excellent. Hence the clusters based on workers' reputation communities are obtained, from which the community of workers with high reputation are found.

Discovering the Workers' Preference Community. This paper introduces the preference characteristics to build relations among workers, and divides workers into communities according to their task preference characteristics.

According to the clustering effects, we determine the quantity of clusters and get the distribution of each clusters in communities of workers' preference,

$$
CBP_i = \{\pi_{c,j}^{\hat{L}_p} | c, j \in J; i \in L_p; \pi^i \in \overline{\theta'_p}\}
\tag{2}
$$

where L_p means the crowd of workers in preference communities, $\pi_{c,k}^{\hat{L}_p}$ is the center node of cluster p, and θ'_p is the crowd distribution model in the cluster.

The Assessment of Workers' Activity. Similarly, we divide workers into "Less active", "Normal" and "Highly active". Finally, we obtain the distribution of communities based on workers' activity and discover the latent highly active community.

Constructing a Worker Model. We use $w_i \rightarrow \{\pi^i, Rpt_i, Act_i, CBR_i, CBP_i, CBA_i\}$ storage worker model, where π^i is the ability matrix, Rpt_i is the reputation value, Act_i is the activity, CBR_i is the worker clusters based on reputation, CBP_i is the worker clusters based on preference community, and CBA_i is the worker clusters based on activity.

3.2   Generating the Recommended List

According to the procedures above, the relatively stable high-quality community and highly active community can be found from historical data. Moreover, when the platform receives the new task set, combined with the pull mechanism in task assignment, it is easier to discover the latent characteristics of a new task through the characteristics of the workers who accept it, and to match them to the specific preference community.

In the process of recommending workers in the real world, some latent characteristics of clustered workers should be considered more, and crossover analysis based on clusters classified in accordance with different standards is used to obtain the optimal worker list that meets various criteria.

4   The Experiments and Their Results Analysis

In experiments, we uses the public data collected by AMT (WS-AMT). In order to illustrate the scientificity and validity of the Recommendation, the experiments aim to answer the following 2 questions:

Q2: How to construct a worker model and discover the latent worker communities?
Q3: What is the performance of this method proposed in this paper?

4.1   Experimental Design and Result Analysis

Experiment 1 (constructing a worker model). Based on WS-AMT dataset, the experiment employs Bayesian Network model to build worker ability matrix that describes the distribution rule of workers' answers to historical tasks.

After K-means clustering, workers are divided into 6 clusters with obvious distribution characteristics. We define these clusters as workers' preference communities. Figure 1 shows the visualized results of center nodes in each preference communities. The igher the value on the diagonal, the higher precision a worker has in completing corresponding type of tasks. For example, workers in community 2 perform better to complete tasks of type 3 or type 5.

In addition, when constructing a worker model, it is necessary to comprehensively consider the characteristics of workers' reputation, activity and preference.

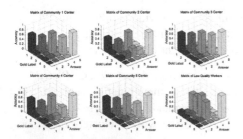

Fig. 1. Visualized matrix of center nodes in workers' preference communities

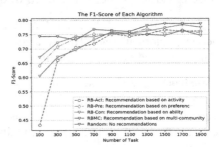

Fig. 2. Aggregation results of recommended data generated

Experiment 2 (evaluating algorithm). In the experiment, we select Top-10 workers list to generate recommendations, the RBMC algorithm is evaluated and compared with three recommendations based on traditional indicators.

From Fig. 2 we can see that the algorithm accuracy is improved after we considered anyone of workers' characteristic of precision, activity and preference. However, the RBMC that considers both worker behaviors and community characteristics has higher values than other algorithms.

5 Conclusion and Prospect

The focus of this paper is a new recommendation of workers based on multi-community collaboration, aiming to recommend a group of workers suitable for completing tasks on crowdsourcing platforms through worker behavior analysis and community classification. The experimental results show that, in terms of various indexes, the RBMC proposed in this paper performs better obviously than the traditional recommendations based on a single characteristic.

In the future, we will try to optimize recommendation process so as to make it more real time, and optimize tag aggregation algorithm to improve the aggregation precision.

References

1. Kucherbaev, P., Daniel, F., Tranquillini, S., Marchese, M.: Crowdsourcing processes: a survey of approaches and opportunities. IEEE Internet Comput. **20**(2), 50–56 (2016)
2. Howe, J.: The rise of crowdsourcing. Wired Mag. **14**(6), 1–4 (2006)
3. Wang, Z., Sun, H., Fu, Y., Ye, L.: Recommending crowdsourced software developers in consideration of skill improvement. In: 2017 32nd IEEE/ACM International Conference on Automated Software Engineering (ASE), pp. 717–722 (2017)
4. Zhang, Y., Qian, Y., Wang, Y.: A recommendation algorithm based on dynamic user preference and service quality. In: 2018 IEEE International Conference on Web Services (ICWS), pp. 91–98 (2018)
5. Qiuyan, Z., Yuan, Z., Chen, L.I., Yueyang, L.I.: Task recommendation method based on workers' interest and competency for crowdsourcing. Syst. Eng. Theory Pract. **37**, 3270–3280 (2017)
6. Liao, Z., Zeng, Z., Zhang, Y., Fan, X.: A data-driven game theoretic strategy for developers in software crowdsourcing: a case study. Appl. Sci. **9**(4), 721 (2019)
7. Hu, H., Zheng, Y., Bao, Z., Li, G., Feng, J., Cheng, R.: Crowdsourced POI labelling: location-aware result inference and task assignment (2016)
8. Mao, K., Yang, Y., Wang, Q., Jia, Y., Harman, M.: Developer recommendation for crowdsourced software development tasks. In: 2015 IEEE Symposium on Service-Oriented System Engineering, pp. 347–356 (2015)
9. Nilashi, M., Ibrahim, O., Bagherifard, K.: A recommender system based on collaborative filtering using ontology and dimensionality reduction techniques. Expert Syst. Appl. **92**, 507–520 (2018)
10. Zhang, X., Su, J.: An approach to task recommendation in crowdsourcing based on 2-tuple fuzzy linguistic method. Kybernetes **47**(8), 1623–1641 (2018)
11. Ye, B., Wang, Y.: CrowdRec: trust-aware worker recommendation in crowdsourcing environments. In: 2016 IEEE International Conference on Web Services (ICWS), pp. 1–8 (2016)
12. Kim, H.C., Ghahramani, Z.: Bayesian classifier combination. In: Artificial Intelligence and Statistics, pp. 619–627 (2012)

Analysis of Resource Allocation of BPMN Processes

Francisco Durán[1]([✉]), Camilo Rocha[2], and Gwen Salaün[3]

[1] University of Málaga, Málaga, Spain
duran@lcc.uma.es
[2] Pontificia Universidad Javeriana, Cali, Colombia
[3] University of Grenoble Alpes, LIG, CNRS, Grenoble, France

Abstract. The approach for the modelling and analysis of resource allocation for business processes presented in this paper enables the automatic computation of measures for identifying the allocation of resources in business processes. The proposed analysis, especially suited to support decision-making strategies, is illustrated with a case study of a parcel ordering and delivery by drones that is developed throughout the paper. BPMN models are represented in Maude.

1 Introduction

This work presents first steps towards the development of a formal and automatic approach to resource allocation analysis for business process models. The approach comprises a formal yet executable specification in rewriting logic [3], a logic of concurrent computation, of a significant and expressive subset of the *Business Process Model and Notation* (BPMN) extended with time features and resources. By being executable in the Maude system [1], the specification supports the concurrent simulation of a process with different types of resources and with multiple replicas for any given workload. The analysis techniques for resource allocation use Maude's rewriting tools for evaluating expected values in the executable model — such as charge, occupancy, and usage percentage — by mechanically generating automatic simulations. The output of the automatic analysis can then be used to quantitatively assess the efficiency of the business process model, and thus guide a re-design or re-allocation of resources.

The overall idea is that multiple concurrent executions of a process compete for shared resources. Models are analyzed by observing how the resources' usage evolve over time when varying the workload and the number of available resources. This is done without an implementation of the system running on real resources: the input to the automatic analysis task is a BPMN model of the process workflow, enriched with a description of its timing behavior and resource

F. Durán was partly funded by project *PGC2018-094905-B-I00* (Spanish MINECO/FEDER), and by U. Málaga, Andalucía Tech. C. Rocha was partly supported by Colciencias-EcosNord project "FACTS: Foundational Approach to Cognition for Today's Systems" (63561).

S. Yangui et al. (Eds.): ICSOC 2019, LNCS 11895, pp. 452–457, 2019.
https://doi.org/10.1007/978-3-030-33702-5_35

availability. The BPMN models are described by means of activity and collaboration diagrams, four types of gateways (namely, inclusive, exclusive, parallel, and event-based), loops, unbalanced processes, event handling, and message-passing. The timing aspects of the models are specified by associating durations to each flow and task in the workflow, which can be sampled from a probability distribution function. Resource usage is specified by providing the amount of resources available and the resources required for the execution of tasks.

The usefulness of the approach is illustrated with an experiment, which supports the claim that such an analysis can help in detecting resource usage problems, thus ultimately leading to the improvement of the business process by optimizing its resource allocation. In particular, the experiment presented in this paper identifies low-level occupancy of resources and undesirable patterns of resource usage. They encompass sequential dependencies and bottlenecks provoked by some highly used resources that may induce performance fall-downs.

2   Business Process Model and Notation

Figure 1 presents a process describing a parcel ordering and delivery by drones. This BPMN process is presented as a collaboration diagram consisting of two pools, one for the client and another one for the order management and the delivery process; they are represented as lanes. This process includes different kinds of gateways, probabilities for choice gateways, stochastic functions for time associated to tasks, a loop, and unbalanced structures.

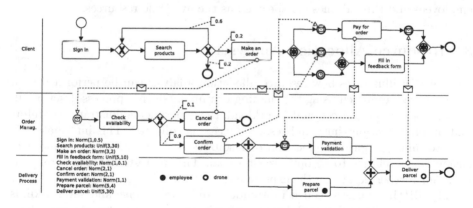

Fig. 1. Running example: parcel delivery by drones.

As usual, start and end events are used, respectively, to initialize and terminate processes. A task represents an atomic activity that has exactly one incoming and one outgoing flow. A task may have a duration (expressed as a stochastic expression) and may produce an event message. A sequence flow describes two nodes executed one after the other, i.e., by imposing an execution order with possible delays.

The timing information associated to tasks and flows (durations or delays) is described either as a literal value or sampled from a probability distribution function. Gateways (*exclusive, inclusive, parallel,* and *event-based*) are used to control the divergence and convergence of the execution flow. Gateways with one incoming (resp., outgoing) branch and multiple outgoing (resp., incoming) branches are called *splits* (resp., *merges*). Event-based split gateways may have a default branch fired by a timeout. Workflows with looping behavior are supported, as well as unbalanced workflows.

Data-based conditions for split gateways are modeled using probabilities associated to outgoing flows of exclusive and inclusive split gateways. For instance, notice the exclusive split after the Search products task in the Client lane of the running example, which has outgoing branches with probabilities 0.6, 0.2, and 0.2, specifying the likelihood of following each corresponding path.

Instead of implicitly associating resources to lanes, resources are explicitly defined at the task level, which is more general. A task that requires resources can include, as part of its specification, the number of required instances (or replicas) of a resource. The process in Fig. 1 relies on employees for parcel packing and drones for parcel delivery. Notice the colored circles at the bottom-right corner of the Prepare parcel and Deliver parcel tasks, indicating that one instance of the employee resource and another one of the drone resource are required, respectively, for the tasks completion. Several tasks could compete for the same resources (not the case in this example). Furthermore, since multiple instances of a process may be executed concurrently, all instances also access and compete for the shared resources. At the bottom-right corner of Fig. 1, a total of two employees and three drones are specified as the available resources.

3   Resource Allocation Analysis

This section illustrates how resource allocation analysis can be performed with the proposed approach using the running example. Given a process description, a specification of resources, and a workload, the experiments illustrate how information on execution times and resource usage is collected. This information is used to find the optimal allocation of resources that minimizes costs and execution times relative to an optimization goal. The interested reader is referred to [2] for further details on the experiments.

The BPMN subset encoded in Maude is quite expressive and several kinds of properties can be computed, including timing and resource-based ones. These properties are meaningful when executing multiple instances of a process that compete for the shared resources. As for *timing properties*, the approach presented in this paper allows the computation of average execution times (AET) of a process, its variance (Var), and the average synchronization time (AST) for merge gateways, representing the time elapse from the arrival of the first token through one of its incoming flows to its activation. Synchronization times make sense only for parallel and BPMN 1.0 inclusive gateways, since there is no waiting/synchronization time for the other gateways.

The following *resource-based properties* are computed:

- The global time usage of all replicas of each resource R (GTU$_R$).
- The average GTU of resource R (GTU$_R^1$).
- The average usage percentage for a resource R (UP$_R^1$).

To quantify these properties, Maude rewriting capabilities are used in order to simulate and extract analysis results on a given BPMN process.

Table 1. Experimental results for the running example (2 employees, 3 drones)

Num. inst.	AET	Var	AST$_{g8}$	AST$_{ee}$	Total time	Resources						Anal. time
						GTU$_e$	GTU$_e^1$	UP$_e^1$	GTU$_d$	GTU$_d^1$	UP$_d^1$	
100	106	72	58	58	326	271	135	41	853	284	87	5 s
200	185	134	71	139	670	514	257	38	1892	630	94	26 s
400	284	173	98	237	1132	994	497	43	3270	1089	96	189 s
800	506	294	145	459	2217	1867	933.6	42	6525	2171	98	1233 s
1600	891	473	240	844	4187	3714	1857	44	12428	4142	98	7909 s

Table 1 summarizes experimental results on execution times and resource usage on the parcel order and delivery example (Fig. 1). They were carried out on an iMac with 3,2 GHz Intel Core i5 and 8 GB. All simulations were performed assuming a given workload with a number of instances (1st column) and an exponentially distributed interarrival time ($\lambda = 4$). Columns 2–6 contain, resp., the average execution time (AET), its variance (Var), the average synchronization time for the parallel merge at the end of the delivery process lane (AST$_{g8}$), the average synchronization time for the end events (AST$_{ee}$), and the total time to complete the execution of all instances. The next six columns show results on resource usage for employees and drones. The final column gives the overall time needed to complete the analysis. All times are logical units, except the ones in the last column that are given in seconds. Other information, such as the duration of each task and the synchronization time of merge gateways, is also collected.

These experiments consist of 100, 200, 400, 800, and 1600 instances for 2 employees and 3 drones. Note that the average execution and synchronization times, as their variance, clearly increase with the number of instances. This is because the more tokens compete for resources, the more time it takes to execute the process and for the tokens to reach the synchronization points. Note the relationship between AET and AST$_{ee}$ times, showing an unbalance between the two lanes: the client lane terminates earlier than the other lane, which exhibits a bottleneck because of the demand on the resources.

The GTU increases with the number of executed instances. These times are particularly interesting because they can be materialized as costs (e.g., cost of a resource, salary of an employee/all employees). In relation with usage percentage (UP), the results indicate that the employees are "underused" since they work around 40% of the time, in contrast to the drones that are constantly busy and used about 90% of the time for delivering parcels. This may suggest an inappropriate allocation of resources. It is worth observing that, although the number of instances clearly affects all computed times, the results for resource usage (UP) are quite stable and a small number of instances is enough for obtaining a good approximation of these percentages.

Resource allocation impacts execution times (AET) and resource usage (UP) of a process. Figure 2 focuses on average execution time and depicts the results when the number of employees and drones vary for a fixed number of executions (400). The objective here is to reduce the average execution time for completing the process: the quicker the parcel is delivered, the more satisfied the client is. It can be observed that, independently of the number of employees, execution times are not satisfactory with 1 or 2 drones (between 400 and 800 time units). The time becomes reasonable for more than 3 drones (less than 300 time units) and tends to stabilize. It is also worth noting that, given its low usage rate, the number of employees does not impact significantly the execution time. For more than six drones, only going from one to two employees makes a significant impact in the AET values.

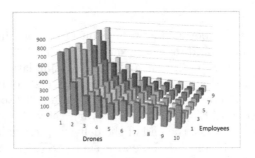

Fig. 2. Average execution time (400 instances)

Figure 3 gives a different point of view of resource usage by concentrating on each resource replica. Figure 3 (left) shows that employees are close to 100% usage only if there is 1 or 2 instances of that resource and at least 4 or 8 drones, respectively. If the number of employees increases, the usage percentage quickly drops, reaching a low level (e.g., 14% for 4 employees and 2 drones). This percentage slightly increases with the number of drone replicas (e.g., 34% for 4 employees and 5 drones), but remains low (around 30%). Figure 3 (right) shows that the drone usage is always quite high whatever the number of employees is. With only 1 or 2 drones, the usage percentage is almost at 100% and slightly decreases with 4 drones. When there are 6 drones and 1 employee, the percentage is still about 60%. Another interesting fact is that the number of employees barely impacts the drone usage percentage. For example, with 4 drones, the usage percentage is around 90% for any number of employees.

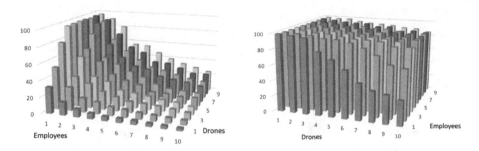

Fig. 3. Average percentage usage per employee (left) and drone (right) (400 instances)

References

1. Clavel, M., et al.: All About Maude - A High-Performance Logical Framework. LNCS, vol. 4350. Springer, Heidelberg (2007). https://doi.org/10.1007/978-3-540-71999-1
2. Durán, F., Rocha, C., Salaün, G.: A Note on Resource Allocation Analysis of BPMN Processes, July 2018. http://maude.lcc.uma.es/BPMN-R
3. Meseguer, J.: Conditional rewriting logic as a unified model of concurrency. Theor. Comput. Sci. **96**(1), 73–155 (1992)

Services at the Edge

Joint Operator Scaling and Placement for Distributed Stream Processing Applications in Edge Computing

Qinglan Peng[1], Yunni Xia[1(✉)], Yan Wang[2], Chunrong Wu[1], Xin Luo[3(✉)], and Jia Lee[1]

[1] Software Theory and Technology Chongqing Key Lab, Chongqing University, Chongqing, China
xiayunni@hotmail.com
[2] Department of Computing, Macquarie University, Sydney, NSW 2109, Australia
[3] Chinese Academy of Sciences, Chongqing Institute of Green and Intelligent Technology, Chongqing, China
luoxin21@gmail.com

Abstract. Distributed Stream Processing (DSP) systems are well acknowledged to be potent in processing huge volume of real-time stream data with low latency and high throughput. Recently, the edge computing paradigm shows great potentials in supporting and boosting the DSP applications, especially the time-critical and latency-sensitive ones, over the Internet of Things (IoT) or mobile devices by means of offloading the computation from remote cloud to edge servers for further reduced communication latencies. Nevertheless, various challenges, especially the joint operator scaling and placement, are yet to be properly explored and addressed. Traditional efforts in this direction usually assume that the data-flow graph of a DSP application is pre-given and static. The resulting models and methods can thus be ineffective and show bad user-perceived quality-of-service (QoS) when dealing with real-world scenarios with reconfigurable data-flow graphs and scalable operator placement. In contrast, in this paper, we consider that the data-flow graphs are configurable and hence propose the joint operator scaling and placement problem. To address this problem, we first build a queuing-network-based QoS estimation model, then formulate the problem into an integer-programming one, and finally propose a two-stage approach for finding the near-optimal solution. Experiments based on real-world DSP test cases show that our method achieves higher cost effectiveness than traditional ones while meeting the user-defined QoS constraints.

Keywords: Edge computing · Distributed stream processing · Operator placement · Operator replication

1 Introduction

Recent years have witnessed the prosperity of Internet of Things (IoT) devices and novel mobile applications. Now we are surrounded by different kinds of IoT

© Springer Nature Switzerland AG 2019
S. Yangui et al. (Eds.): ICSOC 2019, LNCS 11895, pp. 461–476, 2019.
https://doi.org/10.1007/978-3-030-33702-5_36

devices, *e.g.*, smart phones, tablets, wearable devices, smart household appliances, *etc.* These devices keep producing data and generating requests for event handling day and night [20]. Such unbounded data and events should be properly analyzed and handled on time, especially when applications are latency-sensitive. A bicycle-sharing system is a good example of such latency-sensitive applications, where the borrowing and returning events of the shared bicycles should be collected and summarized in a timely manner for guaranteeing prompt responses to queries of available bicycles. Augmented reality (AR) is another good example, where objects or human faces in the video or pictures captured by mobile camera should be recognized, analyzed, and augmented as fast as possible to avoid congestions between user-machine interactions. Traditional cloud computing can be ineffective for hosting such latency-sensitive applications because by deploying services and providing data caching at the remote cloud ends, cloud users may frequently experience high latency and congestions. In contrast, the edge computing paradigm can be highly capable and efficient in supporting them due to the fact that user data are managed at the edge of Internet, where mobile core networks are alleviated from problems of congestion and edge servers are usually located near data sources for highly-reduced latency and communication overhead [17].

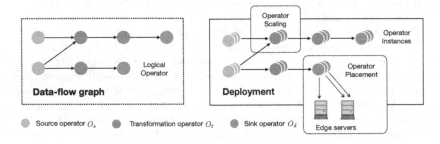

Fig. 1. A data-flow graph example and its deployment.

The above-mentioned latency-sensitive applications can usually be viewed as typical distributed stream processing (DSP) systems [12], where the underlying business processes can be described as *data-flow graphs* with the help of control-flow, and the corresponding events can thus be handled by continuously flowing through the operators according to the structure of data-flow graphs. Figure 1 shows an example of a data-flow graph and its deployment. There are three type of operators: (1) *source operators*, which are in charge of reading data or receiving events; (2) *transformation operators*, which perform transformations on data or events (*e.g.*, map, reduce, join, and filter); and (3) *sink operators*, which could be end users or other information systems. The processed data or events are finally consumed by them.

A major limitation of the existing studies in this direction lies in that they usually assume that the topological structure of the data-flow graph is pre-given and thus address the operator placement problem in a static way [3,18]. However, for many real-world DSP engines and systems, *e.g.,* Apache Storm and Flink, operators can be scalable at run-time because multiple replicas of an operator are allowed to be instantiated to increase throughput and avoid the single-point-failures. As shown in Fig. 1, when deploying a DSP application, for one logical operator in the data-flow graph of this application, multiple operator instances can be launched and they can be placed to different edge resources. Therefore, the cost-effective joint operator scaling and placement of operators in the data-flow graph of an edge-oriented DSP application with guaranteed quality-of-service (QoS) becomes a key challenge.

Therefore, within this paper, instead of assuming pre-given and static data-flow graphs, we consider configurable ones and the resulting problem of joint operator scaling and placement for DSP applications on the edge computing platforms. To this end, we propose a queuing-network-based model for the estimation of the response time and formulate the joint problem into an integer-programming problem. Moreover, we propose a combination of a Binary-Genetic-Algorithm (BGA)-based method and a bottleneck-analysis-based solution refinement for identifying high-quality near-optimal solutions. Experiments based on real-world DSP test cases clearly show that our method significantly outperforms traditional ones in terms of response time and cost.

2 Related Work

Operator placement refers to assigning the stream processing operators in a DSP application to different machines [14]. It has been widely acknowledged that placing the stream operators of IoT applications to edge, where is close to the user data is generated, can speed up the applications, reduce the load of cloud data centers and save more communication bandwidths [7]. According to the latest Cisco global cloud index [15], by 2021, 75% of data produced by human, machines, or things will be stored or processed at the edge.

However, it has been proven that such an operator placement problem on heterogeneous edge resources is NP-hard [2]. Therefore, how to develop efficient and elegant methods or algorithms for the edge-oriented operator placement problem has become a hot issue, and many efforts were paid to this field. For example, Cai et al. [3] investigated the fluctuation of request rate of complex-event-processing (CEP) applications in the edge computing environment, then they proposed a predictive algorithm which is capable of adjusting the placement of operators on the fly. On the other hand, Silva Voith et al. [18] considered a mixture resource pool with both edge and cloud servers and proposed a latency-aware operator placement method. Likewise, Renart et al. [7] also considered a mixture resource pool and they developed a programming model, which is capable of splitting mobile applications dynamically across the edge and the cloud online, to optimize the end-to-end latency, bandwidth consumption and messaging cost. Amarasinghe et al. [1] targeted at minimizing the end-to-end latency, they formulated the operator placement problem into a constraint satisfaction problem and employed Gecode solver to acquire placement plans. While

Hiessl *et al.* [9] considered various QoS metrics, including response time, availability, enactment, and migration cost, to build their system model. Then they employed a simple additive weighting method to aggregate these metrics and the IBM CPLEX tool to solve the optimal placement problem.

A careful investigation into the aforementioned studies shows that they are still limited in two ways: (1) many studies, *e.g.*, [3,16] and [19], assumed that the data-flow graph of DSP applications is pre-given and thus no operator scaling is permitted. However, as an important feature in real-world DSP engines, operator scaling has strong impacts to user-perceived QoS and deployment cost; (2) various existing methods, *e.g.*, [5] and [18], only considered a single path or a combination of multiple paths in building their QoS model. However, the performance of an operator instance might be interfered by operator instances in other paths; thus, evaluating the QoS of a DSP system by modeling it to tandem queues may suffer from the loss of accuracy. To overcome these limitations, we consider configurable data-flow graphs and propose a queuing-network-based QoS model for the estimation of the response time of a DSP application. Based on the proposed model, we formulate the joint operator scaling and placement for DSP applications in edge computing into an integer-programming problem and develop a two-stage method to solve it.

3   System Model and Problem Formulation

In this section, we first propose a queuing-network-based model for the estimation of the response time of DSP applications on edge computing, then we formulate the joint operator scaling and placement into an integer-programming problem. Table 1 lists the notations used in our system model.

3.1   System Model

The data-flow graph of a DSP application can be described as a directed acyclic graph $G = (O, S)$, where $O = \{o_1, o_2, ..., o_n\}$ is the set of logical event processing operators, $S = \{s_{(i,j)} | i \neq j \land i, j \in [1, n]\}$ the streams of events flowing between logical operators [9].

As shown in Fig. 1, there are three type of operators in a data-flow graph, *i.e.*, source operators O_s, transformation operators O_t, and sink operators O_d [18]. Note that, a data-flow graph may contain multiple source operators and sink operators. Unbounded events enter the DSP system continuously from O_s, then wait to be processed by flowing through O_t, and are finally consumed by end users or other information systems at O_d. We use o_i^c to denote the required amount of computation of processing an event at o_i, which can be measured by the count of instructions, o_i^m the required memory for running o_i itself. Figure 1 also shows an example of scaling and placing the operators in a data-flow graph to edge resources. As we can see in this figure, multiple operator instances are allowed to be launched for a single logical operator and they can be deployed to different edge servers [4]. We use $p = \{p_1, p_2, ..., p_n\}$ to denote the operator

Table 1. List of notations

Notation	Description	Notation	Description
γ_i	Output rate of events at logical operator o_i	$o_{(i,j)}$	j-th operator instance for o_i
λ_i	Input rate of events at logical operator o_i	o_i^c	Required amount of computation of processing an event at o_i
$\lambda_{i,j}$	Input rate of events at operator instance $o_{(i,j)}$	o_i^m	Required memory for running o_i itself
$\mu_{(i,j,k)}$	Event processing rate of operator instance $o_{(i,j)}$ at edge server e_k	p	Operator scaling plan for a data-flow graph
$\rho_{(i,j,k)}$	Event processing strength of operator instance $o_{(i,j)}$ at e_k	p_i	Parallelism number of a logical operator o_i
ψ_i	Ratio of the number of input events to output events of o_i	$s_{(i,j)}$	An event stream flows from o_i to o_j
$\omega_{(i,j)}$	Probability of an output event emitted by o_i flows through o_j	$q_{(i,j,k)}$	Average queue length of an operator instance $o(i,j)$ at edge server e_k
$b_{(i,j)}$	Bandwidth between edge servers e_i and e_j	x	Operator placement plan for a data-flow graph
c_i	Average size of an event at o_i	$x_{(i,j,k)}$	Function to identify whether $i_{(i,j)}$ is placed to server e_k
e_i	i-th edge server in resource pool	D	User-defined response time constraint
m	Available edge servers count in a resource pool	O_s	Set of source operators in a data-flow graph
m_k	Required memory for server e_k	O_t	Set of transformation operators in a data-flow graph
n	Logical operators count in a data-flow graph	O_d	Set of sink operators in a data-flow graph
$l_{(i,j)}$	Latency between edge servers e_i and e_j	$\mathbb{R}(p,x)$	Estimated response time of the joint operator scaling and placement solution
o_i	i-th logical operator in a data-flow graph	$\mathbb{C}(p,x)$	Estimated cost of the joint operator scaling and placement solution

scaling plan of a data-flow graph, where p_i is the parallelism number of a logical operator o_i, and the operator instances of o_i can thus be represented as $o_i = \{o_{(i,1)}, o_{(i,2)}, ..., o_{(i,p_i)}\}$.

For an event stream $s_{(i,j)}$ which connects o_i and o_j, the probability of an output event emitted by o_i flows through o_j is determined by $\omega_{(i,j)}$. For a logical operator o_i, the ratio of the number of input events to the number of output events is determined by its selection rate ψ_i. $\omega_{(i,j)}$ and ψ_i can be empirically obtained from the log files of the DSP system [11,18]. We use λ_i and γ_i to denote the input and output rates of events at o_i respectively, and λ_i can be calculated as follows:

$$\lambda_i = \begin{cases} \gamma_k, & \exists s_{(k,i)} \in S \wedge o_k \in O_s \\ \sum_{s_{(i,j)} \in S} \lambda_i \times \psi_i \times \omega_{(i,j)}, & o_i \notin O_s \end{cases} \tag{1}$$

where

$$\gamma_i = \lambda_i \times \psi_j, \qquad o_j \notin O_d, \tag{2}$$

the event arrival rate at each operator can thus be calculated in a recursive way.

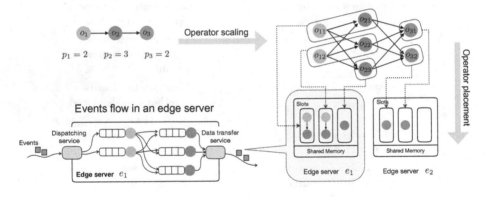

Fig. 2. An example of joint operator scaling and placement.

A DSP application can be deployed to the resource pool constructed by heterogeneous edge servers, *e.g.*, base stations, wireless access points, on-board computers, *etc*. These servers are usually distributed around end users, and we use a 3-tuple $R = (E, B, L)$ to denote the configuration of a resource pool, where $E = \{e_1, e_2, ..., e_m\}$ is the set of available edge servers, $B = \{b_{(i,j)}|i, j \in [1, m]\}$ is the bandwidth between edge servers, and $L = \{l_{(i,j)}|i, j \in [1, m]\}$ is the latency between them. We use e_i^m to denote the available memory of edge server e_i, use e_i^c to denote the computing capability of e_i, which can be measured by million of instructions per second (MIPS), and e_i^p the price per unit time of hiring such an edge server.

An edge server with multi-core processors can support multiple operator instances at the same time. We use slots count to represent how many operator instances can be accommodated to an edge server, the number of slots of edge server e_i is denoted as e_i^s. Figure 2 shows an example of scaling logical operators in a data-flow graph and placing the corresponding operator instances to the slots of different edge servers. Note that, the operator instances deployed to the same server share the host's memory, and operators can be bundled together and to placed into one slot, e.g., the *SlotSharingGroup* function in Apache Flink. According to the Burke theorem, slots with bundles of operator instances can be seen as a tandem queue.

The system described above can be modeled as a Jackson queuing-network. We use x to denote the placement plan, and $x_{(i,j,k)} \in \{0,1\}$ is the indicator of whether $o_{(i,j)}$ is placed into server e_k. The event input rate of an operator instance $\lambda_{(i,j)}$ can be calculated as $\lambda_{(i,j)} = \lambda_i/p_i$. We use $\mu_{(i,j,k)}$ to denote the event processing rate of $o_{(i,j)}$ at edge server e_k, the event processing strength $\rho_{(i,j,k)}$ of $o_{(i,j)}$ at e_k can thus be calculated as:

$$\rho_{(i,j,k)} = \frac{\lambda_{(i,j)} \times o_i^c}{e_k^c}. \tag{3}$$

Therefore, the average queue length of an operator instance $o_{(i,j)}$ at edge server e_k is:

$$q_{(i,j,k)} = \frac{\rho_{(i,j,k)}}{1 - \rho_{(i,j,k)}}. \tag{4}$$

We use c_i to denote the average event size at o_i, the required memory m_k for server e_k can thus be calculated as:

$$m_k = \sum_{i=1}^{n} \sum_{j=1}^{p_i} x_{(i,j,k)} \times q_{(i,j,k)} \times c_i + o_i^m. \tag{5}$$

According to the Little's law, given the scaling plan p and placement plan x, the expected response time for the events to finish their processing steps in a data-flow graph is:

$$\mathbb{R}(p,x) = \sum_{i=1}^{n} \sum_{j=1}^{p_i} \sum_{k=1}^{m} \frac{x_{(i,j,k)} q_{(i,j,k)}}{\lambda_i} + \sum_{s_{(i,j)} \in S} \frac{\omega_{(i,j)}}{p_i p_j} \times \sum_{g \in E_i} \sum_{h \in E_j} \left[\frac{c_i}{b_{(g,h)}} + l_{(g,h)} \right],$$

$$\tag{6}$$

where $E_i = \{c_k | k \in [1,m] \land j \in [1,p_i] \land x_{(i,j,k)} = 1\}$ is the set of hired edge servers whose purpose is to accommodate all operator instances of o_i. And finally, the total cost of hiring edge servers can be calculated as:

$$\mathbb{C}(p,x) = \sum_{k=1}^{m} w(k) \times e_k^p, \tag{7}$$

where $w(k)$ is the function to identify whether server e_k is hired, $w(k) = 1$ if $\sum_{i=1}^{n} \sum_{j=1}^{p_i} x_{(i,j,k)} > 0$, otherwise 0.

3.2   Problem Formulation

Based on the system assumption and configuration, we have interest to know, for a given data-flow graph of a DSP application, how to find the joint operator scaling and placement plan with the minimal cost while fulfilling the user-defined response time constraint. The resulting problem of joint operator scaling and placement can be formulated as follow:

$$Min: \quad \mathbb{C}(p, x) \tag{8}$$

$$s.t: \quad \mathbb{R}(p, x) \leq D \tag{9}$$

$$\sum_{i=1}^{n} \sum_{j=1}^{p_i} q_{(i,j,k)} \leq e_k^m, \qquad \forall e_k \in E \tag{10}$$

$$\sum_{i=1}^{n} \sum_{j=1}^{p_i} x_{(i,j,k)} \leq e_k^s, \qquad \forall e_k \in E \tag{11}$$

$$p_i \geq 1, \qquad i \in \{1, 2, ..., n\} \tag{12}$$

where D is the user-defined response time constraint. Equations (8) and (9) indicate that the target of our problem is to minimize the cost of hiring edge servers while meeting user-defined response time constraint. Equations (10) and (11) are the memory and slot constraints of edge servers, *i.e.*, the slots and memory consumed by the operator instances placed in the same edge server should not exceed the capacity of that server. Equation (12) is the functional constraint, *i.e.*, each logical operator should be implemented by at least one operator instance.

4   Proposed Joint Scaling and Placement Approach

According to [2] and [8], both the operator scaling and placement problems are NP-hard. In this section, we first propose a Binary-Genetic-Algorithm (BGA) based method to find the preliminary solutions in polynomial time complexity, then we perform a bottleneck-analysis-based refinement (BAR) to them for the improvement of resource utilization and response-time reduction. Figure 3 shows the process of our proposed two-stage approach.

4.1   BGA-Based Method for Preliminary Solution

Genetic Algorithm (GA) [6] is a kind of evolutionary algorithm capable of finding the near-optimal solutions of complex optimization problem by means of simulating the evolution of species. The original GA is designed for solving continues problem, rather than discrete integer-programming ones such as operator placement or workflow scheduling. Therefore, we employ BGA and design a novel encoding scheme and fitness evaluation strategy for it to solve the problem preliminarily.

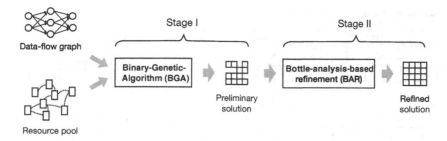

Fig. 3. The process of proposed two-stage approach.

The encoding operation aims at representing a feasible joint solution in a BGA-solvable way. In the binary encoding scheme, each segment in a chromosome contains a series of binary digits whose decimal meaning is the index of a possible operator-slot combination which will be needed for fitness evaluation. Figure 4 shows an example of encoding. The encoded solution is illustrated in Fig. 2, where there are 2 available edge servers in resource pool and thus the chromosome has 2 segments. There are 3 logical operators in the data-flow graph and $\{o_1, o_2\}$ are allowed to be deployed as a bundle to one slot. The status of slots range from $\{0, 1, 2, 3, 4\}$, where 0 indicates the current slot is idle and 4 indicates that a bundle of operator instances for o_1 and o_2 is placed. Each edge server has 3 slots and thus the length of each segment is $\lceil \log_2 u(3, 1, 3) \rceil$, where $u(n, b, k)$ is the function to identify how many operator-slot combinations there will be for server e_k and it can be calculated as follows:

$$u(n, b, k) = \frac{(n + b + e_k^s)!}{e_k^s!(n+b)!}, \tag{13}$$

where b is the number of bundle operators, and the corresponding operator-slot combination for fitness evaluation can be generated from index with the time complexity of $O(n + b)$ [13]. As shown in Fig. 4, this process can be regarded as finding the unique combination from a virtual mapping table.

To find the desired joint solution that fulfills user-defined latency and cost expectation, we design a fitness function with lower values being better as:

$$f(c) = \begin{cases} \mathbb{R}(c.p, c.x), & F(c) = 1 \wedge R(c.p, c.x) > D \\ \frac{\mathbb{C}(c.p, c.x)}{\mathbb{C}_T} \times D, & F(c) = 1 \wedge R(c.p, c.x) \leq D \\ +\infty, & F(c) = 0 \end{cases} \tag{14}$$

where c denotes a joint solution, $c.p$ and $c.x$ denote the scaling and placement plan respectively, $F(c)$ the function to identify whether a joint solution c satisfies the constraint based on Eqs. (10), (11), and (12), $\mathbb{R}(c.p, c.x)$ the estimated response time of solution c based on Eq. (6), $\mathbb{C}(c.p, c.x)$ the cost of hiring edge servers based on Eq. (7), and $\mathbb{C}_T$ the total cost of available edge servers. To guarantee the monotonic property of the fitness function, we scale the total cost to $(0, D]$ and associate the fitness values of those unfeasible solutions with infinity.

Binary encoding

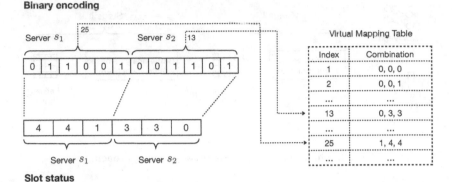

Fig. 4. An example of binary encoding scheme.

Suppose that the population size and iteration time are k and l respectively. The complexity of population initialization, fitness evaluation, crossover, and mutation are $O(km(n+b))$, $O(klm(n+b))$, $O(km)$, and $O(km)$ respectively. Thus the total time complex of the proposed BGA-based method is $O(klm(n+b))$.

4.2   Bottleneck-Analysis-Based Solution Refinement

To further refine the preliminary solutions yielded by BGA, we perform a bottleneck analysis to identify the key logical operator of the DSP system, and employ a best-fit-decreasing-(BFD)-based method to find suitable slots for accommodating the newly instantiated key operator instance. The philosophy for doing so is that there are still idle slots for hired servers in preliminary solutions and they can be utilized to further improve the response time. The major problem is to find where is the bottleneck of current system, *i.e.,* the key logical operator which can reduce more response time if we launch more instances to it, and how many operator instances should be launched for it to which idle slots. The key logical operators usually have longer queue lengths than others, thus we find the logical operator with the longest queue length as the bottleneck of current system. Then, we launch a new instance to it and try to assign it to an available slot with the highest processing capability. This loop will repeat until all idle slots are utilized or no further operator can be instantiated to any idle slots.

Algorithm 1: Bottleneck-analysis-based Refinement

Input: Scaling plan p; Placement plan x; Set of idle slots S ; Logical
      operator set O; Edge resources pool $R = \{E, B, L\}$

Output: Refined scaling plan p and placement plan x

1 $S \leftarrow$ rank S according to edge servers' CPU capability in descending
    order ;

2 $B \leftarrow \varnothing$

3 **while** $|S| \neq 0$ **do**

4 | **if** $|B| = |O|$ **then**

5 | | **break**;

6 | $Q \leftarrow \varnothing$;

7 | **foreach** $x_{(i,j,k)} \in x$ **do**

8 | | **if** $x_{(i,j,k)} = 1$ **then**

9 | | | $q \leftarrow$ evaluate the queue length according to Eq.(4);

10 | | | $Q[i] \leftarrow O[i] + q$;

11 | $i \leftarrow \min(Q[j])$ *where* $j \in \{1, 2, ..., n\} \wedge j \notin B$;

12 | $St \leftarrow S$; $s \leftarrow St.pop()$; $p_i \leftarrow p_i + 1$; $x' \leftarrow x$; $x'_{(i,p_i,s)} \leftarrow 1$;

13 | **while** $F(x') = 0 \vee T(x) < T(x')$ **do**

14 | | **if** $|St| = 0$ **then**

15 | | | $B \leftarrow B \cup \{i\}$; $x' \leftarrow x$; $s \leftarrow \varnothing$;

16 | | | **break**;

17 | | $x'_{(i,p_i,s)} \leftarrow 0$;

18 | | $s \leftarrow St.pop()$;

19 | | $x'_{(i,p_i,s)} \leftarrow 1$;

20 | $x \leftarrow x'$;

21 | $S \leftarrow S - s$;

22 **Return** p, x;

Algorithm 1 shows the process of such a bottleneck-analysis-based solution refinement, short for BAR. It starts with ranking all available slots by their hosts' CPU capability. Then, it initializes B, which denotes the logical operators that can not be instantiated in any slot, with empty set. The main loop aims at finding the bottleneck of the current solution (as shown in lines 6–11) and tries to launch a new instance to available slots in a best-fit-decreasing way (as shown in lines 12–21). The time complexity of ranking all available slots is $O(m \log m)$, finding the bottleneck of the current solution is $O(m \log m)$, and the attempt to launch a new operator instance for the current bottleneck is $O(m)$. Therefore, the complexity of the BAR method is $O(m \log m + m(m \log m + m)) = O(m^2 \log m)$, and the total time complexity of our approach is $O(m^2 \log m + klm(n + b)) = O(m^2 \log m + mn)$.

5 Experiments

To validate the performance of the proposed method, we conduct a series of case studies based on real-world DSP applications and edge server configurations. The proposed algorithms are implemented using Matlab and the experiment environment is implemented on top of Simpy, which is a process based discrete event simulation framework. We evaluate the performance of our method and baselines in terms of response time and deployment cost.

5.1 Experiment Settings

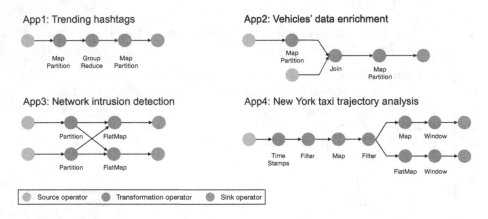

Fig. 5. Data-flow graphs of the real-world DSP applications.

Figure 5 shows the data-flow graphs of 4 real-world DSP applications, *i.e.*, (1) trending hashtags for social media; (2) data enrichment for vehicles information; (3) intrusion detection for IT security or network; and (4) trajectory analysis for the taxi in New York city. The amount of required computation, *i.e.*, o_i^c, for processing per event at each logical operator and its average size, *i.e.*, c_i, are measured by running these applications at Apache Flink (version 1.7.2). The response time constraint of these four applications is set to 160 ms, 300 ms, 400 ms, and 630 ms, respectively.

We consider there are four different types of edge servers in an edge resource pool in terms of computation capacity, *i.e.*, tiny, small, medium, and large; Table 2 shows their configurations. 100 servers are selected to build up an edge resource pool to support the DSP applications, each of which randomly follows one of the above four configurations. As [18] did, the bandwidths between edge servers are generated by normal distribution with a mean value of 300 Mbps [10], and the latencies between them are generated from a uniform distribution between 0.085 ms and 3.576 ms. The price of edge servers follows the latest Amazon EC2 server pricing which is pay-as-you-go with one hour billing interval.

Table 2. Configuration of edge servers

Type	Model	Cores	CPU speed	RAM	Price (cent)
Tiny	Raspberry Pi 2	4	474 MIPS @ 1 GHz	1 GB	2.55
Small	Advantech EIS-D210	4	3,846 MIPS @ 1.5 GHz	4 GB	5.1
Medium	ZTE ES600S	8	32,885 MIPS @ 2.8 GHz	32 GB	38.4
Large	Inspur NE5260M5	16	27,135 MIPS @ 2.1 GHz	64 GB	76.8

The event input rates are set to range from 50 to 500 to verify the effectiveness of the proposed method and baselines under different user request loads. Each case is performed 50 times and the average response time and cost are reported.

5.2 Baseline Approaches

We consider the simplex BGA and two state-of-the-art DSP operator placement approaches, *i.e.,* ODRP and GS+RTA, as baselines:

- **BGA**: it takes the preliminary solution yielded by our BGA-based method (as illustrated in Sect. 4.1) as the final joint scaling and placement solution, no further refinement is performed;
- **ODRP** [4]: it considers the worst end-to-end delay from the source to sink as the response time of a data-flow graph, then formulates the joint operator replication and placement as an integer-linear-programming problem, and finally employs IBM CPLEX optimizer to solve it;
- **GS+RTA**: RTA [3] is a heuristic method to shorten the response time of data-flow graph by improving the placement of the path with the largest end-to-end delay. Because it does not consider the scaling of operators, we implement a greedy scaling strategy for it and name it as GS+RTA.

5.3 Comparison of Response Time

Results: Figure 6 compares the response time of the joint operator scaling and placement solution obtained by our proposed BGA+BAR and baselines at different event arrival rates. It can be clearly seen that the response time constraint violation rates of both BGA+BAR and ODRP are zero, while it is 5.26% and 11.84% for BGA and GS+RTA, respectively. Our proposed BGA+BAR also can deliver a shorter response time than BGA and GS+RTA (*i.e.,* 3.64% lower than BGA on average in four applications, and 10.56% lower than GS+RTA).

Analysis: BGA+BAR outperforms BGA, because the proposed BAR method is capable of eliminating the inherent drawbacks of the employed genetic algorithm and further improving the quality of solutions by performing a bottleneck-analysis-based refinement. BGA+BAR outperforms GS+RTA, because the meta-heuristic method that we have employed is capable of breaking out of local optima and finding solutions with higher quality. The reason why ODRP delivers the lowest response time is that it regards the worst end-to-end delay as the

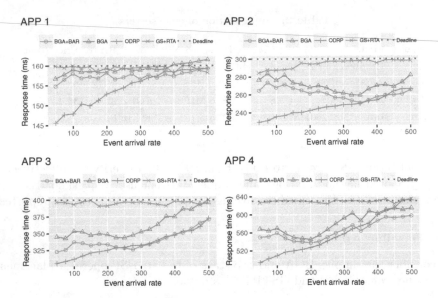

Fig. 6. Response time evaluation.

response time. However, this is considered too conservative and it is inefficient to find cost-effective solutions especially when the response time constraint is met. In contrast, our QoS model considers the whole data-flow graph by employing the queuing-network-theory to evaluate its response time, which makes our model more objective and thus capable of yielding more cost-effective solutions.

5.4   Comparison of Cost

Results: Figure 7 shows the comparison of cost between our method and baselines at different event arrival rates. It is easy to see that BGA+BAR achieves the lowest cost in all cases (*i.e.*, 39.56% lower than ODRP on average in all four Apps, and 30.85% lower than GS+RTA on average).

Analysis: The reasons of why BGA+BAR yields more cost-effective solutions than baselines lie in threefold: (1) we employ queuing-network, which takes all event flowing paths in a data-flow graph into consideration, instead of only considering the shortest path, to build our QoS model. Therefore, our model is capable of estimating the response time more objectively; (2) the proposed binary encoding scheme for BGA can significantly reduce the search space by introducing the unique operator-slot combination and virtual mapping table mechanism; (3) the proposed BAR method does not invest any new edge resources to the current resource pool. Therefore, the solutions yielded by BGA+BAR have the same cost as those of BGA but have lower response time and higher resource utilization.

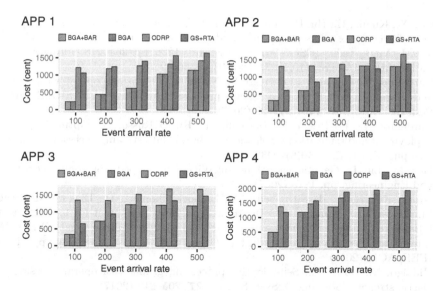

Fig. 7. Cost evaluation.

6 Conclusion and Further Work

This paper targets at the joint operator scaling and placement problem for DSP applications in edge computing environments. We consider that the data-flow graphs of DSP applications are configurable instead of static, and propose a queuing-network-based model to evaluate the response time and cost of a joint scaling and placement solution. Then, we formulate the proposed problem into an integer-programming problem and develop a two-stage approach to solve it. Experiments based on real-world datasets have demonstrated that our methods can achieve lower cost while meeting user-defined QoS constraint than baselines.

In our further studies, the following concerns will be addressed: (1) the fluctuation of event arrival rate and edge server performance should be well analyzed and further predicted to generate joint solutions with higher quality; (2) heavy-tailed distributions, *e.g.,* pareto distribution, are suitable for modeling the process of events arrival and being processed, some stochastic approaches should be investigated for the further improvement of the accuracy of our system model.

References

1. Amarasinghe, G., de Assuno, M.D., Harwood, A., Karunasekera, S.: A data stream processing optimisation framework for edge computing applications. In: 2018 IEEE 21st International Symposium on Real-Time Distributed Computing (ISORC), pp. 91–98. IEEE (2018)
2. Benoit, A., Dobrila, A., Nicod, J.M., Philippe, L.: Scheduling linear chain streaming applications on heterogeneous systems with failures. Future Gener. Comput. Syst. **29**(5), 1140–1151 (2013)

3. Cai, X., Kuang, H., Hu, H., Song, W., Lü, J.: Response time aware operator placement for complex event processing in edge computing. In: Pahl, C., Vukovic, M., Yin, J., Yu, Q. (eds.) ICSOC 2018. LNCS, vol. 11236, pp. 264–278. Springer, Cham (2018). https://doi.org/10.1007/978-3-030-03596-9_18

4. Cardellini, V., Grassi, V., Lo Presti, F., Nardelli, M.: Optimal operator replication and placement for distributed stream processing systems. ACM SIGMETRICS Perform. Eval. Rev. **44**(4), 11–22 (2017)

5. Cardellini, V., Lo Presti, F., Nardelli, M., Russo Russo, G.: Optimal operator deployment and replication for elastic distributed data stream processing. Concurr. Comput. Pract. Exp. **30**(9), e4334 (2018)

6. Gen, M., Lin, L.: Genetic algorithms. In: Wiley Encyclopedia of Computer Science and Engineering, pp. 1–15 (2007)

7. Gibert Renart, E., da Silva Veith, A., Balouek-Thomert, D., Dias de Assuncao, M., Lefèvre, L., Parashar, M.: Distributed operator placement for IoT data analytics across edge and cloud resources. In: CCGrid 2019 - 19th Annual IEEE/ACM International Symposium in Cluster, Cloud, and Grid Computing, pp. 1–10. IEEE/ACM (2019)

8. Hidalgo, N., Rosas, E.: Self-adaptive processing graph with operator fission for elastic stream processing. J. Syst. Softw. **127**, 205–216 (2017)

9. Hiessl, T., Karagiannis, V., Hochreiner, C., Schulte, S., Nardelli, M.: Optimal placement of stream processing operators in the fog. In: 2019 IEEE 3rd International Conference on Fog and Edge Computing (ICFEC), pp. 1–10. IEEE (2019)

10. Hu, W., et al.: quantifying the impact of edge computing on mobile applications. In: Proceedings of the 7th ACM SIGOPS Asia-Pacific Workshop on Systems, p. 5. ACM (2016)

11. Kaur, N., Sood, S.K.: Efficient resource management system based on 4vs of big data streams. Big Data Res. **9**, 98–106 (2017)

12. Mai, L., et al.: Chi: a scalable and programmable control plane for distributed stream processing systems. Proc. VLDB Endow. **11**(10), 1303–1316 (2018)

13. Myrvold, W., Ruskey, F.: Ranking and unranking permutations in linear time. Inf. Process. Lett. **79**(6), 281–284 (2001)

14. Nardelli, M., Cardellini, V., Grassi, V., Presti, F.L.: Efficient operator placement for distributed data stream processing applications. IEEE Trans. Parallel Distrib. Syst. **30**(8), 1753–1767 (2019)

15. Networking, C.V.: Cisco Global Cloud Index: Forecast and Methodology, 2016–2021. Cisco Public, San Jose (2018). White paper

16. Pietzuch, P., Ledlie, J., Shneidman, J., Roussopoulos, M., Welsh, M., Seltzer, M.: Network-aware operator placement for stream-processing systems. In: 22nd International Conference on Data Engineering (ICDE 2006), pp. 49–49. IEEE (2006)

17. Shi, W., Cao, J., Zhang, Q., Li, Y., Xu, L.: Edge computing: vision and challenges. IEEE Internet Things J. **3**(5), 637–646 (2016)

18. da Silva Veith, A., de Assunção, M.D., Lefèvre, L.: Latency-aware placement of data stream analytics on edge computing. In: Pahl, C., Vukovic, M., Yin, J., Yu, Q. (eds.) ICSOC 2018. LNCS, vol. 11236, pp. 215–229. Springer, Cham (2018). https://doi.org/10.1007/978-3-030-03596-9_14

19. Taneja, M., Davy, A.: Resource aware placement of iot application modules in fog-cloud computing paradigm. In: 2017 IFIP/IEEE Symposium on Integrated Network and Service Management (IM), pp. 1222–1228. IEEE (2017)

20. Yang, S.: Iot stream processing and analytics in the fog. IEEE Commun. Mag. **55**(8), 21–27 (2017)

Graph-Based Optimal Data Caching in Edge Computing

Xiaoyu Xia[1], Feifei Chen[1], Qiang He[2(✉)], Guangming Cui[2], Phu Lai[2],
Mohamed Abdelrazek[1], John Grundy[3], and Hai Jin[4]

[1] Deakin University, Burwood, Australia
{xiaoyu.xia,feifei.chen,mohamed.abdelrazek}@deakin.edu.au
[2] Swinburne University of Technology, Hawthorn, Australia
{qhe,gcui,tlai}@swin.edu.au
[3] Monash University, Clayton, Australia
john.grundy@monash.edu
[4] Huazhong University of Science and Technology, Wuhan, China
hjin@hust.edu.cn

Abstract. In an edge computing environment, edge servers are deployed
at base stations to offer highly accessible computing capacities and services to nearby users. Data caching is thus extremely important in edge
computing environments to reduce service latency. The optimal data
caching strategy in the edge computing environment will minimize the
data caching cost while maximizing the reduction in service latency. In
this paper, we formulate this edge data caching (EDC) problem as a constrained optimization problem (COP), prove that the EDC problem is
$\mathcal{NP}$-complete, propose an optimal approach named IPEDC to solve the
EDC problem using the Integer Programming technique, and provide a
heuristic algorithm named LGEDC to find near-optimal solutions. We
have evaluated our approaches on a real-world data set and a synthesized
data set. The results demonstrate that IPEDC and LGEDC significantly
outperform two representative baseline approaches.

Keywords: Optimization · Edge computing · Data caching

1 Introduction

Over the last decade, the world has witnessed an exponential growth of mobile
traffic over the internet, which is predicted to expand by 1,000 times over the
coming decade with a huge increase in Internet of Things (IoT) connected devices
[1]. The enormous network traffic load often causes network congestion that
significantly impacts users' quality of experience, especially service latency. To
attack this challenge, edge computing, a new distributed computing paradigm,
has emerged to allow computing capacities such as CPUs, memory and storage
to be distributed to *edge servers* at the edge of the cloud [2]. Each edge server is
powered by one or more physical servers and deployed at base stations that are
geographically close to users. Mobile and IoT app vendors can hire computing
capacities on edge servers so that they can host their services to offer their app

© Springer Nature Switzerland AG 2019
S. Yangui et al. (Eds.): ICSOC 2019, LNCS 11895, pp. 477–493, 2019.
https://doi.org/10.1007/978-3-030-33702-5_37

users low service latency [3]. Such services are referred to as *edge services* in the remainder of this paper.

As an increasing number of mobile devices start to access edge services, a large proportion of the rapidly growing mobile traffic will go through edge servers. Enormous data will be transmitted by edge servers. Caching data, especially popular data such as viral videos and photos from Facebook, on edge servers will minimize the latency in users' data retrieval. Users can retrieve data from a nearby edge server instead of retrieving it from the cloud if the data is cached on that edge server. This is especially important for latency-sensitive applications, e.g., gaming, navigation, augmented reality, etc. Popular data often accounts for a large percentage of the mobile traffic data over the internet. Thus, caching popular data on edge servers can significantly reduce the traffic load on the internet backbone. It is expected to reduce mobile traffic data by 35% [4]. From an app vendor's perspective, it can also considerably reduce data transfer costs by decreasing the volume of data transferred from the cloud to its users.

Given a piece of popular data, a straightforward solution is to cache it on all the edge servers in a particular area for nearby app users to access. This way, the latency in all app users' data retrieval can be minimized. However, based on the pay-as-you-go pricing model, the app vendor will need to hire substantial resources on edge servers for caching the data. This incurs excessive *caching cost* and is impractical for most, if not all, app vendors. Thus, from an app vendor's perspective, it is critical to find an optimal data caching strategy that minimizes the caching cost incurred while guaranteeing the low latency in its users' data retrieval. We refer to this data caching problem in the edge computing environment as an *edge data caching* (EDC) problem. While existing research investigates data caching in the edge computing environment from either the network infrastructure provider's or users' perspectives, we make the first attempt to study the EDC problem based on graph from the app vendor's perspective.

In this work, we make the following major contributions:

- We model and formulate the EDC problem as a constrained optimization problem (COP) from the app vendor's perspective.
- We prove that the EDC problem is $\mathcal{NP}$-complete based on the minimum dominating set problem.
- We develop an optimal approach named IPEDC for solving the EDC problem with the Integer Programming technique.
- We develop a heuristic approach named LGEDC for finding near-optimal solutions to the EDC problem efficiently in large-scale scenarios.
- We evaluate our approaches against two representative baseline approaches with experiments conducted on both real-world data and synthesized data.

The rest of paper is organized as follows. Section 2 motivates this research with an example. Section 3 discusses our approaches for solving the EDC problem. Section 4 evaluates the approaches experimentally. Section 5 reviews the related work. Section 6 concludes this paper and points out future work.

2   Motivating Example

Video services accounted for 54% of the total internet traffic in 2017 and the ratio is expected to grow to 79% by 2022 [5]. Thus, a representative example of data cached on edge servers is video data. App vendors such as YouTube currently store their video data on their servers in the cloud. When a video goes viral over the internet, a large number of mobile YouTube users make requests for it. This creates immense pressure on the service in the cloud. Caching this piece of data on edge servers, especially in areas with high user density, brings it closer to the users and reduces the latency of data retrieval.

In an edge computing environment, edge servers can communicate with their neighbor edge servers and share their computing capacities and storage via high-speed links [6] (*server adjacency constraint*). This allows workloads in a particular area to be balanced across the edge servers covering that area [6]. Thus, the edge servers in a particular area can be modeled as a graph where a *node* represents an edge server and an *edge* represents the link between two edge servers. Moreover, the coverage areas of adjacent edge servers often intersect to avoid blank areas not covered by any edge servers. A user in the intersection area can connect to one of the edge servers covering this user (*server coverage constraint*).

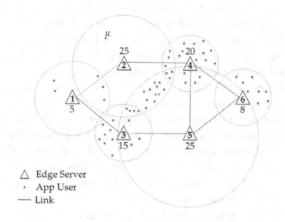

Fig. 1. An example EDC scenario

Figure 1 presents an example area with six edge servers, i.e., $\{v_1, ..., v_6\}$, each covering a specific geographic area. The number next to each edge server is the number of app users covered by that edge server. Let us assume a YouTube video goes viral and it is predicted that a large number of mobile YouTube users in this area will request this video. Please note that there is a large body of research work available on the prediction of popular videos [7] and thus in this research we assume that the number of mobile YouTube users who will request this popular video can be predicted. From YouTube's perspective, caching this video on all the edge servers can easily accommodate all the mobile YouTube users in this area. However, it is usually not cost-effective considering that YouTube will pay for the resources on the edge servers hired for caching the data, e.g., storage and bandwidth. Thus, the data caching strategy must minimize the data caching cost and ensure that all the app users in this area can retrieve the video from one of the edge servers. This edge data caching (EDC) problem is inherently a constrained optimization problem (COP).

The data caching cost and data retrieval latency can be evaluated using a variety of metrics. A user's data retrieval latency consists of two components: the latency between the user and its nearby edge server, and the latency between edge servers. As the first component is very small and not influenced by the data caching strategy, it is not considered in the formulation of the data caching strategy. To quantify the optimization objective and constraints in the COP in a generic manner, we measure the data caching cost using the number of cached data replicas and the data retrieval latency using the number of hops, i.e., links between edge servers. For example, the cost of caching the video on all the six edge servers in Fig. 1 is 6. The *server adjacency constraint* requires that all the users must be able to retrieve the data from an edge server less than two hops. For example, this constraint holds for the u in the top left corner if the video is cached on v_1, v_2 or v_4 and it does not hold if the video is only cached on v_3, v_5 and/or v_6. The rationale behind this constraint is that edge servers can communicate with their neighbor edge servers, but they are not designed or linked to route (potentially large) data across multiple hops. Based on the generic metrics for data caching cost and data retrieval latency, specific pricing policies and latency models can be integrated into our COP model. For example, knowing the size of the data to be cached and the prices for the storage and bandwidth for caching the data, the data cache cost can be calculated based on the number of cached data replicas.

There might be multiple caching strategies that minimize the data caching cost while fulfilling the latency constraint for every app user. Different edge servers usually cover different numbers of app users, depending on the user density in their coverage areas. Thus, one of those caching strategies is to maximize the total latency reduction across all the covered app users. From YouTube's perspective, the other optimization objective is thus to maximize the benefit produced by the cached data replicas, which is measured by the total reduction in data retrieval latency for all the app users.

The model and approach proposed in this research are generic and applicable to various apps. Thus, data are cached on edge servers in whole and we do not consider the situation where data can be partially cached, e.g., video segments. In addition, the scale of the EDC problem in the real-world scenarios can be much larger than the example presented in Fig. 1. Finding an optimal solution to a large-scale EDC problem is not trivial.

3   Our Approach

3.1   Definitions

In this research, the n edge servers in a particular area are modeled as a graph. For each edge server v_i, the graph has a corresponding node. For each pair of linked edge servers (v_i, v_j), the graph has a corresponding edge e_t. We use $G(V, E)$ to represent the graph, where V is the set of nodes in G and E is the set of edges in G. *In the remainder of this paper, we will speak inter-changeably of an edge server and its corresponding node in graph G, denoted as v.* The notations adopted in the paper are summarized in Table 1.

As discussed in Sect. 2, we formulate the EDC problem in a generic manner by measuring the data retrieval latency by the number of hops between edge servers and the data caching cost by the number of cached data replicas.

Compared with cloud's virtually unlimited computing capacities, an edge server usually has limited computing capacities due to its size limit [8,9]. At runtime, many app vendors will need to hire the computing capacities for hosting their services and caching their data for their own app users. Thus, an app vendor is unlikely to hire a huge amount of computing capacities on an edge server for caching a lot of its data. It is more cost-effective for most, if not all, app vendors to cache the most popular data on edge servers to serve its nearby users. Thus, in this paper, we investigate the scenarios where data is processed and cached individually. The model and the approaches proposed will build the foundation for more sophisticated edge caching scenarios, e.g., caching multiple data.

Table 1. Summary of notations

Notation	Description
b_u	the maximum benefit for user u
$b_{u,j}$	the benefit of caching replica on server v_j for app user u
CU	the set of users covered by the selected edge server set S
cu_i	the set of users covered by edge server v_i
$d_{i,j}$	the distance from server v_i to server v_j
d_T	the threshold of distance
d_u	the minimum distance from app user u to retrieve replica
$E = \{e_1, e_2, ..., e_m\}$	finite set of links between edge servers
G	the graph presenting a particular area
$R = \{r_1, r_2, ..., r_n\}$	the set of binary variables indicating cache replicas on edge servers
S	the set of selected servers to cache data replica
$U = \{u_1, u_2, ..., u_k\}$	finite set of users
$V = \{v_1, v_2, ..., v_n\}$	finite set of edge servers

Given a piece of data and a set of edge servers v_i $(1 \leq i \leq n)$, a data caching strategy is a vector $R = <r_1, ..., r_n>$, where r_i $(1 \leq i \leq n)$ denotes whether the data is cached on edge server v_i:

$$r_i = \begin{cases} 0 & \text{if data is not cached on edge server } v_i \\ 1 & \text{if data is cached on edge server } v_i \end{cases} \tag{1}$$

In graph G, the distance between two nodes v_i and v_j is the number of hops on the shortest path between them. Thus, given an app user u, its data retrieval latency is measured by the number of hops between the edge server covering u and the nearest edge server with the data in its cache.

$$d_u = \min\{d_{i,j}, r_j = 1, v_j \in V\}, \forall u \in U_i \tag{2}$$

The main objective of edge data caching is to ensure a low data retrieval latency for app users. Thus, R must fulfill the *latency constraint* - every app user must be able to retrieve the data from an edge server within a certain number of hops:

$$d_u < d_T, \forall u \in U_i \tag{3}$$

As discussed in Sect. 2, each edge server can only communicate with its neighbors. Thus, there is $d_T = 2$. However, this can be relaxed, e.g., $d_T = 3, 4, ...$, if the high latency incurred is considered acceptable by the app vendor and new techniques enable data to be transmitted through multiple edge servers rapidly.

To evaluate and compare different data caching strategies, we use the concept of data caching benefit, which is calculated based on the reduction in data retrieval latency measured by the number of hops reduced by cached data. The caching benefit produced by caching data on v_j for user u covered by v_i denoted by $b_{u,j}$, is calculated as follows:

$$b_{u,j} = \begin{cases} 0 & \text{if } d_{i,j} \geq d_T \\ d_T - d_{i,j} & \text{if } d_{i,j} < d_T \end{cases} \tag{4}$$

In the edge computing environment, an app user $u \in U$ might be covered by multiple edge servers. App user u can retrieve the data from any of those edge servers that have the data in the cache. Thus, the data caching benefit produced by the data caching strategy for an app user u is:

$$b_u = \max\{r_j * b_{u,j}, v_j \in V\} \tag{5}$$

From the app vendor's perspective, one of the optimization objectives is to minimize the data caching cost incurred by R and measured by the number of cached data replicas:

$$\text{minimize } cost(R) \tag{6}$$

The second optimization objective is to maximize the data caching benefit, measured by the total reduction in all users' data retrieval latency produced by R based on (5):

$$\text{maximize } benefit(R) \tag{7}$$

3.2   Edge Data Caching Optimal Model

The EDC problem can be modeled as a constrained optimization problem (COP). One of the two optimization objectives can be prioritized over the other with the Lexicographic Goal Programming technique, depending on the app vendor's preference.

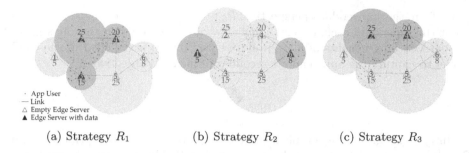

- · App User
- — Link
- △ Empty Edge Server
- ▲ Edge Server with data

(a) Strategy R_1 (b) Strategy R_2 (c) Strategy R_3

Fig. 2. Example data caching strategies

A COP consists of a finite set of variables $X = x_1, \ldots, x_n$, with domain $D_1, \ldots, D_n$ listing the possible values for each variable in X, and a set of constraints $C = c_1, c_2, \ldots, c_t$ over X. A solution to a COP is an assignment of a value to each variable in X from its domain such that all constraints in C are satisfied. The COP model for the EDC problem is formally expressed as follows.

For a graph $G = (V, E)$, where $V = \{v_1, .., v_n, \}$ and $E = \{e_1, ..., e_m\}$, there are a set of variables $R = \{r_1, .., r_n\}$, where $D(r_i) = \{0, 1\}, \forall i \in \{1, ..., n\}$, r_i being 1 if the a data replica is cached on the ith node, 0 otherwise. The constraints for the COP model are:

$$b_u = \max(r_i * b_{u,i}), \forall u \in \{1, ..., k\}, \forall i \in \{1, ..., n\} \tag{8}$$

$$1 \le b_u \le 2, \forall u \in \{1, ..., k\} \tag{9}$$

Constraint family (8) is converted from (5). It ensures that every app user will always retrieve the data from the nearest edge server. Constraint family (9) enforces the latency constraint to ensure that every app user can retrieve the data from an edger server within 2 hops.

There might be multiple solutions fulfilling (8) and (9). In Fig. 2(a) and (b), two possible data caching strategies are $R_1 = \{0, 1, 1, 1, 0, 0\}$, which caches the data on v_1, v_2, and v_3 and $R_2 = \{1, 0, 0, 0, 0, 1\}$, which caches the data on v_1 and v_6. Both R_1 and R_2 fulfill (8) and (9). However, R_2 caches two data replicas, incurring a lower data caching cost than R_1. Thus, the below objective function that minimizes the total number of data replicas cached over G is included in the COP model to capture the app vendor's first optimization objective:

$$\min \sum_{i=1}^{n} r_i \tag{10}$$

The app vendor's second optimization objective also needs to be captured by the COP model. Let us assume two solutions as demonstrated in Fig. 2(b) and (c), $R_2 = \{1, 0, 0, 0, 0, 1\}$, which caches the data on v_1 and v_6, and $R_3 = \{0, 1, 0, 1, 0, 0\}$, which caches the data on v_2 and v_4, both fulfilling the latency constraint and achieving the app vendor's first optimization objective. However, compared with v_1 and v_6, v_2 and v_4 cover more app users, 39 versus 13 in total. Thus, R_3 allows more app users to retrieve the data from edge servers directly.

Thus, from the app vendor's perspective, R_3 produces more caching benefits than R_2 at the same data caching cost. The below objective function that maximizes the data caching benefits of all app users based on (5) is included in the COP model to capture the app vendor's second optimization objective:

$$\max \sum_{u=1}^{k} b_u \tag{11}$$

Integer Programming problem solvers, e.g., IBM CPLEX Optimizer[1] and Gurobi[2], can be employed to solve the above COP. The optimal solution is the data strategy that achieves both (10) and (11) while fulfilling (8) and (9). In this paper, objective (10) (minimize the total number of data replicas) is prioritized over objective (11) (maximize the data caching benefits) as an example for discussion. In real-world applications, objective (11) can be given a higher priority than (10) if the app vendor is willing to minimize its app users' latency at a high data caching cost.

Given multiple data to be cached over time, multiple COPs need to be solved to find one data caching strategy for each piece of data. Those COPs share the same G. Thus, the shortest distance between every two nodes in G can be pre-computed offline to facilitate rapid calculation of (2) as well as app users' cache benefits (5) at runtime.

3.3   Problem Hardness

In this section, we demonstrate that the COP of EDC is $\mathcal{NP}$-complete by proving the following theorems.

Theorem 1. *The COP of EDC is in $\mathcal{NP}$.*

Proof. As there are $(nk + k)$ constraints in total, any solution to the COP can be validated in polynomial time by checking whether the solution satisfies the constraint group (8) and (9). Thus, the COP of EDC is in $\mathcal{NP}$.

Theorem 2. *The COP of EDC is $\mathcal{NP}$-complete.*

Proof. To prove this problem is $\mathcal{NP}$-complete, we introduce the minimum dominating set problem (MDS). MDS problem is known to be $\mathcal{NP}$-complete. Given an undirected graph $G = (V, E)$, where $|V| = n$ and $|E| = m$. The metrics $C_{n,n}$ presents the connection between vertices. $C_{i,j} = 1$ if v_i and v_j are connected, otherwise $C_{i,j} = 0$. The formulation is displayed below:

$$object : \min \sum_{i=1}^{n} v_i \tag{12a}$$

$$s.t. : v_i \in \{0,1\}, i = \{1,..,n\} \tag{12b}$$

$$\sum_{j=1}^{n} C_{i,j} \geq 1, \forall i \in \{1,...,n\} \tag{12c}$$

---

[1] https://www.ibm.com/analytics/cplex-optimizer.
[2] http://www.gurobi.com/.

Now we prove that the minimum dominating set problem can be reduced to an instance of the EDC problem. The reduction is done in two steps: (1) let each edge server cover only one app user; (2) let each app user be covered by only one edge server. Due to the reduction, objective (8) can be ignored because the total user benefits are always the same with the same number of servers selected for caching this data. Given an instance $MDS(v, e, C_{n,n})$, we can construct an instance $EDC(r, e, B_{n,k})$ with the reduction above in polynomial time while $|r| = |v|$ and $n = k$, where $B_{n,k}$ is the benefit matrix from (4). In this case, any solution s satisfying objective (12a) and constraint (12b) also satisfies objective (10). Moreover, the constraint (12c) means that for each vertex v_i not in the solution s, there exists at least one neighbour of v_i in s. From this point, user u covered by vertex v_i can obtain benefit $b_u \geq 1$. Thus, if the solution s fulfills constraint (12c), it also fulfills constraints (8) and (9). Therefore, the COP of EDC is reducible from MDS and it is $\mathcal{NP}$-complete.

3.4   A Near-Optimal Algorithm

Finding the optimal solution to the $\mathcal{NP}$-complete EDC problem is intractable in large-scale scenarios. Thus, this section proposes a heuristic algorithm for finding a near-optimal solution to large-scale EDC problems efficiently.

A naive and straightforward heuristic is to always cache data on the edge server with the most app users. However, selecting an edge server with many neighbor edge servers allows the app users covered by those neighbor edge servers to retrieve cached data within one hop. Based on this heuristic, we present a link-oriented greedy algorithm, namely $LGEDC$, that always selects the node with the most edges in G to cache the data. The pseudo code is presented in Algorithm 1. In the worst-case scenario, LGEDC selects no more than n edge servers, while the computational complexity of the function $selectMaximumEdgsServer$ is $O(n)$. Thus, the computational complexity of LGEDC is $O(n^2)$.

EDC problem has two objectives (10) and (11). Here, we select the prioritized objective (10) (minimize the total number of data replicas) to calculate the approximation ratio of LGEDC. The approximation ratio can be calculated based on Theorem 3.

Theorem 3. *LGEDC is $O(n)$-approximation.*

Proof. Let us assume that the optimal solution OPT selects k edge servers to cache data. Figure 3 presents a worst-case EDC scenario, where n edge servers are linked as a circle and each edge server covers its own group of distinct app users. In this case, Algorithm 1 will select $v_1, v_2, ..., v_{n-2}$ to cache data, as the app users in v_n covered by v_n can be served by v_1, the app users covered by v_{n-1} can be served by v_{n-2}. The solution S of LGEDC selects at most $n-2$ edge servers to cache data. Thus, there is $\frac{|S|}{|OPT|} = \frac{n-2}{k}$, and LGEDC is $O(n)$-approximation.

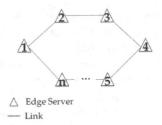

Fig. 3. The worst-case in LGEDC

Algorithm 1. LGEDC Algorithm

1: Initialization:
2: $CU, S \leftarrow \varnothing$
3: End of initialization
4: **repeat**
5:      $v \leftarrow$ selectMaximumEdgesServer()
6:      $S \leftarrow S \cup \{v\}$
7:      $CU \leftarrow CU \cup cu_i$
8: **until** $CU = U$

4 Experimental Evaluation

We conducted two sets of experiments to evaluate the performance of IPEDC and LGEDC. The COP discussed in Sect. 3 is solved with IBM's CPLEX Optimizer. All the experiments are conducted on a machine equipped with Intel Core i7-8550 processor (8 CPUs, 1.8 GHz) and 8 GB RAM, running Windows 10.

4.1 Baseline Approaches

In these experiments, we evaluate the performance of our approaches against two representative baseline approaches, namely *Random* and *Greedy-Covered-Users*:

- *Random*: This approach randomly selects edge servers, one after another, to cache data until the latency constraint (3) is fulfilled.
- *Greedy-Covered-Users (GU)*: This approach always selects the edge server that covers the most app users to cache data until the latency constraint (3) is fulfilled.

4.2 Experimental Settings

Data Sets: Two sets of experiments are conducted, one on the public real-world EUA data set[3] [2] and the other on a synthetic data set. The latter is synthesized to simulate more general EDC scenarios. In the experiments on the synthesized data set, a certain number of edge servers are randomly distributed within a particular area with app users generated also randomly. In the experiments, edges are randomly generated according to the edge density to ensure the graph is connected.

Parameter Settings: To comprehensively evaluate IPEDC and LGEDC, we vary two parameters in the experiments to simulate different EDC scenarios, as presented in Table 2. This way, we can also evaluate how the changes in the parameters impact the performance of our approaches. Every time a parameter varies, the experiment is repeated 100 times and the results are averaged:

---

[3] https://github.com/swinedge/eua-dataset.

- The number of edge servers (n). This parameter impacts the size of graph G and varies from 10 to 40 in steps of 10.
- Edge density (d). In the second set of experiment,s given n edge servers in a particular area, a total of e edges are generated randomly according to the edge density calculated with $d = e/n$. This parameter impacts the density of graph G and varies from 1 to 3 in steps of 0.5.

Performance Metrics: Four metrics are used in the experiments for the evaluation, three for effectiveness and one for efficiency: (1) Data Caching Cost *cost*, the lower the better; (2) Data Caching Benefit *benefit*, the higher the better; (3) Benefit per Data Replica *bpr*, the higher the better; (4) Computation Overhead *time*, the lower the better.

According to (11), *cost* is calculated by summing the benefits of all app users. Thus, to stabilize the impact of the number of app users, we always select or generate a total of 100 app users in the experiments set #2.

Table 2. Parameter settings

	Number of edge servers	Edge density	Data set
Set #1	10, 20, 30, 40	1	Real-World
Set #2.1	10, 20, 30, 40	1	Synthetic
Set #2.2	10	1, 1.5, 2, 2.5, 3	Synthetic

4.3   Experimental Results

The results of the experiments are shown in Figs. 4, 5 and 6, corresponding to Set #1, #2.1 and #2.2.

Effectiveness: Fig. 4 presents the results of experiment set #1. Overall, of all the four approaches, **IPEDC achieves the highest benefit per replica at the lowest data caching cost, while LGEDC is the second lowest in cost with the second highest in benefit per data replica.** Figure 4(b) shows that IPEDC achieves the lowest data caching benefit. In the experiments, objective (10) is prioritized over (11). With the priority to minimize the data caching cost, retrieving data from edge servers via one hop is more preferable. Thus, IPEDC will aim for a solution that barely fulfills (9), i.e., a solution that suffices to allow the most users to retrieve data from edge servers via one hop. Figure 4(a) shows that **the average data caching costs achieved by IPEDC and LGEDC are much lower than other two approaches,** 7.71 for IPEDC and 14.43 for LGEDC versus 19.44 for GU and 19.14 for Random. Figure 4(a) also shows that, as the number of edge servers increases from 10 to 40, the data caching cost achieved by IPEDC increases from 3.48 to 11.14 on average, much slower than LGEDC (5.01 to 24.01), Random (6.78 to 31.98) and GU (6.57 to 32.7).

Figure 4(b) shows that the increase in the number of edge servers will increase the data caching benefits achieved by all four approaches, from 497.13 to 1164.28 for IPEDC, 530.30 to 1289.99 for LGEDC, 612.17 to 1397.02 for GU and 579.48 to 1368.11 for Random. Figure 1(c) demonstrates **the significant advantage of IPEDC over the other approaches in achieving cost-effective data caching strategies**. On average, it outperforms LGEDC by 54.54%, GU by 84.09% and Random by 90.83%. As the number of edge servers increases, the benefits per replica achieved by all approaches decrease. The increase in the number of edge servers deployed in a specific area increases the connectivity between the edge servers. This increases app users' chances of retrieving data via one hop, which lowers the average benefit produced by each data replica.

Figure 5 depicts the results from experiment Set # 2.1. Overall, **IPEDC achieves the highest data per replica at the lowest data caching cost** again. Its advantage over the other approaches is significant. In this set of experiments, the edge servers are set up in a similar way as Set #1. Therefore, the

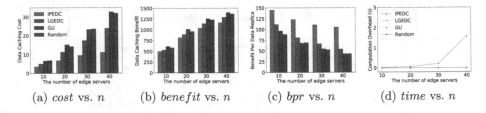

(a) *cost* vs. *n*   (b) *benefit* vs. *n*   (c) *bpr* vs. *n*   (d) *time* vs. *n*

Fig. 4. Experiment Set #1

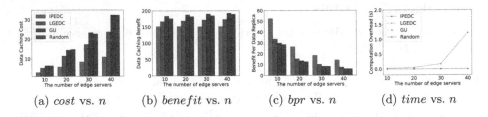

(a) *cost* vs. *n*   (b) *benefit* vs. *n*   (c) *bpr* vs. *n*   (d) *time* vs. *n*

Fig. 5. Experiment Set #2.1

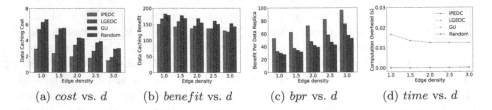

(a) *cost* vs. *d*   (b) *benefit* vs. *d*   (c) *bpr* vs. *d*   (d) *time* vs. *d*

Fig. 6. Experiment Set #2.2

results shown in Fig. 5(a) are similar to those shown in Fig. 4. However, Fig. 5(b) shows that the **data caching benefit does not increase** with the increase in the number of edge servers. The reason is that, unlike experiment Set #1, the number of app users in experiment Set #2.1 does not increase. Thus, the data caching benefit does not increase accumulatively as in Fig. 4(b). This is also the same reason for the rapid decrease in the benefit per data replica demonstrated in Fig. 5(c).

Figure 6 shows the results in experiment Set #2.2 where the graph density varies. In terms of the average data caching cost and benefit per data replica, **IPEDC outperforms the other approaches** with large margins, 44.17% against LGEDC, 55.81% against GU and 56.77% against Random on average in data caching cost, 45.85% against LGEDC, 83.25% against GU and 89.30% against Random on average in benefit per data replica. Interestingly, Fig. 6 shows that **the edge density impacts the approaches in a very different way** from the number of edge servers. Figure 6(a) shows that as the edge density increases from 1.0 to 3.0, the data caching cost achieved by IPEDC decreases from 2.92 to 1.47. This is because the increase in the edge density allows each edge server to be linked to more edge servers. This increases the app users' chances of retrieving data from edge servers via one hop. IPEDC does not need to cache as many data replicas to ensure that all app users are served by edge servers within one hop. As a result, the average data caching cost decreases. For the same reason, the data caching benefit decreases, as demonstrated in Fig. 6(b). The increase in the connectivity between edge servers also allows more app users to be able to retrieve data via one hop. As a result, the benefit per data replica increases, as demonstrated in Fig. 6(c), from 52.84 to 96.60 for IPEDC, from 32.70 to 75.25 for LGEDC, from 29.82 to 57.46 for GU and from 27.74 to 52.73 for Random.

Overall, **IPEDC significantly and consistently outperforms all other approaches, with LGEDC second**, in formulating cost-effective data caching strategies, especially in EDC scenarios where edge servers are highly connected.

Efficiency: Figures 4(d), 5(d) and 6(d) present the average computation times taken by the four approaches to find a solution to the EDC problem. We can see in Figs. 4(d) and 5(d) that the **computation overhead of IPEDC increases rapidly** when the number of edge servers increases. When there are 40 edge servers to consider, IPEDC takes 1–2 s to find the optimal solution in Fig. 4(d). This excessive computation overhead is inevitable in large-scale EDC scenarios because IPEDC tries to find the optimal solution to the $\mathcal{NP}$-complete EDC problem. Thus, **IPEDC is suitable for solving EDC problems with reasonable sizes, while LGEDC is suitable for solving large-scale EDC problems**. The results in Fig. 6(d) indicates that IPEDC is also very efficient in EDC scenarios where edge servers are highly connected.

4.4 Threats to Validity

Construct Validity. The major threat to construct validity is the two baseline approaches used for comparison. Due to the innovation of the EDC problem in the edge computing environment, we chose two basic naive approaches as baselines in our evaluation. As those baseline approaches are relatively simple, IPEDC and LGEDC tend to achieve better experimental results. Thus, there is a threat that the comparison does not suffice to comprehensively evaluate IPEDC and LGEDC. To minimize this threat in the experiments, we changed two parameters, as presented in Table 2, to simulate various EDC scenarios. In this way, we could evaluate our approaches by not only comparison to the baseline approaches, but also demonstrate how the changes in the parameters impact the performance of the approaches.

External Validity. The major threat to external validity is whether IPEDC and LGEDC can be generalized and applied in other application scenarios in the edge computing environment. To tackle this threat, we measure the performance of our approaches in a generic way - using the number of reduced hops for effectiveness evaluation and the number of data replicas for efficiency evaluation. In this way, the results of the evaluation can be interpreted based on specific models of data retrieval latency and data caching cost. In addition, we ran the experiments on a real-world data set and a synthetic data set. We also varied two parameters to vary the size and the complexity of the EDC problem. This way, the representativeness and comprehensiveness of the evaluation are ensured. The above measures allowed us to ensure that the results were generalized, which reduced the threat to external validity.

Conclusion Validity. The main threat to conclusion validity is the lack of statistical tests, e.g., chi-square tests. We could have conducted chi-square tests to draw conclusions. However, we ran the experiment for 100 times in experiments and averaged the results each time we changed a parameter. This led to a large number of test cases, which tend to result in a small p-value in the chi-square tests and lower the practical significance of the test results [10]. For example, in experiment Set 2, there were a total of 1,300 runs. This number is not even close to the number of observation samples that concern Lin et al. in [10]. Thus, the threat to the conclusion validity due to the lack of statistical tests might be high but not significant.

5 Related Work

Edge computing is an extension of cloud computing with distributed computing resources and services at the edge of the cloud [11]. With the deployment of edge servers, the problem of computation offloading arises. It has been well studied with consideration of edge servers' energy efficiency [12], offloading cost [13] and so forth.

In the last few years, researchers have been investigating the challenges raised by data caching in the edge computing environment. Conventional approaches for data caching are not suitable in the edge computing environment and cannot be applied directly. Thus, new ideas and techniques are being proposed and investigated. An optimal auction mechanism was introduced in [14] that considers the data retrieval and delivery costs. The authors showed computationally efficient approaches for calculating the optimal decisions of cache allocation and user pays. Halalai et al. [15] proposed Agar, a caching system, from the erasure-coded perspective. They designed Agar based on a dynamic programming algorithm for optimally caching data chunks with consideration of data popularity and network latency.

Instead of data caching optimization across edge servers, some researchers study how to integrate edge servers' internal caches and external caches. In [16], the authors proposed Cachier, a system that minimizes data retrieval latency by coordinating the loading balance between edge servers and the cloud in a dynamical manner. The authors of [17] integrated in-network caching and edge caching to guarantee the quality of time-sensitive multimedia transmissions over the 5G wireless network. They also provided three hierarchical edge caching mechanisms, including a random hierarchical caching approach, a proactive hierarchical caching approach and a game-theory-based hierarchical caching approach. Zhang et al. [18] proposed an architecture to enhance edge caching by using computation resources of edge servers. They presented a caching scheme by implementing smart vehicles as edge servers to provide external caches.

To the best of our knowledge, our work is the first attempt to solve the Edge Data Caching (EDC) problem from the app vendor' perspective in the edge computing environment. We also realistically and innovatively solve the EDC problem in a generic manner to minimize the data caching cost and maximum the data caching benefit with the server coverage constraint and the server adjacency constraint.

6   Conclusion

In this paper, we formulated the new Edge Data Caching (EDC) problem in the edge computing environment as a constrained optimization problem from the app vendor's perspective. To find an optimal solution, we proposed IPEDC, an approach based on the Integer Programming technique with two optimization objectives: (1) to minimize the data caching cost measured by the number of cached data replicas; and (2) to maximum the data caching benefit measured by the total reduction in app users' data retrieval latency. However, we also proved that the EDC problem is $\mathcal{NP}$-complete. We then provided a heuristic approach named LGEDC for finding near-optimal solutions to the EDC problem. We conducted extensive experiments based on a real-world data set and a synthetic data set to evaluate the performance of IPEDC and LGEDC in different EDC scenarios. The results demonstrate that IPEDC significantly outperforms all other approaches in formulating cost-effective EDC solutions, while LGEDC solves large-scale EDC problems efficiently.

This research has established the foundation for the EDC problem and opened up a number of research directions. In our future work, we will first consider the problem of caching multiple data at the same time for an app vendor. Other issues that can be investigated include data popularity, security constraints, etc.

Acknowledgement. This research is partially funded by Australian Research Council Discovery Projects (No. DP170101932 and DP180100212).

References

1. Osseiran, A., et al.: The foundation of the mobile and wireless communications system for 2020 and beyond: challenges, enablers and technology solutions. In: IEEE 77th Vehicular Technology Conference (VTC2013-Spring), pp. 1–5 (2013)
2. Lai, P., et al.: Optimal edge user allocation in edge computing with variable sized vector bin packing. In: Pahl, C., Vukovic, M., Yin, J., Yu, Q. (eds.) ICSOC 2018. LNCS, vol. 11236, pp. 230–245. Springer, Cham (2018). https://doi.org/10.1007/978-3-030-03596-9_15
3. Tran, T.X., Hosseini, M.-P., Pompili, D.: Mobile edge computing: recent efforts and five key research directions. IEEE COMSOC MMTC Commun. Front. **12**(4), 29–33 (2017)
4. M. ETSI.: Mobile edge computing - introductory technical white paper (2014)
5. Cisco visual networking index: global mobile data traffic forecast update, 2017–2022 (2019). https://www.cisco.com/c/en/us/solutions/collateral/service-provider/visual-networking-index-vni/white-paper-c11-738429.html
6. Chen, L., Zhou, S., Xu, J.: Computation peer offloading for energy-constrained mobile edge computing in small-cell networks. IEEE/ACM Trans. Netw. **26**(4), 1619–1632 (2018)
7. Tatar, A., De Amorim, M.D., Fdida, S., Antoniadis, P.: A survey on predicting the popularity of web content. J. Internet Serv. Appl. **5**(1), 1–20 (2014)
8. Chen, M., Hao, Y., Lin, K., Yuan, Z., Hu, L.: Label-less learning for traffic control in an edge network. IEEE Netw. **32**(6), 8–14 (2018)
9. Wang, S., Zhang, X., Zhang, Y., Wang, L., Yang, J., Wang, W.: A survey on mobile edge networks: convergence of computing, caching and communications. IEEE Access **5**, 6757–6779 (2017)
10. Lin, M., Lucas Jr., H.C., Shmueli, G.: Research commentary-too big to fail: large samples and the p-value problem. Inf. Syst. Res. **24**(4), 906–917 (2013)
11. Yannuzzi, M., et al.: A new era for cities with fog computing. IEEE Internet Comput. **21**(2), 54–67 (2017)
12. Wang, F., Xu, J., Wang, X., Cui, S.: Joint offloading and computing optimization in wireless powered mobile-edge computing systems. IEEE Trans. Wirel. Commun. **17**(3), 1784–1797 (2018)
13. Yao, H., Bai, C., Xiong, M., Zeng, D., Fu, Z.: Heterogeneous cloudlet deployment and user-cloudlet association toward cost effective fog computing. Concurr. Comput. Pract. Exp. **29**(16), e3975 (2017)
14. Cao, X., Zhang, J., Poor, H.V.: An optimal auction mechanism for mobile edge caching. In: 38th IEEE International Conference on Distributed Computing Systems (ICDCS), pp. 388–399 (2018)
15. Halalai, R., Felber, P., Kermarrec, A.-M., Taïani, F.: Agar: a caching system for erasure-coded data. In: 37th IEEE International Conference onDistributed Computing Systems (ICDCS), pp. 23–33 (2017)

16. Drolia, U., Guo, K., Tan, J., Gandhi, R., Narasimhan, P.: Cachier: edge-caching for recognition applications. In: 37th IEEE International Conference onDistributed Computing Systems (ICDCS), pp. 276–286 (2017)
17. Zhang, X., Zhu, Q.: Hierarchical caching for statistical qos guaranteed multimedia transmissions over 5G edge computing mobile wireless networks. IEEE Wirel. Commun. **25**(3), 12–20 (2018)
18. Zhang, K., Leng, S., He, Y., Maharjan, S., Zhang, Y.: Cooperative content caching in 5g networks with mobile edge computing. IEEE Wirel. Commun. **25**(3), 80–87 (2018)

Load-Aware Edge Server Placement for Mobile Edge Computing in 5G Networks

Xiaolong Xu[1], Yuan Xue[1], Lianyong Qi[2(✉)], Xuyun Zhang[3], Shaohua Wan[4], Wanchun Dou[5(✉)], and Victor Chang[6]

[1] School of Computer and Software, Nanjing University of Information Science and Technology, Nanjing, China
njuxlxu@gmail.com, xueyuannuist@gmail.com
[2] School of Information Science and Engineering,
Qufu Normal University, Qufu, China
lianyongqi@gmail.com
[3] Department of Electrical and Computer Engineering, University of Auckland,
Auckland, New Zealand
xuyun.zhang@auckland.ac.nz
[4] School of Information and Safety Engineering,
Zhongnan University of Economics and Law, Wuhan, Hubei, China
shaohua.wan@ieee.org
[5] State Key Laboratory for Novel Software Technology,
Nanjing University, Nanjing, China
douwc@nju.edu.cn
[6] School of Computing & Digital Technologies,
Teesside University, Middlesbrough, UK
Victor.Chang@xjtlu.edu.cn

Abstract. Edge computing is a promising technique for 5G networks to collect a wide range of environmental information from mobile devices and return real-time feedbacks to the mobile users. Generally, the edge servers (ESs) are both contributing in macro-base station (MABS) sites for large-scale resource provisioning and micro-base station (MIBS) sites for light-weighted resource response. However, to lower the investment of construing the edge computing systems in the MIBS sites, limited number of ESs are employed, since there is an intensive distribution of MIBSs in 5G networks. Thus, it remains challenging to guarantee the execution efficiency of the edge services and the overall performance of the edge computing systems with limited ESs. In view of this challenge, a load-aware edge server placement method, named LESP, is devised for mobile edge computing in 5G networks. Technically, a decision tree is constructed to identify the MIBSs served by a definite ES and confirm the data transmission routes across MIBSs. Then, the non-dominated sorting genetic algorithm II (NSGA-II) is employed to obtain the balanced ES placement strategies. Furthermore, simple additive weighting (SAW) and multiple criteria decision making (MCDM) techniques are leveraged to recognize the optimal ES placement strategy. Finally, the experimental evaluations are implemented and the observed simulation results verify the efficiency and effectiveness of LESP.

© Springer Nature Switzerland AG 2019
S. Yangui et al. (Eds.): ICSOC 2019, LNCS 11895, pp. 494–507, 2019.
https://doi.org/10.1007/978-3-030-33702-5_38

Keywords: 5G networks · Edge computing · Edge server placement

1 Introduction

Nowadays, with the development of Internet of Things (IoT), the increment rate of smart mobile device scale has reached a ninety-two percent per year since 2006 [1]. Cellular providers intend to enhance mobile applications which require high quality and low latency to these mobile devices [2]. However, considering the spectrum technologies in the fourth generation (4G) networks, the remaining spectrum resources are insufficient to support the harsh requirements for the delay and the bandwidth from mobile applications such as telesurgery, health monitoring and transportation cruise control, which compels providers to surmount the lack of the spectrum resources [3].

Aiming to remedy the shortage of spectrum resources, cellular providers employ a brand-new spectrum technology called the millimeter-wave (mm-Wave) in 5G, which is capable of taking full advantage of spectrum resources [4]. Technically, the wave length of the mm-wave is 1 m to 10 mm, which results in 5G bandwidth reaching up to 273.5 GHz. Nevertheless, the attenuation degree of mm-Wave signal is severely impacted by fog/cloud conditions [5]. For the sake of decreasing the attenuation of the mm-Wave signal and make use of spectrum resources, the base stations in 5G are divided into macro base stations (MABSs) and micro base stations (MIBSs) in line with their coverage [6]. Then, arranging MIBSs intensively increases the spectrum density and improves the spectrum efficiency.

As massive 5G smart applications appear continuously, it is approximately impossible to deal with computation-intensive services locally due to the limited computing resources in smart mobile devices [7]. Thus, mobile devices ask for the computing resources provided by the cloud platform to execute the services [8]. In spite of that the pressure for mobile devices to handle services is relieved by the cloud, the quality of experience (QoE) for users is hard to satisfy, especially for the real-time applications like virtual reality (VR) games. Therefore, edge computing, as a significant paradigm, is utilized to shorten the delay and make users experience the applications real-timely. Detailedly, edge computing endows the computing resources to edge servers (ESs), the gathered applications on the network edge are in a position to obtain the resources in the ES close by.

On account of that mobile applications are usually in the vicinity of MIBSs, ESs are co-located with MIBSs, which are seen as the edge nodes (ENs) to cooperate with MABS for executing the applications. Nonetheless, MIBSs are arranged intensively because of its relatively narrow range. With a view to the high cost of purchasing ESs, it is unpractical to equip each MIBS with an ES, which makes some tasks offloaded to a distant ES and generates unbearable delay for users. In addition, the finite computing resources in ESs are unable to handle such abundant tasks, which makes some services wait in the queue of ESs and severely affects the efficiency of service execution. Hence, to ensure the stability and the performance of ESs, it is urgent to achieve the load balance of ESs. Given these facts, it is a truly difficult challenge to realize the reasonable ES placement for improving the performance of all ESs by reducing the transmission delay and achieving load balance. A load-aware edge server placement method named as LESP, is devised for edge computing in 5G networks in this paper. In conclusion, the primary contributions are presented as follows.

- A decision tree is structured to record the routings of edge services according to the balanced distribution of load.
- Non-dominated sorting genetic algorithm II (NSGA-II) is used to formulate the appropriate balanced ES placement strategies.
- Simple additive weighting (SAW) and multiple criteria decision making (MCDM) are adopted to select the optimal ES placement strategy.
- Simulation experiments are conducted to confirm the efficiency of the devised method LESP.

The remaining part of this paper is divided into five sections. The system model is shown in Sect. 2. A load-aware edge server placement method is designed in Sect. 3. The simulation experiment results and the comparison analysis are conducted in Sect. 4. Related Works are summed up in Sect. 5. Conclusions are outlined in Sect. 6.

2   System Model

In this section, the overview of the ES placement framework in 5G networks is presented first. Then, according to the specific ES placement strategy, transmission delay and load balance analyses are conducted. Finally, the ES placement problem is formulated as a multi-objective optimization problem.

2.1   Resource Model

In 5G networks, multiple macro-base stations (MABSs) are deployed to provision services for mobile applications and the MABS covers several micro-base station (MIBS) to improve the service quality [9]. With wireless signals, the MIBSs receive service requests from mobile devices. In Fig. 1, the framework for supporting edge computing in 5G networks is shown. In the range of the MABS, several MIBSs are deployed to receive service requests. Assume that there are Q MIBSs in the range of the MABS, denoted as $M = \{m_1, m_2, \ldots, m_Q\}$. As MIBSs fail to meet the process requirements of massive services, the computing and storage capacity of MIBSs are extended through realizing the cooperative placement of ESs and MIBSs. Thus, the ESs are co-located with the specific MIBSs for helping process transmitted services, denoted as $S = \{s_1, s_2, \ldots, s_N\}$. Notably, the number of ESs is not equal to the number of MIBSs. Besides, with the virtualization technique in edge computing, the capacity of the ES is measured by the number of virtual machines (VMs) in the ES, denoted as φ_n [10,11]. Provided that all VMs in the ES are occupied, unprocessed edge services need to wait for the completion of the services in the previous round.

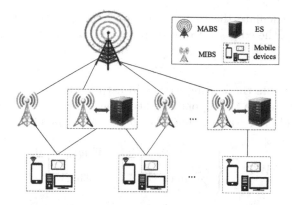

Fig. 1. An edge computing framework in 5G networks.

2.2   Transmission Delay Model

The transmission delay is composed of the transmission time from the MIBS to the destination ES, the waiting time of the edge services in the ES, the service execution time of the ES and the transmission time of the feedbacks.

In view of that not all MIBSs are cooperating with the ES, we first adopt a binary variable B_Q^N to judge whether the q-th ($q = 1, 2, \ldots, Q$) MIBS m_q is co-located with the n-th ($n = 1, 2, \ldots, N$) ES s_n.

$$B_q^n = \begin{cases} 1, & \text{if } m_q \text{ is cooperatively placed with } s_n, \\ 0, & \text{otherwise.} \end{cases} \tag{1}$$

The time consumption of data transmission from the MIBS to the destination ES is calculated by

$$DT_q = (1 - B_q^n) \cdot \frac{ds_q}{\theta} \cdot \omega_q, \tag{2}$$

where ds_q represents the data size of the edge service in m_q and θ represents the data transmission rate between MIBSs. In addition, ω_q is the number of passing MIBSs in the process of data transmission.

By means of the virtualization technique, the resource units in ESs are normalized as VMs. Therefore, the service execution time in s_n is

$$ET_q = \frac{ds_q}{ru_q \cdot \rho}, \tag{3}$$

where ru_q represents the VMs demanded by the edge service transmitted from s_n and ρ is the processing power of each VM.

In order to calculate the waiting time of the edge services in the ES, the waiting rounds of the edge services need to be calculated first, which is shown as

$$R = wr_n, \tag{4}$$

where wr_n represents the waiting rounds in n-th ES s_n.

Let ET_r denote the corresponding execution time of processing all services in the z-th round. The waiting time of edge services offloaded from s_n is calculated by

$$WT_q = \begin{cases} 0, & \text{if } wr_n = 0, \\ \sum_{r=1}^{R-1} \max(ET_r), & \text{otherwise.} \end{cases} \tag{5}$$

The transmission time of feedbacks from s_n is calculated by

$$FT_q = \frac{ds'_q}{\theta} \cdot \omega_q, \tag{6}$$

where ds'_q is the data size of the processing results of the edge service offloaded from m_q.

The total transmission delay of the edge service in m_q is calculated by

$$D_q = DT_q + ET_q + WT_q + FT_q. \tag{7}$$

The average delay for all edge services is calculated by

$$A = \frac{1}{Q} \cdot \sum_{q=1}^{Q} D_q. \tag{8}$$

2.3   Load Balance Model

The load balance conditions of ESs are measured by the load balance variance. Specifically, the occupy conditions of ESs and the number of running VMs are described. F_n is a binary variable to judge whether s_n is occupied, which is calculated by

$$F_n = \begin{cases} 1, & \text{if } s_n \text{ is occupied,} \\ 0, & \text{otherwise.} \end{cases} \tag{9}$$

Besides, P_q^n is a binary variable to judge whether the edge service in m_q is offloaded to s_n for execution, which is defined by

$$P_q^n = \begin{cases} 1, & \text{if } m_q \text{ offloads the service to } s_n, \\ 0, & \text{otherwise.} \end{cases} \tag{10}$$

Consequently, the number of running ESs is calculated by

$$\xi = \sum_{n=1}^{N} P_q^n. \tag{11}$$

The resource utilization of s_n is measured by the usage of VM instances, which is calculated by

$$RU_n = \frac{1}{\varphi_n} \sum_{q=1}^{Q} P_q^n \cdot \varepsilon_q, \tag{12}$$

where ε_q is the number of VMs required by the edge service in m_q.

Thus, the average resource utilization of ESs is calculated by

$$U = \frac{1}{\xi} \sum_{n=1}^{N} RU_n. \tag{13}$$

The load balance variance of s_n is calculated by

$$b_n = (RU_n - U)^2. \tag{14}$$

Then, the average load balance variance of occupied ESs in 5G networks is calculated by

$$B = \frac{1}{\xi} \sum_{n=1}^{N} b_n \cdot F_n. \tag{15}$$

2.4 Problem Formulation

In this paper, the ES placement is defined as a multi-objective optimization problem. We minimize the transmission delay in (8) and the load balance variance in (15), which is given as

$$\min A, \min B. \tag{16}$$

$$s.\, t. \quad N \le Q, \tag{17}$$

$$\sum_{q=1}^{Q} \varepsilon_q \le \sum_{n=1}^{N} \varphi_n. \tag{18}$$

3   A Load-Aware Edge Server Placement Method

In this section, the routing confirmation of edge services is presented first. Then, NSGA-II is adopted for the multi-objective optimization problem. Finally, SAW and MCDM are used to select the optimal ES placement strategy.

Algorithm 1. Routing Confirmation of edge services in MIBSs

Require: M, S, an empty decision tree
Ensure: Routing confirmation of edge services
    Set $flag_q$ (q=1, 2, ..., Q) as 0
    Co-locate each ES with a random MIBS
    for the edge server s_n in S **do**
        for the MIBS m_q in M **do**
            if s_n is co-located with m_q **then**
                Offload the edge service in m_q to s_n
                Insert m_q into the decision tree
                m_q.flag $= 1$
            else
                Calculate the distance between s_n and m_q
            end if
        end for
    end for
    for the MIBS m_q in M **do**
        if m_q.flag $= 0$ **then**
            Seek out the minimum distance
            Calculate the depth difference g between the subtrees
        end if
        if $\mid g \mid \leq 1$ **then**
            Offload the service and insert m_q into the current subtree
        else
            Offload the service and insert m_q into the opposite subtree
        end if
    end for
    return Routing confirmation of edge services

3.1 Routing Confirmation of Edge Services

Aiming to offload the edge services from MIBSs to ESs, the transmission routings of edge services need to be confirmed. As all ESs have been placed, decision trees are used to record the routes of edge services from MIBSs. A two-dimensional matrix is set up and for each ES, the distance between the ES and every MIBS is entered into the matrix. The MIBS with the smallest distance value offload the edge services to the ES. Provided that there are more than one ES which have the same distance with a certain MIBS, the number of MIBSs connected to each ES is compared and the edge service in the MIBS is offloaded to the ES which connects the few MIBSs.

The specific routing confirmation of edge services is presented in Algorithm 1. First, the flag of each MIBS is initialized as 0, which means the MIBS has not been traversed. Then, every ES is co-located with a MIBS randomly. The MIBSs which are co-located with an ES offload the edge service to the co-located ES. Finally, other MIBSs determine the offloading destination ES according to the ES load situation.

3.2 Edge Server Placement Strategy Generation Based on NSGA-II

In order to minimize the transmission delay and the load balance variance of all ESs, NSGA-II is used to solve the multi-objective optimization problem in (16). Firstly, the ES placement strategy is encoded, which is known as a gene. As a gene represents a placement strategy of a certain ES, multiple genes represent the placement strategy of all ESs, which constitute a chromosome. The integer coding method is adopted and the ESs are encoded by 1, 2, ..., N.

Aiming at select optimal solutions in a chromosome, fitness functions work as the standards. As shown in Sect. 2, the transmission delay and the load balance variance are the standards to select the appropriate solution. For further selection, the size of population H, the crossover capacity R_c and the mutation capacity R_m and the maximum iteration times V are determined.

Based on the existing population, crossover and mutation operations are conducted to generate new solutions. The crossover in this paper is single-point crossover, which means that two chromosomes swap genes around a predetermined intersection. Through combining two chromosomes, a better chromosome is obtained. In addition, the genes are modified randomly to generate chromosomes which have higher fitness values, known as mutation operation. During the mutation operation, each gene has the same possibility to modify.

For $2H$ solutions after the crossover and mutation operation, the selection operation is conducted to select H solutions. Specifically, the fitness functions of each solution are calculated based on the model.

According to the usual dominating principle, the solutions are sorted and the selection operation is conducted. The population generates non-dominated layers and each placement strategy owns a crowding distance respectively. Through the comparison of the crowding distances, the appropriate individuals are used to form the next population, which is calculated by

$$j_g = j_g^D + j_g^L = |D^{j+1} - D^{j-1}| + |L^{j+1} - L^{j-1}|, \tag{19}$$

where j_g represents the j-th ES placement strategy. j_g^D as well as j_g^L represents the objective functions. D_{j+1} and L_{j+1} represent the objective values of the $j+1$-th placement strategy. D_{j-1} and L_{j-1} represent the objective values of the $j-1$-th placement strategy.

3.3 Edge Server Placement Strategy Selection Using SAW and MCDM

For the last generated chromosome, SAW and MCDM are employed to select the optimal ES placement strategy. The transmission delay is normalized as

$$V(D) = \begin{cases} \frac{D^{\max} - D}{D^{\max} - D^{\min}}, D^{\max} - D^{\min} \neq 0, \\ 1, D^{\max} - D^{\min} = 0, \end{cases} \tag{20}$$

where D^{max} and D^{min} represent the maximum and minimum transmission delay of the solutions in the last population respectively.

Moreover, the load balance variance is normalized as

$$V(L) = \begin{cases} \frac{L^{\max} - L}{L^{\max} - L^{\min}}, L^{\max} - L^{\min} \neq 0, \\ 1, L^{\max} - L^{\min} = 0, \end{cases} \tag{21}$$

where L^{max} and L^{min} represent the maximum and minimum load balance variance of the solutions in the last population respectively.

Aiming to achieve the optimization of normalized transmission delay and load balance, the utility value of the h-th solution needs to calculated, which is shown as

$$V(C_h) = w_1 V(D) + w_2 V(L), \tag{22}$$

where w_1 and w_2 are the weight of transmission delay and load balance variance respectively.

Based on the utility value of the solution, the optimal strategy is selected by

$$V(C) = \max_{h=1}^{H} V(C_h)(1 \leq h \leq H). \tag{23}$$

3.4 Method Overview

In this paper, a load-aware edge server placement method is devised to minimize the transmission delay and the load balance variance. The specific procedure of this method is shown in Algorithm 2. First, a decision tree is structured and the routing of edge services is determined. Then, NSGA-II is adopted to generate balanced ES placement strategies. Finally, SAW and MCDM are utilized to identify the optimal ES placement strategy from the generated population.

Algorithm 2. Load-aware edge server placement

Require: M, S
Ensure: The optimal edge server placement strategy
    $e = 1$
    while $e \leq E$ **do**
        Complete routing confirmation by Algorithm 1
        $e = e + 1$
    end while
    Obtain balanced ES placement strategies by NSGA-II
    for $h = 1$ to H **do**
        Calculate utility values by formulas (20-22)
    end for
    Select the optimal ES placement strategy by formula (23)
    return The optimal edge server placement strategy

---

4   Experimental Evaluation

In this section, the efficiency and effectiveness of LESP are verified by conducting simulation experiments. Firstly, the parameter settings are presented in Table 1. Then, the comparative methods are introduced. Finally, the influences of different MIBS scales on the transmission delay and load balance variance performance of LESP and the comparative methods are evaluated.

Table 1. Parameter settings

Parameter description	Value
The total number of MIBSs	200
The number of VMs in each edge server	40
The number of VMs required by each MIBS	[1, 7]
The transmission rate between MIBSs	5000 Mb/s
The execution capacity of edge server	2000 MHz
The scales of MIBSs	5, 10, 15, 20, 25, 30

4.1   Simulation Setup

We adopt 5 different ES scales in the experiments and the number of ESs is set to 5, 10, 15, 20, 25 and 30. To more intuitively evaluate the performance of LESP, two comparative methods are utilized, which are shown as follows.

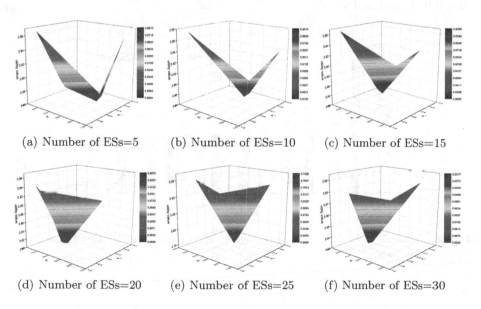

(a) Number of ESs=5   (b) Number of ESs=10   (c) Number of ESs=15

(d) Number of ESs=20   (e) Number of ESs=25   (f) Number of ESs=30

Fig. 2. The utility value of solutions at different MIBS scales.

- *Greedy-D*: Each MIBS offloads its edge service to the nearest ES. Considering that the nearest ES is likely to have no spare computing resources, the edge service is offloaded to a neighbor ES with enough needed computing resources. The system would repeat this procedure until all edge services have been offloaded.
- *Greedy-L*: Each MIBS offloads its edge service to the ES which has most idle computing resources. Provided that several ESs have the similar resource usage, the service is offloaded to the ES which is nearest to the resource MIBS. This procedure is repeated until all edge services have been offloaded.

4.2 Performance Evaluation

When the MIBS scales are 5, 10, 15, 20, 25 and 30 respectively, the weight of $V(D)$ and $V(L)$ in the formula (22) are changed, which are from 0 to 1. In Fig. 2, as the weight of $V(D)$ and $V(L)$ change, the utility value alters correspondingly. Considering that there is a linear relationship between the two weights and the utility value, the utility value graph is divided into two sections and there is a minimum utility value. By means of comparing utility values, the most balanced ES placement strategy is selected. The solution with the maximum utility value is selected as the optimal ES placement strategy.

4.3 Comparison Analysis

For different MIBS scales, the comparisons between LESP and comparative methods are presented. The transmission delay and the load balance variance are functioned as two key criteria. The corresponding experimental results are shown in Figs. 3 and 4.

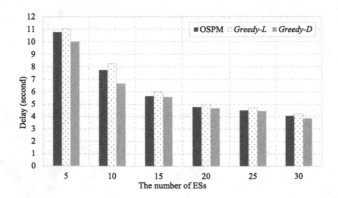

Fig. 3. Comparison of the delay for different MIBS scales between OSPM and comparative methods.

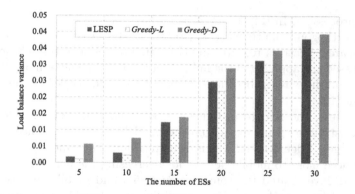

Fig. 4. Comparison of the load balance variance for different MIBS scales between OSPM and comparative methods.

(1) Comparison of Transmission Delay. In the experiment, the processing efficiency of each ES is defined as equal. Therefore, with the determination of edge service routings, the service execution time is the same in LESP, Greedy-D and Greedy-L. In Fig. 3, as the size of the ES expands, the transmission delay decreases because MIBSs are more likely to offload edge services to a close ES than to a remote ES. Nevertheless, Greedy-L aims to minimize load balance variance and the edge services are likely to be offloaded to relatively remote ES, achieving the balanced distribution of load and high transmission delay. Intuitively, LESP is less capable of optimizing transmission delay than Greedy-D and is more effective than Greedy-L in the aspect of optimizing transmission delay.

(2) Comparison of Load Balance Variance. The load balance variance is measured by the occupancy of VM instances. When the ES scale is small, the data waits for limited computing resources in the ES in the queue and the total number of rounds processed by the ES is large. In Fig. 4, as the number of ES increases, more computing resources are vacated and the total round of service execution decreases. In contrast to Greedy-L, Greedy-D is designed to minimize transmission delay. In Greedy-D, the edge services are offloaded to the nearest ES whose VMs are all occupied, making the destination ES overload. Intuitively, the ability to optimize load balancing of LESP is inferior to Greedy-L and superior to Greedy-D.

5   Related Work

Nowadays, as the wireless and mobile communication technologies develop rapidly, the number of smart mobile devices increased dramatically. These smart mobile devices, which possess numerous compute-intensive applications, lead to a large quantity of data needed to be processed [12,13]. However, smart mobile devices are unable to deal with the data for its limited computing resources. Therefore, the 5th generation mobile network (5G), as a novel paradigm, is proposed to help devices offload the data to the remote infrastructures such as the cloud for processing. In [14], Islam et al. probed into a radio access technology called non-orthogonal multiple access (NOMA). NOMA can relieve the pressure from the scarce spectrum resource in 5G for its greater spectrum efficiency. Niu et al. discussed the applying of the millimeter wave (mm-wave) in 5G. The small cell access and the wireless backhaul are investigated to accelerate the mm-wave deployment [13].

Nevertheless, the remote distance between smart mobile devices and the remote infrastructure generates an unbearable delay for users. Hence, edge computing emerges. Edge servers, which own the computing and storage capabilities, are placed close to mobile devices for decreasing the delay [15,16]. In [17], Nunna et al. investigated the combination of 5G and mobile edge computing. In addition, Rimal et al. considered providing mobile edge computing (MEC) capabilities of integrated fiber-wireless (FiWi), making MEC fit in 5G [18]. If all computing tasks are offloaded to the edge servers without planning. The efficiency of edge servers is influenced hugely [19,20]. Therefore, it is significant to realize the optimal edge server placement to achieve the load balance and improve the delay.

6   Conclusion and Future Work

Edge computing emerges as an appropriate paradigm in 5G networks to collect environmental parameters and return processing results to users. As the number of edge services increases, chances are that the execution efficiency of edge services is hardly to guarantee with limited ESs. In this paper, we formulate the ES placement problem as a multi-objective problem. A load-aware edge server placement method named LESP is devised. To demonstrate that LESP is efficient and feasible, the performance of LESP is evaluated through experimental simulations.

In the future, we will improve LESP to adapt to the real scene. The different processing capacities of ESs will be specified and the corresponding offloading strategies will be revised.

Acknowledgment. This work was supported by the National Key Research and Development Program of China (No. 2017YFB1400600). Besides, this research is supported by the National Natural Science Foundation of China under grant no. 61702277, no. 61872219 and no. 616722763. This research is also supported by College Students' Enterprise and Entrepreneurship Education Program of NUIST, CSEEEP.

References

1. Chen, M., Qian, Y., Hao, Y., Li, Y., Song, J.: Data-driven computing and caching in 5G networks: architecture and delay analysis. IEEE Wireless Commun. **25**(1), 70–75 (2018)
2. Sun, S., Rappaport, T.S., Shafi, M., Tang, P., Zhang, J., Smith, P.J.: Propagation models and performance evaluation for 5G millimeter-wave bands. IEEE Trans. Veh. Technol. **67**(9), 8422–8439 (2018)

3. Gringoli, F., Patras, P., Donato, C., Serrano, P., Grunenberger, Y.: Performance assessment of open software platforms for 5G prototyping. IEEE Wireless Commun. **25**(5), 10–15 (2018)
4. Skouroumounis, C., Psomas, C., Krikidis, I.: Heterogeneous FD-mm-wave cellular networks with cell center/edge users. IEEE Trans. Commun. **67**(1), 791–806 (2019)
5. Ordonez-Lucena, J., Ameigeiras, P., Lopez, D., Ramos-Munoz, J.J., Lorca, J., Folgueira, J.: Network slicing for 5G with SDN/NFV: concepts, architectures, and challenges. IEEE Commun. Mag. **55**(5), 80–87 (2017)
6. Duan, P., Jia, Y., Liang, L., Rodriguez, J., Huq, K.M.S., Li, G.: Space-reserved cooperative caching in 5G heterogeneous networks for industrial IoT. IEEE Trans. Industr. Inf. **14**(6), 2715–2724 (2018)
7. Rodrigues, T.G., Suto, K., Nishiyama, H., Kato, N.: Hybrid method for minimizing service delay in edge cloud computing through VM migration and transmission power control. IEEE Trans. Comput. **66**(5), 810–819 (2016)
8. Li, H., Ota, K., Dong, M.: Learning IoT in edge: deep learning for the internet of things with edge computing. IEEE Netw. **32**(1), 96–101 (2018)
9. Kim, Y., Kwak, J., Chong, S.: Dual-side optimization for cost-delay tradeoff in mobile edge computing. IEEE Trans. Veh. Technol. **67**(2), 1765–1781 (2017)
10. Boulogeorgos, A.A.A., et al.: Terahertz technologies to deliver optical network quality of experience in wireless systems beyond 5G. IEEE Commun. Mag. **56**(6), 144–151 (2018)
11. Li, M., Yu, F.R., Si, P., Zhang, Y.: Green machine-to-machine communications with mobile edge computing and wireless network virtualization. IEEE Commun. Mag. **56**(5), 148–154 (2018)
12. Beyranvand, H., Lévesque, M., Maier, M., Salehi, J.A., Verikoukis, C., Tipper, D.: Toward 5G: FiWi enhanced LTE-A HetNets with reliable low-latency fiber backhaul sharing and WiFi offloading. IEEE/ACM Trans. Networking **25**(2), 690–707 (2016)
13. Mozaffari, M., Kasgari, A.T.Z., Saad, W., Bennis, M., Debbah, M.: Beyond 5G with UAVs: foundations of a 3D wireless cellular network. IEEE Trans. Wireless Commun. **18**(1), 357–372 (2019)
14. Richardson, T., Kudekar, S.: Design of low-density parity check codes for 5G new radio. IEEE Commun. Mag. **56**(3), 28–34 (2018)
15. Lyu, X., Tian, H., Ni, W., Zhang, Y., Zhang, P., Liu, R.P.: Energy-efficient admission of delay-sensitive tasks for mobile edge computing. IEEE Trans. Commun. **66**(6), 2603–2616 (2018)
16. Ning, Z., Kong, X., Xia, F., Hou, W., Wang, X.: Green and sustainable cloud of things: enabling collaborative edge computing. IEEE Commun. Mag. **57**(1), 72–78 (2019)
17. Bi, S., Zhang, Y.J.: Computation rate maximization for wireless powered mobile-edge computing with binary computation offloading. IEEE Trans. Wireless Commun. **17**(6), 4177–4190 (2018)
18. Wang, R., Yan, J., Wu, D., Wang, H., Yang, Q.: Knowledge-centric edge computing based on virtualized D2D communication systems. IEEE Commun. Mag. **56**(5), 32–38 (2018)
19. Wang, K., Yin, H., Quan, W., Min, G.: Enabling collaborative edge computing for software defined vehicular networks. IEEE Network **99**, 1–6 (2018)
20. Hou, W., Ning, Z., Guo, L.: Green survivable collaborative edge computing in smart cities. IEEE Trans. Industr. Inf. **14**(4), 1594–1605 (2018)

PAPS: A Framework for Decentralized Self-management at the Edge

Luciano Baresi, Danilo Filgueira Mendonça, and Giovanni Quattrocchi(✉)

Dipartimento di Elettronica, Informazione e Bioingegneria,
Politecnico di Milano, Milan, Italy
{luciano.baresi,danilo.filgueira,giovanni.quattrocchi}@polimi.it

Abstract. The emergence of latency-sensitive and data-intensive applications requires that computational resources be moved closer to users on computing nodes at the edge of the network (edge computing). Since these nodes have limited resources, the collaboration among them is critical for the robustness, performance, and scalability of the system. One must allocate and provision computational resources to the different components, and these components must be placed on the nodes by considering both network latency and resource availability. Since centralized solutions could be impracticable for large-scale systems, this paper presents PAPS (Partitioning, Allocation, Placement, and Scaling), a framework that tackles the complexity of edge infrastructures by means of decentralized self-management and serverless computing. First, the large-scale edge topology is dynamically partitioned into delay-aware communities. Community leaders then provide a reference allocation of resources and tackle the intricate placement of the containers that host serverless functions. Finally, control theory is used at the node level to scale resources timely and effectively. The assessment shows both the feasibility of the approach and its ability to tackle the placement and allocation problem for large-scale edge topologies with up to 100 serverless functions and intense and unpredictable workload variations.

Keywords: Edge computing · Serverless computing · Resource management · Service placement · Geo-distributed infrastructures

1 Introduction

The advent of mobile computing and the Internet of Things (IoT) is paving the ground to new types of applications. For most real-time, interactive applications, the latency from devices to cloud data centers can be prohibitive, and the transport and analysis of exponentially larger volumes of data may result in bottlenecks and consequently low throughput. Edge computing aims to fill this gap by means of densely-distributed computing nodes. Locality and decentralization mitigate network latency and helps reduce the amount of data that is transported to and processed by centralized servers.

The management of these geo-distributed infrastructures poses significant challenges. One must provision and allocate computational resources to the various components, but these components must be placed on edge nodes by taking

S. Yangui et al. (Eds.): ICSOC 2019, LNCS 11895, pp. 508–522, 2019.
https://doi.org/10.1007/978-3-030-33702-5_39

into account both latency and resource availability. The analysis of current work-load, availability of resources, and performance of application components is key for the efficient placement of components and the allocation of resources, but it must be carried out in a timely manner for the entire topology. Network latency and time-consuming decisions, typical of centralized approaches, may jeopardize the overall effectiveness, especially with highly volatile workloads—a likely-to-happen scenario with densely distributed edge nodes that serve the needs of mobile/IoT devices.

On a parallel thread, serverless computing [2,11] is emerging as a novel cloud computing execution model that allows developers to focus more on their applications and less on the infrastructure. The user must only submit the application logic (stateless functions) to be executed. In turn, the provider offers dedicated containers for its execution and is in charge of resource allocation, capacity planning, and function deployment.

This paper proposes PAPS (Partitioning, Allocation, Placement, and Scaling), a framework for tackling the automated, effective, and scalable management of large-scale edge topologies through decentralized self-management and serverless computing. The approach partitions the large-scale edge topology into delay-aware network communities. Community leaders then tackle the joint allocation of resources and the placement of serverless functions—w.r.t both SLAs and the aggregate demand for each function. Finally, edge nodes exploit control theory to scale required containers timely while also giving valuable feedback to community leaders.

A prototype implementation of PAPS allowed us to assess the proposal on a set of experiments. Obtained results witness the feasibility of the approach and its ability to tackle the placement and allocation problem for large-scale edge topologies with up to 100 distinct functions and intense and unpredictable fluctuations of the workload. To the best of our knowledge, this is the first work that tackles the orchestration of such a high number of geo-distributed nodes and application components.

The rest of the paper is organized as follows. Section 2 presentes the context and introduces PAPS. Sections 3, 4, and 5 describe the self-management capabilities provided by PAPS at system, community, and node levels. Section 6 discusses the evaluation, Sect. 7 surveys related approaches, and Sect. 8 concludes the paper.

2   Context and PAPS

This paper focuses on a MEC topology [7,12] composed of a finite set of geo-distributed nodes $\mathcal{N}$. Figure 1 presents such a topology, where mobile and IoT devices access the system through cellular base stations. Each station is connected to a MEC node $i \in \mathcal{N}$ through the *fronthaul network*. MEC nodes in $\mathcal{N}$ are interconnected through the *backhaul network*. The total propagation delay $D_{i,j}$ between an end-user device that accesses the system through the base station co-located with the MEC node $i \in \mathcal{N}$ and that is served by the MEC node $j \in \mathcal{N}$ is defined as:

$$D_{i,j} = \begin{cases} \gamma_i + \delta_{i,j}, & \text{if } i \mathrel{!}= j \\ \gamma_i, & \text{if } i = j \end{cases} \qquad (1)$$

where γ_i and $\delta_{i,j}$ are respectively the fronthaul and backhaul propagation delays.

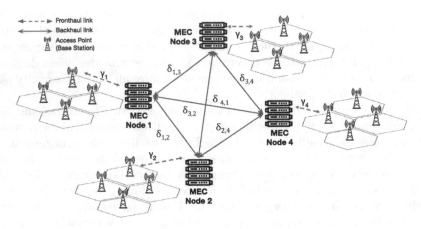

Fig. 1. Example topology of geo-distributed MEC nodes.

Our framework targets the dynamic allocation and placement of the containers required for the execution of serverless functions [2]. Even if the allocation model of different serverless vendors can vary [6], typically functions are given access to a fixed CPU share proportional to their memory requirement. In addition, we assume a deployment descriptor for each function that provides the memory required by the container in charge of executing the function and the SLA between the MEC operator and the application provider, that is, the owner of the function to execute.

The SLA associated with each function is specified through: a *Response Time* (RT_{SLA}), which states the upper limit for the round trip time between the arrival of a request to execute a function, its execution, and the returned value (if the invocation is synchronous), and a *Maximum Execution Time* (E_{MAX}), which limits its execution time. The latter is a common attribute in cloud-based serverless computing platforms, and it is key for us to guide the decision on the joint allocation and placement of the function.

In this context, for a given topology $\mathcal{N}$ and a set of admitted functions $\mathcal{F}$, the adaptation problem is twofold: one must decide *how many* containers are needed for each function and *where* (onto which nodes) should each container be placed. Each allocated container works as a server for a specific function $f \in \mathcal{F}$. Most vendors of serverless solutions try to use existing containers, if possible, and allocate new ones as soon as they are needed. In contrast, if one queued requests for a short period Q, resources (containers) may become available, and thus the number of used resources may decrease. The perceived response time is then defined as:

$$RT = D + Q + E \qquad (2)$$

where D represents the total propagation delay (see Eq. 1), Q the queuing time, and E the execution time. MEC operators must scale the number of containers allocated to each function $f \in \mathcal{F}$ and place them onto MEC nodes in $\mathcal{N}$ to minimize the difference between RT and RT_{SLA}. The goal is twofold: (i) to maximize the efficient use of resources, and thus the number of functions and users that can be admitted into the system; (ii) to prevent SLA violations.

This paper introduces PAPS, a framework to manage the allocation and placement problems in large-scale edge systems. Figure 2 shows that the self-management capabilities provided by PAPS work at three different levels: system, community, and node level. The next three sections describe how each level works in detail.

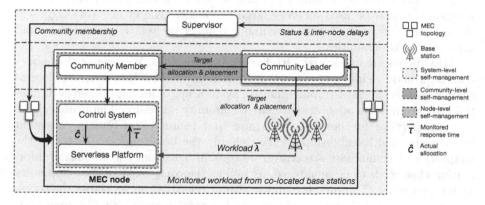

Fig. 2. PAPS in a nutshell.

3 System-Level Self-management

Self-management at system level aims to tackle the complexity of managing the large scale decentralized infrastructure by partitioning it into delay-aware network *communities*. In complex networks, a network is said to have a *community structure* if its nodes can be (easily) grouped into (potentially overlapping) sets of nodes such that each set is densely connected internally [14]. PAPS extends this definition and considers a set of logically interconnected MEC nodes, whose propagation delay from one another is below a threshold, as a *delay-aware* network community.

These communities provide a reduced space in which a solution to the placement and allocation problem can be computed. Furthermore, they allow for the decentralization of resource management (w.r.t. a single orchestrator) and its localization within distinct geographical areas.

The definition of these communities may follow different approaches. PAPS assumes the availability of a *supervisor* that has a global view of the MEC topology and uses a dedicated search algorithm to create communities. This algorithm takes the maximum inter-node delay (D_{MAX}) and the maximum community size (MCS) as parameters. The former is used to produce a sub-graph (G_{DA}). Each of its vertices maps to a node in the MEC topology, and an edge exists between two vertices if the network delay between their respective MEC nodes is lower than D_{MAX}. The second parameter limits the number of MEC nodes that can belong to a community, and it is useful to limit the complexity of community-level self-management.

The produced sub-graph G_{DA} in then used to feed the algorithm in charge of creating the communities. In particular, we adopt the SLPA method [14], whose complexity is $O(t * n)$, where t is a predefined maximum number of iterations (e.g. $t \leq 20$) and n is the number of nodes. Since the complexity is linear, the solution can also be used for very large topologies. Xie et al. [14] suggest a modest value ($t = 20$) for the maximum number of iterations needed to find good quality communities.

MEC nodes are co-located with fixed infrastructures. We assume that nodes and inter-node delays are expected to remain stable. However, topological changes caused by catastrophic failures, system upgrades, and other eventualities may require the adaptation of the community structure. The primary goal of the supervisor is, therefore, to ensure that communities remain consistent in their size and membership. While defining the best approach to tackle the adaptation of community structures, we took into account the amount of information that needs to be monitored, as well as the complexity of the community search procedure. The presence and health of the MEC nodes across the topology can be obtained through light-weight *heartbeat* messages sent by each node to the supervisor. This approach is commonly adopted in distributed systems of different scales and does not prejudice the scalability of the proposed solution.

The supervisor harnesses its global system view to tackle the adaptation of the community structure. We model the system-level adaptation as a master-slave MAPE loop [13] in which: *Monitoring* is performed by all nodes through heartbeat messages that contain the inter-node delay to all other nodes; the supervisor performs *Analysis* and *Planning* by deciding when and how to adapt the community structure in the advent of topological changes; *Execution* means that each affected node adapts by updating its community membership.

4   Community-Level Self-management

Self-management at community-level aims to ensure that the MEC nodes in the community operate under feasible conditions, that is, it aims to minimize the likelihood of SLA violations to occur and, if they occur, to react to bring the community back to its equilibrium.

Inter-community Allocation. A first challenge that emerges when the MEC system is partitioned into communities refers to resource allocation to shared community members. This is to say that one must decide the share of resources that each overlapping community gets from its common members. One trivial, but possibly inefficient, solution is to privilege one community and give it all the "shared" resources: disadvantaged communities might need more resources while the common members might be underutilized by the privileged community. Since changes to the workload are expected to happen frequently, and without any warning, resources from common nodes must flow from one overlapping community to the other to prevent SLA violations.

PAPS tackles this problem by weighting the aggregate demand and capacity of each overlapping community. The aggregate demand refers to the number of containers needed to cope with the aggregate workload. The latter refers to the rate of requests that come from the base stations co-located with MEC nodes whose network latency w.r.t. the common node is below the inter-node delay threshold (D_{MAX}), plus a proportional demand share from the base station(s) co-located with the common node itself. The aggregate capacity, in turn, refers to the sum of the resources from the previous nodes, excluding the common node. A share of the capacity of the common node is then allocated to each overlapping community proportionally to their aggregate demand-capacity ratio.

Algorithm 1 details our inter-community allocation approach. This procedure is greedily performed for all MEC nodes in the topology that belong to two or more overlapping communities.

Algorithm 1. CapacityDemandRatio($community, node, D_{MAX}$)

1: $neighborsInRange \leftarrow$ GETNEIGHBORS($community, node, D_{MAX}$)
2: $aggDemand \leftarrow 0$, $aggCapacity \leftarrow 0$
3: **for all** $n \in neighborsInRange$ **do**
4:     $aggDemand \leftarrow$ GETAGGREGATEDEMAND(n)
5:     $aggregateCapacity \leftarrow$ GETAGGREGATECAPACITY(n)
6: **end for**
7: $ovCount \leftarrow$ GETOVERLAPPINGCOUNT($node$)
8: $demandShare \leftarrow$ GETDEMAND($node$) / $ovCount$
9: $aggDemand \leftarrow aggDemand + demandShare$
10: **return** $aggDemand$ / $aggCapacity$

Intra-community Allocation and Placement. The intra-community allocation aims to distribute resources among member nodes given the aggregate demand and capacity within the community. Each community has a leader responsible for solving the joint allocation and placement problem introduced in Sect. 2. Such a *centralization within decentralization* (i) allows the placement problem to be solved in a single step for the whole community, and (ii) eliminates the need for a more complex coordination protocol. More importantly, the leader-based approach allows the placement problem to be solved by well-known centralized optimization techniques.

The complexity of the container placement problem implies high-resolution time and prevents communities to promptly adapt to workload fluctuations. Before a solution is computed, the workload may have significantly changed, and limit the efficiency and efficacy of the solution. Pro-active adaptation could be used to mitigate this problem. For example, if the workload is character-ized by a well-known probabilistic distribution (e.g., a Poisson distribution), the allocation problem might then benefit from techniques such as queueing theory to predict the number of containers that are needed to keep the response time below a threshold. Unfortunately, the decentralized infrastructure model makes the previous assumption less realistic. Not only users can freely enter and exit different areas, but the aggregate workload to be served by each MEC node is limited compared to typical cloud data centers and thus may vary more abruptly. Because of this, PAPS favors a reactive adaptation approach for solving the joint allocation and placement problem.

Our solution draws inspiration from the Ultra-Stable system architecture [10]. The community-level self-management acts as the second control loop in the Ultra-Stable system. When workload fluctuations are significant enough to impact or to throw the node-level self-management out of its limits, the community-level self-management provides the community with a new allocation and placement solution. In turn, the node-level self-management works as the primary feedback loop in the Ultra-Stable system. Through its sensors, the MEC node monitors subtle changes in the environment (i.e., in the actual workload for each function). It accordingly responds, through its actuators by changing the actual number of containers hosted for each function. Hence, the community-level placement does not target a single solution, but a solution space in which the scaling of containers at node-level ultimately takes place.

The community-level self-management consists of an instance of the *regional planner* MAPE loop [13]. Each community member takes advantage of its priv-ileged position within the MEC topology to *monitor* and *analyze* the workload coming from adjacent base stations (see Fig. 1). The number of containers needed to cope with a given workload while satisfying the SLA is determined at the node level by using a feedback loop with a short control period—compatible with the container start-up time (i.e., up to a few seconds). In turn, the community leader extrapolates this information to *plan* for the number of containers needed to satisfy the SLA given the aggregate workload over a longer control period—compatible with the time needed to compute the optimal placement (i.e., up to a few minutes).

Informed load balancers composing the community infrastructure use the computed optimal allocation and placement to route the workload coming from different base stations to their respective destinations (i.e., MEC nodes).

Each affected node in the community *executes* the plan with the update of the target allocation. Depending on how the new placement solution diverges, community members may have to remove/add function(s).

Our decentralized solution provides each MEC node with the freedom to decide the actual number of containers it hosts for each placed function based on monitored workload, SLA, and available computing resources. As the workload fluctuates, the response time deviates from its target value, and the node-level controller takes care of the timely creation and termination of containers to optimize resource usage while preventing SLA violations. The community-level solution is enforced by members in case of resource contention until a new optimal allocation and placement solution is enacted by the community leader.

Optimal Container Placement. PAPS is agnostic about the formulation of the optimal allocation and placement problem. In this paper, we formulate it as a mixed integer programming (MIP) problem as follows:

$$\min_{x} \quad \sum_{i \in \mathcal{N}} \sum_{j \in \mathcal{N}} \sum_{f \in \mathcal{F}} d_{i,j} * x_{f,i,j} \tag{3a}$$

$$\text{subject to} \quad d_{i,j} * x_{f,i,j} \leq x_{f,i,j} * D_f \qquad \forall i \in \mathcal{N}, \forall j \in \mathcal{N}, \forall f \in \mathcal{F} \tag{3b}$$

$$\sum_{i \in \mathcal{N}} \sum_{f \in \mathcal{F}} c_{f,i} * m_f * x_{f,i,j} \leq M_j \qquad \forall j \in \mathcal{N} \tag{3c}$$

$$\sum_{j \in \mathcal{N}} c_{f,i} * x_{f,i,j} = c_{f,i} \qquad \forall i \in \mathcal{N}, \forall f \in \mathcal{F} \tag{3d}$$

where the decision variable $0 \leq x_{f,i,j} \leq 1$ denotes the fraction of the demand for containers $c_{f,i}$, from any base station co-located with node $i \in \mathcal{N}$, for function $f \in F$, hosted on node $j \in \mathcal{N}$. The objective function (Eq. 3a) minimizes the overall network delay that results from placing containers. The first constraint (Eq. 3b) limits the propagation delay. Specifically, D_f is calculated by using the following equation:

$$D_f = \beta * (RT_{SLA,f} - E_{MAX,f}) \tag{4}$$

where $0 < \beta \leq 1$ defines the fraction of the marginal response time $RT_{SLA,f} - E_{MAX,f}$ for function $f \in F$ that can be used for networking. Conversely, the complement $1 - \beta$ defines the fraction of the marginal response time used for queuing requests for function f hosted on node j:

$$Q_{f,j} = (1 - \beta) * (RT_{SLA,f} - E_{f,j}) \tag{5}$$

where $E_{f,j}$ is the monitored execution time for function f hosted on node j. The queue component $Q_{f,j}$ is particularly important for the control-theoretic solution for scaling containers (see Sect. 5) since it provides an additional margin for the control actuation and thus mitigates the likelihood of overshooting.

The second constraint (Eq. 3c) ensures that the number of containers placed at a node j does not violate its memory capacity M_j. An additional constraint (Eq. 3d) ensures that the required containers for all $f \in \mathcal{F}$ are properly placed.

5   Node-Level Self-management

Self-management at node-level aims to efficiently and effectively scale the containers needed to satisfy the SLA (response time) of each admitted function given the fluctuations in the workload and the target allocation defined by the community leader. With a static allocation of resources, the response time of a function can change due to various reasons: for example, variations in the workload, changes in the execution time (e.g., due to input variation), and disturbances in the execution environment (e.g., at the operating system or hardware level). While some factors are harder to quantify and account for, others can be monitored and taken into account while determining the number of containers needed to prevent SLA violations. Our framework leverages a control-theoretic approach [3] to scale containers at node-level.

The control system is responsible for the deployment of containers onto the pool of virtual machines running on the MEC node. We consider a dedicated controller for each admitted function $f \in F$. Considering a discrete time, for each function, we define $\lambda(k)$ as the function of the measured arrival rate of requests at each control time k, while $\bar{\lambda}(k)$ is the corresponding vector for all admitted functions.

At time k, the function is executed in a $c(k)$ number of containers, while $\bar{c}(k)$ is the vector for all $f \in F$. The disturbances are defined as $\bar{d}$ and cannot be directly controlled and measured. Finally, $\bar{\tau}$ is the system output and corresponds to the response time vector that comprises all functions, whereas $\bar{\tau}^\circ$ corresponds to the vector of the desired response time for each function (or control *set-point*).

In our current set-up, function $\bar{\tau}^\circ(k)$ does not vary over time, that is, we target a constant response time for each function. These values should be less than the agreed SLA to avoid violations. For example, a reasonable target response time for non-critical functions is $0.8 * SLA$, while a lower value like $0.4 * SLA$ implies a more conservative allocation and can be used for safety-critical applications. Moreover, since a response time cannot be measured instantaneously, but by aggregating it over a predefined time window, many aggregation techniques could be used without any change to the model and controller. In our framework, we compute the average of the response time values in $\bar{\tau}$ within each control period, but stricter aggregation functions, such as the $99th$ percentile, could be used given the needs of the service provider.

We also use a characteristic function to model the system with enough details to govern its dynamics. We assume that this function needs not be linear but regular enough to be linearizable in the domain space of interest. Moreover, we consider this function be dependent on the ratio between the number of allocated containers c and the request rate λ. The characteristic function monotonically decreases towards a possible lower horizontal asymptote, as we can assume that once available containers are enough to allow a function to reach the foreseen degree of parallelism, the addition of further containers would provide no benefits in terms of response time. We found that a practically acceptable function is:

$$f\left(\frac{c(k)}{\lambda(k)}\right) = \widetilde{u}(k) = c_1 + \frac{c_2}{1 + c_3 \frac{c(k)}{\lambda(k)}} \qquad (6)$$

where parameters c_1, c_2, and c_3 were obtained through profiling of each function.

As control technique, we rely on PI controllers because they are able to effectively control systems dominated by a first-order dynamic [1] (i.e., representable with first-order differential equations) such as the studied ones. Algorithmically, for each admitted function:

$e := \tau_r^\circ - \tau_r;$ $\qquad\qquad\qquad c := max(min(Kmax, c), Kmin);$

$x_R := x_{R_p} + (1-p)*e_p;$ $\qquad\qquad x_{R_p} := (p-1)/(\alpha-1)*f(c/\lambda) - e;$

$c := \lambda * f_{inv}((\alpha-1)/(p-1)*(x_R + e));$ $\quad e_p := e;$

where e is the error, the p subscript denotes "previous" values, that is, those that correspond to the previous step, f and f_{inv} correspond to the characteristic function and its inverse, respectively, $\alpha \in [0,1)$ and $p \in [0,1)$ are the single pole of the controller and the system respectively, and x_R is the state of the controller. The higher the value of α is, the faster the error converges—ideally to zero—at the expense of a more fluctuating allocation.

At each control step, the function controllers run independently (i.e., without synchronization) to compute the next number of containers for the corresponding function, which is added to vector $\hat{c}$. The number of containers in $\hat{c}$ is not immediately actuated since the sum of required containers could be greater than the entire capacity of the resource pool. Instead, $\hat{c}$ is passed to a contention manager. This component outputs a vector $\bar{c}$, which contains the actual number of containers per function, defined as:

$$\bar{c}(k) = \begin{cases} \hat{c}(k), & \text{if } no \ resource \ contention \\ solveContention(\hat{c}(k)), & \text{otherwise} \end{cases} \qquad (7)$$

where function $solveContention$ scales the values in $\hat{c}$ according to the thresholds defined by the placement solution provided by the community leader (see Sect. 3). The contention manager also updates the state of each controller (variable x_{R_p}) to make it become consistent with the actual allocation.

6   Experimental Evaluation

We created a prototype implementation of the PAPS framework[1] based on Peer-Sim[2]. The implementation was used to evaluate the allocation, placement, and scaling mechanisms of PAPS, given different partitioning of the MEC topology. A node in the topology was implemented as a dynamic pool of threads, where

---

[1] Source code available at: https://github.com/deib-polimi/PAPS.

[2] http://peersim.sourceforge.net/.

Table 1. Results.

			RT		
Test	Conf	V	μ	σ	95th
OPT	10/50	6.4%	84.9	13.9	111.9
CT	10/50	0.6%	74.4	4.9	81.2
OPT	10/75	7.1%	89.6	15.1	113.4
CT	10/75	0.7%	75.6	7.8	81.8
OPT	10/100	8.9%	92.7	18.7	146.8
CT	10/100	0.9%	76.3	8.1	86.0
OPT	25/50	6.8%	92.6	16.7	176.0
CT	25/50	0.9%	75.6	10.7	85.8
OPT	25/75	10.5%	95.1	19.9	210.7
CT	25/75	1.8%	88.1	12.0	101.6
OPT	25/100	11.7%	101.6	23.0	221.3
CT	25/100	2.0%	85.8	20.0	107.3
OPT	50/50	7.4%	114.9	23.6	243.6
CT	50/50	1.4%	77.7	9.9	89.8
OPT	50/75	12.4%	118.9	27.6	260.6
CT	50/75	1.6%	78.7	15.6	91.6
OPT	50/100	14.0%	125.9	29.6	270.6
CT	50/100	2.2%	90.6	17.3	114.7

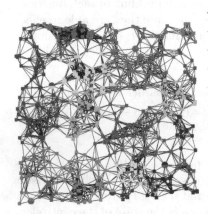

Fig. 3. Communities found in a large scale topology with 250 nodes.

one container is a thread that executes the incoming requests. All the experiments were run using two servers running Ubuntu 16.04 and equipped with an Intel Xeon CPU E5-2430 processor for a total of 24 cores and 328 GB of memory.

The maximum number of containers that can be allocated onto a node depends on its memory capacity and the memory requirements of the functions that are to be deployed: 96 GB and 128 MB, respectively, in our experiments.

First, we assumed a large-scale edge topology of 250 nodes and normally distributed node-to-node latencies. We used the SLPA algorithm to partition the topology in communities of 10, 25, and 50 nodes (parameter MCS) with membership probability $r = 0.35$. Figure 3 shows the partitioning when MCS was set 25. Colored squares represent edge nodes within a single community; those that belong to overlapping communities are rendered with multi-color circles.

Then, we run two types of experiments to evaluate (i) the feasibility, performance, and scalability of the approach and (ii) the benefit of having a multi-layered self-management solution. The first experiment, called $testOPT$, tested the behavior of communities under an extremely fluctuating workload by only using community-level allocation and placement. Each node kept the target resources allocated to each running function constant between two community-level decisions. The second experiment, called *testCT*, used both community-level and node-level adaptations to provide more refined and dynamic resource allocation for the incoming random workload.

For each of the three community sizes, we tested the system with an increasing number of types of functions: 50, 75, 100. Each execution lasted 10 min and tested one of the nine combinations of community sizes and number of functions. For each configuration we executed 5 runs of *testOPT* and 5 runs of *testCT* for a total of 90 experiments.

The control periods of the community-level and node-level self-management were set to 1 min and 5 s, respectively. If no feasible optimal solution is found at the community level, PAPS solves a constraint-relaxed version of the optimization problem of Sect. 4, and the next placement starts after 1 min. Moreover, we set the fraction of the marginal response time β to 0.5 and the value of the pole of the node-level controller (see Sect. 5) to 0.9.

The workloads were generated by using normal distributions for both function execution times (E_k), while inter-arrival rates were generated by using three different scenarios (low, regular, high) that were chosen randomly every 15 s to simulate an extremely fluctuating traffic. Within each scenario, the time between two requests was computed by using an exponential distribution. Finally, the RT_{SLA} of all the functions was set to 120 ms, and ET_{MAX} was set to 90 ms.

Table 1 shows obtained results, where *Test* can be either *testOPT* or *testCT*, *Conf* shows used configuration (e.g., 10/50 means each community had 10 nodes, and there were 50 different function types), V shows the percentage of control periods in which the average response time violated the SLA, while columns μ, σ and 95th show, respectively, the overall average, the standard deviation, and the 95th percentile of the response time of the system aggregated over the five repetitions. If we focus independently on *testOPT* and *testCT*, we can observe that even by increasing the number of nodes and functions the percentage of failures is kept under 14.0% and 2.2%, respectively. These are reasonable values if we consider we used extremely variable workloads (changes every 15 s). Note that the control period used for the community-level decision is four times longer than the time between two scenarios. Instead, if we compare the results of both tests, we can easily notice the benefit of the node-level self-management. The control-theoretical planners reduce the number of violations by one order of magnitude: for example, from 6.4% to 0.6% in configuration 10/50, from 10.5% to 1.8% in configuration 25/75, and from 14% to 2.2% in configuration 50/100. Moreover, on average, the standard deviation and the 95th percentile of the response time are significantly lower in all *testCT* experiments.

The charts of Fig. 4 help better visualize obtained results. Figure 4(a) and (b) show the average response time for *testOPT* and *testCT* with configuration 10/50, where the horizontal line at 120 ms is the SLA. The first chart shows some violations, while the second chart only shows one violation close to 500 s and the response time is more constant (lower standard deviation) given the faster actuation of the node-level manager. Figure 4(c) and (d) show the number of requests (lighter line) and the allocation (darker line) during the execution of

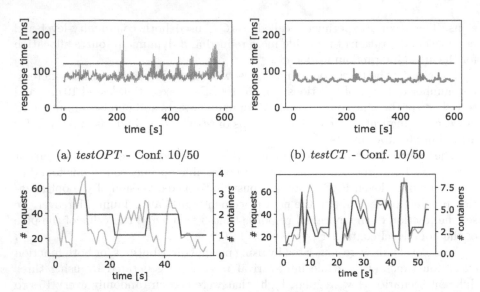

(a) *testOPT* - Conf. 10/50

(b) *testCT* - Conf. 10/50

(c) *testOPT* - Sample of workload and allocation of a function on a node.

(d) *testCT* - Sample of workload and allocation of a function on a node.

Fig. 4. Experiment results.

a function on a single node for the two types of experiments (same configuration as before). *testOPT* exploits a longer control period given the complexity of the optimization problem. Therefore, the allocation is often sub-optimal and quite approximated w.r.t. the actual user needs (workload). On the other hand, the faster adaption used in *testCT* allowed the system to fulfill user needs better and follow the actual workload more closely.

7   Related Work

A few works combine the benefits of serverless and edge computing. Baresi et al. [4] propose a serverless architecture for Multi-Access Edge Computing (MEC). The authors also propose a framework [5] for the opportunistic deployment of serverless functions onto heterogeneous platforms, but they do not tackle the allocation and placement problem across nodes.

The platform proposed by Nastic et al. [9] extends the notion of serverless computing to the edge via a reference architecture to enable the uniform development and operation of data analysis functions. An orchestrator receives the information on how to con the application as high-level objectives and decides how to orchestrate the underlying resources. The implementation of the orchestration is left open.

Nardelli et al. [8] propose a model for the deployment of containerized applications. The number of required containers is defined by the user, the solution acquires and releases virtual machines and places containers onto these machines.

A possibly-new deployment configuration is defined in each adaptation cycle. In contrast, PAPS is in charge of both the target number of containers—to cope with agreed SLAs—and their placement onto MEC nodes. While PAPS works at the level of both nodes and communities, the multi-level formulation proposed in [8] could only be adopted in the latter case.

Zanzi et al. [16] propose a multi-tenant resource orchestration for MEC systems. The authors introduce a MEC broker that is responsible for procuring slices of the resources available in the MEC system to the various tenants based on their privilege level. At each optimization cycle, the broker decides on placing single-component applications onto the MEC node of choice (gold users), or onto any feasible node according to resource availability and network delay. We have instantiated our framework with a similar MEC topology, but our solution tackles the placement of a dynamic number of instances of various serverless functions onto stateless containers. We take into account the response time as SLA and a varying workload from different sources in the topology.

Yu et al. [15] propose a fully polynomial-time approximated solution for tackling the joint QoS-aware application placement and data routing problem in an edge system. Their formulation also admits multiple workload sources across the topology. Differently from PAPS, they focus on the placement of single-instance, single-component applications. While their solution tackles the allocation of bandwidth and the routing of data, it does not consider the allocation of computational resources, which is a crucial requirement in edge-centric systems.

A number of other works tackle the placement of applications onto geo-distributed infrastructures. Due to their combinatorial nature, tackled problems are usually NP-Hard [15], and many of the existing solutions are based on heuristics and approximations. These solutions are demonstrated for a limited number of nodes and applications or do not consider abrupt workload variations. PAPS targets different objectives, where scalability and unpredictable workload are first-class requirements. It tackles the optimal resource allocation and component placement by scaling containers at the node level through control theory.

8 Conclusions and Future Work

This paper presents PAPS, a comprehensive framework for the effective and scalable self-management of large edge topologies that works at different levels. It partitions the edge topology into smaller communities. Each community elects a leader that is in charge of placing and allocating containers for the incoming workload. Each node exploits control theory to scale containers properly and timely. The evaluation demonstrates the feasibility of the approach, its performance under extremely fluctuating workloads, and highlights the benefit of the multi-level solution.

As for future work, we plan to integrate PAPS into a real-world serverless framework and to extend our community-level allocation and placement algorithm to consider also the cost of migrating containers.

References

1. Åström, K.J., Hägglund, T.: PID Controllers: Theory, Design, and Tuning, vol. 2. ISA Research Triangle Park, Durham (1995)
2. Baldini, I., Castro, P., et al.: Serverless computing: current trends and open problems. In: Research Advances in Cloud Computing, pp. 1–20 (2017)
3. Baresi, L., Guinea, S., Leva, A., Quattrocchi, G.: A discrete-time feedback controller for containerized cloud applications. In: Proceedings of the 24th ACM SIGSOFT International Symposium on Foundations of Software Engineering, pp. 217–228. ACM (2016)
4. Baresi, L., Filgueira Mendonça, D., Garriga, M.: Empowering low-latency applications through a serverless edge computing architecture. In: De Paoli, F., Schulte, S., Broch Johnsen, E. (eds.) ESOCC 2017. LNCS, vol. 10465, pp. 196–210. Springer, Cham (2017). https://doi.org/10.1007/978-3-319-67262-5_15
5. Baresi, L., Mendonça, D.F., Garriga, M., Guinea, S., Quattrocchi, G.: A unified model for the mobile-edge-cloud continuum. ACM Trans. Internet Technol. **19**, 29:1–29:21 (2019)
6. Lloyd, W., et. al.: Serverless computing: an investigation of factors influencing microservice performance. In: Proceedigns of the 6th IEEE International Conference on Cloud Engineering, pp. 159–169 (2018)
7. Mach, P., Becvar, Z.: Mobile edge computing: a survey on architecture and computation offloading. IEEE Comm. Surv. Tutorials **19**(3), 1628–1656 (2017)
8. Nardelli, M., Cardellini, V., Casalicchio, E.: Multi-level elastic deployment of containerized applications in geo-distributed environments. In: Proceedings of the 6th IEEE International Conference on Future Internet of Things and Cloud, pp. 1–8 (2018)
9. Nastic, S., Rausch, T., et al.: A serverless real-time data analytics platform for edge computing. IEEE Internet Comput. **21**, 64–71 (2017)
10. Parashar, M., Hariri, S.: Autonomic computing: an overview. In: Unconventional Programming Paradigms, pp. 257–269 (2005)
11. Roberts, M.: Serverless architectures. https://martinfowler.com/articles/serverless.html. Accessed May 2018
12. Several authors: Mobile edge computing (mec); framework and reference architecture. Technical report, ETSI GS MEC, January 2019. http://www.etsi.org/deliver/etsi_gs/MEC/001_099/003/01.01.01_60/gs_MEC003v010101p.pdf
13. Weyns, D., et al.: On patterns for decentralized control in self-adaptive systems. In: de Lemos, R., Giese, H., Müller, H.A., Shaw, M. (eds.) Software Engineering for Self-Adaptive Systems II. LNCS, vol. 7475, pp. 76–107. Springer, Heidelberg (2013). https://doi.org/10.1007/978-3-642-35813-5_4
14. Xie, J., Szymanski, B.K., Liu, X.: SLPA: uncovering overlapping communities in social networks via a speaker-listener interaction dynamic process. In: Proceedings of the 11th IEEE International Conference on Data Mining Workshops, pp. 344–349 (2011)
15. Yu, R., Xue, G., Zhang, X.: Application provisioning in FOG computing-enabled Internet-of-Things: a network perspective. In: Proceedings of the 37th IEEE International Conference on Computer Communications, INFOCOM, pp. 783–791 (2018)
16. Zanzi, L., Giust, F., Sciancalepore, V.: M^2ec: a multi-tenant resource orchestration in multi-access edge computing systems. In: Proceedings of the 19th IEEE Wireless Communications and Networking Conference, WCNC, pp. 1–6 (2018)

Measuring the Fog, Gently

Antonio Brogi, Stefano Forti$^{(\boxtimes)}$, and Marco Gaglianese

Department of Computer Science, University of Pisa, Pisa, Italy
stefano.forti@di.unipi.it

Abstract. The availability of suitable monitoring tools and techniques will be crucial to orchestrate multi-service applications in a context- and QoS-aware manner over new Fog infrastructures. In this paper, we propose FogMon, a lightweight distributed prototype monitoring tool, which measures data about hardware resources (viz., CPU, RAM, HDD) at the available Fog nodes, end-to-end network QoS (viz., latency and bandwidth) between those nodes, and detects connected IoT devices. FogMon is organised into a peer-to-peer architecture and it shows a very limited footprint on both hardware and bandwidth. The usage of FogMon on a real testbed is presented.

Keywords: Fog computing · Lightweight monitoring · Network QoS · Hardware resources · Internet of Things · Peer-to-peer architectures

1 Introduction

In the last decade, Cloud computing has shaped the way in which software services are delivered to their final users, fostering the emergence of computing as the fifth utility (beyond water, electricity, gas, and telephony) [14]. At the same time, the Internet of Things (IoT) has been expanding at a very rapid pace, currently producing about 2.5×10^{18} bytes of data daily [1] and being increasingly often associated to limited computing capabilities at the edge of the network to support IoT-enabled applications [15,32,40]. As a consequence, established deployment models [13] for IoT applications consist typically either of

- *IoT+Cloud* deployments [32] where Things send data to Cloud data centres for further processing/analytics purposes, awaiting for a response, and only minor computation happens locally, or of
- *IoT+Edge* deployments [33] where data is processed locally at the edge of the Internet to determine reactions to sensed events.

On one hand, the IoT+Cloud model gives access to unlimited computing capabilities but often results in high latencies and network congestion [36], which is not tolerable whenever the deployed application has to meet stringent Quality of Service (QoS) requirements (e.g., it is life-, business- or mission-critical). On the other hand, the IoT+Edge model enacts faster responses to sensed events by processing data closer to the IoT sources and it does not require moving large amounts of data through the Internet, as computation is performed directly on edge devices (e.g., access points, routers, personal devices). This results in lower

© Springer Nature Switzerland AG 2019
S. Yangui et al. (Eds.): ICSOC 2019, LNCS 11895, pp. 523–538, 2019.
https://doi.org/10.1007/978-3-030-33702-5_40

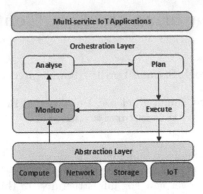

Fig. 1. Fog orchestration layer [9].

latencies and faster response times but shows important shortcomings, especially when data should be collected across different systems or when limited edge capabilities (e.g., battery-powered or resource-constrained devices) cannot satisfy the application (hardware, software, QoS) requirements.

In this context, the Fog computing paradigm emerged aiming at exploiting computation capabilities all through the continuum from the IoT to the Cloud [44]. The Fog relies on the assumption that application (micro-)services should be deployed wherever their (functional and non-functional) requirements can be satisfied at best [17]. The central Cloud is still considered for service deployment, but other intermediary computing capabilities are also used to support computation between edge devices and the Cloud. As a result, for instance, it is possible to reduce the traffic by pre-processing and filtering the data before it is sent to the Cloud, and to substantially reduce response times by suitably placing critical application services closer to the edge of the network.

Bonomi et al. [9] first proposed a software architecture for Fog computing platforms. Particularly, they considered it crucial to implement an orchestration layer for Fog services, as sketched in Fig. 1. The Fog orchestration layer, based on a *Monitor-Analyse-Plan-Execute* (MAPE) loop, was expected to provide dynamic, adaptive life-cycle management of multi-service applications in a distributed manner. Since then, a large amount of research has been devoted to the *Analyse* phase [11] (to informedly decide where to (re-)deploy application services) and some work studied the *Plan* (to identify the actions sequence to (re-)deploy services) and *Execute* (to actually (re-)deploy services) phases combined together [30,35,41]. However, to the best of our knowledge, very little effort went towards designing models and implementing tools covering the *Monitor* phase in Fog computing orchestration platforms [39].

Monitoring is indeed an important part of the Fog orchestration layer and a challenging one to design and implement. It is important because its output can be exploited both to decide where to deploy application services for the first time, as well as to decide when and where to migrate them in case the requirements of one or more services cannot be met at runtime. As a matter of fact, all proposed approaches for the *Analyse* phase require the availability of historical or real-time monitoring data about the available Fog infrastructure to suggest (sub-)optimal multi-service application (re-)deployments. Monitoring is also challenging to implement because it has to deal with various peculiarities of Fog infrastructures, such as (possibly) limited hardware resources and unstable connectivity at the Edge, platform heterogeneity, and node failures.

In this paper, we present FogMon, a first distributed and lightweight prototype monitoring tool for Fog computing infrastructures, capable of measuring and statistically aggregating data about hardware resources (viz., CPU, RAM, HDD) at the available Fog nodes, and end-to-end network QoS (viz., latency and bandwidth) between those nodes, and connected IoT devices. As we will discuss, FogMon is written in C++ and released as open-source software, it is fully configurable by its users and it has been dockerised so to permit deployment across different platforms. Last but not least, it relies upon a two-tier peer-to-peer (P2P) architecture and gossiping protocols to feature some tolerance to node or network failures and to promptly spread monitoring data across the network.

The rest of this paper is organised as follows. We present the design and implementation of FogMon in Sect. 2, and we discuss a case study in Sect. 3, where FogMon was run a real Fog computing testbed consisting of 13 Cloud and Fog nodes. Related work is discussed in Sect. 4, while some concluding remarks are drawn in Sect. 5.

2   Design and Implementation of FogMon

FogMon is an open-source C++ monitoring prototype[1] for Fog computing infrastructures. The tool is made from two types of software agents, viz. *Follower* and *Leader* nodes, as shown in the example topology of Fig. 2. *Follower* nodes are responsible for probing all monitored metrics and are grouped into sets, each set being associated to a *Leader* node.

Leaders, besides monitoring data about their own deployment node, periodically aggregate data gathered from the probing performed by all the *Follower* nodes they manage. Furthermore, *Leaders* are organised into an overlay peer-to-peer network and share data aggregated from their *Followers* with all other *Leaders* through gossiping.

As aforementioned, the current FogMon prototype can monitor:

- overall, used and available *hardware resources* at each node (i.e., CPU, memory, hard disk), which can be used to know whether a node can support a given application service to be deployed,
- average, maximum and minimum *end-to-end network QoS* (i.e., latency and bandwidth) between available Fog nodes, which can be used to know whether a link can suitably support communication among two distinct services, and
- availability of *IoT devices*, which are to be exploited by those services that require sensing from (or acting onto) cyber-physical systems.

---

[1] Available at: https://github.com/di-unipi-socc/FogMon.

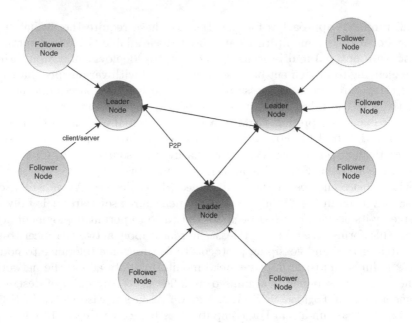

Fig. 2. FogMon topology example.

The current FogMon prototype relies on *Hyperic Sigar* [4] for gathering information about hardware, on ICMP via *ping* to measure end-to-end latency, on *iperf3* [5] and *Assolo* [20] to collect bandwidth probes, and on the C++ *libserialport* [6] to discover connected IoT devices. Communication among *Followers* and *Leaders* is performed through JSON messages (using the tool *rapidjson* [43]) over non-persistent TCP connections. To facilitate its cross-platform deployment, FogMon is released as two Docker images which can be used to build and run the prototype on any Docker-compliant platform.

Figure 3 gives an overview of the packages and classes composing FogMon. The node and the connections package contains the agent classes, which implement the monitoring logic and the TCP interactions, respectively. The storage package is used to handle the SQLite3 database instance local to each *Follower* and *Leader* node. Interfaces and classes prefixed by IMaster or Master are used by the *Leaders*, all other are related to the *Followers*. The iot package contains the classes (and interfaces) which can be instantiated (or extended) to discover and monitor available IoT devices. Finally, the shared package contains the classes in common between *Leader* and *Follower* nodes, which are mainly used for building the JSON messages to be sent via TCP connections.

In what follows, we will describe the *Follower* (Sect. 2.1) and *Leader* behaviour (Sect. 2.2) during the functioning of FogMon, and comment on how the prototype can tolerate hardware or network failures and scale over possibly large infrastructures (Sect. 2.3).

2.1 Follower Nodes

Fog infrastructures are expected to be highly dynamic environments, where *Follower* nodes can leave and join the network at any moment in time, due to their own decision as well as to node or network failures. The topology of the FogMon monitoring network is constructed upon a proximity criterion based on the *latency distance* among *Follower* and *Leader* nodes.

When a new *Follower* joins the environment monitored by FogMon, we assume that, initially, it only knows the address[2] of one (or some) *Leader* node(s). Any new *Follower* joining the network connects to the known *Leader* and retrieves a list of the identifiers of all other available *Leaders*, consequently it measure the latency distance (i.e., the round-trip time) against each of them. According to the obtained measurements, the *Follower* node associates to the closest *Leader*. Doing so guarantees that the latency experienced from each *Follower* to the associated *Leader* is as low as possible and splits *Followers* among the available *Leaders*. Such a procedure is also repeated in case a *Follower* cannot reach the associated *Leader* anymore due to network or node failures. Hereinafter, we refer to the set of *Followers* under the same *Leader* as a *group*.

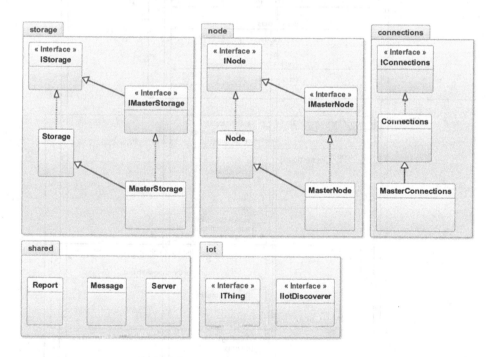

Fig. 3. FogMon classes structure.

---

[2] We assume that *Leaders* act as *superpeers* [24] that are (possibly) deployed to faster, more powerful and more reliable nodes. The known *Leader* node acts as a registry of *Leader* identifiers (viz., IP addresses and ports) of all other *Leaders*, and we assume it to be deployed at a known location.

After joining the network, *Follower* nodes can start their normal functioning as illustrated in Fig. 4. At the *Follower*, a thread dedicated to data reporting, also probes node hardware capabilities and communicates them – along with all other updates – to the associated *Leader* at set intervals. The same thread is also in charge of receiving from the *Leader* updates concerning new *Followers* joining the same group, and new *Leaders* joining the network. Such information is then exploited by a second thread which periodically monitors the network QoS of end-to-end links as follows, by updating the oldest K measurements of latency and bandwidth. Table 1 lists all main parameters that users can set in FogMon.

It is worth detailing the process of bandwidth probing performed by the *Follower* node, as it is important to avoid that monitoring such QoS parameter con-

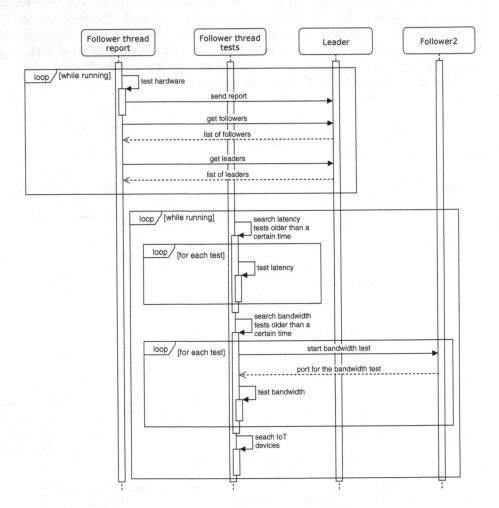

Fig. 4. Overall *Follower* functioning.

gests the Fog network. To tame the effects of iperf3 active[3] – therefore intrusive – bandwidth measurements, FogMon also relies on Assolo passive measurements, which are way less intrusive at the price of some measurement unreliability. To combine the best of the two tools, we follow a hybrid approach like the one of [26]. Particularly, FogMon always runs first an intrusive measurement, and then it exploits the packet dispersion method [21] until the probed value is coherent (up to a set difference) with the last intrusive measurement stored in the database.

Finally, FogMon monitors IoT devices connected[4] to each node along with their description. Latency and bandwidth associated to interaction between a certain node and an IoT device between the considered node and the node to which the IoT device connect[5].

2.2 Leader Nodes

Leaders main purposes are to manage monitoring of all *Followers* in their group (intra-group monitoring), to collect hardware monitoring data from other groups, and to compute estimates of the bandwidth and latency values between *Followers* belonging to distinct groups (inter-group monitoring), based on exchanged data of intra-group measurements.

As aforementioned, *Leaders* collect data from the *Followers* they directly monitor by leveraging a push/pull protocol, in which *Follower* nodes periodically

Table 1. Configurable parameters in FogMon.

Parameter	Description
Report time	The time between two different reports sent by the *Follower*
Test time	The interval waited between two iterations of the QoS tests
Latency time	The number of seconds that have to pass for a latency test to be repeated on the same link
Bandwidth time	The number of seconds that have to pass for a bandwidth test to be repeated on the same link
Heartbeat	The time before a non-responding *Follower* is eliminated from those in the group of a *Leader*

---

[3] Active bandwidth measurements consist of sending as many bytes as possible over a certain end-to-end link and measuring the ratio between the employed time and the amount of transmitted data. Despite being very reliable, this approach tends to make unstable the connectivity between the considered nodes.

[4] Currently, the prototype discovers IoT devices connected through serial ports, any other standard (e.g., Bluetooth, ZigBee) can be supported by extending the IoT package of FogMon.

[5] IoT devices directly connected to a node are assumed to reach it with negligible latency and infinite bandwidth.

report their probed data. When needed, *Leaders* can also request specific data *on-demand*. Additionally, each *Leader* stores data on the hardware of all nodes by leveraging gossiping protocol involving all other *Leaders*. The exploited gossiping protocol, based on [23], is proven to guarantee that any new piece of information is spread to every other node in the super-peers network, in a logarithmic number $O(\log L)$ of communication rounds in the number L of available *Leaders*, with a linearithmic number $O(L \log L)$ of messages. Particularly, at every set interval of time, each *Leader* selects another random *Leader* and sends the complete report about its group of *Followers*. At the end of this operation, the *Leader* also eliminates the *Followers* that did not send any report within the set heartbeat time.

As aforementioned, inter-group network QoS values are approximated by *Leader* nodes. For what concerns the latency $\ell_{A,B}$ between two *Followers* A and B referring to distinct *Leaders* $L1$ and $L2$ respectively, FogMon computes it as:

$$\ell_{A,B} = \ell_{A,L1} + \ell_{L1,L2} + \ell_{L2,B}$$

Such an approximation assumes that the latency between *Leaders* is always higher with respect to the latency between each *Follower* node and its *Leader*. The assumption is reasonable as per the proximity criterion that is used to build up the FogMon network.

Analogously, the available bandwidth capacity $\beta_{A,B}$ from node A to node B is approximated as the maximum of outgoing bandwidth of A and the maximum of the incoming bandwidth of B:

$$\beta_{A,B} = \min_{k,h}(\max(\beta_{A,k}), \max(\beta_{h,B}))$$

Such an approximation assumes that common access technologies (e.g., xDSL, 3G, 4G) are asymmetric and represent a bottleneck in the communication, especially among nodes that reside at the edge of the Internet. Again, this is a reasonable assumption as per the current technological trend, where we expect the upload (or download) bandwidth of one of the considered peers to cap their communication capacity.

2.3   Remarks

Before presenting some quantitative results on the behaviour of FogMon over a real testbed, we briefly comment here on the fault-tolerance and scalability properties of the approach.

First, the replication of monitored data at each *Leader* node and the eventual consistency of such data achieved through gossiping make our system capable of resisting to failures of some *Leader* nodes. Indeed, in such an event, *Followers* can join the group of a new (different) *Leader* and start again their monitoring activity. Also, it is worth mentioning the fact that each group can run autonomously from others, so that the approach also tolerates temporary network disruptions between *Leaders*.

As far as *scalability* is concerned, the two-tiered architecture of FogMon contributes to mitigating the complexity of monitoring large-scale infrastructures. The most expensive measurement in our approach is the monitoring of network QoS – particularly bandwidth – which requires to perform, in principle, $O(N^2)$ measurements, where N is the number of available nodes. Now, considering a network of N nodes to be monitored, with L *Leaders* among them ($L \leq N$), each *Leader* will approximately manage $O(\frac{N}{L})$ nodes overall. Thus, $O(\frac{N^2}{L^2})$ QoS measurements will be performed within every single group. By suitably setting[6] $L = O(\sqrt{N})$, the originally quadratic complexity of monitoring end-to-end QoS becomes linear in the number of nodes, i.e. $O(\frac{N^2}{L^2}) = O(\frac{N^2}{(\sqrt{N})^2}) = O(N)$.

3   Case Study

To experiment our FogMon prototype, we have exploited the testbed Fog network sketched in Fig. 5, which consists of 3 public Cloud virtual machines (VMs) on Amazon AWS and 3 on Microsoft Azure, 1 private Cloud VM on the Cloud datacentre of the University of Pisa, 4 RaspberryPi3 B+, and 3 other RaspberryPi3 deployed in private homes[7].

The nodes of the testbed feature different networking technologies. Namely:

- node A relies on ADSL Internet access with a nominal speed of 7 Mbps and 1 Mbps in download and upload, respectively,
- node B relies on VDSL Internet access with a nominal speed of 70 Mbps and 20 Mbps in download and upload, respectively,
- node C relies on VDSL Internet access with a nominal speed of 20 Mbps and 3 Mbps in download and upload, respectively,
- nodes $D1$–$D4$ are within the Gigabit LAN of the Department of Computer Science, and reach out the university datacentre through fibre links.

After the initialisation of the FogMon overlay, the groups reported in Table 2 were formed, and monitoring of the network started. For the purposes of this case study, we considered and experimented with three different configurations of FogMon parameters, as shown in Table 3. Throughout the experiments we

---

[6] In real large-scale settings, it is up to the infrastructure manager to guarantee a sufficient number of *Leaders* is available in the Fog network monitored by FogMon. More precisely, we expect *Leaders* to be deployed either to Cloud nodes or to Fog nodes that naturally manage a subset of *Followers* (e.g., gateways, building servers, ISP switches).

[7] The VMs on AWS feature 1 vCPU, 1 GB of RAM and 8 GB of storage, and run Amazon Linux 2, based on RedHat Enterprise Linux and CentOS. The VMs on Microsoft Azure feature 1 vCPU, 4 GB of RAM and 7 GB of storage, and run Debian 9.9. The VM on the university datacentre features 1 vCPU, 2 GB of RAM and 30 GB of storage, ad runs Ubuntu 18.04. RaspberryPi3 nodes feature a Cortex-A53 (ARMv8) 64-bit SoC 1.4 GHz processor, 1 GB of RAM and 16 GB of storage, and run Raspbian 4.14, but for node A which runs Fedora 28.

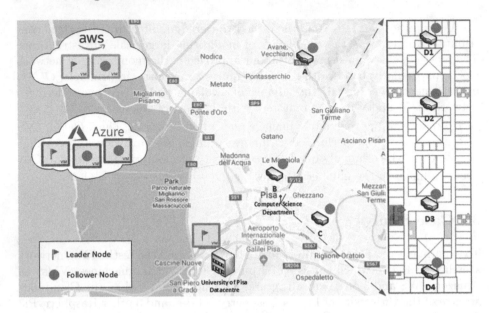

Fig. 5. FogMon testbed.

Table 2. Groups formed in the experimental testbed.

Leader	Followers
Unipi Datacentre	A, B, D1, D2, D3, D4
AWS Cloud	AWS Follower, C
Azure Cloud	Azure Followers

keep fixed other parameters[8] as they have shown not to significantly affect the performance of FogMon over our testbed.

The goal of this case study was two-fold, aiming at assessing the *footprint* of FogMon on hardware and bandwidth and aiming at evaluating the *accuracy* of the obtained measurements. First, we wanted to actually measure FogMon footprint on both hardware resources and bandwidth. Over three consecutive hours of functioning, the prototype has shown a very contained impact on hardware resources and on bandwidth usage as shown in Table 4.

More detailedly, CPU consumption stayed on average around 2% on all the available nodes, whilst RAM consumption settled on a constant value of 3 MB, both for the *Leader* and *Follower* agents. When it comes to bandwidth, we exploited the *bmon* [3] tool to retrieve information on how much data was sent or received from our nodes. We focussed our analyses on the home nodes as all other connections featured Gigabit speeds, thus bandwidth usage from FogMon

---

[8] With reference to Table 1, reporting time was set to 30 s, latency time was set to 30 s and heartbeat time was set to 120 s.

Table 3. FogMon configurations.

Config	Test time	Bandwidth time
config1	30 s	600 s
config2	20 s	300 s
config3	10 s	60 s

Table 4. FogMon footprint on hardware and bandwidth.

Resource	Consumption			
	config1	config2	config3	avg
CPU	1.5%	1.8%	2%	1.75%
RAM	3 MB	3 MB	3 MB	3 MB
Down/Up Bandwidth	0.5/0.9%	1.2/3.6%	1.5/4.3%	1.1/2.9%

was affecting them only negligibly. Similarly to hardware footprint, the bandwidth footprint of FogMon on nominal connection speeds was contained, settling on average around 1.1% for the download and on 2.9% for the upload.

For what concerns measurements accuracy, we focussed on the error related to bandwidth and latency. We first run our prototype FogMon throughout 3 h with a single *Leader* node – at the University of Pisa datacentre – so to obtain actual end-to-end measurements for all node couples (having all other nodes running the *Follower* agent). When comparing the collected values with the ones obtained in the settings of Fig. 5, the average errors of latency and bandwidth proved to be bound by 14% and 18%, respectively, in all three parameter configurations. Overall, for inter-group measurements, the error is always bound by 5% (both for latency and bandwidth), whilst for inter-group estimated values it never exceeds 25%. It is worth noting that, if considering QoS profiles for latency (e.g., ≤ 5 ms, 5–15 ms, 15–20 ms) and bandwidth (e.g., ≤ 7 Mbps, 7–20 Mbps, 20–50 Mbps), the monitoring accuracy substantially grows and gets closer to 95%.

4   Related Work

While quite many tools have been proposed to monitor Cloud environments, only few efforts have been devoted so far to specifically monitor Fog infrastructures, as pointed out by Taherizade et al. [39] in their comprehensive review.

Some monitoring tools, like Ganglia [27] or DARGOS [31] (are intended to) monitor node resources, and do not measure inter-node latency or bandwidth.

GMonE [29] aims at offering a comprehensive monitoring suite for (IaaS, PaaS and Saas) Cloud platforms. However, GMonE does not monitor end-to-end network QoS nor IoT, and it has not been adapted to run over heterogeneous (Fog, multi-Cloud) deployment environments. Similarly, Zenoss [7] is a commercial agent-less monitoring platform targeting VM, application, and service monitoring in Cloud environments. End-to-end network QoS monitoring is only offered for latency measurements through plug-in extensions, and limited support is given to deal with failure scenarios typical of Fog infrastructures. Still, no support is offered for detecting connected IoT devices.

Zabbix [38] is an agent-based tool designed to monitor network resources. While Zabbix is quite resource efficient with a small footprint, there are some concerns on its stability and robustness [34]. Nagios Core [8], originally conceived for the Cloud, is a tool that can be used to monitor both node hardware resources and network QoS capabilities, like end-to-end bandwidth. While its extensibility [22] could suggest its consideration for Fog monitoring, there are some concerns on its ease of configuration and scalability [28]. Amazon AWS offers the possibility to deploy its CloudWatch Agent [2] to on-premises servers. This permits extending the Amazon Cloud infrastructures with Fog nodes. However, CloudWatch Agent does not monitor end-to-end network QoS metrics.

Only a couple proposals have been recently put forward to specifically monitor Fog infrastructures. Brandón et al. [10] have recently prototyped a Python framework (FMonE) that is capable of monitoring node resources across Fog infrastructures. FMonE however does not monitor end-to-end network QoS metrics, nor interactions with the IoT, which are instead needed for realizing QoS-aware orchestration of Fog services [12,39]. Also Souza et al. [37] have proposed a monitoring tool for Fog infrastructures that is capable of monitoring some node resources and end-to-end latency (but not bandwidth).

Table 5 summarises the dimensions supported by the aforementioned monitoring tools. Summing up, to the best of our knowledge, none of the available tools for Cloud or Fog infrastructure monitoring is capable of measuring all metrics and information collected and aggregated by **FogMon** on hardware resources

Table 5. Overview of available monitoring tools (extended from [39]).

Ref	Hardware				Network QoS		Non-functional reqs.		
	CPU	Ram	Disk	IoT	Latency	Bandwidth	Scalable	Robust	Non-intrusive
Nagios Core [8]	✓	✓	✓	✗	✓	✓	✗	✗	~
DARGOS [31]	✓	✓	✓	✗	✗	✗	✓	✗	✓
Zenoss [7]	✓	✓	✓	✗	✓	✗	✓	✗	✓
Ganglia [27]	✓	✓	✓	✗	✗	✗	✓	✓	~
Zabbix [38]	✓	✓	✓	✗	✓	✓	✓	✗	✓
Lattice [16]	✓	✓	✓	✗	✗	✗	✓	✓	✓
FMonE [10]	✓	✓	✓	✗	✗	✗	✓	✓	✓
GMonE [29]	✓	✓	✓	✗	✓	✓	–	–	–
Osmotic [37]	✓	✓	✗	✗	✓	✗	–	✗	✓
CloudWatch [2]	✓	✓	✓	~	✗	✗	✓	✓	✓
FogMon	✓	✓	✓	✓	✓	✓	✓	✓	✓

✓ means support, ✗ no support, ~ partial support, - information not available (viz., CPU, RAM, HDD), on end-to-end network QoS parameters (viz., latency and bandwidth) and on available IoT devices, in a scalable, robust, and non-intrusive manner.

5   Concluding Remarks

In this paper, we delved into the architecture and the implementation of a prototype distributed monitoring tool for Fog infrastructures, FogMon, focussing on the methods it exploits to probe and monitor some relevant metrics, and we run some experiments with the prototype by performing a series of tests within an actual testbed. FogMon constitutes a first step towards collecting and aggregating those data on Fog infrastructures that will be needed to perform dynamic and adaptive life-cycle management of Fog services. FogMon can monitor hardware resources of the available nodes (viz., CPU, RAM, HDD), end-to-end network QoS (viz., latency and bandwidth) between Fog nodes, and discover available IoT devices.

Notably, FogMon shows a very small footprint both on hardware resources and on network bandwidth. Moreover, a peer-to-peer architecture – avoiding single points of failure – has been employed to make FogMon tolerant to some node and network failures.

Naturally, many lines for future work are possible by extending the current version of FogMon. Particularly, we intend to:

- exploit FogMon to actually feed predictive tools for Fog application deployment or management (e.g., FogTorchΠ [12] or FogDirMimc [19]), and to assess the quality of their predictions,
- reduce the error on inter-group bandwidth measurements by also exploring alternative methods for approximating bandwidth probing among *Leader* nodes (e.g., via matrix completion techniques [18, 25, 42])
- include a (topology-aware) *Leader* election mechanism so to fully automate the creation of the network overlay,
- assess the scalability and fault-tolerance of the prototype over a large-scale Fog infrastructure, while exploring the possibility of reducing the number of replicas of the monitored data, and
- further engineer the prototype and extend it with some authentication mechanism so to being able to verify that a node entering the network can be actually trusted.

Acknowledgements. This work has been partly supported by the project *"DECLWARE: Declarative methodologies of application design and deployment"* (PRA_2018_66), funded by University of Pisa, Italy, and by the project *"GIÒ: a Fog computing testbed for research & education"*, funded by the Department of Computer Science of the University of Pisa, Italy.

References

1. Cloud key marketing trends for 2017 and ideas for exceeding customer expectations, IBM Marketing (2017)
2. Amazon CloudWatch. https://aws.amazon.com/it/cloudwatch/
3. bmon - portable bandwidth monitor. https://linux.die.net/man/1/bmon
4. Hyperic's system information gatherer (sigar). https://github.com/hyperic/sigar/wiki/overview
5. Iperf. https://software.es.net/iperf/
6. Libserialport. https://sigrok.org/wiki/Libserialport
7. Zenoss (2014). http://www.zenoss.com/
8. Barth, W.: Nagios: System and Network Monitoring. No Starch Press, San Francisco (2008)
9. Bonomi, F., Milito, R., Natarajan, P., Zhu, J.: Fog computing: a platform for internet of things and analytics. In: Bessis, N., Dobre, C. (eds.) Big Data and Internet of Things: A Roadmap for Smart Environments. SCI, vol. 546, pp. 169–186. Springer, Cham (2014). https://doi.org/10.1007/978-3-319-05029-4_7
10. Brandón, Á., Pérez, M.S., Montes, J., Sanchez, A.: Fmone: a flexible monitoring solution at the edge. Wirel. Commun. Mob. Comput. **2018**, 15 (2018)
11. Brogi, A., Forti, S., Guerrero, C., Lera, I.: How to Place Your Apps in the Fog-State of the Art and Open Challenges. preprint arXiv:1901.05717 (2019)
12. Brogi, A., Forti, S., Ibrahim, A.: How to best deploy your fog applications, probably. In: 2017 IEEE 1st International Conference on Fog and Edge Computing (ICFEC), pp. 105–114. IEEE (2017)
13. Brogi, A., Forti, S., Ibrahim, A., Rinaldi, L.: Bonsai in the Fog: an active learning lab with Fog computing. In: 2018 Third International Conference on Fog and Mobile Edge Computing (FMEC), pp. 79–86. IEEE (2018)
14. Buyya, R., et al.: A manifesto for future generation cloud computing: research directions for the next decade. ACM Comput. Surv. (CSUR) **51**(5), 105 (2018)
15. CISCO: the internet of things: Extend the cloud to where the things are. Cisco White Paper (2015)
16. Clayman, S., Galis, A., Mamatas, L.: Monitoring virtual networks with lattice. In: 2010 IEEE/IFIP Network Operations and Management Symposium Workshops (NOMS Wksps), pp. 239–246. IEEE (2010)
17. Dastjerdi, A.V., Buyya, R.: Fog computing: helping the internet of things realize its potential. Computer **49**(8), 112–116 (2016)
18. Du, W., Liao, Y., Tao, N., Geurts, P., Fu, X., Leduc, G.: Rating network paths for locality-aware overlay construction and routing. IEEE/ACM Trans. Networking (TON) **23**(5), 1661–1673 (2015)
19. Forti, S., Ibrahim, A., Brogi, A.: Mimicking FogDirector application management. Software-Intensive Cyber-Phys. Syst. **34**(2–3), 151–161 (2019)
20. Goldoni, E., Rossi, G., Torelli, A.: Assolo, a new method for available bandwidth estimation. In: 2009 Fourth International Conference on Internet Monitoring and Protection, ICIMP 2009, pp. 130–136. IEEE (2009)
21. Hu, N.: Network monitoring and diagnosis based on available bandwidth measurement. Technical report, Carnegie-Mellon University, Pittsburgh, PA School of Computer Science (2006)
22. Issariyapat, C., Pongpaibool, P., Mongkolluksame, S., Meesublak, K.: Using Nagios as a groundwork for developing a better network monitoring system. In: 2012 Proceedings of PICMET 2012 Technology Management for Emerging Technologies (PICMET), pp. 2771–2777. IEEE (2012)

23. Jelasity, M.: Gossip. In: Di Marzo Serugendo, G., Gleizes, M.P., Karageorgos, A. (eds.) Self-organising Software. NCS, pp. 139–162. Springer, Berlin (2011). https://doi.org/10.1007/978-3-642-17348-6_7

24. Jesi, G.P., Montresor, A., Babaoglu, O.: Proximity-aware superpeer overlay topologies. IEEE Trans. Netw. Serv. Manag. 4(2), 74–83 (2007)

25. Liao, Y., Du, W., Geurts, P., Leduc, G.: DMFSGD: a decentralized matrix factorization algorithm for network distance prediction. IEEE/ACM Trans. Networking (TON) 21(5), 1511–1524 (2013)

26. Marttinen, A., et al.: Estimating kpis in deployed heterogeneous networks. IEEE Commun. Mag. 54(10), 158–165 (2016)

27. Massie, M.L., Chun, B.N., Culler, D.E.: The ganglia distributed monitoring system: design, implementation, and experience. Parallel Comput. 30(7), 817–840 (2004)

28. Mongkolluksamee, S., Pongpaibool, P., Issariyapat, C.: Strengths and limitations of Nagios as a network monitoring solution. In: Proceedings of the 7th International Joint Conference on Computer Science and Software Engineering (JCSSE 2010), Bangkok, Thailand. pp. 96–101 (2010)

29. Montes, J., Sánchez, A., Memishi, B., Pérez, M.S., Antoniu, G.: GMonE: a complete approach to cloud monitoring. Future Gener. Comput. Syst. 29(8), 2026–2040 (2013)

30. Noghabi, S.A., Kolb, J., Bodik, P., Cuervo, E.: Steel: Simplified development and deployment of edge-cloud applications. In: 10th {USENIX} Workshop on Hot Topics in Cloud Computing (HotCloud 18) (2018)

31. Povedano-Molina, J., Lopez-Vega, J.M., Lopez-Soler, J.M., Corradi, A., Foschini, L.: Dargos: a highly adaptable and scalable monitoring architecture for multi-tenant clouds. Future Gener. Comput. Syst. 29(8), 2041–2056 (2013)

32. Rahimi, M.R., Ren, J., Liu, C.H., Vasilakos, A.V., Venkatasubramanian, N.: Mobile cloud computing: a survey, state of art and future directions. Mobile Networks Appl. 19(2), 133–143 (2014)

33. Satyanarayanan, M., et al.: Edge analytics in the internet of things. IEEE Pervasive Comput. 14(2), 24–31 (2015)

34. Simmonds, E., Harrington, J.: SCF/FEF Evaluation of Nagios and Zabbix Monitoring Systems, pp. 1–9 (2009). www.scopus.com, cited By: 2

35. Skarlat, O., Bachmann, K., Schulte, S.: Fogframe: Iot service deployment and execution in the fog. KuVS-Fachgespräch Fog Comput. 1, 5–8 (2018)

36. Song, Y., Yau, S.S., Yu, R., Zhang, X., Xue, G.: An approach to QoS-based task distribution in edge computing networks for IoT applications. In: 2017 IEEE International Conference on Edge Computing (EDGE), pp. 32–39. IEEE (2017)

37. Souza, A., Cacho, N., Noor, A., Jayaraman, P.P., Romanovsky, A., Ranjan, R.: Osmotic monitoring of microservices between the edge and cloud. In: 2018 IEEE 20th International Conference on High Performance Computing and Communications; IEEE 16th International Conference on Smart City; IEEE 4th International Conference on Data Science and Systems (HPCC/SmartCity/DSS), pp. 758–765 (2018)

38. Tader, P.: Server monitoring with zabbix. Linux J. 2010(195), 7 (2010)

39. Taherizadeh, S., Jones, A.C., Taylor, I., Zhao, Z., Stankovski, V.: Monitoring self-adaptive applications within edge computing frameworks: a state-of-the-art review. J. Syst. Softw. 136, 19–38 (2018)

40. Vögler, M., Schleicher, J.M., Inzinger, C., Dustdar, S.: Diane-dynamic IoT application deployment. In: 2015 IEEE International Conference on Mobile Services, pp. 298–305. IEEE (2015)

41. Wöbker, C., Seitz, A., Mueller, H., Bruegge, B.: Fogernetes: deployment and management of fog computing applications. In: NOMS 2018–2018 IEEE/IFIP Network Operations and Management Symposium, pp. 1–7. IEEE (2018)
42. Xie, K., et al.: Sequential and adaptive sampling for matrix completion in network monitoring systems. In: 2015 IEEE Conference on Computer Communications (INFOCOM), pp. 2443–2451. IEEE (2015)
43. Yip, M.: Rapidjson-a fast json parser/generator for c++ with both sax/dom style api. THL A29. https://github.com/miloyip/rapidjson (2015)
44. Yousefpour, A., et al.: All one needs to know about fog computing and related edge computing paradigms: a complete survey. J. Syst. Architect. **98**, 289–330 (2019)

Mobile Apps with Dynamic Bindings Between the Fog and the Cloud

Dionysis Athanasopoulos[1]([✉]) [iD], Mitchell McEwen[2], and Austen Rainer[1] [iD]

[1] School of EEECS, Queen's University Belfast, Belfast, UK
{D.Athanasopoulos,A.Rainer}@qub.ac.uk
[2] DXC Technology, Wellington, New Zealand
mmcewen3@dxc.com

Abstract. The back-ends of mobile apps usually use services executed on remote (e.g., cloud) machines. The transmission latency may though make the usage of remote machines a less efficient solution for data that need short analysis time. Thus, apps should further use machines located near the network edge, i.e., on the Fog. However, the combination of the Fog and the Cloud introduces the research question of when and how the right binding of the front-end to an edge instance or a remote instance of the back-end can be decided. Such a decision should not be made at the development or the deployment time of apps, because the response time of the instances may not be known ahead of time or cannot be guaranteed. To make such decisions at run-time, we contribute the conceptual model and the algorithmic mechanisms of an autonomic controller as a service. The autonomic controller predicts the response time of edge/remote instances of the back-end and dynamically decides the binding of the front-end to an instance. The evaluation results of our approach on a real-world app for a large number of datasets show that the autonomic controller makes efficient binding-decisions in the majority of the datasets, decreasing significantly the response time of the app.

Keywords: Fog · Mobile back-end · Autonomic control-loop · Predictive model

1 Introduction

Amelia is an avid eBay user, always ready to snap up a bargain. And generally enjoys the thrill of a bidding fight right up to the final moments. She wants to buy a nearly new Xbox but she finds it difficult to decide on the best bidding price. Thus, she downloaded on her phone an auction app that predicts bidding prices [1]. However, Amelia complains she lost some final-moment bidding fights due to delays in the app response.

What Amelia does not know is that data collected on her phone are moved to the Cloud and the output of the analysis is sent back to her. While the Cloud offers powerful machines for efficient data-analytics, the latency of the transmission may make the usage of the Cloud a less efficient solution for data that need short analysis time [2]. To make apps more efficient, service instances (i.e., replicas) of a back-end should be further deployed on the Fog. The Fog constitutes machines located near the network

© Springer Nature Switzerland AG 2019
S. Yangui et al. (Eds.): ICSOC 2019, LNCS 11895, pp. 539–554, 2019.
https://doi.org/10.1007/978-3-030-33702-5_41

edge (e.g., laptops, small-scale data-centers) [3]. The combination of the Fog and the Cloud though introduces the research question of when and how the right binding of the front-end of an app to an edge or a remote instance can be decided[1].

Concerning the first part of the question, bindings should not be decided at the development or the deployment time of apps (as the state-of-the-art does), because the response time of instances may not be known ahead of time or cannot be guaranteed. Thus, we face the challenge of deciding the binding of the front-end at run-time. Regarding the second part of the question, we consider that the response time of an instance depends on the execution time of the instance on a machine and on the network latency to reach out the machine[2]. Thus, we face the challenge to predict the response time of instances based on the input datasets and the machines used for deploying the instances. On top of that, the efficiency challenge of predicting response times from a large number of datasets is raised, since the number of the datasets increases over time.

To address the above challenges, we contribute the conceptual model and the algorithmic mechanisms of an *autonomic controller-as-a-service* (one for each back-end) that is deployed on the Fog and further acts as a proxy between the front-end and the back-end instances[3]. Each time the front-end interacts with the autonomic controller, the latter dynamically predicts the response time of the instances and decides the binding of the front-end to an instance. To do it in an autonomic manner, the controller follows the *control loop* of self-adaptive software [4]. Specifically, the controller monitors the past invocations to the instances, analyses a few *representative* (addressing the efficiency challenge) input datasets, (re-)builds *predictive models* of the response time of the instances, and dynamically decides the binding of the front-end to an instance.

To evaluate our approach, we implement a research prototype of the autonomic controller-as-a-service of the auction app (Fig. 1). A large number of datasets, collected from the UC Irvine machine-learning repository [5], is given as input to the app. The experimental results show that the autonomic controller makes efficient binding-decisions in the majority of the datasets, decreasing significantly the response time of the app.

The rest of the paper is structured as follows. Section 2 describes the related approaches and compares them against ours. Sections 3 and 4 specify the conceptual model and the algorithmic mechanisms of the controller. Section 5 presents the evaluation of our approach. Section 6 discusses the threats to the validity of our work. Section 7 summarizes our contribution and discusses future directions of our research.

2   Related Work

The approaches that use the Fog and the Cloud for the execution of mobile apps have focused on the development or the deployment time of apps. Concerning the non-automated approaches, [6] provides suggestions for mapping back-ends to machines

---

[1] The front-end includes the programming clients that interact with the service back-end.

[2] The locally stored datasets are synchronized to the remote storage. We do not consider the synchronization time in the current work.

[3] We assume at least an edge and a remote instance have been pre-deployed (whose endpoints are registered to the controller). We leave as future work the decision of the number of instances.

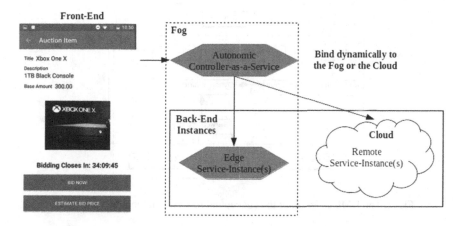

Fig. 1. Auction app extended with the autonomic controller and multiple back-end instances.

at deployment time. The suggestions mainly aim at reducing the network latency, the energy consumption and the financial cost of renting machines. [7] proposes a methodology for assessing the security level of deployment plans.

Regarding the automated approaches, [8–10] generate deployment plans that minimize the network latency, the delay of machines to serve apps and the renting cost, respectively. [11,12] generate deployment plans that minimize the network usage. [13,14] produce deployment plans that reduce the power consumption. [15] generates deployment plans based on the renting cost and the end-users' budgets. [16] selects machines at deployment time based on their ranking with respect to the delay of machines and the power consumption. [17] regenerates deployment plans via modeling the delay of machines as a function of the elapsed discrete-time. Finally, [18] regenerates deployment plans when the latency of back-ends exceeds a time threshold.

Overall, only two approaches monitor the app execution to regenerate deployment plans [17,18]. However, [17,18] are reactive (i.e., they suspend the app execution) and lay between apps and operating systems (e.g., redeployment engines). Contrarily, our approach runs at the application layer and pro-actively (without suspending the app execution) self-decides the binding of the front-end.

3   Conceptual Model of Autonomic Controller-as-a-Service

The autonomic controller-as-a-service (Fig. ?) mainly consists of its API (Sect. 3.1), its dynamic binding-mechanism (Sect. 3.2) and its control loop (Sect. 4).

3.1   API of Autonomic Controller

The API offers all of the operations of the back-end. From the Web-service technology perspective, an API is exposed by using the REST [19] or the SOAP [20] protocol. We define the notion of the API in a generic manner as follows.

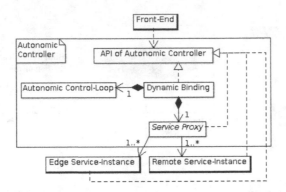

Fig. 2. The UML diagram of the conceptual model of autonomic controller.

Definition 1. *Each operation of the API of an autonomic controller corresponds to a programming method[4] of the API of the back-end. Each operation accepts/returns a (possibly empty) set of input/output parameters.*

Given that the XML/JSON schemas of input/output parameters can be easily transformed to programming objects (e.g., JAXB[5]), we define the notion of the parameter based on the object-oriented paradigm as follows.

Definition 2. *A parameter p is characterized by a name and a built-in or complex data-type. A complex data-type is a group of parameters or a reference to another parameter.*

Returning to the auction app, we assume the back-end uses the k-means clustering algorithm [22]. The single operation of the API accepts the following parameters: a dataset and the numbers of clusters and algorithm iterations. The last two parameters have a built-in data-type (`int`), while the first parameter has the complex data-type of a list of multi-dimensional data-points (`List<Double[] dataPoint> dataset`). In turn, a data-point is a parameter that has a complex data-type too. The latter is defined by a vector of coordinates, where each coordinate has a built-in data-type (`Double`).

Based on Definition 2, a parameter has a hierarchical structure. However, only the leaves of the structure carry actual data-values. Returning to our example, while a two-layer structure is formed, only the second/lowest layer (`Double[] dataPoint`) contains actual data (a.k.a., the coordinates of data-points). Our approach pre-processes multi-layer parameters and converts them to a set of unstructured ones. We define the notion of the unstructured parameter as follows.

Definition 3. *The unstructured parameters of a multi-layer parameter p is the set of the leaf data-types $\{x\}$ of p. Each unstructured parameter x is defined by a tuple (n, c) that consists of the name n and the cardinality c of the corresponding leaf data-type. The cardinality c equals to product of the cardinalities of the grouping structures that are met in the path followed to reach n from the root node of p.*

---

[4] The programming methods are explicitly defined in a SOAP-based API or they can be determined by parsing the suffix of the URI of the API in a RESTful API [21].

[5] https://docs.oracle.com/javase/tutorial/jaxb/intro/index.html.

The multi-layer parameter, $p = List < Double[] \, dataPoint > dataset$, in our example is converted to the singleton set, $\{x\} = \{(dataPoint, c)\}$, where c is the cardinality of the list structure (the list is the only node that precedes x in the path from the root)[6]. Hereafter, we use the term parameter to refer to an unstructured parameter.

3.2 Dynamic Binding-Mechanism of Autonomic Controller

The dynamic binding-mechanism comprises the components of the Dynamic Binding, the Autonomic Control-Loop and the Service Proxy, as depicted in Fig. 2.

The Dynamic Binding implements all of the operations of the API of the back-end. In particular, the implementation of the operations of the Dynamic Binding handles calls from the front-end to the operations of the back-end. The Dynamic Binding first pre-processes the input data (to form the unstructured parameters), following uses the Autonomic Control-Loop to predict the response time of the edge/remote instances and then finds the instance that has the lowest predicted response-time. Finally, the Dynamic Binding uses the Service Proxy[7] to forward an operation call to the selected instance. To this end, the Dynamic Binding instantiates the target parameters of the operation of the selected instance via considering the one-to-one mapping between the parameters of the called operation of the controller API and the parameters of the mapped operation of the selected instance. The mapping exists because the controller API is the same with that of the edge and remote instances.

4 Autonomic Control-Loop

The autonomic control-loop of the controller extends the generic Monitor-Analyze-Plan-Execute and Knowledge loop (MAPE-K) of self-adaptive software as follows [4]. Our Monitoring mechanism records the response time of the invocation of edge/remote instances, i.e., the elapsed time between when the invocation is made and when the response is returned back. In other words, the response time is the sum of (i) the execution time of an instance on a machine and (ii) the network latency. The Analysis mechanism (re-)constructs predictive models of response times and expresses them as a function of the input parameters (Sect. 4.1). A separate model is constructed for each instance because instances are usually deployed on different machines. The Planning mechanism dynamically (re-)creates groups of parameter values and stores a representative value for each group, along with the corresponding monitoring response-times (Sect. 4.2). The mechanism uses the constructed models and the stored parameter-values to predict response times and select the instance that has the lowest predicted response-time. The Execution mechanism invokes the selected instance via implementing a proxy. The latter firstly instantiates the target parameters of the invoked operation

---

[6] If the cardinality is not declared in parameter schemas, then our approach considers a large pre-defined value as an artificial cardinality.

[7] The relationship between the Dynamic Binding and the Service Proxy is UML composition (depicted by filled diamond) so as to hide the edge/remote instances from the front-end.

of the instance via considering the one-to-one mapping that exists between the parameters of the called operation of the controller API and the parameters of the mapped operation of the instance (Sect. 3.2). Finally, the constructed predictive-models, the groups of parameter values and the monitoring response-times are stored as the Knowledge of the loop.

4.1 Analysis Mechanism

We firstly define the notions of predictive model and prediction error used by the mechanism. We also specify the algorithmic steps and the time complexity of the mechanism.

The mechanism constructs a separate predictive-model for each instance and especially, for each operation of an instance, as defined below.

Definition 4 (Predictive model of an operation). *The predictive model, p_{op}, of an operation, op, of a service instance is defined by the tuple, $\left(x[D, N], \widehat{y}[D], y(x) \right)$:*

- $x[D, N]$*: D past values of each one of the N input parameters of op*
- $\widehat{y}[D]$*: D monitoring response-times of op*
- $y(x)$*: a polynomial function of x that predicts the response time of op.*

Definition 5 (Prediction error for an operation). *The prediction error, e, for the response time of an operation op, of a service instance for the current values, $x[N]$, of the input parameters of op, equals to the relative distance of the predicted (for x) response-time, y, from the monitoring response-time, $\widehat{y}$, of op: $e = \frac{|y(x) - \widehat{y}|}{\widehat{y}}$.*

Analysis Algorithm. Considering that polynomials describe the performance of programs well [23], the algorithm builds polynomial functions to predict response times. A widely used technique to build polynomials is the regression technique [24]. However, it takes all possible variable combinations forming long expressions with possibly unneeded terms. To build compact expressions, greedy techniques have been proposed [24,25]. We extend the sparse-term technique of [25]. Our technique further selects the term that is dominant (i.e., it has the lowest prediction-error) and confident (i.e., its prediction error is higher than a threshold).

The algorithm steps are specified in Algorithm 1. Algorithm 1 accepts as input the current values of the input parameters, the past and the current monitoring response-times and the polynomial function of the predictive model of an operation of a service instance. The inputs of Algorithm 1 further include a threshold ω of the lowest prediction-error. Algorithm 1 initially calculates the prediction error (Algorithm 1 (1–4)). If the error is higher than ω, Algorithm 1 rebuilds the predictive model via fitting all of the possible single-variable terms to the past and the current response-times (Algorithm 1 (8)). To fit a term to the response times, Algorithm 1 applies the linear least-square regression-technique [24] (Algorithm 1 (5–10)). Finally, Algorithm 1 selects and returns the term that is dominant and confident (Algorithm 1 (11–20)).

Algorithm 1. Analysis Mechanism

Input: $x[D, N], \widehat{y}[D], y(x), \omega$
Output: $y(x)$

1: $e \leftarrow \frac{|y(x[D,N]) - \widehat{y}[D]|}{\widehat{y}[D]}$;
2: **if** $e > \omega$ **then**
3:      $T \leftarrow \text{FIT}(x, \widehat{y})$;
4:      $y(x) \leftarrow \text{SELECT}(T, x, \widehat{y})$;

5: **function** FIT($x[D, N], \widehat{y}[D]$): T
6:      **for all** $1 \leq j \leq N$ **do**
7:          $y(x) \leftarrow a * x^b$
8:          FIND $a, b : \sum\limits_{i=1}^{D} (y(x[i, j]) - \widehat{y}[i])^2$ is minimized
9:          $T.\text{ADD}(y(x))$;
10: **end function**

11: **function** SELECT($T, x[D, N], \widehat{y}[D]$): $y(x)$
12:      **for all** $y(x) \in T$ **do**
13:          **for all** $1 \leq i \leq D$ **do**
14:              $e \mathrel{+}= \frac{|y(x[i, N]) - \widehat{y}[i]|}{\widehat{y}[i]}$;
15:          $\overline{e} \leftarrow \frac{e}{|D|}$;
16:          **if** $\overline{e} < min$ and $\overline{e} \geq \omega$ **then**
17:              $min \leftarrow \overline{e}$;
18:              $min_y \leftarrow y(x)$;
19:      $y(x) \leftarrow min_y$;
20: **end function**

Time Complexity. The complexity scales with the numbers D (parameter values) and N (fitted terms), $\mathcal{O}(N * D)$. Since N is much lower than D (we use a sparse-term technique, which is time efficient), the complexity is captured by the expression, $\mathcal{O}(N * D) \approx \mathcal{O}(D)$. Moreover, the complexity does not scale with the number of the back-end instances (even if Algorithm 1 is repeated for each instance), because this number is expected to be (in the order of tens or lower) much lower than D (Sect. 4.2).

4.2 Planning Mechanism

We firstly define the notion of the partition used by the mechanism. We also specify the algorithmic steps of the mechanism, along with its time complexity.

The mechanism partitions the domain of the values of each parameter and stores a representative value for each partition. Each partition is defined as an one-dimension interval. The partitions of a parameter are a set of intervals with consecutive integer-endpoints, as defined below.

Definition 6 (Partitions of the values domain of a parameter). *Let x_{min} and x_{max} be the min and the max domain values of a parameter, x. The set, r, of the Q partitions of the domain values of x is:*

$$r = \left\{ r_1, \ldots, r_j, \ldots, r_Q \right\}, \; where:$$

$$r_1 = \left[x_{min}, \; x_{min} + len(x) \right]$$

$$r_j = \left[x_{min} + len(x) * (j-1) + 1, x_{min} + len(x) * j \right], \; j \in [2, Q-1]$$

$$r_Q = \left[x_{min} + len(x) * (Q-1), \; x_{max} \right]$$

The partition length that is used in Definition 6 is defined as follows.

Algorithm 2. Planning Mechanism

Input: $x[N], r[N], v[N], \{instances\}, \{y(x)\}$
Output: *instance*

1: PARTITION(r, v, x);
2: *instance* ← SELECT({*instances*}, x, {$y(x)$});

3: **procedure** PARTITION($r[N], v[N], x[N]$)
4:    **for all** $1 \leq i \leq N$ **do**
5:        $adjustment$ ← false;
6:        **if** $x[i] > x_{max}[i]$ **then**
7:            $x_{max}[i] \leftarrow x[i]$;
8:            $adjustment$ ← true;
9:        **else if** $x[i] < x_{min}[i]$ **then**
10:            $x_{min}[i] \leftarrow x[i]$;
11:            $adjustment$ ← true;
12:        **if** $adjustment$ = true **then**
13:            $l \leftarrow \frac{x_{max}[i] - x_{min}[i]}{Q}$;
14:            $r_1[i] \leftarrow \left[x_{min}[i], x_{min}[i] + l \right]$;
15:            $v_1[i] \leftarrow$ UPDATE($v_1[i], r_1[i]$);
16:            **for all** $2 \leq j \leq Q$ **do**
17:                $r_j[i] \leftarrow \left[x_{min}[i] + l * (j-1) + 1, x_{min}[i] + l * j \right]$;
18:                $v_j[i] \leftarrow$ UPDATE($v_j[i], r_j[i]$);
19:            $r_Q[i] \leftarrow \left[x_{min}[i] + l * Q, x_{max}[i] \right]$;
20:            $v_Q[i] \leftarrow$ UPDATE($v_Q[i], r_Q[i]$);
21:            **for all** $1 \leq j \leq Q$ **do**
22:                **if** $x_j[i].c \in r_j[i]$ **then**
23:                    **if** $|v_j[i]| = 0$ **then**
24:                        $v_j[i] \leftarrow$ ADD($v_j[i], x_j[i].c$);
25: **end procedure**

Definition 7 (Partition length). *Let x_{min} and x_{max} be the min and the max domain values of a parameter, x, and Q be a number of partitions. The partition length $len(x)$ is calculated by dividing the range of values of x in Q equally-sized intervals:* $\left\lceil \frac{x_{max} - x_{min}}{Q} \right\rceil$

The representative values (one for each partition) of parameter are defined below.

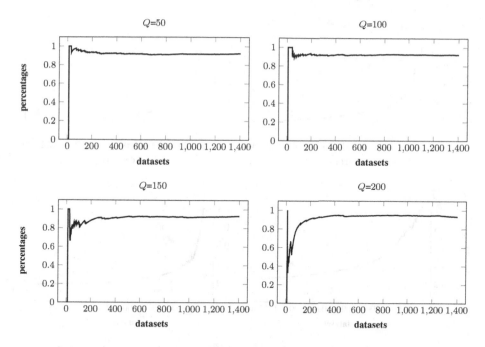

Fig. 3. The percentages of the correct binding-decisions for the auction app.

Definition 8 (Representative values of parameter). *Let r be the set of the partitions of the domain values of a parameter x. The Q representative values of the Q partitions are defined by the set, $v = \left\{ x_1.c, \ \ldots, \ x_j.c, \ \ldots, \ x_Q.c \right\}$, where $x_j.c \in r_j$.*

The Planning mechanism dynamically (re-)defines the partitions (see below) whenever a new parameter-value arrives that is not represented by an existing partition.

Planning Algorithm. Algorithm 2 accepts as input the current values of the input parameters of an operation of an API, along with the existing partitions of the parameters. The inputs of Algorithm 2 further include the available instances of the API and the set of the polynomial functions of the current predictive-models of the instances. If the current values of the parameters do not belong to the existing partitions, Algorithm 2 redefines the partitions by adjusting their endpoints (Algorithm 2 (5–11)) and accordingly redistributing their representative values[8] (Algorithm 2 (13–20)). Algorithm 2 adds the current values of the parameters to the proper partitions only if the partitions do not contain values (Algorithm 2 (21–24)). Algorithm 2 predicts the response times of the instances for the current parameter-values and returns back the instance that has the lowest predicted response-time (see Footnote 8).

---

[8] Due to the algorithmic simplicity, we do not specify the functions UPDATE, ADD and SELECT.

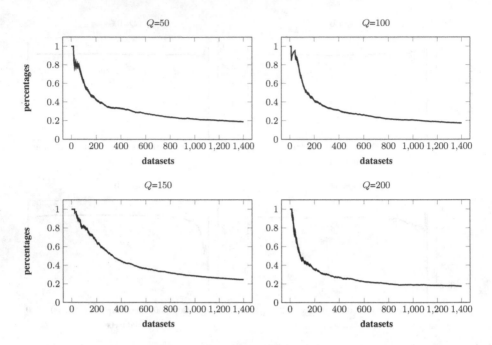

Fig. 4. The percentages of the datasets used for rebuilding predictive models.

Time Complexity. The complexity scales with the numbers N (parameters), Q (parameter partitions), Q (parameters values) and service instances, $\mathcal{O}(N * Q^2)$. Since the number of the instances of a single back-end is expected to be (in the order of tens) much lower than the numbers of the other factors (e.g., Q ranges in the order of hundreds), the complexity does not asymptotically scale with the number of instances.

5   Experimental Evaluation

We evaluate our approach on five benchmarks (Sect. 5.1). Prior to presenting the results, we set up below our experiments.

We extended an existing auction app[9] with a data-analytics back-end that uses the k-means clustering algorithm. We implemented a research-prototype (in Java) of the autonomic controller and we exposed it as a RESTful Web service. Datasets collected from UC Irvine machine-learning public repository[10] were given as input to the app. We used all of the datasets where the number (resp., dimensions) of the data points in the respective dataset was less than 12000 (resp., 12). We did it due to the computational constraints of the used machines. As also the evaluation results show in Sect. 5.1, the usage of extra datasets from the repository would have been redundant. In that way, we concluded to use 1456 datasets. We run the experiments 1456 times, each time adding

---

[9] https://github.com/jagmohansingh/auction-system.
[10] http://archive.ics.uci.edu/ml/index.php.

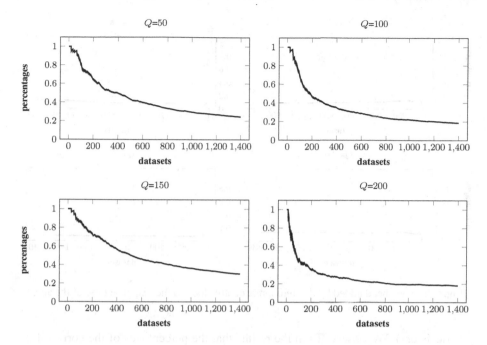

Fig. 5. The percentages of the monitoring response-times used for rebuilding predictive models.

an extra dataset, starting with one dataset and progressing with the remaining datasets in a random order.

The front-end of the app runs on a mobile phone[11], the edge instance and the autonomic controller on a laptop[12] (connected to the same LAN with the mobile phone), and the remote instance on a virtual machine deployed to the Google cloud[13]. All of the instances of the service back-end are exposed as RESTful Web services. We do not present experiments that use multiple edge/remote instances, since the complexity of our approach does not asymptotically scale with the number of instances (Sect. 4.2).

5.1   Evaluation Results

B1. *How many binding decisions are correct?*

For each dataset given as input to the controller, the latter makes a binding decision between the edge and the remote instances. We repeated this experiment for different numbers Q of partitions (Q affects how many times the predictive models are reconstructed). Figure 3 depicts the percentages of the correct binding-decisions (i.e., the number of the correct decisions is divided by the number of all of the

---

[11] 1.9 GHz CPU, 4 GB RAM, Android 8.0.

[12] 2.70 GHz CPU, Intel Core i5-5257U, 64-bit Windows 10 Home, 8 GB RAM.

[13] 2.2 GHz 2 vCPU, Intel Xeon E5 v4 (Broadwell) platform, 7.5 GB RAM, Windows server 2016 (the cost of renting a more powerful machine for our experiments was very high).

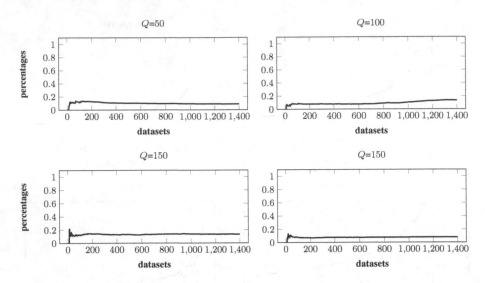

Fig. 6. The overhead added by the autonomic control-loop to the response time of the app.

decisions). We observe from the results that the percentages of the correct decisions are increasing with the increase of the number of the datasets and are finally
stabilized at the 90% of the total number of the decisions.

B2. *How many datasets are used for rebuilding predictive models?*
We present in Fig. 4 the percentages of the datasets that are used for rebuilding
the predictive models in the previous experiment (i.e., the number of the used
datasets is divided by the number of all of the datasets). The percentages of the
used datasets for rebuilding models decrease with the increase of the number of
the provided datasets. Especially, a small percentage (20%–30%) of the total number of the datasets is used for rebuilding models. Thus, the inclusion of extra
datasets from the repository in the experiment for rebuilding models would have
been redundant.

B3. *How many monitoring response-times are used for rebuilding predictive models?*
Figure 5 depicts the percentages of the monitoring response-times of the
edge/remote instances used in the previous experiments (i.e., the number of the
used response-times is divided by all of the monitoring response-times). The percentages of the used response-times decrease with the increase of the number
of the provided datasets. Especially, a small percentage (20%–30%) of the total
number of the monitoring response-times is used. Note that the curves of the percentages of the used datasets and the used response-times (Figs. 4 and 5) are anal-
ogous.

B4. *What is the overhead to the response-time of the app added by our approach?*
We present in Fig. 6 the percentages of the overhead to the response time of the app
added by the autonomic mechanisms (i.e., the execution time of the mechanisms is
divided by the response time of the app). The overhead comes to the 10%–15% of
the response time of the app. Note that the overhead is higher in the first datasets

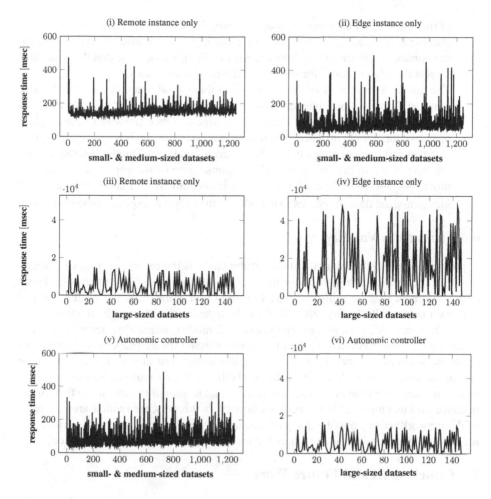

Fig. 7. The response time of the app when it uses the edge/remote instances or the controller.

because the reconstruction of the predictive models and the parameter partitions occur more frequent for these datasets.

B5. *What is the improvement to the response time of the app?*

To examine the improvement, we divide the datasets into small-, medium-, and large-sized datasets. We consider that the size of a dataset equals to the number of the datapoints of the dataset[14]. The first two charts of Fig. 7 present the response times of the app when it uses the remote instance only or the edge instance only for small- and medium-sized datasets. The next two charts present the response times of the app for large-sized datasets[15]. The last two charts present the response times

---

[14] We define the equally-sized intervals of the dataset sizes, (1, 4000], (4000, 8000] and (8000, 12000], which correspond to small-, medium-, and large-sized datasets, respectively.

[15] The scale of the y-axis in the first two charts is different from the scale in the next two charts.

of the app when it uses the controller. Comparing Fig. 7(vi) against Fig. 7(iii), we observe that the controller selects the remote instance for large-sized datasets. On the contrary, comparing Fig. 7(v) against Fig. 7(ii), we observe that the controller selects the edge instance for small- and medium-sized datasets.

The above observations verify our intuition that Cloud machines are much more efficient than Fog machines on large-sized datasets. Since the controller selects for small- and medium-sized datasets the edge instance (instead of the original option of the remote instance), the response time of the app is improved. To quantify that improvement, we calculate for each small- and medium-sized dataset the percentage of the decrease of the response time of the app by using the formula, $\frac{y_{remote}-y_{edge}}{y_{remote}}$. Overall, the average improvement over all of the small- and medium-sized datasets comes to the 50% of the original response-time of the app.

6 Threads to Validity

A possible threat to the internal validity of the study is the exclusion from the experiments of the datasets that have more than 12000 datapoints and 12 dimensions. However, this threat may be mitigated based on the observation from the results that our approach needs only the first 20%–30% of the datasets to stabilize the number of the correct binding-decisions. Regarding the external validity, our study does not explicitly associate the built predictive-models to the software/hardware properties of machines or to the machine/network load. To reduce this threat, our approach builds separate predictive-models for each service instance. Additionally, each model is built as a function of the response time of an instance that is equal to sum of the execution time of the instance on a machine and of the network latency. In this way, the models are indicative of the network latency and the delay of machines to serve apps at the time periods and the network locations when and where the monitoring measurements were made.

7 Conclusions and Future Work

We contributed with the specification of the conceptual model and the algorithmic mechanisms of an autonomic controller for edge/remote instances of a mobile backend. The evaluation results showed that the number of the correct binding-decisions is the 90% of the total number of decisions, the number of the monitoring data (datasets and response times) used for reconstructing predictive models is the 20%–30% of the total number of data, the added overhead comes to the 10%–15% of the response time of an app, and the app response-time is decreased to the 50% of its original response-time.

A future research-direction is to consider the synchronization time (spent by the edge/remote instances for storing datasets) in the construction of predictive models. Another direction is to explicitly associate the predictive models to the machine and the network properties/load. A final direction is to enhance the autonomic controller with the capability to dynamically (de-)register service instances that are (not) available on the Fog and the Cloud.

Acknowledgments. The work was partially funded from the Victoria University of Wellington in New Zealand. We further express many thanks to Prof. B. Pernici for her valuable reviews.

References

1. Kaur, P., Goyal, M., Lu, J.: Pricing analysis in online auctions using clustering and regression tree approach. In: Cao, L., Bazzan, A.L.C., Symeonidis, A.L., Gorodetsky, V.I., Weiss, G., Yu, P.S. (eds.) ADMI 2011. LNCS (LNAI), vol. 7103, pp. 248–257. Springer, Heidelberg (2012). https://doi.org/10.1007/978-3-642-27609-5_16
2. Plebani, P., et al.: Information logistics and fog computing: the DITAS approach. In: International Conference on Advanced Information Systems Engineering, pp. 129–136 (2017)
3. Varghese, B., et al.: Realizing edge marketplaces: challenges and opportunities. IEEE Cloud Comput. **5**(6), 9–20 (2018)
4. Kephart, J.O., Chess, D.M.: The vision of autonomic computing. IEEE Comput. **36**(1), 41–50 (2003)
5. Dheeru, D., Karra Taniskidou, E.: UCI machine learning repository (2017)
6. Ashouri, M., Davidsson, P., Spalazzese, R.: Cloud, edge, or both? Towards decision support for designing IoT applications. In: International Conference on Internet of Things: Systems, Management and Security, pp. 155–162 (2018)
7. Brogi, A., Ferrari, G.L., Forti, S.: Secure cloud-edge deployments, with trust. CoRR, abs/1901.05347 (2019)
8. Brogi, A., Forti, S.: Qos-aware deployment of IoT applications through the fog. IEEE Internet Things J. **4**(5), 1185–1192 (2017)
9. Deng, R., Lu, R., Lai, C., Luan, T.H., Liang, H.: Optimal workload allocation in fog-cloud computing toward balanced delay and power consumption. IEEE Internet Things J. **3**(6), 1171–1181 (2016)
10. Brogi, A., Forti, S., Ibrahim, A.: Deploying fog applications: how much does it cost, by the way? In: International Conference on Cloud Computing and Services Science, pp. 68–77 (2018)
11. Mohan, N., Kangasharju, J.: Edge-fog cloud: a distributed cloud for Internet of Things computations. In: Cloudification of the Internet of Things, pp. 1–6 (2016)
12. Mohan, N., Kangasharju, J.: Edge-fog cloud: a distributed cloud for Internet of Things computations. CoRR, abs/1702.06335 (2017)
13. Brogi, A., Forti, S., Ibrahim, A.: How to best deploy your fog applications, probably. In: International Conference on Fog and Edge Computing, pp. 105–114 (2017)
14. Gupta, H., Dastjerdi, A.V., Ghosh, S.K., Buyya, R.: iFogSim: a toolkit for modeling and simulation of resource management techniques in the Internet of Things, edge and fog computing environments. Softw. Pract. Exp. **47**(9), 1275–1296 (2017)
15. Tran, D.H., Tran, N.H., Pham, C., Kazmi, S.M.A., Huh, E.-N., Hong, C.S.: OaaS: offload as a service in fog networks. Computing **99**(11), 1081–1104 (2017)
16. Guo, X., Singh, R., Zhao, T., Niu, Z.: An index based task assignment policy for achieving optimal power-delay tradeoff in edge cloud systems. In: IEEE International Conference on Communications, pp. 1–7 (2016)
17. Yousefpour, A., Ishigaki, G., Jue, J.P.: Fog computing: towards minimizing delay in the Internet of Things. In: IEEE International Conference on Edge Computing, pp. 17–24 (2017)
18. Saurez, E., Hong, K., Lillethun, D., Ramachandran, U., Ottenwälder, B.: Incremental deployment and migration of geo-distributed situation awareness applications in the fog. In: ACM International Conference on Distributed and Event-Based Systems, pp. 258–269 (2016)
19. Richardson, L., Ruby, S.: Restful Web Services, 1st edn. O'Reilly, Sebastopol (2007)
20. Erl, T.: Service-Oriented Architecture: Concepts, Technology, and Design. Prentice Hall, Upper Saddle River (2005)
21. Fokaefs, M., Stroulia, E.: Using WADL specifications to develop and maintain REST client applications. In: 2015 IEEE International Conference on Web Services, pp. 81–88 (2015)

22. Smola, A.J., Vishwanathan, S.V.N.: Introduction to Machine Learning. Cambridge University Press, Cambridge (2008)
23. Goldsmith, S., Aiken, A., Wilkerson, D.S.: Measuring empirical computational complexity. In: International Symposium on Foundations of Software Engineering, pp. 395–404 (2007)
24. Huang, L., Jia, J., Yu, B., Chun, B.-G., Maniatis, P., Naik, M.: Predicting execution time of computer programs using sparse polynomial regression. In: International Conference on Neural Information Processing Systems, pp. 883–891 (2010)
25. Athanasopoulos, D., Pernici, B.: Building models of computation of service-oriented software via monitoring performance indicators. In: International Conference on Service-Oriented Computing and Applications, pp. 173–179 (2015)

Re-deploying Microservices in Edge and Cloud Environment for the Optimization of User-Perceived Service Quality

Xiang He[✉], Zhiying Tu[✉], Xiaofei Xu[✉], and Zhongjie Wang[✉]

School of Computer Science and Technology, Harbin Institute of Technology,
Harbin, China
september_hx@outlook.com,
{tzy_hit,xiaofei,rainy}@hit.edu.cn

Abstract. Deploying microservices in edge computing environment shortens the distance between users and services, and consequently, improves user-perceived service quality. Because of resource constraints of edge servers, the number and Service Level Agreement (SLA) of microservices that could be deployed on one edge server are limited. This paper considers *user mobility*, i.e., location changes of massive users might significantly result in deterioration of user-perceived service quality. We propose a method of looking for an optimized microservice re-deployment solution by means of *add*, *remove*, *adjust*, and *switch*, to make sure service quality that massive users perceive always conforms to their expectations. Three algorithms are adopted for this purpose, and an experiment in real-world edge-cloud environment is also conducted based on *Kubernetes* to re-deploy microservice systems automatically.

Keywords: Microservices · Edge and cloud environment · Service system re-deployment · Service quality · User mobility

1 Introduction

Recently, lots of research have been conducted on *Cloud - Edge - Mobile devices* architecture in Edge Computing. In such architecture, the distance between users and services can be shortened by deploying services on edge servers. Microservices architecture and container technology have been adopted so that the services can be easily deployed, and services can be migrated to a cloud-native architecture [1], which makes the system adapt to the user demand changes.

User demands cannot remain unchanged all the time. *User mobility, functional requirement changes*, and *quality expectation changes* are typical changes in user demands. Deployment of microservices in cloud and edge environment should make changes accordingly to keep users satisfied. In this paper, we consider *user mobility* as the trigger of microservice system re-deployment.

In this paper, the following factors are considered: (1) *Multi-services*: A service system is composed of many services with different functionalities and SLAs,

© Springer Nature Switzerland AG 2019
S. Yangui et al. (Eds.): ICSOC 2019, LNCS 11895, pp. 555–560, 2019.
https://doi.org/10.1007/978-3-030-33702-5_42

and a user might need to request two or more services to satisfy his needs; (2) *Multi-SLAs*: Each microservice in the system might offer different SLAs; at a certain time, its SLA is deterministic, but it would switch to another SLA after re-deployment; (3) *Multi-users*: Massive users are simultaneously requesting services, and it is necessary to keep the quality of service that a service system offers always above their expectations; (4) *Resource constraints*: Computing resources offered by each edge server is different and limited.

Our work is to look for an optimized re-deployment solution, and the main contributions of the paper are listed below:

- We define the optimization problem of microservice system evolution which takes multi-services, multi-SLA, and multi-users into consideration. This extends traditional placement research to make it more fit for real world.
- We use Genetic algorithm (GA), heuristic algorithm (HA) and Artificial Bee Colony algorithm (ABC) to look for an optimized re-deployment solution. A set of experiments are conducted under four representative user mobility scenarios and the results have validated algorithm performance.
- We develop a tool based on docker and Kubernetes to execute a re-deployment solution in real-world edge-cloud computing environment, which empowers a service system the capacity of automatic and continuous re-deployment.

The remainder of this paper is organized as follows. Section 2 introduces definitions. Section 3 describes algorithms. Section 4 details the experimental and protosystem. Section 5 reviews related work. Section 6 concludes the paper.

2   Problem Formulation

Definition 1 (Service). The set of services are describes as S. A service s is described as a set of triple $\{(l_{sla}, r, n)\}$, and for each $s \in S$: id is the unique id which is used to distinguish different instances of the same service with the same SLA on one server; r is how much computing resources s needs to offer the quality level l_{sla}; n is the maximum number of users that one instance of s with l_{sla} can serve concurrently.

Definition 2 (Cloud/Edge Server Node). E stands for a set of server nodes, and a node is described as $e = (type, r, loc)$: $type \in \{EDGE, CLOUD\}$ is the type of e (might be an edge server or a cloud server); r is the total computing resources e can be provided for service instances; loc is the geographic location of e (*latitude* and *longitude*). It is important to notice the difference between cloud and edge nodes: computing resources in a cloud node is much more sufficient than an edge node.

Definition 3 (Re-deployment operations on microservice instances). $O^I = \{adjust, add, remove, retain\}$ is used to describe four types of re-deployment operations on a microservice instance: *adjust* means adjusting the quality level of an instance; *add* means creating a new instance; *remove* means deleting an instance; *retain* means keeping unchanged.

Definition 4 (Re-deployment operations on users). $O^U = \{switch, keep\}$: *switch* stands for switching a user's request on a service to another; *keep* means keeping a user on the same instance before and after.

Problem Definition. A service system evolves from time t to $t + \delta$ by a set of operations on users $OU = \{o^U | o^U \in O^U\}$ and a set of operations on microservice instances $OI = \{o^I | o^I \in O^I\}$. The δ means that the service system doesn't keep evolving all the time, only be triggered when most of the user demands are not satisfied. The optimization problem is described below:

$$minC_e = min(\sum_{o^I \in OI} cost(o^I) + \sum_{o^U \in OU} cost(o^U))$$

$$\text{s.t.} \begin{cases} f(u_i, eu_{ij}) * sla(eu_{ij}) >= sla(u_i, s_j), & \forall s_j \in S, \forall u_i \in U(t + \delta) \\ \sum_{inst\ on\ e_k} r(inst) <= r_{design}(e_k), & \forall e_k \in E(t + \delta) \\ 1 \leq ns(inst) \leq ns_{design}(inst), & \forall inst \in Inst(t + \delta) \end{cases} \quad (1)$$

where $Inst$ denotes the set of instances, eu_{ij} is an instance of service s_j and a user u_i's request on s_j is to be satisfied by eu_{ij}. $f()$ is a function for *attenuation coefficient* of quality level *w.r.t.* the distance between a user and a service instance. $r()$ get the amount of computing resources that $inst$ requires, and $ns()$ gets the actual number of users that $inst$ is serving, while $ns_{max}()$ gets the maximal number of users that $inst$ can serve concurrently.

The first constraint assures that the quality level that each user could be satisfied. The second constraint assures that the total resources do not exceed the maximal resource offering by the node. The number of users that each instance serves cannot exceed the maximal number that the instance can serve concurrently, which is assured by the last constraint.

3   Algorithms

In ABC, to initialize the population, one server node is picked up randomly from the candidate list for every service that each user requests. An instance with the lowest cost to accept the user will be chosen, and the result is treated as the *nectar*. In the *employed bees* phrase, a non-empty service instance will be chosen, and all users it serves will be dispatched to other instances. In the *onlooker bees* phrase, some nectar will be picked randomly and dispatched to other instances on nodes randomly. The abandoned food sources will be replaced by solutions randomly generated in the scout bees phrase.

In GA, the initialization process is the same as ABC. The gens represent the instances that are chosen for the user demand for every service. Some of the genes will be randomly chosen, and they will be adapted to other instances on the nodes which are in their candidate lists, and exchanging parts of the gens between two solutions is treated as the crossover.

The heuristics algorithm is based on the following heuristic rules: (1) Assign each user to the server node that is the most closest to him; (2) Existing instances will be considered first. Or the cost of *add* and *adjust* is compared, and the operation with the lower cost will be chosen; (3) User demands that cannot satisfied by the closest server node will be assigned to the next closest node; (4) When there are no enough computing resources, existing instances will be merged, and instances that have no user will be removed.

4   Experiments and Prototype

4.1   Experiments Setup

In the experiments, the cellular layout is used to place edge servers. The costs of all operations come from the average time (seconds * 10) of necessary Kubernetes operations. It is noteworthy that Kubernetes doesn't support dynamic resource allocation for pods, the *adjust* operation has to be split into one *remove* and one *add*. The cost of *switch* operation is calculated by the time that 1 MB data needed to transfer with 100 Mbps. The costs for *add, remove, adjust, retain, switch*, and *keep* used here are 68, 25, 94, 0, 0.8, and 0.

There are three main scenarios: (1) *Group to Group*: Users are gathered in some specific locations (i.e., they are in the form of groups;) and after their moves, they are in re-grouped; (2) *Random to Group*: Users are distributed randomly, and after their moves, they are gathered in groups; (3) *Group to Random*: Users are gathered in groups, and then they disperse all over the area.

4.2   Scenario 1: Group to Group

In this experiment, we evaluate our algorithms with the scenario 1. We generate three basic scenes: Scene 1, Scene 2 and Scene 3. They are three different situations that users gather together. Three experiments were conducted: moving from Scene 1 to 2, from Scene 2 to 3, and from Scene 3 to 1. The results are shown in Fig. 1. The x-axis stands for the number of users in the experiment, and the y-axis is the cost of the evolution plan that algorithm generated.

As shown in Fig. 1, the cost of evolution is linearly and positively correlated with the number of users. As the number of users grows, more user connections should be switched from the old server node to the new one, and more service instances must be deployed on server nodes. It shows that our ABC algorithm performs better than the GA and HA in all three situations. Both HA and ABC have a huge improvement compared to GA.

4.3   Scenario 2 and 3: Random to Group and Group to Random, and Continuous Evolution

In this experiment, we explore the situations of moving from random to group and from group to random with 10000 users and the number of server nodes that the users are grouped by differs from 1 to 7. The performance of the algorithms in the situation of *continuous evolution* is also explored.

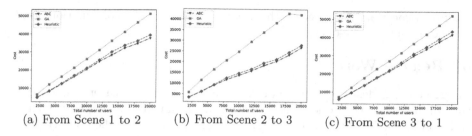

(a) From Scene 1 to 2   (b) From Scene 2 to 3   (c) From Scene 3 to 1

Fig. 1: Re-deployment cost $w.r.t.$ number of users in scenario 1

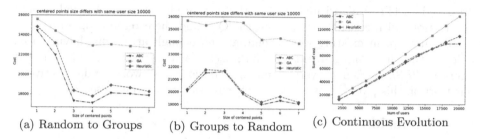

(a) Random to Groups   (b) Groups to Random   (c) Continuous Evolution

Fig. 2: Re-deployment cost in scenarios 2&3 and continuous evolution

The results in Fig. 2(a) and (b) show the ABC still performs better than GA and HA in these two situations. The x-axis is the number of cluster nodes and the y-axis is the cost of evolution plan generated by the algorithms.

For continuous evolution, we execute the re-deployment algorithm three times: Scene 1 to 2, then 2 to 3, and back to 1. And the cost in total is the sum of the cost. Figure 2(c) shows that ABC performs better than GA and HA. It means ABC does not overlook the global cost of the continuous evolution while trying to find the best solution to part of the problem, and the stability of the algorithm and the deployment of the service system are guaranteed.

4.4   Prototype

The prototype system is built with *Docker* and *Kubernetes*. Because the user location awareness is beyond our work, it will not detailed here.

As listed in Sect. 3, there are four types of operations that we need to implement, i.e., *add, remove, adjust* and *switch*. It's easy to implement the *switch* operation by proxy and gateway on each node, so we only illustrate how to do *add, remove* and *adjust* operations in K8s with the command tools *kubectl*. We assume that all the configuration files required by K8s are prepared in advance.

For *add* operation, the configuration file that related to the desired service will be used by *kubectl* with node-selector attribute. What to mention is we should label the pod with the instance that is generated by the algorithm. For *remove* operation, the pod id, which is associated with the instance id label, is passed to the command tool. Unfortunately, K8s doesn't support dynamic resource allocation now, thereby the *adjust* operation is the combination of *add* operation and *remove* operation.

5   Related Work

Zhang et al. [2] designed a framework for dynamic service placement based on control and game theoretic models, aiming at optimizing hosting cost dynamically in Geographically Distributed Clouds. Selimi et al. [3] studied service placement in Community networks to improve the quality of experience. Mahmud et al. [4] proposed a QoE-aware application placement policy. Wang et al. [5] proposed an ITEM algorithm to solve the service placement of Virtual Reality applications with consideration about the QoS and the economic operations.

To sum up, in existing works there are no enough attentions having been paid to the changing demands of *multi-users* in a *multi-service* system that offers *multi-SLAs*. Being a very common scenario in real world and objective of our work in this paper, it is a significant extension to current research.

6   Conclusions

This paper considers user mobility to re-deploying microservices in edge and cloud environment, which can improve user-perceived service quality. Considering the challenges of *multi-services*, *multi-users* and *multi-SLAs*, and by six types of basic operations and three strategies, our methods could identify an optimized re-deployment solution effectively. And a prototype tool has been developed. Other types of user demand changes will be considered in future work.

Acknowledgment. Research in this paper is partially supported by the National Key Research and Development Program of China (No. 2017YFB1400604), the National Science Foundation of China (61802089, 61772155, 61832004, 61832014).

References

1. Balalaie, A., Heydarnoori, A., Jamshidi, P.: Microservices architecture enables DevOps: migration to a cloud-native architecture. IEEE Softw. **33**(3), 42–52 (2016)
2. Zhang, Q., Zhu, Q., Zhani, M.F., Boutaba, R., Hellerstein, J.L.: Dynamic service placement in geographically distributed clouds. IEEE J. Sel. Areas Commun. **31**(12), 762–772 (2013)
3. Selimi, M., Cerdà-Alabern, L., Sánchez-Artigas, M., Freitag, F., Veiga, L.: Practical service placement approach for microservices architecture. In: 2017 17th IEEE/ACM International Symposium on Cluster, Cloud and Grid Computing (CCGRID), Madrid, pp. 401–410 (2017)
4. Mahmud, R., Srirama, S.N., Ramamohanarao, K., Buyya, R.: Quality of Experience (QoE)-aware placement of applications in Fog computing environments. J. Parallel Distrib. Comput. (2018)
5. Wang, L., Jiao, L., He, T., Li, J., Mühlhäuser, M.: Service entity placement for social virtual reality applications in edge computing. In: IEEE INFOCOM 2018 - IEEE Conference on Computer Communications, Honolulu, HI, pp. 468–476 (2018)

Short Papers

Short Papers

Mapping Business Rules to LTL Formulas

Isaac Mackey[(✉)] and Jianwen Su

Department of Computer Science, University of California, Santa Barbara, USA
{isaac_mackey,su}@cs.ucsb.edu

1 Introduction

A business service consists of a set of business processes. A service enactment is formed by the set of process instances serving a client. Business service *rules* are conditions restricting enactments derived from policies, regulations, and service-level agreements with clients. The problem of service provisioning [3] includes monitoring enactments to detect violations of rules at run-time. We develop a solution to service provisioning by modeling rules with quantitative time constraints and automatically generating finite state machines (FSMs) as run-time monitors. A key step is translating a class of "simple" rules to linear temporal logic (LTL), where known algorithms [4] can translate LTL formulas to FSMs. The central problem of this approach is the rule translation problem: *Given a rule over a service, construct an equivalent LTL formula.*

A *service schema* S is a finite set of process names. Each process *instance* is tagged with a timestamp for its completion. A *service enactment* η of a service schema S is a mapping $\eta : S \to 2^{\mathbb{N}}$ such that for each $p \in S$, $\eta(p)$ is a finite set representing the timestamps of instances of p. Business rules are formula constructed by the following logic language. A *(timed) process atom* is an expression "$p@x$", where p is a process name and x is a variable, that indicates an instance of process p happens at timestamp x. A *gap atom* is an expression "$x \leqslant_n y$" or "$x \geqslant_n y$" (x, y are variables and $n \in \mathbb{Z}$) representing the condition $x+n \leqslant y$, $x+n \geqslant y$, resp. A *constraint* is a finite conjunction of atoms. A *rule* is a statement of implication from one constraint to another. The intent of a rule $\phi \to \psi$ is to require that each set of process instances in a service enactment satisfying the constraint ϕ can be extended to satisfy ψ.

We translate rules into linear temporal logic, i.e. formulas built recursively from process names in a service schema S and the following connectives/operators:
$$\varphi := p \mid true \mid false \mid \neg\varphi \mid \varphi \vee \varphi \mid \varphi \wedge \varphi \mid \varphi \to \varphi \mid \mathsf{X}\varphi \mid \mathsf{Y}\varphi \mid \mathsf{F}\varphi \mid \mathsf{P}\varphi$$
where $p \in S$, *true, false* are Boolean values, and $\neg, \vee, \wedge, \to$ are Boolean operators, and X (*next*), F (*future*), Y (*yesterday*), and P (*past*) are temporal operators [1, 2]. For convenience, we use X^i ($i \in \mathbb{Z}$) for i consecutive X operators when $i \geqslant 0$ and i consecutive Y operators when $i < 0$.

Given an enactment η of a service schema S, the *trace* π_η of η is defined as follows: if κ is the largest timestamp in η, then $\pi_\eta = \pi_\eta[0]...\pi_\eta[\kappa]$ where for each $i \in [0..\kappa]$ and each $p \in S$, $\pi_\eta[i](p) = true$ if $i \in \eta(p)$. The technical problem studied

© Springer Nature Switzerland AG 2019
S. Yangui et al. (Eds.): ICSOC 2019, LNCS 11895, pp. 563–565, 2019.
https://doi.org/10.1007/978-3-030-33702-5

here is: Given a set of rules R over a service schema S, is there an LTL formula φ such that for each enactment η of S, η satisfies every rule in R iff $\pi_\eta, 0 \models \varphi$?

2   Mapping Rules to LTL

Consider a business rule Initial Deposit: each client should make a payment no later than three days after a Schedule process responds to the client's request:

$$r_{\text{ID}} : \{\text{Request@}x, \text{Schedule@}y, y \geqslant_0 x\} \rightarrow \{\text{Payment@}z, y \leqslant_0, y \geqslant_3 z\}$$

Let φ_{L} and φ_{R} be the constraint at the left- and right-hand-side (resp.) of r_{ID}. There is a natural (faithful) representation of φ_{L} and φ_{R} as acyclic, undirected graphs. A rule $\phi \rightarrow \psi$ (over a service schema) is *simple* if $\phi \cup \psi$ is acyclic and there is exactly one variable shared by ϕ and ψ. Thus, we represent a simple rule where variable y is shared as a *tree* rooted at node y. r_{ID} is shown below as the graphs for φ_{L} and φ_{R} with their common node connected by a dashed line.

Fig. 1. A tree-like representation of the Initial Deposit rule, where y is a shared variable

We translate these constraints by observing that an edge labeled $\{y \geqslant_0 x\}$ can be captured by operators $\mathsf{X}^0\mathsf{P}$, and $\{y \leqslant_0 z, y \geqslant_3 z\}$ by operators $\bigvee_{0 \leqslant i \leqslant 3} \mathsf{X}^i$. The translations of φ_{L} and φ_{R} with respect to y are

$$\tau_{\varphi_{\text{L}}, y} = \text{Schedule} \wedge \mathsf{P}\,\text{Request, and } \tau_{\varphi_{\text{R}}, y} = \text{Schedule} \wedge \bigvee_{0 \leqslant i \leqslant 3} \mathsf{X}^i \text{Payment}$$

r_{ID} expresses a property of all sets of Request and Schedule instances with appropriate timestamps. This corresponds to a property of all instants of a trace that satisfy Schedule $\wedge$ P Request. To reflect this coverage, the implication is placed in the scope of the G operator. Then the translation of r_{ID} is

$$r_{\text{ID}}^{LTL} : \mathsf{G}((\text{Schedule} \wedge \mathsf{P}\,\text{Request}) \rightarrow \bigvee_{0 \leqslant i \leqslant 3} \mathsf{X}^i \text{Payment}).$$

Let $r : \phi_{\text{L}} \rightarrow \phi_{\text{R}}$ be a simple rule with a shared variable y. $\tau_{\varphi_{\text{L}}, y}$ and $\tau_{\varphi_{\text{R}}, y}$ are attained by traversing the graphs of ϕ_{L} and ϕ_{R} from the root y, converting gap atoms into LTL operators. Then the translation $\gamma(r)$ of r is $\mathsf{G}(\tau_{\phi_{\text{L}}, y} \rightarrow \tau_{\phi_{\text{L}}, y})$. Let S be an arbitrary service schema and R an arbitrary set of simple rules over S. It can be shown that all enactments η of S, η satisfies R iff $\pi_\eta, 0 \models \bigwedge_{r \in R} \gamma(r)$.

References

1. Lichtenstein, O., Pnueli, A., Zuck, L.: The glory of the past. In: Parikh, R. (ed.) Logic of Programs 1985. LNCS, vol. 193, pp. 196–218. Springer, Heidelberg (1985). https://doi.org/10.1007/3-540-15648-8_16
2. Pnueli, A.: The temporal logic of programs. In: 18th Annual Symposium on Foundations of Computer Science, 1977, pp. 46–57. IEEE (1977)
3. Su, J., Wen, L., Yang, J.: From data-centric business processes to enterprise process frameworks. In: EDOC 2017, pp. 1–9. IEEE (2017)
4. Vardi, M.Y.: Reasoning about the past with two-way automata. In: Larsen, K.G., Skyum, S., Winskel, G. (eds.) ICALP 1998. LNCS, vol. 1443, pp. 628–641. Springer, Heidelberg (1998). https://doi.org/10.1007/BFb0055090

A SDN/NFV Based Network Slicing Creation System

Meng Wang, Bo Cheng$^{(\boxtimes)}$, and Junliang Chen

State Key Laboratory of Networking and Switching Technology,
Beijing University of Posts and Telecommunications, Beijing, China
{mengwang,chengbo,chjl}@bupt.edu.cn

Abstract. The next-generation network system is envisioned to be a multi-service network supporting different applications with multiple requirements. In this vision, Network SLicing (NSL) is considered a key mechanism to create multiple virtual networks over the same physical infrastructure. However, it is a challenging problem to deploy NSL with great flexibility. In this paper, we propose a novel SDN/NFV based NSL creation system, which includes the design domain, execution domain, and infrastructure domain. With these components, tenants can create NSL freely via an easy-to-use UI on a web browser.

Keywords: Network slicing · 5G · SDN · NFV

1 Introduction

The emerging fifth-generation (5G) network is expected to support a multitude of applications with diverse performance requirements. Recently, Network SLicing (NSL) [2] has been introduced as a promising solution to address this challenge. NSL is a concept that enables the operator to provide multiple dedicated virtual networks over a common network infrastructure. In this situation, NSL [1] is facing a rapid change by embracing Software Defined Networking (SDN) and Network Function Virtualization (NFV).

Although some excellent works have been done on NSL, there are still some existing problems. Firstly, most of the current NSL systems are specific and NSLs are difficult to reuse. Secondly, an NSL provider has to deploy NSL instances for multiple tenants. Thirdly, although there are many NFV management and orchestration systems, few of them can orchestrate network service by integrating both SDN and NFV. Given these facts, we propose a novel SDN/NFV based NSL creation system.

2 System Overview

As Fig. 1 shows, our proposed NSL creation system consists of three main domains: design domain, execution domain, and infrastructure domain. In this

© Springer Nature Switzerland AG 2019
S. Yangui et al. (Eds.): ICSOC 2019, LNCS 11895, pp. 566–568, 2019.
https://doi.org/10.1007/978-3-030-33702-5

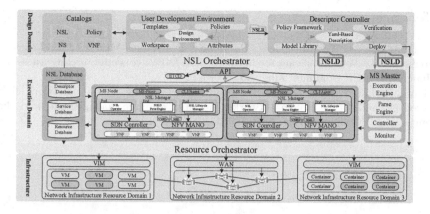

Fig. 1. The architecture of SDN/NFV based NSL creation system.

architecture, we mainly focus on the transport network and core network, ignoring the RAN domain for simplicity.

At the design domain, there are multiple sub-services available in catalogs. Tenants can use sub-services to design their own NLS in a drag-and-drop way. After designing, the NLS Descriptor (NSLD) is generated.

As Fig. 1 shows, NSLD is delivered to the execution domain. It is a service execution environment designed to manage the NSL life cycle. This microservice architecture based domain is distributed and self-organized.

At the infrastructure domain, there are multiple VIMs and Wide Area Networks (WANs) connecting them. In this domain, NSL instances belonging to different tenants run simultaneously in multiple VIMs.

3   Conclusion

In this paper, we propose a novel SDN/NFV based NSL creation system. The design domain provides an easily-operating service design environment. The execution domain is a distributed and self-organized service execution environment with multi-tenancy support. The infrastructure domain contains multiple network infrastructure resource domains. Tenants can create NSL with great flexibility and full automation.

Acknowledgement. This work was supported in part by the National Key Research and Development Program of China No.2017YFB1400603, Natural Science Foundation of China No.61772479.

References

1. Ordonez-Lucena, J., Ameigeiras, P., López, D., Ramos-Muñoz, J.J., Lorca, J., Folgueira, J.: Network slicing for 5G with SDN/NFV: concepts, architectures, and challenges. IEEE Commun. Mag. **55**, 80–87 (2017)
2. Zhang, H., Liu, N., Chu, X., Long, K., Aghvami, H., Leung, V.C.M.: Network slicing based 5G and future mobile networks: mobility, resource management, and challenges. IEEE Commun. Mag. **55**, 138–145 (2017)

Neural Adaptive Caching Approach for Content Delivery Networks

Qilin Fan[1(✉)], Hao Yin[2], Qiang He[3], Yuming Jiang[4], Sen Wang[1],
Yongqiang Lyu[2], and Xu Zhang[5]

[1] Chongqing University, Chongqing, China
fanqilin@cqu.edu.cn
[2] Tsinghua University, Beijing, China
[3] Swinburne University of Technology, Melbourne, Australia
[4] Norwegian University of Science and Technology (NTNU), Trondheim, Norway
[5] Nanjing University, Jiangsu, China

Keywords: Caching · Deep Reinforcement Learning ·
Quality of Service

1   Introduction

The last few years have witnessed an explosive growth in Internet traffic, stemming mainly from the streaming of high-quality multi-media contents. Such a significant growth has promoted the applications of Content Delivery Networks (CDNs). Today's CDN providers still use some well known cache eviction algorithms such as LRU, FIFO, LRU(m) due to their simplicity for implementation to guarantee the content availability. However, these conventional cache eviction algorithms may suffer major performance degradation for the two primary reasons. First, for the performance analysis on the existing cache eviction algorithms, it is generally assumed that the content requests follow a fixed Zipf popularity distribution, referred to as the Independent Reference Model (IRM). However, it has been observed that the performance under synthetic versus real data traces can vary quite greatly. Second, the majority of existing content eviction algorithms develop fixed control rules for making eviction decisions based on access time, frequency, size or their simple combinations. These rules do not generalize to different network conditions and traffic patterns.

To overcome the aforementioned limitations, in this paper, we propose a neural adaptive caching approach, called NA-Caching, that combines the benefits of the Recurrent Neural Network (RNN) and Deep Reinforcement Learning (DRL) to strengthen the representation learning of content requests and make adaptive caching decisions online with the objective of maximizing the long-term average hit rates. The experimental results driven by real-traces demonstrate that NA-Caching outperforms several candidate methods.

© Springer Nature Switzerland AG 2019
S. Yangui et al. (Eds.): ICSOC 2019, LNCS 11895, pp. 569–570, 2019.
https://doi.org/10.1007/978-3-030-33702-5

2   Methodology

We introduce a novel NA-Caching approach for the adaptive cache management. First, we adopt the GRU framework to learn the feature embedding of contents. There are two categories of features in focus: the contextual features that would be variant over time and the semantic features that would not change. The Mean Relative Squared Error (MRSE) is utilized as our loss function when applied to heavy-tailed data. Second, we utilize Deep Q-Network (DQN) to tackle the adaptive cache management online for the individual cache server from its own experiences. Under a regular Reinforcement Learning (RL) framework, the sequential decision-making problem is modeled using the Markov Decision Process (MDP) formulation. The deep version of RL adopts Deep Neural Networks (DNN), known as Deep Q-Network (DQN) as Q-function to approximate the action values $Q(s_t, a_t|\theta)$, where the term θ are the parameters of the Q-network and (s_t, a_t) represents a state-action pair. The DQN can be trained by minimizing the square of Temporal Difference (TD) error:

$$L(\theta) = \mathbb{E}[(y_t - Q(s_t, a_t|\theta))^2] \tag{1}$$
$$y_t = r_t + \gamma \max_{a'} Q(s_{t+1}, a'|\theta^-) \tag{2}$$

where y_t is the target value, θ^- are the parameters used to compute the target network. Specifically, the DRL agent derives an action a_{base} randomly from the set of base cache management solutions with ϵ probability. We also adopt the prioritized experience replay method to learn more efficiently.

3   Experimental Evaluation

The dataset is collected by a video provider company in China, which spans 2 weeks and covers 1.4 million distinct videos. To compute the results given the limited computing resources, we sample and pick 10,000 videos randomly in the experiment. We separate the traces into two periods: (i) the warm-up period represents the input of the prediction of video popularity; (ii) the test period starts immediately after the warm-up period. We compare the performance of NA-Caching with RANDOM, FIFO, LRU, PopCaching, Optimal benchmarks.

Evaluation results shows that NA-Caching significantly outperforms RANDOM, LRU, FIFO in terms of average hit rates under various cache percentages. When the cache percentage is lower than 1%, the performance gap between NA-Caching and Optimal is around 10%. As the cache percentage increases, this gap reduces. In addition, we observe that the marginal benefit of cache percentage diminishes gradually. It means that the increase in the cache capacity will no longer improve the cache hit rate significantly, and the cache hit rate is now limited by the distribution of the content popularity. We also observe that NA-Caching maintains a relatively stable cache hit rate. On average, NA-Caching outperforms PopCaching, RANDOM, FIFO, LRU by 5.1%, 30.8%, 30.6% and 16.0% respectively.

Personal Service Ecosystem (PSE) and Its Evolution Pattern Analysis

Haifang Wang[✉], Yao Fu, Zhongjie Wang, Zhiying Tu, and Xiaofei Xu

School of Computer Science and Technology,
Harbin Institute of Technology, Harbin, China
{wanghaifang,rainy,tzy_hit,xiaofei}@hit.edu.cn, fy777@foxmail.com

Abstract. To profile users, based on user's behavior logs, we present a novel model called Personal Service Ecosystem (PSE) for delineating a user's preferences and a method of recovering PSE (*PSER*). We define nine sub-patterns to describe the local (short-term) evolution of the preferences. Aggregating local evolution sub-patterns together, we give six types of global evolution patterns. A systematic empirical study is conducted, which illustrates the usability of the models and methods.

Keywords: Personal Service Ecosystem (PSE) · User preference · Evolution analysis · Evolution patterns · User behavior logs

1 Introduction

A PSE looks like an "electron cloud", i.e., multi-layer concentric tracks, and services are distributed on different tracks in terms of the "intimacy" with the user in a specific time slot. A PSE is divided into a set of non-overlapping sectors based on domains these services belong to. And there exist intensive *co-use* relationships among these services (called service network). In a PSE, services, tracks, the percentage of different domains, and the network structure among services, jointly depict the preferences and habits of a user. To model a user's preference by a PSE, **RQ1: in terms of a user's behavior logs of a given time slot, how is such a PSE recovered from the logs?**. To capture the evolution of user preferences [1], the variations of PSEs of multiple successive time slots are well analyzed. By a comprehensive observation on the evolutions, we find these evolutions follow some common patterns. **RQ2** tries to identify **what types of evolution patterns of user preference exist**. In terms of the identified global evolution patterns, **RQ3: how can we judge which specific evolution pattern an object in PSEs follows?**.

To answer **RQ1**, a method called *PSER* for recovering PSE from user behavior logs is presented. *PSER* identifies all the involved services, the domains and the underlying *co-use* relationships among services, calculates the "intimacy" of each service based on the duration and frequency of the usage, and then each service is allocated to a specific track of the PSE based on the "intimacy". *PSER*

© Springer Nature Switzerland AG 2019
S. Yangui et al. (Eds.): ICSOC 2019, LNCS 11895, pp. 571–572, 2019.
https://doi.org/10.1007/978-3-030-33702-5

measures the percentages of the domains and the weight attached to each *co-use* relationship between two services. To address **RQ2**, we identify six types of global evolution patterns for the objects in PSEs, including *refugee pattern, periodic pattern, stable pattern, fluctuant pattern, emergency pattern, zombie pattern*. To answer **RQ3**, for a set of successive time slots, multiple PSEs can be recovered. We present nine sub-patterns along with three parameters to delineate the local evolution of an object in PSEs. Then, the global evolution of an object can be expressed as a set of sequential sub-patterns with specific parameter values. Based on the six types of global evolution patterns, several rules are listed to judge which type of global evolution pattern an object may follow.

In experiments, to collect user behavior logs, we developed an App which was installed on Android smartphones by 50 volunteers. One representative user is shown in Fig. 1. Differences of users on services, domains and service network are highlighted, which illustrates the usability of PSE. The evolution analysis of PSEs is further studied, and details are not tried in words here.

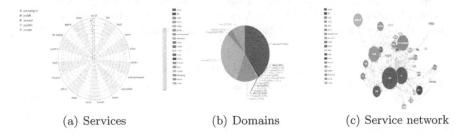

(a) Services   (b) Domains   (c) Service network

Fig. 1. PSE of one representative user for a specific time slot

2   Conclusion

This paper presents a novel model to profile users, an approach for recovering a PSE, six types of global evolution patterns of objects in PSEs, and a set of rules to predicate the global evolution pattern a member in PSEs follows. A empirical study is conducted, which proves the usability of the model and methods.

Acknowledgment. Research in this paper is partially supported by the National Key Research and Development Program of China (No 2017YFB1400604), the National Science Foundation of China (61772155, 61832014, 61832004).

Reference

1. Wang, H., Wang, Z., Xu, X.: Time-aware customer preference sensing and satisfaction prediction in a dynamic service market. In: Sheng, Q.Z., Stroulia, E., Tata, S., Bhiri, S. (eds.) ICSOC 2016. LNCS, vol. 9936, pp. 236–251. Springer, Cham (2016). https://doi.org/10.1007/978-3-319-46295-0_15

Adaptive Mobile Business Process Monitoring Service with Enhanced NFV MANO

Giovanni Meroni, Marouan Mizmizi, Pierluigi Plebani[✉], and Luca Reggiani

Dipartimento di Elettronica, Informazione e Bioingegneria,
Politecnico di Milano, Piazza Leonardo da Vinci, 32 - 20133 Milan, Italy
{giovanni.meroni,marouan.mizmizi,
pierluigi.plebani,luca.reggiani}@polimi.it

1 Introduction

The transmission of monitoring data collected by the smart devices paired with the artifacts is crucial to properly monitor business processes not confined within an organization premises. In this scope, the recent advancements brought by the 5G networks can be helpful [3], as the Network Function Virtualization (NFV) Management and Orchestration (MANO) gives the possibility to create virtual networks able to guarantee Quality of Service (QoS) requirements. At the same time, the limitation of current NFV MANO implementations concerns the time-invariant nature of those requirements. In fact, based on how the business process is executed, QoS requirements may change over time.

In this context, expressing only static requirements would limit the designer of the monitoring system to balance between the cost of an always high-rate/low-latency configuration and the risk of being unable to receive timely information in case of configuration with a lower cost.

The goal of this work is two-fold. Firstly, we provide a method to identify the QoS requirements of the network connectivity used to transmit the monitoring data, where these QoS requirements can be automatically derived from a mobile business process model properly decorated with location and time-varying monitoring requirements. Secondly, we discuss the limitations of current NFV MANO specifications with the aim of contributing in the advancement of this type of infrastructure by also allowing the enforcement of dynamic QoS requirements.

2 A Method for Specifying Slicing Requirements

In the monitoring process relying on a 5G mobile network, for each network device participating in the process, a set of QoS constraints has to be defined. Such constraints are related to the specific activities currently running during the process execution. In addition, they are dependent on the location where and the time when the activities are executed.

This work has been funded by the Italian Project ITS Italy 2020 under the Technological National Clusters program.

S. Yangui et al. (Eds.): ICSOC 2019, LNCS 11895, pp. 573–574, 2019.
https://doi.org/10.1007/978-3-030-33702-5

To derive time- and location-dependent slicing requirements, we propose to consider in the process model: (i) information on the location where activities are supposed to be executed classifying them in three categories: trajectory-based, path-based, and area-based; (ii) information on the duration of activities and time dependencies. In particular, Time-BPMN [2] is adopted as an extension of the Business Process Model and Notation (BPMN) modeling language with specific constructs to define temporal constraints for each activity, and temporal dependencies among activities; and (iii) the QoS requirements that should be satisfied for the involved networked devices. Here, for each activity in a process, four states are defined: Init, when the process is instantiated; Ready, when the activity is ready to be started; Running, when the activity is being executed; Terminated, when the activity has been ended. For each state, it is then possible to define the requirements that must hold.

Once time, location, and QoS information has been included to extend the process model, slicing requirements are generated to configure an NFV MANO. To this aim, we developed an application[1] that automatically defines slicing requirements compliant to the ETSI GS NFV-MAN specifications for Virtual Link Descriptor (VLD) files [1] starting from the extended process model.

3   Improving NFV-MANO for Dynamic Requirements

Based on our study, we can conclude that the following modifications should be introduced into the NFV MANO specifications to support time- and location-varying QoS requirements. (i) The descriptor for physical networks, base stations and machines should include location tags. Thus, the NFV MANO would know where these components are located and which areas they can serve. (ii) The VLD should explicitly support the definition of time- and location-dependent information. Therefore, the time for a network slice instantiation could be formalized and be known by the NFV MANO. At the same time, only the infrastructure components serving the requested area would be affected. (iii) Resources should be allocated, updated and forecast according to the information provided by the processes. To this aim, future NFV MANO should include a resource scheduler capable of also dynamically taking into considerations issues on the infrastructure (i.e., low network coverage area) thanks to the position information, and either anticipating counteractions or alerting the users thanks to the time information.

References

1. ETSI, NFVISG: GS NFV-MAN 001 V1. 1.1 Network Function Virtualisation (NFV); Management and Orchestration (2014)
2. Gagné, D., Trudel, A.: Time-BPMN. In: CEC 2009, pp. 361–367. IEEE Computer Society (2009)
3. Li, S., Xu, L.D., Zhao, S.: 5G Internet of things: a survey. J. Ind. Inf. Integr. **10**, 1–9 (2018)

---

[1] Source code available at https://bitbucket.org/polimiisgroup/qos5g-bpmn2vld.

SATP: Sentiment Augmented Topic Popularity Prediction on Social Media

Weizhi Gong, Zuowu Zheng, Xiaofeng Gao$^{(\boxtimes)}$, and Guihai Chen

Shanghai Key Laboratory of Scalable Computing and Systems,
Department of Computer Science and Engineering,
Shanghai Jiao Tong University, Shanghai 200240, China
{gongwz,waydrow}@sjtu.edu.cn,{gao-xf,gchen}@cs.sjtu.edu.cn

Abstract. In this paper we propose a topic popularity prediction model to quantifiy popularity more accurately with senmantic information and incorporates sentiment ino popularity prediction.

Keywords: Topic popularity prediction · Sentiment analysis · Popularity quantification · Social media

1 Introduction

Most existing topic popularity prediction models measure popularity simply using forwarding or view count, ignore semantic relation between posts and topic, which may lead to inccuracy. Therefore, we propose a model to quantify popularity more accurately with posts' semantic information and incorporate sentiment into popularity prediction.

2 Model Construction

For the input of a series of posts about a certain topic, we aim to output the predicted popularity.

We first quantify the topic popularity using posts' forwarding number weighted by words' relevance WR to the topic. We use the idea of PageRank [1] to calculate word w's relevance to the topic $WR(w)$ in post d, defined in Eqn. (1):

$$WR(w_i) = \frac{1-\theta}{|d|} + \theta \cdot \sum_{j \to i} \frac{\rho(w_i, w_j)}{\sum_{k \to j} \rho(w_k, w_j)} \cdot WR(w_j), \tag{1}$$

where $|d|$ is the length of the post that contains w_i, $\rho(w_i, w_j)$ is distance between word w_i and w_j, which is a linear combination of their semantic distance calculated by *Word2Vec* and lexical distance.

We then use MPQA subjective lexicon [3] to evaluate sentiment intensity of the subjective words and tag 64 most popular emojis with their sentiment

© Springer Nature Switzerland AG 2019
S. Yangui et al. (Eds.): ICSOC 2019, LNCS 11895, pp. 575–577, 2019.
https://doi.org/10.1007/978-3-030-33702-5

intensity. With the sentiment intensity of subjective words and emojis, we create dataset to train the hybrid architecture [2] of Bi-LSTM and convolutional network to calculate sentiment intensity of a certain post. After getting popularity and sentiment time series, we use convolutional network to learn their dependence and learn the history influence information of each time period and use Autoregressive model to predict future popularity.

3   Experiments

We test our model on the Twitter data from Dec. 23, 2017 to Mar. 19, 2018 on different topics. Here we use result of topic Gun Control and Trump as an example to illustrate performance of our model. We evaluate the accuracy of each prediction using *Mean Square Error (MSE)*, the result is shown in Fig. 1 and Tab. 1.

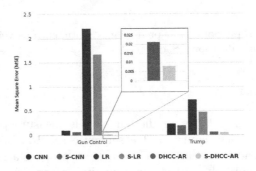

Fig. 1. Prediction performance of each model on each topic, the horizontal ordinate represents two topics, the vertical ordinate represents *MSE*. The "S" prefix means combining with sentiment intensity

Table 1. Improvement of prediction for each network when combining sentiment

S-CNN/CNN	S-LR/LR	S-DHCC-AR/DHCC-AR
21.39%	29.10%	38.71%

4   Conclusions

In this paper we propose a topic popularity prediction model, *SATP*. This model quantifies popularity using semantic information, making the quantification more accurate and explainable. We use the idea of Autoregressive for popularity prediction. To incorporate sentiment into prediction, we use *CNN* to learn sentiment and popularity's data dependence and history influence. We evaluate *SATP* on Twitter dataset by comparing mean square error (*MSE*).

Acknowledgement. This work was supported by the National Key R&D Program of China [2018YFB1004703]; the National Natural Science Foundation of China [61872238, 61672353]; the Shanghai Science and Technology Fund [17510740200]; the Huawei Innovation Research Program [HO2018085286]; the State Key Laboratory of Air Traffic Management System and Technology [SKLAT M20180X]; and the Tencent Social Ads Rhino-Bird Focused Research Program.

References

1. Gao, T., Bao, W., Li, J., Gao, X., Kong, B., Tang, Y., Chen, G., Li, X.: DANCINGLINES: an analytical scheme to depict cross-platform event popularity. In: Hartmann, S., Ma, H., Hameurlain, A., Pernul, G., Wagner, R.R. (eds.) DEXA 2018. LNCS, vol. 11029, pp. 283–299. Springer, Cham (2018). https://doi.org/10.1007/978-3-319-98809-2_18
2. Wang, C., Jiang, F., Yang, H.: A hybrid framework for text modeling with convolutional rnn. In: ACM SIGKDD International Conference on Knowledge Discovery and Data Mining, pp. 2061–2069 (2017)
3. Wilson, T., Wiebe, J., Hoffmann, P.: Recognizing contextual polarity in phrase-level sentiment analysis. In: Conference on Human Language Technology and Empirical Methods in Natural Language Processing, pp. 347–354 (2005)

A Hierarchical Optimizer for Recommendation System Based on Shortest Path Algorithm

Jiacheng Dai, Zhifeng Jia, Xiaofeng Gao$^{(\boxtimes)}$, and Guihai Chen

Shanghai Key Laboratory of Scalable Computing and Systems,
Department of Computer Science and Engineering,
Shanghai Jiao Tong University, Shanghai 200240, China
{daijiacheng,fergusjia}@sjtu.edu.cn,
{gao-xf,gchen}@cs.sjtu.edu.cn

Abstract. Top-k Nearest Geosocial Keyword (T-kNGK) query on geosocial network is defined to give users k recommendations based on some keywords and designated spatial range, and can be realized by shortest path algorithms. However, shortest path algorithm cannot provide convincing recommendations, so we design a hierarchical optimizer consisting of classifiers and a constant optimizer to optimize the result by some features of the service providers.

Keywords: Geosocial network · Keyword query · Spatial query

1 Problem Statement

Top-k Nearest Geosocial Keyword Search Query (T-kNGK) works on a geosocial network. A T-kNGK query's task is to recommend k service providers (SP's) that best meet the user's requirement (keywords and location). Shortest path algorithms are used to solve this problem. We simply take the length of the shortest path between user u and SP v as the basis for recommendation. A geosocial network [1] is a weighted undirected graph $G = (V, E, W, K, L)$. We give a simple instance Fig. 1 to illustrate its structure and contents. The weight of an edge shows the intimacy between users or rating for SPs (mapped to $[0, 1]$). Each SP v has a keyword set $k_v \in K$ and location $l_v \in L$. The process of a T-kNGK query is shown in Fig. 2 (together with the Hierarchical Optimizer). The defect of T-kNGK query is that it seems to be unconvincing since it only references one comment (one path) due to shortest path algorithm. Therefore, we should optimize the results of T-kNGK query to enhance reliability and avoid extreme bad cases.

© Springer Nature Switzerland AG 2019
S. Yangui et al. (Eds.): ICSOC 2019, LNCS 11895, pp. 578–580, 2019.
https://doi.org/10.1007/978-3-030-33702-5

2   Hierarchical Optimizer

Constant Optimizer We try to let the SP's with more comments get higher score and reduce the score of SP's who have few comments. We define multiplier α to calculate the new score $Score_c$. $\alpha_{s_i} = 1 + \frac{1}{\beta}(\frac{count_{s_i} - average}{average - min_{1 \leq j \leq n}\{count_{s_j}\}})^\gamma$ when $count_{s_i} < average$ and $\alpha_{s_i} = 1 + \frac{1}{\beta}(\frac{count_{s_i} - average}{max_{1 \leq j \leq n}\{count_{s_j}\} - average})^\gamma$ when $count_{s_i} \geq average$, where $average = \frac{\Sigma_{j=1}^n count_{s_j}}{n}$, β and γ are adjustable parameters and $count_{s_i}$ is the number of comments of SP s_i. Finally, $Score_c = \alpha_{s_i} \times ratings_{s_i}$.

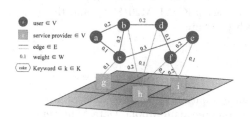

Fig. 1. An instance of geosocial network

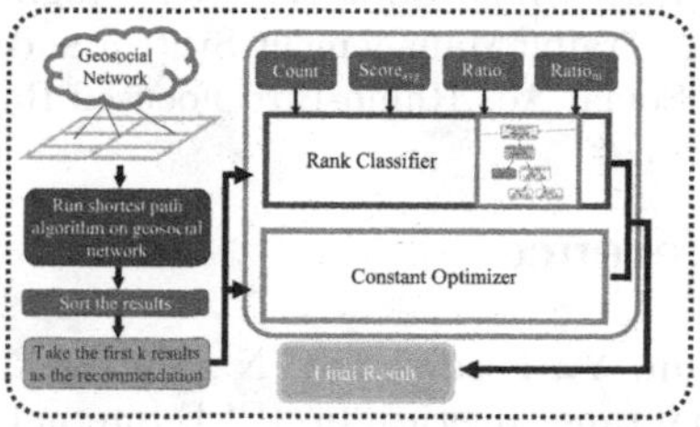

Fig. 2. The optimized T-kNGK query

Rank Classifier We defined four features to train a classifier which ranks the SP's from 1 to 5: "Matched Keyword Ratio" $Ratio_m = \frac{|k_q \cap k_{s_i}|}{|k_q|}$, "Specific Keyword Ratio" $Ratio_s = \frac{|k_q \cap k_{s_i}|}{|k_{s_i}|}$, "Count of Ratings" $Count_{s_i}$, "Average Score" $Score_{avg_{s_i}}$.

In the Hierarchical Optimzer, we first use Rank Classifier to rank the SP's we get from the shortest path algorithm and sort them by their rank. Then we use Constant Optimizer to calculate $Score_c$ and sort the SP's of the same rank by $Score_c$. Thus, we got the optimized results.

3   Experiments and Results

We use Yelp dataset (over 3 GB and has over 6.5 million reviews) which contains all the data we need in the T-kNGK query and the hierarchical optimizer. For Constant Optimizer, we set $\beta = 5$ and $\gamma = 2$. For Rank Classifier, we choose random forest with accuracy of 82%. We use 80% of the data to train the model and 20% to test the model. First, we run shortest path algorithm on the geosocial network built on Yelp dataset and get some raw result. Then we use our Hierarchical Optimizer to re-order the raw results and get ideal result. One of our optimized result is shown in Fig. 3.

	NO.1 Old NO.2	NO.2 Old NO.1	NO.3 Old NO.5	NO.4 Old NO.3	NO.5 Old NO.4	NO.6 Old NO.9	NO.7 Old NO.10	NO.8 Old NO.8	NO.9 Old NO.6	NO.10 Old NO.7
Rank	5	5	5	5	5	5	4	2	0	0
$Score_c$	4.800	4.581	4.350	4.325	4.078	2.886	3.941	2.645	2.342	1.789
Path length	0.01	0.01	2.126	2.12	2.126	2.498	2.501	2.497	2.495	2.495
$Ratio_{ep}$	0.167	0.167	0.167	0.125	0.208	0.042	0.208	0.083	0.042	0.042
$Ratio_c$	0.228	0.8	0.4	0.6	1.0	0.1	0.4	0.2	0.057	0.133
Count	1090	35	80	74	28	75	106	12	51	20
$Score_{avg}$	4	5	4.5	4.5	4.5	3	4	3	2.5	2
User rate	5	5	5	5	1	2	4	2	1	1

Fig. 3. The result of optimization

Acknowledgments. This work was supported by the National Key R&D Program of China [2018YFB1004703]; the National Natural Science Foundation of China [61872238, 61672353]; the Shanghai Science and Technology Fund [17510740200]; the Huawei Innovation Research Program [HO2018085286]; the State Key Laboratory of Air Traffic Management System and Technology [SKLAT M20180X]; and the Tencent Social Ads Rhino-Bird Focused Research Program.

Reference

1. Sun, Y., Pasumarthy, N., Sarwat, M.: On evaluating social proximity-aware spatial range queries. In: IEEE International Conference on Mobile Data Management (MDM), KAIST, Taejeon, South Korea, pp. 72–81 (2017)

Author Index

Printed in the United States
By Bookmasters